Mediation

Chs. 14, 15.

Mediation
The Roles of Advocate and Neutral

Dwight Golann

Suffolk University

Jay Folberg

University of San Francisco

ΛSPEN

PUBLISHERS

76 Ninth Avenue, New York, NY 10011
http://lawschool.aspenpublishers.com

© 2006 Aspen Publishers, Inc.
a Wolters Kluwer business
http://lawschool.aspenpublishers.com

Aspen Publishers
Attn: Permissions Department
76 Ninth Avenue, 7th Floor
New York, NY 10011-5201

Printed in the United States of America.

1 2 3 4 5 6 7 8 9 0

ISBN 0-7355-4016-0

Library of Congress Cataloging-in-Publication Data

Golann, Dwight.
  Mediation : the roles of advocate and neutral / Dwight Golann, Jay Folberg.
    p. cm.
  Includes bibliographical references and index.
  ISBN 0-7355-4016-0 (pbk. : alk. paper)
    1. Mediation — United States.   2. Dispute resolution (Law) — United States.
3. Compromise (Law) — United States.   4. Mediation.   I. Folberg, Jay, 1941-
II. Title.

KF9084.G648 2006
347.73'9 — dc22

2006008987

About Aspen Publishers

Aspen Publishers, headquartered in New York City, is a leading information provider for attorneys, business professionals, and law students. Written by preeminent authorities, our products consist of analytical and practical information covering both U.S. and international topics. We publish in the full range of formats, including updated manuals, books, periodicals, CDs, and online products.

Our proprietary content is complemented by 2,500 legal databases, containing over 11 million documents, available through our Loislaw division. Aspen Publishers also offers a wide range of topical legal and business databases linked to Loislaw's primary material. Our mission is to provide accurate, timely, and authoritative content in easily accessible formats, supported by unmatched customer care.

To order any Aspen Publishers title, go to *http://lawschool.aspenpublishers. com* or call 1-800-638-8437.

To reinstate your manual update service, call 1-800-638-8437.

For more information on Loislaw products, go to *www.loislaw.com* or call 1-800-364-2512.

For Customer Care issues, e-mail *CustomerCare@aspenpublishers.com*; call 1-800-234-1660; or fax 1-800-901-9075.

Aspen Publishers
a Wolters Kluwer business

To my wife, Helaine, who has taught me how much dispute resolution depends on the learning of psychology and the art of understanding people.

To my children, Ross, Lisa, and Rachel, who taught me the necessity of mediation.

SUMMARY OF CONTENTS

CONTENTS

CHAPTER 4
BARRIERS TO SETTLEMENT   69

PART II

THE MEDIATION PROCESS   93

CHAPTER 5
AN OVERVIEW OF MEDIATION   95

CHAPTER 11
REPRESENTING CLIENTS: DURING THE PROCESS   277

PART IV

PUBLIC POLICY, ETHICS, AND LAW   301

CHAPTER 12
PUBLIC POLICY AND ETHICAL ISSUES   303

CHAPTER 13
THE LAW OF MEDIATION   **343**

PART V

PREFACE

This book is based on three key assumptions: First, to represent clients effectively, the next generation of lawyers must be able to mediate effectively. Second, new lawyers are much more likely to encounter mediation as advocates or advisors than as professional neutrals. Finally, textbooks should be interesting to read, bring together the latest and best writing on the process, and lend themselves to interactive teaching.

Our book, therefore, has a different emphasis from most other texts on mediation. It focuses on *legal* mediation — substantial disputes involving legal claims, in which the disputants are likely to hire attorneys. It also looks at mediation primarily from the perspective of a lawyer representing a client, rather than from the viewpoint of a mediator or a party.

This book includes examples drawn from actual disputes to illustrate the readings and pique students' interest. The introductory chapter in Part II, for example, features the comments of practicing lawyers on how they use mediation in a variety of settings. It also includes accounts of how two high-profile disputes were mediated, one involving a student death and the other the Microsoft antitrust case. The readings on mediation techniques and about ethical issues are also interspersed with examples from practice.

The book includes questions designed to provoke critical thinking about the readings and stimulate class discussion. The text is practical, while grounded in theory, and lawyer-focused, but enriched by interdisciplinary knowledge. Accompanying role-plays allow students to apply the readings and bring the text material to life. These role-plays again center largely on the types of disputes in which students are likely to find themselves as practicing lawyers — cases with significant legal claims, as opposed to neighborhood quarrels or purely personal conflicts. There is also a comprehensive bibliography to give readers access to a variety of writings by scholars in the field.

This is the first mediation book to include video as an integral part of the teaching materials. Instructors receive a two-hour "Teaching DVD" that contains eighteen professionally filmed video excerpts. The selections are drawn from the authors' own work, as well as from leading mediation videos. The excerpts show experienced lawyers and neutrals performing in some of the same role-plays featured in the teaching materials, which allows students to see how experienced professionals deal with the same challenges that they face.

We begin the book with an overview of the disputing universe. It shows that actual legal disputes, unlike the appellate cases that characterize first-year texts, are not preordained or neatly packaged. Instead, they arise as aspects of a near-endless universe of human conflict. Because mediation is a process of assisted negotiation, we next provide readings that explain the basic concepts of bargaining, analyze choices of style, and present a framework for effective negotiation. Part I of the book concludes with a chapter devoted to the strategic, cognitive, and emotional barriers that often make settlement difficult, creating an intellectual backdrop for our exploration of how mediation can assist the settlement process.

Part II, on mediation technique, begins with examples of mediation in action, then goes on to describe the principal styles of commercial mediation that lawyers are likely to encounter, as well as no-caucus and transformative approaches. We then examine the mediation process itself in depth, covering both traditional and alternative models and focusing on the methods mediators use to deal with process, emotional, and merits-based barriers.

Perhaps the most practical section of the book is Part III, which focuses on how lawyers can represent clients in mediation. This unit is based on the authors' extensive experience in conducting commercial and family mediations. Contrary to the image presented in some texts, we begin from the premise that commercial mediators commonly do in fact exercise "power" in legal mediation. We argue that this phenomenon presents both a challenge and an opportunity for lawyers, since they can enhance their bargaining effectiveness by drawing on their neutral's influence. We describe, again with numerous case examples, how good lawyers can become active participants in mediation, enlisting mediators to overcome common barriers to settlement and achieve a client's goals.

In Part IV we analyze policy issues in mediation, including its impact on the development of the law and its use in situations where a disputant may be disadvantaged by culture, gender, or spousal violence. We also analyze ethical issues, seeking to bring general principles to life for class discussion by presenting issues encountered by practicing lawyers and neutrals.

Finally, the book examines how mediation is applied in specific contexts, ranging from court-connected programs and family disputes to victim-offender reconciliations and international cases. We conclude with a look at how students entering practice are likely to see mediation evolve.

We have deliberately chosen very recent writings on mediation so that teachers will not need to prepare supplements in order to assign entirely up-to-date material. Readings have been carefully edited to keep the material interesting and lively. We also take advantage of new technology and of students' increasing preference for electronic and video formats. Items that have traditionally gone into a paper appendix now appear on the book's Web site. This makes the book easier to carry without sacrificing depth, allows readers to download specific rules or laws for discussion or study, and permits us to update the book's appendix between editions as new rules and standards are promulgated.

A note about form: In order to focus discussion and conserve space, we have substantially edited the readings and have deleted most footnotes, references, and case citations. Deletions of material are shown by three dots, but omitted footnotes and other references are not indicated. The footnotes we have retained in excerpts carry their original numbers, while our own footnotes appear with either asterisks or sequential numbering, as appropriate.

This book is the culmination of our combined decades of teaching, practicing, and shaping dispute resolution in legal contexts. Although our formal acknowledgments follow, we are grateful to the many students and lawyers we have had the pleasure of teaching and from whom we have learned much about what works in a dispute resolution text.

April 2006

D.G.
J.F.

ACKNOWLEDGMENTS

This mediation book evolved from our comprehensive coursebook, *Resolving Disputes: Theory, Practice, and Law*, which we wrote with Lisa Kloppenberg and Thomas Stipanowich. This book has grown to become a text of its own, but it would not exist without Lisa and Tom's collaboration in creating the survey text. We are grateful for their continuing encouragement and friendship. We benefited from their enthusiasm for this project, and we look forward to partnering with them in the future.

We are thankful for the support and assistance we have each received from the staffs and librarians of the law schools at Suffolk University and the University of San Francisco, especially from Diane D'Angelo and Richard Buckingham. Special thanks go to the anonymous reviewers, whose comments on the draft text were insightful and very helpful in refining the contents of this book. We are most grateful to the students and lawyers whom we have trained and worked with in mediation. They have inspired us and guided what we have selected here to present to the next generation of lawyers.

Finally, we are indebted to the many authors and publishers who have granted their permission for us to edit and include parts of their publications. More specifically, we thank the following sources for permission to publish excerpts of their work:

Aaron, Marjorie C., At First Glance: Maximizing the Mediator's Initial Contact, 20 Alternatives 167, 184 (2002). Copyright © 2002. Reprinted with permission of John Wiley & Sons, Inc.

Aaron, Marjorie C., Mediation Practice Do's and Don'ts (2001). Reprinted with permission of the author.

Aaron, Marjorie Corman, and David P. Hoffer, Decision Analysis as a Method of Evaluating the Trial Alternative, in Dwight Golann, Mediating Legal Disputes. Copyright © 1996. Reprinted by permission of Dwight Golann.

Abramson, Harold, Mediation Representation: Advocating in a Problem-Solving Process. Copyright © 2004 by the National Institute for Trial Advocacy (NITA). Reprinted with permission from the National Institute for Trial Advocacy. Further reproduction is prohibited.

Ambrose, Stephen E. Reprinted with permission of Simon & Schuster Adult Publishing Group from Undaunted Courage: Meriwether Lewis, Thomas Jefferson, and the Opening of the American West by Stephen E. Ambrose. Copyright © 1996 by Ambrose-Tubbs, Inc.

Arnold, Thomas, Client Preparation for Mediation, 15 Corporate Counsel Quarterly 52 (April 1999). Copyright 1999. Reprinted by permission of the author.

Arnold, Tom, "20 Common Errors in Mediation Advocacy," 13 Alternatives 69 (1995). Copyright © 1995. Reprinted with permission of John Wiley & Sons, Inc.

Dawson, Roger. Reprinted, with permission of the publisher, from Secrets of Power Negotiating, 2nd ed. © 2001 Roger Dawson. Published by Career Press, Franklin Lakes, NJ. All rights reserved.

Delgado, Richard, "ADR and the Dispossessed: Recent Books About the Deformalization Movement," 13 Law & Soc. Inquiry 145. Copyright © 1988 by University of Chicago Press. Reprinted with permission.

Donahey, M. Scott, "The Asian Concept of Conciliator/Arbitrator: Is It Translatable to the Western World?" 10 Foreign Investment L.J. 120 (1995). Reprinted with permission.

Dunnigan, Alana, Comment — Restoring Power to the Powerless: The Need to Reform California's Mandatory Mediation for Victims of Domestic Violence, 37 USF L. Rev. 1031-1053 (2003) Copyright 2003. Reprinted by permission.

Fisher, Roger, William Ury, and Bruce Patton, "Getting to Yes." From Getting to Yes 2nd ed. by Roger Fisher, William Ury, and Bruce Patton. Copyright © 1981, 1991 by Roger Fisher and William Ury. Reprinted by permission of Houghton Mifflin Company. All rights reserved.

Fisher, Tom, "Advice by Any Other Name..." 29 Conflict Resolution Quarterly 107 (2001).

Fiss, Owen M., "Against Settlement." Reprinted by permission of The Yale Law Journal Company and William S. Hein Company from The Yale Law Journal, Vol. 93, pp. 1073-1090.

Folberg, Jay, et al., "Mediation and Domestic Abuse." Divorce and Family Mediation. Copyright 2004. Reprinted with permission of The Guilford Press.

Folberg, Jay, et al., "Transformative Mediation Principles and Practices in Divorce Mediation," in Divorce and Family Mediation. Copyright 2004. Reprinted with permission of The Guilford Press.

Freedman, Lawrence R., and Michael L. Prigoff, "Confidentiality in Mediation: The Need for Protection," Ohio St. J. Disp. Resol. 2 37-38. Copyright 1986. Reprinted by permission.

Friedman, Gary, and Jack Himmelstein, "Choosing Mediation," in A Guide to Divorce Mediation by Gary Freidman and Jack Himmelstein. Copyright 2005, Workman Publishers. Reprinted by permission of the authors.

Friedman, Gary J., and Himmelstein, Jack, "The Heart of Mediation: Resolving Conflict Through Understanding." Copyright 2006. Reprinted by permission of the authors.

Galanter, Marc, "Reading the Landscapes Disputes: What We Know and Don't Know (And Think We Know) About Our Allegedly Contentious and Litigious Society," 31 UCLA L. Rev. 4. Copyright 1983. Reprinted by permission of the author.

Golann, Dwight, "A Basic Mediative Strategy," in Mediating Legal Disputes. Copyright © 1986 Dwight Golann. Reprinted with permission.

Golann, Dwight, "Cognitive Barriers to Effective Negotiation," ADR Currents 6, 6 (September 2001). Copyright 2001. Reprinted by permission.

Golann, Dwight, "The Death of a Claim: Loss Reactions in Bargaining," 20 Negot. J. 539 (2004). Copyright 2004. Reprinted by permission of Blackwell Publishers.

Golann, H. Scarlett, and Dwight Golann, "Why Is It Hard for Lawyers to Deal with Emotional Issues?" by H. Scarlett & D. Golann, published in Dispute Resolution, Volume 9, No. 2, Winter 2003. © 2003 by the American Bar Association.

Goodpaster, Gary, "A Primer on Competitive Bargaining" J. Disp. Resol. 325,342-344, 375-377. Copyright 1996. Reprinted by permission of Gary Goodpaster.

Green, Eric, and Jonathan Marks, "How We Mediated the Microsoft Case," Boston Globe. Copyright © 2001 by Globe Newspaper Co. (MA). Reproduced with permission of Globe Newspaper Co. (MA) in the format Textbook via Copyright Clearance Center.

Grillo, Tina, "The Mediation Alternative. Reprinted by permission of The Yale Law Journal Company and William S. Hein Company from The Yale Law Journal, Vol. 100, pp. 1545-1610.

Hagar the Horrible cartoon. Copyright © 2000 King Feature Syndicate. Reprinted by permission.

Haynes, John, Mediating Divorce: Casebook of Strategies for Successful Family Negotiation. Copyright © 1989. Reprinted with permission of John Wiley & Sons, Inc.

Hermann, Michele, "New Mexico Research Examines Impact of Gender and Ethnicity in Mediation," published in Disp. Resol. Mag. Vol. 1 Fall 1994. © 1994 by the American Bar Association. Reprinted by permission.

Hughes, Scott H., "A Closer Look: The Case for a Mediation Confidentiality Privilege Still Has Not Been Made," published in Disp. Resol. Mag. Vol. 5, Winter 1998. © 1998 by the American Bar Association. Reprinted by permission.

Keating, J. Michael, "Mediating in the Dance for Dollars," 14 Alternatives 71 (Summer 1996). Copyright © 1996. Reprinted with permission of John Wiley & Sons, Inc.

Kichaven, Jeffrey, "How Advocacy Fits in Effective Mediation," 17 Alternatives 60 (1999). Copyright © 1999. Reprinted with permission of John Wiley & Sons, Inc.

Laflin, James, and Robert Werth, "Unfinished Business: Another Look at the Microsoft Mediation: Lessons for the Civil Litigator," 12 Cal. Tort Rep. 88-92 (April 2001). Copyright 2001. Reprinted by permission of James Laflin.

Lax, David A., and James K. Sebenius. Reprinted with the permission of The Free Press, a Division of Simon & Schuster Adult Publishing Group, from The Manager as Negotiator: Bargaining for Cooperation and Competitive Gain by David A. Lax and James K. Sebenius. Copyright © 1986 by David A. Lax and James K. Sebenius. All rights reserved.

Lieberman, Jethro K., and James F. Henry, "Lessons from the Alternative Dispute Resolution Movement." University of Chicago Law Review by Lieberman & Henry. Copyright 1986 by University of Chicago Law School. Reproduced by permission of University of Chicago Law School in format Textbook via Copyright Clearance Center.

Levin, Arnie. Cartoon. © The New Yorker Collection 1982 Arnie Levin from http://cartoonbank.com. All rights Reserved.

Lipsky, David B., and Ronald L. Seeber, "Patterns of ADR Use in Corporate Disputes," *Dispute Resolution Journal* 54,66 (February 1999). Copyright 1999. Reprinted by permission of the American Arbitration Association.

Love, Lela P., "The Top Ten Reasons Why Mediators Should Not Evaluate," Florida State University Law Review 24,937-948 (1997). Copyright © 1997. Reprinted by permission of The Florida State University Law Review.

Lowry, L. Randolph, "To Evaluate or Not — That Is the Question!" 2 Resolutions 2 (Pepperdine University) (Winter 1997). Copyright 1997. Reprinted by permission of the author.

McGuire, James E., "Certification: An Idea Whose Time Has Come," published in Disp. Resol. Mag. Vol. 10 Summer 2004 © 2004 American Bar Association. Reprinted by permission.

Menkel-Meadow, Carrie, "Toward Another View of Legal Negotiation," UCLA Law Review 31:754-841. Copyright 1984. Reprinted by permission of Carrie Menkel-Meadow.

Mnookin, Robert H., "Why Negotiations Fail: An Exploration of Barriers to the Resolution of Conflict," Ohio St. J. Disp. Resol. 8 235-43, 238-49. Copyright 1993. Reprinted by permission.

Mnookin, Robert H., Scott R. Peppet, and Andrew S. Tulumello. Reprinted by permission of the publisher from Beyond Winning: Negotiating to Create Value in Deals and Disputes by Robert H. Mnookin, Scott R. Peppet, and Andrew S. Tulumello, pp. 37-43, Cambridge, MA: The Belknap Press of Harvard University Press, Copyright © 2000 by the President and Fellows of Harvard College.

Nelken, Melissa. Excerpted from Understanding Negotiation, with permission. Copyright 2001 Matthew Bender & Company, Inc., a member of the LexisNexis Group. All rights reserved.

O'Connor, Theron, Planning and Executing an Effective Concession Strategy. Reprinted with permission of the author.

Olivella, Miguel A., Jr., "Toro's Early Intervention Program, After Six Years, Has Saved $50 M," 17 Alternatives 81 (1999).

Peppet, Scott R., "Contract Formation in Imperfect Markets: Should We Use Mediators in Deals?" Ohio St. J. on Disp. Resol. 38:283. Copyright 2004. Reprinted by permission.

Price, Marty, "Personalizing Crime: Mediation Produces Restorative Justice for Victims and Offenders," published in Disp. Resol. Mag., Vol. 7, Fall 2000 © 2000 by the American Bar Association. Reprinted with permission.

Reno, Janet. This excerpt from "The Federal Government and Appropriate Dispute Resolution: Promoting Problem Solving and Peacemaking as Enduring Values in Our Society" is reprinted from Into the 21st Century: Thought Pieces on Lawyering, Problem Solving and ADR, 19 Alternatives 16 (January 2001). Copyright © 2001. Reprinted with permission of John Wiley & Sons, Inc.

Riskin, Leonard, "Retiring and Replacing the Grid of Mediator Orientations," 21 Alternatives to the High Costs of Litigation 69 (April 2003). Copyright © 2003. Reprinted with permission of John Wiley & Sons, Inc.

Rosenberg, Joshua D., "Interpersonal Dynamics: Helping Lawyers Learn the Skills, and the Importance of Human Relationships in the Practice of Law," University of Miami Law Review, 55 1225-83. Copyright 2004. Reprinted by permission.

Ross, David S., "Strategic Considerations in Choosing a Mediator: A Mediator's Perspective," 2 J. Alt. Disp. Res. in Emp. 7 (Spring 2000). Copyright 2000. Reprinted by permission of CCH, Inc.

Rule, Colin, Online Dispute Resolution for Business: B2B, Ecommerce, Consumer, Employment, Insurance, and Other Commercial Conflicts. Copyright © 2002. Reprinted with permission of John Wiley & Sons, Inc.

Rummel, R.J., The Conflict Helix. Copyright © 1991 by Transaction Publishers. Reprinted with permission.

Salem, Richard, "Emphatic Listening." Beyond Intractability. Eds. Guy Burgess and Heidi Burgess. Conflict Research Consortium, University of Colorado, Boulder. Posted July 2003, http://www.beyondintractability.org/essay/emphatic_listening.

Shell, G. Richard, "The Second Foundation: Your Goals and Expectations," from Bargaining for Advantage by G. Richard Shell, copyright © 1999 by G. Richard Shell. Used by permission of Viking Penguin, a division of Penguin Group (USA) Inc.

Shell, G. Richard, "Step Four: Closing and Gaining Commitment," from Bargaining for Advantage by G. Richard Shell, copyright © 1999 by G. Richard Shell. Used by permission of Viking Penguin, a division of Penguin Group (USA) Inc.

Smith, Robert M., "Advocacy in Mediation: A Dozen Suggestions," 26 San Francisco Att'y 14 (June/July 2000). Copyright © 2000 by the Bar Association of San Francisco. Reprinted with permission.

Steinstra, Donna, "Demonstrating the Possibilities of Providing Mediation Early and by Court Staff," published in Court-Annexed Mediation: Critical Perspectives on State and Federal Programs. © 1998 American Bar Association. Reprinted by permission

Technology Mediation Services, "High Tech and Intellectual Property Disputes." Reprinted by permission of Technology Mediation Services, LLC.

Welsh, Nancy A., "Making Deals in Court-Connected Mediation: What's Justice Got to Do with It?" 79 Wash U. Law Q. 787, 817-26 (2001). Copyright 2001. Reprinted by permission.

Welsh, Nancy A., and Barbara McAdoo, "Alternative Dispute Resolution in Minnesota — An Update on Rule 114," published in Court-Annexed Mediation: Critical Perspectives on State and Federal Programs, pp. 203-212. © 1998 American Bar Association. Reprinted by permission.

Wissler, Roselle P., "To Evaluate or Facilitate? Parties' Perceptions of Mediation Affected by Mediator Style," published in Disp. Resol. Mag. Vol 7, Winter 2001. © 2001 by the American Bar Association. Reprinted by permission.

Wittenberg, Carol A., Susan T. Mackenzie, and Margaret L. Shaw, "Employment Disputes," in Dwight Golann, Mediating Legal Disputes, pp. 441-456 (1996). Copyright 1996. Reprinted by permission.

PART
I

INTRODUCTION

CHAPTER
1

The Origins of Disputes

"I found the old format much more exciting."

Legend has it that the use of lawyers in court evolved from disputants hiring gladiators to fight in their place. Referring to lawyers as "modern-day gladiators" is, however, a misnomer. It is the parties who bear most of the costs, risks, and injuries of modern legal combat. Today people have options to resolve disputes other than traditional litigation, and to advise and represent clients successfully, lawyers must be skilled in using these techniques. The adage that, to someone with only a hammer, everything looks like a nail suggests the limitations of an attorney who only knows how to litigate or a gladiator who knows only how to fight. The purpose of this book is to provide the knowledge to counsel clients about an increasingly popular alternative to legal combat — mediation — as well as the ability to represent clients effectively in the mediation process.

A. The Nature of Disputing in America

Most of the disputes that clients will bring you will barely resemble the cases you encountered in your first-year courses in law school. In place of a clearly defined contest between named parties over narrow issues, practicing lawyers typically deal with inchoate mixtures of grievances, emotions, and justifications. Clients are usually clear about the heroes and villains in their disputes, but many of the other key facts are in doubt. Lacking a precise appellate record, attorneys typically work with, and must make decisions based on, witnesses with fallible memories and documents that are incomplete. In many situations, lawyers must rely heavily on experience and intuition to assess what a client's dispute is really about and how it may unfold in court.

The disputes that you encounter in practice will depend on the path you choose. If you become a transactional lawyer, you will help clients to evaluate and structure potential deals and then will be called on to negotiate terms that give them the greatest advantages and least possible risk. Clients will respect you for steering them away from conflict and will value your ability to bring disparate parties together into productive agreements and deal with the disagreements that are inevitable in any long-term relationship. Knowing when and how to use mediation to accomplish this will distinguish you as a lawyer.

If you become an inside counsel to a corporation or nonprofit organization, you will negotiate regularly as well, both with your counterparts in other entities and with colleagues in your own office. You may be surprised to learn that experienced corporate counsel operate not only as constant negotiators, but also at times as "Mediators with a small 'm'." What this means is that many find that a major aspect of their work is to resolve disagreements and disputes between people within their organization. Inside lawyers often find that they in fact have multiple "clients," in the form of different personalities and constituencies within their company. Unless their constituencies can agree on a common course of action, it is very difficult for attorneys to produce a coherent legal policy or negotiate effectively with outsiders. Corporate lawyers thus often find themselves playing the role of "honest broker," using mediative skills to forge a consensus among their multidimensional clients.

Even if you assume the traditional role of civil litigator, the disputing landscape you encounter will bear little resemblance to the case law in the typical law school textbook. First, clients seldom know the precise issue that must be resolved, the opposing arguments, or the remedies available to them. Second, most of the disputes that clients bring to litigators never become court cases. Good lawyers perform an important screening function, measuring their client's grievances against the requirements of the law and, perhaps even more critically, the client's larger interests.

Does the client have a viable legal theory? Will discovery produce factual evidence that supports his argument? Will the client be willing to persevere after his initial anger and frustration have died down, and does he have the resources to do so? Is it even in the client's long-term interest to be involved in litigation? Is a court likely to side with him, and, if it does, will the potential defendant be able to satisfy a judgment? Just as very few screenplays ever become movies, the large majority of potential legal cases fall by the wayside long before they reach a courtroom!

Indeed, the rate of trial in the United States is very small, and the absolute number of trials is declining. Of all civil cases filed in the federal court system, less than 2 percent actually reach trial. Trial rates in state courts are substantially higher, but in 2002 still averaged only 16 percent. Even allowing for cases that are decided on the merits without a trial, for example through motions for summary judgment, *the large majority of civil cases are never adjudicated on the merits*. Indeed professional legal groups, as well as scholars, are debating the causes and implications of what has come to be called "the vanishing trial" (see, e.g., Galanter 2004; Lande 2005).

There is an important qualification when considering the small percentage of disputes that are adjudicated. The possibility of going to trial has an impact on the decisions of litigants that is out of proportion to the actual frequency of courtroom decisions. The wish to avoid the "fire" of trial is a major factor in motivating parties to choose the "frying pan" of settlement. In other words, we bargain in the "shadow of the law" (Mnookin and Kornhauser 1979). Decisions about whether, and on what terms, to settle a dispute are thus heavily influenced by predictions and concerns about what a court will do if an agreement is not reached.

B. How Disputes Arise

Where do legal disputes come from, and what determines whether a potential legal claim ever reaches a lawyer's desk? In the excerpt that follows, Professor Marc Galanter discusses how individual grievances may or may not ripen into disputes, and how only a small proportion of disputes ever become legal cases, in a process that he calls the "dispute pyramid."

❖ Marc S. Galanter, Reading the Landscape of Disputes: What We Know and Don't Know (and Think We Know) About Our Allegedly Contentious and Litigious Society

31 UCLA L. Rev. 4, 12-20, 22-27 (1983)

1. The Lower Layers: The Construction of Disputes

...Disputes are not discrete events like births or deaths; they are more like...illnesses and friendships, composed in part of the perceptions and understandings of those who participate in and observe them. Disputes are drawn from a vast sea of events, encounters, collisions, rivalries, disappointments, discomforts and injuries. The span and composition of that sea depend on the broad contours of social life. For example, the introduction of machinery brings increases in non-intentional injuries; higher population densities and cash crops bring raised expectations and rivalry for scarce land; advances in knowledge enlarge possibilities of control and expectations of care. Some things in this sea of "proto-disputes" become disputes through a process in which injuries are perceived, persons or institutions responsible for remedying them are identified, forums for presenting these claims are located and approached, claims are formulated acceptably to the forum, appropriate resources are invested, and attempts at diversion resisted. The disputes that arrive at courts can be seen as the survivors of a long and exhausting process. In this view, the arrival of matters at the doors of lawyers and courts is a late stage in an extended process by which the dispute has crystallized out of the sea of proto-disputes....

We can visualize the early stages of the process as the successive layers of a vast and uneven pyramid. A pioneering inquiry by Felstiner, Abel and Sarat (1981) provides a useful conceptual map of these lower reaches. We begin, in effect, with all human experience which might be identified as injurious. This should alert us to the subjective and unstable character of the process, for what is injurious depends on current and ever-changing estimations of what enhances or impairs health, happiness, character and other desired states. Knowledge and ideology constantly send new currents through this vast ocean.

Some experiences will be perceived as injurious. (Felstiner et al. call these *perceived injurious experiences*.) Among these perceived injurious experiences, some may be seen as deserved punishment, some as the result of assumed risk or fickle fate[,] but a subset is viewed as violations of some right or entitlement caused by a human agent (individual or collective) and susceptible of remedy. These, in Felstiner's terminology[,] are *grievances*. Again, characterization of an event as a grievance will depend on the cognitive repertoire with which society supplies the injured person and his idiosyncratic adaptation of it. He may, for example, be liberally supplied with ideological lenses to focus blame or to diffuse it. When such grievances are voiced to the offending party they become *claims*. Many will be granted. Those claims not granted become *disputes*. That is, a dispute exists when a claim based on a grievance is rejected in whole or in part. Using this terminology lets us attempt a crude sketch of the lower layers of the pyramid.

First, a very large number of injuries go unperceived. Breaches of product warranties and professional malpractice may be difficult to recognize and go undiscovered. Even if the injury is discovered, the injured may not perceive that he has an entitlement that has been violated, the identity of the responsible party, or the presence of the remedy to be pursued. The perception of grievances requires cognitive resources. Thus [one study] found that both higher income and white households perceive more problems with the goods they buy and complain more both to sellers and to third parties than do poor or black households. It seems unlikely that this reflects differences in the quality of the goods purchased. Similarly, . . . better educated respondents experience more problems of infringement of their constitutional rights.

Even where injuries are perceived, a common response is resignation, that is, "lumping it." In the most comprehensive study available, Miller and Sarat (1981) report that over one-quarter of those with reported "middle range" (i.e., involving the equivalent of $1,000 or more[1]) grievances did not pursue

---

1. *Note:* The $1,000 threshold in the Miller and Sarat study would be roughly $2,400 today. To arrive at the current equivalent of the dollar numbers quoted in this reading, multiply by 2.4. — Eds.

the matter by making a claim. This proportion was fairly uniform across subject matters (with the striking exception of discrimination problems; almost three-quarters did not move from grievance to claim). Of course this figure is not a precise measure of the phenomen[on] of "lumping it" because it may include individuals who took other forms of unilateral action — like exit, avoidance or self-help. . . . Also, some populations have a higher proclivity for "lumping it": e.g., low income consumers. . . . "Lumping it" is done not only by naive victims who lack information about or access to remedies, but also by those who knowingly decide that the gain is too low, or the cost too high, including the psychic costs of pursuing the claim . . .

Exit and avoidance — withdrawal from a situation or relationship by ~~Exit~~ moving, resigning, severing relations, etc. — are common responses to many kinds of troubles. Like "lumping it," exit is an alternative to invoking any kind of organized remedy system, although its presence as a sanction may support the working of other remedies. The use of "exit" options depends on a number of factors: on the availability of alternative opportunities or partners and information about them; on bearable costs of withdrawal, transfer, relocation, and development of new relationships; on the pull of loyalty to previous arrangements; and on the availability and cost of other remedies. Disputes are also pursued by various kinds of self-help such as physical retaliation, seizure of property, or removal of offending objects. The amount of self-help in contemporary industrial societies has not been mapped, but it evidently occurs very frequently. [S]tudies portray self-help as a major component of disputing in American neighborhoods.

The most typical response to grievances, at least to sizable ones, is to make a claim to the "other party" — the merchant, the other driver or his insurer, the ex-spouse who has not paid support, etc. Thus, Miller and Sarat found that over 70% of those who experienced "middle range" grievances made claims for redress. Aggrieved consumers make claims in about the same proportion. Some claims may be granted outright, but a large number are contested in whole or part. It is this contest that Felstiner labels a dispute. Miller and Sarat found that about two-thirds of claims lead to disputes. A large portion of disputes are resolved by negotiation between the parties. Almost half of the disputes in the Miller and Sarat survey ended in "agreement after difficulty" which I take as indicating the occurrence of negotiation. "Negotiation" ranges from that which is indistinguishable from the everyday adjustments that constitute the relationship to that which is "bracketed" as a disruption or emergency.

Some disputes are abandoned by their initiators. [A study that] coined the term "clumpit" for those who make a claim but don't persist, found that more than one-quarter of all consumers with problems abandoned their claims. Similarly, a study of medical malpractice claims found that 43% were dropped without receiving any payment.

Other disputes are heard by the school principal, the shop steward or the administrator — i.e., in forums that are part of the social setting within which the dispute arose. Such "embedded forums" range from those which are hardly distinguishable from the everyday decision making within an institution ("I'd like to see the manager") to those which are specially constituted to handle disputes which cannot be resolved by everyday processes. We know that such forums process a tremendous number of disputes. We have no count of them, but we do have some idea of the conditions under which they flourish. Resort to embedded forums is encouraged where there are continuing relations between the disputants....

These data about disputing are taken from surveys of individuals or households. They tell us about the grievances, claims, and disputes of individuals in their non-business capacities (i.e., as householder, consumer, citizen, spouse, neighbor, etc.) but not in their business or professional lives. There are other disputants: businesses, organizations and units of government. We have an even dimmer picture of their patterns of disputing...

2. The Upper Layers: Lawyers and Courts

The pyramid imagery imparts to the process of dispute construction and transformation a stability and a solidity that are illusory. Changes in perceptions of harm, in attributions of responsibility, in expectations of redress, in readiness to be assertive — all of these affect the number of grievances, claims and disputes. New activities, based on new technologies, and new knowledge may change notions of causal agency. Some parts of the pyramid are more solid than others. In matters like automobile accident claims and post-divorce disputes, there are many cues about how to perceive the problems: it is "common knowledge" how to proceed; social support for complaining is readily forthcoming; there are occupational specialists ready to receive the matter and pursue it on a routine and standardized basis. Other parts are more volatile and shifting.

We can imagine a frontier of perceived grievances moving over time. As the span of human control expands[,] so do attempts to extend accountability. Claims for compensation for rainfall from cloud seeding and "wrongful birth" claims are examples of the growing edges of the world of dispute, where the borders between fate, self-blame, and specific or shared human responsibility are blurred and disputed. These areas of blurring and contest are eventually resolved. But it should be noted that the area of recognized disputes contracts as well as expands. Claims may become subject to routine reimbursement and removed from the disputing process. Other sorts of claims may lose their standing, such as claims to honor or racial superiority, or claims to privacy by officials.

As we trace the movement of disputes up the pyramid and laterally from one forum to another, it is useful to recall that the dispute does not remain unchanged in the process. The disputes that come to courts originate elsewhere and may undergo considerable change in the course of entering and proceeding through the courts. Disputes must be reformulated in applicable legal categories. Such reformulation may restrict their scope. Diffuse disputes may become more focused in time and space, narrowed down to a set of discrete incidents involving specified individuals. Or, conversely, the original dispute may expand, becoming the vehicle for consideration of a larger set of events or relationships. The list of parties may grow or shrink; the range of normative claims may be narrowed or expanded; the remedy sought may change; the goals and audiences of the parties may alter. In short[,] the dispute that emerges in the court process may differ significantly from the dispute that arrived there, as well as from "similar" disputes that proceed through other settings.

Lawyers are often viewed as important agents of this transformation process. They help translate clients' disputes to fit into applicable legal categories. But lawyers may also act as gatekeepers, screening out claims that they are disinclined to pursue. [A Wisconsin study of the handling of consumer disputes] found that lawyers tended to defuse consumer claims, diverting them into mediative channels rather than translating them into adversary claims. Those disputes that are not resolved by negotiation or in some embedded forum may be taken to a champion or a forum external to the situation. Recourse to any such third party is relatively infrequent across the whole range of disputes. [A Milwaukee study] found that the proportion of problems that were taken to any third party was 3%.... As stakes increase, so does resort to third parties.... Yet for a very large portion of the population (47% of non-users; 40% of multiple users) lawyers are regarded as a last resort that should not be used until one has "exhausted every other possible way of solving the problem."

Some of those who consult lawyers, as well as a few who don't, get to court. Miller and Sarat report that about 11% of disputants (approximately 9% when those with post-divorce problems are excluded) took their middle range disputes to court.... In the mostly smaller consumer disputes...the use of courts virtually disappears. Overall, 9% of American adults report having had experience in a major civil court and 14% in a minor civil court. This includes parties, witnesses, jurors, and observers....

There may be very little use of litigation to adjust relations among whole classes of major organizational actors such as large manufacturing corporations, financial institutions, educational and cultural institutions, political parties, etc. Macaulay found manufacturers reluctant to intrude litigation into relationships with their customers and suppliers.... Such potential suitors can afford, and are likely to make extensive use of, skilled professional help to channel their affairs so as to prevent trouble. Similarly, when trouble emerges, they are likely to be equipped to make sophisticated choices of alternatives to litigation to resolve difficulties through bargaining, mediation or arbitration....

Like other kinds of remedy-seeking, litigation requires information and skills. Complaints to all third parties come disproportionately from the better educated, better informed and more politically active households.... In order to understand the distribution of litigation, we must go beyond the characteristics of individual parties to consider the relations between them. Are the parties strangers or intimates? Is their relationship episodic or enduring? Is it single-stranded or multiplex?

In the American setting, litigation tends to be between parties who are strangers. Either they never had a mutually beneficial continuing relationship, as in the typical automobile injury case, or their relationship — marital, commercial, or organizational — is ruptured. In either case, there is no anticipated future relationship. In the American setting, unlike some others, resort to litigation is viewed as an irreparable breach of the relationship. However, where parties are locked into a relationship with no chance of exit, such as divorced parents, or inmates and institutional managers, litigation may proceed side-by-side with the continuation of that relationship...

3. The Litigation Process: Attrition, Routine Processing, Bargaining and Settlement

Of those disputes which are taken to court, the vast majority are disposed of by abandonment, withdrawal, or settlement, without full-blown adjudication and often without any authoritative disposition by the court. In fact, of those cases that do reach a full authoritative disposition by a court, a large portion does not involve a contest. They are uncontested either because the dispute has been resolved, as in divorce, or because only one party appears. Over 30% of cases in American courts of general jurisdiction are not formally contested. This predominance of uncontested matters in American courts is long-standing.

Many cases are withdrawn or abandoned because the mere invocation of the court served the initiator's purpose of harassment, warning or delay. . . . The official system may be invoked, or invocation may be threatened, in order to punish or harass, to demonstrate prowess, to force an opponent to settle, or to secure compliance with the decision of another forum. The master pattern of American disputing is one in which there is actual or threatened invocation of an authoritative decision maker. This is countered by a threat of protracted or hard-fought resistance, leading to a negotiated or mediated settlement, often in the anteroom of the adjudicative institution.

Questions

1. Have you ever been asked by a family member, friend, or neighbor to give advice about a potential legal claim? Did you see a legal issue? What advice did you give, and what did your "client" do?
2. Can you think of an example of a situation in which someone might suffer a legal injury but not realize that he has been injured?
3. Can you think of a situation in which someone realizes that he has been injured, but cannot identify the perpetrator? Or knows that he has a potential claim and can identify the likely defendant, but nevertheless decides to "lump it"?
4. Do you know of situations in which a case appears to have been brought for a purpose other than obtaining a court judgment? What was the apparent purpose?
5. During your childhood, how did your family deal with conflict? Do you think that your upbringing has in any way influenced your own instinctive response to disputes? In what ways?

C.   The Spectrum of Dispute Resolution Options

Assuming a dispute develops far enough to reach your desk as a practicing lawyer, what options will you have to deal with it? In fact, attorneys can use a variety of processes to achieve their clients' goals. The most common options fall along a spectrum that appears in Figure 1. At one end is direct negotiation, at the other a court trial.

Figure 1.
Dispute Resolution Spectrum

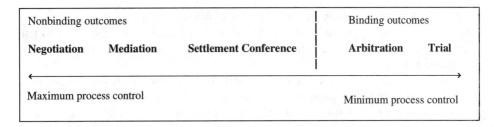

Negotiation and trial are polar opposites. Parties who opt for trial have relatively little control over either the process or the outcome: The proceeding is a formal and public one, conducted under detailed procedural and evidentiary rules, with a judge in control. A third party — either a judge or jury — decides the outcome and in doing so is bound to follow established legal principles. By contrast, the process at the other end of the spectrum — negotiation — gives parties maximum control over both the process and its outcome. Direct bargaining is an informal process, generally conducted in private and without set rules. Parties are free to agree to whatever outcomes they wish, subject to the limits of contract law and public policy if they seek to enforce their agreement.

In between direct negotiation and trial is a continuum of alternative dispute resolution (ADR) processes. The continuum moves from processes that have characteristics very similar to negotiation to ones that closely resemble a trial. Mediators, for example, assist negotiators in reaching a settlement but do not have the power to require disputants to reach agreement or to impose a decision on them. For that reason, mediation is on the nonbinding side of the spectrum. Judicial settlement conferences are also nonbinding, but as conducted by some judicial officers they take on a coercive, "arm-twisting" tone that makes them less than completely voluntary. Other processes, such as neutral evaluation, are also available but have become less popular than mediation in recent years.

On the other side of the divide are binding processes. In arbitration, a third-party neutral has the power to decide the outcome over the objection of a party, in essence acting as a private judge. Arbitration permits more party control than a trial; however, because the parties must agree to enter the process and can, within very broad bounds, specify the procedure the arbitrator will follow and the substantive standards on which she will base her decision. Once parties have agreed to arbitrate, however, the arbitrator's decision is fully binding.

There are several other ADR processes that could be put on the nonbinding side of this spectrum, carrying names such as "early neutral evaluation" and "mini-trial." The variety of nonbinding processes is nearly infinite, limited only by what the parties can create, agree upon, and afford. However, mediation has become by far the most popular nonbinding process aside from direct negotiation, and it is the one on which we focus in this book.

D. Conclusion

Given that lawyers have several options for dispute resolution, the challenge is to select the right approach for a particular client's problem and then to use that process effectively. Each ADR process has particular strengths and weaknesses.

Litigation culminating in a trial is still the forum of choice when it is important to know what happened — the availability of evidentiary discovery and examination of witnesses at trial are designed to find historical truth. Adjudication can provide a party with a court order to enforce a financial obligation or compel specific performance of an agreement. Judicial decisions can establish precedent, nurture the growth of the common law, and shape rules of conduct for the future. Lawsuits may also establish social values or rally people behind a principle or a cause. Finally, the litigation process can be used strategically to create the conditions for successful negotiation. Of course the irony is that most of these advantages are potentially a two-way street: Each reason for you to pursue litigation can also be a reason for your opponent to do so. The ultimate curse may be to have a case in which both your client and the other side are sure that they are right and determined to persevere!

Mediation is a more appropriate choice when potential litigation costs are high relative to the amount in controversy, one or both parties cannot bear the risk of an adverse result, or the dispute is time sensitive. It is also likely to be appealing when standard adjudication remedies do not meet the disputants' real needs, the parties want a voice in shaping the final outcome, or confidentiality is a significant consideration. Given the rapidly shrinking number of trials and changes in the legal culture supporting ADR, you are much more likely to represent clients in mediation than at trial. Indeed, an increasing number of lawyers now say that they settle more cases through mediation than through direct negotiation. For that reason, understanding the mediation process, and how to use it effectively on behalf of clients, is important for you, whatever path your career may take.

The most direct and inexpensive path to resolving a dispute, however, remains negotiation, and mediation itself is in essence a process of assisted negotiation. Bargaining is therefore a lawyer's first option for dispute resolution and will form the foundation for our study of mediation. The next two chapters examine the process of negotiation.

CHAPTER
2

An Introduction to Negotiation

Negotiation is the process of communication we use to get something we want, when another person has control over whether or how we can get it. If we could have everything we wished, materially and emotionally, without the concurrence of anyone else, there would be no need to bargain, but because of our interdependence there is a pervasive need to do so. Everyone bargains as part of modern life, and negotiation is at the core of what lawyers do in representing clients.

A. Negotiation Styles and Approaches

Legal negotiators use varying styles and approaches. Lawyer styles correlate closely with their view of the goal of the process — what they are seeking to achieve — and their relationship to others in it — whether the other side is viewed as a partner or opponent. Many terms are used to describe styles of negotiating. For purposes of introducing the process, we focus on two basic categories: competitive and cooperative.

A *competitive* negotiator assumes that the purpose of bargaining is to obtain the best possible result for her client at the expense of the other side. A competitive negotiator is likely to think that the negotiation process involves a limited resource, or fund, that must be distributed between competing parties — in effect, a fixed "pie." She sees this "pie" as consisting primarily, if not exclusively, of money and assumes that a dollar more for her opponent is necessarily a dollar less for her own client. The goal is to pay as little as possible (if a buyer or defendant) or obtain as much as possible (if a seller or plaintiff). From a competitor's perspective the parties' relationships and other intangibles are either absent or relatively unimportant. A competitive bargainer, in other words, sees negotiation much as a litigator sees a trial — someone must win and someone must lose, and the competitor's central mission is to win. This approach is also known as "distributive" or "zero-sum" bargaining, since the negotiators see the task as to distribute a limited resource between them, and as "positional" negotiation, because competitive bargainers tend to trade positions in a gradual progression toward compromise.

An example of a competitive bargaining situation is one in which a lawyer represents a client whose car has been damaged by another motorist. The attorney is bargaining with the insurer of the other driver, and neither bargainer expects to deal with the other in the future. Both sides have an interest in conducting the bargaining process efficiently, but otherwise the lawyer and the adjuster are likely to see their sole goal as to agree on a dollar amount the company will pay the insured to give up his claim. In these circumstances they are likely to assume that a better settlement for one will necessarily be worse for the other.

A *cooperative* bargainer, by contrast, does not view negotiation "pies" as fixed. Cooperative bargainers work to identify interests and examine differences in how the parties value items. They then search jointly with the other negotiator for a solution that will best satisfy both parties' interests. This approach is frequently called "integrative" bargaining, because it emphasizes integrating the parties' needs to find the best joint solution. It is also referred to as "interest-based" or "problem-solving" negotiation, because the participants' goal is to satisfy people's underlying interests, and they see conflict as a problem to be solved rather than as a cause for battle.

A classic situation that calls for cooperative bargaining is an effort by two businesses to form a joint venture. Cooperative bargainers would first ask what special resources and capabilities each partner could bring to the deal (e.g., Does Partner A have special expertise in marketing, while Partner B has more strength in design? Does one have good access to financing, while the other has unused office space?). The negotiators would also ask whether either partner had particular needs, for example, for one an assured stream of income, and for the other cutting-edge technology. Cooperative bargainers would focus on finding terms that best exploit each partner's abilities and minimize weaknesses, creating the strongest possible future partnership.

Cooperative and competitive bargaining are not mutually exclusive: Working to "bake the biggest possible pie" does not, in itself, say how the final pie will be divided. Savvy competitive negotiators, for example, will look earnestly for ways to "expand the pie" and at the same time get the biggest possible piece. Competitors, however, are likely to see pie-expansion as the less important goal. Cooperators, by contrast, would emphasize creating the best deal and then look for a principle that both partners saw as fair to divide the benefits, rather than trying to outfox the other side and get the lion's share. In practice, cooperative and competitive approaches may be mixed or sequenced, depending on the setting, subject matter, and personalities of the negotiators. Still, the concepts of cooperative and competitive styles provide a paradigm for understanding the dynamics of negotiation.

There are important styles of bargaining that go beyond either cooperative or competitive, and which might be seen as more intense versions of each approach. So-called *adversarial* bargainers view negotiation as a kind of war and believe that all is fair in winning it. They are willing, for example, to renege on tentative deals, misrepresent their authority, make empty threats, and lie about facts that cannot be checked, if such tactics seem likely to win them a better outcome.

By contrast, *problem-solving* bargainers employ intensely cooperative tactics. Problem solvers focus almost exclusively on finding solutions that will maximize the value of the deal for both parties. They are extremely reluctant to become involved in trying to obtain a better outcome for their client than the other side and insist on using genuinely neutral principles to accomplish the task of allocating benefits. For simplicity, we will discuss bargaining styles in terms of "cooperative" and "competitive," but will also refer to adversarial and problem-solving techniques.

1. Competitive Approach

❖ Gary Goodpaster, A Primer on Competitive Bargaining
J. Disp. Resol. 325, 342-44, 375-377 (1996)

One cannot understand negotiation without understanding competitive behavior in negotiation. It is not that competing is a good way to negotiate; it may or may not be, depending on the circumstances. Understanding competition in negotiation is important simply because many people do compete when they negotiate, either by choice or happenstance.

In competitive negotiation or distributive bargaining, the parties['] actual or perceived respective aims or goals conflict. In this context, the negotiator's aim is to maximize the realization of its goals. Since the goals conflict, either in fact or supposition, one party's gains are the other party's losses. Therefore, a negotiator's goal is to win by gaining as much value as possible from the other party.... Not only is the competitive negotiator out to gain as much as he or she can, but he or she will take risks, even the risk of non-agreement, to secure a significant gain.

The competitive negotiator adopts a risky strategy which involves the taking of firm, almost extreme positions, making few and small concessions, and withholding information that may be useful to the other party. The intention, and hoped-for effect, behind this basic strategy is to persuade the other party that it must make concessions if it is to get an agreement. In addition to this basic strategy, competitive negotiators may also use various ploys or tactics aimed at pressuring, unsettling, unbalancing or even misleading the other party to secure an agreement with its demands.

In an important sense, the competitive negotiator plays negotiation as an information game. In this game, the object is to get as much information from the other party as possible while disclosing as little information as possible. Alternatively, a competitive negotiator sometimes provides the other party with misleading clues, bluffs, and ambiguous assertions with multiple meanings, which are not actually false, but nevertheless mislead the other party into drawing incorrect conclusions that are beneficial to the competitor.

The information the competitive negotiator seeks is the other party's bottom line. How much he will maximally give or minimally accept to make a deal. On the other hand, the competitive negotiator wants to persuade the other side about the firmness of the negotiator's own asserted bottom line. The competitive negotiator works to convince the other party that it will settle only at some point that is higher (or lower, as the case may be) than its actual and unrevealed bottom line.

In skillful hands the bargaining position performs a double function. It conceals, and it reveals. The bargaining position is used to indicate — to unfold gradually, step by step — the maximum expectation of the negotiator, while at the same time concealing, for as long as necessary, his minimum expectation.

By indirect means, such as the manner and timing of the changes in your bargaining position, you, as a negotiator, try to convince the other side that your maximum expectation is really your minimum breaking-off point....Since you have taken an appropriate bargaining position at the start of negotiations, each change in your position should give ever-clearer indications of your maximum expectation. Also, each change should be designed to encourage or pressure the other side to reciprocate with at least as much information as you give them, if not more.

Taking a firm position and conceding little will incline the other party to think the competitor has little to give. Thus, if there is to be a deal, then the other party must give or concede more.

1. Pure bargaining, haggling, and just trading figures

When the parties are apart and have no reason, other than their mutual choice, to settle at any particular point between them, they are in a "pure bargaining" situation. It is easy to see how the simple negotiation game...can degenerate into a contest of haggling or just trading figures. The parties' positions — the particular dollar figures they are offering — are not connected to any reason or rationale. Basically, both buyer and seller are seeking to maximize gains. Each attempts to accomplish this by seeing how far the other party can be pushed.

Often this happens in competitive bargaining, particularly with unsophisticated competitive bargainers and usually in the late and ending stages of a negotiation. When it occurs, the "take as much as you can" grab is transparent and signals that the parties, or at least one party, is bargaining just to win as much as possible. Automobile dealers' sales practices exemplify this phenomenon. A new car dealer usually pegs an asking price to a manufacturer's suggested retail sticker price and to items the dealer adds to the car. Once those starting prices are left behind, the dealer and buyer usually just trade dollar figures until they reach one they are both comfortable with. Similarly, travelers who visit native markets or bazaars, or those who visit flea markets or garage sales in this country, sometimes experience much the same kind of trading. Offers and counteroffers are thrown back and forth, each party testing the other party's resolve to stick with a figure by refusing to budge further or threatening to walk away. In essence, bargaining in this fashion is really nothing but a contest of firmness or a game of chicken.

2. Focal points or mutually prominent alternatives

It is revealing to analyze a pure bargaining situation where two equally competitive negotiators bargain with each other. Once the bargaining parties have assured their bottom lines or reservation values and have staked out their respective positions on the bargaining range, nothing inherently seems to impel settlement at any particular point between the positions, except each party's expectations regarding what the other side in fact will accept. This is problematic, however, for with each guided by expectations and knowing that the other is too, expectations become compounded. A bargain is struck when somebody makes a final, sufficient concession. Why does he concede? Because he thinks the other will not. "I must concede because he won't. He won't because he thinks I will. He thinks I will because he thinks I think he thinks so. . . ." There is some range of alternative outcomes in which any point is better for both sides than no agreement at all. To insist on any such point is pure bargaining, since one always would take less rather than reach no agreement at all, and since one always can recede if retreat proves necessary to agreement. Yet if both parties are aware of the limits to this range, any outcome is a point from which at least one party would have been willing to retreat and the other knows it! . . .

Because people bargain competitively for various reasons, negotiators and mediators need to understand competition in negotiation in order to respond appropriately. Some people bargain competitively without giving much conscious attention to the matter. Others compete in response to the other party's competitive behavior. In this response, they follow the common pattern that a particular kind of behavior elicits a similar behavior in response. In other words, one party frames the negotiation as a contest, and the other party picks up the competitive cues and behaves accordingly. Further, people naturally incline to competitive bargaining when they are non-trusting. In such situations, in order to avoid putting themselves at risk, non-trusting people act guardedly and adopt elements of the competitive strategy, for example, withholding information or misrepresenting a position. Finally, one can readily imagine ambiguous bargaining situations, in which at least one party is non-trusting, quickly devolving into a competitive negotiation between both parties. The non-trusting party acts defensively, and the other party senses this as competitive behavior and, therefore, acts in a similar fashion.

Negotiators, however, can also consciously adopt a competitive strategy. Negotiators are most likely to compete purposefully when

- the parties have an adversarial relationship;
- a negotiator has a bargaining power advantage and can dominate the situation;
- a negotiator perceives an opportunity for gain at the expense of the other party;
- the other party appears susceptible to competitive tactics;
- the negotiator is defending against competitive moves; or
- there is no concern for the future relationship between the parties.

This list suggests that competitive bargaining most likely occurs in situations such as labor and lawsuit negotiations, insurance and similar claims-type settlements, and in one-time transactions between a relatively experienced party and a relatively inexperienced party. One would, for example, expect to see it in sales transactions where the parties will probably not see each other again.

Representative bargaining or bargaining for a constituency may also prompt competitive bargaining even when there will be future negotiations between equally sophisticated parties. The negotiator's accountability may override relationship concerns and reasons for cooperation. The concerned audience, consisting of a client, constituency, coalition partner, or other phantom party at the table, is, in effect, looking over the negotiator's shoulder. The negotiator, therefore, takes positions and makes moves she believes her client either expects or would approve. International negotiations between countries, union-management, lawsuit negotiations, and negotiations between different parties in interest-group coalition negotiations sometimes evidence this pattern.

Aside from circumstantial or situational pressures, there are some parties who bargain competitively because they believe that is the way to conduct business. There are also parties who are simply predisposed to bargain competitively and will incline to do so opportunistically in any bargaining situation if possible.

Finally, it is important to note that one can bargain competitively in a negotiation on some issues and cooperatively on others. In other words, a negotiator can selectively use competitive strategy or tactics on particular issues, while using a cooperative or problem-solving strategy on other issues. In such a case, extracting gain competitively may not greatly endanger future relationships. . . .

Obviously, competitive bargaining covers a continuum of behaviors from the simplest, unreflective adversarial actions to highly conscious and virtually scripted contests. As such, competitive bargaining moves are natural responses in some negotiation situations and advantageous or profitable actions in others. . . .

Questions

1. What seem to be the most significant advantages of adopting a competitive approach to bargaining?
2. What are the most likely weaknesses of this style?

2. Cooperative Approach

As we have noted, bargainers have another option — to adopt a cooperative approach, seeking to meet each others' needs in a solution valuable to both. In their best-selling book, *Getting to Yes*, Roger Fisher, William Ury, and Bruce Patton (1991) suggest that "you can change the game." They prescribe a problem-solving, interest-based approach. The five basic elements of this approach are as follows:

1. *Separate the people from the problem.* The negotiators should focus on attacking the problem posed by the negotiations, not each other, although they should also separately consider how to deal with human factors in bargaining.
2. *Focus on interests not positions.* Distinguish positions, which are what you want, from interests, which are *why* you want them. Focus on the "why," not the "what." Then look for mutual or at least nonopposed interests.
3. *Invent options for mutual gain.* Even if the parties' interests differ, there may be bargaining outcomes that will advance the interests of both. The story is told of two sisters who are trying to decide which of them should get the only orange in the house. Once they realize that one sister wants to squeeze the orange for its juice, and the other wants to grate the rind to flavor a cake, a "win-win" agreement that furthers the interests of each becomes apparent.

4. *Insist on objective criteria.* Not all disputes and negotiations lend themselves to a "win-win" outcome. The negotiation between the owner of a damaged car and an insurer is one example. Fisher, Ury, and Patton suggest that the parties first attempt to agree on objective criteria to determine the outcome. Thus, instead of negotiating over the value of a destroyed car, both parties might agree that the standard "blue book" price will determine the settlement amount. "Commit yourself to reaching a solution based on principle, not pressure."

5. *Know your Best Alternative To a Negotiated Agreement (BATNA).* The reason you negotiate with someone is to produce better results than you could obtain without negotiating. If you do not know the best you are likely to obtain without negotiating, you may accept an offer you should reject or may reject an offer better than you can otherwise get. Your BATNA is the measure to decide if you are better off agreeing to a negotiated outcome or pursuing your alternatives, whether they be a trial or a deal with someone else. Your BATNA is the basis of comparison to protect you from bad negotiating.

   Note: This last principle applies equally to both types of bargaining. Competitors, even more perhaps than cooperators, should keep their best alternative in mind so that their desire to "win" does not prevent them from accepting a deal that is objectively better than they could achieve elsewhere.

Note: Interests in Bargaining

The most important aspect of cooperative bargaining is that the negotiators focus on the parties' underlying interests rather than on the positions they take. Interest-based bargainers begin with the assumption that a party's position is simply one way (and often not the most efficient or effective one) to achieve a need or interest. What might these interests be? In most disputes parties have multiple interests of varying intensities. They fall into four basic categories: process, personal, relational, and economic.

Process interests.   People have a "process" interest in having disagreements resolved by a fair procedure. This usually includes the opportunity to tell their story and have the feeling that they have been understood, even if not agreed with. A good negotiator will sometimes address an opponent's process interest by listening quietly while he vents angry emotions or accusations, then demonstrating, for example by summarizing what has been said, that while the listener does not agree with what the speaker has said, he has heard and taken pains to understand it — so-called "active listening" (e.g., "So if I understand you correctly, you believe that . . . ."). Participants may also feel an interest in having a negotiation proceed under predictable rules and having their wishes considered in the process of drafting a settlement.

Personal interests.   Most people have a personal interest in feeling respected as professionals and as human beings, in being physically and financially secure, and in being seen as acting consistently with what they have said and done in the past and in accordance with moral standards. Negotiators can address these personal interests, for example, by agreeing to ground rules that participants will treat each other courteously. A mediator, as we will see, might address this same interest by telling a lawyer in front of a client that she has done an excellent job of presenting a legal argument, or by remarking to an executive that she has shown the ability to see the "bigger picture" in the dispute.

A bargainer might satisfy an angry party's process interest by hearing him out, but could meet his personal interests by going farther, to acknowledge that given how the speaker sees the situation, his feelings seem appropriate (e.g., "We don't see the facts the same way you do, but I understand that you believe you were denied the promotion because of your gender. Given how you see the situation, I can understand why you are very angry with the company.").

Relational interests. The parties may also have an interest in preserving or creating a cooperative relationship. This is particularly true in contractual disputes, since the very existence of a contract indicates that the parties once saw a benefit in working together, but it can also be true in disputes that arise from less formal connections. Examples of situations with relational interests include divorce and child custody disputes, land-use controversies between neighbors, and disagreements between companies and longtime customers.

In some cases, good negotiators can succeed in repairing the parties' rupture. Bargainers do not need to reconcile disputants to achieve a useful result, however. In a divorce, for example, parents benefit from a visitation arrangement that preserves their relationships with their children, and in a land-use dispute, parties may be able to minimize friction by trading use restrictions on property.

Economic interests. Disputants also have economic interests. This is obviously true whenever parties remain in a working relationship with each other, for example owners and contractors in an ongoing building project or managers and employees in a unionized company. Even when parties expect no future relationship, they often can benefit from settling in a way that minimizes their economic losses.

One example is taxes. A divorcing couple may be able to minimize tax burdens by putting alimony into the form of a lump-sum transfer rather than periodic payments. By adjusting the way in which settlement terms are structured and characterized, bargainers can sometimes create significant tax savings in other kinds of settlements. A party may have nontax interests as well, such as a concern that a settlement payment be made in a particular fiscal year because it will affect the company's financial reporting. The fact that courts usually do not address these concerns opens opportunities to arrange gains through interest-based negotiation.

Problem 1

Assume that you are counsel for a party in a role-play assigned by your instructor. As part of your preparation to negotiate, you must make decisions about each of the following issues:

- Will you make a first offer? If so, what will it be?
- Will you talk with the other side before specific settlement terms are mentioned? If so, about what?
- What pattern of bargaining do you expect after each side has mentioned specific terms?
- If discussions reach an impasse, what approaches would you consider using to revive the process?

(a) Please answer these questions from the perspective of a cooperative negotiator.
(b) Please answer the same questions from the viewpoint of a competitive negotiator.

Questions

3. You are planning to buy a new car upon graduation. You are living in a metropolitan area and have many dealers to choose from. You plan to have your local mechanic service the vehicle and don't expect problems with it (if you did, you would look to the manufacturer), so you don't expect to see the dealer after the sale. You are preoccupied with the bar exam and don't want to do the bargaining yourself.

   Luckily, you have the option of asking either of two relatives to serve as your negotiator in this transaction. Your sister Jill is an avid shopper who enjoys the give and take of haggling and bargains assertively for the last dollar (to tell the truth, she can be somewhat argumentative at times). Your cousin Brian is much more agreeable and accommodating. He thinks that it is important to meet both sides' needs in a deal and find an outcome that seems fair to both. Which relative would you ask to negotiate for you to buy the car?

4. Assume that you are still bargaining for a car after graduation, but your plans have changed. You will be moving to a small community in which dealers are few and far between. Moreover, you can't afford a new car yet, and so are looking for a vehicle three to five years old. You expect to return to the seller for routine maintenance and servicing. Which relative would you choose for this negotiation?

5. If your choices in questions 3 and 4 differed, or at least were a closer call in one scenario than the other, what does this say about your personal view about whether one bargaining style is more effective than another, and when?

Converting an adversarial process to an interest-based one may not always be possible, but when it occurs even bitter adversaries can reap gains. Consider the following account of how Microsoft and a business partner settled a lengthy court case.

❖ **Jim Carlton, Microsoft, Stac End Battle With Pact,**
  a "Win-Win" Cross-Licensing Agreement

The Wall Street Journal (June 22, 1994)

In a surprise ending to a bitter battle, Microsoft Corp. and Stac Electronics signed a broad cross-licensing agreement, settling their patent infringement dispute and giving Microsoft a 15% stake in Stac.

The move caught Wall Street off guard. Analysts had anticipated protracted legal appeals over a Los Angeles federal jury's verdict of $120 million against software behemoth Microsoft for using technology patented by little Stac. The same jury in February awarded $13.6 million against Stac for alleged use of Microsoft trade secrets. Moreover, Stac's chairman and chief executive officer, Gary Clow, had launched inflammatory attacks on Microsoft and its chairman, William Gates.

Under terms disclosed yesterday, both companies agreed to drop their claims in exchange for cross-licensing all of their existing patents, as well as future ones over the next five years. Those patents cover a technology that compresses software data on computer storage disks.

Royalties of $43 Million

The pact calls for Microsoft to pay Stac license royalties totaling $43 million over 43 months, while also investing $39.9 million for a 15% equity stake in Stac. . . .

The total $82.9 million outlay represents a victory for Microsoft, which had already charged $120 million for the jury award in its fiscal third quarter and now gets to credit much of the difference in the current period. Microsoft also comes out on top, analysts say, because it gets access to what they consider Stac's more reliable compression technology. "Instead of a long and drawn out legal process, it's done and behind them," said Merrill Lynch analyst Stephen T. McClellan.

Stac also comes out ahead: It gets a significant cash infusion without a long appeals process to collect money from Microsoft. Indeed, Mr. Clow said the $82.9 million being turned over by Microsoft represents more than Stac would have gotten had the $120 million been paid, today, since income taxes and Stac's own $13.6 million penalty would have whittled the final amount to about $64 million. Stac also gets an alliance with the most powerful player in the software industry. "This demonstrates it is possible to do win-win deals," Mr. Clow said.

Mr. Clow's current demeanor is a dramatic turnabout from just a few weeks ago, when he appeared on CBS's "Eye to Eye With Connie Chung" to describe his competition against Microsoft Chairman Bill Gates as "like a knife fight." Mr. Gates, the subject of a profile on the show, walked out of an interview when Ms. Chung asked him about Mr. Clow's charges. Yesterday, Mr. Clow backpedaled from his earlier criticisms, saying, "This is not personal. This [settlement] makes good business sense going forward. In doing battle . . . I gained a high degree of respect for Microsoft."

"More Fun Than Disagreeing"

Microsoft executives, too, expressed no hard feelings. "This is a lot more fun than disagreeing," said Michael Brown, Microsoft's vice president of finance. Paul Maritz, a Microsoft senior vice president, said the company wanted to get the case over to end "any uncertainty in the minds of our customers" over Microsoft products that may have contained the offending compression code. . . .

Questions

6. What could each side in the Microsoft-Stac dispute have obtained by pursuing litigation? What, exactly, did they gain from settling?
7. If a settlement made so much sense, why do you suppose the two sides did not reach agreement years earlier? What seems to have triggered the rapprochement?

3. Problem-Solving Approach

The type of integrated negotiation that led to the Microsoft-Stac agreement involved problem-solving thinking on the part of the parties' lawyers and executives. Although problem solving is quite similar to interest-based bargaining, it has become an increasingly popular term for an imaginative and intense form of that approach. Professor Carrie Menkel-Meadow has been a leading proponent of the concept of problem solving, and is co-author of *Mediation: Practice, Policy, and Ethics* (with Lela Love and Andrea Schneider, Aspen, 2006) and in the following reading describes it in depth.

❖ **Carrie Menkel-Meadow, Toward Another**
View of Legal Negotiation: The Structure of Problem Solving

31 UCLA L. Rev. 754-841 (1984)

1. Identifying the Parties' Underlying Needs and Objectives

Unlike the adversarial model[,] which makes assumptions about the parties' desires to maximize individual gain, problem solving begins by attempting to determine the actual needs of particular clients. . . .

Ascertaining the client's needs will, of course, begin with the initial interview. [I]n thinking ahead to the negotiation which might occur, a lawyer might begin by asking the client such general questions as "how would you like to see this all turn out?" or "what would you like to accomplish here?" before channel[ing] the client's objectives in directions the lawyer knows are legally possible. The client may be the best source of ideas that go beyond what the court or the legal system might commonly permit. Once the client's ideas are brought to the surface, the lawyer can explore the needs they are meant to satisfy, and the legal and nonlegal consequences of these and other solutions.

Since so many legal problems are reduced to monetary solutions, consideration of the economic needs and objectives of the client faced with a dispute or transaction is a good place to begin. What are the monetary requirements now — compensation, return on investment, liquidity for payment? What might be the future monetary needs? What is the money needed for? Are any cheaper means available? Are there cash substitutes that are available and acceptable? What are the tax consequences of payment/ receipt now? Later? What payment structure is desirable — lump sum, installments? Why? What are the transaction costs or solution costs of negotiation as opposed to litigation?

Next the lawyer might consider that with which she is most familiar — the legal issues. What legal regulations govern the parties' situation? Must there be an admission of liability? Is a legal judgment necessary? Why? Is a formal document evidencing agreement desirable or required? What are the likely future legal consequences of actions taken? What are the parties likely to do if one of them breaches an agreement? What assets will be available in the future for legal action, if necessary?

The negotiator might consider how any solution affects the client's relationship to others. What are the social needs of the parties? How do others feel about this dispute or transaction? Will family members, friends, business associates, employers, employees be affected by actions taken by the parties? If not affected now, how will any of these people feel if things change in the future?

The negotiator might also ask the client to consider the personal feelings generated by the dispute or transaction. What are the psychological needs of the parties? Does one desire vindication, retribution, power? Why? What will be the long-term psychological consequences of satisfying or not satisfying these needs? How risk-averse are the parties? What are their motivations for pursuing their aims in the negotiation? How might some of these feelings change if they forego litigation now or if they insist on obtaining some advantage?

Finally, the negotiator might also consider the ethical concerns of the parties. How fair do they desire to be with each other? What are the consequences of acting altruistically or dishonestly now? In the future? Will there be feelings of guilt later for "taking advantage" of the other side?

For each of these basic categories of needs the negotiator should also consider how the needs may change over the long run. . . .

Ideally, this framework for determining the parties' needs must be considered from both parties' perspectives. At the very least, it should encourage lawyers and clients to consider whether all the potential needs presented by a negotiation have been canvassed. . . .

In negotiation, as in counseling, the lawyer should be certain that she acts with full knowledge of the client's desires. Within the suggested framework, the lawyer ranks the client's preferences in terms of what is important to the client rather than what the lawyer assumes about the "typical" client.

In order to engage in problem-solving negotiation the lawyer must first ascertain her clients' underlying needs or objectives. In addition, the lawyer may want to explore whether there are unstated objectives, pursue those which she thinks appropriate to the situation, or probe the legitimacy and propriety of particular goals. It should be noted, however, that the lawyer's role in exploring latent concerns or discussing the propriety of objectives can come dangerously close to the role of the lawyer in the adversarial model who imposes his own values or makes assumptions about what the client wants to accomplish. Finally, in order to pursue solutions that will be advantageous for both parties, the lawyer must ascertain the likely underlying needs and objectives of the other party. The client is a primary source for this information, but the lawyer should pursue other sources throughout the negotiation process.

2. Creating Solutions

a. Meeting the Parties' Needs.

Having identified the parties' needs[,] one can begin the search for solutions with those that are suggested by the parties or that otherwise directly meet the parties' needs. . . .

c. Just or Fair Solutions.

. . . Because problem-solving negotiations are likely to result in a greater number of potential solutions not contemplated in advance, the client in such negotiations is more likely to become involved in evaluating proposals. This will be particularly true where a client's objectives or needs may change over time, or need to be reevaluated as new proposals are forthcoming. Thus, the increased fluidity and emphasis on the parties' underlying interests may result in greater client involvement in the legal negotiation process. One of the key differences between the conventional adversarial model and the problem-solving model is the extent to which the parties and their lawyers engage in a continually interactive negotiation process, using the opportunity to seek new solutions rather than simply moving along a predetermined linear scale of compromise. . . .

Conclusion

This article has outlined a systematic approach to legal negotiation premised on the notion that agreements will be more effective when the parties conceive of their purposes as solving the problem or planning the transaction, rather than winning or gaining unilateral advantage. The creative problem-solving approach outlined here depends on two structural components: (1) identifying the parties' underlying needs and objectives, and (2) crafting solutions, first by attempting to meet those needs directly, and second, by attempting to meet more of those needs through expanding the resources available. By utilizing such a framework for negotiations, the parties should recognize the synergistic advantage of such an approach over the adversarial and manipulative strategies of zero-sum negotiations. Parties should be able to achieve solutions to disputes that would not have been possible in court-ordered resolutions. . . .

The attraction of the problem-solving approach to negotiations is that it returns the solution of the problem to the client and forces the lawyer to perform her essential role in the legal system — that of solving problems. By using her professional expertise to canvas possible solutions to the problems and by constantly referring back to the client's real needs and objectives, the lawyer can make the negotiation process more responsive, while at the same time reducing the client's desire for potentially destructive unilateral victory. By utilizing a problem-solving approach the lawyer may be able to avoid the analog of iatrogenic illness, refusing to make worse or increase the costs of the legal problem by her intervention. The client will not then experience his dispute or transaction as getting worse simply because of his entrance into the legal system....

Questions

8. In what ways does problem-solving bargaining differ from cooperative or interest-based techniques? If the difference is a matter of emphasis, what seems to be the emphasis?
9. Should clients be able to decide how cooperative or problem-solving they want their attorney to be when negotiating on their behalf?
10. What happens if an attorney's interest, for example in maintaining good relations with a lawyer with whom she interacts regularly, comes into conflict with a client's wish to get the best possible deal in a particular case regardless of relationships?

4. Adversarial Approach

Competitive bargainers differ in the way they seek to achieve their goals. Many are what might be called "honorable competitors." They approach negotiation the way an ethical litigator approaches a trial. Honorable litigators do their very best to win — and beat the other side. But an ethical trial lawyer is courteous with opponents and treats his word as his bond. He will not assent, for example, to allow in evidence that he thinks will work to his client's disadvantage, but if he does give his word, he will not renege on it. Similarly, a good trial lawyer will conduct hard-hitting cross-examination but will not slip in evidence improperly, even when doing so might make points with a jury. To use a sports metaphor, an "honorable competitive" bargainer is like a player who does his utmost to win but never commits cheap fouls or calls a ball in when it is out of bounds.

Some bargainers, however, seek an advantage by using tricky, dishonest, and discourteous tactics. These we call "adversarial" bargainers. The following excerpts, highlighted from a longer book, provide a mixture of competitive and adversarial advice.

❖ Roger Dawson, Secrets of Power Negotiating
Career Press (2d ed. 2001) [The following are excerpted highlights from the book.]

You have probably heard that the objective of a negotiation is to create a win-win solution. It is a creative way that both you and the other person can walk away from the negotiating table feeling that you've won....Oh, sure! That could happen in the real world, but it doesn't happen enough to make the concept meaningful....

Power Negotiating takes a different position....You play Power Negotiating by a set of rules, just like the game of chess. The big difference between negotiating and chess is that, in negotiating, the other person doesn't have to know the rules. The other person will respond predictably to the moves that you make....

[Chapter by chapter the author sets out the "gambits" of power negotiating and comments on them. He includes some tactics that he identifies as unethical in order to alert the reader and describes "Negotiating Pressure Points," some of which are included in the following list.]

- **Flinch at Proposals:** Power Negotiators know that you should always flinch — react with shock and surprise at the other side's proposals.... They may not expect to get what they are asking for; however, if you do not show surprise you're communicating that it is a possibility.
- **Use the Vise Technique:** The Vise is another very effective negotiating gambit and what it will accomplish will amaze you.... Respond to a proposal or counter-proposal with the Vise Technique: "You'll have to do better than that."
- **Don't Let the Other Side Know You Have the Authority to Make a Decision:** Your higher authority should be a vague entity and not an individual.... Don't let the other person trick you into admitting that you have authority.
- **Don't Fall into the Trap of Thinking That Splitting the Difference Is the Fair Thing to Do:** Splitting the difference doesn't mean down the middle, because you can do it more than once.
- **The Red Herring:** With the Red Herring, the other person makes a phony demand that he will withdraw, but only in exchange for a concession.
- **Cherry Picking:** Let's say that you're buying a piece of land in the country, and the seller is offering it for $100,000 with 20 percent down and the balance due over ten years with 10 percent interest added. You might ask the owner to quote his or her lowest price for an all-cash deal. He or she might agree to $90,000 for all cash. Then you ask what the lowest interest rate would be for a 50 percent down transaction. The owner quotes you seven percent. Then you Cherry Pick the best features of both components of the deal and offer $90,000 with 20 percent down and the balance carried by the owner with seven percent interest added.
- **Nibbling:** Power Negotiators know that by using the Nibbling Gambit, you can get a little bit more even after you have agreed on everything. You can also get the other person to do things that she had refused to do earlier. It works because the other person's mind reverses itself after it has made a decision.
- **Escalation:** Raising demands after both sides reach an agreement.
- **The Fait Accompli:** If you have ever sent someone a check for less than they're asking and marked the back of the check "Payment in full is acknowledged," you have used the Fait Accompli Gambit. It's when one negotiator simply assumes the other will accept the assumed settlement rather than go to the trouble of reopening the negotiations. It works on the principle that it's a lot easier to beg forgiveness than it is to get permission.
- **Ultimatums:** Ultimatums are very high-profile statements that tend to strike fear into inexperienced negotiators... An ultimatum is a powerful pressure point, but it has one major flaw as a gambit: If you say that you are going to shoot the first hostage at noon tomorrow, what had you better be prepared to do at noon tomorrow? Right. Shoot the first hostage. Because

if 12:01 P.M. rolls around and you haven't done that, you have just lost all of your power in negotiation.

Question

11. Would an attorney's reputation for cooperation and integrity present a particular attraction to a client who wants to hire the attorney to engage in hard bargaining or sharp tactics on her behalf? How should an attorney respond in such a case? For an interesting real-life example, see David McKean and Douglas Frantz's *Friends in High Places: The Rise and Fall of Clark Clifford* (1995).

B. A Combined Approach — Creating and Claiming Value

As we have seen, even cooperative bargainers must divide the negotiation "pie" as well as enlarge it. The challenge of carrying out both tasks in the same process is often difficult even for the best negotiators, creating what is known as the "negotiator's dilemma." In the next reading Professors David Lax and James Sebenius explore this problem.

❖ David A. Lax and James K. Sebenius, The Manager as Negotiator: Bargaining for Cooperation and Competitive Gain

The Free Press 29-35 (1986)

The Negotiator's Dilemma: Creating and Claiming Value

We assume that each negotiator strives to advance his interests, whether they are narrowly conceived or include such concerns as improving the relationship, acting in accord with conceptions of equity, or furthering the welfare of others. Negotiators must learn, in part from each other, what is jointly possible and desirable. To do so requires some degree of cooperation. But, at the same time, they seek to advance their individual interests. This involves some degree of competition.

That negotiation includes cooperation and competition, common and conflicting interests, is nothing new. In fact, it is typically understood that these elements are both present and can be disentangled. Deep down, however, some people believe that the elements of conflict are illusory, that meaningful communication will erase any such unfortunate misperceptions. Others see mainly competition and take the cooperative pieces to be minimal. Some overtly acknowledge the reality of each aspect but direct all their attention to one of them and wish, pretend, or act as if the other does not exist. Still others hold to a more balanced view that accepts both elements as significant but seek to treat them separately. [W]e argue that all these approaches are flawed.

A deeper analysis shows that the competitive and cooperative elements are inextricably entwined. In practice, they cannot be separated. This bonding is fundamentally important to the analysis, structuring, and conduct of negotiation. There is a central, inescapable tension between cooperative moves to create value jointly and competitive moves to gain individual advantage. This tension affects virtually all tactical and strategic choice. Analysts must come to grips with it; negotiators must manage it. Neither denial nor discomfort will make it disappear.

Warring Conceptions of Negotiation

Negotiators and analysts tend to fall into two groups that are guided by warring conceptions of the bargaining process. In the left-hand corner are the "value creators" and in the right-hand corner are the "value claimers."

Value Creators

Value creators tend to believe that, above all, successful negotiators must be inventive and cooperative enough to devise an agreement that yields considerable gain to each party, relative to no-agreement possibilities. Some speak about the need for replacing the "win-lose" image of negotiation with "win-win" negotiation, from which all parties presumably derive great value....

Communication and sharing information can help negotiators to create value jointly. [T]he drive to create value by discovering joint gains can require ingenuity and may benefit from a variety of techniques and attitudes. The parties can treat the negotiation as solving a joint problem; they can organize brainstorming sessions to invent creative solutions to their problems. They may succeed by putting familiar pieces of the problem together in ways that people had not previously seen, as well as by wholesale reformulations of the problem.

Roger Fisher and Bill Ury give an example that concerns the difficult Egyptian[–]Israeli negotiations over where to draw a boundary in the Sinai. "This appeared to be an absolutely classic example of zero-sum bargaining, in which each square mile lost to one party was the other side's gain. For years the negotiations proceeded inconclusively with proposed boundary lines drawn and redrawn on innumerable maps. On probing the real interests of the two sides, however, Egypt was found to care a great deal about sovereignty over the Sinai while Israel was heavily concerned with its security. As such, a creative solution could be devised to "unbundle" these different interests and give to each what it valued most. In the Sinai, this involved creating a demilitarized zone under the Egyptian flag. This had the effect of giving Egypt "sovereignty" and Israel "security." This situation exemplifies extremely common tendencies to assume that negotiators' interests are in direct opposition, a conviction that can sometimes be corrected by communicating, sharing information, and inventing solutions....

We create value by finding joint gains for all negotiating parties. A joint gain represents an improvement from each party's point of view; one's gain need not be another's loss. An extremely simple example makes the point. Say that two young boys each have three pieces of fruit. Willy, who hates bananas and loves pears, has a banana and two oranges. Sam, who hates pears and loves bananas, has a pear and two apples. The first move is easy: they trade banana for pear and are both happier. But after making this deal, they realize that they can do still better. Though each has a taste both for apples and oranges, a second piece of the same fruit is less desirable than the first. So they also swap an apple for an orange. The banana-pear exchange represents an improvement over the no trade alternative; the apple-orange transaction that leaves each with three different kinds of fruit improves the original agreement — is a joint gain — for both boys.

The economist's analogy is simple: Creativity has expanded the size of the pie under negotiation. Value creators see the essence of negotiating as expanding the pie, as pursuing joint gains. This is aided by openness, clear communication, sharing information, creativity, an attitude of joint problem solving, and cultivating common interests.

Value Claimers

Value claimers, on the other hand, tend to see this drive for joint gain as naive and weak minded. For them, negotiation is hard, tough bargaining. The object of negotiation is to convince the other guy that he wants what you have to offer much more than you want what he has; moreover, you have all the time in the world while he is up against pressing deadlines. To "win" at negotiating — and thus make the other fellow "lose" — one must start high, concede slowly, exaggerate the value of concessions, minimize the benefits of the other's concessions, conceal information, argue forcefully on behalf of principles that imply favorable settlements, make commitments to accept only highly favorable agreements, and be willing to outwait the other fellow.

The hardest of bargainers will threaten to walk away or to retaliate harshly if their one-sided demands are not met; they may ridicule, attack, and intimidate their adversaries. . . . At the heart of this adversarial approach is an image of a negotiation with a winner and a loser: "We are dividing a pie of fixed size and every slice I give to you is a slice I do not get; thus, I need to claim as much of the value as possible by giving you as little as possible."

A Fundamental Tension of Negotiation

Both of these images of negotiation are incomplete and inadequate. Value creating and value claiming are linked parts of negotiation. Both processes are present. No matter how much creative problem solving enlarges the pie, it must still be divided; value that has been created must be claimed. And, if the pie is not enlarged, there will be less to divide; there is more value to be claimed if one has helped create it first. An essential tension in negotiation exists between cooperative moves to create value and competitive moves to claim it. . . .

The Tension at the Tactical Level

The tension between cooperative moves to create value and competitive moves to claim it is greatly exacerbated by the interaction of the tactics used either to create or claim value.

First, tactics for claiming value (which we will call "claiming tactics") can impede its creation. Exaggerating the value of concessions and minimizing the benefit of others' concessions presents a distorted picture of one's relative preferences; thus, mutually beneficial trades may not be discovered. Making threats or commitments to highly favorable outcomes surely impedes hearing and understanding others' interests. Concealing information may also cause one to leave joint gains on the table. In fact, excessive use of tactics for claiming value may well sour the parties' relationship and reduce the trust between them. Such tactics may also evoke a variety of unhelpful interests. Conflict may escalate and make joint prospects less appealing and settlement less likely.

Second, approaches to creating value are vulnerable to tactics for claiming value. Revealing information about one's relative preferences is risky . . . The information that a negotiator would accept position A in return for a favorable resolution on a second issue can be exploited: "So, you'll accept A. Good, Now, let's move on to discuss the merits of the second issue." The willingness to make a new, creative offer can often be taken as a sign that its proposer is able and willing to make further concessions. Thus, such offers sometimes remain undisclosed. Even purely shared interests can be held hostage in exchange for concessions on other issues. Though a divorcing husband and wife may both prefer giving the wife custody of the child, the husband may "suddenly" develop strong parental instincts to extract concessions in alimony in return for giving the wife custody.

In tactical choices, each negotiator thus has reasons not to be open and cooperative. Each also has apparent incentives to try to claim value. Moves to claim value thus tend to drive out moves to create it. Yet, if both choose to claim value, by being dishonest or less than forthcoming about preferences, beliefs, or minimum requirements, they may miss mutually beneficial terms for agreement.

Indeed, the structure of many bargaining situations suggests that negotiators will tend to leave joint gains on the table or even reach impasses when mutually acceptable agreements are available.

Note: The Importance of Differences in Creating Joint Gains

One of the key points of value creation is somewhat counterintuitive: Improving deals depends on discovering what parties value differently, not what they value the same. At the simplest level, differences in parties' valuation of items are the motivating force in bargaining.

If, for example, I am selling you my used car and we both value the car at the same price — $10,000 — then neither one of us is highly motivated to make a deal. I will be no happier if I obtain the money than if I keep the car, and you feel the same way about obtaining the car. If, however, I am planning to move after law school to Manhattan, where garaging a car would be expensive, I may value the car at only $5,000. If you are planning to move to a rural community when you graduate, this car may be just what you need to get to work and suddenly seem to you to be worth $12,000 or more. We now both feel much more motivated to carry out a sale, but it is the difference in how we value the car, not the fact that we value it similarly, that drives the transaction.

A difference in valuation is the simplest kind of variation that allows negotiators on both sides to leave a transaction feeling better off — that is, to construct "win-win" deals. Lax and Sebenius (2002) have identified other differences that can be used to increase the value of negotiated agreements. They include the following:

- *Differences in relative valuation or priorities* can lead to exchanges, directly or by "unbundling" differently valued interests. The apple-and-orange fruit exchange, noted above, is an example of differences in relative valuation that create trading value, as is the simpler example of the car sale.
- *Differences in tolerance for risk and risk aversion* motivate deals and give rise to insurancelike arrangements. A risk-adverse plaintiff, for example, may prefer to take a sure $500,000 settlement rather than opt for a trial in which he has a 70 percent chance of winning $1 million, but a 30 percent chance of winning nothing at all. At the outset of cases, many plaintiffs enter into contingent fee agreements with their lawyers. Contingent agreements are a kind of insurance, in which litigants pay a percentage of any recovery in return for the lawyer's agreement to bear the cost of litigation, a risk that the lawyer can spread over her entire docket.
- *Differences in time preference* can lead to patterns of payments or other actions over time. If a corporation wants to book a recovery quickly to solve a cash flow problem, for example, and an insurance company with large reserves cares more about the amount of the payment than its timing, both sides are better off if the insurer makes a quick, discounted payment.
- *Different capabilities* can be combined. In a joint venture, for example, a corporation with a strong production capacity might combine forces with a company having sophisticated marketing abilities to enhance profitability for both.
- *Differences in cost/revenue structure* can create cost-saving trades. Imagine, for instance, that a company making business accounting software has hired a contractor to install a lighting system. The system is inoperable, however, because of poor work by a subcontractor. One option would be for the software maker to hire another entity to replace the system and then sue the contractor for the cost. Another might be to exchange goods and services, as well as making a money payment. The original contractor may be able to obtain replacement equipment at a discount, and if the contractor could use software services provided by the company, it could provide them at very low cost.
- *Differences in forecasts* can lead to contingent agreements when the items under negotiation are uncertain, or when a party feels that it will fare better if it bears part of the other's risk. If, for instance, an executive looking for a job has a very optimistic view of her abilities, she may agree to a relatively low salary with a large potential bonus. Indeed, the very fact of the bonus may make her perform better, increasing the deal's value for both parties.
- *Other differences*, such as the value of personal reputation, attitudes of constituencies, and concepts of fairness, can also be fashioned into joint gains. If, for example, a law firm is being threatened with a suit for sexual harassment, it may be willing to pay more if the settlement is cast as payment for wrongful termination, and an accused partner may be more willing to depart quietly if he is allowed to resign than if he is fired.

Questions

12. Are the suggestions made by Lax and Sebenius as applicable to the settlement of legal disputes, in which relationships are usually ruptured, as to deal-making, where the parties contemplate a future beneficial connection?
13. Which of the above differences are most likely to be of use in settling legal controversies?

C. Choosing an Effective Approach

1. Cooperation Versus Competitiveness — Who Decides?

If a client retains an attorney with a reputation for cooperation and instructs him during a negotiation to drop his cooperative pattern and pursue adversarial tactics, can the lawyer refuse? Generally clients are entitled to choose the objective of negotiation, while lawyers may use their professional judgment to select how to attain the client's objective. In real life, of course, it is sometimes not so simple. In litigation matters the lawyer owes the client an ethical obligation of zealous advocacy in pursuit of the client's interests. Some scholars interpret the ethical norms to mean that "the final authority on important issues of strategy rests with the client; and the client may discharge his lawyer at will, but the lawyer has only limited ability to withdraw from representation" (Gilson and Mnookin 1995, 550). Mnookin and Gilson believe that a lawyer who wishes to pursue a cooperative approach may not be able to do so in the litigation context, or at least that the client calls the negotiation shots. They point out that the client can fire the lawyer at will if the lawyer seems more cooperative than the client wishes, but that ethical norms do not always allow the lawyer to quit if the client insists on a more aggressive strategy.

A different perspective is offered by Professor Robert J. Condlin, who distinguishes between the reality of what lawyers do in negotiation and what the ethical rules appear to demand. The distinction, according to Condlin, is really between ends and means. Clients have control over the end result desired, and lawyers choose the means. "Lawyers are persons in their own right, with moral and political rights and obligations of their own, and even though they must take direction from their clients, they need not do everything asked. For example, the duty of deference distinguishes between questions of ends and questions of means, and reserves to lawyers the tactical and technical decisions of how best to advance client objectives" (Condlin 1992, 71).

According to Condlin, lawyers must be substantively competitive in negotiating for clients but can choose their own personal style. A competitive, or even adversarial, attorney can adopt a cordial and respectful persona when bargaining, though this can be a difficult distinction to maintain. Condlin refers to the tug between a client's wishes for the lawyer to defect from a pattern of cooperation and the lawyer's desire for long-term cooperation as the "bargainer's dilemma." Clients tend to view litigation and some deals as a one-round game. Lawyers usually view their negotiation with other lawyers as unlimited multiple rounds, where any defection will bring future retaliation and a blemished reputation. Hence the "bargainer's dilemma."

As a lawyer negotiating for clients, you do have a choice whether to take a cooperative or competitive approach. Also recall that the choice of how to fulfill clients' interests depends on circumstances. Cooperation may be the best way to meet the needs of a client if an integrative outcome will allow each party to get what they want most, while a competitive approach risks eliminating most of the value in the deal. In the context of a bitter lawsuit, however, both sides may be irrevocably committed to competing.

2. *Negotiating Within Your Comfort Zone*

The previous sections refer to different approaches to negotiation. Being cooperative or competitive, problem-solving or adversarial, is at least in part a matter of choice. The choice you make depends on a number of factors: The subject of the negotiation, the interrelation between issues, the past or anticipated future relationship between the parties or the attorneys, the customs of the community in which the negotiation occurs, the amount of time available, and the amount at stake may all influence your approach. The biggest factor, however, is your own comfort zone, formed by your ethical standards, personality, and values. Choosing a style that does not fit you, if not a recipe for failure, is likely to make your work as a negotiator difficult and unsatisfying. To succeed as a professional and find satisfaction in what you are doing, you must negotiate within your personal zone of comfort, in terms of practicality, concern for relationships, and ethics.

Defining our negotiating comfort zone is not always an easy task. It is common to wish to be liked rather than disliked. We know that we are more likely to be liked when we are cooperative and giving than when we are competitive and taking. However, we also know that winners are admired, and we want to be respected for vigorously representing our clients' interests. Students without legal experience may share the view popularized in movies and television series of good lawyers as hard-charging and aggressive. The dramatic, adversarial presentation of jury trials in movies may also be transposed in our minds to other settings. As a result, many students have a latent fear that their preference for cooperation and friendliness will not serve them or their clients well in negotiation.

Other students may have enjoyed competition and winning in sports and other contests. We know that law students are a self-selected group of achievers who have succeeded, at least academically, and made it into law school through a competitive admissions process. Competition appears to be encouraged by the legal system, while cooperation and generosity may be viewed as virtuous but less-valued qualities. So it is understandable that some students feel that negotiation should be approached as a professional game in which their competitive qualities are to be let loose and rewarded with success.

How lawyers behave in negotiation and what they do is not fully known. The privacy and confidentiality surrounding most negotiations prevent outsiders from even knowing that the process occurred. So we must rely on self-reported accounts of success. However, few lawyers ever seem to feel that they have lost a negotiation, or to admit it if they have. (There appear to be no books on "How I Failed as a Negotiator.") The few statistical studies of whether particular negotiation styles are effective almost all are based on lawyer self-reporting, in which attorneys rate their own performance without the benefit of objective criteria or observation. Such data give new lawyers little guidance on what is successful in negotiation and how to weigh competing tensions and negotiate effectively within their comfort zone.

We believe that both competitive and cooperative styles can be effective approaches to negotiation if done well, with integrity, and in the right situation. Being an effective competitive negotiator does not require the use of tricks or deceit, and being a cooperative bargainer need not involve being a pushover. Cooperative and problem-solving attorneys, in particular, can be extremely successful.

Mediation, ironically, can make both competitive and cooperative approaches more successful, or at least less risky. As we will see, the framework of mediation can protect competitive bargainers from failure caused by overreaching while insulating cooperative negotiators from the risk of having their openness exploited. The chapters that follow show how the mediation process accomplishes this, and how attorneys of all types use mediation to maximize their effectiveness as bargainers.

CHAPTER
3

Negotiation — Step by Step

The negotiation process varies greatly, depending on the situation and the personalities and approaches of the participants. This said, good bargainers tend to proceed through a series of stages, and knowing these stages will help you understand how the process should work. The stages are:

1. Preparing and setting goals,
2. Interacting initially,
3. Exchanging information,
4. Bargaining,
5. Moving toward closure,
6. Reaching impasse or agreement, and
7. Finalizing an agreement.

In the early stages the activities and tasks within the competitive and cooperative approaches are very similar. (See Table 1.) Also, the labels "competitive" and "cooperative," like all one-word descriptions, are too simple; adversarial and problem-solving, positional and interest-based, or distributive and integrative may better capture the behavioral contrasts. Still, this model may help you understand the differences between the two "families" of negotiation philosophy.

Table 1.
Negotiation Chart

Stage	Competitive or Adversarial Approach	Cooperative or Problem-Solving Approach
1. Preparing and setting goals	➤ Planning and research ➤ Counseling client about negotiation ➤ Assessing the power of each party ➤ Identifying alternatives and setting goals ➤ Devising tactics	➤ Planning and research ➤ Counseling client about negotiation ➤ Assessing the needs of each party ➤ Identifying alternatives, interests, and potential options to satisfy them ➤ Setting goals

Stage	Competitive or Adversarial Approach	Cooperative or Problem-Solving Approach
2. Interacting initially	➤ Setting a tone ➤ Establishing authority ➤ Possibly stating positions	➤ Setting a tone ➤ Establishing rapport and trust ➤ Possibly explaining needs and interests
3. Exchanging information	➤ Asking questions ➤ Offering self-serving data and standards ➤ Trading for information	➤ Offering mutual disclosure ➤ Discussing interests ➤ Exploring relevant data
4. Bargaining	➤ Stating initial positions, usually exaggerated ➤ Arguing over facts and relevant principles ➤ Making concessions ➤ Maneuvering for tactical advantage	➤ Agreeing on an agenda for discussion ➤ Identifying needs and developing options ➤ Identifying principled criteria and discussing views of fairness ➤ Exploring possible trades and packages
5. Moving toward closure	➤ Using power and threats ➤ Creating deadlines ➤ Evaluating offers	➤ Examining alternatives ➤ Agreeing on a time frame ➤ Proposing adjustments
6. Reaching impasse or decisions	➤ Possible impasse ➤ Compromising and splitting the difference ➤ Adding conditions	➤ Possible, but less likely, impasse ➤ Reaching mutual decisions through joint invention and packaging ➤ Creating alternative outcomes
7. Finalizing the agreement	➤ Preparing opposing drafts ➤ Negotiating over drafts ➤ Getting approval and ratification if necessary	➤ Memorializing terms ➤ Working from a single text ➤ Getting approval and ratification if necessary

Questions

1. Have you found that negotiations in which you have been involved go through predictable stages? Did this depend on the nature of the issue, the identities of the bargainers, or something else? What seemed determinative?

2. Could a "single-text" approach, listed in Stage 7 and described later in this chapter, be used earlier in the process to formulate choices, bargain, and reach decisions? For a fascinating application of the single-text procedure to reach a groundbreaking agreement between Israel and Egypt, see Jimmy Carter's *Keeping Faith: Memoirs of a President* (1982).

A. Preparing to Negotiate

Watching a good negotiator or hearing about an effective negotiation can give the impression that negotiating skill comes easily and that success results primarily from quick thinking and intuition. However, success in negotiation, like skill in the courtroom and other disciplines, comes mainly from careful planning, research, and other preparation, especially for less-experienced practitioners. The following excerpts describe two key aspects of the planning process: identifying your alternatives to agreement and setting high goals.

1. Identifying Alternatives

One key aspect of planning is to identify the minimum terms that you will accept. As Fisher, Ury, and Patton point out, this should flow from identifying your *"Best Alternative To a Negotiated Agreement"* in any situation.

❖ **Roger Fisher, William Ury, and Bruce Patton, Getting to Yes**
Penguin 97-106 (1991)

When you are trying to catch an airplane your goal may seem tremendously important; looking back on it, you see you could have caught the next plane. Negotiation will often present you with a similar situation. You will worry, for instance, about failing to reach agreement on an important business deal in which you have invested a great deal of yourself. Under these conditions, a major danger is that you will be too accommodating to the views of the other side — too quick to go along. The siren song of "Let's all agree and put an end to this" becomes persuasive. You may end up with a deal you should have rejected.

The Costs of Using a Bottom Line

Negotiators commonly try to protect themselves against such an outcome by establishing in advance the worst acceptable outcome — their "bottom line." If you are buying, a bottom line is the highest price you would pay. If you are selling, a bottom line is the lowest amount you would accept. You and your spouse might, for example, ask $200,000 for your house and agree between yourselves to accept no offer below $160,000.

Having a bottom line makes it easier to resist pressure and temptations of the moment.... But the protection afforded by adopting a bottom line involves high costs. It limits your ability to benefit from what you learn during negotiation.... A bottom line also inhibits imagination. It reduces the incentive to invent a tailor-made solution which would reconcile differing interests in a way more advantageous for both you and them.... Moreover, a bottom line is likely to be set too high.... In short, while adopting a bottom line may protect you from accepting a very bad agreement, it may keep you both from inventing and from agreeing to a solution it would be wise to accept....

Is there an alternative to the bottom line? Is there a measure for agreements that will protect you against both accepting an agreement you should reject and rejecting an agreement you should accept? There is.

Know Your BATNA

When a family is deciding on the minimum price for their house, the right question for them to ask is not what they "ought" to be able to get, but what they will do if by a certain time they have not sold the house. Will they keep it on the market indefinitely? Will they rent it, tear it down, turn the land into a parking lot, let someone else live in it rent-free on condition they paint it, or what? Which of those alternatives is most attractive, all things considered? . . .

The reason you negotiate is to produce something better than the results you can obtain without negotiating. What are those results? What is that alternative? What is your BATNA — your Best Alternative To a Negotiated Agreement? *That* is the standard against which any proposed agreement should be measured. That is the only standard which can protect you both from accepting terms that are too unfavorable and from rejecting terms it would be in your interest to accept.

Your BATNA not only is a better measure but also has the advantage of being flexible enough to permit the exploration of imaginative solutions. Instead of ruling out any solution which does not meet your bottom line, you can compare a proposal with your BATNA to see whether it better satisfies your interests.

The Insecurity of an Unknown BATNA

If you have not thought carefully about what you will do if you fail to reach an agreement, you are negotiating with your eyes closed. . . . Even when your alternative is fixed, you may be taking too rosy a view of the consequences of not reaching agreement. You may not be appreciating the full agony of a lawsuit, a contested divorce, a strike, an arms race, or a war. . . .

As valuable as knowing your BATNA may be, you may hesitate to explore alternatives. You hope this buyer or the next will make you an attractive offer for the house. You may avoid facing the question of what you will do if no agreement is reached. You may think to yourself, "Let's negotiate first and see what happens. If things don't work out, then I'll figure out what to do." But having at least a tentative answer to the question is absolutely essential if you are to conduct your negotiations wisely. Whether you should or should not agree on something in a negotiation depends entirely upon the attractiveness to you of the best available alternative.

Formulate a Trip Wire

Although your BATNA is the true measure by which you should judge any proposed agreement, you may want another test as well. In order to give you early warning that the content of a possible agreement is beginning to run the risk of being too unattractive, it is useful to identify one far from perfect agreement that is better than your BATNA. Before accepting any agreement worse than this trip wire package, you should take a break and reexamine the situation. Like a bottom line, a trip wire can limit the authority of an agent. "Don't sell for less than $158,000, the price I paid plus interest, until you've talked to me."

A trip wire should provide you with some margin in reserve. If after reaching the standard reflected in your trip wire you decide to call in a mediator, you have left him with something on your side to work with. You still have some room to move.

Making the Most of Your Assets

Protecting yourself against a bad agreement is one thing. Making the most of the assets you have in order to produce a good agreement is another. How do you do this? Again the answer lies in your BATNA. The better your BATNA, the greater your power. [The authors suggest that a negotiator should attempt to improve her alternative or search out a better one to increase her negotiating power.]

Consider the Other Side's BATNA

You should also think about the alternatives to a negotiated agreement available to the other side. They may be unduly optimistic about what they can do if no agreement is reached. Perhaps they have a vague notion that they have a great many alternatives and are under the influence of their cumulative total. The more you can learn of their alternatives, the better prepared you are for negotiation. Knowing their alternatives, you can realistically estimate what you can expect from the negotiation. If they appear to overestimate their BATNA, you will want to lower their expectations. . . .

When the Other Side Is Powerful

If the other side has big guns, you do not want to turn a negotiation into a gunfight. The stronger they appear in terms of physical or economic power, the more you benefit by negotiating on the merits. To the extent that they have muscle and you have principle, the larger a role you can establish for principle the better off you are.

Having a good BATNA can help you negotiate on the merits. You can convert such resources as you have into effective negotiating power by developing and improving your BATNA. Apply knowledge, time, money, people, connections, and wits into devising the best solution for you independent of the other side's assent. The more easily and happily you can walk away from a negotiation, the greater your capacity to affect its outcome.

Developing your BATNA thus not only enables you to determine what is a minimally acceptable agreement, it will probably raise that minimum. Developing your BATNA is perhaps the most effective course of action you can take in dealing with a seemingly more powerful negotiator.

Questions

3. What is your "BATNA" likely to be in litigation? Is there ever any alternative but to obtain a court judgment on the merits?

4. What alternatives might a party have in a situation in which she is bargaining to create a contract with a potential business partner?
5. In real life, should there ever be a difference between a party's BATNA and its bottom line? Can you think of a situation in which a litigant might rationally decide to accept a settlement that is not as good as the most likely outcome in adjudication, taking into account the legal costs involved in going to trial? What would explain such a decision?

Time, trial, witnesses, lost bus ops.

2. Setting Goals

Setting high goals is identified with a competitive approach to negotiation. It is often assumed, in other words, that setting a high goal for oneself necessarily means imposing a low one on one's negotiating partner. This is not necessarily true, however. It is quite possible for negotiators jointly to set the goal of finding the potentially elusive set of terms that best satisfy each person's interests — a task that is cooperative in intent but often difficult to achieve in practice. The following reading stresses the importance of goal setting for both cooperative and competitive bargainers.

❖ **G. Richard Shell, Bargaining for Advantage: Negotiation Strategies for Reasonable People**

Viking 24-34 (1999)

Goals: You'll Never Hit the Target If You Don't Aim

In Lewis Carroll's Alice's Adventures in Wonderland, Alice finds herself at a crossroads where a Cheshire Cat materializes. Alice asks the Cat, "Would you tell me please, which way I ought to go from here?" The Cat replies, "That depends a good deal on where you want to get to." "I don't much care where — [,]" says Alice. "Then it doesn't matter which way you go," the Cat replies, cutting her off.

To become an effective negotiator, you must find out where you want to go — and why. That means committing yourself to specific, justifiable goals. It also means taking the time to transform your goals from simple targets into genuine — and appropriately high — expectations. . . . Our goals give us direction, but our expectations are what give weight and conviction to our statements at the bargaining table. We are most animated when we are striving to achieve what we feel we justly deserve.

Expectations in negotiation are a function of a number of factors, including our previous successes and failures in similar negotiations, prevailing market prices and standards, past practices, information about the other party's alternatives and frame of reference, our potential for a future relationship with the other side, and our basic personality. . . . The more time we spend preparing for a particular negotiation and the more information we gather that reinforces our belief that our goal is legitimate and achievable, the firmer the expectations grow. . . .

Negotiations are no different from other areas of achievement. What you aim for often determines what you get. Why? The first reason is obvious: Your goals set the upper limit of what you will ask for. You mentally concede everything beyond your goal, so you seldom do better than that benchmark.

Second, research on goals reveals that they trigger powerful psychological "striving" mechanisms. Sports psychologists and educators alike confirm that setting specific goals motivates people, focusing and concentrating their attention and psychological powers.

Third, we are more persuasive when we are committed to achieving some specific purpose, in contrast to the occasions when we ask for things half-heartedly or merely react to initiatives proposed by others. Our commitment is infectious. People around us feel drawn toward our goals. . . .

Goals versus "Bottom Lines"

Most negotiating books and experts emphasize the importance of having a "bottom line," "walkaway," or "reservation price" for negotiation. Indeed, the bottom line is a fundamental bargaining concept on which much of modern negotiation theory is built. It is the *minimum acceptable level* you require to say "yes" in a negotiation. By definition, if you cannot achieve your bottom line, you would rather seek another solution to your problem or wait until another opportunity comes your way. When two parties have bottom lines that permit an agreement at some point between them, theorists speak of there being a "positive bargaining zone." When the two bottom lines do not overlap, they speak of a "negative bargaining zone". . . .

A well-framed goal is quite different from a bottom line. As I use the word, "goal" is your *highest legitimate expectation* of what you should achieve.

Researchers have discovered that humans have a limited capacity for maintaining focus in complex, stressful situations such as negotiations. Consequently, once a negotiation is under way, we gravitate toward the single focal point that has the psychological significance for us. Once most people set a firm bottom line in a negotiation, that becomes their dominant reference point as discussions proceed. They measure success or failure with reference to their bottom line, and it is very difficult to psychologically re-orient themselves toward a more ambitious bargaining goal. . . .

What is the practical effect of having your bottom line become your dominant reference point in a negotiation? Over a lifetime of negotiating, your results will tend to hover at a point just above this minimum acceptable level. . . . Meanwhile, someone else who is more skilled at orienting himself toward ambitious goals will do much better. . . . To avoid falling into the trap of letting our bottom line become our reference point, be aware of your absolute limits, but do not focus on them. Instead, work energetically on formulating your goals — and let your bottom line take care of itself. . . .

Orient firmly toward your goal in the planning and initial stages of negotiation, then gradually re-orient toward a bottom line as that becomes necessary to close the deal. With experience, you should be able to keep both your goal and your bottom line in view at the same time without losing your goal focus. Research suggests that the best negotiators have this ability. Meanwhile, during the actual negotiation, you should strive to determine what the other side's bottom line is as best you can — and not allow yourself to be too swayed by the other party's aspirations. If, in the end, you must make adjustments to your high expectations to close a deal, you can take care of that later.

If setting goals is so vital to effective preparation, how should you do it? Use the following simple steps:

1. Think carefully about what you really want — and remember that money is often a means, not an end.
2. Set an optimistic — but justifiable — target.
3. Be specific.
4. Get committed. Write down your goal and, if possible, discuss the goal with someone else.
5. Carry your goal with you into the negotiation.

Set an Optimistic, Justifiable Target

When you set goals, think boldly and optimistically about what you would like to see happen. Research has repeatedly shown that people who have higher expectations in negotiations perform better and get more than people who have modest or "I'll do my best" goals, provided they really believe in their targets....

Once you have thought about what an optimistic, challenging goal would look like, spend a few minutes permitting realism to dampen your expectations. *Optimistic goals are effective only if they are feasible; that is, only if you believe in them and they can be justified according to some standard or norm* ... [N]egotiation positions must usually be supported by some standard, benchmark, or precedent, or they lose their credibility....

Commit to Your Goal: Write It Down and Talk About It

Your goal is only as effective as your commitment to it. There are several simple things you can do that will increase your level of psychological attachment to your goal. First, as I suggested above, you should make sure it is justified and supported by solid arguments. You must believe in your goal to be committed to it.

Second, it helps if you spend just a few moments vividly imagining the way it would look or feel to achieve your goal. Visualization helps engage our mind more fully in the achievement process and also raises our level of self-confidence and commitment....

Third, psychologists and marketing professionals report that the act of writing a goal down engages our sense of commitment much more effectively than does the mere act of thinking about it. The act of writing makes a thought more "real" and objective, obligating us to follow up on it — at least in our own eyes....

Notes and Questions

6. Should there ever be a difference between one's goals and one's expectations in bargaining? When?
7. Does the advice to set high expectations only work if the other side does not follow the same advice? Will high expectations by both sides lead to

frequent impasses? Is there a way for two highly optimistic negotiators to reach agreement?

8. If expectations in negotiation are, in part, a function of previous success and failures, as Shell suggests, how does a new lawyer set expectations? Would a client be best advised to seek out a lawyer who has had well-known success in trials and negotiations?

9. For an in-depth, scholarly discussion of the role of aspirations in settlement negotiations, see Korobkin (2002). Both Shell and Korobkin conclude that high aspirations may help negotiators reach better results, but at the cost of a greater risk of impasse and personal dissatisfaction in not fully achieving the expectations created by these aspirations.

3. A Preparation Checklist

The following checklist expands on the concepts developed in the previous excerpts and includes points from the selections that follow. Using a checklist is a way to discipline your thinking and provides an inventory of questions from which you can choose, depending on the case and the time available. Even limited preparation, you will find, is much better than none at all!

A. Strategy

1. Information:
- What data would be helpful to us in reaching a good settlement? What questions or steps will elicit it?
- What information is the other side likely to ask for?
- What information will they need to respond favorably to our proposals? Can we provide it, or help them obtain it?
- What should we be willing to reveal? What must we be careful to protect?
- Is there a basis for trading information?

2. Alternatives:
- What is our best alternative to an agreement?
- Can we improve the reality of that alternative?
- What is our worst outcome, if there is no agreement?
- Can we improve the other side's perception of the attractiveness of our alternative?
- What are their best alternative and their worst outcome?
- Can we diminish the value of their best and worst alternatives, or the way they perceive it?

3. Principles:
- What principles can we cite as to why our desired outcome is fair?
- Which principles are likely to be most persuasive to the other side?
- What standards will they cite? How can we rebut them?

4. Interests:
- What are ours? How do we rank their relative importance?
- What appear to be their interests? How do they see their relative importance?
- How do they see our interests? Should we attempt to change or enlarge their perspective?

- Are there potential solutions that would accommodate both sides' interests? What might be the best possible fit of terms?

5. **Communication:**
   - Should we communicate with the other side, either before the first meeting or before we begin to negotiate?
   - If so, should the communication be focused on building trust or on substance? What message do we want to send?
   - What theme or story will best present our perspective?
   - Are there special issues, such as culture or language, that we should consider?

6. **Relationships:**
   - Will the right people be at the table? Should we seek anyone out?
   - What kind of relationship do we want with the other side, at the bargaining table and afterwards?
   - Should I or my client attempt to create working relationships with specific members of the other team? How should we do this?
   - What message do we want to leave with the other side at the end of our first meeting?
   - Are there any problems in the relationship that need to be resolved?

B. Bargaining

7. **Process:**
   - What style of bargaining is likely to be most effective? What style is the other side likely to employ?
   - Should we change style, or expect a change, as the process goes forward?
   - What process, in terms of structure or stages, do we want? What is the other side likely to expect?
   - What roles should I, my client, and any other team members play? How should we interact and coordinate with each other?
   - What agenda should we propose? What agenda do they expect?
   - How can we influence the process, style, and agenda?

8. **Goals:**
   - What are our goals in the process: an interest-based solution, best result for our side, or something else? What would a good overall result look like?
   - What should we set as our highest achievable goal?
   - How can we explain or justify it, to ourselves and to the other side?
   - How can we strengthen our commitment to our goal?
   - What is the minimum that we will accept?
   - What "trip wire" should we set above the minimum?

9. **Tactics:**
   - If we anticipate a positional process:
     - Should we make the first offer? How quickly?
     - What should it be?
     - What message do we want to send by our offer?
     - What pattern of concessions is most likely to get us to our goal? What pattern is the other side likely to use?
   - If we want to stimulate an interest-based solution:
     - How should we encourage a process that brings out interests?
     - That identifies good solutions?

10. Final Terms:
- Do we need any specific terms in the final agreement? Is the other side likely to insist on particular terms?
- Should we prepare a draft agreement?
- Will we or the other side need to get approval for a settlement? How should we provide for that in the negotiation process?

B. Initial Interaction

How we feel about people with whom we negotiate is critical to whether an agreement will be reached. Just as you may feel that you can quickly "read" the character and trustworthiness of those you face, so others are forming a quick impression of you. Bargaining partners may begin to form an impression of you before you actually meet. As you gain experience, your reputation in the community may precede you, and the Internet opens your public history for all to see.

Almost all negotiators communicate and interact at least somewhat before they begin substantive bargaining, if only to exchange greetings and introductions. Although Americans are famous for wanting to "get down to business," in all but the most adversarial situations even lawyers exchange a bit of "small talk" before they begin to negotiate. These initial nonsubstantive interactions can have a significant impact on the later bargaining.

Trust is more likely to develop between negotiators if they see one another as similar. Similarities in backgrounds, experience, values, tastes, or group identity help develop rapport and smooth the way to trust. There is a balance between engaging in "small talk" and getting to substantive issues, but to a degree that you might not have appreciated, time devoted to establishing personal connections is usually time well spent.

❖ Roy Lewicki et al., Essentials of Negotiation
McGraw-Hill/Irwin 116-117 (3d ed. 2004)

Although there is no guarantee that trust will lead to collaboration, there is plenty of evidence to suggest that mistrust inhibits collaboration. People who are interdependent but do not trust each other will act tentatively or defensively. Defensiveness usually means that they will not accept information at face value but instead will look for hidden, deceptive meanings. When people are defensive, they withdraw and withhold information. Defensive people also attack their opponent's statements and position, seeking to defeat their position rather than to work together. Either of these responses is likely to make the negotiator hesitant, cautious, and distrustful of the other, undermining the negotiation process.

Generating trust is a complex, uncertain process; it depends in part on how the parties behave and in part on the parties' personal characteristics. When people trust each other, they are more likely to share information [and] communicate accurately their needs, positions, and the facts of the situation.

In contrast, when people do not trust each other, they are more likely to engage in positional bargaining, use threats, and commit themselves to tough positions. As with defensiveness, mistrust is likely to be reciprocated and to lead to unproductive negotiations. To develop trust effectively, each negotiator must believe that both she and the other party choose to behave in a cooperative manner; moreover each must believe that this behavior is a signal of the other's honesty, openness, and a similar mutual commitment to a joint solution.

A number of key factors contribute to the development of trust between negotiators. First, people are more likely to trust someone they perceive as similar to them or as holding a positive attitude toward them. Second, people often trust those who depend on them: Being in a position to help or hurt someone (who can do the same in return) fosters mutual trust. Third, people are more likely to trust those who initiate cooperative, trusting behavior. Acting in a cooperative, trusting manner serves as an invitation to others, especially if the invitation is repeated despite initially contentious behavior from the opponent. Fourth, there is some evidence that giving a gift to the other negotiator may lead to increased trust. Finally, people are more likely to trust those who make concessions. The more other people's behavior communicates that they are holding firm in their fundamental commitment to their own needs at the same time as they are working toward a joint solution, the more negotiators are likely to find their conduct trustworthy, in the spirit of the best joint agreement.

Given that trust has to be built during the negotiation, tone-setting and other opening moves are crucial. The more cooperative, open, and non-threatening the opening statements and actions of a party are, the more trust and cooperation are engendered in the other party. Once a cooperative position is established, it is more likely to persist. If cooperative behavior can be established at the very beginning, there is a tendency for parties to lock into this cycle and make it continue. Finally, opening moves not only help set the tone for the negotiation but also begin the momentum. The longer the cycle of trust and cooperation continues, the easier it would be to reestablish it should the cycle break down.

Note: The Importance of "Small Talk" in Bargaining

Professor Janice Nadler has reported on an interesting experiment in which students at Northwestern and Duke Law Schools tested the impact of "small talk" on bargaining. (Nadler 2004) The following are excerpts from her comments:

> The experiment involved an email negotiation over the purchase of a new car between students at the two law schools. It contained both distributive and integrative elements; although both parties were motivated to claim as much value for themselves as possible, they had different priorities as to specific terms. One set of students simply began to negotiate. Another group of students, however, were told to have an initial "getting to know you" telephone conversation with their partner lasting five to ten minutes. The participants were told that they should not talk about business (i.e., the negotiation); the

goal was simply to "break the ice." The content of the chats was often trivial (e.g., "The weather is nice here in Chicago." "Yes, it is nice here, too.") Regardless of whether there was small talk, all of the negotiations took place exclusively via e-mail.

The negotiators who had a "getting-to-know-you" conversation prior to negotiating via e-mail reached superior economic outcomes and markedly better social outcomes than negotiators who did not talk on the phone....Only 9 per cent of the "Small Talk" pairs failed to reach agreement, while nearly 40 per cent of the others failed to reach agreement.

Why did this occur? Negotiators who did not engage in small talk reported feeling more competitive and less cooperative toward their counterpart than negotiators who did engage in small talk. The "Small Talk" group exchanged significantly more information about their relative priorities on issues than the other group, and their information sharing was reciprocated more often.

The "Small Talk" group was also less likely to talk about their alternatives to reaching agreement (such as buying their car at another dealership). Students who did not chat first found the process of e-mail communication more difficult, ending up feeling significantly more angry, annoyed, and cold toward their opponent. In a related phenomenon, negotiators who engaged in small talk formed an impression of their counterpart as significantly more accomplished, skilled, effective, and perceptive than negotiators who did not. Finally, "Small Talk" bargainers left the negotiation with significantly more trust in their counterparts than the other group.

Nadler concluded that cooperation helped participants solve the "negotiator's dilemma." The getting-to-know-you telephone calls made the bargainers' subsequent e-mail negotiations proceed more smoothly by creating rapport that helped them trust each others' good intentions. The negotiators who engaged in small talk agreed (albeit tacitly) to share enough information to determine what kind of agreement would satisfy both their needs. In Nadler's view, the study documents the importance for lawyers of establishing rapport when negotiating with another lawyer who is an "unknown quantity."

Question

10. In her article Professor Nadler suggests: "[O]utside of the negotiation context, social psychologists have shown that using flattery (even when people suspect the flatterer has ulterior motives) and humor, and mentioning points of similarity, can facilitate good feelings and relationship building, thereby engendering the kind of cooperation and trust that leads to discovery of mutually profitable negotiated solutions." If "schmoozing" is one form of social grease that makes deals happen, can you think of other ways to create rapport?

C. Exchanging Information

The task of finding out all that you can about the other side — their needs, their arguments, their BATNA, and other factors affecting their approach to bargaining — pervades the entire negotiation process. Similarly, disclosing and managing information in your control that may shape the other side's perceptions is also important. Exchanging information is listed as a separate step to emphasize its importance in bargaining. A hallmark of effective negotiators, whether competitive or cooperative, is their ability to listen, their propensity to ask questions, and their desire to gather information continually. Indeed, information often is power in negotiation. In one empirical study, for example, effective bargainers were found to ask more than twice as many questions as average ones (Rackham and Carlisle 1978). Good competitive lawyers devote much of the negotiation process to bargaining over information, often before they make any actual offers. Experienced cooperative lawyers also exchange information, but in an open and collaborative manner.

If you can learn what is in the mind and heart of the other bargainer, you can make a personal connection, satisfy his needs, and get what you want at the lowest possible cost. If you actively allow others to openly express themselves, they usually will give you useful data. The more you talk, the less you can listen and learn. The key lesson here is an easy one: Talk less and listen more. When you do speak in a negotiation, do so in a way that elicits information or that helps shape the process. Indeed, sometimes giving out information is the best way to encourage others to provide it to you.

❖ Melissa L. Nelken, Understanding Negotiation
Anderson Publishing 68-71 (2001)

In the course of the negotiation, you will try to learn things about the other party's case, and about his perception of your case, that you don't know when the negotiation starts. He, of course, will do the same with you. Another important aspect of preparation, then, is deciding what you need to find out before you actually make a deal. Without considering what information you need to gather in the early stages of the negotiation, you will not be able to gauge how well the actual situation fits the assumptions you have made in preparing to negotiate. You may have overestimated how much the other party needs a deal with you, or underestimated the value he places on what you are selling. Only careful attention to gathering information will enable you to adjust your goals appropriately. In addition to what you want to learn, you also have to decide what information you are willing, or even eager, to divulge to the other party — for example, the large number of offers you have already received for the subject property — and what information you want to conceal — for example, the fact that none of those offers exceeds the price you paid for the property originally. Managing information is a central feature of distributive bargaining, and you have to plan to do it well.

A beginning negotiator often feels that she has to conceal as much as possible, that virtually anything she reveals will hurt her or be used against her.... [Y]ou are more likely to feel this way if you have not thought through your case and [considered] how to present it in the best light that you realistically can. If you choose when and how you will reveal information, rather than anxiously concealing as much as possible, you gain a degree of control over the negotiation that you lack when you merely react to what your counterpart says or does. Increasing the amount of information you are prepared to reveal, and reducing the amount you feel you absolutely must conceal, will help you make a stronger case for your client. In addition, the more willing you are to share information that the other party considers useful, the more likely you are to learn what you need to know from your counterpart before you make a deal.

Using Outside Sources

As part of your preparation, you need to consult outside sources of information to help you understand the context of a given negotiation. You will need data about the subject of the negotiation — market prices, alternate sources of supply, industry standards, market factors affecting the company you are dealing with, and so on. In addition, information about the parties and their representatives from others who have negotiated with them in the past will be helpful in planning your strategy. You will also want to learn about any relevant negotiation conventions, for example, the convention in personal injury litigation that the plaintiff makes the first demand....

Bargaining for Information

A central aspect of distributive [or competitive] bargaining is bargaining for information. In the course of planning, you have to make certain working assumptions about the motives and wishes of the other side, as well as about the factual context of the negotiation. In addition, we all have a tendency to "fill in" missing information in order to create a coherent picture of a situation. For a negotiator, it is imperative to separate out what you know to be true from what you merely believe to be true by testing your assumptions during the early stages of the negotiation. Otherwise, you risk making decisions based on inaccurate information and misunderstanding what the other side actually tells you....

Many negotiators forget that they start with only a partial picture of the situation, and they push to "get down to numbers" before learning anything about the other side's point of view.... The most obvious way to gather that information is by asking questions, especially about the reasons behind positions taken by the other party. Why does a deal have to be made today? How good are her alternatives to settlement with you? What is the basis for a particular offer? Asking questions allows you to test the assumptions that you bring to the negotiation about both parties' situations. Questions also permit you to gauge the firmness of stated positions by learning how well supported they are by facts. In addition, the information you gather can alert you to issues that are important (or unimportant) to your counterpart, opening up possibilities for an advantageous settlement if you value those issues differently.

In addition to asking questions, you have to learn to listen carefully to what the other party says, to look for verbal and nonverbal cues that either reinforce or contradict the surface message conveyed. If someone tells you that he wants $40,000-50,000 to settle, you can be sure that he will settle for $40,000, or less. If he starts a sentence by saying, "I'll be perfectly frank with you...," take whatever follows with a large grain of salt and test it against other things you have heard. Asking questions is only one way to gather information, and not always the most informative one....

One of the most effective and underutilized methods of bargaining for information is silence. Many inexperienced negotiators, especially lawyer-negotiators, think that they are paid to talk and are not comfortable sitting quietly. If you can teach yourself to do so, you will find that you often learn things that would never be revealed in response to a direct question. [I]t is useful to keep in mind that if you are talking, you probably aren't hearing anything you do not already know. Therefore, silence is truly golden....

Sharing Information

All that has been said so far about integrative bargaining suggests that lawyers will only be able to do a good job if they share substantive information about their clients' needs and preferences and look for ways to make their differences work for them in the negotiation. According to Follett (1942, p. 36), "the first rule ... for obtaining integration is to put your cards on the table, face the real issue, uncover the conflict, bring the whole thing into the open." This is a far cry from the bargaining for information that characterizes distributive negotiations, where each side seeks to learn as much as possible about the other while revealing as little as it can. The more straightforward and clear the negotiators' communications are, the fewer obstacles there will be to recognizing and capitalizing on opportunities for mutual gain.... Of course, the need to share information in order to optimize results creates risks for the negotiators as well....

Strategic Use of Information

There is also anxiety because the amount of shared information needed for integrative bargaining to succeed may be more than a distributive bargainer wants to reveal. For example, a distributively-inclined buyer may prefer that his counterpart think that time of delivery, which he does not care much about, is very important to him, so that he can exact concessions on other aspects of the deal by "giving in" to a later delivery to accommodate the seller.... The fear of being taken advantage of often results in both sides' taking preemptive action focused on "winning" rather than on collaborating. Sometimes such strategies are effective; but they are also likely to impede or prevent what could be a fruitful search for joint gains.

Questions

11. Are there times when active listening, or responding to a question with a question, should not be used? When would you find these techniques annoying or counterproductive?
12. In addition to allowing you to listen more effectively, your silence will often prompt the other person to "fill the void" by speaking. The silence should be accompanied by continued eye contact to convey an expectation or invitation for more information. Have you used this method with friends or a family member? Do you think you are susceptible to this technique when used by others?

D. Bargaining

At the bargaining stage the cooperative and competitive approaches to negotiation diverge even more clearly. As we have seen, a competitive bargainer usually assumes that the goal is to obtain the biggest possible piece of a fixed pie and therefore focuses on orchestrating a pattern of concessions that will lead to the best outcome for his side. Such bargainers think of bargaining in terms of a positional "dance," with appeals to principle and fairness used mostly to bolster positions. By contrast, a cooperative or problem-solving bargainer gives top priority to identifying interests and devising options to satisfy them. This difference in goals inevitably shapes the bargaining tactics of different negotiators.

1. Competitive Approach

As we discussed in the prior chapter, competitive negotiators are likely to attach importance to who makes the first offer and what that offer should be. A competitor's goal in making a first offer is to set up an "anchor" that influences the other side's view of what would be a fair compromise and/or what it will take to get a deal. Once each side has made an initial offer, competitive bargainers face the challenge of deciding on a pattern of concessions that will lead to the best possible outcome for their client. Competitors almost always make concessions in a reciprocal pattern, moving up or down in response to corresponding moves by their opponent. The timing, amount, and characterizations of concessions are a form of communication. By varying these factors, each side sends the other signals about its intentions, offering enough to keep the other party "in the game" while at the same time seeking to deceive the opponent about exactly how far the offeror is willing to go to get an agreement. The following excerpt gives advice on how bargainers should structure the "dance" of concessions in a competitive process.

❖ Theron O'Connor, Planning and Executing an Effective Concession Strategy

Bay Group International (2003)

Negotiation is the process for reaching an agreement — pure and simple. Well, maybe not so simple and maybe not so pure[,] either. The process may be competitive; it may be collaborative; or, as in most cases, it may have significant elements of both. Negotiators typically aspire to maximize the satisfaction of their own interests and, at the same time, they must respond to the interests of and build a sustainable relationship with the other side. As with any process, negotiation is comprised of a number of moving parts which must be carefully managed and integrated — value must be anchored, framed and positioned; ambitious aspirations must be set; data must be handled in a disciplined way to ensure that only appropriate information is divulged to the other side and that the full range and depth of the other side's interests are uncovered; emotions and behavior must be rigorously controlled to both convey confidence and instill trust; and, finally, concessions typically have to be made in order to reach a meeting of the minds.

It is the concession piece of the negotiation process — the bargaining, the give-and-take, the "horse-trading," what the parties are willing to give up in order to reach an agreement — that will be discussed here. There are two principal sets of tasks to consider. The first is how to create the most advantageous negotiation context within which a concession strategy can be implemented. . . . The second critical consideration is how to effectively handle the *execution* of the concession strategy or plan once the context has been established. This piece will focus upon the execution phase.

It should be noted that the many parts of the negotiation process are not strictly sequential. Rather, they occur and reoccur throughout the negotiation and must be attended to iteratively. That is particularly true of concession patterns. Often attention to concessions is mistakenly deferred until late in the game and concessions are used tactically, rather than strategically, as a closing tool.

Once a desirable negotiating context has been established, the concession strategy can be executed. Whether to concede, when to concede, what to concede, how to concede are among a number of important considerations to keep in mind in dealing with concessions. Skilled negotiators develop plans for managing the process of making concessions, and thereby exert more control over the negotiation process. Conceding without a plan can doom you to failure in negotiation.

Concessions Should Be Made Only as Required

Notwithstanding that a sophisticated concession strategy has been developed — replete with creative and cost effective negotiables — no concessions should be made unless they are demanded by the other side. If the other side is willing to accept the initial proposal, then there has probably been a failure to accurately gauge the unexpectedly high value perception of the other side and a failure to take a sufficiently ambitious opening position. That error ought not to be compounded by then freely granting concessions from the largesse that has been built into the plan. While this should go without saying, there is often the temptation to "throw something in" simply because it is unexpectedly still there.

Concessions Should Be Made Slowly and Reluctantly

At the early stages of the negotiation, the focus should be on continuing to shape and influence the value perception of the other side and continuing to uncover and evaluate their wants and needs. With the range of reason advantageously set, it is imperative to hold the line and show resolve with respect to the value proposition and opening position. Reluctance to make concessions early on tends to increase their value in the mind of the other negotiator when they are in fact granted. Care should be taken, however, not to communicate too aggressive and inflexible a stance.

Try Not to Be the First to Make a Concession

If possible, get the other party to move first. Take the time to test the resolve of the other side by asking for concessions and suggesting ways that interests might be satisfied by them. First concessions can carry strong signals as to the flexibility of the other negotiator and can help calibrate the distance between the party's positions. Do not hesitate to make a concession, however, if it seems necessary to keep the negotiation going.

Get Something in Return for Any Concession

Concessions should be made in the context of trades or exchanges rather than given simply to see if the other side's point of satisfaction might be found. Demanding a concession in return both reinforces the value of what is being conceded and signals the resolve of the negotiator making the concession. It also helps to build the process of give and take and stimulate movement toward agreement.

First Concede Low Cost Negotiables That Represent High Value to the Other Side and Vice Versa

Having prioritized and ranked those things which might be offered to satisfy the wants and needs of the parties, it is important to evaluate each opportunity in terms of what might be offered that would be perceived to provide the highest possible value to the other side at the lowest cost. Likewise, in seeking concessions from the other side, it is important to seek concessions of high perceived value at comparatively low cost to them.

Use a Concession Pattern Designed to Leverage Fundamental Interests

Concession patterns communicate predictable messages to the other side. Holding firm and making one big concession at the end sends one message; making one large early concession and then holding firm sends another message. Making incremental but growing concessions sends one message; making incremental but diminishing concessions sends another message. Driving value early on and then executing a concession pattern of a large concession first and then progressively smaller ones often can be the most powerful pattern of all. It communicates resolve, then flexibility, and then diminishing returns moving toward closure.

Conclusion

It is critical to the ultimate success of the negotiation to deal with the concession process early on — even prior to initial contact — both to build the most advantageous context and to develop a strategy for execution of the concession plan. The context-building activities — anchoring, framing, positioning, setting high opening targets, discovering interests and nego-tiables, and managing emotions and behaviors — help to develop a robust value proposition and to stretch the range-of-reason within which an optimal outcome can be achieved.

Concession execution guidelines help to ensure that the negotiator will not give up too much too soon and that an appropriate balance will be maintained between self-interested competitiveness on the one hand and relational collaboration on the other. The concession execution guidelines are:

No Concession Unless Needed
Get the Other Party to Make First Concession
Concede Slowly and Reluctantly
Get Something in Return
Concede to High Value from Low Cost/Vice-Versa
Use Advantageous Pattern

Rigorous integration of both phases, building context and concession execution — from beginning to end — create the highest likelihood of successful negotiation.

_____

This discussion may suggest that toughness is the most desirable quality in a bargainer. After all, if a negotiator begins with an extreme position and makes concessions grudgingly, she will have the benefit of the "anchoring" effect and there will be little risk of giving up value unnecessarily. Moreover, it is always possible to become more reasonable, but usually very difficult to move from an initial position of reasonableness to an extreme. Still, there are potential risks to adopting an extreme approach to first offers or concessions. These risks are dramatically illustrated by the following account of a bargaining session that occurred in a high-stakes case, in which a group of working-class families sued major corporations over groundwater pollution that they believed had caused the deaths of their children from leukemia.

❖ Jonathan Harr, A Civil Action
Vintage Books 277-279 (1996)

After a few minutes, the lawyers took their assigned seats at the table. Schlichtmann began talking about how he and his partners took only a few select cases and worked to the exclusion of all else on those. (This was Schlichtmann's way of saying there was no stopping them.) He said he wanted a settlement that would provide for the economic security of the families, and for their medical bills in the future. The families, he continued, weren't in this case just for money. They wanted an acknowledgment of the companies' wrongdoing, Schlichtmann said, a full disclosure of all the dumping activities.

"Are you suggesting there hasn't been a full disclosure?" Facher asked. "No," said Schlichtmann, who was suggesting exactly that, but now made an effort to avoid confrontation. "But as part of a settlement, we want a disclosure that the judge will bless." Another condition of settlement, he added, was an agreement that the companies clean their land of the toxic wastes, and pay the costs for cleaning the aquifer.

None of the defense lawyers had touched any of the food or drink. As Schlichtmann spoke, he saw Facher reach for a bowl of mints on the table and slowly unwrap the foil from one. Facher popped the mint into his mouth and sucked on it, watching Schlichtmann watch him.

Schlichtmann talked for fifteen minutes. Then Gordon laid out the financial terms of the settlement: an annual payment of $1.5 million to each of the eight families for the next thirty years; $25 million to establish a research foundation that would investigate the links between hazardous wastes and illness; and another $25 million in cash.

Cheeseman and his partners took notes on legal pads as Gordon spoke. Facher examined the pen provided courtesy of the Four Seasons, but he did not write anything on his pad. Facher studied the gilt inscription on the pen. It looked like a good-quality pen. These figures, he thought, were preposterous. They meant that Schlichtmann did not want to settle the case, or else he was crazy. Maybe Schlichtmann simply wanted to go to trial. This opulent setting, and Schlichtmann sitting at the table flanked by his disciples like a Last Supper scene, annoyed Facher. Where was Schlichtmann getting the money for all this?

When Gordon finished, silence descended.

Finally Facher stopped studying the pen. He looked up, and said, "If I wasn't being polite, I'd tell you what you could do with this demand."

Cheeseman had added up Gordon's figures. By Cheeseman's calculations, Schlichtmann was asking a total of four hundred ten million over thirty years. "How much is that at present value?" Cheeseman asked Gordon.

Gordon replied that he would rather not say. "Your own structured-settlement people can tell you that."

Facher took a croissant from the plate in front of him, wrapped it in a napkin, and put it into his pocket. That and the mint he had consumed were the only items the defense lawyers had taken from the sumptuous banquet that Gordon had ordered.

Cheeseman and his partners asked a few more perfunctory questions about the terms of disclosure, which Schlichtmann answered. Facher had gone back to studying the pen. "Can I have this?" he said abruptly, looking at Schlichtmann.

Schlichtmann, appearing surprised, nodded. Facher put the pen into his breast pocket. "Nice pen," he said. "Thank you."

Then Facher got up, put on his coat, and walked out the door. Frederico, who had not uttered a word, followed him.

Cheeseman and his partners stood, too, and in a moment, they followed Facher.

Schlichtmann and his colleagues sat alone on their side of the table. Gordon looked at his watch. The meeting had lasted exactly thirty-seven minutes, he announced. "I guess we're going to trial," Gordon added.

Schlichtmann was surprised, but only for a moment. He looked at his colleagues and shrugged. "We're going to get a jury in two weeks," he said. "The pressure's on them."

Conway got up and paced the room and smoked a cigarette. He didn't feel like talking. There was nothing to discuss. They'd gotten nothing out of this so-called settlement conference, not even information from the other side. He put on his coat and, along with Crowley, walked up Tremont Street back to the office.

Questions

13. How did Schlichtmann go wrong? What advice offered by Shell about justification for high demands and by Goodpaster on competitive bargaining might have been helpful to Schlichtmann in making his demand? What would you have done differently than Schlictmann in this situation?

14. Might local custom and the experience of opposing counsel, as well as their evaluation of the legal case, have been contributing factors to the defense walkout?

2. Cooperative Approach

How would a cooperative or problem-solving negotiator approach the task of exchanging offers to obtain an agreement? Professor Menkel-Meadow suggested in the prior chapter that such a bargainer would see the entire purpose of the process differently, and this in turn should affect the tactics the negotiator would employ. In the next reading Professors Mnookin, Peppet, and Tulumello propose a way to generate value-creating bargains as part of a cooperative approach.

❖ **Robert H. Mnookin, Scott R. Peppet, and Andrew S. Tulumello, Beyond Winning: Negotiating to Create Value in Deals and Disputes**

Harvard University Press 37-43 (2000)

Generate Value-Creating Options

[Looking] for value-creating trades . . . is not as easy as it might appear. Many negotiators jump into a negotiation process that inhibits value creation. One side suggests a solution and the other negotiator shoots it down. The second negotiator proposes an option, only to be told by the first why it can't work. After a few minutes of this, neither side is willing to propose anything but the most conventional solutions. This method mistakenly conflates two processes that should be engaged in separately: generating options and evaluating them.

It often helps to engage in some sort of brainstorming. The most effective brainstorming requires real freedom — however momentary — from practical constraints. [There are two ground rules for brainstorming:]

- No evaluation
- No ownership

Premature evaluation inhibits creativity. We are all self-critical enough, and adding to our natural inhibitions only makes matters worse. When brainstorming, avoid the temptation to critique ideas as they are being generated. This includes avoiding even congratulatory comments about how great someone else's idea is, murmurs of approval, and backslapping. When you signal such approval, you send the implicit message that you're still judging each idea as it is generated — you're just keeping the *negative* comments to yourself. That does not encourage inventiveness. The goal is to liberate those at the table to suggest ideas. One person's idea may seem crazy, but it may prompt another person to suggest a solution that might otherwise have been overlooked. There will be time enough for evaluation. The idea behind brainstorming is that evaluation should be a separate activity, not mixed with the process of generating ideas.

The second ground rule of brainstorming is: *no ownership of ideas*. Those at the table should feel free to suggest anything they can think of, without fear that their ideas will be attributed to them or used against them. Avoid comments such as: "John, I'm surprised to hear you suggest that; I didn't think you believed that idea made much sense." John should be able to suggest an idea *without believing it*. Indeed, those at the table should feel free to suggest ideas that are not in their best interests, purely to stimulate discussion, without fear that others at the table will later take those ideas as offers.

In preparing for negotiations, brainstorming is often employed behind the table with colleagues in order to generate ideas. For many negotiators, however, it may feel very dangerous to engage in this activity with someone on the other side. Our own experience suggests, nevertheless, that by negotiating process clearly, brainstorming can also be productive across the table.

How do you convey these ground rules to the other side? You can get the point across without sounding dictatorial or rule-obsessed. Just explain what you're trying to achieve and then lead by example.... Generating these possible options may broaden the parties' thinking about the terms of their negotiated agreement....

What happens to interest-based, collaborative problem-solving when you turn to distributive issues? Some negotiators act as if problem-solving has to be tossed overboard when the going gets tough. We could not disagree more. In our experience, it's when distributive issues are at the forefront that problem-solving skills are most desperately needed....

Sometimes, of course, you won't be able to find a solution that satisfies both sides. No matter how hard you try, you will continue to disagree about salary, the amount to be paid in a bonus, or some aspect of a dispute settlement. Norms may have helped move you closer together, but there's still a big gap between the two sides. What should you do?

Think about process. How can you design a process that would fairly resolve this impasse? In a dispute settlement, you might be able to hire a mediator to address the distributive issues that are still open. Is there anyone both sides trust enough to decide the issue? Could you put five possible agreements into a hat and pick one at random?

Procedural solutions can often rescue a distributive negotiation that has reached an impasse. They need not involve complicated alternative dispute resolution procedures that cost money and time. Instead, you can often come up with simple process solutions that will resolve a distributive deadlock and allow you to move forward.

Changing the Game

Not everyone approaches negotiation from a problem-solving perspective. The basic approach described [here] — with its emphasis on the sources of value creation and the importance of a problem-solving process — obviously departs from the norm of adversarial haggling. To be a problem-solver, a negotiator must often lead the way and change the game....

Conclusion

The tension between value creation and value distribution exists in almost all negotiations. But as our teaching and consulting have shown us, many people tend to see a negotiation as purely one or the other. Some people see the world in zero-sum terms — as solely distributive. We work hard to demonstrate to people that there are nearly always opportunities to create value. Others believe that, with cooperation, the pie can be made so large that distributive questions will disappear. For these negotiators, we emphasize that there are always distributive issues to address....

The problem-solving approach we have suggested here will not make distributive issues go away or this first tension of negotiation disappear. But it does outline an approach that will help you find value-creating opportunities when they exist and resolve distributive issues efficiently and as a shared problem....

Question

15. If this approach will not make distributive issues go away, how do you think the authors would deal with them?

E. Moving Toward Closure

As the bargaining process continues, negotiators often find it more and more difficult to make concessions or identify additional value-creating trades. All the easy, obvious moves have been made, and yet a gap may well remain. There are many ways to manage the process of bridging the final gap between bargainers. This section explores two of the most common methods.

1. Seeking Inventive Solutions

❖ Roger Fisher, William Ury, and Bruce Patton, Getting to Yes
Penguin 171-175 (1991)

[H]ow do you reach closure on issues? We don't believe that there is any one best process, but here are some general principles worth considering:

Think about closure from the beginning. Before you even begin to negotiate, it makes sense to envision what a successful agreement might look like. This will help you figure out what issues will need to be dealt with in the negotiation and what it might take to resolve them. Imagine what it might be like to implement an agreement. What issues would need to be resolved? Then work backwards. Ask yourself how the other side might successfully explain and justify an agreement to their constituents. ("We will be in the top 10 percent of all electrical workers in Ontario." "We are paying less than the value given by two out of three appraisers.") Think about what it will take for you to do the same. Then ask yourself what kind of an agreement would allow you both to say such things. Finally, think about what it might take to persuade the other side — and you — to accept a proposed agreement, rather than continuing to negotiate.

Keep these questions in mind as your negotiation progresses, reshaping and filling in your vision as more information becomes available. Focusing on your goal in this way will help to keep your negotiation on a productive track.

Consider crafting a framework agreement. In negotiations that will produce a written agreement, it is usually a good idea to sketch the outlines of what an agreement might look like as part of your preparation. Such a "framework agreement" is a document in the form of an agreement, but with blank spaces for each term to be resolved by negotiation....

Whether or not you start your negotiation with a framework agreement, it makes sense to draft possible terms of an agreement as you go. Working on a draft helps to keep discussions focused, tends to surface important issues that might otherwise be overlooked, and gives a sense of progress. Drafting as you go also provides a record of discussions, reducing the chance of later misunderstanding. If you are working with a framework agreement, drafting may involve no more than filling in the blanks as you discuss each term; or, if you have yet to reach consensus, it may involve drafting alternative provisions.

Move toward commitment gradually. As the negotiation proceeds and you discuss options and standards for each issue, you should be seeking a consensus proposal that reflects all the points made and meets each side's interests on that issue as well as possible. If you are as yet unable to reach consensus on a single option, try at least to narrow the range of options under consideration and then go on to another issue. Perhaps a better option or a trade-off possibility will occur later. ("All right. So perhaps something like $28,000 or $30,000 might make sense on salary. What about the starting date?")

To encourage brainstorming, it is a good idea to agree explicitly that all commitments are tentative.... At the top of a framework agreement, for example, you might write: "Tentative Draft — No Commitments."

The process of moving toward agreement is seldom linear. Be prepared to move through the list of issues several times, going back and forth between looking at particular issues and the total package. Difficult issues may be revisited frequently or set aside until the end, depending on whether incremental progress seems possible. Along the way, avoid demands or locking in. Instead, offer options and ask for criticism. ("What would you think of an agreement along the lines of this draft? I am not sure I could sell it to my people, but it might be in the ballpark. Could something like this work for you? If not, what would be wrong with it?")

Be persistent in pursuing your interests but not rigid in pursuing any particular solution. One way to be firm without being positional is to separate your interests from ways to meet them. When a proposal is challenged, don't defend the proposal; rather explain again your underlying interests. Ask if the other side can think of a better way to meet those interests, as well as their own. If there appears to be an irresolvable conflict, ask if there is any reason why one side's interests should have priority over the other's.

Unless the other side makes a persuasive case for why your thinking is incomplete and should be changed, stick to your analysis. When and if you are persuaded, modify your thinking accordingly, presenting the logic first. ("Well, that's a good point. One way to measure that factor would be to . . .") If you have prepared well, you should have anticipated most arguments the other side might raise and thought through how you think they should affect the result.

Throughout, the goal is to avoid useless quarreling. Where disagreements persist, seek second-order agreement — agreement on where you disagree. Make sure that each side's interests and reasoning are clear. Seek differing assumptions and ways to test them. As always seek to reconcile conflicting interests with external standards or creative options. Seek to reconcile conflicting standards with criteria for evaluating which is more appropriate or with creative trade-offs. Be persistent.

2. Splitting the Difference and Dealing with Impasse

One deceptively simple technique often used for closing remaining money differences and employed by both competitive and cooperative negotiators is "splitting the difference." Professor Richard Shell discusses this tactic under a category he refers to as "softer closing tactics" and offers additional advice on what to do if the negotiation reaches impasse.

❖ G. Richard Shell, Bargaining for Advantage: Negotiation Strategies for Reasonable People

Viking 189-195 (1999)

. . . Perhaps the most frequently used closing technique is splitting the difference. Bargaining research tells us that the most likely settlement point in any given transaction is the midpoint between the two opening offers. People who instinctively prefer a compromise style like to cut through the whole bargaining process by getting the two opening numbers on the table and then splitting them right down the middle. Even in cases in which the parties have gone through several rounds of bargaining, there often comes a time when one side or the other suggests that the parties meet halfway between their last positions. In situations in which the relationship between the parties is important, this is a perfectly appropriate, smooth way to close.

Why is splitting the difference so popular? First, it appeals to our sense of fairness and reciprocity, thus, setting a good precedent for future dealings between the parties. . . . Each side makes an equal concession simultaneously. What could be fairer than that? Second, it is simple and easy to understand. It requires no elaborate justification or explanation. The other side sees exactly what you are doing. Third, it is quick. For people who do not like to negotiate or are in a hurry, splitting the difference offers a way out of the potentially messy interpersonal conflict that looms whenever a negotiation occurs.

Splitting the difference is such a common closing tactic that it often seems rude and unreasonable to refuse, regardless of the situation. This is taking a good thing too far, however. There are at least two important situations in which I would hesitate to split the difference.

First, you should be careful that the midpoint being suggested is genuinely fair to your side. Experienced hagglers know that most deals end up halfway between the two opening offers, so they open aggressively. If you have opened at a reasonable price rather than an aggressive one, the midpoint is likely to favor the other party by a big margin. So don't split the difference at the end if there was a lack of balance at the beginning. Hold out for a fair price that achieves your goals.

A second time when splitting may be ill advised is in the early stages of [situations where you are concerned both about the outcome and the relationship]. When a lot of money or an important principle is on the line and relationships matter, quick resort to a simple-minded closing gambit such as splitting may leave everyone worse off than necessary. It is nevertheless tempting to split because this tactic appears so transparently fair....

When the gap between offers is too wide to split, another friendly way to close is to obtain a neutral valuation or appraisal.... If the parties cannot agree on a single appraiser, they can each pick one and agree to split the difference between the two numbers given by the experts.

What Happens If Negotiations Break Down?

The concession-making stage of bargaining sometimes ends with no deal rather than an agreement. The parties reach an impasse. In fact, a no deal result is sometimes the right answer. There are many reasons for bargaining breakdowns. In some cases, negotiators escalate their commitment to their prior positions and pride gets in the way of continuing with bargaining. In addition to escalation problems, sometimes the parties start too far apart to close the gap. Many times there are miscommunications, misunderstanding, and simple bad chemistry that the parties fail to overcome. Now what?

Accommodating people usually think that impasse is a bad thing. After all, people tend to get emotional when there is a bargaining breakdown, and interpersonal conflict usually bothers accommodators and avoiders. But the truth is otherwise: Impasse can often be helpful. A break in the negotiation causes parties to seriously reevaluate their expectations. They can return with clearer priorities and new solutions. And, as discussed above, walkouts are useful ways of signaling the issues of critical importance. Far from being anyone's fault, one party sometimes plans an impasse as part of its opening strategy — regardless of what the other side does.

That said, what can you do to get negotiations restarted once impasse occurs? I will touch on a few techniques below that I think work well.

Jump-Starting the Negotiation Process

Perhaps the easiest way to overcome impasse is to leave yourself a back door through which to return to the table when you get up to leave it. "In light of the position you have taken," you might say as you pack your bags, "we are unable to continue negotiations at this time." An attentive opponent will pick up on your use of the words "at this time" and tactfully ask you later if the time has come to reinitiate talks. This back door also allows you to contact the other side at a later date without losing face.

If the other negotiator leaves in a genuine fit of anger, he may not be very careful about leaving a back door open. If so, you should consider how you can let him back in without unnecessary loss of face. You must, in one expert's phrase, build him a "golden bridge" across which to return to the table. Such bridges include "forgetting" that he made his ultimatum in the first place or recalling his last statement in a way that gives him an excuse for returning. When miscommunication is the problem, a simple apology may be enough to get the parties back on track. If the relationship has deteriorated beyond apologies, changing negotiators or getting rid of intermediaries altogether may be necessary. . . .

The worst impasses are the products of emotional escalation that builds on itself: My anger makes you angry, and your response makes me even angrier . . . When people begin to fight over something, they tend to lose sight of the real issues. A deal is possible, but no one can make a move without losing face. What are the parties to do? The solution to this sort of collision, in business deals as well as wars, is what I call the "one small step" procedure. One side needs to make a very small, visible move in the other side's direction, then wait for reciprocation. If the other party responds, the two can repeat the cycle again, and so on. . . .

Egypt's late Prime Minister, Anwar Sadat, used the "one small step" technique to deescalate the Arab-Israeli conflict when he flew to Jerusalem on November 19, 1977 and later met with Prime Minister Menachem Begin. By simply getting off a plane in Israel — a very small step indeed — Sadat demonstrated his willingness to recognize Israel's existence. This move eventually led to the Camp David peace accords and Israel's return of the Sinai Peninsula to Egypt.

An executive once told me a bargaining story that nicely sums up how the "one small step" process can work in everyday life. Two parties were in a complex business negotiation. Both were convinced that they had leverage, and both thought that the best arguments favored their own view of the deal. After a few rounds, neither side would make a move. Finally one of the women at the table reached in her purse and pulled out a bag of M&M's. She opened the bag and poured the M&M's into a pile in the middle of the table.

"What are those for?" asked her counterparts.

"They are to keep score," she said.

Then she announced a small concession on the deal — and pulled an M&M out of the pile and put it on her side of the table. "Now it's your turn," she said to the men sitting opposite. Not to be outdone, her opponents put their heads together, came up with a concession of their own — and pulled out two M&M's. "Our concession was bigger than yours," they said. The instigator of the process wisely let the other side win this little argument and then made another concession of her own, taking another M&M for herself.

It wasn't long before the parties were working closely together to close the final terms of the deal. . . . Any similar mechanism that restarts the norm of reciprocity within the bargaining relationship will have a similar, helpful effect. . . .

Questions

16. Have you ever split the difference to conclude a negotiation or sale? Looking back, was that the best way to resolve the issue? Are you now sure you were not manipulated into an outcome that was more favorable to the other side?
17. Do you agree with Shell that impasse can often be helpful? If so, when? Why would anyone plan an impasse as part of their negotiating strategy?

F. Finalizing an Agreement

Even after decisions are made about how a case will be settled or a deal structured, the lawyer's work is not complete. In their relief at reaching a settlement, negotiators may neglect the important task of deciding how the agreement will be worded and the remaining details determined. A lack of clarity here can result in later arguments about what was decided or in a tentative deal unraveling. Relationship, legal, and practicality issues can arise in finalizing a negotiated agreement. The following reading discusses these issues.

❖ **Charles B. Craver, Effective Legal Negotiation and Settlement**

Lexis 212-218 (4th ed. 2001)

Leave Opponent with Sense They Got Good Deal

As the overall terms are being finalized, negotiators should remember how important it is to leave their opponents with the feeling they got a good deal. If their adversaries are left with a good impression, they will be more likely to honor the accord and more likely to behave cooperatively when the parties interact in the future. Some advocates attempt to accomplish this objectively by making the final concession on a matter they do not highly value. Even a minimal position change at this point is likely to be appreciated by the other side. Others try to do it by congratulating their opponents on the mutually beneficial agreement achieved. Individuals must be careful, however, not to be too effusive. When negotiators lavish praise on their opponents at the conclusion of bargaining interactions, those individuals tend to become suspicious and think they got a poor deal.

Take Time to Review Agreement

When bargaining interactions are successfully concluded, many participants are anxious to terminate their sessions and return to other client matters. As a result, they fail to ensure a clear meeting of the minds. If both sides are not in complete agreement, subsequent misunderstandings may negate their bargaining efforts. To avoid later disagreements, the participants should take the time to review the specific terms agreed upon before they adjourn their discussions. In most instances they will encounter no difficulties and will merely reaffirm the provisions they have achieved.

Endeavor to Draft Final Agreement

Once ... a final accord has been achieved, many negotiators are readily willing to permit opposing counsel to prepare the settlement agreement. While this may save them time and effort, it is a risky practice. [Each negotiator] would probably use slightly different terminology to represent his or her own perception of the matter. To ensure that their client's particular interests are optimally protected, bargainers should always try to be the one to draft the operative document.

No competent attorney would ever contemplate the omission of terms actually agreed upon or the inclusion of items not covered by the parties' oral understanding. Either practice would be wholly unethical and would constitute fraud. Such disreputable behavior could subject the responsible practitioner and his or her client to substantial liability and untoward legal problems. Why then should lawyers insist upon the right to prepare the final accord? It is to allow them to draft a document that unambiguously reflects their perception of the overall agreement achieved by the parties.

Each provision should be carefully prepared to state precisely what the drafting party thinks was mutually agreed upon. When the resulting contract is then presented to the other party for execution, it is quite likely that it would be reluctant to propose alternative language, unless serious questions regarding the content of particular clauses were raised. Doubts tend to be resolved in favor of the proffered document. This approach best ensures that the final contract will most effectively protect the interests of the party who drafted it.

Review Opponent's Draft Carefully

If negotiators are unable to prepare the ultimate agreement, they should be certain to review the terms of the document drafted by the other side before they permit their client to execute it. They should compare each provision with their notes and recollections of the interaction, to be positive that their understanding of the bargaining results is accurately represented. They should be certain that nothing agreed upon has been omitted and that nothing not agreed upon has been included. If drafters suggest that certain new terms are mere "boilerplate," reviewers should make sure those terms do not alter the fundamental substantive or procedural aspects of their agreement.

Unabashed Questioning of Drafts

Agreement reviewers should not hesitate to question seemingly equivocal language that may cause future interpretive difficulties or challenge phrases that do not appear to describe precisely what they think was intended by the contracting parties. ... Bargainers should never permit opponents to make them feel guilty about changes they think should be made in finally prepared agreements. It is always appropriate for non-drafting parties to be certain that the final language truly reflects what has been achieved through the negotiation process. If the other side repeatedly objects to proposed modifications because of the additional work involved, the participant suggesting the necessary alterations can quickly and effectively silence those protestations by offering to accept responsibility for the final stages of the drafting process. It is amazing how expeditiously these remonstrations cease when such an easy solution to the problem is suggested!

Tact in Questioning

When negotiators reviewing draft agreements discover apparent discrepancies, they should contact their opponents and politely question the pertinent language. They should not assume deliberate opponent deception. It is always possible that the persons challenging the prepared terminology are mistaken and that the proposed terms actually reflect what was agreed upon. . . . It is also possible that the drafting parties made honest mistakes that they would be happy to correct once they have examined their notes of the bargaining interaction. Even when document reviewers suspect intentional deception by drafting parties, they should still provide their opponents with a face-saving way out of the predicament. The best way to accomplish the desired result is to assume honest mistakes and give the drafters the opportunity to "correct" the erroneous provisions. If reviewers directly challenged an opponent's integrity, the dispute would probably escalate and endanger the entire accord.

Vigilance Against Underhanded Tactics

In recent years, a few unscrupulous practitioners in the corporate area have decided to take advantage of the drafting stage of large documents to obtain benefits not attained during the negotiation process. They include provisions that were never agreed upon, or modify or omit terms that were jointly accepted. They attempt to accomplish their deceptive objective by providing their opponents with copies of the agreement at the eleventh hour, hoping that time pressure will induce their unsuspecting adversaries to review the final draft in a cursory manner. Lawyers who encounter this tactic should examine each clause of the draft agreement with care to be certain it represents the actual accord achieved. If necessary, they should completely redraft the improper provisions. If their proposed terms are rejected by opposing counsel, they should insist upon a session with the clients present to determine which draft represents the true intentions of the parties. When this type of meeting is proposed, deceitful drafters are likely to "correct" the "inadvertent misunderstandings" before the clients ever get together. . . .

Addressing Unforeseen Ambiguities and Problems

On some occasions, ambiguities or actual disagreements may be discerned during this stage. Negotiators should not allow these difficulties to destroy their previous progress. When good faith misunderstandings are found, the advocates should strive to resolve them before they terminate their current interaction. At the conclusion of [this stage], the parties tend to be in a particularly accommodating frame of mind. They feel good about their bargaining achievements and are psychologically committed to a final accord. It is thus a propitious time to address newly discovered problems. If they do not deal with these issues now, they are likely to encounter greater difficulties when these questions arise at a later date.

Note: Ratification and Approval

In many situations, the final authority to sign the agreement rests with someone who has not been directly involved in the negotiation. Resolving labor-management controversies, for example, may require getting ratification from union members, and some corporate issues require a vote of stockholders. Disputes involving municipalities and other public bodies may require final approval of elected councils or boards. In such situations bargainers should agree at the outset on the approval or ratification process for any deal and on steps to ensure that the bargainers have the confidence of the final decision makers. Good faith deposits or penalty provisions if approval is not forthcoming may help guard against last-minute manipulations and disappointments.

The need for approval can give adversarial bargainers an opportunity to reopen negotiations and "nibble" at what was thought to be an agreed deal. As a bargainer, you should get clarification of who has ultimate authority and whose signature is necessary to create an enforceable agreement before you make any commitments. Alternatively, you may agree to limit the review to an up-or-down, all-or-nothing decision. The most effective way to ensure that "stakeholders" or other absent parties ratify a deal is to involve those with final authority in the bargaining process. If this is not feasible, you may want to build in requirements for interim approval or endorsement along the way. If stakeholders become invested in the process, they will be more inclined to concur than if they are presented with a fait accompli.

One method used by mediators can also be of help in direct negotiation, particularly when ratification may be required. It is the "single-text" approach, which involves agreeing on a provision or section and then circulating that section for approval before the next is written. This approach became famous due to its use by President Jimmy Carter in mediating the Camp David negotiations between Egypt and Israel (Carter 1982). The resulting document grows section by section, with buy-ins by all parties along the way. The completed agreement then reflects a joint effort, and the decision makers feel ownership of the result. Of course the pieces of an agreement are interrelated. and final approval must await the completed document, so there is no guarantee that a single-text agreement will be finally accepted. The process, however, makes success much more likely, while providing early signals of any difficulty.

This ends our brief introduction to the complex and fascinating process of negotiation. We now explore the hidden barriers and obstacles that often frustrate the settlement of legal disputes.

CHAPTER
4

Barriers to Settlement

If all negotiations were successful, then the dispute resolution pyramid described by Professor Galanter in Chapter 1 would have its top half lopped off. Either disputants would reach an accommodation with their opponents directly, or lawyers would negotiate satisfactory resolutions on their behalf, making it unnecessary for a party ever to file a case in court, much less go to trial. However, conflicts — in particular, legal disputes — often do fail to settle initially, leading to many court cases being filed. We now know that the large majority of legal cases are never adjudicated, implying that most litigants do eventually reach some kind of resolution short of trial. However, this may not occur for months or years, and while the dispute is pending, all the parties are likely to incur significant costs, both directly in terms of fees for legal services and indirectly in anxiety and disruption of their personal or business lives.

Negotiations fail, or stall, for a wide variety of reasons. One useful way to think about this issue is to focus on the specific barriers that make it difficult for lawyers and clients to bargain effectively. In the readings that follow, we examine four common types of barriers to successful bargaining: strategic, principal-agent, cognitive, and emotional.

A. Strategic and Principal-Agent Barriers

❖ Robert H. Mnookin, Why Negotiations Fail:
An Exploration of Barriers to the Resolution of Conflict

8 Ohio St. J. Disp. Resol. 235-243, 238-249 (1993)

Conflict is inevitable, but efficient and fair resolution is not. Conflicts can persist even though there may be any number of possible resolutions that would better serve the interests of the parties. . . . In our everyday personal and professional lives, we have all witnessed disputes where the absence of a resolution imposes substantial and avoidable costs on all parties. Moreover, many resolutions that are achieved — whether through negotiation or imposition — conspicuously fail to satisfy the economist's criterion of Pareto efficiency. Let me offer a few examples where, at least with the benefit of hindsight, it is easy to identify alternative resolutions that might have left both parties better off.

My first example involves a divorcing family in California who were part of a longitudinal study carried out by Stanford psychologist Eleanor Maccoby and me. Mary and Paul Templeton spent three years fighting over the custody of their seven-year-old daughter Tracy after Mary filed for divorce in 1985. Mary wanted sole custody; Paul wanted joint physical custody. This middle-income family spent over $37,000 on lawyers and experts. In the process, they traumatized Tracy and inflicted great emotional pain on each other. More to the point, the conflict over who would best care for their daughter damaged each parent's relationship with Tracy, who has suffered terribly by being caught in the middle of her parents' conflict. Ultimately the divorce decree provided that Mary would have primary physical custody of Tracy, and Paul would be entitled to reasonable weekend visitation. The parents' inability to negotiate with one another led to a result in which mother, father, and daughter were all losers.

A conflict between Eastern Airlines and its unions represents another conspicuous example of a lose-lose outcome. In 1986, Frank Lorenzo took over Eastern, then the eighth largest American airline, with over 42,000 employees and about 1,000 daily flights to seventy cities. For the next three years, Lorenzo, considered a union buster by organized labor, pressed the airline's unions for various concessions, and laid off workers to reduce costs. The unions retaliated in a variety of ways, including a public relations campaign suggesting Eastern's airplanes were being improperly maintained because Lorenzo was inappropriately cutting costs. In March 1989, labor-management skirmishes turned into all-out war. Eastern's machinists went on strike, and the pilots and flight attendants initially joined in. The ensuing "no holds barred" battle between Lorenzo and the machinists led to losses on both sides.

Soon after the strike began, to put pressure on the unions and to avoid creditor claims, Eastern's management filed for bankruptcy, hired permanent replacements for the strikers, and began to sell off assets. While the pilots and flight attendants held out only a few months, the machinists union persisted in its strike, determined to get rid of Lorenzo at whatever cost. In one sense, they succeeded, for in 1990 the bankruptcy court forced Lorenzo to relinquish control of Eastern. It turned out to be a pyrrhic victory for the union, however, for on January 18, 1991, Eastern Airlines permanently shut down operations.

The titanic struggle between Texaco and Pennzoil over Getty Oil provides another example of a bargaining failure, although of a somewhat more subtle sort. Here, both corporations survived, with a clear winner and loser; Texaco paid Pennzoil $3 billion in cash to end the dispute in 1988. The parties reached settlement, however, only after a year-long bankruptcy proceeding for Texaco and protracted legal wrangling in various courts. While the dispute dragged on, the combined equity value of the two companies was reduced by some $3.4 billion. A settlement before Texaco filed for bankruptcy would have used up fewer social resources and would have been more valuable to the shareholders of both companies than the resolution created by the bankruptcy court about a year later.

My last example is an Art Buchwald story — but it isn't a laughing matter, at least, not for Buchwald. He and his partner, Alain Bernheim, submitted Buchwald's two and a half page "treatment" for a story called "King for a Day" to Paramount Pictures pursuant to contracts providing that Bernheim would produce any film based on the story idea and that Buchwald and Bernheim would each share in the profits. In 1989, Buchwald and Bernheim sued Paramount for breach of contract. They claimed that the studio had based Eddie Murphy's film, "Coming to America[,]" on their treatment but had failed to give them their due. After three years of bitter litigation, a trial judge awarded Buchwald $150,000 and Bernheim $750,000. In the initial newspaper accounts, both sides claimed victory, but this is hardly an example of "win-win." Paramount claimed to be the winner because the legal fees of the plaintiffs' lawyers exceeded $2.5 million and the total recovery of only $900,000 was a small fraction of the $6.2 million Buchwald and Bernheim had requested in their final arguments. As it turns out, Buchwald and Bernheim will not have to pay the full legal fees because of a contingency arrangement with their law firm, but Buchwald has acknowledged that his share of out-of-pocket expenses alone exceeds $200,000 and that as a consequence, he will have no net recovery. On the other hand, Buchwald ridiculed Paramount's claim of victory. How, he asked, could it be a victory for a defendant to pay out nearly $1 million in damages, and, in addition, have legal fees of its own in excess of $3 million? Seems like lose-lose to me.

On her death bed, Gertrude Stein was asked by Alice B. Toklas, "What is the answer? What is the answer?" After a long silence, Stein responded: "No, what is the question?" Examples like these, and I am sure you could add many more of your own, suggest a central question for those of us concerned with dispute resolution: Why is it that under circumstances where there are resolutions that better serve disputants, negotiations often fail to achieve efficient resolutions? In other words, what are the barriers to the negotiated resolution of conflict?

Barriers to the Negotiated Resolution of Conflict

. . . I am not attempting [here] to provide a comprehensive list of barriers or an all-encompassing classification scheme. Instead, my purpose is to show that the concept of barriers provides a useful and necessarily interdisciplinary vantage point for exploring why negotiations sometimes fail. After describing these barriers and their relevance to the study of negotiation, I will briefly suggest a variety of ways that neutral third parties might help overcome each of these barriers.

Strategic Barriers

The first barrier to the negotiated resolution of conflict is inherent in a central characteristic of negotiation. Negotiation can be metaphorically compared to making a pie and then dividing it up. The process of conflict resolution affects both the size of the pie, and who gets what size slice.

The disputants' behavior may affect the size of the pie in a variety of ways. On the one hand, spending on avoidable legal fees and other process costs shrinks the pie. On the other hand, negotiators can together "create value" and make the pie bigger by discovering resolutions in which each party contributes special complementary skills that can be combined in a synergistic way, or by exploiting differences in relative preferences that permit trades that make both parties better off. Books like "Getting to Yes" and proponents of "win-win negotiation" emphasize the potential benefits of collaborative problem-solving approaches to negotiation which allow parties to maximize the size of the pie.

Negotiation also involves issues concerning the distribution of benefits, and, with respect to pure distribution, both parties cannot be made better off at the same time. Given a pie of fixed size, a larger slice for you means a smaller one for me. Because bargaining typically entails both efficiency issues (that is, how big the pie can be made) and distributive issues (that is, who gets what size slice), negotiation involves an inherent tension — one that [has been] dubbed the "negotiator's dilemma." In order to create value, it is critically important that options be created in light of both parties' underlying interests and preferences. This suggests the importance of openness and disclosure, so that a variety of options can be analyzed and compared from the perspectives of all concerned. However, when it comes to the distributive aspects of bargaining, full disclosure — particularly if unreciprocated by the other side — can often lead to outcomes in which the more open party receives a comparatively smaller slice. To put it another way, unreciprocated approaches to creating value leave their maker vulnerable to claiming tactics. On the other hand, focusing on the distributive aspects of bargaining can often lead to unnecessary deadlocks and, more fundamentally, a failure to discover options or alternatives that make both sides better off. A simple example can expose the dilemma. The first involves what game theorists call "information asymmetry." This simply means each side to a negotiation characteristically knows some relevant facts that the other side does not know.

Suppose I have ten apples and no oranges, and Nancy Rogers has ten oranges and no apples. (Assume apples and oranges are otherwise unavailable to either of us.) I love oranges and hate apples. Nancy likes them both equally well. I suggest to Nancy that we might both be made better off through a trade. If I disclose to Nancy that I love oranges and don't eat apples, and Nancy wishes to engage in strategic bargaining, she might simply suggest that her preferences are the same as mine, although, in truth, she likes both. She might propose that I give her nine apples (which she says have little value to her) in exchange for one of her very valuable oranges. Because it is often very difficult for one party to know the underlying preferences of the other party, parties in a negotiation may puff, bluff, or lie about their underlying interests and preferences. Indeed, in many negotiations, it may never be possible to know whether the other side has honestly disclosed its interests and preferences. I have to be open to create value, but my openness may work to my disadvantage with respect to the distributive aspect of the negotiation.

Even when both parties know all the relevant information, and that potential gains may result from a negotiated deal, strategic bargaining over how to divide the pie can still lead to deadlock (with no deal at all) or protracted and expensive bargaining, thus shrinking the pie. For example, suppose Nancy has a house for sale for which she has a reservation price of $245,000. I am willing to pay up to $295,000 for the house. Any deal within a bargaining range from $245,000 to $295,000 would make both of us better off than no sale at all. Suppose we each know the other's reservation price. Will there be a deal? Not necessarily. If we disagree about how the $50,000 "surplus" should be divided (each wanting all or most of it), our negotiation may end in a deadlock. We might engage in hardball negotiation tactics in which each tried to persuade the other that he or she was committed to walking away from a beneficial deal, rather than accept less than $40,000 of the surplus. Nancy might claim that she won't take a nickel less than $285,000, or even $294,999 for that matter. Indeed, she might go so far as to give a power of attorney to an agent to sell only at that price, and then leave town in order to make her commitment credible. Of course, I could play the same type of game and the result would then be that no deal is made and that we are both worse off. In this case, the obvious tension between the distribution of the $50,000 and the value creating possibilities inherent in any sale within the bargaining range may result in no deal.

Strategic behavior — which may be rational for a self-interested party concerned with maximizing the size of his or her own slice — can often lead to inefficient outcomes. Those subjected to claiming tactics often respond in kind, and the net result typically is to push up the cost of the dispute resolution process. (Buchwald v. Paramount Pictures Corp. is a good example of a case in which the economic costs of hardball litigation obviously and substantially shrunk the pie.) Parties may be tempted to engage in strategic behavior, hoping to get more. Often all they do is shrink the size of the pie. Those experienced in the civil litigation process see this all the time. One or both sides often attempt to use pre-trial discovery as leverage to force the other side into agreeing to a more favorable settlement. Often the net result, however, is simply that both sides spend unnecessary money on the dispute resolution process.

The Principal-Agent Problem

The second barrier is suggested by recent work relating to transaction cost economics, and is sometimes called the "principal[-]agent" problem. Notwithstanding the jargon, the basic idea is familiar to everyone in this room. The basic problem is that the incentives for an agent (whether it be a lawyer, employee, or officer) negotiating on behalf of a party to a dispute may induce behavior that fails to serve the interests of the principal itself. The relevant research suggests that it is no simple matter — whether by contract or custom — to align perfectly the incentives for an agent with the interests of the principal. This divergence may act as a barrier to efficient resolution of conflict.

Litigation is fraught with principal[-]agent problems. In civil litigation, for example — particularly where the lawyers on both sides are being paid by the hour — there is very little incentive for the opposing lawyers to cooperate, particularly if the clients have the capacity to pay for trench warfare and are angry to boot. Commentators have suggested that this is one reason many cases settle on the courthouse steps, and not before: for the lawyers, a late settlement may avoid the possible embarrassment of an extreme outcome, while at the same time providing substantial fees.

The Texaco/Pennzoil dispute may have involved a principal[-]agent problem of a different sort. My colleague Bob Wilson and I have argued that the interests of the Texaco officers and directors diverged from those of the Texaco shareholders in ways that may well have affected the conduct of that litigation. Although the shareholders would have benefited from an earlier settlement, the litigation was controlled by the directors, officers, and lawyers whose interests differed in important respects. A close examination of the incentives for the management of Texaco in particular suggests an explanation for the delay in settlement.

The directors and officers of Texaco were themselves defendants in fourteen lawsuits, eleven of them derivative shareholder actions, brought after the original multi-billion dollar Pennzoil verdict in the Texas trial court. These lawsuits essentially claimed that Texaco's directors and officers had violated their duty of care to the corporation by causing Texaco to acquire Getty Oil in a manner that led to the multi-billion dollar Texas judgment. After this verdict, and for the next several years, the Texaco management rationally might have preferred to appeal the Pennzoil judgment and seek complete vindication, even though a speedy settlement for the expected value of the litigation might have better served their shareholders. Because they faced the risk of personal liability, the directors and officers of Texaco acted in such a way as to suggest they would prefer to risk pursuing the case to the bitter end (with some slight chance of complete exoneration) rather than accept a negotiated resolution, even though in so doing they risked subjecting the corporation to a ten billion dollar judgment. The case ultimately did settle, but only through a bankruptcy proceeding in which the bankruptcy court eliminated the risk of personal liability for Texaco's officers and directors.

Overcoming Strategic Barriers: The Role of Negotiators and Mediators

The study of barriers can do more than simply help us understand why negotiations sometimes fail when they should not. It can also contribute to our understanding of how to overcome these barriers. Let me illustrate this by using the preceding analysis of four barriers briefly to explore the role of mediators, and to suggest why neutrals can often facilitate the efficient resolution of disputes by overcoming these specific barriers.

First, let us consider the strategic barrier. To the extent that a neutral third party is trusted by both sides, the neutral may be able to induce the parties to reveal information about their underlying interests, needs, priorities, and aspirations that they would not disclose to their adversary. This information may permit a trusted mediator to help the parties enlarge the pie in circumstances where the parties acting alone could not. Moreover, a mediator can foster a problem-solving atmosphere and lessen the temptation on the part of each side to engage in strategic behavior. A skilled mediator can often get parties to move beyond political posturing and recriminations about past wrongs and to instead consider possible gains from a fair resolution of the dispute.

A mediator also can help overcome barriers posed by principal/agent problems. A mediator may bring clients themselves to the table, and help them understand their shared interest in minimizing legal fees and costs in circumstances where the lawyers themselves might not be doing so. In circumstances where a middle manager is acting to prevent a settlement that might benefit the company, but might be harmful to the manager's own career, an astute mediator can sometimes bring another company representative to the table who does not have a personal stake in the outcome....

Note: Professor Mnookin's article also describes cognitive and perceptual barriers, which are discussed below.

B. The Role of Perceptions

The key to mastering both negotiation and mediation is to be aware that those in conflict and who want something from one another often see the same situation very differently. It is these differences that give root both to the conflict and to the possibility of agreement. We assess conflict and evaluate a case or the worth of an item differently because of differing perceptions. It is because of such differences in perceptions that people bet on horse races, wage war, and pursue lawsuits.

A classic Japanese story, on which the film *Rashomon* is based, illustrates the ancient literary awareness of the role of perceptions and how the truth as seen through one person's eyes may be very different from another's. Through divergent narratives, the story and the film explore how the power of perceptions may distort or enhance different people's memories of a single event, in this narrative the death of a Samurai warrior. Each tells the "truth" but perceives it very differently. The film, like the story, is unsettling because, as in much of life, no single truth emerges.

A more contemporary film, *The War of the Roses*, captures different truths as perceived by a divorcing couple. Early in the story, Oliver and Barbara Rose reveal to their respective lawyers their perspectives on the marriage and how their family home should be divided. Each sees the marriage relationship and what's fair differently, as filtered through his or her own experience, values, and selectivity. Is there any doubt, based on such different perceptions, that a war between the Roses would follow?

❖ Warren Adler, The War of the Roses
Stonehouse Press 51-76 (1981)

[*Oliver Rose's perception:*] "She just upped and said, 'No more marriage.' Like her whole persona had been transformed. Maybe it's something chemical that happens as forty gets closer."

He had . . . been a good and loving husband. He had nearly offered "faithful" to complete the triad but that would have discounted his two episodes with hookers during conventions in San Francisco and Las Vegas when the children were small. My God, she had everything she could possibly want....

What confused him most was that he had not been warned. Not a sign. He hated to be taken by surprise.

"And the house?" Goldstein asked.

"I don't know. Say half the value. After all, we did it together. Half of everything is okay with me...."

[*Barbara Rose's perception:*] "He's like some kind of animal. Almost invisible. He leaves early, before we get up, and comes home late, long after we've gone to bed. He doesn't take his meals at home...."

"You think it's fair for me to have devoted nearly twenty years to his career, his needs, his wants, his desires, his security. I gave up my schooling for him. I had his children. And I devoted a hell of a lot more time to that house than he did. Besides, the house is all I have to show for it. I can't match his earning power. Hell, in a few years he'll be able to replace its value. I'll just have cash. Well, that's not good enough. I want the house. I want all of it. It's not only a house. It's a symbol of a life-style. And I intend to keep it that way. That's fair...."

"It's my house. I worked my [—] off for it," she said.

The following reading further develops the concept that conflict is subjective and flows from different perceptions in the minds of people. Rummel's "subjectivity principle" may help to explain the *War of the Roses* and many other conflicts that would otherwise defy understanding and resolution.

❖ R. J. Rummel, The Conflict Helix
Transaction Publishers 13-23 (1991)

The Subjectivity Principle

Perceived reality is your painting. You are the artist. You mix the colors, draw the lines, fix the focus, achieve the artistic balance. Reality disciplines your painting; it is your starting point. As the artist, you add here, leave out there; substitute color, simplify; and provide this reality with a point, a theme, a center of interest. You produce a thousand such paintings every moment. With unconscious artistry. Each a personal statement. Individualistic.

Now, most people realize that their perception of things can be wrong, that they may be mistaken. No doubt you have had disagreements with others on what you all saw or heard. And probably you have heard of eyewitnesses who widely disagree over the facts of a crime or accident. Some teachers who wish to dramatically illustrate such disagreement have staged mock fights or holdups in a classroom. A masked man rushes in, pointing some weapon at the teacher; demands his wallet; and with it hastily exits, leaving the class stunned. Then each member of the class is asked to write down what he saw and heard. Their versions usually differ widely.

But, of course, such are rapidly changing situations in which careful observation is difficult. Surely, you might think, if there were time to study a situation or event you would perceive it as others do. This is easy enough to test. Ask two people to describe in writing a furnished room, say your living room, or a car you may own. Then compare. You will find many similarities, but you should also find some important and interesting differences. Sometimes such differences result from error, inattentiveness. However, there is something more fundamental. Even attentive observers often will see things differently. And each can be correct.

There are a number of reasons for this. First, people may have different vantage points and their visual perspectives thus will differ. A round, flat object viewed from above will appear round, from an angle it will appear an ellipse, from the side a rectangle. This problem of perspective is acute in active, contact sports such as football or basketball. From the referee's line of sight there is no foul, but many spectators (especially the television audiences who see multiple angles and instant replays) know they saw an obvious violation.

But people can compare or change perspectives. Were this all, perception would not be a basic problem. The second reason for different perceptions is more fundamental. You endow what you sense with meaning. The outside world is an amorphous blend of a multitude of interwoven colors, lights, sounds, smells, tastes and material. You make sense of this complex by carving it into different concepts, such as table, chair, or boy. Learning a language is part of learning to perceive the world.

You also endow this reality with value. Thus what you perceive becomes good or bad, repulsive or attractive, dangerous or safe. You see a man running toward you with a knife as dangerous; a calm lake as peaceful; a child murderer as bad; a contribution to charity as good. And so on.

Cultures are systems of meanings laid onto reality; to become acculturated is to learn the language through which a culture gives the world unique shape and evaluation. A clear example of this is a cross, which to a Christian signifies the death of Jesus for mankind as well as the whole complex of values and beliefs bound up in the religion. Yet, to non-Christian cultures a cross may be meaningless: simply two pieces of wood connected at right angles....

Besides varying perspectives and meanings, a third reason for different perceptions is that people have unique experiences and learning capacities, even when they share the same culture. Each person has his own background. No two people learn alike. Moreover, people have different occupations, and each occupation emphasizes and ignores different aspects of reality. Simply by virtue of their separate occupational interests, the world will be perceived dissimilarly by a philosopher, priest, engineer, union worker, or lawyer.

Two people may perceive the same thing from the same perspective, therefore, but each through their diverse languages, evaluations, experience, and occupations, may perceive it differently and endow it with personal meaning. Dissimilar perspective, meaning, and experience together explain why your perception will often differ radically from others.

There is yet an even more basic reason: what you sense is unconsciously transformed within your mental field in order to maintain a psychological balance. This mental process is familiar to you. People often perceive what they want to perceive, what they ardently hope to see. Their minds go to great pains to extract from the world that which they put there. People tend to see things consistent with their beliefs. If you believe businesspeople, politicians, or bureaucrats are bad, you will tend to see their failings. If you like a person, you tend to see the good; hate him and you tend to see the worst. Some people are optimists, usually seeing a bottle half full; others are pessimists, seeing the same bottle half empty.

Your perception is thus the result of a complex transformation of amorphous sensory stimuli. At various stages your personal experience, beliefs, and character affect what you perceive. . . . Independent of the outside world's powers to force your perception, you have power to impose a perception on reality. You can hallucinate. You can magnify some things to fill your perception in spite of what else is happening. Think of the whisper of one's name.

What you perceive in reality is a balance between these two sets of powers: the outside world's powers to make you perceive specific things and your powers to impose a certain perception on the world. This is the most basic opposition, the most basic conflict. Its outcome is what you perceive reality to be. . . . The elements of The Subjectivity Principle are perception, mental field, and balance: your perception is a balance between the powers of your mental field and the outside world. It is a balance between the perception you tend to impose on the outside world and the strength of what is out there to force its own reality on you. It is a balance between what you unconsciously want to perceive and what you cannot help but perceive. . . .

This balance that envelopes your mental field changes with your interest and concentration. Its shape and extension will depend on your personality and experience. And, of course, your culture. No wonder, then, that you are likely to perceive things differently from others. Your perception is subjective and personal. Reality does not draw its picture on a clean slate — your mind. Nor is your mind a passive movie screen on which sensory stimuli impact, to create a moving picture of the world. Rather, your mind is an active agent of perception, creating and transforming reality, while at the same time being disciplined and sometimes dominated by it. . . .

You and I may perceive reality differently and we both may be right. We are simply viewing the same thing from different perspectives and each emphasizing a deferent aspect. Blind men feeling different parts of an elephant may each believe they are correct and the others wrong about their perception. Yet, all can be correct; all can have a different part of the truth.

Notes and Questions

Rummel's subjectivity principle explains how we process the information and stimuli around us through the filters of our experience, needs, and biases. The complexity of our environment and our minds prevents us from taking it all in whole, so we focus selectively on some stimuli and ignore others. We develop shortcuts in our perceptual systems that allow us to function and process information more quickly and make timely decisions. These mental shortcuts, known as "heuristics," can serve us well in allowing us to respond as needed. However, they come at a risk that our selectivity can, on occasion, distort reality as seen by others. The different ways we process information can lead to conflict based on our different perceptions of reality.

1. Can you recall a conflict you have experienced that might be better understood in light of the subjectivity principle?
2. Is the conflict between Barbara and Oliver Rose really over their house, or something else? If the division or ownership of the house is the overt conflict, what is the underlying conflict or "hidden agenda"? Can lawyers

negotiate over what may be an underlying conflict about gender roles? Can they do something about each spouse's need for recognition?

C. Psychological Traps

Lawyers, it is thought, help clients in part by providing professional objectivity. Although they advocate vigorously for clients, attorneys usually do not have a direct stake in the outcome, which makes it easier for them to maintain the clear thinking and rationality so important to successful outcomes. This is the common wisdom about why, other than their technical skills and special access to the court system, lawyers "add value" in a dispute — but is it true?

The readings that follow describe specific cognitive forces that can distort one's ability to assess conflicts accurately and bargain effectively. As lawyers, we can often recognize partisan biases in our clients, but we are easily fooled by our own errors of perception. The longer we work with a client on a case or a deal, the more we share the same reality as our client — distorted or not. As a result, lawyers may become no more able than clients to objectively analyze the strengths or weaknesses of a case, or to make good bargaining decisions.

It will be helpful for you in representing clients to understand some of the psychological factors likely to affect a disputant's assessment of the value of a case and influence how she negotiates. The following section explains and applies these psychological concepts to a lawyer's tasks of evaluating a case, conducting discovery, and negotiating a settlement. It also provides groundwork for our later discussion of how lawyers can use mediation to deal with such obstacles.

❖ Dwight Golann, Cognitive Barriers to Effective Negotiation

6 ADR Currents 6 (September 2001)

Students at Harvard Law and Business Schools are preparing to negotiate over a personal injury law suit. Before they begin, the students are told to make a private assessment of the plaintiff's chances of winning based on their confidential bargaining instructions. What the students don't know is that there is nothing confidential about their information: Representatives of the plaintiff and defendant have received exactly the same instructions. Since both sides have the same data, they should logically come out with the same answer — but this is not what occurs. In fact, hundreds of law and business students told to negotiate for the plaintiff assessed her chances of winning at nearly 20 percent higher than did the students assigned to the defense. When they were asked to estimate the damages that a jury would award the plaintiff if she did win, again based on identical case files, there was a similar disparity: Plaintiff bargainers estimated her damages at almost 50 percent ($100,000) higher than defense negotiators. [See Figure 1.]

Figure 1
Case Assessments Based on Identical Information

Will your client win?

	Plaintiff Counsel	Defense Counsel	Total
Business students	61%	57%	118%
Law students	65%	52%	117%

What damages will the plaintiff receive if she does win?

	Plaintiff Counsel	Defense Counsel
Business	$286,000	$189,000
Law	$264,000	$188,000

What caused the distortions in this example? It was not that the negotiators were operating on different facts about the case, since they all had the same information. Nor was it due to their lack of experience. When the author posed the same problem to experienced litigators who mediated cases in a state court program, they showed a similar pattern: Lawyers assigned to represent the plaintiff were consistently more optimistic about the likelihood of success and the amount of any verdict than defense counsel who received the same file. Experiments in other settings also confirm the existence of a strong "advocacy effect" in case evaluation.

In real-life negotiations, lawyers on opposing sides do operate on the basis of sharply differing assessments of the odds of winning in court. Even allowing for the inevitable "puffing" that occurs in bargaining, both sides are likely to honestly believe that they have a better than even chance of prevailing, or at least to value the likely outcome very differently. These variances in perception obviously can affect the outcome of a negotiation, since bargainers who assess a case differently will find it very hard to agree as to what constitutes a "fair" settlement. These and other hidden barriers to successful negotiation lie in the domain of cognitive psychology, the science of how people assimilate information and make decisions. We will focus on four common cognitive obstacles that pose challenges even for experienced negotiators and mediators.

Selective Perception

The first factor that explains the disagreements of the Harvard students as well as problems that arise in real-life bargaining, is that negotiators often miss key data in the case that would be apparent to an outsider. This phenomenon, known as "selective perception," happens in this way: Whenever we encounter a new problem, we must interpret a stream of unfamiliar, often conflicting data. We respond by instinctively forming a hypothesis about the situation; we then organize what we later see and hear with the help of that image. The problem is that our hypothesis also operates as a filter, protecting us from conflicting data by automatically screening it out — which in turn reinforces the belief that our initial view was correct.

Selective perception is a universal phenomenon. Henry David Thoreau was probably thinking about it when he said, "We see only the world we look for." Every piece of litigation involves a story, and lawyers usually hear only one version of that story from their client. Based on this data, they tend to form a hypothesis about the dispute. In many instances selective perception then takes over to "protect" both lawyers and clients from the dissonance of conflicting evidence.

Optimistic Overconfidence

Assessing the value of a legal case requires predicting events that are uncertain, for example, how an unknown jury will react to evidence that may or may not be admitted. These assessments are often unreliable. For one thing, people are consistently overconfident about their ability to assess uncertain data. Why is this? The problem is that when we don't know something — even a fact that we aren't expected to have at our fingertips — either we are embarrassed to admit our ignorance or simply feel a competitive urge to be right. So we give a more precise answer than our knowledge can support: We are overconfident, in other words, about our ability to assess uncertainty.

There is a related problem. When people in an uncertain situation are asked to estimate the likelihood of a good or bad outcome, they consistently underestimate the chances of an unfavorable result. The reason, it appears, is that we like to believe that we are in control of events and thus able to bring about good results, even when we cannot. These tendencies become even stronger when the person making the judgment acquires a personal stake in the outcome. In psychological experiments, for example, subjects who have wagered that a horse will win a race are typically more confident, both about their ability to handicap races and about the chance that their chosen horse will win, than are people who have not placed a bet.

How do these forces affect negotiations over lawsuits? Lawyers are often asked to estimate the likely outcome of court proceedings at a point when they have little basis for offering an accurate assessment. In such situations, to maintain their reputations as expert litigators and avoid appearing ignorant to a client or another lawyer, they are likely to offer an overoptimistic estimate, and to have more confidence in the correctness of their forecast than their knowledge supports. To make matters worst, both lawyers and clients "bet" on their cases by investing substantial amounts of time and money in them, thus accentuating the inherent tendency to err.

Loss Aversion

No one likes to lose, whether the issue is money or an abstract legal argument. Recent studies have made us aware, however, of just how strongly feelings of loss can affect bargaining decisions. The results of this research require modification of one of the pillars of modern negotiation — the search for "win-win" terms. Creating interest-based bargains is certainly valuable, but it turns out to be even more important that neither side in a negotiation feel that it has "lost."

To understand the impact of loss on bargaining, consider the following experiment: Stanford students who had expected to attend a seminar without charge were told after they arrived that because of unexpected expenses, they would each have to pay $20. They could, however, spin a roulette wheel, with three chances in four of not having to pay the $20 and one chance of having to pay $100. These odds discouraged gambling: Since the average cost of spinning the wheel was $25, the smart choice was to pay the $20. However, a large majority of students chose to spin the wheel. Having expected to pay nothing, they apparently experienced the demand for $20 as an unwelcome loss, and were willing to take an unreasonable risk to avoid it.

This phenomenon, known as "loss aversion," affects legal bargaining, because litigants usually enter negotiations with a clear view about what is the "right" settlement in their case. In effect, they carry a mental benchmark about the expected settlement value, a figure that is often distorted by optimistic overconfidence and includes recovery of their legal expenses. For example, the plaintiff in a case that is objectively valued at $75,000 may honestly believe that it is worth $90,000. Since he has had to pay $25,000 in legal expenses to pursue justice, the plaintiff may have a "fair" settlement benchmark of $115,000 in mind. The defendant, however, may well see the same case as being worth only $60,000, even before factoring his costs of defense. In situations like this one, no settlement is possible, either through direct negotiation or mediation, unless at least one party accepts an outcome that is significantly worse than his internal sense of what is fair. This inevitably produces strong feelings of loss. To avoid that loss, litigants often elect to spin the roulette wheel of litigation.

Reactive Devaluation

Imagine that you are defense counsel in a lawsuit. Your opponent is demanding that you pay $100,000 to settle, but appears sure that you will never agree. Now you decide to offer that sum. Is your adversary pleased? To the contrary, her first reaction is likely to be that she has undervalued the case: it must be worth more than $100,000, because you are the enemy and would never offer her a fair deal. We all have a tendency to reject offers made by anyone we see as an adversary, a phenomenon known as "reactive devaluation." Our instinctive response to an opponent's offer is reminiscent of Groucho Marx, who vowed never to join any club that would have him as a member.

In conclusion: Advice about negotiation often focuses on conscious strategy and tactics. In fact, some of the most important factors affecting our judgments, and those of our negotiating partners, operate beneath the surface of our minds, outside our awareness. Knowing that these forces exist, and how to deal with them, will make you a more effective negotiator.

❖ Richard Birke, Settlement Psychology: When Decision-Making Processes Fail

18 Alternatives 203 (December 2000)

[A]t each phase of the litigation/settlement process, pervasive psychological traps may impede lawyers' ability to make decisions that effectively maximize client values. This article describes a few of the most well-established psychological phenomena that occur during the litigation/settlement process.

Why We Form Initial Estimates That Favor Our Side: Availability and Anchoring

The most common way to form an estimate of the value of something unknown is to compare it to the value of something known. If a person wants to know what her house is worth, she may look to the price at which a similar house sold recently. So it is with litigation.

When clients describe cases and ask for estimates of strength and value, the lawyers try to recall cases that relate to the one described by the client. Unfortunately, the cases that come to mind do so because they are memorable and relatively unusual, not because they are run-of-the-mill. Thus, when a client describes his tort case against a restaurant, his lawyer is likely to flash for a moment on the McDonald's coffee cup case [multi-million dollar jury verdict for coffee being too hot]. When the client describes a sexual harassment claim, the lawyer might think of any of a number of such cases recently in the news. When the lawyer compares his or her client's case to a notorious case, he or she distorts its value as a result of the Availability heuristic. The attorney, like all people, doesn't have the memory to retain every bit of information that comes before him or her, so the mind selects the most vivid to remember. The vividness of the image or the ease with which it can be recalled distorts its representativeness. This is why people tend to believe, incorrectly, that there is more annual rainfall in Seattle than in northern Georgia, that shark attacks lead to more deaths than falling airplane parts, or that murder is more common than suicide.

Of course, a good lawyer understands that the case the client described is not the McDonald's coffee cup case. She understands that this client's case is probably worth less than that one, so she adjusts from the McDonald's verdict downward. The question is whether she adjusts far enough. Research suggests that she will not adjust sufficiently because of something called the Anchoring effect: that decision makers will become anchored on reference points with highly attenuated or even nonexistent links to the decision at hand. For example, people — many with legal training — have been asked questions such as, "What are the odds that the temperature in San Francisco is higher or lower today than 578 degrees?"

Of course, everyone says the odds are 100% that the temperature is lower than 578 degrees. But when they are then asked to estimate the true San Francisco temperature, their estimates are invariably higher than the true temperature. When asked the likelihood that the temperature is higher than 1,000 degrees below zero, they answer 100%. If then asked the true temperature, the distortion is toward the low side. Of course, these temperatures are absurdities and are entirely unrelated to the true temperature of any place on this planet. Nevertheless, they affect the responses given. Thus, when a lawyer recalls a notorious case like McDonald's Corp.'s for torts, Mitsubishi Motor Corp. or Baker & McKenzie for sexual harassment, or some locally notorious case after a client has begun to recount the facts of his case, rest assured that it has a distorting effect on the lawyer's initial case evaluation. When availability causes a case to pop to mind as comparable, the odds are that the mind will anchor on it and insufficiently adjust.

The best cure is to check base rates. Checking a database of awards in the local jurisdiction will yield a better estimate of case value than will reliance on experience and adjustment from seemingly comparable cases. Data always trumps intuition.

Why We Think We Always Win: Biases and Positive Illusions

The mere fact that the client hires a particular lawyer often triggers a "bias of perspective" exacerbated by "positive illusions." . . . Perspective biases cause lawyers to overestimate the rightness of their side, and also to feel more confidence in their assessments. . . . Thus, when a client comes to his lawyer's office and tells his or her side of the case, the lawyer may know that there is another side of the story and may try to withhold evaluation until he or she hears it, but experiments indicate that the lawyer will form an opinion favorable to the client and be more confident in that opinion than the lawyer would be if he or she were not a partisan.

Perspective biases are reinforced by positive illusions — unrealistic optimism, exaggerated perceptions of personal control and inflated positive views of the self. For example, people tend to overestimate the probability that their predictions and answers to trivia questions are correct. There are a great many studies that indicate lawyer overconfidence. One study, conducted at a recent American Bar Association meeting, found that on average lawyers rated themselves in at least the top 80th percentile on such qualities as ability to predict the outcome of a case, honesty, negotiation skills and cooperativeness. This high degree of self-regard leads to an inflated sense of the value of a case.

These biases are difficult to correct, but if the goal is a realistic estimate of case value, lawyers should realize that their healthy self-images may lead to distorted images of how much a case is worth, and how likely they are to win. Finding a brutally honest colleague to act as "devil's advocate" may be a worthwhile investment of time. . . .

The next four principles, "Biased Assimilation," "Confirmation Bias," the "Certainty Effect," and the principle of "Commitment and Consistency," occur primarily during discovery.

Why Discovery Makes Us Overconfident: Biased Assimilation and Confirmation Biases

Operating in tandem, assimilation biases and confirmation biases distort both the search for information and the valuation of information found. As the lawyer begins discovery, he or she has a theory of the case — a plan of attack or defense that is discussed with the client. As the attorney gathers cases and information, he or she sorts the information into three categories: helpful, harmful, or neutral. The psychology of biased assimilation suggests this lawyer will interpret cases and evidence in a way that supports the conclusion he or she wants, whether the information actually supports that conclusion or not. If the information is favorable, he or she will overweight its relevance and applicability. If the information is harmful, the attorney may concede that it is harmful but will underweight its harmful effects. If the information is neutral, he or she will tend to see it as marginally helpful.

Finally, if the information contains information that is part helpful and part harmful, the attorney will tend to overweight the helpful parts and underweight the harmful parts, concluding that the information is of net positive value. This often causes a distortion in the valuation of the evidence. If both sides have done this, the case may be difficult to settle. Moreover, experienced attorneys rarely start case research by canvassing the entire legal literature to determine the state of the law and the relative power of all of the related areas of law. It would be hard to justify billing too many hours doing general research. Instead, the lawyers try to go straight to research directly bearing on their clients' cases. They are biased and have incentives in favor of confirming that which they already believe to be true.

The same, of course, is true of lawyers processing cases. When they hope a proposition is true (e.g., a theory of liability or a defense), they will see supporting information as strong and negating information as weak. This is biased assimilation. Furthermore, because they tend to look for and find corroborating information first, their theories tend to be mentally reinforced. This is a confirmation bias.

In order to reduce the negative effects of these biases, it may make some sense to think about the "anti-thesis" before doing research. Ask yourself what the case looks like to the other client, and consider doing a little bit of research into their case-in-chief before starting your own. If you think about your research as rebutting their case (as opposed to building yours), you may retain a view of the case closer to the one that a neutral judge or juror might hold. If you can have such a neutral view, you will be more likely to settle earlier for an amount that would approximate an average verdict.

Why We Spend Too Much for Information: The Certainty Effect [and Commitment]

As attorneys approach the middle of the discovery process they face decisions whether to gather more information on a particular point or to spend the time and money on another aspect of the case or another case. The certainty effect suggests that when people already have a great deal of information about an issue, they will spend more resources to establish that point than is warranted by the prospective value of the new information. Studies of decision making have found that increasing the probability of winning a prize by a fixed amount, say 5%, has more impact on people when it changes the probability from 95% to 100%, than when it changes the probability from 25% to 30% or 65% to 70%. Stated another way, people are willing to pay a premium to change a high probability into a certainty. The certainty effect may cause lawyers who are "pretty sure" that they have uncovered all information to spend more in the search for information than is warranted by the value of the information uncovered. . . . Discovery exacerbates a tendency to escalate commitment to initial courses of action. The concept of "sunk costs" causes people who have invested in a course of action to make economically irrational choices to promote their desired outcome. . . .

Why We Fail to Treat Similar Offers in Similar Ways: Framing

Not all offers are alike, but some only differ in the way that they are phrased. Empirical studies of attorneys suggest that particular phrasings, or "framings," can affect a lawyer's willingness to accept an offer. Experimental and real-world data demonstrate that losses have more impact on choices than do equivalent gains. For example, most people think that a 50% chance of gaining $100 is not sufficient to compensate for a 50% chance of losing $100. In fact, people typically need a 50% chance of gaining $200 or $300 to offset the 50% chance of losing $100.

The theory further asserts that decision makers are risk averse when faced with medium-to-high probability gains and risk seeking when faced with medium-to-high probability losses. By framing a settlement offer as a gain and the trial as a risk, the person making the offer may increase his chances of getting the offer accepted, relative to a framing in which the settlement is seen as partial compensation for a loss and a trial as a risky way to perhaps eliminate the whole loss. Furthermore, the tendency to think of gains and losses so differently may lead to a heightened aggressiveness when the bargaining is viewed as an attempt to minimize losses rather than maximize gains. . . .

How People Manipulate Each Other — Tools of Social Influence

Notwithstanding the aforementioned obstacles, people do make deals. They manage, somehow, to persuade the other side to accept offers. They use tools of social influence. The psychological literature on topics related to persuasion is abundant — and as yet has been rarely adapted over to legal settings. A handful of the best-known tools of social influence are scarcity, authority, liking, social proof, and reciprocation. These are familiar, so the descriptions are brief.

Scarcity is the extra boost of desire one feels for something that will disappear after deadlines pass, opportunities disappear, or something becomes unavailable. Experience suggests that "exploding offers" are accepted more often than offers that ostensibly don't expire.

Authority captures the ways in which the trappings of authority promote certain behaviors. Stanley Milgrom's famous experiments showed that when an experimenter ordered subjects to administer painful electrical shocks to innocent people, that the subjects' willingness to cause pain in others was correlated with the trappings of authority of the experimenter. If the experimenter wore a white lab coat and other "scientific" emoluments, the subjects were more willing to obey the cruel commands. These experiments stand as a "shocking" reminder of the lengths to which people will go to please or placate someone perceived to be an authority figure. Liking is somewhat the opposite of reactive devaluation. Naturally, people think more kindly of offers made by people they like, but this may not always yield the best results for a client.

Social proof is the tendency to confirm the rightness of choices or actions by reference to observations of others in similar settings. People view a behavior as correct in a given situation to the degree that they see others performing it. Sometimes following the pack will yield a good result, but in other circumstances, this method of choice may result in a lemming-like march over a cliff.

Finally, the *tendency to reciprocate* should not be underestimated. Even uninvited favors and gifts leave people with a sense of indebtedness. In negotiation, there is a strong norm that the recipient of a concession from the other side should make a concession of her own, even if the initial offer from the other side was extreme and the concession not particularly meaningful. The tendency to reciprocate is not in itself problematic, but when the person on the receiving side reciprocates a relatively trivial concession with a more meaningful one, such as a significant reduction of an already-reasonable request, she may be committing a negotiation error....

Lawyers, like all professionals, aspire to make rational decisions and to maximize their clients' outcomes. However, all decision makers, including lawyers, depart from the rational path to best outcomes. Fortunately, psychologists have shown that some of these departures are systematic, and by understanding that they exist and seeing how they operate, decision makers might be able to avoid or overcome the obstacles to best outcomes. For lawyers who settle the vast majority of the cases they handle on behalf of millions of people — many of whom are emotionally engaged in the conflict and rely on their lawyers for advice — this is an area of study of enormous importance. There are no simple answers for how to handle all of this psychology, but that is as it should be — the lawyer's mind is a complicated place.

The psychological factors described above may work against one another when bargainers make tactical decisions. For example, there are differing views about the advantages and disadvantages of making the first offer in a negotiation, because several of these perceptional elements come into play. If you make the first offer, particularly when the values involved are uncertain or without ready comparisons, you can take advantage of the "anchoring bias" created by your offer. However, reactive devaluation, which may be at a peak near the beginning of negotiations, may cause the other side to radically discount your offer because of suspicion.

Another psychological factor to consider is what Professor Birke describes as the tendency to reciprocate concessions made by others. This tendency helps explain why negotiators tend to settle midway between the initial "not unreasonable" offers made by each side. With this in mind, a bargainer may respond to a first offer with a relatively extreme counteroffer, so that the midpoint of compromise will be closer to him. Although negotiation need not proceed in this extreme manner, attempts to manipulate perceptions and exploit cognitive errors can trigger conflicting tendencies.

Questions

3. Do you think that knowing about the potential for these cognitive errors will help you to avoid being affected by them? For example, how might you overcome, or at least minimize, selective perception in your own thinking or that of your client?

4. If a lawyer is to follow a client's wishes regarding settlement, what is the lawyer's role if he is aware that the client is suffering from cognitive distortions? Must the lawyer agree to an outcome acceptable to a client if he is aware that the client's view is being influenced by cognitive errors?

5. How might you counter cognitive error and perceptual distortion that would influence an opponent to reject an otherwise acceptable settlement, for example, the tendency of an opponent to reject even a reasonable offer because of her suspicion of any offer coming from you?

D. The Role of Emotions

Cognitive and perceptual distortions affect negotiations even when everyone involved is calm and attempting to think rationally. But what if the people involved are not calm — in fact, are in the grip of strong emotions? Strong feelings are common in legal cases. Disputants often do not talk about their feelings because they are embarrassed to do so, have been told that emotions are irrelevant, or are not even conscious that an emotional issue exists. Still, feelings stirred by personal clashes between participants, combined with forces generated by the dispute itself, are the primary obstacles to settlement in many cases.

The judgment of disputants can be overwhelmed by a variety of strong emotions, ranging from guilt to frustration, sadness, and anger. An accident victim or an employer charged with discrimination, for example, is likely to have intense feelings about her case. Even if the dispute itself is not inflammatory, people often become angry over events that occur during litigation. A party may be enraged, for example, by a perceived snub, or a lawyer may become angry when an opponent uses "hardball" bargaining tactics. The *War of the Roses* excerpt is only one example of how strong feelings can disrupt communication and produce irrational decision making. This often means that bargainers must navigate through a treacherous mixture of emotional crosscurrents. Thus, Professor Lawrence Susskind, talking about efforts to resolve public controversies (Kolb 1994), cautioned that:

> I don't assume some perfect rationality from everybody in the room. I assume, first, that emotion will overcome logic during the course of the process. Almost everybody will often do things that, if they thought about them beforehand and were asked "Would you do that?" they'd say, "No." But they — we — will do it anyway, because emotion dominates logic.

Joshua Rosenberg, a law professor and psychologist, relates emotional intelligence and the skill of building good relationships to successful bargaining. In the reading below he describes the ways in which emotions can interfere with negotiators' effectiveness, and how much of this interference is unconscious.

❖ **Joshua D. Rosenberg, Interpersonal Dynamics:**
Helping Lawyers Learn the Skills, and the Importance of Human
Relationships in the Practice of Law

55 U. of Miami L. Rev. 1225-1283 (2004)

[M]ost lawyers and academics vastly overestimate the importance of reason and logic. We tend to view them as both the primary motivator of our own behavior and the primary tool to change the thinking and behavior of others. Although they are important, they are only one part of the puzzle. There are important differences between the kind of dispassionate reasoning and analysis in which lawyers and law students engage while sitting at desks at home, in the office, or in the library, and the kind of activities in which we engage when we are dealing in real time with real people. Real time, real life interactions implicate emotions, learned patterns of behavior, habituated perspectives and frames of reference, and other human, but not reasoned, responses.

The reactions to emotions occur whether or not the person is aware of either the reaction or the emotion, and they significantly impact the outcome of most negotiations and most other interpersonal interactions. People who become anxious may tend to over-accommodate the other by inappropriately giving in on the substance of the discussion, or may tend to talk too much (or too little) in an unconscious effort to forestall that anxiety. People who become irritated may tend to become slightly belligerent or withdrawn in ways that can harm their interactions. Any feelings are likely to trigger unconscious patterns of thought and behavior that will inevitably influence an interaction. . . .

It is not just how we think about what we perceive that is tainted by our feelings. Our very perceptions themselves are determined, in part, by our feelings (and thoughts). As an initial matter, emotions precipitate changes in the autonomic nervous system. These changes include increasing the heart rate, changing breathing patterns, skin changes such as perspiration or blushing, and redirecting blood flow (anger has been found to direct blood to the hands, presumably for combat; fear has been shown to redirect blood to the legs, presumably for running). At a micro level, these changes in the autonomic nervous system change not only our ability to think, but also our ability to act and perceive. Along with our thoughts, our blood flow, and our energy, the focus of our attention, and our ability to take in data are significantly changed by our emotional state. Not only our behavior, but also our perceptions become both differently focused and less accurate. . . .

Although no one doubts that thinking impacts our behavior, the extent to which the exact opposite is also true is worth noting. What we do significantly impacts both how we think and what we think about. In order to make this point to students, I have conducted in some negotiation classes a simple experiment in which some students are chosen for each of two groups, and the remaining students (who have previously, and secretly, been instructed on how to act) are designated as "observers" of each group. Each group, with its designated "observers," is sent to a different room and asked to toss pennies to see how close they can get them to the wall. One group's tossing is met with complete silence by its "observers," who pretend to busy themselves with note taking. The other group receives constant praise from its "observers" (for example, for their ability to get pennies close to the wall, for their good form, etc.). Not surprisingly, the second group invariably continues long after the first group stops.

When asked why they stopped, the first group typically replies that they had other things to do (such as "reviewing" the reading they were supposed to have done for that day's class). When asked why they continued for as long as they did, the second group typically responds with statements such as "it reminds me of when I was a kid, so it brings back fond memories" or "it was fun," or simply "you told us to." None in the second group responds that she continued because she was getting cheered on by others, and none in the first group suggests or believes that she stopped because her "observers" were silent. Each group thought differently about the tossing they had done, and each individual had very reasonable and logical thoughts about why she did what she did. In each case, however, these thoughts were the result of their behavior, rather than its cause. . . .

Students have pointed out that penny-throwing was more enjoyable for the group that had the active and engaged observers than it was for the group that had silent note-takers, so that the decision of one group to continue while the other group quickly quit is entirely "reasonable." My point, however, is not about whether the behavior of both groups appears reasonable to an objective observer. It is instead that those who participated were not thinking about their own behavior in that way. They may have been acting according to known principles of behavioral psychology, but they thought they were acting for other reasons entirely.

In addition to affecting our thoughts, how we act also affects our emotions. We all know that there are certain activities that make us feel better (sports, relaxation, being with close friends and family, etc.) and others that make us feel worse (some kinds of legal work, being with certain people — sometimes family, etc.). More recently, researchers have shown that merely adopting certain postures or facial expressions has immediate impact on emotions, regardless of the reason the postures are adopted and regardless of whether the positions are physically comfortable, uncomfortable, stressful or relaxing. Similarly, how we act while experiencing emotions significantly impacts the course of those emotions, regardless of the way that our behavior impacts on others who might be the cause or target of those emotions.

Again, while lawyers may not toss pennies at work, they do engage in many behaviors which impact their thoughts, feelings, and future behaviors. They may begin to engage in logical argument and continue to do so long after it has become useless, they may begin to agree with another and tend to keep doing so, or to keep talking about topics that have outlived their utility, and they often adopt physical positions and attitudes that impact not only their emotions and thinking, but also the reactions of others.

Result: Interacting Systems and Self-Fulfilling Prophecies

Basically, our thoughts, feelings, behaviors and perceptions influence each other. We react to our perceptions of the world around us while our own behavior impacts on the world. Of course, the patterns of our behavior, thoughts, perceptions and feelings are far from random. We tend to learn patterns of thought, feeling, and behavioral reactions in childhood. In adulthood we tend to engage in those patterns we learned as children, often resulting in "self-fulfilling prophecies" that tend to reinforce those same old patterns. Basically, because of our particular frame of reference (thoughts, feelings, etc.), we expect people to act in certain ways, and we act toward them in ways that tend to precipitate the behaviors we expect. When people do act in the ways we expected, we interpret that behavior in line with our expectations, and we react in certain predictable ways (which tend to confirm to us the validity of our earlier expectations).

Negotiation experts are aware of the significant impact of self-fulfilling prophecies on negotiations, but the actual impact of these patterns extends well beyond "negotiations," to encompass most of our interactions in life. To demonstrate how frequently, extensively and unconsciously these self-fulfilling prophecies direct us, I often discuss in class the person P at a party who looks at person AC and thinks she is arrogant and cold, and then looks at person FW and thinks he is friendly and warm. It is almost inevitable that by the end of the event, P's initial perspective will prove (to P, at least) correct (regardless of the actual personality of either AC or FW). In all likelihood, P will approach and be receptive to FW, who in response will likely act friendly. On the other hand, in what P believes is simply self-protection, she will likely retreat from AC, who in turn will be less likely to act warmly toward P. P will then leave the party unaware of how her own feelings and beliefs impacted her behaviors, or of how her own behaviors impacted AC and FW, but acutely (albeit inaccurately) aware of her own insight and ability to predict human behavior. These self-fulfilling prophecies and other generally unconscious learned responses significantly impact the outcome of most negotiations and most other interpersonal interactions.

Human Communication: Colliding Systems

As all of the above suggests, despite our typical estimation to the contrary, we are often unaware of the actual causes (and unintentional consequences) of our own behavior, thinking, emotions, and perceptions. We are not sufficiently self-aware to realize how many of our patterns of acting and thinking are ingrained, unconscious or triggered by our autonomic nervous system rather than by reason. Communication, of course, is a two way street, and much of the time we are even more misguided about what is headed toward us than we are about where we ourselves are going. Just as we incorrectly believe that we understand our own behavior better than we do, we also (and to a much greater degree) wrongly believe that we understand others much better than we actually do. . . .

As an initial matter, researchers have concluded that the single greatest weakness of most negotiators is that they too often fail to even consider the thinking and emotions of others. Perhaps even more significantly, when we do attempt to consider the thinking and feelings of others, we usually get it wrong. We often attribute to them moods, goals or motivations that simply are not there, or we exaggerate the significance of one of many reactions they may be having and forget that, like our own, their reactions might be both dynamic and complex.

While we tend to be accepting of situational factors that impact our own behavior, we tend to be unaware of, and inattentive to, the impact of such situational factors on others. As a result, we tend to think of ourselves as more sympathetic, as having a better case, or as being a better person than the one with whom we are dealing. In turn, this often leads us to devalue the other's case and proposals, and to fail to reach agreements that are available and would have been in our client's (or our own, as the case may be) best interest.

Basically, we tend to assume, too often inaccurately, that the message we take from the other is actually the message they intended to send. We vastly underestimate not only the impact of our own perspectives, feelings and thinking on the message we take in, but also the role of simple miscommunication.

Compounding the problem of our misperceptions of others is the fact that we are basically unaware that the problem even exists. Research clearly shows that more than 98% of us are unable to tell when others are lying or telling the truth. We are essentially equally likely to believe those who are lying as we are to believe those who are telling the truth, and we are equally likely to disbelieve those who are actually telling the truth as we are to disbelieve those who are actually lying. Interestingly, and typically, I have never met a person who believes that she is a part of that 98% majority....

Establishing and Maintaining Connection

The ability to establish and maintain some "connection" with any person I work with is important for several reasons. As an initial matter, the extent of my influence on any person depends, in part, on that person's feelings toward me. In addition, the personal connection between two people is often an important part of what can enable them to engage in creative problem-solving and collaborative bargaining in the midst of conflict. Significant research on negotiation shows that one of the essential components of successful collaborative negotiating is the ability to refocus discussion away from areas of disagreement onto areas of commonality and agreement, and the ability to establish those areas of commonality and connection is a key aspect of the ability to focus on them....

The ability to establish and maintain connection with another is not easy to learn, and many of those who are well liked do not necessarily have to work hard at it. Nonetheless, to the extent we dismiss the ability as completely due to genetics and natural disposition, we do ourselves, and our ability to improve, an injustice. There are behaviors that can increase connection to others, and they can be learned....

Questions

6. Have you seen any examples, in real life or in an exercise in this course, of how emotional intelligence contributed to successful negotiation?
7. Do you think that such intelligence can be taught?
8. If you served on your school's curriculum committee, how would you assess the pros and cons of offering a course on "Interpersonal Skills for Law Students"? Would you vote to create such a course?

Strategic, principal-agent, cognitive, emotional, and other issues can make it hard for bargainers to reach agreement even when they have a joint interest in doing so, as in deal-making or transactional negotiations. When people are embroiled in a dispute, however, such obstacles become much larger, often making it impossible for disputants to bargain at all. Mediation has become an increasingly popular way to overcome barriers to negotiation, making it possible for lawyers and clients to achieve settlements and avoid the cost and disruption of litigation. We now examine how the mediation process does this, and how lawyers can take advantage of its qualities.

PART
II

THE MEDIATION PROCESS

CHAPTER
5

An Overview of Mediation

A. Introduction

1. The Process of Mediation

a. What Is Mediation?

Mediation is a process of assisted negotiation in which a neutral person helps people reach agreement. The process varies depending on the style of the mediator and the wishes of the participants. Mediation differs from direct negotiation in that it involves the participation of an impartial third party. The process also differs from adjudication in that it is consensual, informal, and usually private: The participants need not reach agreement, and the mediator has no power to impose an outcome.

In some contexts you may find that this definition does not fully apply. The process is sometimes not voluntary, as when a judge requires litigants to participate in mediation as a precondition to gaining access to a courtroom. In addition, mediators are not always entirely neutral; a corporate lawyer, for instance, can apply mediative techniques to help colleagues resolve an internal dispute, despite the fact that he is in favor of a particular outcome. Occasionally mediation is required to be open to the public, as when a controversy involves governmental entities subject to "open meeting" laws. And finally, a mediator's goal is not always to settle a specific legal dispute; the neutral may focus instead on helping disputants to improve their relationship.

There is an ongoing debate within the field about what "mediation" should be. To some degree, this results from the different goals that participants have for the process: Some focus only on settlement and seek to obtain the best possible monetary terms. Others seek to solve a problem or repair a relationship. Still other participants use mediation to change people's attitudes. The increasing application of mediation to areas such as family and criminal law also raises serious questions of policy. This text focuses on "civil" mediation, involving legal disputes outside the area of collective bargaining, since this is what you are most likely to encounter in law practice. However, to give you a sense of what mediation may become, we also present other perspectives on the process.

b. What Do Mediators Do?

Mediators apply a wide variety of techniques. Depending on the situation, a settlement-oriented mediator may use one or more of the following approaches, among others:

• Help litigants design a process that ensures the presence of key participants and focuses their attention on finding a constructive solution to a dispute.
• Allow the principals and their attorneys to present legal arguments, raise underlying concerns, and express their feelings directly to their opponents, as well as hear the other side's perspectives firsthand.
• Help the participants to focus on their interests and identify imaginative settlement options.
• Moderate negotiations, coaching bargainers in effective techniques, translating communications, and reframing the disputants' positions and perceptions in constructive ways.
• Assist each side to assess the likely outcome if the case is litigated, and to consider the full costs of continuing the conflict.
• Work with the disputants to draft a durable agreement and, if necessary, to implement it.

c. What Is the Structure of Mediation?

Because mediation is informal, lawyers and clients have a great deal of freedom to modify the process to meet their needs. In practice, good neutrals and advocates vary their approach significantly to respond to the circumstances of particular cases. That said, a typical mediation of a legal dispute is likely to proceed through a series of stages.

Premediation

Before the disputants meet to mediate, the neutral often has conversations with the lawyers, and sometimes also with the parties, to deal with issues such as who will attend the mediation and what information the mediator will receive beforehand. Lawyers can use these contacts to start to build a working relationship with the mediator and educate him about their client's perspective on the dispute and obstacles that have made direct negotiations difficult.

The Opening Session

Most mediations begin with a session in which the parties, counsel, and mediator meet together. The content and structure of a joint session can vary considerably, depending on the goals of the process. When mediation is focused on reaching a monetary settlement, the joint session is likely to be dominated by arguments of lawyers, perhaps followed by questions from the neutral. If the goal of the process is to find an interest-based solution or to repair a ruptured relationship, then the mediator is much more likely to encourage the parties themselves to speak and to attempt to draw out underlying issues and emotions.

Private Caucusing and No-Caucus Models

After disputants have exchanged perspectives, arguments, and questions, most commercial mediators adjourn the joint session in order to meet with each side individually in private "caucuses." The purpose of caucusing is to permit disputants, counsel, and the mediator to talk candidly together. Keeping the parties separated, with communications channeled through the mediator, also allows the neutral to shape the disputants' dialogue in productive ways.

When the mediation process is focused on monetary bargaining, the participants usually spend most of their time separated, with the mediator shuttling back and forth between them, and in unusually contentious cases parties may not meet together at all. If, however, parties are interested in exploring an interest-based resolution or repairing a broken relationship, then the mediator is much more likely to encourage them to meet so that they can work through emotions, explore options, and learn to relate productively with each other. Mediators who handle family disputes often prefer to remain in joint session during the entire process, and some mediators are experimenting with no-caucus formats in general civil cases.

Joint Discussions

Even when a mediation is conducted primarily through private caucusing, neutrals sometimes ask the disputants to meet with each other for specific purposes, for instance, to examine the tax issues in a business breakup or to deal with a difficult emotional issue in a tort case. In most mediations, whether or not conducted through caucusing, the lawyers or parties also meet at the end of the process to sign a memorandum of agreement or decide on future steps.

Follow-up Contacts

Increasingly the mediation process is not limited to the specific occasions on which the mediator and disputants meet together. If a dispute is not resolved at a mediation session, then the neutral is likely to follow up with the lawyers or parties. Depending on the situation, the mediator may facilitate telephone or e-mail negotiations, or convene additional face-to-face sessions.

2. The Value of Mediation

Although litigants are sometimes compelled to enter mediation, the process can only be successful to the extent that disputants find it effective. What, in the eyes of parties and their lawyers, are the potential benefits of going to mediation? Consider the comments and data that follow.

a. Viewpoints of Lawyers

Diane Gentile, Dayton

My practice is focused on employment law. These claims deal with one of the most important aspects of peoples' identity — their work. In addition, they often involve serious allegations of wrongdoing. Both sides in these disputes often have good reason to want a confidential solution. One example [is] a case I handled involving a worker and supervisor. Several years before[,] the two had had a consensual intimate relationship, but the worker later accused her supervisor of sexual harassment. For the employer, the claim was a potential nightmare. The fact that the supervisor had at first denied the existence of the earlier relationship made it even more difficult. Moreover, because the employer was a nonprofit organization that depended in part on public funds, the potential for negative publicity could have crippled the organization. As soon as we received notice of the plaintiff's suit we suggested mediation. After nine hours of difficult discussions we had a resolution, and the organization's relief was limitless.

Mediation is effective in part because it allows the parties to talk about many things that will never be considered relevant by a court. When they are allowed to speak freely, often in private to a mediator offering a sympathetic ear, material just spills out, and afterward people are often much more willing to compromise. Mediation also allows for nonlegal relief, which is particularly important in employment cases: changes to a file to reflect a voluntary quit rather than termination, for example, or agreement on what the company will say to a future employer asking for a reference.

*Mary Alexander, San Francisco, Former President, American Trial
Lawyers Association*

My practice focuses on personal injury cases, including auto accident, product liability, and defective design claims. Years ago we settled cases only on the courthouse steps, but courts in California now push parties to mediate long before trial. Often a case will not settle at court-ordered mediation, but the process gets lawyers talking and often leads to an agreement.

The single most useful service provided by mediators in my practice is to provide a reality check for clients. People often come into a lawyer's office with very real injuries, but unrealistic expectations about what they can obtain from the court system. They have heard somewhere about a large award and assume that it is typical, when in fact it is not. Clients are often in dire financial straits and physical pain, making it hard for them to listen to a lawyer's warnings about trial risk. When a mediator, especially a former judge, explains the realities of present-day juries — often in language that turns out to be very similar to what I had said earlier — it makes a real impression. Clients are able to become more realistic, and to accept a good offer when it appears. Even if the courts did not order it, I would elect to mediate almost every significant case.

Stephen Oleskey, Boston

I use mediation extensively in commercial cases to deal with a wide variety of obstacles. My goals depend on the nature of the situation. In one recent case, for example, the problem was anger: The parties had been talking off and on for two years, but both were so upset that they could not focus productively on settlement. At the same time, with several hundred million dollars at stake, neither side could bear the risk of a winner-take-all trial. Mediation created the context for a rational discussion of the merits and risks. In another case, we used mediation to get a group of corporate and political stakeholders to come to the same place and focus intensively on a case that some of them had not previously thought through. Occasionally, I've used a mediator to give a message to a client — or the other side's client — that was hard for a lawyer to deliver. In a few cases, it's been the way that the mediator has framed the discussions: her choice of what issues to focus on, or the statement that, "We'll stay here until midnight if we have to, to get this done," that tells the parties that this is the time to make the difficult choices, put all their money on the table, and work out a deal if possible.

Katherine Gurun, General Counsel, Bechtel Corporation

Our business involves complex construction and engineering projects. It is built around long-term relationships with suppliers and partners. Things inevitably go wrong — equipment fails, customers encounter financial problems, and so on. We have to resolve these issues, but in a way that keeps our relationships healthy. Mediation has become our most powerful and successful process for accomplishing this.

The flexibility of mediation is its most useful quality. In the disputes we encounter, the complex nature of the issues almost always requires several sessions, often spread over a period of months. During adjournments, people can confer with their organizations and the mediator can work on one or both sides. Overall, ADR has reduced our litigation costs phenomenally; just as important, it avoids the management distraction caused by formal litigation.

We also use mediation in international disputes. Here cultural differences are an important consideration. Many of our foreign partners are in mediation for the first time, and it's particularly important to find a neutral who "knows both sides of the fence." Asian executives seem especially comfortable with the mixture of joint and private meetings, because the structure accommodates their preference for conferring and reaching a consensus within the team at each point in the process. Europeans sometimes seem troubled by mediation's lack of formality, but I find that its adaptability is what makes the process so effective.

Paul Bland, Washington, D.C.

There are two major situations in which I find mediation helpful as a litigator for a public interest organization. The first is when we challenge widespread practices; for example, a group of HMOs flagrantly violating a statute. Inside counsel sometimes cannot believe that their organization has violated any law, simply because all of their peers are doing the same thing. In such cases I ask for mediation with a former judge or well-regarded private lawyer — someone who can convincingly tell the other lawyer that her client has a genuine problem.

Another indicator for mediation is when I suspect that defense counsel is not being candid with his own client. Many firms I encounter are completely ethical — they fight hard but fair. Some lawyers, however, seem to "milk" clients, playing on defendants' instinctive belief that they've done nothing wrong and billing them unnecessarily for a year or two. Mediation can be the best way to get the truth to an unrealistic client. I often have to work to get such cases into mediation. I have resorted to coming up to a defense counsel, in the presence of his client, and saying, "This looks like a perfect case for mediation." Or I might write to defense counsel and make an explicit request that he transmit the letter to his client. The hardest part of mediation is sometimes to get the other side into the process.

Patricia Lee Refo, Phoenix, Former Chair, ABA Section of Litigation

My caseload consists primarily of large commercial disputes. We use mediation in most of our cases — I sometimes joke that we lawyers have worked ourselves into a place where we can't settle cases by ourselves anymore! I don't believe that a bad settlement is better than a good trial. I am convinced, though, that in the right situation, a mediator can add a great deal of value. Sometimes the problem is that both sides have the same facts, but they view them very differently. A mediator may not be able to convince a client to change his viewpoint, but she can make the client understand what the other side can do with the facts at trial. It's often the first time the client has heard the reaction of someone who comes to the case completely fresh.

There are also issues in business cases over which people become quite invested and emotional — for example, did someone violate an agreement in bad faith. Mediation allows clients to vent their feelings in private, making it easier for them to compromise later in the process. I recently encountered a mediator who said that he didn't "do venting." I find that aspect of the process often to be crucial, and I won't use neutrals who can't handle it. Mediators can also be helpful by "cutting to the chase," focusing on the few issues that will really matter at trial. This frees parties from arguing over every point, and moves them toward making settlement decisions.

Harry Mazadoorian, Connecticut

I've used mediative methods often in working out business relationships. Insurers, for example, often make investments in joint venture and partnership deals. It's impossible to predict the future, and as the project goes on and circumstances change, issues often arise about how the parties should share unexpected benefits and responsibilities. I remember one alternative energy venture that nearly broke down when money ran short and additional contributions were required from the participants. At first the lawyers focused on parsing the language of the contract, but as we talked I was able to persuade them to explore options that redistributed costs so that each partner could bear them most easily, and potential benefits in ways that they would be felt most strongly. Once the partners dropped their focus on legalese and looked instead at their specific needs, the conflict was quickly resolved. The greatest music to my ears in these situations was always to hear an executive say, "I just don't know how to get this done." I knew that if I could get the attention of high-level decision makers — ideally, get top people from both sides to sit down at lunch and commit to trying to work it out — success was nearly assured.

b. Business Perspectives

One of the first companies to make aggressive use of mediation was the Toro Corporation, which produces a wide variety of consumer goods, including lawn mowers, snow blowers, and other power tools, and as a result receives personal injury claims. Toro's national mediation counsel describes the results of its program.

❖ **Miguel A. Olivella Jr., Toro's Early Intervention Program, After Six Years, Has Saved $50 M**

17 Alternatives 81 (1999)

[In 1991 the Toro Corp. implemented] a pre-litigation alternative dispute resolution program that featured nonbinding mediation as its corner-stone.... Most of the claims diverted to the program [at the outset arose] in the products liability or personal injury areas....

How the Program Works

When Toro gets word of a claim against it or one of its many subsidiaries, a paralegal in the Toro legal department is assigned the matter. The legal assistant promptly contacts the claimant's counsel and schedules a meeting to take place as soon as possible at a location convenient to both the claimant and counsel. The purpose of the meeting is to elicit information about the claim and the claimant's expectations. Documentation supporting the claim is requested [usually in the form of medical and wage records]. An in-house Toro engineer typically accompanies the legal assistant to this initial meeting to inspect the product.... Following this meeting, the legal assistant ... engages in settlement discussions with the claimant's counsel. If the negotiations don't produce a settlement, the claim is referred to Toro's national mediation counsel, who suggests to claimant's counsel ... nonbinding mediation. This offer is almost universally accepted. The mediation is typically scheduled within one month.... Mediations typically last the better part of a day....

The Results

After almost eight years and hundreds of claims, this process has resulted in a 95% settlement rate. [The program has gradually been expanded to include] commercial matters and breach of contract. . . . It is virtually impossible to think of any form of litigable claim that the Toro legal department must confront that is not sent to the program. . . . Comparing data on costs before and after the program was implemented, the total cost of handling a claims file from the time it was opened until the time it was closed decreased from $115,620 to $30,617 . . . a 74% drop. And the average file's lifespan was reduced to three months from two years. . . . With 636 claims opened and closed between 1992 and 1996 . . . the program translates into an overall savings for Toro exceeding $50 million. . . . That doesn't include [savings in more recent years or] the roughly $6 million in insurance savings realized during the first three years of the program. We're just getting warmed up.

Questions and Notes

1. If you were Toro's outside counsel and were consulted when the company was considering whether to implement an ADR program, what concerns might you reasonably have had about its effects? Why do you think these concerns did not materialize?
2. If you were consulted by a client injured by a Toro product, would you advise her to participate in the Toro process? What factors would be important in your decision?
3. One issue that Toro faced was to persuade plaintiff counsel that the invitation to mediate was not merely a pretext for "free discovery" or "below market" settlements. To overcome such suspicions, Toro developed a list of references — plaintiff lawyers who had worked with Toro and could vouch for its sincerity.

In recent years researchers have questioned companies about their use of ADR. The following is a summary of what one survey found.

❖ David B. Lipsky and Ronald L. Seeber, Patterns of ADR Use in Corporate Disputes

54 Disp. Resol. J. 66 (February 1999)

We asked respondents a range of questions designed to gauge the extent of ADR use [by large U.S. corporations.] Nearly all our respondents reported some experience with ADR, with an overwhelming 87% having used mediation and 80% having used arbitration at least once in the past three years. . . . We conclude that ADR has made substantial inroads into the fabric of American business, with counsel overwhelmingly preferring mediation (63%); arbitration was a distant second (18%) . . . . [N]early all corporations have experience with ADR, but a much smaller number of companies use mediation and arbitration frequently.

Why Do Corporations Use ADR?

One of the more significant forces driving corporations toward ADR is the cost of litigation and the length of time needed to reach a settlement. All else being equal, ADR is widely considered cheaper and faster....Cost reduction may be the most widely cited reason for choosing ADR, but corporations report other reasons as well....We found that many of the answers related to the parties' desire to control their own destinies — to have some control over the path to resolution....The most often cited reason to use mediation (identified by 82% of the respondents) was that it allows the parties to resolve the dispute themselves....

Eighty-one percent of those surveyed said that mediation provided a more satisfactory process than litigation, 67% said that it provided more satisfactory settlements, and 59% reported that it preserved good relationships. In sum, these responses indicate that mediation provides not just an alternative means to conventional dispute resolution but a superior process for reaching a resolution....Large corporations that have faced intense competitive pressures...appear more likely to have strong pro-ADR policies. Also, corporations that have adopted cutting-edge management strategies seem likelier to be pro-ADR. By contrast, smaller, more profitable corporations...are more likely to favor litigation. When corporations use mediation frequently or very frequently, the dominant reason they do not use it is because opposing parties won't agree to it....

The Future of ADR

In general, a large majority of the respondents in our survey believe that they are "likely" or "very likely" to use mediation in the future — 38% and 46%, respectively. They were more cautious about the use of arbitration.... If these projections are accurate, the use of ADR by U.S. corporations will grow significantly.

———————

The trends noted in this reading continue. A 2004 survey of corporate general counsel found that the respondents had mixed attitudes toward binding arbitration, but supported the use of mediation. Asked "What is your company's attitude toward nonbinding mediation clauses in its [domestic business] agreements?", the respondents gave these answers:

Strongly Favor	31%
Slightly Favor	29%
Neutral	25%
Slightly Disfavor	8%
Strongly Disfavor	7%

General counsel at large companies were the most likely to support mediation clauses, with 35 percent strongly favoring and only 1 percent strongly disfavoring their use. (For full survey results, see *Corporate Counsel Litigation Trends Survey Results* at *www.fulbright.com*.) We discuss the issues raised by contractual mediation clauses in Chapter 12.

c. Is It Right for Every Dispute?

No one would argue that mediation is appropriate for every controversy. Even those who generally favor its use agree that the process may not be effective in the following situations, among others:

- A disputant is not capable of negotiating effectively. This may occur, for example, because the person lacks legal counsel or is suffering from a personal impairment.
- One side in the controversy feels the need to establish a legal precedent. A party may need a judicial decision to use as a benchmark for settling similar cases.
- A litigant may require a court order to control the conduct of an adversary.
- One of the disputants is benefiting from the existence of the controversy. For example, a party may be using the litigation process to inflict pain on the other, or is maintaining a defense in court to delay making a payment for business reasons.
- A party needs formal discovery to evaluate the strength of its legal case.
- A crucial stakeholder refuses to join the process.

To some commentators, mediation is inherently unjust. They argue that the very informality of the process allows both neutrals and parties to express prejudice that is suppressed by more formal procedures. Mediation, it is argued, also facilitates case-by-case resolutions that siphon off pressure for law reform. Other critics concede that ADR may be useful generally, but sharply object to its application to specific areas, for example in divorce litigation. Some contend, for example, that by suggesting that legal standards are only one point of reference, ADR opens the way to the exploitation of unsophisticated parties. Such criticism is particularly strong in situations where participation in mediation is mandatory, as when parents in a dispute over child custody are required to go through ADR as a precondition to obtaining access to a judge. Other writers have suggested that minorities tend to do less well in certain forms of mediation. Still another issue is whether ADR gives an advantage to "repeat players" such as corporations and insurers. And some studies have called into question a basic premise of court-related mediation programs — that they reduce the duration of cases. All of these critiques raise significant policy issues, which are discussed in more depth in Chapter 13.

3. Examples of Mediation in Action

a. Death of a Student

Note: Confidentiality is one of the most important attributes of mediation. The facts in the following account that have not previously been published have been approved by attorneys for both parties.

In August 1997 Scott Krueger arrived for his freshman year at the Massachusetts Institute of Technology. Five weeks later, he was dead. In an incident that made national headlines, Krueger died of alcohol poisoning following an initiation event at a fraternity. Nearly two years later Krueger's parents sent MIT a demand letter stating their intent to sue. The letter alleged that MIT had caused their son's death by failing to address what they claimed were two long-standing campus problems: a housing arrangement that they said steered new students to seek rooms in fraternities, and what their lawyer called a culture of alcohol abuse at fraternities.

MIT's lawyers saw the case as one that could be won. An appellate court, they believed, would rule that a college is not legally responsible for an adult student's voluntary drinking. Moreover, under state law the university could not be required to pay more than $20,000 to the Kruegers (although that limit did not apply to claims against individual university administrators). MIT officials felt, however, that a narrowly drawn legal response would not be in keeping with its values. They also recognized that there were aspects of the institution's policies and practices — including those covering student use of alcohol — that could have been better. MIT's president, Charles M. Vest, was prepared to accept responsibility for these shortcomings on behalf of the university, and felt a deep personal desire for his institution to reach a resolution with the Krueger family. MIT also recognized that defending the case in court would exact a tremendous emotional toll on all concerned. The Kruegers would be subjected to a hard-hitting assessment of their son's behavior leading up to his death, while MIT would be exposed to equally severe scrutiny of the Institute's culture and the actions of individual administrators. Full-blown litigation in a case of this magnitude was also sure to be expensive, with estimated defense costs well in excess of $1 million.

The question, as MIT saw it, was not whether to seek to engage the Kruegers in settlement discussions, but how. The university decided to forego a traditional legal response and reply instead with a personal letter from President Vest to the Kruegers, which noted the university's belief that it had strong legal defenses to their claims, but offered to mediate.

The Kruegers responded with intense distrust. Tortuous negotiations ensued. The parents eventually agreed to mediate, but only subject to certain conditions: At least one session would have to occur in Buffalo, where the Kruegers lived. MIT would have to offer a sincere apology for its conduct; without that, no sum of money would settle the case. There would be no confidentiality agreement to prevent the parents from talking publicly about the matter, while at the same time any settlement could not be exploited by MIT for public relations purposes. The Kruegers would have the right to select the mediator. And, President Vest would have to appear personally at all the mediation sessions. The university agreed to most of the conditions and the mediation went forward.

MIT's lawyers believed that it was important that the Kruegers' lawyers and the mediator understand the strength of the university's defenses, but plaintiff counsel knew that subjecting the Kruegers to such a presentation would make settlement impossible. To resolve the dilemma, the lawyers bifurcated the process. The first day of the mediation, which the Kruegers would not attend, would focus on presentations by lawyers and would be held in Boston. One week later the mediation would resume at a conference center located a 40-minute drive outside Buffalo, this time with the Kruegers present. Their counsel selected that location so that "no one could leave easily." On the second day the Kruegers would personally meet President Vest, and the parties would begin to exchange settlement proposals.

Counsel had agreed that the mediator, Jeffrey Stern, should begin the day by having a private breakfast with Mr. and Mrs. Krueger and their lawyers. The Kruegers vented their anger, first to Stern and later to President Vest. "How could you do this?" they shouted at Vest, "You people killed our son!" They also challenged Vest on a point that bothered them terribly: Why, they asked him, had he come to their son's funeral but not sought them out personally to extend his condolences? Vest responded that he had consulted with people about whether or not to approach the Kruegers and was advised that, in light of their anger at the institution, it would be better not to do so. That advice was wrong, he said, and he regretted following it.

Vest went on to apologize for the university's role in what he described as a "terrible, terrible tragedy." "We failed you," he said, and then asked, "What can we do to make it right?" Mrs. Krueger cried out again at Vest, but at that point her husband turned to her and said, "The man apologized. What more is there to say?" Their counsel, Leo Boyle, later said that he felt that, "There's a moment . . . where the back of the case is broken. You can feel it. . . . And that was the moment this day." The mediator gradually channeled the discussion toward what the Kruegers wanted and the university could do.

Hard bargaining followed, much of it conducted though shuttle diplomacy by the mediator. In the end the parties reached agreement: MIT paid the Kruegers $4.75 million to settle their claims and contributed an additional $1.25 million to a scholarship fund that the family would administer. Perhaps equally important, President Vest offered the Kruegers a personal, unconditional apology on behalf of MIT that no court could have compelled and that would not have been believed if it were. At the conclusion of the process Vest and Mrs. Krueger hugged each other. For MIT the settlement, although expensive, made sense: It minimized the harm that contested litigation would have caused to the institution. And, most important, the university felt that it was the right thing to do.

What did the mediator contribute to the process? During the first day, Stern questioned both lawyers closely about the legal and factual issues, creating a foundation for realistic assessments of case value later in the process. The initial money offers put forth by each party were far apart, but the mediator put them into context so that neither side gave up in frustration. According to plaintiff counsel Brad Henry, Stern's greatest contribution was probably the way he responded to the Kruegers' feelings: "What he did most masterfully was to allow a lot of the emotion to be directed at him. He allowed it almost to boil over when it was just him with the Kruegers, but later he very deftly let it be redirected at President Vest and the university. . . . He also prepared Charles Vest for the onslaught. . . . Mediation can be like a funeral — especially with the death of a child. He mediated the emotional part of the case, and then let the rest unfold on its own."

Questions

4. What barriers appear to have made it difficult for the parties in the Krueger case to negotiate with each other directly?
5. What did the Kruegers obtain in mediation that they could not have won at trial?

b. United States et al. v. Microsoft Corporation

In one of the highest-profile antitrust cases in U.S. history, the Justice Department, later joined by several states, sued the Microsoft Corporation, arguing that it had monopolized certain markets in computer software. While the case was pending, judges twice ordered the parties into mediation processes, which are described in the following readings.

❖ **James Laflin and Robert Werth, Unfinished Business: Another Look at the Microsoft Mediation: Lessons for the Civil Litigator**

12 Cal. Tort Rep. 88-92 (April 2001)

On November 18, 1999, twelve months into a case that was eventually to last eighteen, U.S. District Judge Thomas Penfield Jackson announced the appointment of Richard A. Posner, the Chief Judge of the Seventh Circuit Court of Appeals in Chicago, to serve as mediator in the Microsoft antitrust case. . . . Posner was neither a practiced diplomat nor experienced mediator. However, he brought other credentials to the table. He had gained recognition as one of the most capable, influential members of the federal bench, and a recognized authority in the field of antitrust law. . . .

Posner's mission as a mediator was to induce Microsoft and the government to shed what he referred to as "emotionality" and come to a rational compromise. At the outset, the parties met for lunch at a private club, in what would turn out to be the only face-to-face meeting of the entire mediation process. In attendance were lawyers representing Microsoft, the Justice Department and three attorneys general representing the nineteen states who joined as plaintiffs in the suit. In describing the protocol, Posner indicated he would refrain from evaluating the strength of either side's case, "try to deflate unrealistic expectations" and keep all talks in confidence. Each side was asked "to make a detailed presentation of the facts and remedies it would consider." Posner promised to devote himself almost full time to the process.

To mitigate "emotionality" Judge Posner ordered separate meetings for at least the first month, the government each Monday, Microsoft each Tuesday. Two months later the process had evolved into a form of shuttle diplomacy interspersed with the judge's email inquiries seeking additional information. He began, in the words of one Microsoft negotiator, "growling at the other side, growling at us." After two months of work Posner outlined the first draft of a settlement proposal. Over the next several months, some nineteen draft proposals were exchanged via Posner, who edited them into his own language and emailed them either to Microsoft's General Counsel, or the chief of the Justice Department's Antitrust Division. Copies went to the chair of the association of the nineteen state attorneys general.

By mid-February, negotiations had stalled. Neither side believed that the other was open to a compromise, and both sides were often confused. At Microsoft, this was reflected by [General Counsel] Bill Neukum[,] who said of Posner, "You keep asking yourself, 'Is he wearing his hat as a mediator, trying to motivate people to narrow their differences and come together, or is he speaking as the Chief Judge of the Seventh Circuit, who's an expert on antitrust law?'" Compounding this confusion, neither side could be sure whether, or which, terms contained in the successive draft proposals originated with Judge Posner or came directly from their adversary.

From late February 2000 through the end of March, Posner had extensive telephone conversions with Microsoft, sometimes with [Chairman William] Gates directly, and with Justice Department attorneys, in which successive draft agreements were negotiated and refined. In early March Gates seemed close to accepting the deal reflected in draft fourteen, which Posner forwarded to the Justice Department and the states. The states were given ten days to accept, or Posner would terminate the process. The state attorneys general made it clear that Joel Klein [chief of the Justice Department team] was not their spokesperson and responded separately to the proposal. The states were angry with both Posner and Klein. As one state official said, "Posner was more interested in dealing with Gates and Klein and didn't perceive that he had nineteen other parties to the lawsuit.... He got enamored of talking to Gates. And he's not a mediator by training, and lacked basic mediation skills."

Posner was prepared to summon the parties to Chicago for direct face-to-face negotiations starting on March 24th. Their options would be to accept the basic terms contained in the most recent draft, or face termination of the mediation. More emails and telephone conversations between Posner and the two sides ensued. Meanwhile, the states had communicated their disapproval of parts of draft eighteen and added further conditions. Posner now realized he would have to negotiate with the nineteen state attorneys general to develop a single government proposal. Then, even if that could be accomplished, he would still have to negotiate the divide between the government stakeholders and Microsoft. That night he telephoned Microsoft and Klein and announced that his mediation effort was over.

The Microsoft case went to trial and the court found that Microsoft had violated antitrust laws. Judge Jackson ordered a breakup of the company, and Microsoft appealed. Several months later the court of appeals upheld some of the trial court's findings of antitrust violations, rejected others, and disapproved the court's breakup remedy. Criticizing the conduct of the trial judge, particularly his decision to talk privately with a reporter, the appeals court appointed a new judge to preside over the case. Other changes had occurred: While the appeal was pending, a new president had taken office and the Justice Department had announced that it would no longer seek a breakup of the company. Before resuming hearings, the second trial judge again referred the Microsoft case to mediation. The following reading summarizes its results.

❖ Eric Green and Jonathan Marks, How We Mediated the Microsoft Case

The Boston Globe A23 (November 15, 2001)

Mediators never kiss and tell. But within the bounds of appropriate confidentiality, lessons can be learned from the three-week mediation marathon that led to Microsoft's settlements with the Department of Justice and at least nine states. Federal District Judge Colleen Kollar-Kotelly took over the case after the Court of Appeals partially affirmed the prior judge's findings that Microsoft had violated antitrust laws.... Neither the mediation nor the settlements would have happened if Kollar-Kotelly had not acted to suspend litigation and order settlement negotiations. The judge's Sept. 28 mandate was blunt: "The Court expects that the parties will...engage in an all-out effort to settle these cases, meeting seven days a week and around the clock, acting reasonably to reach a fair resolution." The court gave the parties two weeks to negotiate on their own, ordering them to mediation if they couldn't reach agreement by then. The court bounded its "24/7" timetable by ordering the parties to complete mediation by Nov. 2.... Tight timetables command attention. In mediation, just as in negotiation, time used tends to expand to fit time available. A firm deadline gets the parties to focus....

We are both mediators, with 40 years of combined experience.... But we are not experts in the applicable law or the disputed technology.... Even had we had such expertise, our objective would not have been to try to craft our own settlement solution and sell its merits to the parties. We believed that the only chance of getting all or most parties to a settlement was for us to work intensively to help them create their own agreement. Our "job one" was to facilitate and assist in the gestation, birth, and maturing of such an agreement. We had to be advocates for settlement — optimistic and persistent — but not advocates for any particular settlement....

Reaching a settlement required working with adversarial parties with very different views about a large number of technologically and legally complicated issues. When we arrived on the scene, the parties had begun exchanging drafts of possible settlement terms.... After initial separate briefings, we moved the process into an extended series of joint meetings, involving representatives of the Antitrust Division, the state attorneys general and their staffs, and Microsoft. No party was left out of the negotiations. The bargaining table had three sides....

Throughout most of the mediation the 19 states and the federal government worked as a combined "plaintiffs" team. We worked to ensure the right mix of people, at the table and in the background. The critical path primarily ran through managing and focusing across-the-table discussions and drafting by subject matter experts — lawyers and computer mavens — with knowledge of the technological and business complexities gained through working on the case since its inception. The critical path also required working with senior party-representatives who could make principled decisions about priorities and deal breakers.

[As a result of the mediation, Microsoft, the Justice Department, and ten state attorneys general reached agreement.] Even as settlement advocates we have no quarrel with the partial settlement that was achieved.... Successful mediations are ones in which mediators and parties work to identify and overcome barriers to reaching agreement . . . Successful mediations are ones in which, settle or not, senior representatives of each party have made informed and intelligent decisions. The Microsoft mediation was successful.

Note: The remaining nine attorneys general filed objections to the settlement with the trial judge, but both the trial and appeals courts upheld its terms.

Questions

6. Consider the mediation of the student death case described previously. What goals, other than avoiding litigation costs, did the university seem to have in proposing mediation?
7. What did the student's family appear to be seeking from the process?
8. Neutrals reveal their own definition of mediation by the manner in which they practice it. Looking at the techniques that Judge Posner applied, what appeared to be his concept of how mediation should work?
9. In what ways did mediators Green and Marks view the process differently?
10. Marks and Green emphasize the importance of deadlines. Do you think the judge could have achieved the same settlement result by setting a firm trial date and ordering the parties to negotiate with each other directly?

4. The Evolution of Legal Mediation

The public thinks of dispute resolution primarily in terms of court trials. Access to courts to remedy wrongs and enforce legal rights is central to American democracy. We have fashioned a system of rules to ensure fair trials and provide a finely tuned system of public justice. However, litigation, with all of its procedural protections, is slow, costly, and relatively inflexible. The process is also centered on lawyers, restricting the roles and expression of the disputing parties. The remedies available through adjudication are limited to what can be enforced through courts. Most commonly, a court judgment to resolve a dispute consists of ordering one party to pay money to another.

In part because of these limitations, alternatives to adjudication have long existed. Mediation has probably existed for nearly as long as humans have lived together — think, for example, of a parent seeking to help children resolve an argument, or a village elder who assists community members to settle a quarrel. There are many examples in history of the use of mediative processes. Thousands of years ago, Chinese villagers were accustomed to resolving disputes through the assistance of respected leaders, and commercial disputes were mediated in England before the Norman invasion (Pei 1999).

Modern American mediation began in response to the rise of organized labor. Following initiatives in several states, Congress in 1898 authorized railroads and their unions to invoke mediation and in 1913 created a permanent Board of Mediation and Conciliation to deal with such cases. Labor mediation expanded greatly in the first half of the twentieth century (Neumeier 2002), and the process also began to be applied to other types of legal disputes. By the early 1920s, for example, mediation programs for civil cases existed in courts in New York, Minneapolis, Cleveland, and other cities. Following the Second World War, legal reformers began to promote the use of mediation in other subject areas, with special emphasis on using mediation to lower the frequency of divorce (Cole et al. 2001).

Civil mediation received a powerful boost during the late 1970s from prominent jurists who believed that the justice system was in crisis (Nolan-Haley 2001). Although some have argued that this concern was overstated (Galanter 1983), it led judges, academics, and bar leaders, among other responses, to advocate increased use of ADR (Sander 1976). During the same period, leaders at the local level argued for the use of mediation to deal with neighborhood disputes, and support continued to grow for applying mediation in family cases (Folberg and Taylor 1984).

During the 1980s, courts and litigators increasingly experimented with using mediation to resolve general civil litigation. At first, lawyers approached the process cautiously, concerned that their willingness to mediate would be interpreted by opponents as weakness. Bar leaders and judges, however, continued to voice support for the process, and equally important, U.S. corporations began to throw their weight behind the use of ADR as a means to reduce the cost of litigation and the risk of uncertain jury verdicts. Some 4,000 companies, for example, have signed a formal pledge by which they undertake to consider using ADR in appropriate cases before resorting to traditional litigation, and more than 1,500 law firms have signed a similar pledge (see *www.cpradr.org*). In 1990 Congress mandated that every federal district court in the nation create a litigation delay control plan that incorporated ADR, and in 1998 it reaffirmed that requirement. By the mid-1990s most state and federal courts had established court-connected ADR programs for a wide variety of civil disputes, and mediation quickly became by far the most popular process used in such programs (Stienstra et al. 1996). The 1990s also saw federal and state government agencies using mediation more frequently to resolve public disputes. As one measure of the growth of the process, by the end of the decade states had enacted more than 2,000 statutes that mentioned mediation (Cole et al. 2001).

As the use of mediation became more widespread, some commentators questioned whether the process, particularly as applied in court-connected programs, might stifle law reform (Delgado 1988), condemn low-income groups to a second-class form of justice, prejudice abused women and children (Grillo 1991), disadvantage the powerless, or provide an unfair advantage to repeat players such as corporations and insurers. At the same time, new data called into question some of the premises of the mediation movement, for example, that court ADR programs would speed the processing of cases (Kakalik et al. 1996), although other studies found that mediation did generate significant savings of time and money (Stienstra et al. 1997; Stipanowich 2003). We explore these policy issues more deeply in Chapter 13. None of these criticisms, however, has prevented mediation from growing rapidly in popularity.

B. Goals and Mediator Styles

1. Goals for the Process

When you participate in mediation as an advocate, what will be your goal for the process? The answer may seem simple: to settle a legal dispute. But the question is often more complex. Many disputes involve issues, interests, and potential solutions that go beyond the legal issues that lawyers typically consider or the remedies that courts can grant. When a dispute arises from an important relationship, for example, repairing the rupture could be more significant to a client than how the current controversy is resolved. In addition, lawyers are sometimes drawn into disputes in which the legal issues are relatively unimportant, as in the example of the corporate counsel in the "viewpoints" section who described managing bargaining between partners in a joint venture. The goals that you pursue in mediation thus may change greatly from one situation to another, and these differences will in turn influence your choice of a neutral and structure for the process. As a lawyer representing clients, you may have one or more of the following purposes in deciding to mediate.

Resolve a Legal Claim on the Best Possible Monetary Terms

When litigators enter mediation, their goal is usually to settle a legal dispute. Most trial lawyers take a narrow approach to the process: They discuss only the legally relevant facts and issues and set as their goal to obtain the highest (for the plaintiff) or lowest (for the defendant) possible monetary payment in return for ending the case. When litigators talk about mediation, they often reflect this perspective. One lawyer, for example, has said that, "The effective advocate approaches mediation as if it were a trial . . . the overwhelming benefit of mediation is that it can reduce the cost of litigation" (Weinstein 1996). Perhaps in response, commercial mediators often see their primary role as to facilitate distributive bargaining. One successful New England neutral, for example, has written that, "In the typical civil mediation, money is the primary (if not the only) issue" (Contuzzi 2000), while a leading Southern mediator has said that, "The goal of resolution is always the same: allowing the parties to negotiate to a 'reasonable ballpark,' in which they, with the help of the mediator, identify 'home plate' based on what a jury will consider 'a reasonable verdict range'" (Max 1999).

In the typical commercial dispute, then, litigants and their counsel are likely to enter the process assuming that it will focus primarily on legal arguments and principled/positional bargaining over money. Although this kind of negotiation often produces less-than-optimal results, a mediator can do a great deal to assist parties even when money is the only issue over which the disputants are willing to bargain.

Example: An inexperienced plaintiff's lawyer was representing an automobile accident victim in negotiations with the defendant's insurer. The victim had suffered broken bones, with out-of-pocket damages totaling $6,000. Requested by the defendant's adjuster to make a settlement demand, the plaintiff counsel asked for $1.2 million. The adjuster was incredulous: In her experience, plaintiff lawyers rarely demanded more than ten times the "out-of-pockets." She refused to "dignify" the plaintiff's "wild number" with a response, and the result was a complete breakdown of talks.

The case went to mediation. In a private meeting with the plaintiff and his counsel, the mediator asked about their goals in the negotiation. The lawyer said that he was willing to be flexible, and the client indicated that he was seeking a much more modest amount than the $1.2 million demand might suggest. The neutral asked the plaintiff lawyer to make a new offer at a much lower level. She offered to tell the adjuster that the plaintiff had done this only to accommodate the mediator's request that both sides "cut to the chase," and that the plaintiff expected the defendant to respond in a similar vein. Three hours later the case settled at $27,500.

Develop a Broad, Interest-Based Resolution

As we have seen, parties to legal disputes often have interests that go far beyond money, and settlements that respond to these concerns can provide greater value to disputants than a purely monetary outcome. Some lawyers employ mediation to facilitate interest-based bargaining and obtain creative resolutions. One text for corporate attorneys, for example, emphasizes that "The process creates an opportunity to explore underlying business interests [and] offers the potential for a 'win-win' solution..." (Picker 2003), while another describes the process as providing "a framework for parties to ...privately reveal to the mediator in caucus sensitive interests that may assist the mediator to facilitate broad solutions" (CPR Institute, Scanlon ed. 1999).

Example: A company that processed hazardous chemical waste and one of its residential abutters had been embroiled for years in a series of disputes over the company's applications for licenses to expand its operations. They eventually agreed to mediate. Although the parties at first focused exclusively on the meaning of certain state hazardous waste regulations, the mediator noted that the abutter became most angry when he mentioned the company's practice of parking large trucks filled with waste on the street across from his house. The company insisted that such situations resulted from unpredictable traffic jams at the plant, but the abutter maintained that the problem showed the company's basic callousness about its neighbors' safety.

As he spoke with the parties, the mediator found that the company also wanted to end the practice, and could do so if it could widen its driveway to accommodate two trucks at a time. This was impossible because the driveway was wedged against the abutter's land. That land was not, however, being used. As part of an overall settlement, the mediator convinced the abutter to convey a narrow strip of his unused land to the company. The company in turn agreed to widen its driveway, thus solving the truck parking problem for everyone and increasing the value of the abutter's remaining land.

Repair the Parties' Relationship

Attorneys sometimes enter mediation not so much to obtain specific terms of settlement as to repair the parties' relationship. When parties enter litigation they typically sever any prior connection between them, but many supporters of mediation believe, in the words of Professor Lon Fuller, that "mediation has as its primary goal the repair of the troubled relationship" (Fuller 1971).

> *Example:* An Austrian company that marketed a process to stop soil erosion along river banks and a principal officer of its U.S. affiliate were in a dispute. The plaintiff was the founder of the company, who had trained the other protagonist, a young American woman, to create a subsidiary to sell his process in the United States. The woman modified the process in the belief that the original version would not fit the American market. This triggered a violent disagreement with the founder. Faced with the prospect of resolving the dispute or declaring bankruptcy, the shareholders and executives agreed to meet.
>
> The founder arrived at the mediation, and sat rigid and silent as others talked. When the mediator asked him to give his perspective on the situation, he refused: His position was stated in a letter that everyone had received. What else needed to be said? Still, the mediator asked if he would read the letter aloud in order to insure that everyone heard him clearly. As the founder began to read, feelings began to show under his stolid exterior. The woman responded angrily, and they began to argue. It seemed to be a classic daughter/mentee-grows-up-and-challenges-father/mentor situation. Eventually the two went to a corner and talked animatedly for more than an hour. Afterward, in a calmer atmosphere, the mediator led the principals through a discussion of the challenges facing the firm and how they might solve them. Under the leadership of a new CEO not linked to either of the protagonists, painful changes were agreed to and the company survived.

Change the Parties' Perspectives

In a still broader view, the purpose of the mediation process is not to obtain any specific outcome. Instead its focus is to assist parties in transforming their perspectives on the dispute and each other, a change that may or may not lead to an improvement in their relationship. Advocates of this perspective, known as "transformative" mediation, argue that the disputants should be allowed to take charge of the mediation process, with the mediator serving simply as a resource to facilitate their conversations. This approach is described in more detail below.

Choices among Goals

Although a particular mediation can have more than a single purpose, one can think of possible goals for the process as falling along a continuum (see Figure 1).

Figure 1.
Potential Goals in Mediation

| Monetary result | Interest-based solution | Repair of relationship | Transformation of perspectives |

←———→

How likely is it in practice that if an attorney seeks one of these goals, he will be able to achieve it — how often, in other words, can parties in a civil mediation expect to leave the process with a purely monetary settlement, an interest-based solution, or a relationship repair?

The answer will be heavily influenced by the nature of the case, the attitudes of clients and counsel, and the skills and goals of the mediator. Relationship repair in mediation is often not feasible; in most automobile tort cases, for example, there is no prior relationship to revive. Even when a dispute does arise from a relationship, the parties often litigate bitterly before mediating, and in such situations repairing the relationship is very difficult. Sometimes, however, both sides recognize that it is in their interest to heal their rupture. This is most common in settings where the parties' past connection has been strong and their alternatives to relating are not attractive. One example of such a situation is a quarrel between a divorcing couple over how they will parent their children. Relationships can be important in commercial settings as well; partners in small businesses, like the Austrian-American venture described above, may have a strong interest in seeking a repair of a troubled relationship because neither is able to buy out the other, and continued conflict will destroy the enterprise. A study of mediations of larger civil disputes arising from relationships (excluding unionized labor and divorce cases) are shown below in Figure 2.

Figure 2.
Outcomes of Legal Mediation in "Relationship" Cases

Repair of relationship	Money & integrative term, but no repair	Money terms only	Impasse
17%	30%	27%	27%

←——————————————————————————————→

In other words, when parties mediate a legal dispute arising from a significant prior relationship with a mediator open to imaginative solutions, there appears to be approximately a 15 to 20 percent chance that the process will culminate in a repair of the parties' relationship, a 30 percent chance of a settlement that has at least one significant integrative term in addition to money,[1] a 25 to 30 percent probability of a settlement consisting solely of a monetary payment, and a 25 to 30 percent likelihood of impasse. Interestingly, focusing only on those cases that settled, agreements with at least one significant integrative term (either a relationship repair or another nonmoney term) totaled 47 percent, a much higher percentage than settlements that consisted only of a monetary payment (27 percent) (Golann 2002).

As a lawyer you are likely to encounter many situations in which your client's only stated goal is to end its relationship with an adversary on the best possible

---

1. Examples of integrative terms in business disputes included an agreement among parties breaking up a partnership that one partner would have the exclusive use of certain billing software, or that the ex-partners would continue to share office space. In employment cases, companies agreed to terms such as temporarily maintaining the health coverage of a departing employee or changing records to reflect a voluntary quit rather than a termination, and employees sometimes agreed never to apply for employment with the company again. Releases of liability and confidentiality agreements were not counted as integrative terms in the survey because they were typically assented to as a matter of course.

terms. The data suggest, however, that in cases that arise from a prior relationship, more often than not it is feasible to obtain an agreement that includes some term of significant value to the parties in addition to money, and that in a small but appreciable portion of cases, it is possible to repair the parties' relationship.

Questions

11. In what kinds of legal cases would you expect the parties to have a weak or nonexistent prior relationship?
12. In what types of disputes are the parties likely to find it very difficult or costly to sever their connection?

2. Mediator Styles

One key issue that you will confront when representing clients in mediation is selecting the neutral. There is now a wide choice of mediators in most communities, and different neutrals have widely varying styles. Depending on the dispute and the personalities and needs of the participants, you may want a mediator with a particular approach to the process. Indeed, experienced lawyers sometimes select a mediator with an eye to finding a person who can work well with the *other party* to the dispute, giving them the best chance of reaching a successful resolution. The following readings describe a method for classifying mediators according to their view of the issues in a dispute and their style in addressing them.

a. Classifying Styles

It is possible to classify mediators according to the goals they pursue and the methods they use to achieve them and to show the results graphically. The following reading demonstrates how this can be done.

❖ Leonard L. Riskin, Retiring and Replacing the Grid of Mediator Orientations

21 Alternatives 69 (April 2003) and 12 Alternatives 111 (Summer 1994)

[A decade ago, there was] a vast and diverse array of processes . . . called mediation. Yet there was no accepted system for distinguishing among the various approaches. As a result, there was great confusion in the field about what mediation is and what it should be. . . . Looking back, I like to think about this confusion in terms of three gaps between mediation theory — that is, what the well-known writings and training programs, mainly those focusing on civil, non-labor mediation, said mediators did or should do — and mediation practice — that is, what mediators actually did.

First, mediation theory held that mediators don't evaluate, make predictions about what would happen in court, or tell parties what to do. In practice, however, many mediators evaluated and told people what to do. Second, mediation theory said that mediation was intended to address the parties' underlying interests or real needs, rather than, or in addition to, their legal claims. Quite commonly, however, mediations in civil disputes — especially those that were in the litigation process, or might be — were narrow and adversarial. The third disparity between theory and practice concerned self-determination. The "experts" touted mediation's potential for enhancing self-determination. Yet in practice, many mediation processes did not fulfill that promise.

These gaps between theory and practice produced a number of problems. The most salient problem concerned evaluation [a mediator's decision to give an opinion as to the likely outcome of the case in adjudication, or to propose terms of settlement]: Sometimes parties went into a mediation thinking they were not going to get an evaluation, but got one nevertheless — without consenting to it or preparing for it. And sometimes the reverse happened: Parties who thought they would get an evaluation, because they were analogizing mediation to some judicial settlement conferences, didn't get one. Similarly, parties who entered a mediation thinking it would focus either broadly or narrowly often were surprised to find the opposite focus. And some mediators gave short shrift to party self-determination by exercising extensive control of the focus and even the outcome.

For all these reasons, great ambiguity suffused most conversations about mediation. In addition, many parties, potential parties, lawyers, and mediators did not recognize the existence of numerous choices about what would happen in a mediation and that someone would make those choices, either explicitly or implicitly. [To address these problems, I proposed a system for classifying mediator orientations.] It focused primarily on two of the gaps: evaluation by the mediator and problem-definition (which was my vehicle for addressing the tendency of many commercial mediators to focus on positions, in the form of claims of legal entitlements, rather than underlying interests). . . .

. . . The classification system [started] with two principal questions: 1. Does the mediator tend to define problems narrowly or broadly? 2. Does the mediator think she should evaluate — make assessments or predictions or proposals for agreements — or facilitate the parties' negotiation without evaluating? The answers reflect the mediator's beliefs about the nature and scope of mediation and her assumptions about the parties' expectations.

Problem Definition

Mediators with a narrow focus assume that the parties have come to them for help in solving a technical problem. The parties have defined this problem in advance through the positions they have asserted in negotiations or pleadings. Often it involves a question such as, "Who pays how much to whom?" or "Who can use such-and-such property?" As framed, these questions rest on "win-lose" (or "distributive") assumptions. In other words, the participants must divide a limited resource; whatever one gains, the other must lose. The likely court outcome — along with uncertainty, delay and expense — drives much of the mediation process. Parties, seeking a compromise, will bargain adversarially, emphasizing positions over interests.

A mediator who starts with a broad orientation, on the other hand, assumes that the parties can benefit if the mediation goes beyond the narrow issues that normally define legal disputes. Important interests often lie beneath the positions that the participants assert. Accordingly, the mediator should help the participants understand and fulfill those interests — at least if they wish to do so.

The Mediator's Role

The evaluative mediator assumes that the participants want and need the mediator to provide some directions as to the approximate grounds for settlement — based on law, industry practice, or technology. She also assumes that the mediator is qualified to give such direction by virtue of her experience, training, and objectivity.

The facilitative mediator assumes the parties are intelligent, able to work with their counterparts, and capable of understanding their situation better then either their lawyers or the mediator. So the parties may develop better solutions than any that the mediator might create. For these reasons, the facilitative mediator assumes that his principal mission is to enhance and clarify communications between the parties in order to help them decide what to do. The facilitative mediator believes it is inappropriate for the mediator to give his opinion, for at least two reasons. First, such opinions might impair the appearance of impartiality and thereby interfere with the mediator's ability to function. Second, the mediator might not know enough — about the details of the case or the relevant law, practices, or technology — to give an informed opinion.

Mediators usually have a predominant orientation, whether they know it or not, based on a combination of their personalities, experiences, education, and training. Thus, many retired judges, when they mediate, tend toward an evaluative-narrow orientation.

Yet mediators do not always behave consistently with the predominant orientations they express.... In addition, many mediators will depart from their orientations to respond to the dynamics of the situation.... [As an] example: an evaluative-narrow mediator may explore underlying interests (a technique normally associated with the broad orientation) after her accustomed narrow focus results in a deadlock. And a facilitative-broad mediator might use a mildly evaluative tactic as a last resort. For instance, he might toss out a figure that he thinks the parties might be willing to agree upon, while stating that the figure does not represent his prediction of what would happen in court.... Many effective mediators are versatile and can move from quadrant to quadrant (and within a quadrant), as the dynamics of the situation dictate, to help parties settle disputes....

I appreciate the insight of Professor George Box: "All models are wrong. Some are useful." No graphic can capture the rich complexity of real life. Nevertheless, I hope that this grid will be useful.

Role of Mediator: Evaluative/Directive

EVALUATIVE NARROW	EVALUATIVE BROAD
FACILITATIVE NARROW	FACILITATIVE BROAD

Problem Definition: Narrow (left)

Problem Definition: Broad (right)

Role of Mediator: Facilitative/Elicitive

Professor Riskin has modified his grid by replacing the word "evaluative" with "directive" and "facilitative" with "elicitive" (the "broad" versus "narrow" continuum remains the same). He explains his reasons for doing so as follows.

> First, the terms "directive" and "elicitive" more closely approximate my goals for this continuum, which [are] to focus on the impact of the mediator's behavior on party self-determination. Second, the term "directive" is more general and abstract than "evaluative" and therefore may cover a wider range of mediator behaviors.... Using the terms "directive" and "elicitive" also can help us recognize that mediators can direct (or push) the parties toward particular outcomes through "selective facilitation" — directing discussion of outcomes the mediator favors, while not promoting discussions of outcomes the mediator does not favor — without explicitly evaluating a particular outcome. (Riskin 2003d)

Most writing on mediator styles continues to use evaluative-facilitative terminology. To avoid using inconsistent terms, therefore, we use those terms in this book. Students interested in exploring the issue of mediator style more deeply, however, should read Professor Riskin's 2003 articles, referenced in the bibliography.

Question

13. Have you seen a demonstration or video of the mediation process? Using the "Riskin grid" shown in the reading, how would you classify the mediator(s) whom you most observed?

b. Do Mediators Have a Single Style?

Do legal mediators use a single goal orientation and style throughout their practice? If not, do they at least maintain a consistent approach during a single mediation? To investigate this issue, one of the authors asked several respected legal mediators to mediate a case in a role-play format while being filmed. The experiment found, as Professor Riskin suggests, that good neutrals do not maintain a single orientation, but instead adapt their approach to fit the circumstances of a dispute. Indeed, neutrals typically changed their approach repeatedly during a single caucus meeting with a party. All of the mediators began in a broadly facilitative mode, asking about the parties' business and personal interests, but they were usually met with narrowly evaluative comments from the lawyers. In response, the mediators remained facilitative, but acceded to counsel's narrow subject-matter orientation. Periodically during the process, however, mediators would return to a "broad" orientation, asking about the client's interests and suggesting nonmonetary solutions.

This experiment confirms Riskin's observation that successful legal mediators are not consistently either facilitative or evaluative. The neutrals in the study did become increasingly evaluative over the course of each mediation, but their advice usually focused on the bargaining situation: They offered opinions, for instance, about how the other side was probably seeing the situation and what negotiating approach was most likely to be effective ("If you make that offer, I'm concerned that they will react by . . ."). As each of the filmed role-plays continued, the mediator became more willing to ask questions or make comments that suggested a view, or at least skepticism, about the disputants' legal arguments. However, when a neutral did make an evaluative comment about a legal issue, he almost always framed it in general terms ("The evidence on causation seems thin . . . I'm concerned that a court might . . ."). Overall, changes in the style of each mediator appeared to be determined much more by the personalities and tactics of the parties and lawyers than by tendencies of the neutral. Lawyer advocacy and client attitudes, in other words, counted for more than a mediator's preferred technique in determining what occurred during each mediation process.

Questions

What type of mediator would you select if you were a lawyer representing the following clients?

14. The family of the deceased MIT student.
15. The chemical company in the abutter-chemical company case.
16. The plaintiff in the "$1.2 million demand" personal injury mediation.

3. Mediative Approaches and Techniques

This section examines forms of mediation that you are likely to encounter in practice. As ADR has evolved, a wide variety of approaches to mediation have gained a measure of acceptance. Most lawyer-mediators focus on civil cases — that is, legal cases involving the kinds of tort, contract, property, and statutory claims that you have studied in law school, as opposed to marital or collective bargaining disputes. We refer to such neutrals as "commercial" mediators. Commercial mediators almost all use a caucus-based format, and the discussion tends to focus on legally relevant facts and issues and monetary offers. Mediators who specialize in mediating divorce and other disputes between family members, by contrast, usually avoid caucusing and place more emphasis on the parties' nonmonetary interests. The setting in which mediation occurs — for example, whether it is an all-day affair conducted by a private provider or a time-limited event ordered by a court — may also have a major impact on how the process unfolds. The readings below give a flavor of several models, beginning with commercial mediation and going on to processes that focus on money bargaining, understanding and interest-based solutions, and transformation of perspectives.

a. Commercial Mediation

Mediators who focus their practice on commercial disputes tend to use similar methods to conduct the process. The following two readings describe these techniques.

❖ Dwight Golann, A Basic Mediative Strategy
Mediating Legal Disputes 39-59 (1996)

In order to be effective, a mediator needs to have a strategy. Your overall goal is to stimulate constructive negotiations. You have been called in, however, because the parties are unable to negotiate effectively on their own, and a general call to reasonableness will rarely be enough to resolve the situation. Some discussions of mediation list a variety of roles which a mediator can take on, ranging from translator to agent of reality to scapegoat. Simply to list a mediator's functions does not, however, help one to select the right approach at a specific point. If people are not negotiating effectively with each other, it is because they are being frustrated by one or more barriers. As you prepare for mediation, then, you should ask yourself two questions:

- What obstacles are preventing the parties from settling this dispute themselves?
- What strategy is most likely to overcome the barriers and help the parties negotiate?

Your understanding of what is keeping the parties apart will deepen over the course of a mediation, and the obstacles themselves may change as the process goes forward. Ideally, your strategy would be unique to each case; in practice, however, this may not be possible. Many mediators use a similar sequence of techniques to deal with the barriers that are most likely to be present and customize their approach as they go along.

This section sets forth a simple six-step strategy that works effectively in less complex situations. It assumes a number of factors, for example that the parties have agreed to mediate and that the right people are in the room. We suggest that you use the strategy set out here as a "default" framework, applying other approaches as your skills grow and circumstances demand it. The strategy is [shown in Table 1.]

1. Create a Settlement Event

Problem: Procrastination and lack of focus. Many cases don't settle as quickly as they could because the parties or their negotiators are unwilling to raise the topic of settlement. This may be due to tactical concerns — the fear of suggesting a lack of confidence in one's legal case, for instance, or of appearing overeager to bargain. Disputants also delay negotiations, however, because they are reluctant to confront unpleasant realities, such as problems that have arisen with their legal arguments. Another common cause of delay is that cases drop out of the daily consciousness ("off the radar screens") of the people whose decisions are needed to resolve them. When this occurs, settlement discussions may never begin, or go on unproductively for months or years.

Response: Create a settlement event. The very scheduling of a mediation is a powerful tactic for dealing with the barrier of procrastination. It creates a focus on the dispute by the key players, a mutual recognition that it is appropriate to compromise, and a sense of deadline ("If not now, when?"). This "focus" aspect is very significant. Simply by agreeing to mediate, each side sends the other a signal that it is willing to invest resources in exploring a settlement, and thus impliedly is ready to compromise. It is easier for each party to move because it has some assurance that its own painful concessions will be reciprocated.

Mediators can also work in advance to ensure that the right people participate in the process. Negotiators sometimes suggest mediation in order to get a key person on the other side, for example a CEO or plaintiff's counsel, to focus on the dispute. If necessary, the mediator can also create a "train is leaving the station" effect to prod a reluctant party to make a difficult decision. ("I think we should go as long as necessary — I'm not going to ask you to come back another day....") Mediators can either enhance or detract from the feeling of a "settlement event" by how they manage the process.

2. Allow the Participants to Argue and Vent

Problem: Unresolved process and emotional needs. If parties do not settle through direct negotiation, it may be because one or more of them want something other than the settlement terms they are discussing. In addition to money, for example, a litigant may be looking for an experience — the opportunity to appear before a neutral person, state his grievance to an adversary, and know that he has been heard. In addition to arguing substantive issues, participants often also want to express strong feelings about what

Table 1.
A Basic Mediation Strategy

Problem	*Responses*
1. Lack of Focus	• Create a "settlement event." • Arrange for decision makers to attend. • Ensure that they have adequate information. • If necessary, propose deadlines.
2. Need to Vent Arguments and/or Emotions	• Provide disputants with a "day in court." • Help them to express their feelings. • Encourage participants to listen to opponents.
3. Positional Bargaining	• Ask for offers. • Clarify opponents' intentions and explain ambiguous moves. • Advise negotiators about the likely impact of tactics.
4. Hidden Nonlegal Issues	• Probe for psychological obstacles. • Seek out opportunities for gain. • Solicit ideas for addressing problems and exploiting opportunities. • Encourage candor and imaginative thinking.
5. Lack of Realism About Alternatives	• Reality test: Question legal and factual issues. • Lead disputants through a case analysis. • Bring out the monetary and other costs of conflict. • Challenge the litigants' views and point out neglected issues. • If necessary, offer a prediction of the likely outcome if the dispute is adjudicated.
6. Inability to Close	• Help participants to avoid bargaining confrontations. • Reframe their options and choices. • Play "confidential listener." • Find new issues to unfreeze impasse. • Offer a "mediator's proposal."

happened. People enter litigation expecting to have the opportunity to speak out, only to learn that the legal process does not usually provide any hearing on the merits, and that their emotions are relevant only to the extent that they serve a strategic purpose. Until disputants feel adequately heard out, however, they are often unwilling to consider settling. Equally important, parties in legal conflicts frequently stop listening to each other except for the limited purpose of making their case. As a result, both sides often miss important data about the origins of the dispute and possibilities for settlement.

Response: An opportunity to speak and feel heard. This aspect of the strategy has three elements: One is to give disputants some elements of a "day in court." The second is to provide a means for them to vent personal feelings. The third is to help each participant hear what the other is saying. The first aspect usually occurs primarily in joint session, while the second and third can happen either in joint session or during private caucuses.

Although mediation is not a court session and mediators are certainly not judges, they can give parties the opportunity during an opening session to present their legal case. Such presentations assist the settlement process in several ways. First, parties are able to see their lawyer argue their case or can do so themselves. In addition, each side hears a direct statement of the strengths of the other's case. The mediator, of course, will not decide the dispute and may never express an opinion about the merits, but the absence of a decision does not prevent the process from being effective. After such presentations and the discussions that follow, disputants often feel more ready to move on to settlement.

The experience of arguing the merits also facilitates the rest of the process by focusing participants on the facts of the controversy and relevant principles. Through the way she moderates the opening session, the mediator also delivers a message that discussing issues and standards in a rational manner, rather than simply stating positions, is the most productive way to negotiate. Parties' knowledge that the mediator will be listening also encourages both sides to assess their facts and theories more carefully and edit out extreme contentions.

In addition to responding to participants' wish to argue legal issues, this aspect of the process often has an emotional component. The need to express strong feelings to one's adversaries or a neutral person is a very human one, felt by CEOs as much as by mail room clerks. Through their lawyers' presentations at the opening session, and perhaps by making comments themselves, parties can partially vent their feelings about the dispute and each other. This may also occur during caucuses. After they have experienced being heard out, disputants often gradually become less upset and angry, making it easier for them to consider settlement.

Novice mediators are often uncomfortable dealing with strong emotions, or worry about unleashing psychological issues with which they are not trained to deal. As a result, they often squelch emotional venting or even skip the opening session altogether. This is almost always a mistake. Unless a disputant appears to be dangerous or psychologically troubled, a mediator can achieve a great deal simply by allowing the parties to talk about their feelings and differences in a safe and controlled environment. The emotional and psychological aspects of mediation are discussed in more depth in Chapter 8.

3. Moderate the Bargaining

Problem: Positional tactics leading to impasse. Negotiators often have trouble reaching a settlement because they use a positional approach to bargaining and cannot successfully manage the resulting "dance" of numbers. One or both sides may, for example, try to claim value by locking themselves into a position, or bargainers may become angry as they feel that they are being pushed to make more than their fair share of concessions. The result often is an impasse.

Response: Become the moderator. When this kind of problem arises, a mediator can coach or advise each side, or lead them through the reciprocal steps needed to reach agreement. A mediator might begin by asking the party who last received a concession or who seems the least upset to make a new offer. (Techniques for moderating positional bargaining are discussed in the article "Mediating in the Dance for Dollars" below and in Chapter 7.)

Having restarted the process, a mediator can give a party advice about how a concession is likely to be received by the other side. She can also explore privately where each side intends to go ("I'll communicate that, but can you give me a private sense of what you'd be willing to do if they *did* make a six-figure offer?"). The mediator can then suggest a strategy to move toward a goal. Concurrently, she can remind the bargainers of the need to justify their positions with facts and arguments, and of the value of focusing on interests.

A mediator's presence helps positional negotiators make offers with less fear that they will be led down a slippery path to a one-sided compromise. In addition, by verifying for each side that their adversary is also "feeling pain," the neutral helps to overcome the tendency of disputants to devalue offers made by their opponent. Indeed, disputants often seem more sensitive to which side is losing more than to their own gains, and take surprising comfort from knowing that their opponent is feeling pain as well! Through such tactics, often mixed with continuing discussions of the merits and the consequences of failing to agree, a mediator can often orchestrate a pattern of reciprocal concessions that moves toward settlement.

4. Probe for and Address Hidden Issues

Problem: Disregard of hidden costs of disputing and missed opportunities. Parties in legal disputes tend to view their situation through a narrow and often distorted lens: They focus almost exclusively on legal issues, even when the conflict appears to be driven primarily by other factors. Even as a mediator discusses litigation options and bargaining proposals, therefore, she should be thinking about what other issues may be keeping the parties apart. These might include the following:

Psychological and emotional issues. Parties often fall into impasse because of psychological or emotional factors. Those emotions, and the parties' inhibitions about expressing them, may be so strong that they will not raise the issue in joint session. Especially in business disputes, parties often appear at mediation with their "game faces on," presenting logical arguments while emotions boil underneath the surface. Simply giving disputants an opportunity to vent their feelings is not enough in these cases. Participants are so reluctant to mention emotions, or so unconscious of them, that they resist discussing feelings even in the privacy of a caucus.

Feelings of loss. Lawsuits almost always impose losses on all of the parties. This is most clear when the parties shared a beneficial relationship, as is true of most contract cases and family disputes. But it is also true even in cases in which the parties had no past relationship, such as most auto accident claims: Simply being in a state of conflict can impose severe costs on litigants in the form of lost time and anxiety. These costs are usually not mentioned in negotiation because the legal system regards them as irrelevant. But they often leave disputants with the feeling that accepting even a rational settlement will involve a serious loss, and the phenomenon known as loss aversion then distorts their bargaining decisions.

Unexploited opportunities for gain. We know that repairing a relationship or satisfying other underlying interests is one of the rewards of effective bargaining. Litigators, however, often find it very difficult to identify and exploit opportunities for value creation, because they are conditioned by their roles as legal warriors to look only at remedies that a court can award, which are almost always restricted to money damages.

Response: Identify and address hidden issues. The next step in a mediator's basic strategy is thus to look for the hidden non-legal issues that are contributing to the dispute or that that could be exploited for mutual gain, then foster a process that addresses them. The neutral should begin to do this even as he is carrying out other tasks. He should look for clues that a hidden issue is present, such as strong emotions, irrational arguments, or a past relationship between the parties. In most cases, the mediator should approach these issues in the privacy of the caucus. He can encourage the participants to address hidden issues in constructive ways or, if necessary, offer solutions himself.

5. Test the Parties' Alternatives; If Necessary, Evaluate the Adjudication Option

Problem: Lack of realism about the outcome in adjudication. Legal disputes differ from other controversies in that one or more of the parties has the option to obtain a binding decision in adjudication. The issue of how an adjudicator will decide the case if it does not settle is usually treated by participants as a key factor in bargaining. Parties sometimes appreciate the weaknesses in their case, and even disputants who honestly disagree about the likely outcome in court may compromise in order to avoid the costs of litigation. In most cases, however, litigants suffer from "optimistic overconfidence," overestimating their chance of prevailing in adjudication. This makes it hard even for well-intentioned negotiators to reach an agreement that they both believe is fair.

First response: Reality test. Mediators can help to solve merits-based problems by "reality testing" — that is, by assisting each side to understand the weaknesses in its litigation option. Reality testing is a key part of most mediation strategies; the question is how best to go about it. At the outset mediators typically limit themselves to asking general questions that will draw out the parties' evidence and arguments. If, for instance, a party has emphasized its strength on liability issues but has avoided discussing the damage claims in a case, the neutral may ask about the neglected issue. Whenever possible, mediators should stress that their question has been raised by the other side; they, in other words are the bearer of the unwelcome question, but not its instigator.

Discussing the merits can help to narrow the gap between litigants for several reasons. First, it may genuinely change peoples' views about the strength of their case, or resolve disagreements between a client and lawyer. In addition, if a disputant is aware of a particular problem but has been hoping that the other side would not notice it, a mediator's question will signal that the weakness is apparent to its adversary or the neutral, and so also to a future judge or jury. Finally, even if a frank discussion does not shake a party's views, the process may convince it that compromise will be necessary and provide a face-saving excuse for what the party realizes it must do to settle.

There is a tension inherent in reality testing between being pointed enough to prompt decision makers to confront a problem, and being so tough that they conclude that the neutral has taken sides with their opponent. A mediator's questions should therefore progress gradually, from open-ended queries ("Have you thought about...?") to more pointed comments ("They are resisting making a higher offer because they believe that you won't be able to establish causation...What can I tell them?")

If a diplomatic approach is not enough, a mediator should consider using "harder" reality testing. Hard testing is a matter of degree. It involves going beyond asking questions, even skeptical ones, to express the opinion that a participant's view of the case is not accurate, without however stating the mediator's own opinion on the issue. Examples include:

> "Perhaps you're right.... Have you seen juries in this area award that level of damages?... Regularly?"
> "I'm having trouble following your argument on that issue. Give me a chance to think about it some more."

Alternative response: Offer evaluative feedback. In some cases even reality testing will not be adequate. This can occur for a wide variety of reasons. For example, participants may be wedded to an unrealistic viewpoint, or may need a better approximation of a "day in court," or require explicit help from the mediator to justify a settlement to a superior. In such situations mediators have the option to go further, offering a specific opinion about how a court is likely to decide the entire case or a key issue in dispute. Evaluations can be structured in a variety of ways. Examples include:

- "I understand your argument on liability but, frankly, given the law in this state, I'd be concerned about whether you can get your emotional distress claim in."
- "My experience with Judge Jones is that she usually denies summary judgment in this kind of situation."
- "If the plaintiff prevails on liability, what I know of Houston juries suggests that they would value damages here at somewhere between $125[,000] and $150,000."

Properly performed, a neutral evaluation can be helpful in producing an agreement, but one that is poorly done or badly timed can derail the settlement process. A deeper discussion of the appropriateness of evaluation in mediation appears in Chapter 9.

6. Offer a Settlement Proposal

Problem: Closing the final gap. Often even the combination of tactics described above will not produce agreement.

Responses: Play confidential listener and if necessary make a "mediator's proposal."
At this point, a mediator should press the parties more strongly. One approach
is to play *confidential listener*. Here the mediator asks each side whether it is
willing to tell the neutral privately the most that it would do to settle. Mediators
ordinarily don't expect to be told a party's true "bottom line." Indeed, asking
for a final position is often counterproductive, because it may lead a party to
commit to unrealistic terms. Taking each side's statement with a grain of salt,
the mediator can give both of them guidance about the gap between them.

Either as an alternative or a follow-up to confidential listener, mediators
have the option of making a *mediator's proposal*. Here the mediator suggests a
set of terms that he thinks may be acceptable to all of the disputants. In doing
so, the neutral is not necessarily evaluating the merits of the case: More
important than what might happen at some future trial is the mediator's
practical assessment of what each side is willing to do at that moment to reach
agreement. Equally important, the package should be presented as the
mediator's proposal. Because of the phenomenon of reactive devaluation, any
idea advanced by a party will be subject to suspicion, but the same terms
coming from the mediator are likely to be received more positively. The
process by which a mediator presents a proposal is crucial. The ground rules
should be that: (1) If all sides accept the proposal, they have an agreement but
(2) If a party rejects the proposal, it never learns whether its adversary would
have accepted it. Thus litigants know that they will only have to make this
difficult concession if it actually brings them a settlement, and that if the effort
fails, their adversary will never know that they were willing to compromise
further. Because of these psychological factors, a mediator's proposal will
often break an apparent impasse and produce agreement. Even if it doesn't,
the proposal may prompt parties to rethink their positions and restart direct
bargaining.

Conclusion

This six-step strategy can produce success in many situations. No limited
strategy, however, can overcome all the subtle obstacles that prevent
disputants from settling. Experienced mediators therefore use these techniques as a foundation, modifying their approach to deal with the obstacles
presented in specific disputes.

Here are more specific suggestions about commercial mediation technique,
presented in the form of "do's" and "don'ts."

❖ Marjorie C. Aaron, Do's and Don'ts of Mediation Practice
11 Disp. Resol. Mag. (Winter 2005)

Preliminary Meetings and Telephone Conferences

Do's

In a preliminary meeting or telephone conference with one or all of the
parties and/or counsel,

do explore process options and interests...

do probe the issue of authority...

do in some complex, highly emotional, or very large stakes cases, ... meet privately with each party and their counsel before the mediation session.... Remember, unlike in a court or arbitration context, there is no prohibition against a mediator contacting one or both parties separately to discuss any question or issue in the case....

do really listen, building trust and developing intuition.... Being a successful mediator sometimes means having the nose and ear of a psychologist. You are also making a personal connection with the people involved. At some point in the process, you may be asking them to accept difficult suggestions. This is a lot easier if they have grown to like and trust you.

Don'ts

don't accept the attorneys'/parties' suggestion regarding the process they prefer ("Three hours will be enough.... It's a simple case.") without asking basic questions about the status of the dispute, the complexity of the issues, and what is at stake.

don't accept the attorneys' assurances that they will have authority at the mediation session. Probe further, particularly where an insurance company holds the purse strings, to ensure that someone with true "worst case authority" will be present...

don't offer any opinion, or show skepticism or favor about the claims or defenses raised in the case....

Initial Joint Session

At the initial joint session (there may well be other meetings between the parties as the process continues), the mediator plays many roles: moderator, master of ceremonies, evaluator, questioner, alter ego, persuader, deal maker. It is important that you:

Do's

do set an appropriate tone with an opening statement. The degree of formality or informality of your statement will vary, but in just about every case, you should:

- Remind the parties and counsel of the confidentiality of the mediation process.
- Remind the parties that they own the process. Its outcome is theirs to determine.... The mediator does not have the power to hand down a decision.
- Ask the parties and counsel to try to listen objectively to the other side's presentation. Suggest that rather than scribbling responses, they try to imagine how a jury listening for the first and only time would view the dispute.
- If appropriate, explain that you may help them to evaluate settlement options and the parties' alternatives to settlement. But *don't* raise the evaluation possibility in the joint session opening unless it is clear, based upon preliminary meetings or conferences, that it is likely to be necessary.

do develop an opening "patter" that fits your personality, your philosophy, and covers general process issues and questions, but be prepared to alter it to fit the parties, the chemistry, and the tone of the case...

do listen and take notes during the presentations, even if you have heard it all before...

do ask questions to focus the issues. You might use questions to demonstrate where the parties agree on the facts or the law, and the sources of disagreement. Ask questions gracefully, without indicating bias. Ask as if simply trying to understand. Make some effort to balance the questions directed at each side...

do try to ask questions or comments that anticipate the reactions or feelings of the side listening to the presentation. Thus, if the speaking lawyer or party has said something outrageous or insulting, you might want to reframe or note that you understand this is an issue in dispute and that the other (listening) party would most likely disagree...

do consider using active listening techniques from time to time, restating how you understand the party's perspective as expressed, but maintain neutrality in the process.

do make sure that all parties and counsel feel they have been given an opportunity to make all of their arguments and say their piece in the joint session.

Don'ts

don't act like a judge, or permit the parties or counsel to treat you like one.

don't allow cross-examination or disruptive interruptions or objections.

don't lose control of the proceeding, unless the parties have "taken over" to engage in real dialogue and problem solving.

don't indicate in any way that counsel could have done a better job of analyzing the case, advising their clients, or preparing for the mediation...

don't, except in unusual circumstances, omit a joint session...

don't interrupt the presentations too much. This is a judgment call...

don't, by a question or statement in joint session, make one side's case stronger. This will buy you an enemy on the other side. In private session, you may point out how the other side's case could be even stronger and note that they will probably figure this out before trial.

Private Caucuses

Do's

do start the private caucuses by asking the parties and counsel what they are thinking, and what they might want to say that they were not comfortable saying in the joint session.

do feel freer to empathize with each party's perspective, while still maintaining neutrality in the dispute. You can express your understanding of why the other side seems like the "bad guys" to them given the history or context....This is called manipulation, or perhaps the groundwork for effective manipulation. It is clearly part of the mediation process...

do pay attention to the negotiation styles of all parties and counsel...

do help the parties see that, whatever the past perceived injury or wrong, they are now faced with a decision problem that involves choices going forward. Can they find a settlement that serves their interests better than the alternatives?

do ask each party in private caucus how they believe the other sees the dispute, and what they think the other party would consider a fair settlement.

do ask how they evaluate the strengths and weaknesses of the other side's case, of their own case, if their analysis of the merits seems to be driving settlement positions.... Try to get a sense of the settlement range that would be acceptable to both sides...

do ask the parties to begin focusing on solution options, including but not limited to dollars. In some cases, you may suggest a number of options for them to think about and tinker with. Then it is your job to shuttle back and forth, trying to put a deal together.

do keep the numbers and the options rolling. Keep up the pressure and the momentum. If people must eat, it's generally best to order in.

don't allow the parties to dig in on a position or a number as a matter of ego. Turn it around: "It takes someone older and wiser to unlock this one...." Make the ego play the other way.

do wait to evaluate until you see no other way to achieve progress toward settlement.... Make sure, before you evaluate, that the party would like to hear what you think of the case...

do provide any evaluation *very, very gently*. Provide it in private session only. Couch your evaluation in terms of what an average jury might do.... Don't argue.... Try to prevent an unfavorable evaluation from turning a party or its counsel against you...

do have patience. You will be in the fifth round of shuttle diplomacy and one of the parties will be arguing against your evaluation on the gravel issue. You must listen. You *cannot* say, "You simpleton. Didn't you hear what I said? Your gravel isn't worth beans." [B]e patient and try to segue from the gravel issue to the question at hand.

Don'ts

don't ask for anyone's bottom line, at least not until the end of a long day, and certainly not in joint session.... Most of the time, they won't tell you the truth and if they announce their (fake) bottom line, they may become entrenched...

don't assume that you will be delivering an evaluation. An evaluation on the merits may be unnecessary and unhelpful. Explore all other paths to settlement first.... Don't deliver an inconsistent evaluation (on the numbers) to both sides. It is always tempting to tell both sides they have a terrible case and find an easy settlement in the middle. That may settle one case, but it will quickly ruin your reputation as a mediator...

don't lose momentum, or give up on the bidding. Too often, a party tells the mediator, "This is my final number, don't come back with anything else," and the mediator obeys. *Never* believe a number is final until the parties have walked out the door (threatening to walk out isn't good enough)....

Settlement

do write up the deal then and there, no matter how tired and edgy people are, no matter if counsel would rather shake hands and go home with assurances that "We all have the same understanding." Drafting should be done with the assistance of both lawyers ...

do, if possible, include a provision stating that the agreement is valid and enforceable.... Obtain signatures of all parties and, preferably, counsel as well.

do go home and relax. Have a fattening dessert. You've earned it. Contemplate a good mediation war story, concealing names and details to preserve confidentiality, of course!

Questions

17. What goals is a mediator using the "Basic Strategy" or the "Do's and Don'ts" approach seeking?
18. Using Professor Riskin's grid, how would you classify the style of a mediator applying the above advice: broad or narrow? facilitative or evaluative?

b. "Pure Money" Mediation

The techniques described above can be used not only to bargain over money, but also to seek out solutions that meet the deeper interests of the parties. In many legal disputes, however, the only issue that the parties recognize, or at least the only one that they are willing to negotiate over, is money. Even when disputants are open to discussing other issues, lawyers in mediation often spend much of their time exchanging offers couched primarily in monetary terms. In such situations, counsel may choose a mediator at least in part based on the neutral's ability to facilitate money bargaining, a process that is explored in the following reading.

❖ J. Michael Keating, Mediating in the Dance for Dollars
14 Alternatives 71 (September 1996)

Virtually every conflict involves a struggle over resources. Litigation, which characteristically transmutes wrongs into dollars, is full of "distributive" disputes.... What does a mediator do when the dispute consists largely (if not solely) of a monetary demand and offer, with no future relationship at stake, as in personal injury and some contractual disputes? ...

Even when parties are fully conscious of the need to reach some sort of accommodation, they are reluctant to begin bargaining: They worry about sending the wrong signal or being exploited by the other party. The mediator can provide both guidance and safety in these situations, principally through the use of the caucus. In an initial round of caucuses, a mediator will want to explore with parties the general nature of their demand or offer, gauge the flexibility of each party, and understand each party's level of sophistication about the negotiation. It is not even necessary to emerge from this first round of caucuses with a new offer or demand. You want to begin building empathy and trust with the parties, communicate your understanding of their positions and show you're dedicated to a fair bargaining process that will protect them from exploitation.

Reasonable Anchors

The mediator needs to be endlessly patient in distributive bargaining. Resist the temptation to push immediately for settlement. Reasonable anchors rarely surface immediately. Especially useful in the quest for those anchors is your insistence that parties provide detailed justifications for their demands or offers, and for their rejections of the other side's offers or demands. Part of the mediator's task is to protect the bargaining process by making sure that concessions are responded to in a meaningful way. That can curb, or at least reduce, the fear of exploitation that often inhibits productive bargaining.

Initial concessions in distributive negotiation are usually the largest and tend to come most quickly. As the process continues, concessions shrink and take longer to elicit. Surprisingly, many negotiators seem oblivious to this pattern: They begin with piddling or insulting openings, discouraging the other party from serious bargaining and prolonging the negotiation process. The mediator needs to help the parties think through the likely impact of their initial concessions.

Lengthy Bargaining

...Many people aren't prepared for lengthy bargaining: They prefer to think that their first concession will bring the process to a quick end as the other party gratefully and immediately embraces the new offer. The mediator needs to educate participants about the pace of bargaining and orchestrate its progress. Even in distributive disputes, the mediator must look for ways to introduce integrative elements. The timing of payments, creating of a structured settlement, payment in kind of services, rebates or discounts, are all ways of maneuvering a seemingly inflexible distributive dispute.... If the gap between the parties' positions is small, such a gambit may help close it. One characteristic of a fierce distributive confrontation is the tendency of parties to demonize each other's motivations and behavior. A mediator has to take the venom out of the dialogue....

Many distributive negotiations involve a lump sum divisible into a variety of components. A personal injury case, for example, may include medical expenses, lost wages, pain and suffering, interest, and attorney's fees. Typically, each element is analyzed and subjected separately to the push and pull of bargaining. But parties may place widely different values on each component of the recovery; once such differences become evident, the smart mediator moves back to bargaining over the lump sum. That leaves the parties free to rationalize distribution....

Joint Session

While much of this bargaining process may best be executed in the caucus, if the parties remain significantly apart, the mediator ought to bring them back together in a joint session. The mediator then needs to help them rehearse their differences as calmly as possible, without interpersonal unpleasantness, so both sides understand the nature of (and reasons for) the remaining gap. This may be the most critical point in developing a mutually acceptable bargain....

[Eventually] it is time for the mediator to put a range of numbers, somewhere near the mid-point of the difference between the parties, on the table. It is not the correctness of the range that counts. The aim here is simply to keep the parties' dialogue — their "dance for dollars" — alive. Ideally, the mediator should present the numbers not as an evaluation of what the case is worth, but as sums at which the parties might be able to settle. They may react with outrage, but meanwhile we want the dialogue to continue....

Patience and optimism are always virtues in a mediator, but that's especially true in a distributive dispute. "No gap too wide" is the motto. Therefore, a party's description of a demand or offer is meaningless. I have watched many parties plummet through "bottom lines." The tactic, in the face of a solemn declaration of a party's bottom line, is simply to ignore it and move on.... Mediation is just as relevant in distributive as in integrative situations. In both, the mediator's role is to navigate parties through what looks like stormy and unmanageable negotiation.

Questions

19. Which elements of the "Basic Mediative Strategy" set out above are not mentioned in Keating's "pure money" methodology?
20. What problems might arise if "pure dollar" methods are applied in a dispute that has significant nonmonetary aspects?

c. No-Caucus Approaches

Although commercial mediators typically employ a joint-session-followed-by-caucusing format, some are experimenting with conducting virtually all the process in joint session. Most mediators of marital disputes also do most or all of their work with both parties present, in part to build a better working relationship between the spouses around issues such as parenting, and in part out of concern that caucusing would exacerbate the air of suspicion that often hangs over such cases. Disputes arising from close business relationships have many of the characteristics of a family quarrel and also may lend themselves to the use of a no-caucus format. Some believe that no-caucus techniques should be used not only when a dispute involves a strong relationship, but whenever parties are seeking a better understanding of the situation and creative agreements. The following reading describes this model.

❖ **Gary J. Friedman and Jack Himmelstein, Resolving Conflict Together: The Understanding-Based Model of Mediation**

(forthcoming 2006)

The Understanding-Based Model of Mediation

The overarching goal of this approach to mediation is to resolve conflict through understanding. Deeper understanding by the parties of their own and each other's perspectives, priorities and concerns enables them to work through their conflict together. With an enhanced understanding of the whole situation, the parties are able to shape creative and mutually rewarding solutions that reflect their personal, business and economic interests. To these ends, the mediator meets directly and simultaneously (rather than separately) with both sides and, if the parties desire, with their lawyers present as well. The model shares much in common with a number of other approaches to mediation. For example, we stress the importance of articulating interests that underlie the parties conflicting positions and developing solutions that will serve those interests. There is also much that distinguishes this approach.

Parties' Responsibility and the Non-caucus Approach

In the understanding-based model, the emphasis is on the parties' responsibility for the decisions they will make. Many models of mediation assume that the mediator should take a strong role in crafting a solution to the parties' dispute and persuading them to adopt it. In this approach, the assumption is that it is the parties, not the professionals, who have the best understanding of what underlies the dispute and are in the best position to find the solution. It is their conflict, and they hold the key to reaching a solution that best serves them both.

Meeting together with the parties (and counsel) follows from these assumptions about parties' responsibility. Many other approaches to mediation recommend that the mediator shuttle back and forth between the parties (caucusing), gaining information that he or she holds confidential. Our central problem with caucusing is that the mediator ends up with the fullest picture of the problem and is therefore in the best position to solve it. The mediator, armed with that fuller view, can readily urge or manipulate the parties to the end he or she shapes. The emphasis here, in contrast, is on understanding and voluntariness as the basis for resolving the conflict rather than persuasion or coercion.

We view the mediator's role in the understanding-based approach as assisting the parties to gain sufficient understanding of their own and each other's perspective so as to be able to decide together how to resolve their dispute. The parties not only know first hand everything that transpires, they have control over fashioning an outcome that will work for both. And they also participate with the mediator (and counsel) in designing a process by which they can honor what they each value and help them reach a result that reflects what is important to both of them. As mediators, our goal is to support the parties in working through their conflict together — in ways that respect their differing perspectives, needs and interests as well as their common goals.

To work in this way is challenging for both the mediator and the parties. The parties' motivation and willingness to work together is critical to the success of this approach. Mediators often assume that the parties (and their counsel) simply do not want to work together, and therefore keep the parties apart. In our experience, many parties (and counsel) simply accept that they will not work together and that the mediator will be responsible for crafting the solution. But once educated how staying in the same room might be valuable, many are motivated to do so. If the parties (and the mediator) are willing, working together throughout can be as rewarding as it is demanding.

Role of Law and Lawyers

Mediators tend to be divided in how they approach the role of law in mediation. Some rely heavily on what a court would decide if the case were to go to trial, authoritatively suggesting or implying that law should be the controlling standard used to end the conflict. Other mediators, concerned that the parties might simply defer too readily to the law and miss the opportunity to find more creative decisions, try to keep the law out of mediation altogether.

In this model, we welcome lawyers' participation and we include the law. But we do not assume that the parties will or should rely solely or primarily on the law. Rather, the importance the parties give to the law is up to them. Our goals are 1) to educate the parties about the law and possible legal outcomes and 2) to support their freedom to fashion their own creative solutions that may differ from what a court might decide. In this way, the parties learn that they can together reach agreements that respond to both their individual interests and their common goals, while also being well informed about their legal rights and the judicial alternatives to a mediated settlement.

lawyers'
roles

This approach to the law's place in mediation draws upon lawyers' knowledge and skills in ways both similar to and different from their traditional roles. To participate in this problem-solving approach to mediation requires many lawyers to shift from reliance on a stance of adversary advocacy to one of collaborative support. For some lawyers, this can be a challenge, but a rewarding one. As we view the lawyers' role in mediation, they are there to protect their clients and to inform them about the legal alternative...At the same time, they are also called upon to support their clients' active participation and open dialogue, which may be a stretch for many lawyers. The lawyers also participate by helping their clients design the mediation process and supporting their clients as the parties create the solutions to their conflict that may be quite different from what a court might do but which better serve what they really care about.

In these and other respects, the understanding-based approach seeks to develop and utilize mediation's potential to resolve conflict in ways that honor the parties, their differences and their relationship.

Example: A caucus-oriented mediator took on a case involving the dissolution of a design firm. One of the partners, whose specialty was marketing, had taken an inside position with a large client of the firm, while her partner, who focused on supervising the execution of projects, had decided to continue the business on her own. The two women remained friendly, but the situation had created tension around setting the terms of the remaining partner's buyout of her colleague's interest in the firm. The partner who handled production was anxious at the prospect of becoming solely responsible for the business and plainly felt somewhat abandoned. Her marketing colleague, by contrast, tended to take an everything-will-work-out approach to life, and found it hard to credit her partner's concerns.

The partnership's corporate lawyer recommended that they mediate the issues between them. In light of their long history of working together cooperatively, he suggested that they do so without lawyers present, but with each having a personal attorney available for consultations between sessions. The mediator ordinarily used a caucus-based format, but he decided in this

= more private, rather
than common table

case to keep the two women together throughout their discussions. He felt that with some assistance they could negotiate directly and was concerned that if he held separate meetings it would be taken as a signal that their disagreements were more serious than they were. Most important, the partners themselves expressed a preference for face-to-face discussions. The mediation went forward in a joint-meeting format, although each woman occasionally talked with the mediator privately by telephone. The memo of agreement was written out and initialed in an ice cream shop located under the partnership's offices.

Questions

21. What potential advantages would a no-caucus model provide, as compared to a caucus-based approach, in a typical commercial contract dispute? What drawbacks?
22. Can a no-caucus model be effective when the disputants believe that the only issue in the case is money? If they insist on limiting bargaining to money?
23. In the case example, the mediator had occasional private conversations with each party over the telephone. Although neither party appeared to feel excluded as a result, what concerns might a no-caucus mediator have about this technique?
24. In terms of the "Riskin grid" described previously, how would you chart the style of a mediator who uses the following techniques:
    a. The "dance for dollars" approach outlined by Keating?
    b. The "understanding-based" process described by Friedman and Himmelstein?

d. Transformative Mediation

As mentioned previously, a very different kind of process, known as "transformative" mediation, does not seek to settle cases. Rather, its goal is to create a setting in which participants can, if they wish, change the way in which they view themselves and others in the dispute. The following readings describe the use of transformative techniques, the first to address issues among employees at the U.S. Postal Service (USPS) and the second to deal with divorce disputes. As you read, ask yourself:

- What appear to be the key differences in goals and techniques between transformative and commercial mediation?
- Are there any situations in which a transformative approach could be useful to you as a practicing lawyer?

In the early 1990s the USPS was plagued by worker discontent. The Postal Service is a unionized organization with over 800,000 employees. At the time, the USPS was going through productivity pressures and was seen by many employees as having an authoritarian, command-and-control management culture. But while employees were angry, many were not willing to leave their jobs. They expressed their frustration by filing enormous numbers of grievances under their union contract and complaints of discrimination with the Equal Employment Opportunity Commission, causing major burdens and distractions for Postal Service managers.

In 1994, as part of the settlement of a class action, the Postal Service created a mediation program known as "REDRESS." The program was designed and neutrals were trained based on the transformative model described below. There is anecdotal evidence, however, that many USPS managers did not accept the transformative model and molded the program to achieve the traditional purpose of resolving disputes. (Indeed, the word REDRESS stands for "Resolve Employment Disputes, Reach Equitable Solutions Swiftly.") The following reading describes the results of the REDRESS program.

❖ **Lisa B. Bingham, REDRESS™ at the USPS: A Breakthrough Mediation Program**

1 AC Resol. 34 (Spring 2002)

Some have observed that getting federal agencies to use dispute resolution inst.... of their traditional approaches to conflict is a battle against inertia, like turning a big ship. Yet, the United States Postal Service (USPS), the largest federal civilian employer and second largest civilian employer in the world, implemented a national mediation program for employment disputes arising out of claims of discrimination, named REDRESS™ ... in just eighteen months. Where there is a will, there is a way. Effective July 1999, every postal employee in the country had access to outside neutral mediators. This award-winning program ... uses transformative techniques ... and consists of the following design features:

- Any employee who contacts the Equal Employment Opportunity (EEO) counselor with an informal EEO complaint may request mediation. The program is voluntary for complainants. Respondents, generally USPS supervisors and managers, are required to participate in one mediation session.
- Mediation is generally scheduled within two to three weeks of a request.
- The complainant and respondent may bring any representative they choose, including lawyers, union or professional association representatives, co-workers, friends, or family....
- Mediators do not evaluate the legal merits of or render opinions on the dispute. They do not press for particular settlements or recommend specific outcomes; any settlement is a function of the participants' mutual agreement.
- If there is no resolution, the complainant may return to the traditional EEO process, proceed with investigation, file a formal complaint, and proceed to an administrative hearing.
- At the formal complaint and administrative hearing stage, the complainant may again request mediation under REDRESS II, a new program implemented in 2001 using the same transformative model of mediation....
- From 70 to 75 percent of all employees offered the option to mediate participate in REDRESS.

- The USPS conducts approximately 11,500 REDRESS mediation sessions each year....
- Over 90% of all participants, including complainants, respondents, and their representatives, report they are satisfied or highly satisfied with the REDRESS process and mediators, and over 65% report they are satisfied or highly satisfied with the outcome of mediation. These rates have held steady throughout the period of the program.
- The REDRESS case closure rate is over 80%....
- After REDRESS, the annual rate at which employees filed formal EEO complaints dropped from a high of 14,000 to a low of slightly over 10,000.

REDRESS is now a permanent program at the USPS.

Questions

25. Why do you think that the USPS decided to use this form of mediation as the model for its program?
26. What would be your greatest concern about referring a client to such a process? Are there any steps you could take to minimize this concern?

❖ **Robert A. Baruch Bush and Sally Ganong Pope, Transformative Mediation Principles and Practices in Divorce Mediation**

Divorce and Family Mediation 53-71 (Folberg et al. eds. 2004)

ᴛʀansformative Conflict Theory: The Why and What of Transformative Mediation in Divorce Cases

Why do parties come to divorce mediators, and what is it that mediators can do to best serve them? The parties themselves, as they enter mediation, give varied reasons for their choice, but most fall into the following categories. Saving money and time and avoiding the legal system are at the top of most lists. Reducing hostility and conflict for their own sake and the sake of their children, and developing effective parenting plans, are also important. One party may be more interested in the time-savings and the other in protection of the children. Most all, however, agree that staying out of the legal system is essential. Certainly, with few exceptions, all hope to achieve a fair divorce settlement agreement....

How then are we to understand the "why" of divorce mediation? In our view, all of the above descriptions of clients' goals express their desire to experience a different form of conflict interaction than they have experienced in their private negotiations and than they believe they would find in the legal system.... Rather, they want to come out of the process feeling better about themselves and each other.... This conclusion is the result of insights from the fields of communication, developmental psychology and social psychology, among others. According to that view — what we call "transformative" theory — conflict is about peoples' interaction with one another as human beings. It is not primarily about problem-solving, about satisfaction of needs and interests. Certainly there are problems to be solved at the end of a marriage — the assets to be divided, the parenting plan to be created — and certainly parties want to solve those problems. The reality is, however, that they want to do so in a way that enhances their sense of their own competence and autonomy without taking advantage of the other. They want to feel proud of themselves for how they handled this life crisis, and this means making changes in the difficult conflict interaction that is going on between them, rather than simply coming up with the "right" answers to the specific problems.

. . . When we study perceptions of and attitudes towards conflict, we find that what most people find hardest about conflict is not that it frustrates their satisfaction of some interest or project, no matter how important, but rather that it leads and even forces them to behave toward themselves and others in ways that they find uncomfortable and even repellent. . . . Before the conflict, there is some decent human interaction going on, whatever the context — between people in a family, a workplace, a community. Even divorcing couples were once engaged in some form of decent, even loving, human interaction. Then the conflict arises and, propelled by the vicious circle of disempowerment and demonization, what started as a decent interaction spirals down into one which is negative, destructive, alienating, and demonizing, on all sides. . . .

Given this view of what conflict entails and "means" to parties, where does conflict intervention come into the picture? In particular, what are divorcing couples looking for when they seek the services of a mediator? One fundamental premise of the transformative model is that what bothers parties most about conflict is the interactional degeneration itself, and therefore what they most want from an intervener — even more than help in resolving specific issues — is help in reversing the downward spiral and restoring a more humane quality to their interaction. . . .

But how do parties in conflict reverse the destructive conflict spiral? . . . The first part of an answer to this question is that the critical resource is the parties' own basic humanity: their essential strength, and their essential decency and compassion, as human beings. . . . They move from weakness to strength, becoming (in more specific terms) calmer, clearer, more confident, more articulate and more decisive. They shift from self-absorption to responsiveness, becoming more attentive, open, trusting, and more responsive toward the other party. . . . [T]hese dynamic shifts are called "Empowerment" and "Recognition." Moreover, there is also a reinforcing feedback effect . . . The stronger I become, the more open I am to you. The more open I am to you, the stronger you feel, the more open you become to me, and the stronger I feel. . . . Why "conflict transformation"? Because as the parties make empowerment and recognition shifts, and as those shifts gradually reinforce in a virtuous circle, the interaction as a whole begins to turn the corner and regenerate. . . .

What divorcing parties want from mediators, and what mediators can in fact provide — with proper focus and skills — is help and support for these small but critical shifts by each party. . . . The mediator's primary goals are: (1) to foster Empowerment shifts, by supporting but never supplanting each party's deliberation and decision-making, at every point in the session where choices arise (regarding process or outcome); and (2) to foster Recognition shifts, by encouraging and supporting but never forcing each party's freely chosen efforts to achieve new understandings of the other's perspective.

The transformative model does not ignore the significance of resolving specific issues; but it assumes that, if mediators do the job just described, the parties themselves will very likely make positive changes in their interaction and, as a result, find acceptable terms of resolution for themselves where such terms genuinely exist. . . . The transformative model posits that this is the greatest value mediation offers to families in conflict: it can help people conduct conflict itself in a different way. . . .

This is what we have learned from the parties that we have worked with and studied over all these years. . . . The promise mediation offers is real . . . because wise mediators can support the parties' own work, create a space for that work to go on, and — most important — stay out of the parties' way. . . .

Translating Theory into Practice: How Does the Transformative Mediator Work?

. . . Essential Skills: Avoiding Directive Responses. The mediator "follows" or accompanies the parties. . . . The transformative mediator is not the director of the discussion. . . . He trusts the parties. He has confidence in them — that they know best — that they know what is right for themselves and their children. He will not attempt to substitute his judgment for theirs. He will not try to steer them in the direction of what he thinks is the best arrangement for them and their children. He will not decide what is fair for them. He respects and trusts the parties to make those decisions. The mediator is not trying "to get the parties to do anything." He is not trying to "get them" to talk to each other, to stop arguments for the sake of the children, or to stay out of court. . . . Probing for the "real, underlying issues" is leading, directive, and disrespectful of the party choice about what to talk about. Following the parties in their discussion will highlight all of the issues the parties choose to put out on the table. . . .

The skills employed by the transformative divorce mediator are simple to describe: listening, reflection, summarizing, questions used to open doors, to invite further discussion on a subject raised by the parties, and to "check in" on what the parties want to do at a choice point in the discussion. . . . They are difficult to employ. It is much easier to allow our directive impulses and positive goals for the parties steer us into leading and guiding the discussion and, therefore, the outcomes. It is much more difficult to stay with the parties through their cycles of conversation as they develop strength and understanding and become clear about what they want to do. . . .

---

4. Is There More to Mediation Than Technique?

The discussion so far may give the impression that while mediators' styles vary widely, the differences revolve around choices of tactics. The mediation process, however, involves subtle personal influences that are more important than any particular format or technique.

❖ Daniel Bowling and David Hoffman, Bringing Peace into the Room: The Personal Qualities of the Mediator and Their Impact on the Mediation

16 Negotiation J. 5 (January 2000)

Empirical studies of the mediation process consistently show high rates of settlement, as well as high levels of participant satisfaction. These favorable results seem to occur regardless of mediation styles or the philosophical orientation of the individual mediator (e.g., evaluative vs. facilitative; transformative vs. problem-solving). Indeed, the history of mediation, as well as our own experience, shows that mediation sometimes works even when the mediator is untrained. Is there some aspect of the mediation process — wholly apart from technique or theory — that explains these results?

Some might say that mediation works because it provides a safe forum for airing grievances and venting emotion (that is, it gives people their "day in court"), and this can be done even with an unskilled mediator. Others might point to the use of active listening and reframing — skills that many people have, whether or not they have had any formal mediation training. Still others may focus on the use of caucusing and shuttle diplomacy — again, techniques that do not necessarily require specialized training.

We believe all of these techniques are important. We also believe that mediation training is vitally important. However, there is a dimension to the practice of mediation that has received insufficient attention: the combination of psychological, intellectual, and spiritual qualities that make a person who he or she is. We believe that those personal qualities have a direct impact on the mediation process and the outcome of the mediation. Indeed, this impact may be one of the most potent sources of the effectiveness of mediation.... As mediators, we have noticed that, when we are feeling at peace with ourselves and the world around us, we are better able to bring peace into the room. Moreover, doing so, in our experience, has a significant impact on the mediation process....

Our starting point is to reflect on how we ourselves developed as mediators. For us, and for many of our fellow mediators, the process seems to involve three major "stages." Although we describe these aspects of our development sequentially, for some mediators they may occur in a different order, overlap, or occur to some degree simultaneously.

First, as beginning mediators, we studied techniques [and] looked for opportunities to practice these skills. A period of apprenticeship ensued.... The second stage of our development involved working toward a deeper understanding of how and why mediation works. In seeking an intellectual grasp of the mediation process, we hoped to find the tools with which to assess the effectiveness of various techniques ... and better understand what we were doing, why we were doing it, and the meaning of the process for our clients....

The third stage of our growth as mediators is the focus of this article, and we consider it to be the most challenging frontier of development. For us, the third aspect begins with the mediator's growing awareness of how his or her personal qualities — for better or worse — influence the mediation process.... It is about being a mediator, rather than simply doing certain prescribed steps dictated by a particular mediation school or theory.... More specifically, it is the mediator's being, as experienced by the parties, that sends the message....

The Mediator's "Presence"

This brings us to the heart of our thesis — namely, that there are certain qualities that the mediator's presence brings to the mediation process that exert a powerful influence, and enhance the impact of the interventions employed by the mediator.... Central to this way of looking at mediation is the recognition that the mediator is not extrinsic to the conflict (any more than the therapist is wholly separate from the issues addressed in therapy)....

Subtle Influences

If we accept the view that, notwithstanding impartiality, mediators are inevitably engaged in creating a relationship with the parties, a relationship in which their personal qualities will influence the parties' ability to negotiate successfully — we are led inevitably to the next question: What are the qualities in the mediator that will contribute to a successful relationship with the parties, one that will support reorganization of this conflict "system"?...

In our work as mediators, integration comes in part from developing a strong identification with our role: the transition from feeling that "I am someone who mediates" to realizing that "I am a mediator" — from seeing mediation as work that we do to seeing it as an integral part of our identity.... [T]hese theories suggest that we as mediators "create" the conflict resolution process through our perception of the participants, the conflict, and our role in it as conflict resolvers.... Accordingly, who we are — i.e., the personal qualities we bring into the mediation room — begins to take on larger significance.... The effectiveness of our interventions often arises not from their forcefulness but instead from their authenticity....

Implications for Mediation Practice

... Integration is a quality that we may never fully achieve but are continually developing. It is a quality which, we believe, mediators should foster because (1) it provides a model for the parties — bringing peace, if you will, into the room; and (2) by subtle means which are more easily described than understood, the "integrated" mediator's presence aligns the parties and mediation process in a more positive direction.

Questions

27. Are the qualities described in this reading more compatible with some models of mediation you have read about than with others? Which ones?
28. Focusing on the two mediations in the *Microsoft* case, what quality did Judge Posner appear to "bring into the room"? What did Green and Marks try to project?
29. Does it appear to matter that Posner conducted the process primarily by telephone and e-mail, while Green and Marks met with the parties in face-to-face sessions? Can a mediator communicate a "presence" to the parties without being physically present?

CHAPTER
6

Stages of Mediation

What a mediator does, and how disputants and their lawyers experience mediation, can be thought of in different ways: One is as a *process* that proceeds in stages, like negotiation. The other is in terms of how mediation *responds to specific obstacles* that are preventing the parties from communicating or bargaining effectively. This chapter examines mediation as a process. Later chapters focus on specific obstacles to agreement and how mediation can address them. For purposes of comparison, we look at both caucus and non-caucus models and explore the process from both the perspective of mediators and that of lawyers representing clients in the process.

A. Commercial Mediation

A mediator has almost complete freedom to improvise, and in practice good neutrals use widely varying approaches. As mentioned previously, however, commercial mediation usually takes place in several distinct stages: pre-mediation, the opening session, private caucuses, and joint discussions. These stages, and the goals and methods appropriate to them, are discussed below.

1. Premediation

Before the parties first meet together, mediators may talk with the principal parties' counsel to lay the groundwork for a successful process. Some premediation tasks are mundane, while others can be quite sensitive. They are discussed below.

Performing Administrative Tasks

The mediator or an assistant must carry out administrative tasks, such as arranging for the participants to sign a mediation agreement and obtaining money deposits. The participants must also agree on when and where the process will take place.

Ensuring That the Right People Are at the Table

The mediator and the participants share a common interest in having the right people present to make the process succeed. Usually the right people are those with the motivation and authority to agree to a settlement. Lawyers are the most likely to know about these issues and should bring "people" problems to the neutral's attention in advance. The mediator can then work to ensure that the necessary people are present.

> *Example:* A company that bought a consulting firm sued an accounting firm for allegedly overstating the firm's profits, misleading the company into over-paying for the firm. Counsel for the buyer called the mediator ahead of time to warn her that it was crucial that the buyer's CEO attend the mediation. However, he said, his CEO would not come unless the president of the defendant accounting firm did so as well. And, said counsel, his principal could not commit to attending until the other side also did so, for fear of seeming overeager to settle and suggesting that the CEO's time was less valuable. The mediator called defense counsel, who agreed that it would be very helpful if the principals attended, but also did not want to be the first to say yes. Faced with a "who'll go first" problem, the neutral made a proposal: She asked each side to indicate privately whether it would bring its CEO if the other did as well. Both parties agreed. With the key decision makers present, the mediation went forward to a successful conclusion.

Building a Working Relationship

The premediation stage may be the first time the mediator actually meets the disputants. This is a good opportunity for lawyers to start to build a relationship with the neutral that will allow them to influence the process and ease hard decisions later on. This can be done through meetings or telephone conversations between the mediator, the lawyers, and possibly also the parties.

Starting to Mediate

It may seem strange to talk about mediating before the parties have even met, but in one sense every contact between a mediator and a lawyer or client is part of the process. In certain situations — for example, an angry plaintiff in an employment case or a bereaved widower in a wrongful death action — it may be useful for the mediator to start to work with one or perhaps both parties before the sides meet to mediate. Defense counsel, for example, will often agree to a mediator having a private meeting with an emotional plaintiff or even suggest that he do so, recognizing that doing so may lay the groundwork for progress in the "formal" process.

> *Example:* A professor was stalked for years by a disturbed female student. He asked his university for assistance, but felt that the deans ignored his plight, eventually forcing him to move to a secret location. He complained to the media and then sued the university, demanding compensation for his distress and the right to teach by video in the future. It was clear to the mediator that the professor was extremely distraught over the ordeal.

With the assent of the university's counsel, the mediator arranged to meet with the professor and his lawyer privately before the mediation began. He listened to the professor describe his feelings of anger and betrayal. Several days later the parties met to mediate. The professor was less upset, but still too angry to accept a compromise, and the university remained suspicious that the professor would continue to criticize them in the media even if the case was settled.

Three weeks of telephone diplomacy ensued between the mediator and the lawyers. All the parties then met again, this time on campus rather than at the mediator's office. The mediator shuttled between the offices of the professor and the university president. A settlement was eventually reached that included a rearranged teaching load, a sensitization program for staff about stalking, special monitoring of the stalker when she was released from prison, and a monetary payment.

2. The Opening Session

You will recall that the opening session is the first time in most mediations that the disputants assemble as a group. Both lawyers and parties will ordinarily be present during the opening session, and the mediator will moderate it.

a. Goals

Introduction.   Other than a chat in the waiting room and, in some cases, a premediation meeting, this is probably the first time that the parties, and perhaps also the attorneys, have had the opportunity to meet the mediator or see the neutral in a "formal" role. For both lawyers and mediators, a primary goal at this stage should be for the parties to begin to feel a sense of rapport and confidence in the neutral.

Explanation. The opening session gives mediators an opportunity to explain the process to the participants. Often parties are first-time participants in mediation, and even lawyers may arrive with mistaken expectations about what will occur. Explaining the format and ground rules can thus clear away misconceptions. Even a lawyer who is familiar with a particular mediator's approach will often welcome an explanation, both for the benefit of the client and to confirm key ground rules such as confidentiality.

Exposure to the Issues.   The opening session allows the lawyers to argue the merits of their legal cases directly to the other side. Each party hears a summary of the strengths of the other's case and the weaknesses in its own. This is often the first time that the clients will hear, often in blunt terms, what their opponents will say if the case goes to trial. Alternatively, advocates can use the opening session to explain their client's interests directly to the other disputant.

Performance.   Opening sessions can play a psychological function for attorneys and clients. The lawyers have the chance to show their skills and demonstrate their commitment to their clients' legal arguments. This makes it easier later in the process for lawyers to shift out of a "warrior" mode and toward problem solving, with less concern that their clients will feel that they are no longer committed to the case.

Venting. During the opening session the participants, directly and/or through their attorneys, sometimes express emotions and frustrations, describing their grievances, anger, and other feelings directly to the other side and to the mediator. Attorneys should consider allowing their clients to speak at this point, especially concerning nonlegal and personal issues.

Information Gathering. By listening carefully during the opening session, both the mediator and counsel can sometimes pick up valuable hints about what is blocking agreement.

b. Techniques

Format. The format of an opening session is flexible, but it typically has the following structure:

- Introductions
- The mediator explains the process, ground rules, and housekeeping issues.
- The lawyers, and hopefully also the parties, make statements.
- The participants exchange views and questions.
- The mediator may ask clarifying questions.
- The mediator makes a transition into caucusing.

The most important thing a mediator can do during an opening session is to set a good tone for the process. Counsel should look for a neutral to make the participants feel as comfortable as possible, project a sense of optimism, model good discussion techniques, and perhaps encourage the participants to talk directly with each other. To accomplish this, a mediator needs to keep the following points in mind.

Set an Informal Tone. Neutrals should not manage an opening session like a court hearing, but rather as an informal discussion. The mediator should greet everyone and ordinarily should make small talk at any opportunity. That said, however, a mediator should not put herself in a position that one side may interpret as "chumminess" or bias toward the other, and counsel will want to avoid compromising a mediator's effectiveness by putting her in such a position. For example, unless it has been cleared in advance, one side should not arrive to find the mediator talking with its adversary behind a closed door.

Encourage Informality But Keep Order. The opening session is the first time that the participants are together. Parties are sometimes hostile, and lawyers may feel the need to stake out positions. Participants are often emotional, whether they show it or not. Good mediators will take an informal approach, encouraging a free expression of views and feelings.

Lawyers may feel the need to play an aggressive "warrior" role in front of their clients; if so, they may want to warn the mediator in advance to expect this. The mediator's job is to allow the disputants to have a controlled confrontation if they need one. This includes both confrontation — allowing the participants to express difficult emotions — and control — not permitting the process to degenerate into accusations.

In rare instances it makes sense for lawyers to ask the mediator to avoid the opening session entirely — for example, when the participants' relationship is so bad that a direct exchange seems more likely to inflame them than to promote catharsis. Neither mediators nor attorneys, however, should confuse their personal sense of discomfort about dealing with unpleasant emotions, or the wish to "focus only on the facts and the law," with a judgment that venting feelings will be unproductive. As explained in Chapter 8, with basic ground rules it is almost always possible to allow venting without provoking a damaging confrontation.

The typical opening session in business mediation occurs in a conference room. The participants ordinarily face each other across a table, with the mediator at the head. Attorneys usually prefer to sit next to the mediator, with their clients on the other side. In the right circumstances, however, such as when a lawyer decides to let her client take the lead, the parties may sit next to the neutral.

c. The Mediator's Opening Comments

To help you anticipate what to expect in a legal mediation, here is a transcript of a typical opening statement by a commercial mediator, with comments to explain the thinking behind them:

MEDIATOR: Good morning. I'm _____. I don't know everyone, so before we go any further I'd appreciate it if you would introduce yourself and indicate who you're with.
Comment: It is often useful for counsel and the mediator to sketch the shape of the table and write down each person's name and role.

M: Some of you are probably familiar with mediation, but for others it may be a new experience. Let me describe what we'll be doing, then turn it over to you for opening comments.

Comment: Participants often are doubtful about protocol (e.g., will there be a time limit on statements?). It's best for lawyers to discuss these issues with the mediator in advance, but a confirmation at the outset is also useful.

M: The purpose of mediation is to help people negotiate. My only role here is to help you find a solution to this dispute. I am not a judge, and I have no power to decide this case. By signing the mediation agreement you have agreed that I am disqualified as a witness and will never play any role in this case if it goes to trial. That leaves me entirely free to focus on one thing: Helping you to find a settlement. My goal is that if an agreement is possible — and it usually is — it should not be left on the table because of an accident or misunderstanding.

   In cases like this my experience and that of other mediators is that about three-quarters of the time parties *are* able to reach agreement. That means that the odds of obtaining a settlement are strongly in your favor. The fact that you have all come here is evidence that everyone wants to find a solution and that you are willing to make reasonable compromises to bring it about. However, ultimately it's up to you whether you agree or not.

Comment: Neutrals should promote optimism, but not misstate the terms of anyone's participation.

M: One of the key aspects of this process is that it is confidential. You have all signed the mediation agreement and agreed not to disclose anything said during this process. You've agreed to confidentiality on two levels. First, both sides agree that nothing said here can be used at trial: No one can ask you in court, "Didn't you say 'X' at mediation, and now you're saying 'Y'?" Second, you've agreed that you won't discuss anything said here with outsiders such as a reporter or a neighbor. It's understood that if you are with an organization, you may have to talk with others to confirm a settlement, and if you are an individual you may want to talk with an advisor or family member. But aside from consultations about settlement, no one will discuss what occurs here with anyone outside this room. That gives us more freedom to talk frankly about possible solutions.

Comment: These comments focus on what the parties have agreed to, rather than what the law requires (for more on confidentiality, see Chapter 13). A mediator cannot guarantee what legal rule may be applied in a future proceeding, and participants in a court-related program may be subject to special reporting requirements. Counsel and mediators need to think through these issues so as not to mislead clients about the degree of confidentiality protection.

M: I understand that we have as long as we need [or: until _____ P.M.] today, and if we keep focused I believe that we can get it done. If you don't mind, since this is an informal process, I'll proceed on a first-name basis, and I hope you'll do so with me too.

Comment: Some participants, such as a complainant in a sexual-harassment case or a foreign businessperson, may feel demeaned by being called by first names. If there is a question about this, a mediator will want to check (and a lawyer will do well to warn the neutral) ahead of time how each person wishes to be addressed. If there is doubt, it is best to proceed formally at first.

M: I would like to begin by asking each side to present its perspective on the situation. It's useful for me and for the other side to know your views on the legal issues, but I also would welcome ideas about how we can get to a resolution. I've asked each side to present its views frankly, so everyone knows what will happen if you can't settle this case. But I've asked the lawyers not to give the kind of full-scale presentation that they would at trial. I also hope that you'll avoid personal attacks.

Comment: If the parties are represented by counsel, the attorneys will usually choose to make the opening statements. Again, counsel will want to think through carefully how large a role to take and what tone to set; Chapter 11 explores this issue in depth. Mediators may want to encourage counsel in advance to let their client or another key player speak, or even to be the primary spokesperson. A personal injury plaintiff, for instance, might be asked to describe how her injuries have affected her life. The plaintiff usually speaks first as a matter of convention.

M: Mr. [party] and Ms. [party], I will ask you to take a special role. You each have experienced lawyers who will handle the legal issues. I'd like you to sit back and simply listen. Ask yourself: If I were a judge or juror hearing this story for the first time, and didn't know what actually happened, how would it sound? As you listen, feel free to take notes, but please don't interrupt. I won't take the fact that you are listening politely as meaning that you agree with anything that you're hearing. I know that you disagree, or you wouldn't be here.

Comment: In general, mediators apply a no-interruption rule. But if the participants begin to talk with each other constructively, an experienced neutral will sit back and let it happen. Counsel should think about whether they prefer a format in which each side takes turns or a less structured exchange.

Parties' Opening Comments

M: Does anyone have any questions about the process or what I've said so far? If not, let's go ahead. I'll ask the plaintiff to go first, and then we'll hear from the defense.

Comment: If a lawyer speaks first, when she concludes the mediator might say:

M: Mr. [party], your counsel has covered the legal aspects of this dispute, but I wonder if there is anything of a nonlegal nature you'd like to say, or that you think we should have in mind as we go forward? If you'd rather not, or would like to wait until later, that's fine, but if you do want to say anything, I hope you'll feel free to do so now.

Joint Discussion

M: [*After each side has spoken and replied to the other*] Often, especially when people mediate early in a dispute, there is information that each side needs to know to make a decision about settlement. You should keep in mind that you are each asking the other to make a very difficult decision. If there is something they need to know to make that decision, I'd encourage you to provide it. Does anyone have any questions?

Comment: This is often an ideal setting for a lawyer to gather information that he may need to bargain effectively, and a lawyer who needs data should prompt the mediator to mention this. Parties who "stonewall" during discovery may be more forthcoming in mediation, especially if they are encouraged by the mediator.

M: [*After any discussion has taken place, mediators might ask a few clarifying questions. When parties do not want to talk or fall into repetitive argument, a mediator might say the following:*] It's clear that there is a disagreement about what happened. Given enough time, we might be able to reach conclusions about the facts, but you're here with the goal of avoiding a trial. I suggest that we go forward with discussions and work to reach a resolution.

Transition to Caucuses

M: [*When productive discussions are over:*] At this point, I suggest that we go into caucuses so that I can talk with each of you privately. We do this because it's usually easier for people to discuss the pros and cons of the legal issues and options for settling if the other side is not sitting there listening while they do it. I'll ask the plaintiff side to come with me to the other conference room, and the defense to remain here.

There is an additional rule of confidentiality that applies to the caucusing process. If you tell me in caucus that something is confidential, I will not disclose it to the other side — just like a lawyer's relationship with a client. Even if you don't say anything, if I sense that something is sensitive I will check with you before discussing it with the other side. But it is much easier for me if you flag items that you want to keep confidential.

Comment: If a lawyer does reveal confidential information, she should make a note of it and remind the mediator not to disclose it at the end of the session.

M: I should warn everyone now about one basic rule of caucusing: Time always passes more slowly for whoever is waiting for the mediator! Please keep in mind, though, that if I spend a long time with the other side — and I'm sure that at some point I will — it's usually because I am explaining your point of view and they are disagreeing, or I am asking them questions so that I can bring you their responses. The first caucuses are also usually longer than later ones because there is more new information to cover. I'll be back with you as soon as I can.

d. Common Mistakes

Both mediators and counsel can make mistakes during the opening session. Some common mistakes that novice mediators make include:

- Assuming that the participants understand the process and failing to explain it.
- Giving in to the lawyers' wish to go directly into caucuses.
- Showing frustration at extreme positions taken by disputants.
- Focusing only on the legal issues and discouraging expressions of emotion.
- Asking more pointed questions of one side than the other, raising sensitive issues that the parties have not mentioned, or making any comment that suggests an opinion about the merits. Any of these behaviors can lead one or both parties to believe that the mediator is biased.

The errors that counsel may make are discussed in more depth in Chapters 10 and 11. They include:

- Doing all the talking themselves, and thus missing a chance to have the client speak.
- Focusing on the mediator, and thus losing an opportunity to connect with the other side.
- Adopting an adversarial tone, making the other side unnecessarily hostile.
- Forgetting to ask questions.
- Focusing only on legal issues, when the real obstacles are nonlegal in nature.

3. Private Caucuses

Commercial mediation almost always involves at least some private caucusing, and most litigators enter the process expecting this format. Caucuses are rarely a one-time event; rather, mediators usually move back and forth between the parties. In most commercial cases, once parties go into caucuses they typically remain apart for the rest of the process, spending most of their time separated. Occasionally a commercial mediator will not caucus, usually because the parties are interacting well and prefer to discuss their differences directly. In the partnership breakup mediation described in Chapter 5, for instance, a caucus-oriented mediator met with the partners jointly because they preferred this format.

A mediator's goals and techniques are likely to change as caucusing proceeds. In the first round the neutral's primary goal will usually be to allow the disputants to explain their perspectives, vent feelings in a protective setting, and develop confidence in the mediator. Good mediators typically adopt a restrained role at this stage, focusing on drawing out the disputants rather than pressing their own agenda. As the process goes on, however, commercial mediators are likely to become increasingly active, posing pointed questions and offering advice. During the last stages of caucusing mediators may make specific settlement suggestions and offer opinions about the likely outcome if the case is adjudicated.

There are several reasons for a mediator to progress from restraint to a more active role over the course of mediation. First, as the process continues, participants become increasingly convinced that they have been "heard" and gain confidence in the mediator, making them more willing to listen to suggestions. Second, the mediator learns more about the legal merits, hidden issues, and the personalities of the participants, making her more confident that her advice will be useful. Finally, especially when the process is dominated by arguments and positional bargaining, disputants are likely to become increasingly frustrated and concerned that the mediation will fail, leading them to be much more receptive to a mediator's interventions. The techniques appropriate to each stage of caucusing are explored below. We discuss early, middle, and later caucuses separately.

a. Early Caucuses

Goals

During the first rounds of caucusing, a mediator will typically seek to achieve the following goals.

Make the disputants feel fully heard.   A good mediator's guiding principle in the first round of caucusing, in particular, is that the disputants should feel free to express their feelings, perspectives, and wishes and come away feeling that the neutral is truly interested in understanding their viewpoint. In colloquial terms, parties and lawyers should be able to "have it their way." Lawyers should think about how to use this freedom and caution clients not to misunderstand this to mean that the mediator has taken their side.

Obtain direct access to the principals. The caucus is also the setting in which a mediator can most easily speak directly with parties, in the presence of their lawyer but without communications being filtered through the advocate. The ability to talk with the actual decision makers in a dispute is one of the most valuable aspects of caucusing. It also poses tactical issues for lawyers about how much access they wish to give a mediator to their client, especially when the client does not present himself to best advantage. (We discuss this issue more in Chapter 11.)

Facilitate venting. In the privacy of the caucus, participants often expose emotions that they did not feel comfortable showing in front of their adversaries, particularly if they are prompted by the mediator. Turning to the party with a simple question such as "Mr. Smith, how do you feel about all this?" sometimes unleashes a burst of feelings. At other times, it is necessary for the mediator to talk privately with a party's counsel, or to wait for a later caucus, to access emotional issues. This is discussed further in Chapter 8.

Gather sensitive information. Caucuses are the setting in which a neutral can gather data that the parties are not willing to share with their adversary. Disputants will often be guarded at first, but may become more open as they gain confidence in the neutral and realize that they will have to take risks in order to settle. Lawyers, for their part, should consider what they wish to share with the mediator at this point in the process.

Identify interests and probe for obstacles. Good mediators will attempt during caucuses to diagnose the obstacles blocking a settlement and to encourage disputants to identify their underlying interests. This said, parties are often so focused at first on pressing their legal arguments that they are not open to talking about other issues or alternative ways of viewing the situation. Lawyers faced with a client who is determined to tell the mediator why he is right will usually accede and stress their legal arguments. In such situations, mediators typically allow the disputants to have their say and return to the topic of interests later.

Build trust. In the early caucuses mediators continue to build relationships with the disputants. A neutral will try to give the parties the feeling that she is not judging them and that she respects them, regardless of what may have been said by their adversary or even what they may in fact have done. Mediators also try to project the feeling that, to the extent possible without taking sides, they genuinely want to help each party achieve an acceptable result.

Techniques

With whom to start? A mediator needs to begin somewhere. The convention is to begin with the plaintiff, but there may be a reason to talk with the defense first, for example when the plaintiff has made an offer and is not willing to make another until the defense responds. In this situation, plaintiff counsel should alert the mediator that they think she needs to meet with the defense first. Some disputants will interpret a mediator's decision to change the "plaintiff first" convention as a signal, and neutrals should therefore offer a brief explanation of why they are starting with one side or the other.

Engage the principals.   In contrast to the opening session, in which the attorneys ordinarily do most or all of the talking, during caucuses mediators try to engage the parties. A mediator might, for example, ask a simple factual question such as: "Mr. Smith, can you tell me where you feel the pain?" or, "Ms. Green, I heard your counsel say that you were seeking reinstatement. Do you know if your position has been filled?" A lawyer should prepare clients for this kind of direct questioning.

Start slowly.   Mediators are advised to resist the temptation to "cut to the chase," even when the likely outcome is clear to the neutral (and perhaps also the lawyers). Unless there is a tight time frame, neutrals should be wary of directing the agenda, making suggestions, or using any confrontational tactic during the first round of caucusing. Even evaluative mediators rarely offer opinions about the merits during the first caucus meeting with each side. This is a reflection of the principle — easier to state than to carry out — that if a person wants to help someone attain a difficult objective, they should begin where that person is, both in a substantive and a psychological sense, rather than at the place the helper wants the person to arrive. Counsel faced with an overly aggressive mediator should consider asking her to slow down and stress his client's wish to talk about the dispute before making a decision.

Ask open-ended questions.   Mediators often begin by asking, "Is there anything that you didn't feel comfortable mentioning in the opening session that you think I should know to understand the situation?" or "Tell me how this all began. . . ." Open-ended questions are intended to elicit new information. Leading questions, by contrast, are meant to confirm what the questioner already knows, and often prompt listeners to respond tersely or defensively. Again, counsel should anticipate this and think about what they want their client to tell the neutral.

Experienced mediators will take care to focus their initial questions and comments on the issues raised by the side with whom they are meeting and only later raise the other party's arguments and concerns. Most disputants want to know that their own views and priorities have been considered before they are willing to deal with an opponent's perspective.

Listen carefully.   Mediators must pay attention to what is said, and to what is not. It is important that they listen for changes in wording, tone, or body language that emphasize or contradict what the speaker is saying. If, for example, a person begins to fidget or her face flushes as a topic is brought up, it is usually a signal that she is upset — even if she continues to speak in a normal tone. Bear in mind, however, that although certain mannerisms (e.g., frowning to show disagreement) are widespread among Americans, a person's nationality, social class, professional training, and other factors influence how she communicates.

Show interest.   It is vital that the participants feel "heard out," ideally by their opponents but at a minimum by the mediator. It is therefore important not simply that the neutral listen, but that he do so in a way that demonstrates to the speaker that she has been understood. Mediators can convey this, for example, by taking occasional notes, maintaining eye contact, summarizing key points, and asking if he has understood the speaker (e.g., "So if I'm understanding you correctly, you feel that the defendant never intended to comply with the contract?").

Show empathy. In a private caucus setting, it is easier for mediators to show empathy for a person's situation without worry that the other side will misinterpret their comments. We discuss empathic listening in more depth in the next chapter, but here the most important thing to understand is that for a mediator or lawyer to listen empathically to someone does not mean that she agrees that the speaker's viewpoint is factually correct. Rather, the listener is showing simply that she understands how the disputant feels. A mediator might comment, for example, "This sounds like it has been an awful experience for you..." or "I'm hearing that you were shocked to get the letter of termination."

Keep track of time. Despite being cautioned in advance, participants sometimes become frustrated by the process of waiting in a caucus room. Mediators should keep rough track of the time spent in each caucus and if necessary step out and "touch base" with the people who are waiting. An attorney who sees that her client is becoming restless might seek out the mediator and ask her to say a few words about the status of the process and the reason for the delay.

b. Middle Caucuses

Middle caucuses in commercial mediation are typically devoted to exchanging information and arguments, exploring interests and options, and conducting distributive bargaining. As caucusing progresses, the mediator usually also becomes a more active participant in the discussions.

Encourage the Exchange of Information. We have seen that one of the main reasons people are unable to negotiate successfully is that they do not have enough information. This problem is heightened by the "hide the ball" approach that dominates adversarial litigation. Another common problem is that selective perception makes disputants unable to assimilate even facts that are available to them. During the middle rounds of caucusing, mediators often help parties exchange information and assist each side to understand how the other sees key factors in the dispute.

Ask About Interests. People in disputes that are serious enough to hire lawyers often are not bargaining well. They may also be focusing too narrowly on the limited remedies that courts can provide, especially money. Good mediators try to stimulate interest-based bargaining. As caucusing progresses and people feel that they have had their say about legal issues, they may become more open to considering nonlegal options.

Probe for the Parties' Priorities. In a case in which, for example, an employee is seeking reassignment, an apology, and a monetary award for emotional distress, a mediator might ask: "When I talk with the company, what issue would you like me to give top priority?" Disputants are usually unwilling to say what they would give up, but they may say what is most important to them, which suggests by implication what is less significant.

Control the Flow of Negative Information.   Mediators work hard to translate angry or provocative rhetoric into words that listeners can hear without becoming angry or defensive. If it is impossible to put a statement into acceptable language, the mediator may withhold it until the recipient is able to listen or the speaker has backed off. A lawyer should think about how a mediator is likely to phrase his side's message in the other room and, if he wants a particular emphasis or "spin" to be used, can suggest it to the mediator. If the client is too upset to hear advice, the lawyer may wish to follow the mediator into the hallway and talk with her there.

Reframe the Disputants' Views.   Mediators work to change negotiators' views of a dispute and each other. They do this by explaining to each side the other's perspectives and, equally important, suggesting different ways, or "frames," of seeing a situation. We explore reframing more deeply in Chapter 7.

> *Example:* A neighbor was bitterly opposing a next-door business's plans to expand. He could not understand why the company was insisting as part of the settlement that it be allowed to buy the abutter's property outright. In response the mediator said, "From what they're telling me in the other room, the company is impressed by your tenacity. They're convinced that you'll fight every effort they make to update their licenses, forever. In one sense, it might not be too surprising why they see it that way: You've been filing protests to their applications for years, and you've been successful in delaying a lot of them.
>
> To them, paying you money to drop this particular objection looks like giving you a war chest to fight a new battle next year. I think that's what's motivating their demand. Is there anything we could tell them that would give them some confidence that if they settle without a buyout, they'll be able to live in peace with you in the future?

Moderate the Bargaining Process.   The middle caucuses are the setting in which a mediator is likely to begin to push each side about the compromises they are willing to make to get an agreement. Often parties come to mediation without having engaged in any real negotiations, but they eventually realize that they will have to compromise to achieve a settlement. The first caucus is sometimes too soon to ask a party to make a new offer, but in later rounds of meetings disputants are usually more ready to make and receive proposals. Attorneys should be ready for this, and explain to their client the necessity of preparing alternative proposals and thinking in advance about concessions and options.

Change the Disputants' Assessments of the Merits.   This is also the phase in which a mediator can start to press the parties to assess carefully their alternatives to settlement. Mediators do this, first, by bringing each side's arguments and perspectives to the other and asking how they can respond to them. A neutral might say, for example, "They are challenging your claim for emotional distress, and saying that they don't have any medical records to back it up. In my experience, insurers do need to have 'paper in the file' in order to make a significant payment on this kind of claim. Is there anything that I could use to convince them to give more weight to it?"

As the process goes on, mediators are likely to become increasingly active about reality testing. They will seek to bring the principals into the discussion, at least to listen to the other side's arguments and hear their lawyer's responses. Mediators may probe participants' assumptions about liability, damages, and the out-of-pocket and hidden costs of litigation. Their goal is to make both sides think seriously, perhaps for the first time, about the full costs of litigating the dispute and the possibility that they will lose. Attorneys should be prepared for "hard reality testing." They should warn their clients that the mediator may ask tough questions and assure them that the neutral is pressing their own arguments just as aggressively with their opponent.

Develop Potential Options.   As caucusing progresses, mediators are likely to push the disputants to focus on options for settlement, ask about priorities, and give each party signals about the other's intentions. Disputants who had rejected interest-based options early in the process will sometimes become more open to such solutions later on, as they come to appreciate that it will be very difficult to reach agreement on purely monetary terms.

Encourage Optimism.   As the process goes on, the participants look for cues about how well it is going, particularly when they are isolated from each other. Unless one party is clearly stonewalling, mediators emphasize positive gestures or movements and remind participants that their opponent is there because he wants a settlement too. Attorneys faced with an unhappy or discouraged client can ask a mediator for her assessment of how the process is going and for the emotional "temperature" in the other room. Experienced mediators will pick up the cue, emphasize the positive, and place the situation in the context of what is typical at that stage of the process.

c. Later Caucuses

As the process moves toward closure, the parties will focus less on exchanging information and arguments and more on looking for a settlement. The mediator will help the parties find a mutually acceptable agreement and intervene to avoid an impasse. As the disputants become frustrated with their inability to reach a solution and develop greater confidence in the mediator, they are likely to accept and even welcome a level of intervention that would have been resented at the outset.

Keep Pushing and Exploring.   Commercial mediators will seek to maintain the momentum of the process by keeping the mediation "in session," for example, by ordering food to be brought in rather than breaking for lunch and continuing into the evening. If a lawyer sees his client becoming tired or irritable or feeling pushed too hard, so that continuing the process is more likely to produce impasse than progress, he should ask the mediator to adjourn so that his client can rest and regroup.

Place the Responsibility on the Disputants.   When parties seem to have dug in, mediators may consciously *not* assume the lead in resolving the problem. Instead they may simply describe the situation and ask the disputants what they wish to do. In doing so the neutral is assuming that if disputants are challenged to take responsibility, they will respond by taking initiatives to move the process forward.

In such situations clients are likely to turn to their lawyers, as the professionals in the process, and ask what they should do. Attorneys should be ready for this; they may want to ask the mediator for a "menu" of possible options (discussed below) and then discuss them privately with their clients.

Advise Them.   Eventually most commercial mediators will take the lead and suggest options to restart the process, asking each side to tell them which they prefer. Typical options include:

- A discussion among the principals or the lawyers only (see the next section);
- "Confidential listener" (discussed as part of the basic strategy, in Chapter 5);
- An evaluation of one or more issues;
- A "mediator's proposal" (also discussed as part of the basic strategy); and
- Anything else that seems likely to be helpful.

Offer an Evaluation.   As the process progresses, commercial mediators may well offer explicit feedback about the likely reaction of a judge, jury, or arbitrator to the parties' positions on a particular issue, or even the entire case. This kind of evaluation can be a dangerous tactic, but many mediators find it useful, and lawyers often ask for it. Private caucuses are the setting in which to deliver this kind of opinion, which may be both unexpected and potentially humiliating to the listeners. Evaluation is discussed in more depth in Chapter 9.

Suggest Specific Settlement Terms.   As caucusing continues, commercial mediators often press parties to consider particular terms of settlement. A mediator might test the waters with the "what if?" technique ("If I could get them to go to 'X,' would that be acceptable?"). Or a neutral might characterize the other side's situation, for instance by emphasizing that the opponent also thinks that she has made too many concessions and feels frustrated. At this point lawyers should understand that they may be bargaining with the mediator, as well as with the other side, about what settlement terms the mediator will propose, and send signals as to what is and is not acceptable.

Adjourn and Try Again.   If parties are not able to reach agreement at a first mediation session, a good commercial mediator will not give up, but instead will suggest that they adjourn and think things over. She will call them a day or a week later to ask about their thinking. Often disputants come into mediation with unrealistic expectations, both about the value of their case and about what the other side will be willing to do to settle. A single day may not be enough time to readjust their expectations, giving up the settlement that they think they deserve to attain one that is feasible. Given time to think, rest, and accustom themselves to the situation, however, disputants are sometimes willing to reopen discussions. This may involve a new meeting, "shuttle" diplomacy by telephone, or some other technique. Anticipating such follow-up activity, a lawyer might opt not to push her client hard on the first day, in effect treating the mediation as a multiday process to give her client more time to accept necessary compromises.

Refer the Parties to Another Process.   If the parties truly cannot agree, a mediator may suggest that they enter a different dispute resolution process, such as expert fact-finding. If disagreement over a specific legal issue (e.g., does the contract bar a lost-profits claim?) is the barrier, the mediator can suggest that the parties present that limited issue to the court for decision, then re-enter mediation. If a settlement is genuinely impossible, the mediator may focus on getting the parties into a more efficient process of adjudication, such as arbitration.

d. Common Mistakes

The most common mistakes in conducting caucuses result from the failure to use the techniques described above. These mistakes include the following.

Asking Leading Questions.   Mediators who are tense or unsure of themselves often slip into asking leading questions. The inevitable effect is to cut off the flow of information and sometimes to make the participants defensive. An occasional leading question can be helpful, however, either to tie down an issue or to confirm to the participants that the mediator has assimilated what they have said.

> *Example:* An experienced litigator was participating in a federal court training program for mediators. Unsure of his competence in conducting a caucus, he unconsciously slipped into a cross-examiner's format, asking the plaintiff subtly leading questions ("May I assume that you are seeking reinstatement in your job?"). Asked about his choice of words, the litigator said that he had no idea that he had been "leading his witness."

Saying Too Much.   Mediators are sometimes tempted to reveal confidential "tidbits" that the other side has provided in order to ingratiate themselves with their listeners, or in some other way tell a party what it wants to hear. Sympathizing with a party's complaint that the other side has acted in bad faith is one example of this. Seeming to take sides is almost always a bad idea, if only because listeners are likely to wonder whether the mediator is saying similar things in the other caucus. The opposite error is to give both sides an overly pessimistic assessment in order to scare them into settling. This is ethically wrong and also self-defeating, since lawyers talk with each other and over time a mediator's practices become widely known.

Humiliating a Participant.   A mediator should avoid demeaning any participant. This can occur unintentionally if a neutral confronts a party with a weakness or inconsistency too soon or in a clumsy way. Apart from confining evaluative comments and advice to caucuses, mediators may wish to raise issues that appear especially sensitive with an attorney privately in a hallway conversation, before mentioning them to the client.

Avoiding Direct Meetings.   A mediator usurps the negotiation process when she keeps the parties unnecessarily separated in caucuses. This slows and sometimes distorts communication and may prevent the disputants from rebuilding a fractured relationship.

Giving Evaluations or Other Advice Unnecessarily, or Too Early.   It is natural for a mediator to gradually form an opinion about who has the stronger legal case.

This does not mean, however, that the neutral should disclose his opinion to the disputants. Doing so may shake the participants' faith in the mediator's impartiality. Mediators can create similar problems by advocating settlement packages too early in the process.

Giving Up Too Soon.   Often during mediation a gap will seem unbridgeable, or the parties will threaten to walk out. It is remarkable, however, how often perspectives and positions change over the course of a single mediation. Mediators need to bend with the current, giving the parties a chance to vent their spleens and then urging them to make another effort to settle, and attorneys sometimes need to wait patiently for a change to occur.

> *Example:* A mediator once took on a difficult employment case, which was scheduled to end at 4:30 P.M. so that the plaintiff and his lawyer could fly home. Shortly after 4 P.M., the employer's representative accepted, and then a few minutes later reneged on, a settlement proposal. This occurred after the mediator had disclosed that the plaintiff agreed to the deal, which enraged the plaintiff. The mediator asked the plaintiff whether he wanted to continue. He reluctantly concluded that he did, and the neutral plugged on, using evaluation and teamwork with the obstinate party's counsel. At 9:30 P.M. everyone accepted a slightly modified version of the earlier package.

The Attorney's Role.   If a lawyer sees a mediator making a mistake and alienating her client, she should warn the neutral about this as quickly as possible, either in front of the client (who may appreciate their attorney standing up) or in a private conversation outside the caucus room.

4. Joint Discussions

Many commercial mediators stay in caucus continuously after the opening session, bringing the participants back together only to sign a settlement agreement. In some cases, however, it is more effective to convene the participants to talk or bargain directly with each other. The mediator can either be present as moderator or allow the disputants to talk privately with each other.

Disputants often find it helpful to talk directly with each other, even if only for a limited time or about a single issue. It can be very helpful in addressing an emotional issue, for example, for a party to acknowledge the impact of its actions or even apologize for them. Such words usually have much more effect, however, when one party says them directly to the other than when they are filtered through a mediator. Joint discussions are especially valuable when disputants:

- Will be interacting in the future, as is the case in many marital and small business disputes, and need to learn how to resolve disagreements directly with each other;
- Consider themselves expert negotiators and respond positively to the challenge of "getting a deal done" (executives often have this perspective);
- Are able to agree on the substantive terms of settlement but are concerned about problems in implementing it; or
- Are unable to agree, but the lawyers or particular team members have a good working relationship with each other. In the latter situation, a mediator

might call the attorneys or particular team members together privately and talk with them about the next steps.

One implication of this is that attorneys should remain alert to the option of interrupting the caucusing process to have a joint meeting and should not hesitate to ask a mediator to convene one or advise them about whether the other side would be receptive to talking directly.

a. Goals and Techniques

The mediator's goals in a joint discussion are to promote constructive communication and bargaining, bring the parties to closure, and if there is a settlement, confirm the terms in writing. Ideally the key persons would meet with each other alone. Often, however, either the parties or their lawyers, afraid that something untoward might take place, will ask the mediator to sit in and moderate. Good mediators will convene the meeting, explain any ground rules, and then remain silent — the purpose, after all, is for disputants to talk directly with each other.

Bring Together a Subgroup.   Alternatively, a subgroup of participants, such as the principals, the lawyers, or the experts, can meet privately. In a business dispute, for example, CEOs might meet to discuss how the dispute arose, or CFOs could meet to exchange financial data.

Orchestrate a Meeting.   If disputants cannot talk with each other without assistance, mediators can take a more active role and orchestrate the process. A good example of moderation of joint discussions is the role taken by the neutrals in the second *Microsoft* mediation in Chapter 5. Mediators often convene working groups in consensus-building processes used to deal with pubic controversies, which are described in Chapter 14.

Serve as Moderator or Referee.   If the participants have difficulty talking, the mediator can referee the process. Here the mediator's role is similar to the opening session: intervene as needed to discourage unproductive tactics, but otherwise allow the disputants to run the process.

Push for Closure.   The mediator can use a joint session to encourage disputants to collaborate so as to come up with imaginative ideas to bridge a final gap. Or the neutral can give parties a "pep talk," saying to them that she will be asking them each to make a further, painful compromise to get a deal. The fact that the admonition is delivered jointly underlines to each side that it is not the only one being asked to sacrifice.

Commit the Agreement to Writing.   Once the parties have reached an agreement, mediators should convene the lawyers or disputants in a joint meeting to write up the terms. At this point the lawyers should normally take over the process. One of them may have used "dead time" during caucusing to draft settlement terms or may have them ready on a laptop computer.

If the parties still cannot talk together, a mediator can facilitate the drafting of the settlement document by shuttling back and forth between caucuses. The key is for the disputants to sign a memo of agreement or understanding that outlines the key terms of their settlement before they leave the mediation site. Often disputants will sign a short, handwritten outline that is legally binding but calls for the execution of formal settlement documents to be drawn up and circulated within a specified period of time.

b. Common Mistakes

Controlling the Process Too Closely.   Mediators sometimes allow parties to reconvene but then forfeit most of the benefit of direct talks by controlling the session too tightly. The neutral may, for example, conduct a Socratic dialogue, channeling the participants into answering the questions he poses, or may choke off discussion of a sensitive issue.

Evaluating the Merits.   Evaluating the merits of a dispute in the presence of both sides is almost always a mistake. Litigants who might accept an opinion delivered in the privacy of a caucus will instinctively reject it in the presence of an adversary. A mediator might identify issues in joint session to confirm what they are — for example, are damages in dispute, as well as liability? But she should rarely, if ever, announce what will be seen as a "verdict" in front of both sides.

Failing to Push Recalcitrant Parties to Close.   In an effort to accord the parties self-determination, mediators sometimes allow negotiations to drift. The effect can be to reward procrastination and fail to bring about a settlement even when an agreement is feasible.

B. No-Caucus Processes

Even among mediators who work without caucusing, there is considerable variation in the structure of the process. Some neutrals include both parties and lawyers in their no-caucus sessions, while others prefer to work with the parties alone; the latter model is common in divorce mediation. Some parties in "no-lawyer" processes will consult an attorney between sessions, while others mediate without legal advice. The following reading describes the stages that occur in one such no-caucus approach.

❖ **Gary J. Friedman and Jack Himmelstein, Resolving Conflict Together: The Understanding-Based Model of Mediation**

(forthcoming 2006)

1. Contracting

In the contracting stage the mediator has four principal goals: (1) establishing contact with the participants; (2) explaining the process; (3) clarifying parties' intention and ability to mediate; and (4) negotiating ground rules. Initially, the mediator elicits some basic information about the nature of the dispute while trying to establish contact with each party by seeking actively to understand each participant.

Understanding is key to our approach to mediation, and the authentic effort to have it there from the beginning is crucial. The mediator first ascertains the parties' understanding of mediation and explains the mediation process. Once each party has had the opportunity to say something about their reasons for coming to mediation, and there is some general understanding of the process, a determination needs to be made by both mediator and parties as to the appropriateness of mediation for these parties and for this dispute. The goal here is to emphasize to the parties what it will take to successfully go through mediation. The parties' motivations to be in mediation are critical to laying the groundwork for a successful mediation; and the mediator can help the parties clarify their motivations and make them explicit.

The mediator also sets the tone. In this respect, it is critical to emphasize the importance of understanding as the fundamental ground of the work. The mediator models that in his/her efforts to understand the parties and their counsel, if present. The mediator can also valuably articulate other common principles for the work of mediation. Central to that is the possibility that an agreement might be reached that would be responsive to each of their needs and interests rather than one which would represent a compromise or trade-off, wherein each party can only have his/her needs met at the expense of the other. To that end, what is key is what is important to the parties, rather than the mediator's view of what is best. It is also important to clarify the place of law in the mediation, so that the tendency to defer to law (or to the mediator or the lawyers) does not take over.

If the parties and the mediator reach an initial determination to go forward, they then need to enter an agreement about their working relationship and allocation of responsibility during the mediation process. The mediator and parties (and their attorneys if present) can negotiate working agreements or ground rules that will structure the mediation process. The ground rules that are established during this state may need either to be re-explained or re-established at a later phase of the mediation. At this early point, the parties lack familiarity with mediation, and they may be anxious; these factors can make it difficult to reach a genuine agreement regarding the working relationship. They may too readily and unreflectively agree to whatever the mediator suggests, which would defeat the goal of including them as full participants in the process. Our goal here is to seek genuine agreements about *how* all participants will work together.

2. Defining the Problem

The goal of the mediator and the parties at this next stage is to set out all information necessary to identify the particular issues needing resolution, and the dimensions of those issues. This means identifying all relevant facts, including economic, emotional, and other factors involved in each party's view of the various concerns and issues. It can be helpful to clarify both where the parties agree and where they disagree so that there is some understanding about what still needs to be resolved through the mediation process. Inquiry into agreements already reached clarifies which issues are in dispute. This process of clarifying agreements and disagreements can also provide key information as to how the parties work together, and what they use as a basis for reaching agreement.

The process of defining the problem can be facilitated by the parties (or their counsel) each making outlines or submissions in writing (outside the mediation sessions), identifying all information relevant to the decisions to be made, and bringing that information into the mediation. Depending upon the complexity of the issues and the nature and intensity of the dispute, this can be a fairly simple or a quite complicated process. There needs to be clarity (usually addressed when discussing ground rules) about the confidentiality of information brought into mediation vis-à-vis its possible use in adversary proceedings if the mediation does not conclude with an agreement.

It may also be important for many parties to understand more fully the legal dimensions of issues. When lawyers are present in the mediation, they can play an important role in clarifying the legal issues (with the help of the mediator). For parties that appear without counsel, it can be critical for them to consult with an outside lawyer at this point in the process. The need to understand the detailed information on any particular issue may also involve consulting appraisers, accountants, or others with technical expertise and, where necessary, to bring them into the mediation. The mediator's role in clarifying the applicable law is a controversial issue amongst mediators.

3. Working Through Conflict

Resolving the conflict has two parts. The mediator can help the parties recognize the non-productive patterns of conflict that keep them divided as well as the content of their differences. In the first respect, the mediator focuses not only on what the parties describe as the content of the issues but how the parties talk about these issues. This dual focus on "the *how*" and "the *what*" can be enormously helpful to the effective work of the mediator.

How the parties communicate: As the parties start to deal with the issues they have to decide, it is normal for there to be a significant degree of tension. The mediator can be aware of the patterns that impede constructive communication such as parties locked into blame and recrimination or one party accommodating to the wishes of the other. Where a limiting pattern repeatedly blocks the parties in their effort to move forward, the mediator can work with the parties to identify *how* they are communicating and to find a better way.

What the dispute is about: The second part of working with conflict is for the mediator to help the parties understand what is important to each of them that underlies the dispute and its resolution. As the mediator helps the parties develop the issues, it is important to allow the parties room to explain the significance to them of any particular issue. We have found it helpful to consider three different levels of concerns operating within the mediation setting:

- Concrete Positions
- Needs and Interests
- Meaning and Direction

Concrete positions represent the most concrete level, which often translates into who gets what and who owes whom how much. *Needs and interests* look underneath the concrete level to the reality of the participants — what the underlying function of each concrete concern is for each party. *Meaning*, the deepest of the levels, represents a sense of the importance and significance of those needs and interests to the lives of persons affected by the issues.

When the mediator is trying to understand more fully what is important to each party, the parties may find themselves identifying their real underlying needs and interests for the first time. For this to happen, it is important that each party be willing to assert what is important to him or her and to allow the other to do the same. Often this will entail exploring assumptions or feelings around a particular issue that have not been previously surfaced.

Most people entering mediation are focused on the most concrete level — their positions — and may well need to start there. It is not important at which level the mediator and parties begin, rather that the level be comfortable to the parties. It is also important to remember that just because the focus is on one level does not mean that the other levels are not functioning as well. Appreciation and expression of the different levels can allow for a movement toward agreement that respects what is important to the parties separately and together.

"Going beneath the problem" in this way can help effuse fixed positions. By looking to what is important for each party underlying the positions they are taking, the mediator can validate that level. At the underlying levels there is often more room to meet what is important to both rather than allowing the parties to get caught in the view that one's needs and interests can only be met at the expense of those of the other. In this way, the mediator can focus on the importance of any ultimate resolution being agreeable to all parties and responsive to their underlying needs and interests as well as to their mutual sense of fairness, thus cutting off a needs/interest competition between the parties. In doing so, the mediator can later help the parties make the link between the various needs and interests and solutions that reflect what is important to all parties in the ultimate resolution.

Many times during this stage, with its concomitant strongly divergent viewpoints, the mediator needs to actively help each party recognize and appreciate their own and each other's reality. As the mediator is able to understand each of the parties' separate realities, s/he is modeling understanding the whole problem for the parties. Ideally, through this process the parties will gain an understanding not only of what is important to themselves but also to each other. There is also the opportunity for the mediator, with the parties' permission, to help the parties recognize and appreciate each other's point of view without necessarily agreeing with it. This is a delicate task and needs to be approached with care.

4. Developing and Evaluating Options

Once the parties have ascertained the necessary information and identified what is important to each of them underlying their concrete positions, the mediator can help them to develop options. In doing so, it can prove vital to explore the full range of possibilities. The mediator needs to counteract the tendency of any party to seize upon his or her proposal as the only solution.

Brainstorm first, evaluate later: ...

Creating value: One of the goals at this point is to see whether options might exist that "create value." ...

Evaluation: Ultimately, the options need to be evaluated and the pie divided. Here it is important that the parties look at the options in terms of how they meet all the parties' needs and interests. The challenge for the mediator is to create a context where each party is looking at an option not only in terms of that party's needs and interests but also how well it serves those of the other party.

Including the law: This may also be the time for the mediator to include the legal context, if it has not already been included, without having it control the parties or keep them from using their own sense of fairness as the basis for choices. The mediator's job is to work creatively with the parties to fashion possible resolutions that honor each party and their relationship, as well as the circumstances of their lives. To do so, both the mediator and the parties may have to look beyond the norms of legal rules or customs to the deeper principles and concerns at stake.

Consequences: After surfacing the possible options that may potentially be acceptable to both parties, the mediator can help the parties understand the consequences and implications of each option. This may raise conflict between them that needs to be understood and unraveled in order for the parties to move toward more collaborative and productive ways of exploring the options.

Parties' responsibility: From this perspective, new options may suddenly emerge from either party or the mediator that are more fully responsive to the needs and interests of each party and their mutual sense of fairness. It is particularly important that the mediator draw out the parties as fully as possible and leave the responsibility with them for resolving the conflict, rather than acting as the sole problem solver.

Keeping decision-making open: During this stage, the parties make specific choices regarding the concrete resolution of particular issues. It is important that any agreement reached on any particular issue be viewed as tentative, subject to review upon the resolution of all issues, so that neither party feels that an agreement that has been reached is immutable. This keeps the parties more fluid and open and allows them to reality-test any particular solution over time. The tendency of the parties toward premature closure needs to be counteracted by the mediator, even when it appears that a particular agreement is in sight.

Testing: This is a time for the mediator to explore with the parties whether any particular agreement is realistic and to do this in a way that does not assert the mediator's particular view. The mediator asks the questions of the parties that need to be asked to determine whether they have fully understood the implications of any particular issue. As part of that process, it can be valuable for the parties to look at the impact of any of the alternatives that they are exploring on relevant third parties. It is also important to examine the implications of the agreement over the period of time that it will be in effect.

5. Concluding Agreement

Once a concrete agreement has been reached, the mediator enters into the task of drafting the agreement. In drafting the agreement, it is important to use words which are understandable to the parties and which also reflect as accurately as possible their intentions as to what the agreement is, and how it will take effect. It is also useful to be clear about any areas that can only be resolved in the future, and to articulate a process for resolving these issues.

The parties may profitably have their agreement reviewed by accountants, lawyers, and others to determine whether any input from any of these "experts" affects the parties' views of both the fairness and the practicalities of the agreement. Particularly critical at this juncture is for the parties to use the experts as consultants rather than as "professionals" who take over what the parties should be doing or who inject their views of how the parties should be looking at their lives. The parties need to determine both how they wish to use the expert and what weight to give the expert's view. Mediator contact with reviewing attorneys should also be done with care because of the tendency of both mediator and lawyers to take over at this stage. At the same time, the mediator can recognize ways in which outside attorneys can help each party determine whether the agreement is fair and workable for them.

The mediator should not become attached to the specific agreement reached as being the result that must be adhered to, regardless of its impact on the parties. Flexibility on the part of the mediator and a willingness to continue to explore parties' priorities with them can be helpful in determining whether or not the agreement needs to be modified or altered in any way.

Finally, once the agreement has been fully reviewed (and modified if necessary), then the agreement is executed (signed) by the parties, and the decision is made as to whether or not the agreement shall be entered in court. The parties or their attorneys can take responsibility for preparation and/or filing of the papers in court, if appropriate and if they wish, which can represent a reaffirmation of what has been achieved in their working relationship. But the mediator needs to recognize and safeguard against the possibility of a conflict reemerging in the drafting process. Be mindful, in this respect, that the mediation process resulting in an agreement can represent an important step for each party and the parties together. It frequently marks not the end of a relationship, but the beginning of new ones — both of the parties to themselves and to each other.

Questions

1. What are the key differences between the stages in the commercial and no-caucus processes described above?
2. In what kinds of disputes would you, as an advocate, advise your client to use a commercial format? When might a no-caucus model be more appropriate?
3. What role does the no-caucus model provide for a party's lawyer? Would you be comfortable in that role? Does it raise any concerns?

Note: Choosing the Right Process

After reading about different structures and approaches to mediation, you may be left with the impression that one model is right and the others wrong. We do believe that there are more and less effective ways of conducting mediation, but we also strongly believe that which approach is best will vary from one dispute to another. As counsel to a disputant, one of your most important tasks will be to select the process that best matches your client's needs and preferences. We explore this issue in more depth in Chapter 10. For now, however, you should be aware that decisions about the structure of the process will depend on factors such as the following:

- The client's overall goals: The best possible monetary outcome? Repair of a ruptured relationship? Something else?
- The client's preferences as to process: Is he willing, for example, to confront or at least tolerate strong and angry emotions? Would he be more comfortable in a caucusing format, or can he handle face-to-face discussions about contested issues?
- The client's role: Is she willing to mediate without a lawyer present? Will she present well? Or would she be better off if you do most of the talking?
- The other side's answers to the same questions.
- The preferences and abilities of the mediator: Although you will seek a neutral who meets your preferences, your choice often will be constrained by the need to agree with the other side on a candidate.

CHAPTER
7

Process Skills

The next three chapters probe more deeply into the mediation process, examining the techniques that mediators use to overcome obstacles to settlement and how lawyers can take advantage of a mediator's interventions. We organize the discussion around three topics: process skills, psychological and emotional forces, and merits-based barriers.

A. Premediation Contacts

You now know that a mediator can do a substantial amount before the parties first meet to create the conditions for a successful negotiation. In some contexts this is not possible: If you are a student in a clinic or a lawyer in a court-sponsored program, for instance, you may not have the ability to talk with your mediator before the process begins. If you are dealing with a busy commercial mediator, it may also be impractical to talk in advance. In many cases, however, it is possible for a mediator to contact the disputants ahead of time. If so, a neutral can do preparatory work, and lawyers have the opportunity to begin to shape the neutral's approach to the conflict. As you read, think how you could apply these ideas in a neutral's role, or how, as lawyer for a party, you could use premediation contacts to advance your bargaining agenda.

❖ **Marjorie C. Aaron, At First Glance: Maximizing the Mediator's Initial Contact**

20 Alternatives 167, 184 (2002)

First moves matter. A mediator's strategic choices during the initial contact can encourage the next steps that will produce a successful mediation, or render mediation less likely or less productive. Too often, a mediator receives a telephone call from a lawyer in a case, and without much thought, gathers the essential information needed for a conflict check and scheduling. Trained to listen, the mediator does so, as the lawyer recites his or her version of the case. A tentative date is set, or opposing counsel is contacted to select a date and work out document exchange. [This response is not necessarily harmful, but it] may cause the mediator to miss significant opportunities to enhance her effectiveness, the likelihood of selection as mediator, and achieving a successful resolution.

This article suggests a set of questions a mediator might ask during the first few moments of initial conversation with a contacting lawyer. Based upon the answers to these questions, the mediator can...more strategically choose among next steps....The following are questions for the mediator to ask the contacting lawyer.

Who is opposing counsel? **Before** learning anything but the paltriest information about the type of dispute and the parties, the mediator should ask for the identity of opposing counsel....

I am curious, how did you get my name? Perhaps you have mediated with opposing counsel, who recommended you for this case....The judge may have recommended you. A former student or law school classmate may be an associate at the firm....The mediator must be acutely sensitive to instances where the referral source could raise neutrality issues....

The following questions are safe for initial and for "separate" conversations — and often yield helpful information:

Have you and your client been involved in mediation before? How did it work? Does it raise any concerns for you about mediation in this case? It is very helpful to know what participants' level of experience is and their expectations are going into the mediation. You may learn [for example] that the attorneys' most recent mediations took place with no joint session — only caucusing back and forth. So that's what those attorneys understand mediation to mean.

What is the status of this dispute/case? Is it in litigation? ...Has a trial date been set? When? This information will give you some indication of the lawyers' and parties' current mindset: the dollars that have been spent;...how much entrenchment there has been and whether a relationship repair is likely to be an option; what is motivating the parties; and the time constraints within which you must operate.

How did the case get to mediation? Was it referred by the court? A suggestion by counsel? Initiated by the client? The neutral may learn that only one party is anxious to settle or that the lawyers really want to settle and talked the clients into the process — or vice versa....

If you and opposing counsel were negotiating, without any involvement by the clients, do you think you could settle it without need for mediation? It's so much more elegant than just asking if there's a client problem, and may prompt a richer response.

Can you describe what the dispute is about — just a bare bones description — that both parties would agree upon? Where a "little bit" of case information before a conference call won't jeopardize perceived neutrality (particularly if you have worked with opposing counsel before), you might opt to ask for a limited description....

Please tell me a little bit about the personalities of the people involved and their relationships. Do counsel get along? ...What are the dynamics between the parties? Is there any past history between them...? This is extremely important information for a mediator to have, and it is best obtained in separate conversations. A mediator can safely operate with the hypothesis that there is something or someone dysfunctional at work in a mediated dispute. Otherwise, they would have been able to settle it without mediation. Sometimes, the dysfunction is limited to the negotiation process; often it is not. The mediator is well served by the answers to questions that will help everyone avoid potential minefields created by the human dynamics in the dispute.

Who do you think should be present at the mediation? . . . Anyone who would be a disaster? The answers to these questions can be critically important. Sometimes counsel will have arranged to bring someone with the appropriate level of "authority," but who was directly involved in the decisions leading to the dispute. Counsel are generally receptive to the mediator's — not the other side's — suggestion to rethink their choice of a representative at the mediation. . . .

Although responses to Professor Aaron's questions are very helpful to a mediator, are there any that lawyers might be reluctant to answer?

Problem

1. You represent an entrepreneur who has filed a claim of fraud against a former business partner. After a year of discovery, it is becoming clear to you that your client has little evidence of fraud; the problem seems to be due more to misunderstandings, exacerbated by some less-than-fully-candid statements by the former partner. You have a shot at winning the case, but you now believe that the more likely outcome is a defense verdict. Meanwhile, as the case has continued and legal costs have accumulated, your client has become increasingly entrenched in his position. He simply will not listen to reason. It was all you could do to convince him to mediate.

   Would you be willing to provide this information to the mediator in advance? What might make you more or less inclined to do so?

B. During the Process

Among the most important ways in which mediators can help parties deal with conflict are to:

- Listen to them;
- Reframe communications between them;
- Identify interests and develop options for settlement; and
- If the disputants insist on positional bargaining, manage it successfully.

If you are in the role of a neutral, think about how you can use these skills in your cases — and why applying them may be difficult in practice. As a lawyer selecting mediators, ask whether process issues appear to be obstacles to settlement in your case and, if so, whether various candidates have the skills needed to overcome them.

1. Listening

Most mediators would agree that of all the skills needed to be an effective neutral, the most important is to be a good listener. This is harder than it may seem, especially for those of us who are inclined by temperament and training to identify issues, discard irrelevancies, and make decisions quickly. It is often difficult, as we listen to clashing viewpoints, to restrain our instinctive wish to pass judgment on them. Doing so requires us to put aside, if only temporarily, some important skills we have learned in law school, in favor of a different approach to listening. To understand the importance of listening, consider the following account of America's most famous expedition.

In 1804, acting on orders of President Thomas Jefferson, Meriwether Lewis and William Clark set out on an epic journey across the unexplored American continent. After wintering on the Pacific coast, they began the long trip home. The party reached the Bitterroot Mountains of Idaho, where they expected to recover horses they had left behind with a local tribe. The horses were essential; without them, the party could not survive their passage through the arid mountains. Author Stephen Ambrose describes what happened next. The quotations are taken directly from Captain Lewis's journal of the expedition.

❖ Stephen E. Ambrose, Undaunted Courage
Touchstone Books 361-362 (1996)

That day, the Americans chanced on Chief Cut Nose with a party of six. Cut Nose had been off on a raid the previous fall, but Lewis had heard of him and knew he was regarded as a greater chief than Twisted Hair. The Indians and white men rode on together, and soon encountered Twisted Hair with a half-dozen warriors. It was Twisted Hair who had agreed to keep the Americans' horses through the winter — he had been promised two guns and ammunition as his reward. The captains were naturally delighted to see him. But he greeted the white men very coolly. Lewis found this "as unexpected as it was unaccountable."

Twisted Hair turned to Cut Nose and began shouting and making angry gestures. Cut Nose answered in kind. This continued for some twenty minutes. The captains had no idea what was going on, but clearly they had to break it up. They needed the friendship of both chiefs if they were to get through the next three weeks, and they needed their horses if they were to have any chance of getting over the mountains.

The chiefs departed for their respective camps, still angry with each other. An hour later, [the expedition's interpreter] returned from hunting. The captains invited Twisted Hair for a smoke. He accepted, and through [the interpreter] explained that the previous fall he had collected the expedition's horses and taken charge of them. Cut Nose than returned from his war party and, according to Twisted Hair, asserted his primacy among the Nez Perce. He said Twisted Hair shouldn't have accepted the responsibility, that it was he, Cut Nose, who should be in charge. Twisted Hair said he got so sick of hearing this stuff that he paid no further attention to the horses, who consequently scattered. But most of them were around, many of them with Chief Broken Arm.

The captains invited Cut Nose to join the campfire. He came and "told us in the presents (*sic*) of the Twisted Hair that he the Twisted Hair was a bad old man that he woar two faces." Cut Nose charged that Twisted Hair had never taken care of the horses but had allowed his young men to ride them and misuse them, and that was the reason Cut Nose and Broken Arm had forbidden him to retain responsibility for the animals. The captains said they would proceed to Broken Arm's camp in the morning, and see how many horses and saddles they could collect. This was satisfactory to Twisted Hair and Cut Nose, who had calmed down considerably after being allowed to tell their sides of the story. The next day, everyone moved to Broken Arm's lodge. There the expedition recovered twenty-one horses, about half the saddles, and some ammunition.

Questions

1. What was the "dispute" here?
2. Did either chief change his mind about who was at fault? If not, why was the meeting helpful?
3. If this encounter had been a modern mediation, what would one call the meeting hosted by Lewis and Clark?

❖ Richard Salem, The Benefits of Empathic Listening
Conflict Research Consortium, University of Colorado (2003)

Empathic listening (also called *active* listening or *reflective* listening) is a way of listening. Though useful for everyone involved in a conflict, the ability and willingness to listen with empathy is often what sets the mediator apart from others involved in the conflict.

How to Listen with Empathy

Empathy is the ability to project oneself into the personality of another person in order to better understand that person's emotions or feelings. Through empathic listening the listener lets the speaker know, "I understand your problem and how you feel about it, I am interested in what you are saying and I am not judging you." The listener unmistakably conveys this message through words and non-verbal behaviors, including body language. In so doing, the listener encourages the speaker to fully express herself or himself free of interruption, criticism, or being told what to do. It is neither advisable nor necessary for a mediator to agree with the speaker, even when asked to do so. It is usually sufficient to let the speaker know, "I understand you and I am interested in being a resource to help you resolve this problem." [In the words of Madelyn Burley-Allen], a skilled listener:

- takes information from others while remaining non-judgmental and empathic,
- acknowledges the speaker in a way that invites the communication to continue, and
- provides a limited but encouraging response, carrying the speaker's idea one step forward.

Empathic Listening in Mediation

Parties to volatile conflicts often feel that nobody on the other side is interested in what they have to say. The parties often have been talking at each other and past each other, but not with each other. Neither believes that their message has been listened to or understood. Nor do they feel respected. Locked into positions that they know the other will not accept, the parties tend to be close-minded, distrustful of each other, and often angry, frustrated, discouraged, or hurt.

When the mediator comes onto the scene, she continuously models good conflict-management behaviors, trying to create an environment where the parties in conflict will begin to listen to each other with clear heads. For many disputants, this may be the first time they have had an opportunity to fully present their story. During this process, the parties may hear things that they have not heard before, things that broaden their understanding of how the other party perceives the problem. This can open minds and create receptivity to new ideas that might lead to a settlement. In creating a trusting environment, it is the mediator's hope that some strands of trust will begin to connect the parties and replace the negative emotions that they brought to the table.

Mediator Nancy Ferrell questions whether mediation can work if some measure of empathy is not developed between the parties. She describes a multi-issue case involving black students and members of a white fraternity that held an annual "black-face" party at a university in Oklahoma. At the outset, the student president of the fraternity was convinced that the annual tradition was harmless and inoffensive. It wasn't until the mediator created an opportunity for him to listen to the aggrieved parties at the table that he realized the extraordinary impact his fraternity's antics had on black students. Once he recognized the problem, a solution to that part of the conflict was only a step away....

Guidelines for Empathic Listening

Madelyn Burley-Allen offers these guidelines for empathic listening [the guidelines have been edited]:

1. *Be attentive*. Be interested. Be alert and not distracted.
2. *Be noncritical*. Allow the speaker to bounce ideas and feelings off you. Don't indicate your judgment.
3. *Indicate you are listening by:*
   - Making brief, noncommittal responses ("I see...").
   - Giving nonverbal acknowledgment, for example by nodding your head.
   - Inviting the speaker to say more: for example, "Tell me about it" or "I'd like to hear about that."
4. *Follow good listening ground rules:*
   - Don't interrupt.
   - Don't change the subject, or move in a new direction.
   - Don't rehearse a response in your own head.
   - Don't interrogate with continual questions.

- Don't give advice.
- Do reflect back to the speaker:
  — What you understand.
  — How you think the speaker feels.
5. *Don't let the speaker "hook" you emotionally.* Don't get angry or upset or allow yourself to get involved in an argument.

The ability to listen with empathy may be the most important attribute of interveners who succeed in gaining the trust and cooperation of parties to intractable conflicts and other disputes with high emotional content. . . .

Example: William Webster, a former federal judge who also served as Director of the CIA and FBI, later became a mediator. He was once asked to name the book that he had found most useful in his work as a neutral in complex corporate disputes. Webster's response: "When my wife and I had teenagers, I found Dr. Haim Ginnott's book, *Between Parent and Child*, very helpful . . . and I find it equally useful now." Dr. Ginnott emphasizes how important it is for parents to listen to children empathically, without expressing judgment on what they say. This, Judge Webster was suggesting, is one of the most important skills that a mediator can bring to a dispute — apparently as useful with angry CEOs as with upset children.

❖ Dana L. Curtis, Reconciliation and the Role of Empathy
ADR Personalities & Prac. Tips 53-62 (1998)

Reconciliation

I love and am committed to my work for many reasons, but I most deeply value being a force in helping parties to reconcile. And I treasure the experience of witnessing it occur. Several years ago at a local bar association program on caucus versus non-caucus mediation models, the presenter advocating a caucus model said that parties who seek the commercial mediation services of his organization "just want an efficient settlement." They do not care about shaking hands or being able to go out to dinner with the other parties.

Sadly, when the mediator assumes a dispute is "just about money," the parties may miss the opportunity for reconciliation. Perhaps because of the high value I place on reconciliation, I see its potential in every mediation. While I am partial to a facilitative, face-to-face model of mediation, where the parties' needs and interests, I have also conducted many mediations where I have deferred to the parties (and their lawyers) preference for a more lawyer-focused mediation that utilizes caucus and evaluation. Even in these "efficiency" focused mediations, reconciliation is still a possibility, though the degree, or quality, of reconciliation differs significantly from reconciliation in broadly facilitative mediations.

Even in those cases where the parties are not able to reach resolution, just sitting down with the other party may reduce the anxiety associated with the conflict. As a participant once stated about his adversary at the outset of a mediation, "I'm not looking to become friends. I just want to be able to meet him on the street and not worry about having to walk the other way."

Parties may not be aware of a desire for reconciliation or may have abandoned hope of it, especially if they come to mediation hostile and bitter. Nevertheless, as mediators we can articulate the possibility, let them know that mediation provides them with the chance not only to settle a lawsuit, but also to return to harmony in their lives or relationship.

When we conclude prematurely, often before ever meeting the parties, that reconciliation is not the province of mediation, or the particular mediation that is coming before us, we may foreclose mediation's highest potential. Even in what is considered a classic distributive bargaining mediation — an insurance carrier and a plaintiff in a personal injury case — the parties may desire reconciliation. I have mediated many personal injury matters in which resolution brought reconciliation. In one such case — a products liability case in which a plaintiff, who was paraplegic, sued an automobile manufacturer for injuries she suffered in the rollover of a sports utility vehicle — the plaintiff was able to meet the defendants and their lawyers as human beings. She told them of her experiences and the ways in which her life had changed. They expressed compassion and respect for the way she had dealt with adversity. She, in turn, understood their business considerations and the conflict responsibilities. The case settled for a dollar amount, which represented a significant compromise on the part of all parties. Had it not been for the mutual understanding that occurred on a deeper level, they might have left without a good settlement, feeling equally unhappy. Every mediator has experienced those moments in mediation where one party "feels the first pain of change" — at last truly understands the other's experience.

I've heard teachers of mediation refer to those experiences as "magic." While it might seem magical, it is not. It is the result of a process that leads parties to reconciliation. That process may proceed as follows:

- The parties each have their "stories" of the dispute.
- The parties want to mend the breach between them, or are open to the possibility, although they may not believe it is possible.
- Each party expresses her own view, still believing her view is right or true.
- Each party hears the other's view and begins to understand the other's perspective.
- Each party realizes that all of the truth is not in her corner, in fact more truth may exist than she initially believed.
- While the dissonance between opposing realities is uncomfortable, the parties permit both realities to co-exist for a time.
- If the conflict can be resolved merely through the sharing of information, one or both of the parties may decide that being right is not relevant to the resolution. Or, a party might revise her story to include the other party's. Rarely, a party might realize and, even more rarely, admit she was wrong.
- Where one or both parties believe they were harmed or betrayed by the other, reconciliation requires a deeper mutual understanding and, perhaps, forgiveness of the "wrongdoer."
- Together, the parties focus on the future and on the solution.

There are a number of tools mediators may use to guide the parties on the path toward understanding and reconciliation, but in my view by far the most important and powerful tool is empathy.

Empathy

Empathy is demonstrating in words what you understand the experience of another to be: the external situation, the feelings and the personal meaning of another's experience. To empathize, the listener receives information from the speaker, filters it through herself, a separate human being, and restates what she understands in order to demonstrate that understanding to the speaker.

In some circles, empathy is criticized as being too "touchy-feely" or overly emotional to be useful or even relevant to a serious lawyer mediator in commercial or civil mediation. It is thought to be the domain of the psychologist. In mediation courses, I've encountered initial resistance from judges, lawyers and law students based on empathy's undeserved bad reputation, only to have them embrace it and incorporate it immediately into their practice and personal relationship. They describe the experience in journals: "I watched with amazement what actually happens when people are really heard...." In addition to experiencing empathy, students learn to respect it as a complex skill, not just a "touchy-feely" exercise. Far from being a mysterious, intuitive process, empathy requires a high level of cognitive and emotional maturity.

Empathizing with Feelings

Lawyers and law students in empathy training often shy away from empathizing with the speaker's feelings. One self disclosing student — a litigator of 15 years — joked that he did not have problems identifying the parties' feelings, as he had a broad range of them himself: hungry, sleepy and angry. The obvious antidote is to start monitoring our own feelings and to attach words to them.

Another reason students shy away from feelings is that feelings often must be inferred and they are afraid of making a mistake. Sometimes they do get it wrong. Either way, getting it wrong is not a problem. The speaker merely corrects the perception and moves on. What matters is that the mediator is listening attentively.

What We Do Instead of Empathizing

Some of us believe empathy is saying, "I understand." While it might be true that we understand, when we do not demonstrate understanding, we forego the positive benefits of empathy....

Instead of empathizing, we may also offer advice. Popular literature about male and female differences attributes to males this tendency "to fix" instead of just listen, but many of my women students admit to being fixers, too. Fixers are often shocked that their efforts to help may seem demeaning to the speaker and make her angry. If we are listening empathetically, we are not giving advice, trying to fix anything or solving a problem. While the mediator might offer solutions at a later point in a mediation (and I recognize there are differences of opinion on the issue), doing so before she truly understands both parties' perspectives is problematic.

Another way of responding is with sympathy. A sympathetic response would be "I am terribly sorry for your loss." An empathetic response, on the other hand, eliminates the mediator's feeling and focuses on the party's: "You continue to be deeply sad to have lost your spouse."

Finally, particularly if a mediator wants the parties to empathize with each other, it is important to distinguish between empathy and agreement. Empathy is understanding. By empathizing, we do not adopt the speaker's point of view; we simply demonstrate that we understand it.

At the bottom line, mediation is about change. If we assume the parties are interested only in changing one another's positions vis-[à]-vis numbers, we may lose the opportunity for more meaningful change through reconciliation. We ignore the possibility of building something new out of disagreement; appreciating and accepting differences and agreeing to go on in spite of them; persevering, not giving up and retreating tired and defeated. As mediators, we can lead parties toward reconciliation through a process that is direct, honest, optimistic, forward looking and aggressive in its effort to work things out.

Problems

2. Your client is going through a difficult divorce and has engaged you to negotiate the terms of dissolution of the marriage. Your client and her husband have been separated for two months. They have two children — a boy, seven, and a girl, ten. He is a partner in a local law firm, and she is a teacher who has been a homemaker since the birth of their second child.

    Your client is extremely angry at her spouse. Her feelings are crystallized around an affair he had with a co-worker a year ago. She complains, however, that the husband was never really committed to the marriage. He enjoyed weekend golf more than spending time with their young children; neglected her emotionally; did not attend many of the children's after-school activities, pleading the press of work; and failed to give her any support during the illness and death of her father two years ago. Your client has demanded that you get the maximum possible recovery from him and "not pull punches." She calls you about every second day to describe her most recent run-in with the husband about payments for household expenses and visitation with the children, and regularly sends you documents that she thinks may be helpful in proving his neglect and ability to pay high alimony.

    (a) Do you think that you would have any difficulty listening empathically to this client? Why? What might you do to deal with any problems?
    (b) Would you have any concern about sending your client into mediation? What qualities would you look for in selecting a mediator for this case?
    (c) What, if anything, would you want to tell the mediator in advance about the case?

2. *Reframing*

The root of many disagreements is that people see the same dispute in quite different ways. The "frame" that a person puts on a situation will influence, in particular, whether he will see a proposal for settlement as a net loss or gain. This, in turn, will strongly affect his decision about whether to settle. Helping disputants to reach agreement often requires finding a way to modify their perspectives, or frames, on a controversy, or at least to allow them to appreciate that an opponent honestly sees the same situation differently. One powerful technique for doing so is known as "reframing."

❖ Ken Bryant and Dana L. Curtis, Reframing
(Unpublished, 2004)

To "reframe" a statement (in mediation lingo) is to recast the statement in more neutral terms, giving the speaker, as well as his mediation partner(s), the chance to look at the problem differently, in a more positive way. The new statement offered by the mediator to accomplish this goal is the "reframe."

How It Works

Let's assume for the moment that a mediation participant has made a statement using value-laden (negative) language. The statement is guaranteed to make the other party angry or defensive if simply left floating in air. The task and challenge for the attentive mediator is to quickly find a positive, constructive interpretation of the assertion. (It helps if you simply assume that every behavior, including a rude comment, is appropriate, given some context, or frame.)

Before you can restate or paraphrase, of course, you must be certain you have heard the original statement correctly, which involves a heavy dose of active listening. Your goal is to accurately reflect the message sent by the speaker, while simultaneously molding the statement into an aid for easier communication. In other words, the speaker must be comfortable that you heard what was said, the other party must not be offended by your restatement, *and* the new version (yours) should point the conversation in a constructive direction.

Restating the Message

You might try restating the message by:

- Redirecting the thrust of the negative assertion, i.e., away from persons verbally attacked to problems inherent in the complaint.
- Narrowing or broadening the gist of the allegation by pinpointing a single problem, or generalizing the issues to include basic policy decisions.
- Forming a question: e.g., "Is there a specific issue you would like to work on? Is there another possible explanation for what happened?" *break train of thought*
- Shifting the focus from problems to opportunities: "Recognizing that you feel the status quo is intolerable, do you have some ideas about what changes are needed?"

- Simplifying a complex statement of a dispute, by choosing a single issue which can be addressed immediately.
- Categorizing the speaker's concerns to be dealt with either on a "most important," "easiest to deal with first," or some other useful basis.
- Neutralizing the original statement by excising ad hominem attacks and generalizing the issues, while retaining the essential elements of the message.

It bears repeating: *Confirm the accuracy of your reframe*. You can confirm your reframe by simply asking, "Is that what you meant?" Or, "Have I expressed your concerns accurately?" Additional, and even more effective, confirmation can be obtained by using your powers of observation of the speaker's non-verbal communication. Check the body language: posture, facial expression, muscle tension, skin coloring, and breathing pattern. Remember, studies indicate that more than ninety-three per cent of human communication is non-verbal.

Why Reframe?

Your purpose is not only to change the harsh effect of the words used by the speaker, but also to create a new dynamic in the mediation. Reframes can change the focus of the speaker's statement, and the mediation, from

- Blame and guilt, to problem-solving
- Past to future
- Judgmental to non-judgmental
- Position to interest
- Ultimatum to aspiration

It probably goes without saying that reframing can, by lowering emotional temperature, increase the efficiency of the mediation process.

Reframing as a Joke

Consider that reframing is the essence of a good joke: What seems to be one thing suddenly shifts and becomes something else. Example: "What do Alexander the Great and Smokey the Bear have in common?" (Answer: their middle names). When you reframe a statement, you shift the speaker's perception, even if just a little. The shift can get creative juices flowing and enhance discussions of options for resolution.

"Meaning" Reframe and "Context" Reframe

Meaning

There was a man who was compulsive about cleaning his house. He even dusted light bulbs. He made his family take their shoes off in their living room. His view of fulfillment as a father and husband was reflected in his home's cleanliness. The problem: He was driving his family crazy. The man was asked to visualize his living room rug, white and fluffy, not a spot anywhere. He was in seventh heaven. Then he was asked to realize that his vision meant he was totally alone, and that the people he cared for and loved were nowhere around. He ceased smiling, and felt terrible, until he was asked to visualize "a few footprints" on the carpet. Then, of course, he felt good again. This is a "meaning" reframe, where the stimulus in the world doesn't actually change, but the meaning does.

Context

A father complained that he and his wife hadn't done a very good job in raising their daughter, because the daughter was so stubborn. The father, a successful banker, acknowledged that he had acquired traits involving tenacity and a stubborn quality needed to protect himself. The father was asked to look at his daughter and to realize that he had taught her how to be stubborn and to stand up for herself, and that this gift might someday save her life. Imagine, he was asked, how valuable that quality will be when *his* daughter goes out on a date with a man who has bad intentions. This is a "context" reframe, demonstrating that every behavior in the world is appropriate in some context. Being stubborn may be judged bad in the context of a family, and becomes good in the context of banking and in the context of a man trying to take advantage of a young girl. When faced with an assertion about the meaning of an event or a person's conduct, the mediator might ask, "What *else* might that conduct mean?" A context reframe can be handled by asking, "Where would this behavior be *useful*?"

Finding the appropriate reframe for negative or non-useful assertions during mediation is hard work and takes practice. No two circumstances will be the same. More often than not, you will not be quite sure if your reframe was useful. Sometimes you will know it was not. There is, however, no such thing as failure, only feedback. You will learn as you try different approaches, and your mediation partners will benefit from your dedication to improving your skills.

Perjury, or just hardball? During mediation of a case arising from a failed partnership, the defendant's attorney argued vehemently that the plaintiff's lawyer had committed malpractice in drafting the partnership contract. This accusation inflamed the entire plaintiff side, requiring the mediation to be temporarily adjourned. A few days later the plaintiff lawyer produced a recently signed affidavit in which a key witness not only rebutted the defendant's version of events, but went on to say that the defense lawyer had told him that he would be given free legal counsel if he changed his story, arguably an incentive to perjure himself.

Defense counsel, told by the mediator about this in caucus, stood up and said angrily that he would not stand for being accused that way. The mediator replied that he thought the abetting-perjury innuendo was simply a "high inside fastball," thrown by the other side in response to the defense attorney's own "hardball" charge of malpractice. The defense lawyer, who did not really want to walk out and did not mind being characterized as a tough player in front of his client, accepted the reframing of his adversary's accusation as a sports move and sat down. Both the perjury and malpractice issues tacitly dropped out of the case.

3. Identifying Interests and Developing Options

One of the major themes of this book is that bargainers can create value and smooth the path to settlement by using interest-based techniques. It is also true, however, that competitive bargaining, accompanied by the angry emotions and suspicion that are engendered by conflict, often makes interest-based bargaining very difficult. The mediation process can assist negotiators greatly to move toward a more cooperative process, and in this section we explore how this can occur.

a. Methods to Identify Interests

The Impact of Value Creation on Impasse

Interest-based techniques can help frustrated disputants in several ways. Some of these are obvious, while others are more subtle. Among the useful impacts of value creation are to:

- Overcome hidden barriers,
- Increase the value of settling,
- Diminish feelings of losing, and
- Distract the parties from positional tactics.

Overcome hidden barriers. As discussed in the context of negotiation, [one of the interests of disputants] is in the process itself: the chance to express emotions and to tell their story. By responding to such interests, mediators can diminish obstacles to settlement.

> *Example:* A mediator handling a construction dispute had become familiar with the parties' arguments through premediation discussions. The parties, who were experienced in mediation, asked her to "cut to the chase," skipping the opening session and going directly into caucuses.
>
> After a few hours, however, the parties fell into impasse. The mediator realized that they were stuck because the CEO of the general contractor felt that he had not had the opportunity to explain why, if all the facts were fairly considered, the problems with the job were not his fault. She convened an "opening session" in the middle of the process in which the CEO explained his position at length. After presenting his arguments, the CEO became more open to considering the practicalities of the situation — for example, that litigating to trial would cost as much as a settlement. After a few hours the parties agreed to a compromise payment and settled the case.

Increase the value of settling. If negotiations were analogized to a card game, moving from competitive bargaining to an interest-based approach would amount not merely to dealing each side a new hand, but changing the game altogether. Players who cannot reach an accommodation under the rules of a positional game are often able to succeed when they apply the rules and goals of an interest-based process. As we have seen, negotiators commonly assume that their goals necessarily conflict with those of the other party and that they must therefore bargain over a "fixed pie." If mediation can increase the amount that each side expects to gain from a settlement, agreement will become more attractive. In some cases the impasse occurs at a point where the parties' positions are quite close; in these circumstances, "expanding the pie" by even a modest amount can produce a resolution.

Diminish feelings of losing. Negotiators often make decisions based on subjective perceptions rather than cold logic. In particular, as we saw in Chapter 4, disputants will keep fighting and take unreasonable risks if they see a settlement as a "loss" compared to their prior expectations, but will agree much more readily to results that they see as a "gain." Closely related to this is the psychological need we all have to feel in control of situations. The conflicts and tests of wills that occur during competitive bargaining often threaten negotiators' sense of control, leading them to become rigid. By helping the parties to identify new opportunities, a mediator can give both sides the sense that they can win something through agreement and regain some control over their fate. This makes it much easier for them to compromise. This psychological effect occurs even when, from an outsider's perspective, the added value is not large.

Distract the parties from positional tactics.   Another psychological obstacle to agreement is the tendency of positional bargainers, in particular, to view compromise as giving in to an opponent's will. Zero-sum bargaining will often degenerate into an adversarial contest as each side tries to avoid submitting to the other. By discussing interests rather than positions, a mediator can distract the negotiators and end their psychological contest. In essence, by shifting their discussion to interests, a mediator helps negotiators to stop thinking about the positional conflicts that provoked their impasse.

Identifying Interests

As we have seen, interest-based bargainers achieve agreement by focusing on needs. Parties to legal disputes, however, rarely come into mediation ready to discuss their needs. This may occur because the bargainers are not skilled in cooperative techniques, because the litigation process has focused them on the limited remedies available from a court, because they fear that even mentioning a nonmonetary issue will imply lack of confidence in their legal case, or because the existence of conflict makes it impossible for them to think creatively about their adversaries' concerns. Mediators can help disputants and their counsel to draw out interests through the following steps:

- Ask specifically about interests.
- Listen carefully for clues and references.
- Suggest needs, give examples, and undertake private probes.
- Ask each side about the other's interests.
- Advocate each side's interests to the other.
- Lower the level of pressure.
- Alternate topics.
- Be persistent.

Ask specifically about interests.   It may seem obvious, but given the blinders with which many disputants approach negotiations, a mediator can often accomplish a good deal simply by looking actively for interests that could be addressed in a settlement. A mediator might see underlying issues in the parties' written statements or might ask what, in his own experience, people in the situation they describe may want: What seems to be motivating them to fight, and what, aside from money, might they find attractive in a settlement?

A mediator can refer to this possibility in a general way in the opening session, but will often save specific questions for caucuses, where the principals are more likely to talk candidly. In general, by designating the topic of interests as relevant, a mediator can ease the "negotiator's dilemma," making it easier for participants to discuss interests without compromising their bargaining positions.

There is an issue of timing, however. If a mediator immediately focuses on interests instead of the legal issues in the case, the negotiators may become annoyed that he is not being sufficiently "hardheaded" — a particular risk if the mediator is young. Litigants are often reluctant to discuss "soft" items until they have shown commitment to their legal positions. A neutral can sometimes shorten this process by asking the parties to discuss both their legal arguments and creative solutions — and a proactive lawyer can ask a mediator to prompt both sides to do so. Often, however, mediators will wait until later in the process, after the parties feel fully heard-out on their legal arguments and realize that they are approaching an impasse. Apart from the issue of timing, mediators use open-ended questions, avoid leading ones, and tolerate silence as tools to draw out interests.

Listen carefully for clues and references.   Mediators listen carefully for clues to the existence of interests — a shift in posture, a change in tone, or a gap in a party's presentation that indicates that something lies beneath the surface. A good lawyer can provide such clues or push for an exploration by asking why the opponent is pressing an issue that appears to his side to be counter-productive or illogical.

Example: A failed businessman sued the bank that had foreclosed on his property, claiming that he had been misled by the bank's president during the transaction. As the mediator caucused with the lender's lawyer, the defense attorney asked in an irritated tone why the plaintiff was even bothering to press the suit, given that he had other creditors who would quickly seize any judgment he might obtain. The defense team in fact had threatened to buy up these unsatisfied claims at a few cents on the dollar, so that it could recoup any money that it might eventually be ordered to pay the plaintiff.

The mediator was intrigued, and asked the plaintiff how he planned to deal with his other creditors. The plaintiff lawyer seized on this, mentioning that the plaintiff was also attempting to buy out the debts but did not have the resources to do so, and asked whether the mediator could suggest a way to deal with the problem. A settlement was eventually reached that included the bank's agreement to buy up the plaintiff's debts at a few cents on the dollar and then cancel them.

Suggest needs, give examples, and undertake private probes.   In addition to general questions, a mediator might mention an interest that she thinks a disputant would have in that situation. Or a mediator might tell an anecdote about a situation in which nonlegal interests proved to be the key to a good settlement and ask a party whether he can think of anything that might be included, if only as an "extra," in an agreement. Again, good lawyers will take advantage of the opening created by such situations to suggest or ask questions about underlying needs.

Ask each side to describe the other's interests.   A mediator might ask each side, perhaps as homework while the mediator meets with the other party, to think about what his opponent might value other than money or a release of liability. Mediators find that such a question often feels less threatening to a litigant than being asked about his own needs, and can help each side appreciate the opponent's perspective.

Explain each side's interests to the other.   In situations where the advocates are skilled and the participants have decent personal relationships, mediators — or counsel — may suggest holding a joint meeting, often in the middle of the process, in which either the principals or all of the participants can explain their interests directly to each other. If, however, parties are too hostile or suspicious to talk directly with each other, the neutral can become the channel of communication, exploring and transmitting new ideas. Again, counsel should think about asking mediators to take on this role.

Lower the level of pressure.   Adjourning briefly to allow participants to recharge themselves, or changing the physical setting or configuration (perhaps by having the principals talk in the lobby, or turn to look at a whiteboard rather than at each other) may relax people, making it easier for them to think inventively. A lawyer who sees her client "freezing up" should consider prompting the mediator, perhaps in a private conversation, to propose a change or a break.

Be persistent.   Good mediators are not surprised or offended to be rebuffed when they first ask about interests. It is not unusual for a question about interests to be rejected out of hand in the first caucus, only to be welcomed later in the same case. Persistence is often required to draw out disputants, and if the area seems fruitful or other approaches have hit dead ends, a mediator should be willing to raise the issue more than once.

b. Methods to Develop Settlement Options

As we have seen, a key problem in stimulating creative bargaining is disputants' suspicion that they will open themselves up to competitive demands by the other side. Mediators can help create the conditions for fruitful discussions of options using the following tactics, among others:

- Brainstorm.
- Make an "unacceptable" proposal.

Brainstorm. A mediator's first option is to encourage the kind of brainstorming described by Professors Mnookin, Peppet, and Tulumello in Chapter 4. The point here is that having the mediator present to moderate the process may make disputants more willing to try this technique. If the parties' relationship is good enough, it is best to discuss possible options jointly. Even when parties are not willing to brainstorm together, they may be willing to do so in private caucuses, relying on the mediator to integrate their ideas and filter them to the other side. The tension is between the advantages of exchanging information quickly and accurately and gaining the psychological "high" that occurs when parties realize that their opponent is genuinely interested in a solution, versus the reluctance that people are likely to feel about throwing out ideas in the presence of adversaries.

Make an "unacceptable" proposal. A mediator can sometimes provoke a useful discussion by making a proposal that he knows will be rejected, but which has elements that respond to the parties' interests. The mediator can then invite each side to critique and improve on the proposal. This is a variant of the "single-text" technique described in Chapter 4.

Promote principled techniques. The basic problem, once the parties have developed options, is to discourage them from lapsing into positional bargaining over them. The suggestions made in the next section for dealing with positional tactics apply here as well. If, for example, a negotiator tries to disparage an option to get it more cheaply, a mediator might privately point out the risk that this will disrupt the process, and ask if the bargainer can suggest a neutral principle to govern the allocation.

Present a proposal as the mediator's. Another option is for a mediator to float settlement packages anonymously, for example by taking a party's proposal and presenting it in the other caucus as his own, or by formulating a settlement package himself. This tactic can be risky, however, for two reasons. First, cognitive forces often make parties perceive even neutral proposals as biased against them. Second, if the mediator becomes too active, the parties may lose their initiative and the mediator may become over-invested in his own solution. A mediator should ordinarily be careful to make it clear that he is merely putting out options for consideration, not designating any particular term as the "right" or "fair" outcome in the dispute.

4. Managing Positional Bargaining

Competitive or positional tactics are a common source of bargaining impasse. The problem of "dividing the pie," however large it can be made, exists, as Professors Lax, Sebenius, and Mnookin pointed out, in almost every negotiation. Competitive approaches are therefore present as well in most legal mediation. Positional bargaining is very common but, as we have seen, it is often inefficient and abrasive. Reviewing how the process works suggests some of the reasons positional bargainers often encounter difficulty.

A positional bargainer's first job is to decide on an opening offer or demand. Many disputants, however, refuse to make an offer at all, for fear of being seen as overeager to settle. Competitive bargainers also tend to begin at an extreme position in the hope that a tough opening offer will have an "anchoring" effect and lead to a favorable compromise. But if one side takes an extreme position, the other side is likely to open with an equally unreasonable position, or even to refuse to "dignify" the other side's "insulting" offer with a response. The result is often a stalemate.

Even when positional bargainers manage to start the process, they often fall into impasse. Positional bargainers must engage in a "dance," exchanging reciprocal concessions in order to close the gap between them. At some point in the process, one or both sides are likely to feel that the other has not made an adequate concession, and either refuse to reciprocate or reply with a move so small that the process again stalemates. Mediators faced with an impasse created by positional bargaining may use the following approaches to avoid or mitigate its effects:

- Move the parties into principled or interest-based bargaining.
- Translate or characterize positions.
- Coach disputants in effective tactics.
- Distract parties from their clash of wills.
- Make a mediator's proposal.
- Suggest a tie-breaker process.

Move the parties into principled or interest-based bargaining. A mediator's obvious first approach to positional bargaining is to seek to transform it into a principled or interest-based process. By using his influence over the parties' communications, a neutral can sometimes move parties away from their initial inclination to use positional methods and encourage them to try more cooperative techniques.

If this is not possible, a mediator may opt to facilitate the parties' competitive techniques. The idea of supporting win-lose bargaining may seem contradictory, but the reality is that many negotiators, especially if they have been locked for years in a bitter legal dispute, will continue to think in competitive terms despite a mediator's best efforts to encourage other approaches. When this occurs, the mediator's practical choice is either to facilitate the positional tactics or give up. Neutrals use the following methods to support positional tactics.

Translate or characterize positions. One option is to change the language of positional offers to make them more palatable to the other side. With parties separated in caucuses, mediators can use their control over communications to translate what each side says into more constructive language. Thus if a disputant says, "Tell them we're offering only $2,000 because their case is simply frivolous," the mediator might translate this in the other caucus room as, "Their opening offer is $2,000, but that's just a first move. Let's see where they are willing to go, and then make a decision about whether or not to accept it...." Alternatively, the mediator might say: "They feel that they have a very strong defense. I think that's why their first offer is at the $2,000 level."

Coach the participants in effective tactics. Mediators sometimes coach positional bargainers to reduce the risk that their positional tactics will backfire. Thus, the neutral may work with one side to select a starting offer that will not drive the other side to respond unreasonably. The neutral may, for example, tell one party that if it begins at a relatively realistic number, he will ask the other side to do so as well. Or the neutral might offer to tell the recipient that the offeror intended to begin at a more extreme position, but adopted a more conciliatory stance at the neutral's request — in effect, allowing the offeror to transmit two messages at once.

If a party does make an extreme offer, the mediator may suggest an acceptable interpretation — in effect, reframe it — and ask the recipient to consider making a constructive response ("They saw you as demanding the most you could win in court — in effect at your 'win' position at trial. So they thought they should stay at their 'win' position too, which for them is zero. The challenge for us is to . . . ."). As the participants trade concessions, a mediator/coach will advise them about the other side's likely reactions and dissuade the negotiators from going down a blind alley.

> *Example:* Consider the personal injury mediation described in Chapter 5, in which a plaintiff's lawyer made a demand of $1.2 million based on medical bills of only $6,000. The insurance adjuster, who was experienced in positional bargaining and expected the plaintiff to make an initial demand that was three to ten times the real goal, saw the plaintiff as signaling that he was seeking a six-figure settlement. She refused to respond at all, for fear of dignifying the plaintiff's "wild" number.
>
> The neutral met privately with the plaintiff and counsel. Learning that in fact they were willing to compromise, he asked the plaintiff lawyer to make a new offer at a lower level. He offered to tell the adjuster that the plaintiff had done this only to accommodate the mediator's request that both sides "cut to the chase," and that the plaintiff expected the defendant to respond in a similar vein. The case settled a few hours later for slightly less than $30,000.

In this coaching role a mediator can help to control the anger, frustration, clashes of egos, and other problems often created by positional tactics. Neutrals will sometimes work to build up each side's self-esteem, assuring the negotiators in the presence of their clients that their opponents respect their abilities, and in general working to minimize the impact of feelings on bargaining. The key point to bear in mind is that although positional tactics are often abrasive and inefficient, they are not inherently unethical, and mediation can be used to facilitate competitive bargaining when necessary.

Distract the parties from their clash of wills. A mediator can sometimes distract the parties, thus helping them forget the anger stirred up by positional tactics. Neutrals do this, for example, by telling a story or redirecting them to interest-based terms. Alternatively, the neutral may suggest that the parties take a break and go to lunch, or go home for the day.

Make a mediator's proposal. Parties will often reach a point at which they have completed their planned pattern of concessions, but a significant gap still remains between their positions. Parties can simply split the difference, but at this point the disputants may feel that doing so would simply reward the other side for being unreasonable. Instead, they lock in and attempt to wait out their opponent, producing an impasse. At this point a mediator's proposal, described in Chapter 5 as part of the basic strategy, can be a useful tie-breaker.

Propose a process rather than a result. If there is more than one item in dispute, a mediator might propose a process rather than a result. In a partnership breakup, for instance, a neutral could suggest that office equipment be appraised and each side receive the same total value, that one side divide the remaining issues in equal parts and the other select, or that they take turns choosing an issue on which they will prevail, like sports teams drafting players. Through these and other approaches, a mediator can sometimes help even positional bargainers reach an acceptable result.

This chapter explored process barriers to agreement and the ways in which mediation can overcome them. We next examine how mediation addresses the psychological and emotional obstacles that often block agreement.

CHAPTER

8

Emotional and Cognitive Forces

Disputes often fail to settle because the people involved are emotionally at odds with each other. Strong feelings may be provoked by the incident that gave rise to the dispute or by something that happened afterward. Recall, for example, how the parents of the deceased MIT student became even angrier because the university president, receiving defensive advice, did not greet them at their son's funeral. Strong emotions can disrupt communication, produce irrational decision making, and create other obstacles to agreement.

Even disputants who are not in the grip of strong feelings are often subject to subtle cognitive influences that distort their decision making even when they are perfectly calm. We saw in Chapter 4 that humans fall prey to a variety of cognitive traps, such as selective perception and reactive devaluation, and these unconscious forces are likely to intensify when people fall into conflict. Lawyers and mediators will lead an opposing counsel or party through a logical analysis of an issue, only to be frustrated when he stubbornly refuses to accept the outcome. They may conclude that the person is not being candid with them, when the real obstacle is psychological. We explore in this chapter how mediators and advocates can respond to emotional and cognitive forces that are frustrating bargaining.

A. Emotional Issues

1. Strong Feelings

Both mediators and lawyers can contribute greatly to the process of settlement by dealing with emotional forces. To do so, one does not have to become a pseudo-therapist or take on other inappropriate roles. A person must, however, be willing and able to listen to expressions of strong feelings without becoming flustered or squelching them. The following responses can be effective in dealing with emotional issues:

- Identify the issue.
- Allow venting: Listen, acknowledge, empathize.
- If necessary, trace the issue back to its source.
- Provide, or arrange for, a response.

- If the cause of the problem is continuing, treat it. If it is carried over from past circumstances, distinguish them.
- Extend the process or adjourn for a time.
- If necessary, circumvent dysfunctional participants.

Identify the Issue.   Parties to legal disputes usually arrive at mediation with "game faces" on; they don't show emotions unless they are part of their legal case. A person whose legal claim involves emotional distress, for example, will be willing to describe her feelings, but executives and lawyers typically present calm, "businesslike" faces even when they are boiling inside. A mediator or advocate's first task, therefore, is often to confirm whether strong emotions are present.

A person's feelings may be apparent from her facial expression, body language, tone of voice, or the way she relates to people on the other side of the table. Often, however, a neutral or lawyer has to ask questions to dig out emotional issues. Attorneys or parties can probe for emotions in a joint session, but it is often easier for a mediator to do so in the private setting of a caucus. Options, couched in terms of what a mediator might say, include the following:

- *Open-ended questions.* ("Is there anything you think I should know about that you didn't feel comfortable mentioning in the opening session?")
- *Mildly prompting inquiries.* ("This must have been very difficult for you, Mr. Smith....")
- *Leading questions.* ("I know how frustrating this must have been...." or "You know, if I felt that I'd been fired because of my age, I'd be very angry....Are you?").
- *References to similar events or personal experiences.* Mentioning that one has had a similar experience can make it clear that feelings are a valid topic. Sometimes it is equally persuasive to mention a situation that you have seen. ("It's been my experience that when people have had this happen to them, they often feel ...")
- *Suggestions of possible responses.* You may want to suggest that the disputant could be experiencing a variety of feelings, indicating that the same events affect people differently. This can be less threatening to listeners, because it allows them to explore possibilities and adopt the one that feels most true or capable of being admitted. ("Well, I wasn't exactly angry, but I guess I felt misunderstood...and maybe even cheated!")
- *Inquiries to lawyers.* If a party is not willing to talk about an emotional issue, one can sometimes gather information through a private chat with the party's attorney. ("Jane, I gather from what's been said that Brad is furious about the way this contract turned out....")

The mediator must be willing to accept brush-offs at the outset, remembering that a question that is turned aside at first may be answered later. This is particularly true for mediators, who can gradually build up trust with participants. The right approach, therefore, is to be both diplomatic and persistent.

Example: A mediator was attempting to settle a claim by an auto dealer that a banker had unfairly foreclosed on his loan and driven him into bankruptcy, then sold his property at a bargain price to a business associate. During the first caucus, when the mediator remarked to the plaintiff how crushing the experience must have been, his lawyer interrupted, saying, "Never mind that — I want to know what they'll offer to settle this thing!"

The mediator raised the emotional issue again during a second meeting a week later. This time the auto dealer hesitated and looked at his attorney. Gesturing expansively, the attorney said, "Joe, tell him how you felt when the bank foreclosed on you. . . ." A torrent of feelings about scheming lenders, the unfair way the public views car dealers, and other angry emotions poured out.

Allow Venting: Listen, Acknowledge, Empathize. Once an emotional issue has been identified, you must decide how to deal with it. In some situations, simply allowing the disputants to vent their feelings directly to each other or privately to the mediator is enough to clear the air. An attorney might, for example, warn a mediator that his client has something to get off her chest, asking the neutral to make clear in opening comments that frank expressions of feelings are welcome and to be prepared to draw them out.

If a party does express a strong emotion, someone should respond. The first-level response is simply to acknowledge that the feeling exists. The appropriate reaction will vary depending on the nature of the issue; a lawyer's anger over an opponent's litigation tactics, for example, is very different from the feelings of a victim of sexual abuse. Whether you are in the role of lawyer or neutral, you can often accomplish a good deal by listening to the aggrieved party and simply showing that you have heard and understood her feelings ("I understand that the deposition was a very frustrating experience for you. . . ."). In some cases, you can go further to sympathize with the person's situation.

A listener does not need to agree with a party's view of the facts to sympathize with the party's emotional reaction to them. Indeed, mediators in particular need to be careful to keep the issue of what happened separate from how a disputant feels about it. By characterizing a situation in terms of "if," one can imply gently that there may be other ways of interpreting the underlying facts. You might say, for instance, "If I felt that I'd been cheated by a business partner, I'd probably feel the same way you do," or "I can understand your frustration, given your belief that the company never tried to respond to your complaints. . . ."

Finally, you do not have to *fix* the problem. This is a lawyer's (and beginning mediator's) instinctive reaction to many emotional situations; solutions, after all, are what we are inclined by temperament and training to look for. But many situations are not "fixable" in any conventional sense. It may help instead to think of the role as similar to that of a mourner at a funeral: You cannot change what has happened, but the very fact that you are present and showing concern provides solace to the bereaved.

In summary:

- Listening is valuable in itself.
- Active listening, in which you show that you have understood the speaker, is more effective.
- Express empathy if appropriate, but don't commit yourself to a position on disputed facts.
- You need not have a solution to be helpful on an emotional level.

Retrace the Issue from the Disputant's Perspective.   Often acknowledging or empathizing with the emotion is not enough: The person remains "stuck" in the feeling. When this occurs, it may help to trace the emotion back to the events that stimulated it. A lawyer can sometimes do this through tactful questions, delivered in a tone that suggests that she is genuinely curious to know the answers. Again, it is easier for a mediator to do this because he is not viewed as an adversary. The listener might, for instance, encourage a disputant to describe how the situation developed.

By asking a disputant to trace the history of a dispute from her perspective, you can often discover the reasons for her strong feelings and begin to identify areas in which emotion is affecting her settlement decisions. When a mediator asks about the past, he also allows the party the opportunity to reexamine her underlying assumptions. In addition, by suggesting that the party once had different feelings about the situation, the questioner opens up the possibility that her current state is not how she will feel in the future.

Arrange a Response.   Even more can be accomplished with emotional issues if a mediator brings an adversary into the process in a constructive way. A neutral may, for example, be able to persuade one party to listen to the other express feelings, then acknowledge having heard what was said. Disputants are sometimes able to go even further, to express empathy in the same manner as a neutral. In fact, within the confidential setting of mediation, with the parties communicating directly with each other and with less concern about admitting liability, one disputant may even express regret or apologize to another. In arranging such encounters, one needs to consider the following questions.

Who should speak and who needs to hear? A formal statement from one attorney to another will not have the emotional impact of a sincere statement made by one party directly to another. In some situations, however, a lawyer-to-lawyer format may be the only option available because a direct encounter would risk causing a damaging explosion.

What form should the communication take? If the goal is personal reconciliation, words heard in "real time," and to which the listener can respond, are much more effective than letters or formal statements. Also, to seem sincere, an expression of regret should be offered freely, without asking for anything in return; an offer of an apology linked to a concession ("We'll apologize, if they'll come down into five figures.") is not likely to impress the listener as sincere. If, on the other hand, the listener is focused on vindication ("I just want them to admit that . . ."), then sincerity is less important. In libel cases, for example, injured parties will often demand that a formal retraction be published.

What needs to be said? It is often not necessary for the defendant to admit error or guilt; the plaintiff may be seeking only an expression of sincere regret. Like Mark Twain's dog, who knew the difference between being kicked and being stepped on, persons injured by someone else's negligence are less likely to insist on an apology than people who believe they have been the victims of an intentional act.

Treat Continuing Problems.   Sometimes people are upset not by a past event, but by an opponent's current conduct. If, for example, one side is angry over what it sees as an opponent's improper tactics, the issue should be handled as a process problem. If, by contrast, the irritation is caused by a condition outside the negotiation process, a mediator can approach it as a hidden substantive issue.

> *Example:* A mediator was moderating discussions between a man and a woman who were breaking up their partnership. The mediator pushed to wrap up the case because he knew that the man was anxious to start a new job, and the woman was pregnant. The woman partner, however, canceled a session at the last minute. The mediator learned from a friend that she had been diagnosed with a serious genetic problem that would affect her unborn child, and she was agonizing over it.
>
> Exploring the issue of scheduling gingerly with both partners, the mediator decided that it would make sense to delay the process. An adjournment would create additional issues, however, because the woman was upset that her partner was making efforts to collect the partnership's outstanding bills. The man had meant this as a gesture of assistance, but the woman interpreted it as a maneuver to change the value of the receivables and thus the sale price of the business. The mediator worked out an agreement by which the male partner would handle day-to-day finances under agreed criteria, and there would be a two-week adjournment of the mediation.

Distinguish Feelings Carried Over from the Past. Disputants may react negatively to opponents because of feelings carried over from a different situation. A plaintiff, for example, may be suspicious of statements made by a defense attorney because she once had a bad experience with another lawyer. When past experiences become obstacles to resolving the dispute at hand, a mediator can make progress by taking the following steps:

- Draw attention to the issue in a diplomatic way.
- Identify the source of the inappropriate emotion.
- Help the participant to distinguish the source of the feeling from the present situation.

The mediator, for example, might simply acknowledge the reaction. ("It sounds like you've had a bad experience that's affecting your view of this case.") Alternatively, a mediator might point out objective differences between the two situations, or call attention to facts that support the credibility of the person involved in the current case.

Extend the Process or Adjourn for a Limited Time. Highly emotional disputants, especially at the outset of a case, may need time to work through their feelings. This was brought home to one of the authors accidentally at a conference on mediation. He sat next to a stranger, who turned out to be the chair of the litigation department at a large national law firm. As a speaker extolled the virtues of mediation, the litigator squirmed in his chair and suddenly whispered:

> This is all very fine, but when my clients come in the door they have steam coming out their ears and the other guy in their sights. They expect me to nail his hide to the wall. If I talked about settling they'd fire me and get some jerk who told 'em what they wanted to hear.... So I let them stew for a few months, and send 'em a couple of bills.... Then you can talk sense to them.

Few mediators would suggest waiting for months for feelings to cool or sending anyone an unnecessary bill, but it is sometimes necessary to adjourn a settlement process for a day or a week to give a participant more time to adjust psychologically to the need to compromise. Having the patience and skill to keep the bargaining process going long enough for a party to deal with strong feelings is one effective way to respond to emotional issues.

Circumvent Dysfunctional Participants. The disputant whose feelings are blocking effective bargaining may not be an individual party but rather a lawyer, manager, or other agent for an organization. In one sense, this is an issue of inconsistent interests between a party and a negotiator — an example of the "principal-agent" problem described earlier. But in this case the dysfunctional player is often not aware that what he is doing is inappropriate. When it is impossible to calm a dysfunctional participant, the most effective approach may be to circumvent him. If, for instance, an executive of a corporate party is too angry to bargain effectively, a mediator or lawyer might arrange for a higher-level person from one side to attend and then suggest that the other side reciprocate. If a dysfunctional person cannot be replaced, mediators are likely to separate the combatants in caucuses and edit out comments that would disrupt the process.

Questions

1. Why might a mediator find it easier to identify an emotional obstacle than a lawyer bargaining directly with an opponent?
2. Which of the techniques described above could a lawyer apply with an angry opponent?
3. Which might an attorney apply with her own emotional client?

Note: Apology in Mediation

One of the potentials of mediation is that it provides a setting in which disputants can apologize. In part this is because the process is confidential, making it possible for a party to express regret without concern that her gesture will be thrown back at her if the case does not settle. In part also it is because of the atmosphere created by the process itself — what Daniel Bowling and David Hoffman referred to as a mediator's "presence in the room." In practice, mediators in commercial cases report that it is very unusual for litigants to apologize to each other. When it does occur, however, an expression of regret can have a major impact. Consider this example.

A famous singer wanted to refurbish an old mansion she had just purchased. She decided to hire a well-known contractor who specialized in restorations, draw her vision of what she wanted, and have the contractor execute it. The contractor gave her a price of several hundred thousand dollars for the job. She agreed, and work began. The project, however, rapidly spun out of control. Changes were made, expenses mushroomed, and the eventual cost was more than double the estimate. The singer refused to pay the final bill, and the contractor sued. The parties agreed to mediate.

Each side sat stiffly at a conference table while the mediator made his opening comments. After the singer's lawyer had summarized her legal arguments, the singer herself asked to speak. Looking directly at the contractor, she said that she realized that she bore some of the responsibility for what had happened: She had very much wanted to realize a vision for her new home, but had made the mistake of not using an architect. She felt that while the contractor should have done a better job of explaining the cost of the changes in the project, part of the fault was hers.

As the singer spoke, the contractor visibly relaxed. He responded that he had tried to do his best, but was willing to work to find a fair solution. After a day of hard bargaining, the case settled.

The nature of an apology can be crucial to its effectiveness; indeed, an apology viewed by the listener as insincere can be worse than no apology at all. Professor Jennifer Robbenolt (2003), for example, reported on the results of an experiment that measured the effect of apologies in a scenario in which parties were negotiating over the settlement of an injury claim arising from a pedestrian-bicycle collision. The experiment compared three different responses: (1) a full apology (in which the party both accepts responsibility for what occurred and apologizes for it), (2) a partial apology (in which the apologizer expresses regret for what happened but not does not take personal responsibility), and (3) no apology at all.

The experiment found that "apologies influenced the inclination to accept or reject a settlement offer. The effect of an apology on settlement decisions was complex, however, and depended on the type of apology offered. Only the full, responsibility-accepting apology increased the likelihood that the offer would be accepted. The partial, sympathy-expressing apology, in contrast, increased participants' uncertainty about whether or not to accept the offer." In other words, while full apologies lessened the likelihood that victims would reject offers and go to court, partial apologies did not. A partial apology may be less likely to expose a speaker to future liability, but it appears to make a settlement *less* likely than if no apology were offered at all.

For more discussion of the impact of apology in mediation, and legal issues that an apology may raise, see the articles by Professor Jonathan Cohen and Deborah Levi in the bibliography.

Questions

4. In April 2001 a U.S. spy plane made an unauthorized emergency landing on China's Hainan Island after colliding with a Chinese fighter jet and causing the loss of the Chinese pilot. The Chinese refused to release the 24 American crew members until the United States issued an apology. The U.S. apology read:

> Both President Bush and Secretary of State Powell have expressed their sincere regret over your missing pilot and aircraft. Please convey to the Chinese people and to the family of pilot Wang Wei that we are very sorry for their loss. Although the full picture of what transpired is still unclear, according to our information, our severely crippled aircraft made an emergency landing after following international emergency procedures. We are very sorry the entering of China's airspace and the landing did not

> have verbal clearance, but very pleased that the crew landed safely. We appreciate China's efforts to see to the well being of our crew.

What elements of an apology does this statement contain? How might it have contributed to the release of the U.S. crew?

5. A highly publicized apology from basketball star Kobe Bryant in 2004 played a role in the dropping of criminal rape charges by the recipient of the apology, as well as the settlement of a related civil suit. The apology is set out below. What considerations and motivations, from both sides, prompted the inclusion of the specific wording in the statement? Do the apology, the subsequent dropping of criminal charges, and a negotiated settlement in 2005 that resolved the civil suit concern you? Why?

> First, I want to apologize directly to the young woman involved in this incident. I want to apologize to her for my behavior that night and for the consequences she has suffered in the past year. Although this year has been incredibly difficult for me personally, I can only imagine the pain she has had to endure. I also want to apologize to her parents and family members, and to my family and friends and supporters, and to the citizens of Eagle, Colorado.
>
> I also want to make it clear that I do not question the motives of this young woman. No money has been paid to this woman. She has agreed that this statement will not be used against me in the civil case. Although I truly believe this encounter between us was consensual, I recognize now that she did not and does not view this incident the same way I did. After months of reviewing discovery, listening to her attorney, and even her testimony in person, I now understand how she feels that she did not consent to this encounter.
>
> I issue this statement today fully aware that while one part of this case ends today, another remains. I understand that the civil case against me will go forward. That part of this case will be decided by and between the parties directly involved in the incident and will no longer be a financial or emotional drain on the citizens of the state of Colorado.

6. Compare the Bryant apology with the statement made by the president of MIT in the mediation of the student death claim in Chapter 5. What differences are there between them?

7. During the 2004 Super Bowl halftime show, singer Janet Jackson experienced a notorious "wardrobe malfunction," in which her co-star, Justin Timberlake, pulled away part of her costume, exposing her breast. A week later at the Grammy Awards, Timberlake made this statement about the incident: "I know it has been a rough week on everyone and, umm, what occurred was unintentional, completely regrettable, and I apologize if you guys were offended." Evaluate the quality of Timberlake's statement. Do you think it accomplished its purpose? If you had been his advisor, what would you have advised him about what to say and in what setting to say it?

2. Personal Issues in Dealing with Emotion

In practice, attorneys and mediators often find it difficult to deal with intense emotions. As you read the following dialogue, ask yourself if any of the lawyer's comments describe your own reactions to deeply emotional situations.

❖ Helaine Golann and Dwight Golann, Why Is It Hard for Lawyers to Deal with Emotional Issues?

9 Disp. Resol. Mag. 26 (Winter 2003)

Lawyer: The fact is, I sometimes don't feel that I'm being professional when I work with emotions. It's not what lawyers do.

Psychologist: That's interesting — What *does* make you feel as if you're acting like a professional?

L: Dealing with facts and arguments, analyzing issues, generating strategies and, most important, solving problems....

P: Well, those are clearly professional activities, and they are often invaluable to clients. My only concern would be not to rush into them too soon. In an emotional situation — and people who feel that they've been hurt or treated unfairly are often quite emotional — people *can't really listen until they feel they've been heard.* You might think that you can predict their story because you have heard so many similar ones, but even if you are right, they won't feel heard until they've told it. In fact they may need to review the story with you in order to hear it themselves and become open to different ways of resolving the problem. Rushing to analyze can get in the way of disputants figuring out what is important to them.

L: I do remember one fairly dramatic instance of that from when I was in law practice. It was a tort case brought against a state trooper. The trooper had been chasing a drunk driver on a rainy night, when he went through a stop sign and accidentally hit another motorist. The driver, a high school student, was killed. His family sued the state and I supervised the defense. After two years of litigation we made a substantial settlement offer, but the family refused to discuss it. They said that they wanted to meet the trooper first. We were suspicious. Everyone had been deposed; what was the point? But eventually we agreed.

It was quite a session. The mother of the student read a poem describing what she hoped her son would have accomplished had he lived. His sisters also spoke about who their brother had been. The trooper said he wanted to say something too. He told the family that he didn't feel that he'd driven negligently, but he did feel awful about what had happened. He had three sons himself and had thought about how he would feel if one of them were killed. He had asked to be assigned to desk work, he told the family, because he could no longer do high-speed chases. As the participants walked out, one of the children turned to the trooper. "It's been three years since my brother died," she said, "and now I feel he's finally had a funeral." Two weeks later, they accepted our offer.

I have to say, though, that we agreed to the meeting only because the other side insisted on it. Not many cases are so openly emotional. Litigants usually don't come in asking for a chance to tell their story.

P: That's an unusual and deeply touching example, and yes, you're right that clients are rarely so clear about their emotions and what they need to do to resolve them. Litigants need you to assure them that dealing with emotions is a valid and potentially productive way to spend time, and even then they may initially resist. I sometimes think of people in this situation as being like a tightly-closed fist: One option is to help them strike with that fist. Another is to counsel them about their chances of winning the fight. But it could be even more useful to help them uncurl their fist, so that they can grasp other possibilities. Strategizing with "closed fist" clients who don't know what they feel or why they feel it is often unproductive. The issues they present are often only a smokescreen for other, more important concerns. Lawyers or mediators who charge ahead to focus on legal or bargaining issues may find themselves going off in a direction that the client may later resist or even sabotage. . . .

L: I think it's sitting without doing anything that often strikes us lawyers as meaningless.

P: OK, I'm hearing how important it is to feel that you are *doing something specific* in order to feel like a responsible professional. It's true that usually more is needed than silence; we need to find a way for lawyers to experience listening, and even encouraging the expression of emotions, as an active, professional activity in and of itself. . . .

L: Another problem is that lawyers often feel lost in long discussions about emotions — they seem directionless.

P: It's true that exploring emotional territory makes it difficult to have a clear agenda. Your questions and interventions need to be guided by what emerges as important to the client as she tells her story. Early in my training as a psychologist, for example, I was assigned to interview a client. The session occurred in a special room fitted out with a one-way mirror and a telephone. Behind the mirror was my professor, also with a phone, and the rest of my class. A patient came in and we began to talk, but he only wanted to discuss his hobby, which was scuba diving.

After about twenty minutes of listening to his adventures while diving, I began to worry about demonstrating my therapeutic skills and interrupted the client to ask what had led him to make the appointment. Immediately the phone rang. I picked it up. It was, of course, my professor. He had one question: "*So* . . . what's the matter with scuba diving?" I took the hint and began to listen more closely to the diving talk. Almost immediately it became clear that he was talking about some complex issues, for example, his anxiety over sharing an air tank with his girlfriend. Was it something about her, about their relationship, or was it more about him and past relationships that had compromised his ability to trust? All I needed to do was reflect the questions I began to hear in his story to help him begin to formulate his own answers.

Years later, the part of me that wanted to say, "Why don't you just get a second tank and let's move on to talking about something *important*?" still occasionally rears its head. I can cringe as I review a session and recognize that I failed to hear something that was essential to my client because I was too caught up in trying to be "helpful." Shutting up and listening can be as hard for psychologists as for other professionals, but equally rewarding.

L: Actually, many of us became lawyers to avoid dealing with these messy emotional issues. I've sometimes said that hearing people out is like "draining pus from an infected wound."

P: Ugh — I can understand why you wouldn't be enthusiastic about doing it. That metaphor also helps me understand why I've rarely heard "venting" described by lawyers as anything more than a necessary evil, to be gotten out of the way as quickly as possible. But allowing people to vent emotions doesn't have to be distasteful, and it does have a purpose and goal — it's just that *you* are not the one setting the goal. It might help to imagine a litigant's experience as a dark room filled with noxious fumes; "venting" is an opportunity to open the windows, release the blinding smoke and let in fresh air so your client can think more clearly.

L: Are you saying that venting moves inevitably toward clarity?

P: Not necessarily — people can just spin their wheels and go even deeper into the same old rut. We all know couples who've been having the same argument for years. That's where the active aspect of listening comes in. If it's not clear to you how a disputant got from point A to point B, you can ask for an explanation (e.g., "I hear that A happened and then B, but I'd like to understand better how you are connecting them.") The answer may be even more clarifying for the client than it is for you. If there's a lot of fuzziness about how A led to B, that may be where unarticulated feelings are hiding.

Active listening stays focused on encouraging the client to tell her story fully, but it also offers opportunities for lawyers to use their organizational skills to bring clarity. You might summarize with a statement such as "As I listen to you, I think I'm hearing at least three separate issues here. Please correct me if I'm wrong." By separating and listing the concerns in this way, you are demonstrating your attempt to understand their perspective (including their feelings), but also are introducing clarity and perhaps facilitating movement. Of course, when you ask if you are getting it right, you also have to be prepared to hear that you've got it all wrong!

L: Many of us worry that if we start to let parties express emotions, the situation will blow up. It'll be like uncapping a volcano — lava everywhere! And people will get burned.

P: In fact, no one can cap an emotional "volcano," and even if you could, it might not be a wise course. The pressure is there and denying it may fuel it further. If you don't drain emotional pressures off, they will find their own escape routes — often to fuel more arguments and hardened positions.

If you want to think of emotional release as a volcano erupting, think of your job as allowing the lava to escape, while at the same time channeling it away from the "village" and into a safe area. There are ways to channel flows of feelings so that they do not disrupt the process of settlement or your relationship with the parties. Just by modeling respectful listening yourself and establishing ground rules for how people express themselves, you can channel emotional "lava." Perhaps the most important rule I enforce in working with families is to ask each participant to focus on his own experience, feelings and wishes, without accusing or analyzing the motives of the other side. . . .

L: Again, as I think about it, the more usual problem is that most parties come to mediation with "game faces on." They act as if there is no emotional issue, when I suspect they are simmering inside.

P: Yes, in therapy, too, clamming up is by far the more common and challenging response to emotional turbulence. The listening techniques we've been discussing are the most effective ways I've found to get at buried emotions.

L: The final obstacle is litigators — the people who usually hire legal mediators. One might fairly ask: If the lawyers don't want to get into an emotional issue, how can we do it without offending them?

P: I wonder if you're reading them right? A major problem may be that a litigator's role as an advocate armored for battle often makes it hard for her to explore a client's mixed feelings. I think a mediator could make himself quite valuable as someone prepared to handle the messy emotions that some attorneys don't feel in a position to confront, yet know are preventing a resolution of the dispute.

Question

8. Do you think that any of these factors might lead you to avoid dealing with intense emotions in a legal dispute? Which seem most significant to you?

B. Cognitive Effects

As we have seen, cognitive forces often prevent persons involved in disputes from making good decisions even when they are calm. Some conditions impair a disputant's ability to assess the merits of a case, while others affect peoples' ability to negotiate well. We discuss each of these in turn and describe what mediators do to overcome them. If you are a lawyer dealing with a dispute in which cognitive factors seem important, you may wish to apply, or prompt your mediator to consider, one of these responses.

1. Forces Affecting Assessment of the Merits

Selective Perception

We have learned that once people adopt a certain view of a situation, they are affected by the phenomenon of "cognitive dissonance" — that is, they unconsciously seek to maintain a consistent picture of the world and find it psychologically difficult to consider data that contradict their viewpoint. To avoid such dissonance, the mind unconsciously screens out conflicting information, leaving people with a false sense of certainty. Lawyers fall into this trap when they listen to a client's version of the facts of a dispute and form a viewpoint about what occurred, then disregard conflicting evidence that later comes to light.

One example of selective perception, mentioned in Chapter 4, is an experiment in which law and business students were given "confidential" instructions for the plaintiff or defendant in a case and asked to assess the plaintiff's chances of prevailing and the average verdict if she did. As you will recall, the "confidential" instructions given to the two sides in fact were identical — but the students' assessments were not. Rather, students on each side unconsciously emphasized data that helped their case and ignored facts that hurt it, and as a result came out with sharply different estimates of success.

Mediators use several techniques to minimize the distortions caused by selective perception. They can:

- Ask the parties to state their cases directly to each other, so that each side hears an unfiltered statement of its opponent's views.
- Ask each party to assume the role of a neutral judge or juror as she listens, imagine that she is hearing the case for the first time, and ask herself how the other side's version would sound to someone who did not know what had "really" happened.
- Review the facts and arguments with each side in private, gently questioning them about apparent gaps.
- Emphasize missing facts and issues visually, for instance with markers of different colors on a white board or flip chart.

Optimistic Overconfidence

We also saw that humans consistently overestimate their ability to assess matters about which they are unsure and are likely to be overoptimistic about their chances of prevailing in uncertain situations. This happens in part because disputants tend to view their own case as unique and thus not controlled by the results of similar disputes. People also become more confident about their ability to assess uncertainty if they have made a personal investment in the outcome. Thus, for example, people who place a bet on a horse are surer than those who do not that they know how to pick a winning steed. These forces tend to distort the judgment of both litigants and lawyers, who must assess the outcome of an uncertain "race" — the likelihood of prevailing in court — and also place a large "bet on their horse," in the form of legal expenses and time.

To combat optimistic overconfidence, a mediator can:

- Seek to distance bettors from their "horses" by making the case seem less unique. For example, a mediator might place the claim among a group of similar ones (e.g., all soft-tissue injuries) and ask about the attorney's experience with the group as a whole. The mediator might also ask parties what is exceptional about their case.
- More generally, either encourage an information exchange or ask an overconfident litigant to do research, for example about verdicts in similar cases in that jurisdiction. A thorough search may well generate new data that contradict the unrealistic assessment,
- Offer an evaluative opinion that challenges the unrealistic assumption. (The issues involved in mediators giving evaluations are explored in the next chapter.)

Endowment Effect

People who possess something typically value it more highly than people who do not, a phenomenon known in psychological literature as the "endowment effect." This is a particular problem for owners who are selling an item. The endowment effect makes sellers tend to view whatever they own as "special" and therefore worth much more than very similar items offered by others. Thus, for instance, a homeowner is likely to see her house as significantly more valuable than other homes that would appear identical to a third party, car owners tend to see their vehicles as "better" than others of the same make, and so on. The endowment effect also afflicts buyers, who tend to undervalue what they are bargaining for, but data show that buyers are affected much less severely than sellers.

In negotiations to settle a legal claim, the plaintiff typically offers to give up, or "sell," her claim in return for the defendant agreeing to pay her money. Not surprisingly, the endowment effect leads plaintiff/sellers to value their claims too highly and, to a lesser degree, encourages buyer/defendants to under-estimate their worth. Faced with this situation, a mediator can:

- Lessen the effect on plaintiffs by:
  — Framing the question as a joint problem ("How should we respond to the defense offer?").
  — Creating emotional distance between the plaintiff/seller and the claim being sold, by treating it as an analytic problem and the claim as being in someone else's control ("How would a judge/jury value this case?"), or alternatively by placing it in a larger group ("How do juries value this kind of claim?").
  — Offering an opinion of how a court is likely to value the claim.
- Increase feelings of ownership in defendants by:
  — Treating terms already agreed to as "owned" by the defendant/buyer, to encourage feelings of endowment in the bargaining process itself.
  — Leading a party to imagine how it will feel to "own" the claim.

2. *Influences on Bargaining Decisions*

Cognitive barriers also affect how parties make tactical bargaining decisions, quite apart from how they value legal claims. Again, mediation can attenuate the problem.

Reactive Devaluation

We know that people tend to react negatively to any offer or information presented by an adversary, perceiving ominous overtones in what an outsider would view as an innocent gesture.

Example: A biotech company hired a contractor to install a state-of-the-art heating and air conditioning system in its office building. The installation went badly. In particular, individual rooms' air flow controls were apparently improperly connected to sensors. As a result, some employees had to work in offices heated to only 55 degrees, while others sweltered at 80. The biotech company, frustrated, refused to make the last two payments due under the contract. Two months ago the contractor walked off the job, claiming that the company's decision to withhold payments had prevented him from paying subcontractors. Both sides have claimed large amounts of expenses and lost profits caused by the situation.

After two sessions of mediation and an exchange of expert reports, the contractor has now proposed to go back and finish the work. He proposes that the work on the air flow controls be done by a different subcontractor than the one originally charged with the task. The system's performance will then be checked by a designated independent expert. The contractor has also offered to warranty the system's performance for two years.

To the mediator, this idea seems promising. She has tentatively concluded that the original problem was due in large measure to a personality conflict between the company's physical plant chief and the contractor's job supervisor. The contractor has been in business for more than 20 years and appears to have a real interest in salvaging his reputation, and the expert's credentials are solid. A supervised fix seems much more promising than engaging in more positional bargaining over the parties' rather vague damage claims.

The company, however, reacts negatively to the entire idea. The contractor, they say, is a sleazy fraud who will simply make jury-rigged adjustments so that the system passes initial tests, and then disappear. They note that the expert has his office in the same city as the contractor, and speculate that the two must have an arrangement to refer each other business. They reject the offer out of hand.

To lessen reactive devaluation, a mediator can:

- Discuss the merits of a settlement option in the abstract, before the listener knows whether its opponent has proposed it (that is, before it is "cursed" by having been endorsed by the enemy).
- Offer a proposal as the mediator's own idea. However, such a proposal must appear within the range of fairness to the recipient, or his confidence in the neutral may be shaken. And devaluation may still occur if the listener thinks that the mediator is endorsing an offer that was proposed by the other side.
- Diminish the negative impact of a proposal by offering an opinion that even though an opponent has made it, the mediator believes that it could have advantages for the listener.

Loss Aversion

We have also seen that disputants tend to develop a perception about the "right" outcome in a case regardless of its objective merit, and then measure settlement offers against that subjective standard. If, as is usually the case, the offer falls short of a recipient's internal benchmark, she will experience a sharp sense of loss. Both experimental data and practical experience indicate that people will take unreasonable risks and suffer great pain rather than accept a loss that they perceive as unjustified (Arrow et al. 1995, 54-59). People in the throes of loss aversion, in other words, often reject settlement offers that would appear sensible to an outside observer. To minimize the impact of loss aversion, a mediator can:

- Bear in mind that disputants arrive with internal "loss-win" or "sunk cost" benchmarks, and look out for signs that such standards are distorting their decision making.
- Remember that participants will resist data or arguments that they sense will lead them toward accepting a "loss." Loss aversion, in other words, will often exacerbate selective perception.
- Work to reframe a situation, placing it in different terms so that the disputant loses his "loss" reference point.
- Use charts and other visual techniques to help disputants break away from a win-loss benchmark. If a disputant is being unduly influenced by the money he has spent on a case, for example, a mediator might distinguish past, unrecoverable legal costs from future expenses that can be avoided through settlement by placing each in a different column or in contrasting colors.
- Distract parties from their "loss-gain" calculations.

Example: A corporation sued a supplier over an allegedly defective product. After a year of litigation, the plaintiff's vice president was discussing a defense settlement offer with his outside counsel. The offer made objective sense to the litigator in light of the company's damages and the objective risk of losing at trial, but the executive refused to consider it. He insisted that any recovery had to include not only damages, but also the nearly $50,000 that the company had paid in legal fees to bring the case. Indeed, perhaps because he felt responsible for the decision to sue, the executive seemed to care more about recovering the legal fees than the damages themselves. The company's lawyer was in a bind because she knew that there was no basis for seeking attorneys' fees in a breach-of-warranty case.

"You need to think about this like a hard-headed businessman," she argued. "At the point you came into my office, the defendant was offering you zero. You've made an investment in this case, and you're now being offered a return on it. How does the deal look — money in versus money out? What are the pros and cons of cashing out now, versus investing more and looking for a better payout later?"

After some resistance, the executive began to talk about what should be considered the "capital" in this situation and gradually became less emotional. Eventually, with a few "sweeteners" that obscured the money terms, he decided to take the deal.

It is said, perhaps apocryphally, that Henry Kissinger ascribed his success in bringing about agreements between Arabs and Israelis to "making the deal so complicated that no one could tell who was winning." In essence, it seems, Kissinger used complex proposals to prevent the parties from comparing his settlement proposals with their initial goals and thus seeing them as a loss.

Attraction to Certainty and Familiar Risks

We have seen that disputants are often willing to pay more if they can achieve a certain outcome and dislike even objectively minor risks. Mediators encounter this "premium for certainty" whenever they present a settlement proposal that leaves open even a minor risk in the future. Listeners often react with negativity out of proportion to the actual risk.

People also prefer familiar risks to strange ones. Pedestrians, for example, will find it much easier to take on a commonplace risk like jaywalking across a busy street than an unusual one like walking along a cliff, although the consequence is the same in either case — death — and the familiar risk is actually much greater than the strange one. Mediators and counsel confront this preference for familiar risks whenever a party sees a settlement as making it bear a risk that seems unusual or out of its experience.

In response, mediators can:

- Analyze less-than-certain proposals carefully, so that the listener appreciates that although a risk does exist, it is small in objective terms.
- Reframe an unusual risk in more familiar terms. ("This is really just like giving a warranty....")
- If a settlement does provide certainty, such as a full release of liability that permanently settles all possible legal claims, emphasize this and use it to persuade parties to agree. Disputants are more likely, for example, to agree to even a very painful concession if a lawyer or mediator can assure them that doing so will bring complete peace. ("If you can just take this one last step, you will never have to hear about this case again.")

Questions

9. Thinking back on exercises you have done in this course, does one of the cognitive factors described above appear to have affected the bargaining?
10. Have you ever encountered such reactions in real life?

3. *General Responses to Cognitive Issues*

Apart from the suggestions for responding to specific issues, mediators can use several general techniques to deal with the impact of cognitive forces on negotiations. They should:

- Treat obstacles as psychological, not simply legal, issues.
- Retrace the disputant's analysis.

- Distance current circumstances from prior ones.
- Reframe the situation.
- Ask the person to play out an adversary's role.
- Use humor.

Treat Obstacles as Psychological, Not Simply Legal, Issues. Often when a disputant resists settlement because of a psychological issue, the instinctive response of legally trained mediators is to present more information or argue for settlement more vehemently. This approach is likely to have little impact, because the problem is not a lack of data or arguments. Indeed, arguing may worsen the situation by making the disputant dig in more deeply. Instead, a mediator needs to understand the psychological reasons for the person's resistance and respond to them.

Retrace the Disputant's Analysis. The first step is usually to listen carefully to the explanations offered by the disputant and talk them through, even if they seem illogical, as one would with a purely emotional issue. It may become apparent to the person that her reasoning is flawed, opening the way to a more realistic appraisal. At a minimum the disputant is likely to become less rigid if he feels heard. A listener could, for example, use reflective statements such as "I see, so you assumed that the documents would show _____, and that led you to estimate the damages at _____," while refraining for the moment from pointing out data that contradict the person's assumptions.

Distance Current Circumstances from Prior Ones. Because the problem, particularly with "loss-gain" obstacles, is that a party is using an obsolete or inaccurate frame of reference to make decisions, one effective response is to help the person distance the situation in which she set up the internal benchmark from present circumstances. A mediator could suggest, for example, that the initial assessment was reasonable given what the person knew at the time, but that new data have since come to light. This frees the disputant from having to admit that her earlier judgment was wrong.

Reframe the Decision. A mediator can also place the decision in a new context, in which the feeling of loss is not as strong. For example, changing the frame of reference from a lawsuit to a business context may make it easier for the disputant to let go of an obsolete loss benchmark.

> *Example:* An executive was frustrated because his company was being offered only $30,000 to settle a claim for damages. The offer was far less than the company's $500,000 initial damage estimate, or even the $70,000 it had spent in legal fees. The problem was that discovery had turned up documents in the company's files that contradicted large portions of its damages and also called into question the defendant's basic liability. The case was now in court-ordered mediation.
>
> Rather than telling the executive that his focus on the company's initial valuation of the case was wrong or the money spent on it was illogical, the mediator listened to the executive's reasons for clinging to a six-figure settlement demand. The neutral went on to ask about the history of the litigation and how the problems with the claim had become apparent. It became evident that the executive had personally advocated filing the case and was embarrassed that it now appeared to be a loser.

The mediator commiserated with the executive's situation, suggesting there was no way he could have known that records kept in a subsidiary would contradict what he was told by his staff. The neutral went on to tell a story of having gotten into a similar situation when he was a litigator. He then characterized the issue as a tough business decision: Should one put additional money into a disappointing investment, or close out the venture? Will the additional costs involved in persevering be worth whatever one can reasonably expect to gain, over the current settlement offer? He suggested that he would also be willing to brief the company's management about why it made sense to settle. As the discussion went on, the executive became less tense, and gradually focused on what could be done to get the best possible deal now.

Ask the Person to Play Out an Adversary's Role.   If a party is having difficulty understanding an adversary's perspective because of problems such as reactive devaluation or selective perception, a mediator can try to explain the opponent's position. A more powerful technique, however, may be to ask the recalcitrant party privately to summarize the opponent's arguments, for example by taking on the role of lawyer for the opponent. By playing out an adversary's arguments, disputants are sometimes able to move out of their own framework and see their situation more objectively.

Use Humor to Shake a Disputant Out of a Rigid Stance.   Finally, a mediator can resort to humor, telling a story that illustrates the illogic of life and helps the listener let go of the feeling that the prospective "loss" has great meaning. Humor can also serve as a break in the process, helping a disputant to relax and shake loose from a rigid position. Mediators and lawyers need to be careful about how they use this technique, however; the wrong anecdote can strike a disputant as trivializing an important issue.

Example: A mediator had to convince a real estate investor to contribute to a settlement of a "lender liability" case in which a bank had allegedly swindled a borrower out of a piece of land. The investor had bought the property through a private deal with his friend, the president of the defendant bank, at what he indignantly insisted was a fair-market price. In response, the mediator told the investor a story about a recent appellate case involving the trustees of a church board who were exposed to tort liability for inadvertently violating the privacy of their minister, while they checked on reports that he had appeared nude in the pulpit. The implication was that one could find oneself legally liable despite the best of intentions. The investor laughed, and 20 minutes later agreed to put in the $50,000 needed to close the deal.

C. The Special Problem of Loss Reactions

There is one barrier to settlement that has both emotional and cognitive aspects. It is the strong reaction that some disputants experience at the point they are asked to make serious compromises to settle a claim or defense. At this point parties must, sometimes for the first time, give up a cherished hope or illusion. The following reading discusses what happens in such situations, and how lawyers and mediators might respond.

❖ Dwight Golann, The Death of a Claim: Loss Reactions in Bargaining

20 Negot. J. 539 (2004)

"It's hard. . . . There's a finality about it. . . . When we sign, then it's done. He's really gone." — The widow of a victim of the 9-11 disaster, describing her reluctance to apply for compensation to which she is entitled

Negotiation is not a fully rational process. People in conflict feel intense emotions, and many of these feelings are negative. In order to reach a settlement disputants must compromise, often accepting terms much less favorable than the goals they set at the outset of their dispute. The experience of giving up hopes and settling below expectations is extremely painful, but in addition litigants incur both explicit expenses, in the form of lawyers' fees and other out-of-pocket costs, and implicit expenses such as lost time, distraction and worry. The longer the conflict goes on before settlement is discussed, the more severe these costs will be.

Experienced mediators often remark that the sense of loss that accompanies settlement is the most serious single obstacle they encounter. Such feelings appear in almost all litigation settlements, but they sometimes take on an unusual intensity. Consider the following example:

A sixty-year-old software engineer, James Evans, was terminated by his company. He filed suit, claiming that he had been fired simply because his young manager did not believe that an older employee could do cutting-edge work. Evans asked for more than two million dollars in damages. After more than a year of litigation the employer moved to dismiss Evans' claim, arguing that he had failed to file his charge with his state anti-discrimination agency. As the parties awaited a court hearing on the motion, the company proposed mediation and Evans agreed.

During the parties' initial session, Evans and his lawyer argued strongly that there could be no reason for his firing other than age. The employer, however, maintained that it had terminated Evans based on his performance, presenting mediocre reviews that he had received from the manager. The company also argued that Evans' failure to file charges with his state anti-discrimination agency would require the court to dismiss his lawsuit, regardless of merit. The mediator's private view was that the company's failure-to-file defense was very likely to prevail. However, the employer knew that the court might well delay ruling until trial and thus had an incentive to settle. She began to work with the parties, and made some initial progress.

In the late afternoon, as the negotiations reached the point at which the disputants confronted painful concessions, Evans began to act oddly. He had voiced anger all along at what he saw as his employer's duplicity and ingratitude, but now he began to act erratically. He would discuss legal risks rationally at one point, then a short time later refuse to talk about the case at all, exclaiming that he could not believe that this was happening to him. At one point Evans authorized the mediator to make a substantial concession, but when she returned with a counteroffer he became nearly hysterical, insisting that he had been "crazy" to make any move at all. At still other times he seemed deeply withdrawn, barely responding to the mediator or his counsel's suggestions. Eventually Evans' emotions subsided, he deferred to his lawyer's advice, and the case settled.

This mediation was unusual. The typical money negotiation resembles an uphill slog. But in this case the process was more like a ride on a roller coaster. The employee's emotions were striking not merely because of their variation, but also because they followed a distinct pattern. Indeed, Mr. Evans seemed to go through phases similar to those observed in people mourning the loss of a close relative. In this case, however, the "death" was of something other than a human being.

The Psychology of Grieving

To understand how people deal with feelings of loss during settlement, it is helpful to consider how they respond to very personal losses such as the end of a close relationship. Theorists such as Sigmund Freud and Elizabeth Kubler-Ross developed models of human response to such traumas.

Freud provided the classic analysis of how people respond to the loss of a close relationship. A victim of serious loss, Freud observed, typically goes through an initial period of shock and withdrawal in which he loses all interest in the outside world: During this period the victim often clings to the fiction that the object of his affection — the lost person — continues to exist. Gradually, however, most victims begin to reconcile with reality, realize that the departed person is truly lost, and withdraw their emotional attachment. Freud saw the process of grieving as a kind of internal negotiation, in which the mind of the bereaved reluctantly works out a compromise between its wish that the relationship continue and the realization that it cannot. As this happens the victim gradually gains the ability to form new emotional attachments and go on with life.

Other clinicians have developed models of human response to loss; perhaps the best-known is Elizabeth Kubler-Ross (1969), who described patients' response to being told that they are terminally ill. She reported that such patients typically go through five distinct stages: numbness/denial, anger, bargaining, depression and acceptance.

A person's first reaction to hearing that she will soon die, said Kubler-Ross, is often numbness followed by the urge to deny what is happening — similar to the belief of Freud's patients that their lost love will somehow return. A typical patient, for example, might exclaim, "No, not me, it cannot be true." Kubler-Ross suggested that patients use denial as a defense against the overwhelming feelings of shock that they experience upon hearing their diagnosis. A patient, she reported, will later enter a second phase in which they begin to feel anger at what is happening: "The cry 'Not me!' becomes 'Why me?' In posing this question, however, the patient is not asking for an explanation, but instead is protesting her fate...."

Kubler-Ross found that many terminally-ill patients enter a third stage in which they attempt to negotiate. Since death cannot be avoided, this bargaining is not realistic, but rather is another form of denial. A dying patient, for example, may offer to donate her body to science if she is allowed to extend her life. The fourth stage is depression: When the patient comes to realize that she cannot avoid death, she is likely to become deeply morose. Kubler-Ross's final stage, acceptance, occurs when people accede to the inevitability of their impending death; patients in this phase may exhibit few feelings of any kind. This series of emotions might be termed a "loss reaction."

Loss Reactions in Legal Disputes

How do these psychological findings apply to persons involved in legal disputes? Freud was clear that people can feel intense grief over the loss of an abstraction as well as another human being. He observed that "Mourning is . . . the reaction to the loss of a loved person, or to the loss of *some abstraction which has taken the place of one, such as . . . liberty, an ideal*, and so on." (Emphasis added.) Freud's observation applies readily to legal disputes. A worker who suddenly loses his job, for example, not only is deprived of income but also forfeits social status and his personal identity as a breadwinner or professional. As one writer put it, "From a grief perspective, the worker is saying, 'Two parts of me are about to die.'" (Evans and Tyler-Evans, 2002, p. 91). Defendants in legal disputes also feel loss; a manager charged with discrimination, for instance, might feel that regardless of the outcome, the charge alone will harm his reputation and prospects for advancement in his company.

When a person suffers the loss of an "object" such as a business relationship or an "ideal" such as her self-image, she is likely to react in much the same way as someone grieving over the loss of a personal relationship. Parties to law suits do, in fact, go through distinct phases of mourning. Most examples arise from family disputes, perhaps because they involve disruptions of such intimate relationships. One Florida domestic relations lawyer, for example, reports that clients who are surprised by a spouse's demand for a divorce typically display feelings of denial; they may express incredulity that a demand has been made, and even suggest that their partner is suffering from mental illness. Divorce litigants, of course, also become angry. Some parties, one practitioner says, will demand that their lawyer use scorched-earth tactics and "crucify the offending spouse." As the legal process continues, these same clients may show signs of depression and some eventually reach acceptance, coming to terms with the fact of separation. Parties may also skip over or mix these phases together. One lawyer, for instance, reports that "In one appointment I have seen a client go from anger to sadness back to anger and finally to acceptance."

Although there are virtually no published reports of litigants outside the divorce arena showing loss reactions, they certainly occur. The age discrimination claimant described at the outset, for example, appeared to go through denial, anger, unrealistic bargaining and depression. Litigants in commercial disputes sometimes also display such feelings.

Even if we accept that parties to legal disputes may react like people confronting death or a deep personal loss, however, it is still not clear why these emotions sometimes do not appear until settlement is discussed. The claimant described above, for instance, displayed symptoms during negotiations that took place more than a year after his law suit had been filed. One might think that by the time litigants got to the point of settling their feelings of loss would be substantially resolved. Why do some litigants suffer reactions so long after their loss has occurred? To answer this question, it is necessary to consider the psychology of abnormal reactions to loss.

Abnormal Responses to Loss

Freud found that while most mourners gradually work through their loss, some do not. This latter group remains "stuck," unable to deal with their feelings of deprivation and disabled from moving on. Thus some parents whose son or daughter has died will maintain their child's bedroom untouched for years, a poignant example of unresolved grief. Freud posited that a key reason for this difficulty is that some victims maintain "a strong fixation to the [lost] love-object." Anna Freud spoke of patients who maintain themselves in denial over a loss by "the substitution of a fantasy or an action, or something of that sort; the defensive use of action in order to do away with something painful and unpleasant." By adopting such a strategy — that is, by fixating on a substitute object or cause — a victim can avoid much of the pain inherent in his loss, sometimes for years.

Some civil litigants also fall into this trap. They avoid the feeling of the loss caused by a dispute by investing another "object" with their feelings. Often this object is the lawsuit itself. A terminated employee, for example, may escape some of the pain of losing his job by convincing himself that a court will compensate his injuries. Defendants may also cling to the belief that they will be vindicated in court.

What happens when such disputants must make compromises to settle? If a person has worked through feelings of loss before negotiations begin, she will be emotionally ready to compromise. If, however, the litigant pretended that a loss could be avoided, then she will confront the loss for the first time when she faces a settlement decision. This is exemplified by the poignant words of the wife who would not claim compensation for the death of her husband in the 9-11 disaster: "When we sign, it's done. He's really gone."

Implications for Bargaining

What are the implications of loss reactions for a negotiator or mediator? Most mediators see expressions of emotion as positive events, but there are reasons why both mediators and lawyers should see loss reactions as a potentially serious problem. The first issue involves interpreting the reaction. Disputants suffering from such reactions behave very similarly to adversarial bargainers. "Tough" negotiators will, for example, present cases in a distorted manner and cling stubbornly to viewpoints. Unfortunately, disputants in the grip of denial behave in much the same way. Adversarial bargainers will also sometimes pretend to agree to terms, and then renege once the other side has accepted the offer. Disputants suffering from a loss reaction may engage in similar behavior, making proposals sincerely, but then falling prey to sudden feelings of anger or denial and withdrawing them. This, for example, is what happened in the age discrimination mediation; the plaintiff authorized the mediator to make an offer, but later denounced the same proposal as "crazy." A negotiator who encounters someone in the throes of a loss reaction may interpret his behavior as unethical bargaining, when in fact it is driven purely by emotion.

A second problem arises from the fact that loss reactions are likely to occur not at the outset of a negotiation but much later when disputants must confront painful compromises. At that point the parties are feeling frustrated and want to wind up the process. Even the mediator may feel that the "listening to feelings" stage is, or should be, over. As a result, both mediators and other disputants may either ignore the loss reaction or become angry.

Potential Responses

How should a negotiator or mediator deal with a disputant who is "acting out" because of a loss reaction? The most useful lesson is to be aware of such responses and recognize them when they occur. If a mediator realizes that a loss reaction is happening, she will understand why a disputant is suddenly behaving in an inconsistent, even offensive manner. Opposing counsel should also bear in mind the possibility that their adversary is not being intentionally difficult or duplicitous, but may simply be unable to deal with the sudden realization that she will have to accept a serious loss in order to settle.

Mediators can treat loss reactions with techniques similar to those applied to emotional issues generally. They might, for instance, invite a person to describe the loss he has suffered, listening actively and empathizing with his feelings. A mediator could also work to re-frame how a disputant views the situation. Both neutrals and opposing lawyers should bear in mind that the process of working through a loss reaction may take longer than a single day, and be ready if necessary to adjourn temporarily; this may, for example, explain why divorce mediations typically take weeks or months to complete, while commercial cases settle in a single session. Professionals who encounter sudden, erratic behavior during bargaining should keep in mind the possibility that a disputant is going through a loss reaction, one of the many factors that make resolving disputes a less-than-fully-rational experience.

CHAPTER

9

Merits-Based Barriers

Lawyers who negotiate over legal disputes instinctively apply one of the key lessons of good bargaining practice — not to settle for less than the value of one's best alternative to a negotiated agreement. In legal disputes each side's most obvious alternative to settlement is usually the same: to submit the case to adjudication. But the fact that disputants have the identical alternative does not mean that they agree about its value. In practice, disagreement over the likely outcome in adjudication is a major obstacle to settling disputes.

Litigators tend to assume that if they cannot settle, it is because the other side has misevaluated its case. But as we saw from the discussion of judgmental overconfidence and selective perception, *both* sides in a dispute — as well as their lawyers — commonly miss relevant information and make overoptimistic judgments about the likelihood that they will win. Given this phenomenon, it is understandable why litigants would have trouble settling. If a tort plaintiff, for example, assesses the most likely outcome at trial as a $120,000 verdict, while the defendant is convinced that the average verdict will be $80,000, they do not agree about the value of their alternative to agreement. Indeed, to the extent that a settlement above or below their projected outcome will feel to each litigant like a "loss," we know that strong psychological forces will motivate them to fight on.

The vast majority of cases do settle, however. Many settlements are driven by the reality that under U.S. law, even a winning party cannot usually recover its costs of litigating. If each side in the above example expects to spend $30,000 to litigate, for instance, the plaintiff should be willing to accept $90,000 (120 minus 30) and the defendant to pay $110,000 (80 plus 30). Litigation costs thus transform a gap of $40,000 into an overlap, or zone of potential agreement, of $20,000 (110 versus 90). Of course, the fact that a solution between $90,000 and $110,000 makes financial sense does not mean that the disputants will regard it as fair.

Another factor inducing settlement, however, is risk aversion — the phenomenon that although sides in a case may think that they have a 60 percent chance of winning at trial, they often cannot afford, either financially or psychologically, to sustain a loss. The prospect of a loss may be devastating to the lawyer as well, particularly if he previously assured a client that his case was strong. The risk of losing is so frightening to many litigants and lawyers that they are willing to accept even what feels like an unfair bargain.

Despite the effects of litigation costs and risk aversion, disagreement about the likelihood of success in court often frustrates negotiations over legal claims. In such situations, part of the challenge for lawyers and mediators is to find ways of bringing the parties' assessments of legal issues closer together so that a settlement will seem less unfair, and cost and risk factors will induce them to agree. How can mediation do this?

A. Responses to Lack of Information

One key obstacle to settlement is often a simple lack of information: People sometimes assess their alternatives incorrectly because they do not have enough data, or the data that they do possess are not accurate. Lawyers express this feeling when they protest that, "It's too early to settle; I don't know the case well enough." In other situations, however, the negotiators claim to have all relevant data, but a neutral observer can see that their arguments are laced with gaps and assumptions. It is also possible that each side has information on all points, but their versions conflict with each other.

It is often surprising to an outsider how little litigants know about each other's claims and defenses even after years of discovery. Court rules are designed to give parties full disclosure of relevant information, but in practice discovery often fails to do this, in part because litigants "hide the ball," concealing evidence from each other for as long as possible. Even when parties do learn the legally relevant facts, they often lack information about other important issues. Ordinary discovery proceedings, for example, do not require the principals in a dispute ever to communicate directly with each other. When a litigant does meet a representative of the other side, for example at a deposition, he is usually discouraged from volunteering any information, particularly about the underlying causes of their dispute. As a result, a mediator can often make significant progress simply by arranging for an informal exchange of information among disputants.

> *Example:* A sales manager who had been fired by a computer software company sued his former employer for violating his employment contract. The company maintained that the termination was lawful. The case remained in pretrial discovery for years, then, as trial approached, went to mediation. When the neutral caucused with the parties, it quickly became apparent that a major component of the manager's claims involved stock options in the company, which he believed were very valuable. The manager, however, had never been able to obtain the internal financial reports needed to value the options. He assumed that the company was hiding the data because it expected to "go public," an event that would make his options very valuable.
>
> Questioned about this in caucus, the company's CEO said that he had ordered the data withheld from the plaintiff because, "It's none of his business." In fact, the company was only marginally profitable, and the options were nearly worthless. The mediator suggested to the CEO that if there really was no pot of gold in the stock options, he could help to settle the case by letting the plaintiff know this. The parties agreed to review the financial data, and within an hour the plaintiff understood the true value of the options. A settlement was quickly worked out; among its terms were verification of the company's financial representations and termination of the plaintiff's options.

To solve disagreements over the legal merits that stem from information problems, a mediator can:

- Arrange an exchange of information.
- Obtain new data.
- Moderate a joint discussion.
- Engage a neutral expert.
- Serve as a channel for, or verifier of, confidential facts.
- Direct attention to non-merits information.

Arrange an exchange of information.   As the above example shows, a mediator can often arrange for a more effective exchange of relevant information than occurs in most discovery proceedings. Litigants are usually more forthcoming in the context of mediation because they have a realistic hope of settling the case, wish to cooperate with the neutral, and trust the mediator to shield them from unreasonable demands. In the mediation context, parties will often provide information on a "one-sided" basis without a quid pro quo by the other side, as occurred in the stock options case. Information exchanges are also easier to arrange because the time-limited quality of the mediation process focuses the parties on the task of pulling together data quickly. Finally, the special confidentiality rules that apply in mediation allow disputants to share data with less fear of being harmed if the case does not settle. Some of the techniques described earlier can also be of help: Mediators can identify information that one side lacks and ask the other party, in the interest of settlement and/or as a courtesy to the neutral, to make an effort to obtain it.

Obtain new data. Negotiators often fail to obtain data from their own side that would help the parties settle. This may occur because the inside litigation contact for a corporate party does not see the case as a priority or does not have enough influence to make data retrieval a priority. A party can also encounter frustration when a co-plaintiff or co-defendant procrastinates about collecting facts that the party needs to evaluate its situation. A mediator can often coax special efforts from parties that allow negotiators to get the data from their own side that they need to settle.

Moderate a joint discussion. In some cases disputants have never looked at the relevant information together to understand its significance to the other side. This is particularly true when disputants mediate at the outset of a dispute, when they have not yet conducted full discovery. In these situations a mediator can move the negotiation forward by helping them do so. If the parties can talk civilly with each other, it often makes sense to ask the participants, or a subset of them, to meet for a joint review of an issue. Even when parties are too emotional to negotiate with each other, they may still be able to talk about facts, for example gathering to review a plot plan. Such discussions can expose ignorance and misunderstandings, as well as give parties the experience of working cooperatively with each other.

Engage a neutral expert. Some facts cannot be determined by the parties even with a mediator's help because they require expert analysis. This is true, for example, of scientific issues in environmental disputes, medical questions concerning injuries, and other matters that are outside lawyers' ordinary store of knowledge. In large disputes that can justify the added time and expense, the parties or a mediator can hire a neutral expert to examine an issue and report confidentially to the participants. In an environmental Superfund or mass tort case, for instance, scientific testing might be needed to gather and assess complex data. Such an analyst is similar to a neutral expert designated by a judge, but with the key difference that the conclusions of an expert in mediation are not admissible in court, making litigants more receptive to undertaking the inquiry.

Serve as a channel for, or verifier of, key facts. In a typical negotiation, facts and arguments cannot be used in bargaining without becoming known to the other side and exposed to discovery. In mediation, by contrast, confidentiality guarantees open up possibilities for the exchange of sensitive data. Sophisticated negotiators and neutrals use the special confidentiality rules that often apply to mediation to communicate information about a case while at the same time preserving their "ammunition" for trial. Parties may agree, for example, to allow a mediator to show key financial documents to the other side on the condition that no copies will be made and the originals will be returned at the end of the process.

> *Example:* Two parties' disagreement about a claim turned in large part on the credibility of a defense witness. The defendant allowed the mediator to question the witness in caucus and then give her impressions to the other side. Since the witness had never been deposed, and the time for taking depositions had expired, this allowed the defense to use the witness for settlement purposes without sacrificing its tactical advantage if the case had to be tried.

Direct attention to non-merits information. We have seen that negotiators tend to define "relevance" quite narrowly in legal disputes, focusing on data that would be useful at trial but slighting information about nonlitigation interests. Mediation, by contrast, can help parties to develop data that may be legally irrelevant but that allow them to construct more valuable settlement packages. Even while a mediator is focusing on the merits, he can find ways to help parties exchange a wide variety of useful non-merits data.

B. Intermediate Techniques

Even when litigants have complete information, they are likely to disagree about the value of their litigation alternative, due to cognitive forces such as selective perception and optimistic overconfidence. In addition to the specific responses discussed to deal with cognitive traps, both mediators and bargainers can use the following approaches to influence disputants who have relevant information but appear to be misreading it:

- Ask questions.
- Lead the participants through an analysis of possible outcomes.
- Point out worst-case scenarios.

- Stress transactional costs.
- Lead the parties through a decision analysis.
- Form alliances with some players to convince others.
- Directly challenge skewed assumptions.

Ask questions. The safest approach to a litigant's misevaluation of an issue is to ask questions about the factual and legal assumptions that underlie his view. This is the essence of the tactic referred to as "reality testing." Asking questions is particularly useful at the outset of a case, because one does not need to have his own analysis to pose queries. Mediators can also ask each party to suggest questions to present to the other. Instead of directly confronting an unrealistic party, mediators can also mention an opponent's argument and ask for help in responding to it. ("The other side is arguing that there is no proof of emotional distress — can you give me something that I can use to persuade them about this?")

It is worth stressing that reality testing does not require a mediator to disclose her own opinion about an issue. By phrasing questions carefully, mediators can challenge the parties' viewpoints without appearing biased. To avoid humiliating participants, this kind of questioning is best done privately and by a neutral. This technique can be used by a mediator in joint session, but if so he should take care that parties do not resent being pushed on sensitive issues in front of their adversary. It can also be carried out by a negotiator in direct bargaining, but then it is even more likely to stir resentment. For example, a mediator might:

- Ask a plaintiff, "Can you explain how you calculated your figure of $5 million in lost profits? Are there any documents I could look at to flesh that out?"
- Ask a defendant, "Is there a precedent for your position that a judge will have to throw out the punitive damages claim? The plaintiff says that the circuit court ruled the other way last year. Is he right, or is there anything to the contrary I can show him?"
- Draw attention to a problem that a plaintiff has ignored: "You're looking for $2 million in damages. I can only see insurance coverage of $250,000. How do you think you can collect a judgment that favorable?"

Lead disputants through an analysis of possible outcomes. If initial questions are not enough, mediators will often take an unrealistic disputant through a point-by-point analysis. A typical money damages claim, for instance, has four basic elements: the plaintiff's allegations, affirmative defenses such as statutes of limitations, proof of damages, and collection of a judgment. The mediator can break each of these elements into subquestions; for instance, proving damages may involve issues of evidence, computation, and expert opinion. He can also discuss potential counterarguments, perhaps writing out the issues on a whiteboard or flip chart to dramatize them. This approach can pinpoint problems that are glossed over or forgotten during informal discussion and counteract litigants' persistent tendency to filter out unfavorable information and overweight the importance of the facts they do know.

Point out worst-case scenarios. Although the concept of the best alternative to a negotiated agreement is a very useful one, parties often take it too much to heart. They are likely to focus only on their *best* alternative to a settlement, which usually is seen as a win, ignoring the *most likely* result in litigation or, what is often even more significant, the *worst* possible outcome. This last possibility is sometimes given the acronym "Worst Alternative To a Negotiated Agreement," or WATNA.

Given the tendency of parties to focus on their best outcome and ignore mediocre and worst-case possibilities, mediators often take pains to direct each side's attention to the less-favorable scenarios. A mediator might play on risk aversion, for instance, by probing the impact of a total loss in the case and requesting each lawyer to estimate for his client the risk that it will occur. If counsel says that a complete loss is inconceivable, a mediator or opponent might ask if he has ever lost a similar case, or heard of others doing so. Or one might cite accounts of serious losses drawn from trial reports. Focusing on WATNAs also lets a mediator harness the psychological power of loss aversion and attraction to certainty. If disputants begin to measure an unattractive but certain settlement against the possibility of a total loss, a compromise may seem more attractive.

Mediators can also focus attention on the most likely outcome, which is a mediocre one. In a tort case, for instance, this might be a finding that the defendant is liable but that the plaintiff was contributorily negligent and therefore should receive reduced damages. In doing this, the neutral is seeking to counterbalance the human tendency to focus on reports of dramatic events such as a huge victory or loss, rather than the more common mediocre result.

Stress transactional costs. We noted earlier that because of the impact of transactional costs such as legal fees and distraction, rejecting a settlement offer often does not make financial sense even if a party expects to do somewhat better in adjudication. Parties almost always understand this problem in general terms, but often they have not calculated even approximately how much it will actually cost to pursue their case through trial. A mediator can prompt disputants to discuss a budget for additional litigation using both optimistic and pessimistic scenarios. If cost estimates seem unrealistic, a mediator can use the same techniques as for miscalculations about legal issues: ask questions, go through a formal analysis, and if necessary express skepticism or offer opposing views.

In talking about costs, good mediators make special efforts to ensure that the parties are inclusive in their analysis. A thorough assessment would include not only attorneys' fees, but also the cost of experts, depositions, services such as "rush" trial transcripts, and travel. A good mediator will also help each side think through and experience more vividly the hidden costs of litigation, such as being pulled away from one's occupation and family by the demands of legal war. Participants who are not regularly involved in litigation do not know how painful the process can be; for a one-time participant, even a routine deposition can be a wrenching experience. Good mediators make everyone aware of the hidden costs of disputing and ensure that they consider them in calculating the value of their alternative.

It is often wise to defer the issue of litigation costs until later in the mediation process. Even when negotiators have developed a realistic estimate of costs, they are often unwilling at first to acknowledge them, making comments such as, "I shouldn't have to take less than a fair result just because the justice system is incompetent." Disputants sometimes also refuse to consider litigation costs because they feel that the other side will also save by settling, and there is no reason to compromise more than their adversary. Because of this reluctance, mediators will not usually focus on costs until after the merits have been fully aired, so that no one feels that their substantive arguments have been slighted.

Lead the parties through a decision analysis. "Decision analysis" is a more formal version of the inquiry described above and is often helpful when informal methods fail, especially with "numbers-oriented" litigants such as engineers and CFOs. It is used both by lawyers and by mediators. At a simple level, decision analysis simply involves asking a disputant to place specific percentages on his chances of winning at various stages of the process. A skeptic might point out that if a disputant is not assessing his case accurately, putting the misestimate into numeric form does not make it any more reliable. In fact, though, decision analysis can help a party to think through each of the possible outcomes in a case and understand the combined impact of risk on case value. How to perform a decision analysis is discussed in the next reading.

Form alliances with some players to convince others. Some members of a bargaining team may be more realistic about the value of their case than others. Attorneys are likely to assess court outcomes best, because they have more experience doing so and are less likely to be driven by the emotions engendered by a dispute. Lawyers also know that they risk being held responsible for a bad result, which works against the tendency to be overoptimistic. By posing tough questions in the presence of the entire team or talking with a lawyer alone, a mediator can sometimes identify such disagreements. Indeed, attorneys sometimes will tell a trusted mediator that their client is being unrealistic and ask for help in dealing with him. How mediators and lawyers may work in concert to convince unrealistic clients is explored in Chapter 11, and the ethical issues it raises, in Chapter 13.

Directly challenge assumptions. If other methods fail, a mediator can explicitly indicate that he disagrees with a disputant, but still avoid giving his own opinion. The neutral might emphasize his disagreement in a clear, even blunt manner; for example, "I understand you plan to argue that the company records were altered, but I'm concerned that the jury will see it as an ordinary error, rather than a cover up." For a mediator to directly challenge an opinion after having demonstrated that he has listened to the disputant's arguments can shake a litigant's confidence in his unrealistic viewpoint. Simply indicating disagreement without offering one's own opinion has the additional advantage of not locking the mediator into a position that may become an obstacle later in the process. On the spectrum of facilitation to evaluation, this technique crosses into the evaluative sector; some mediators, however, would describe it simply as a tough form of "reality testing."

As we have indicated, one option to resolve differences in case assessment is to carry out a process known as decision analysis. In the reading that follows, Marjorie Aaron and David Hoffer explain the basics of how to do a decision analysis and why it can be helpful in settling cases.

❖ **Marjorie Corman Aaron and David P. Hoffer, Decision Analysis**
as a Method of Evaluating the Trial Alternative

In D. Golann, Mediating Legal Disputes 307 (1996)

"Decision analysis" provides quantitative evaluation of decisions under conditions of uncertainty. Long used by business people to model business decisions, decision analysis has more recently gained recognition within the legal community as a tool for decision-making in complex litigation. The term "decision analysis" was originally used to refer specifically to the analysis of decision "trees" — tree-shaped models of the decision to be made and the uncertainties it encompasses. We will introduce the very simple terminology used (not surprisingly, decision trees have branches) and will walk the reader through the "how to's" of decision analysis in a litigation/mediation context.

Before turning to the mechanics, it is important to understand the logic behind the method. People commonly use decision analysis to make decisions without even realizing it. (1) They sort out the possibilities — the various things which might occur, (2) consider the costs or gains associated with each possibility, (3) discount each possibility by its probability — the estimated likelihood that it will in fact occur, and (4) finally, weight the overall picture.

Decision analysis adds the most value when costs, opportunities, and probabilities can be valued or estimated, and when the problem is sufficiently complex that the "right" answer may not be intuitive. Many legal (and business) decisions can be materially improved through the design of even a relatively simple decision tree. To model a choice between litigation and settlement, a lawyer can estimate ranges of damage awards and legal fees with some confidence, and she can approximate probabilities of different outcomes based on previous experience with similar cases. Furthermore, most legal decisions are characterized by multiple uncertainties, and decision analysis can be extremely helpful in assessing the relative importance of different issues and stages in a case.

For example, a plaintiff in a complex environmental liability case may have to win several important discovery rulings, survive motions to dismiss and for summary judgment, and succeed in coaching its fact and expert witnesses to testify credibly — all before the case even reaches a jury. In cases where victory is contingent on multiple uncertainties, case value is very hard to assess analytically without the aid of decision analysis. While experienced lawyers can sometimes develop an intuitive sense of what a case is worth, their intuition is usually much less accurate in assessing the impact of a mid-stream change in strategy or particular ruling. Furthermore, intuitive "seat-of-the-pants" valuations are hard to support or explain to clients, and even more so when they are proven wrong. It is for these reasons — accuracy, flexibility, and transparency — that decision analysis can offer significant advantages over traditional "back-of-the-envelope" valuations of cases.

Working with Decision Trees

For legal disputes, decision analysis is used to value the parties' litigation alternatives. A typical decision tree used in litigation typically has two branches: "litigate" or "settle." The settle branch may reflect the other side's most recent offer . . . The litigate branch is generally an extended tree, whose branches represent the different events that may transpire during litigation.

Decision trees are organized chronologically, from left to right. Events are depicted in the tree in the order they are likely to occur. Decision trees contain "nodes." [A "node" represents two or more possible outcomes or choices at a particular point in a case, such as winning or losing at trial.]

The following example represents a situation in which a plaintiff must decide whether to accept a settlement offer of $30,000 or proceed to trial with a chance of recovering $100,000. Assume that you represent the plaintiff, with whom you have a contingent fee arrangement in this lawsuit.

Figure A.

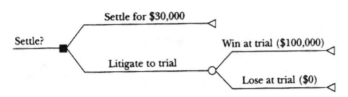

The plaintiff faces two choices — litigate or settle — which are represented by branches. If the plaintiff settles, the inquiry is complete: he will get $30,000 and the dispute will be over. If he chooses to litigate, there are two possible outcomes: win (a payoff of $100,000), and lose (a payoff of $0). For the purposes of this example, all other uncertainties associated with litigation have been ignored. To make this decision intelligently, the plaintiff must assess how likely he is to win if litigation is pursued. The $30,000 settlement offer may be inadequate if the plaintiff has an excellent chance of winning $100,000. However, the offer may be attractive if the chance is low.

Assume that, in the attorney's professional judgment, the plaintiff has a 60% (.6) chance of winning at trial. This probability would be displayed beneath the chance labeled "win." Accordingly, it follows that a probability of 40% (.4) would be displayed beneath the node labeled "lose."

Figure B.

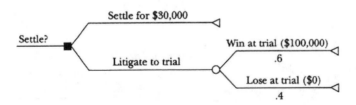

Litigation is apparently preferable to settlement (at least given the current settlement offer) in this case because the probability of winning is more than high enough to warrant gambling at trial. In simple terms, the expected value of a course of action is the average value of taking that course of action many times. If one were to try the identical case one hundred times, and there is a 60% likelihood of a plaintiff's verdict, approximately 60 trials would result in a plaintiff's verdict while 40 would result in a defense verdict. The average recovery would be 60 victories multiplied by $100,000 per victory or $6,000,000, divided by 100 cases, for an average recovery of $60,000.

Walking Through a Slightly More Complex Tree. In more complex cases, there will be more than one layer of nodes, or options. Before the case goes to trial, for example, it may be heard on summary judgment. Thus, there would be a node for summary judgment (granted or denied). Assume a 10% chance that the summary judgment motion will be granted. On the branch of the tree that represents "summary judgment denied," one would find the chance node for liability at trial. Figure C below illustrates how a motion for summary judgment would be interposed between the decision to litigate and the outcome of trial.

Figure C.

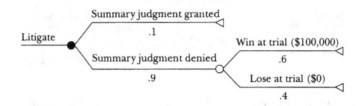

As in all decision trees, the calculations start at the right side. By multiplying the probability of defeat at trial by the payoff, and adding the two figures together, an expected value of $60,000 is calculated (or "rolled back") and displayed next to the node "Summary Judgment denied." Thus, the expected value of the case upon denial of summary judgment is $60,000.

In this case, the plaintiff's expected value of litigation must also take into account the possibility of losing on summary judgment. Thus, the expected value of the litigation is calculated by multiplying the expected value after denial of the motion for summary judgment — $60,000 — by the probability that summary judgment will be denied, 90%. As reflected in figure D below, the expected value of litigation is thus $54,000. The $6,000 difference between this expected value and the expected value in the earlier example reflects the risk that the plaintiff will lose on summary judgment.

Figure D.

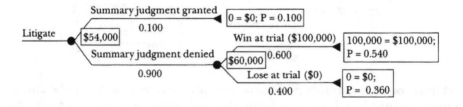

The Analysis Is Only as Good as the Data. It is important to remember that the outcome of any analysis is only as valuable as the input. One must consider carefully the numbers assigned to the range of predicted awards and associated costs at each node. For example, where a party is paying for its attorney's time (not on a contingency fee), lower legal costs should be factored in at the node where summary judgment is granted than at either of the nodes that follow trial. Depending on the level of precision required, one may design a rough-cut model, limiting the range of possibilities and making bold assumptions about damages. Or, one may develop a more refined tree, taking into account numerous possibilities (even if some have low probabilities) and assigning probabilities to different levels of damage awards.

Notwithstanding the inherent imprecision in assigning probabilities to events at trial, the process of designing a decision tree can itself assist in valuing litigation. Thinking through the hurdles to be surmounted in order to prevail can help each side organize its thinking. Furthermore, performing more advanced calculations can identify those issues that have the greatest impact on case value, which can help focus negotiation strategy and research emphasis.

Sensitivity Analysis

Particularly where the parties' assessments on one or two issues diverge widely (from each other's or from the mediator's), it is worth asking how sensitive the case's expected value is to those issues. What if one's assessment of that issue were to change? How much difference would alteration of the assessment make [to case value]? Sensitivity analysis answers such questions, whether done with formal computer-generated graphs or the ubiquitous legal pad and hand calculator.

Before turning to the method, a further explanation of sensitivity analysis is in order. The expected value of a case is derived from its many components. However not all components are equally important; they have different degrees of influence on the expected value. For example, the parties may disagree strenuously on two issues, such as whether a particular witness's testimony would be admitted, or whether lost profits would be the appropriate measure of damages in a business case. Both are uncertainties in the case, and sensitivity analysis could determine how much they matter to the end result. In other words, if one were 100% certain (or 90%, or 70%, or 50%, etc.) that the lost profits measure would be applied, how would that change the expected value? If the expected value is highly sensitive to a given issue, a small change in the probability assigned that issue would lead to a large swing in the expected value of the entire case.

There are two basic and related ways to perform a sensitivity analysis. The first is simply to recalculate the tree, answering the "what if . . . ?" question. Assume that the defendant in the example described earlier disagrees strongly with the assessment of a mere 10% likelihood that the summary judgment motion will be successful. The defendant agrees that summary judgment is a "long shot," but more on the order of 25%. (After all, 10% makes it hard to just-ify the fees for the summary judgment motion.) The mediator might then recalculate the tree, substituting a 25% probability of summary judgment for the original 10%. The resulting change in the expected value would demonstrate its "sensitivity" to the summary judgment issue. Sensitivity analysis can be particularly useful in a mediation context, as discussed in more detail below.

Value of Decision Analysis in Mediation

Decision analysis can play a highly positive role in the discussion, understanding, and impact of the participants' and the mediator's evaluation of the trial alternative. Using decision analysis can [among other advantages]:

- Insure clarity of assessments;
- Reduce perceptions of pressure;
- Provide a rational basis for parting with emotional or extreme cases.

[For example, a] party who has been consistently reassured by counsel that he has a "good case" may be startled (and sobered) to learn that counsel still only assigns it a 55% or 60% chance of success [and therefore a 40 to 45% chance of losing!]. The client may have interpreted counsel's reassurances to mean a 75% or 80% chance of success and justified his vigorous pursuit or defense of the case on that unarticulated assumption. In other instances, a lawyer's assertion that "strong" case is 90 to 95% likely to succeed may cause a more seasoned and realistic client to question the lawyer's judgment and settlement advice.

Decision analysis helps parties escape the feeling that settlement is a personal or corporate concession by transforming it to an individual or business decision. The exercise of creating the decision tree structure and mounting it on a large paper easel or blackboard (or, better yet, on a large computer screen) removes the analysis from the arena of ego and emotion. Working through a decision analysis feels (and is) neutral, rational, and intelligent.

Even where the mediator has provided most of the probability assessments, the decision-analytic method and framework encourages the participants to see themselves as rational actors faced with an important decision problem. While they may not be delighted by the expected value — which they cannot control — the analysis reinforces their control over the settlement decision. When a party decides to adjust its settlement position as a result of the analytical result, that decision feels like an intelligent, rational adoption of the logic of the analysis rather than capitulation to an opponent.

Indeed, it is good practice for a mediator to use decision analysis to formulate his own evaluation of a case, whether or not the method is communicated to the parties. Using decision analysis provides an important check on intuition for the mediator as well.

Technologically Appropriate Choices

For [a lawyer or] mediator who is less than comfortable with high technology, it will be reassuring to learn that decision analysis can be performed on a simple note pad, large easel pad, blackboard, or whiteboard; those who wish to use a computer will find comfort in simple, user-friendly decision analysis software. Using a computer with special decision-tree software is often particularly effective in business disputes because business people tend to have confidence in the computer's ability to generate valuable information. Many learned the principles of decision analysis for business strategy choices in business school. Decision analysis software for evaluating legal/business disputes applies a familiar method in a technology they trust. For other people, who may have had some difficulty embracing the decision-analytic approach or who view computers as alien and suspicious, the pad and the calculator may be the best choice, despite or even because of the slower pace.

C. Evaluation of the Likely Outcome in Adjudication

When bargaining reaches an impasse and the problem seems to stem from disagreements over what will happen in court, many lawyers will ask a mediator to give his opinion about what is likely to occur. Legal issues are not the only topics on which disputants may ask for a mediator's advice. Disputants may also ask a mediator what offer they should make at a particular point, how an offer is likely to be received in the other camp, or what meaning they should assign to an opponent's tactic.

1. Should Mediators Evaluate?

The issue of mediator advice is controversial. Almost no one would argue that mediators should use evaluation as a first resort, and settlement processes that rely solely on evaluation have declined greatly in popularity. Still, the description of commercial mediation techniques assumed that it is appropriate, in some circumstances at least, for a mediator to offer litigants a prediction about the likely outcome of the case if it is adjudicated. Commercial mediators tend to think that offering advice is part of what they have been hired to do, and that in the right circumstances evaluation can be very helpful. Even when parties do not ask for an opinion, commercial neutrals often offer advice on their own initiative. Indeed, in commercial mediation there is often no clear dividing line between the facilitative and evaluative phases of the process.

However, a significant number of neutrals, particularly transformative mediators and mediators trained in family or neighborhood processes, believe that evaluation should not be part of mediation at all. They feel strongly that for a mediator to offer advice, especially about the legal merits or settlement terms, interferes with one of the core values of mediation — the right of parties to make their own decisions about how to proceed and whether to settle. Consider the following perspectives on this issue.

❖ **Lela P. Love, The Top Ten Reasons Why Mediators Should Not Evaluate**

24 Fla. St. U. L. Rev. 937-948 (1997)

. . . The debate over whether mediators should "evaluate" revolves around the confusion over what constitutes evaluation and an "evaluative" mediator. . . . An "evaluative" mediator gives advice, makes assessments, states opinions — including opinions on the likely court outcome, proposes a fair or workable resolution to an issue or the dispute, or presses the parties to accept a particular resolution. The ten reasons that follow demonstrate that those activities are inconsistent with the role of a mediator.

1. *The Roles and Related Tasks of Evaluators and Facilitators Are at Odds*

Evaluating, assessing, and deciding for others is radically different than helping others evaluate, assess, and decide for themselves. Judges, arbitrators, neutral experts, and advisors are evaluators. Their role is to make decisions and give opinions. To do so, they use predetermined criteria to evaluate evidence and arguments presented by adverse parties. The tasks of evaluators include:

finding "the facts" by properly weighing evidence; judging credibility and allocating the burden of proof; determining and applying the relevant law, rule, or custom to the particular situation; and making an award or rendering an opinion. The adverse parties have expressly asked the evaluator — judge, arbitrator, or expert — to decide the issue or resolve the conflict.

In contrast, the role of mediators is to assist disputing parties in making their own decisions and evaluating their own situations. A mediator facilitates communications, promotes understanding, focuses the parties on their interests, and seeks creative problem-solving to enable the parties to reach their own agreement. Mediators push disputing parties to question their assumptions, reconsider their positions, and listen to each other's perspectives, stories, and arguments. They urge the parties to consider relevant law, weigh their own values, principles, and priorities, and develop an optimal outcome. In so doing, mediators facilitate evaluation by the parties.

These differences between evaluators and facilitators mean that each uses different skills and techniques, and each requires different competencies, training norms, and ethical guidelines to perform their respective functions. Further, the evaluative tasks of determining facts, applying law or custom, and delivering an opinion not only divert the mediator away from facilitation, but also can compromise the mediator's neutrality — both in actuality and in the eyes of the parties — because the mediator will be favoring one side in his judgment.

Endeavors are more likely to succeed when the goal is clear and simple and not at war with other objectives. Any task, whether it is the performance of an Olympic athlete, the advocacy of an attorney, or the negotiation assistance provided by a mediator, requires a clear and bright focus and the development of appropriate strategies, skills, and power. In most cases, should the athlete or the attorney or the mediator divert their focus to another task, it will diminish their capacity to achieve their primary goal. "No one can serve two masters." Mediators cannot effectively facilitate when they are evaluating.

2. *Evaluation promotes positioning and polarization, which are antithetical to the goals of mediation....*

3. *Ethical codes caution mediators — and other neutrals — against assuming additional roles....*

4. *If mediators evaluate legal claims and defenses, they must be lawyers; eliminating non-lawyers will weaken the field....*

5. *There are insufficient protections against incorrect mediator evaluations....*

6. *Evaluation abounds: The disputing world needs alternative paradigms....*

7. *Mediator evaluation detracts from the focus on party responsibility for critical evaluation, re-evaluation and creative problem solving....*

8. *Evaluation can stop negotiation....*

9. *A uniform understanding of mediation is critical to the development of the field.* . . .

10. *Mixed processes can be useful, but call them what they are!* . . .

---

2. What Is Evaluation?

One of the issues in this debate is what constitutes "evaluation," as opposed to the less-controversial practice of "reality testing." Consider the following analysis of practice in Australian family mediation.

❖ **Tom Fisher, Advice by Any Other Name**
29 Conflict Resol. Q. 107 (2001)

Within the context of family law mediation [there is a] well documented tension in both practice and in ethical codes between listening and giving advice, between encouraging the client to make decisions, and taking over the decision making process. . . . The Australian community of family law mediators would commonly draw a distinction between providing information, which is acceptable practice, and offering advice, which is not. [However,] it is arguable whether, given the power of a mediator, her suggestions or recommendations may not carry considerable authority. . . .

For example, in a dispute about which parent a child will reside with, a mediator might suggest shared residence. How might this intervention affect the parties, particularly if they know that the mediator is also a psychologist? At first glance, it may appear that simply providing information is less directive and more impartial than offering advice for action. So the mediator might say that recent studies have shown that in general the interests of children of separated parents are best served by frequent contact with their father. Again, how might these words affect party self-determination? In both cases, how impartial might the intervention seem to the mother who has just suggested full residence with herself? . . .

Many mediators are loath to give direct advice, even to clients who indicate they are desperate for it. This reluctance, however well intentioned, may nevertheless mask intervention, used consciously or unconsciously, that is designed to accomplish similar ends. These methods include, among others, creating doubt (usually by posing questions), reframing, and selective facilitation. . . .

Creating doubt

One party might say something like, "I'd rather roast in hell than let that creep see the kids!" A lawyer advising such a client may give direct advice that, according to [legal standards,] children have the right to see both of their parents. A mediator, on the other hand, might seek to create doubt in that party's mind by asking whether the party is familiar with the relevant [law]. Or the mediator might first reframe the comment to manage the emotional content of the message and then might say something like, "I can see you're furious with him for what he's done to you. But what effect would that have on the parenting needs of the children?" In both cases, however, the force of the intervention is somewhat akin to a lawyer's saying, "I must *advise* you that such action is contrary to the interests of the children and the relevant legal principles."

Reframing

Another major formulation is reframing, which occupies an important place in the practical literature and in mediation training courses. Reframing takes the communication of a party and, without abrogating his or her meaning entirely, alters and redirects that meaning to allow for its more constructive use. For example, it can detoxify aggressive language. So when one party says to the other, "Stop sucking at the trough and get a life," the mediator might reframe the outburst as something like, "You'd like Mary to be more self-sufficient." It may shift attention from positions to interests (from "I need the car on Wednesdays" to "So, you need a way to get to the day care center every Wednesday.")

Perhaps the most frequently used and helpful mediator intervention, reframing also carries with it some danger. Because it is an opportunity for the mediator to put words into a client's mouth to forward the mediator's own agenda, the client may experience reframing as manipulative or partisan.

Selective facilitation. Selective facilitation, as originally conceived, refers to how mediator acknowledgment of a party's statement may be used to produce a specific outcome favored by the mediator. For example, there might be an argument over who gets the household appliances, which starts when one former spouse say something like "I'll take the vacuum cleaner, washing machine, microwave, and the dishwasher. You probably never noticed that we had them, since you never did a thing around the house." The other responds with a counterattack on the standard of cleanliness of the house and a homily on the importance of financial contributions to the welfare of the family.

A mediator, particularly one wishing to work in a transformative mode, might choose to ask for mutual emotional acknowledgment from the parties. Perhaps more commonly, the mediator elects to ignore the interchange and say something on the order of "It seems that one area to be dealt with in deciding who gets what is the household appliances." Mediators are almost continuously making choices about what to attend to and what to let pass.

Conclusion. An intervention that casts doubt, reframes, and selectively facilitates communication between parties obviously does not fit [the] definition of giving advice in the narrow sense by recommending a specific course of action. However, it is not simply a process intervention; it is potentially powerful. This kind of intervention forces us to confront [the] critique of the central "myth" perpetuated by mainstream guidelines to mediation practice, that the mediator is a "passive and neutral facilitator." In fact, using such tactics raises the question of the extent to which the mediator is engaging in some sort of dissimulation, using techniques of "deception and manipulation" even if they are intended to help people in conflict view and understand the world around them differently and to help release disputing parties from their self-imposed constraints of limited options. In the end, successful implementation of the balancing act lies with the individual mediator.

Questions

1. Do you think that Professor Love would agree that each of the behaviors described by Tom Fisher is "evaluation"? What might she exclude from this category?
2. Using Fisher's definition, can you think of any time in a role-play or in real life when you have "evaluated" something, even if unintentionally?

3. If a Mediator Does Evaluate, How Should It Be Done?

Assuming that a mediator does evaluate the merits, one key issue is what substantive standard he should apply. There are several possible criteria:

- A mediator can offer a *prediction of what will happen* if a particular issue or the entire matter is adjudicated. Here the mediator is not saying how he personally would decide the issue, but rather is assessing how a judge, jury, or arbitrator in that jurisdiction, with all *their* quirks and foibles, is likely to respond. To put it another way, in this model the mediator is offering a "weather forecast" about the atmosphere in some future courtroom, but not advocating rain. This is the classic form of mediator evaluation.
- Alternatively, a mediator can give an *expert judgment about what happened or a personal view of what is fair*. Here the neutral is assuming the role of advisory arbitrator in the case. This is the most dangerous form of evaluation, because the loser is likely to feel, with some justification, that the neutral has taken sides against him. In any case, the mediator's personal view of a case is almost always irrelevant, since he would be disqualified from sitting in judgment on it.
- Finally, a mediator may not evaluate the legal merits at all, but instead *assess the bargaining situation*. Here the neutral is giving an estimate of what each side needs to do to get an agreement, given the current state of mind of the other party. A neutral might say, for instance, "Given how they are feeling in the other room, my sense is that you'll need to go to six figures if you want a deal today."

The use of decision analysis can make a mediator's evaluation more effective. In the reading excerpted previously, Marjorie Aaron and David Hoffer suggest why:

> The greatest potential harm [in providing an evaluation] is that recipients of the more negative evaluation will thereafter view the mediator as an adversary — as an advocate for the other side or for the evaluation itself. Decision analysis creates a perception of distance between the mediator and the evaluation and thus avoids or mitigates this key risk. Using a decision analysis framework for evaluations shifts the participants' focus literally and figuratively toward the structure of the tree on note pad, blackboard, easel or computer

screen, and toward the task of assigning probability estimates and values at its branches and nodes. These dynamics render it less likely that a negative evaluation will be closely identified with the mediator. Thus despite the evaluation, the mediator's perceived neutrality may remain intact, as is essential in any mediation process.

The following readings discuss how mediators might present evaluations and how parties might react to them.

❖ L. Randolph Lowry, To Evaluate or Not — That Is Not the Question!
2 Resolutions 2 (Pepperdine University) (Winter 1997)

One of the joys of the mediation field is the spirit of debate that takes place regarding approaches to the process. Notable in recent years has been the debate over "evaluation" — the mediator providing an opinion about the case, a perspective on a party's position, or even suggesting an appropriate outcome....I want to suggest that perhaps the question is wrong. In many cases it is not a question as to whether or not evaluation will take place, but more accurately, when and how it does so.

Let me attempt to state the case. First of all, I would contend that all mediators are at least involved in internal "evaluation," in the sense of making judgments on the information presented.... It is the basis on which [they make decisions] regarding the process, the people and the resolution of the problem. Even "facilitative" mediators exercise evaluative judgment internally while deciding how to reframe issues or which areas of questioning to pursue with the objective of bringing the parties to an agreement....

If one concedes the reality that evaluation takes place, then the question changes to whether or not the door is open to reveal the evaluation to the parties.... My strong sense is that mediators not only evaluate internally, but also express some sense of that evaluation during the mediation process. What we argue about, or *should* argue about, is how the evaluation is expressed....

First, evaluation ought to take place at a time when its influence will be greatest. Evaluation is not a tool for the mediator to demonstrate competence. It is not a technique allowing the mediator to manipulate a case in such a way that it comes out as he or she designates. Rather, evaluation is a tool to move parties from positions that have resulted in impasse to positions that are consistent with each other so that a settlement can take place....

Second, the style of evaluation may be critical....

Third, the nature of the evaluation is somewhat affected by the type of relationship the mediator wishes to establish with those involved in the mediation.... While a relationship is important for some, it is not important for others.

Fourth, there may be a strong connection between the nature of evaluation and the type of claim involved in the mediation process. For instance, a claim in which the alternative is extraordinarily clear may allow the mediator greater confidence and promote more willingness to be evaluative. In cases where there is no clear external alternative . . . a basis for evaluation may not exist.

Fifth, the method of evaluation may make a difference as well. For instance, if the case turns on the dollar amount of a damage award, one option would be for the mediator simply to state [her opinion.] An alternative would be to arrive at the same place through a series of questions. . . . For instance, in a personal injury case one might ask,

- "What is the jury verdict range for these kinds of cases?"
- "What is the settlement range for these kinds of cases?"
- "Does the existence of a particular fact increase or decrease the likelihood of being at the top of that settlement range?"
- "If that fact has that influence, does it not then affect the real settlement range?"
- "If that is the real settlement range, does it not seem reasonable to lower your demand so that you . . . attract . . . the insurance company to meet you there . . . ?"

Such questioning can be expressed in an almost indicting spirit or . . . in the spirit of one . . . seeking to understand and massage the process in such a way that parties can come together. In any event, the mediator has never made a statement as to his or her opinion directly, but has reflected it in questions.

While others debate [the] abstract question of whether there is a place for evaluation in mediation, I invite you to join me in a more pragmatic examination of when and how some level of evaluation should be manifested.

Questions

3. Do Professor Lowry's arguments answer any of Professor Love's concerns? Which concerns are not addressed?
4. The Supreme Court of Virginia has adopted the following rule for court mediators:

   The mediator may offer legal information if all parties are present, or separately if they consent, and shall inform unrepresented parties or those parties who are not accompanied by legal counsel about the importance of reviewing the mediator's legal information with legal counsel. Also, the mediator may offer evaluation of strengths and weaknesses of positions only if such evaluation is incidental to the facilitative role and does not interfere with the mediator's impartiality or the self-determination of the parties.

   Does this rule respond to Professor Love's concerns about evaluation? Which ones?

Will a disputant's reaction to an evaluation differ depending on what issue the mediator evaluates, or the reasons the neutral gives for an opinion? Consider the following survey of parties' reactions to evaluation in court-connected mediation programs.

❖ **Roselle P. Wissler, To Evaluate or Facilitate? Parties' Perceptions of Mediation Affected by Mediator Style**

7 Disp. Resol. Mag. 35 (Winter 2001)

Some commentators have argued that if a mediator evaluates the merits of a case instead of using a more purely facilitative approach, the parties will feel that the mediator is less neutral. The parties will also have less opportunity to participate in the mediation process and to determine its outcome, will not gain a better understanding of the other side's position and their own interests, and will be less satisfied with mediation. Four recent studies of mediation in civil and domestic relations cases provide the opportunity to empirically test the effect of mediator style on parties' perceptions....

One of the studies involved 708 general jurisdiction civil trial cases mediated by court-employed attorney-mediators in three Ohio courts. A second study of civil cases involved 698 cases mediated by volunteer attorney-mediators during Settlement Week in four different Ohio courts. The third and fourth studies involved domestic relations cases mediated in 13 Maine courts [and] six Ohio courts. In this article, I report findings that occurred in [two] or more of the studies. No consistent differences were observed in the pattern of findings between the studies of civil cases and the studies of domestic relations cases.

When the mediator evaluated the merits of the case, no negative effects on parties' perceptions of mediation or the mediator were observed in any of the studies. Instead ... parties were more likely to say that the mediation process was fair and the mediator understood their views. They were also more likely to say that they had enough opportunity to express their views, had input in determining the outcome, were satisfied with the outcome and gained a better understanding of their own interests. Importantly, parties who reported that the mediator evaluated the case did not feel more pressure to settle.

In contrast, when the mediator recommended a particular settlement, parties were *less* likely to say that the mediation process was fair and the mediator was neutral [and] parties were more likely to feel pressured to settle.

When the mediator suggested possible options for settlement, parties were more likely to say that the mediation process was fair and that the mediator was neutral and understood their view. By far the strongest and most consistently positive effects on parties' perceptions were observed when the mediator encouraged the parties to express their feelings and summarized what they said. (These actions were examined only in the domestic relations studies.)

In summary, if the mediators evaluated the merits of the case and even made some suggestions about possible settlements, the parties had more favorable perceptions of mediation with virtually no negative repercussions, as long as the mediators did not recommend a specific settlement.

Questions

5. According to Professor Wissler, which kinds of evaluation are likely to lead to negative reactions from litigants, and which are not? Assuming that parties do not object to certain forms of evaluation, does this answer Professor Love's concerns?
6. Imagine that you are the defense counsel in the MIT student death case. Can you imagine circumstances in which you would want the mediator to give an evaluation? If so, what issues would you wish to have evaluated?
7. Now assume that you are counsel for the plaintiffs in the same case. How, if at all, might an evaluation be useful to your side?
8. If you agree with Professor Love, how would you want a mediator to respond to a situation in which you and your opposing counsel disagreed vehemently about the likely outcome at trial, and you thought the other lawyer was being unrealistic? What if your own client appeared to be unrealistically optimistic about the chances of winning in court?

Problems

Read the following exchanges, taken from the mediation of a commercial breach of warranty case. The plaintiff entered the mediation with a demand of $1.5 million, based on out-of-pocket damages of about $250,000; a request for an additional $200,000, representing intangible damages; and a claim that the defendant was subject to trebling of these damages under an unfair business practices statute. The defense has made no offer of settlement. The mediator has formed an initial impression that the plaintiff will face significant obstacles in proving liability, will find it difficult to establish damages beyond the out-of-pocket sum, and has little to no chance of winning its treble damages claim. As to each exchange, ask yourself:

- Is the mediator performing an "evaluation," or merely "reality testing"?
- What issues are being evaluated?
- Is the mediator acting in a manner likely to incur resentment?

1. A Caucus Meeting with the Defense

Mediator: Well, all right, you heard the frustration from the plaintiff side, and you said you were surprised by it. What I'm hearing from [the vice president of the plaintiff company] is that he feels that there has never been a dialogue, acknowledgment of their difficulties and, most importantly to them, I guess, an offer of cash to settle this dispute. I'm hearing from you that you are not willing to make a specific settlement offer at this point. If you can't authorize me to bring back a specific number to the plaintiff . . . what I'd like to have is a feel for the range that you are in that I could communicate to them, so that they would have a sense of where things are going.

Defense counsel: We will respond if they come down to a range of reasonableness, but their demand of $1.5 million is just in the stratosphere. I know that you're experienced, and I'm going to rely on you to digest what our view of the damages are and speak to them and maybe tell them what the real world is like: A million five is just not the real world.

Mediator: Well, what if the plaintiff were willing at this point to accept an amount that would allow them to recoup their out of pocket costs, and were perhaps looking for a little bit extra to put away in case their soft damages become a reality: Would you think that was a more reasonable place for them to be?

Defense counsel: Well, that would be a more reasonable place for them to start, and then we have to discount that number for the risk that they won't be able to prove liability at all.

2. Meeting with the Plaintiff

Plaintiff counsel: The bottom line is — what is their bottom line? What's their offer? That's what we have been trying to get at for two years.

Mediator: I think there is a number that they would pay, which maybe will turn out to be a number that you would accept. But they haven't told me what it is yet. I don't think you're going to find out what they'll pay unless you get past this impasse. I see you as being at an impasse so far because they see you as "up in the clouds," and because you see them as completely recalcitrant "stones" who won't offer a thing. In fact, I don't see them as stones refusing to deal — I think they *will* deal. But they want to have some confidence that they are in the right universe with you, and if I can give them that confidence, then we'll get a number out of them. A better indication of what you're really looking for is what I need.

3. Second Meeting with the Defense

Mediator: What is it going to cost to try this case?

Defense counsel: Oh, about $25,000.

Mediator: Wow, that's a bargain . . . You really think you can do it for that?

Counsel: Most of the discovery is done, and my rates are reasonable.

Mediator: Well, you're going to need an expert . . . They'll get an expert . . . It'll get expensive.

4. Meeting with the Defense Late in the Process

Inside counsel: You don't have to do this now, but if at some point if you could explain to me if you think we are being too optimistic about our chances at trial. I just don't see very much risk here.

Mediator: Well, I think the following . . . So far, the court has been willing to accept the plaintiff's case on their "res ipsa" theory that incidents of this type just don't occur without somebody being negligent. It looks as if the judge will let the case go to the jury on that theory. As a result, I think you run the risk that the jury will seize the appealing simplicity of the plaintiff's argument, and if it does it will find against you. You have a credible, viable defense, and I think that this significantly reduces the likelihood that the plaintiff will prevail. But the likelihood that the other side will win on liability, given their *res ipsa* argument, is probably at least 50-50, and maybe better than that.

Quite apart from the issues of policy raised by the use of evaluation in mediation are the practical questions that it raises for lawyers. As counsel to a disputant, you may encounter the issue in several ways:

- First, do you want your mediator to give an evaluation? If so, at what point in the process, and about what issues?
- Is the other side likely to ask for evaluative feedback? If so, how should you deal with such a request?
- Is the mediator likely to offer evaluative comments on his own initiative? Is there anything you can do to influence his decision?
- What do you want the mediator to know or see before he makes such comments?

We discuss these issues, and how a lawyer can use evaluation in mediation to best advantage, in Chapter 11.

PART
III

THE ADVOCATE'S ROLE

CHAPTER
10

Representing Clients: Preparation

A. Introduction

The next two chapters focus on the lawyer's role in mediation. We have described how the mediation process can facilitate disputants' ability to communicate and bargain with each other. We now explore how advocates can use the process to best advantage.

Lawyers' expectations upon entering mediation, and the tactics they use when working with mediators, are changing in significant ways. A decade ago lawyers approached mediation like the settlement processes with which they were more familiar — direct bargaining and settlement conferences conducted by judges. In the "direct bargaining" model of mediation, each party's assent to mediate is a signal: By committing to engage in an expensive and time-consuming process, parties confirm to each other that they are serious about exploring settlement. Lawyers in the direct bargaining model often see the process, particularly caucusing, as a way to bargain competitively and positionally with less aggravation and risk of impasse than would exist if they were using the same tactics in direct bargaining.

In the "settlement conference" model, attorneys assume that the mediator will set the agenda and control the discussion. They expect to be allowed to argue their cases, then adjourn to caucuses and engage in positional bargaining. In this model the mediator is expected to evaluate the case. Particularly if a mediator gives a "hard" evaluation ("This case is worth "X" dollars"), it is likely to amount to a take-it-or-leave-it offer to both litigants.

These concepts of mediation are still prevalent, but lawyers increasingly approach the process in other ways. They are more likely to expect mediators to play a wide variety of roles. They also see themselves as bargaining not simply with the other side, but also with the mediator, in a three-sided process. Attorneys bargain with neutrals, for example, over what the mediator will say about their offers to their opponent, what she will tell them about the attitudes of persons in the other camp, and whether and how the mediator will employ impasse-breaking tactics such as evaluation or a mediator's proposal.

Mediated negotiations sometimes have more than three sides. Lawyers may view their own client as impaired and unable to make good bargaining or settlement decisions. They sometimes enlist mediators to help persuade, and sometimes manipulate, a "difficult" or "unrealistic" client to make the "right" decision. These lawyers generally see themselves as acting in their clients' best interests. Still, by asking mediators to become allies in their interactions with clients, they make the mediation process much more complex for the neutral. We explore the practical issues raised by these tactics in Chapter 11, and the ethical concerns they present in Chapter 12.

1. Identifying Goals

In planning for mediation, the first important issue to decide at the outset is what goal your client wants to achieve in a case. Is the client seeking the best possible monetary outcome? An imaginative solution? Repair of a relationship? Your goals in mediation will strongly influence the approach you take to the process and how you relate to the mediator.

As we have noted, disputants' goals in mediation vary widely. An organization that advocates the use of ADR in business disputes stresses that: "Mediation provides a framework for parties to ... achieve remedies that may be outside the scope of the judicial process...maintain privacy...preserve or minimize damage to relationships and reduce the costs and delay of dispute resolution" (CPR Institute 1999). By contrast, a prominent tort lawyer, exemplifying a more traditional approach, describes mediation as "an opportunity — a time for you, as the legal representative of your client, to avoid putting your client through the litigation 'mill' ... and get results. ... It is a means of essentially 'selling' your client's lawsuit to a buyer, who buys off the expense and exposure of an ongoing lawsuit. The client has the money to begin the life restructuring process and has avoided the pressures and uncertainties of litigation..." (Kornblum 2004).

If you see your objective as solving a problem or repairing a relationship, you will be inclined to treat the mediator almost as a member of your team, revealing your interests and soliciting the neutral's advice about how to achieve them. If the focus is on relationship repair, both lawyer and mediator may gradually withdraw as the process progresses to give the parties an opportunity to relearn how to communicate positively. If, however, your goal is to obtain the best possible monetary settlement, your relationship with the mediator will be more complex. You can continue to take advantage of the neutral's knowledge, for example, by asking about hidden obstacles, and as long as you employ genuinely principled bargaining techniques, you will be able to work together cooperatively. At the point, however, that you begin to compete with the other side for the best possible terms, your goal and that of the neutral will diverge, because the mediator cannot take sides. Indeed, competitive bargainers talk about "spinning" a mediator to advance their client's objectives.

Legal mediators have significant power, whether or not they decide to use it. Although mediators cannot compel parties to settle, they can greatly influence the *process* of bargaining, opening opportunities for advocates to mold the process to their clients' needs. We believe that whatever their goals, lawyers can use the mediation process to advantage by approaching it actively and keeping in mind its special characteristics.

Questions

1. Which of these concepts of mediation goals felt most appropriate when you began this course? Has your perspective changed?
2. When you enter practice, what goals do you think your clients will want to achieve through mediation?

Problem 1

Your client is a business in a dispute with a supplier of IP services over the quality of the supplier's performance under a contract. Given the expected costs of litigating the issue, you have recommended that the client consider mediating before a complaint is filed, and the client has reluctantly agreed.

The client sees the goal as simply to collect as much as possible for the interruptions in its activities and lost profits caused by the supplier's bad work, damages it has estimated at $1.5 million. The client would also like to recoup as much as possible of the roughly $500,000 it has paid the supplier so far, and secure cancellation of its obligation to pay $200,000 more that is due under the contract terms. You see the merits of the case as doubtful, however; the rupture seems to have been caused more by ambiguities in the scope of work in the contract and the rigid approach taken by the client's IP director, than by lack of competence in the supplier — although the supplier's performance can certainly be faulted. You also doubt that, as a practical matter, the supplier could ever pay the lost profits claim and return of fees that your client is seeking, even if you won. You also see ways in which the supplier could continue to provide services, and think that this would respond to your client's actual injuries much more effectively than a lawsuit.

(a) How would you raise this issue with the client?
(b) What would you say about goals in mediation and the process best suited to accomplishing them?

2. An Overview of Strategy

We believe that over time more lawyers and parties will come to view bargaining primarily as a method of problem solving. At present, however, most attorneys who use mediation are litigators who see the process mainly as a way to facilitate money bargaining. To prepare for what you are likely to encounter in practice, we examine how counsel should approach a mediation process that includes interest-based elements, but is dominated by competitive bargaining over money. To provide you with tools to adapt to the future, we first discuss how to represent a client in a process focused on problem solving.

a. Problem-Solving Approaches

❖ **Harold Abramson, Mediation Representation:**
Advocating in a Problem-Solving Process

NITA 1-3 (2004)

The mediation process is indisputably different from other dispute resolution processes. Therefore, the strategies and techniques that have proven so effective in settlement conferences, arbitrations, and judicial trials do not work optimally in mediation. You need a different representation approach.... Instead of advocating as a zealous adversary, you should advocate as a zealous problem-solver....

[I]n mediation there is no third party decisionmaker, only a third party facilitator. The third party is not even the primary audience. The primary audience is the other side, who is surely not neutral and can often be quite hostile. In this different representational setting, the adversarial approach is less effective, if not self-defeating. Many sophisticated and experienced litigators realize that mediation calls for a different approach, but they still muddle through mediation sessions. They are learning on the job....

As a problem-solver...you do more than just try to settle the dispute. You creatively search for solutions that go beyond the traditional ones based on rights, obligations, and precedent. Rather than settling for win-lose outcomes, you search for solutions that can benefit both sides. To creatively problem-solve in mediation, you develop a collaborative relationship with the other side and the mediator, and participate throughout the mediation process in a way that is likely to result in solutions that are enduring as well as inventive....

You should be a constant problem-solver. It is relatively easy to engage in simple problem-solving moves such as responding to a demand with the question "why?" in order to bring to the surface the other party's interests. But it is much more difficult to stick to this approach throughout the mediation process, especially when faced with an adversarial, positional opponent. Trust the problem-solving approach. And, when the other side engages in adversarial tactics — a frequent occurrence in practice — you should react with problem-solving responses, responses that might even convert the other side into a problem-solver.

Also strive to create a problem-solving process when your mediator does not. Your mediator may fail to follow this approach (even though he professes to foster one) because he lacks the depth of experience or training to tenaciously maintain a consistent approach throughout the mediation process. Or, your mediator may candidly disclose his practice of deliberately switching tactics based on the needs of the parties — a philosophy that...undermines the problem-solving approach.

Finally, for the skeptics who think that problem-solving does not work for most legal cases because they are primarily about money, I offer three responses. First, the endless debate about whether or not legal disputes are primarily about money is distracting. Whether a dispute is largely about money varies from case to case. You have little chance of discovering whether your client's dispute is about more than money if you approach the dispute as if it is only about money. Such a preconceived view, backed by a narrowly focused adversarial strategy, will likely blind you to other parties' needs and inventive solutions....

Second, if the dispute or any remaining issues at the end of the day turn out to be predominately about money, then at least you will have followed a representation approach that may have created a hospitable environment for dealing with the money issues. A hospitable environment can even be beneficial when there is no expectation of a continuing relationship between the disputing parties. Third, the problem-solving approach provides a framework for resolving money issues....

In short, the problem-solving approach provides a comprehensive and coherent approach to representation that can guide you throughout the mediation process. By sticking to this approach, you will be prepared to deal with the myriad of unanticipated challenges that inevitably arise as mediation unfolds.

---

b. Commercial Mediation Processes

Most litigators approach what we call "commercial" mediation in a predominantly adversarial frame of mind. We begin with a reading that focuses on some errors that this mind-set can produce. Inherent in this list, however, are messages about what lawyers can do to be effective in mediation. As you read, ask yourself:

- Have you made any of these mistakes in a role-play exercise? Can you imagine making them in a real case?
- How do Tom Arnold's assumptions about the nature of mediation differ from those of Professor Abramson?

❖ Tom Arnold, Twenty Common Errors in Mediation Advocacy
13 Alternatives 69 (1995)

Trial lawyers who are unaccustomed to being mediation advocates often miss important opportunities. Here are twenty common errors, and ways to correct them.

Problem: Wrong Client in the Room

CEOs settle more cases than vice presidents, house counsel, or other agents. Why? For one thing, they don't need to worry about criticism back at the office. Any lesser agent, even with explicit "authority," typically must please a constituency which was not a participant in the give and take of the mediation. That makes it hard to settle cases.

A client's personality also can be a factor. A "Rambo" who is highly self-confident, aggressive, critical, unforgiving, or self-righteous doesn't tend to be conciliatory. The best peace-makers show patience, creativity and sometimes tolerance for the mistakes of others. Of course, it also helps to know the subject.

Problem: Wrong Lawyer in the Room

Many capable trial lawyers are so confident that they can persuade a jury of anything (after all, they've done it before) that they discount the importance of preserving relationships, as well as the common exorbitant costs and emotional drain of litigation. They can smell a "win" in the court room, and so approach mediation with a measure of ambivalence. Transactional lawyers, in contrast, having less confidence in their trial outcome, sometimes are better mediation counsel. At a minimum, parties should look for sensitive, flexible, understanding people who will do their homework, no matter what their job experience. Good preparation makes for more and better settlements. A lawyer who won't prepare is the wrong lawyer. Good mediation lawyers also should be good risk evaluators and not averse to making reasonable risk assumptions.

Problem: Wrong Mediator in the Room

Some mediators are generous about lending their conference rooms, but bring nothing to the table. Some of them determine their view of the case and like an arbitrator urge the parties to accept that view without exploring likely win-win alternatives. The best mediators can work within a range of styles described by Leonard L. Riskin. As Mr. Riskin described them, these styles fall along a continuum from being totally facilitative, to offering an evaluation of the case, to being highly directive and adjudicative. Ideally, mediators should fit the mediation style to the case and the parties before them, often moving from style to style as a mediation progresses, relatively more facilitative at the beginning and more instructive or directive as the end comes into view. Masters of the questioning process can render valuable services whether or not they have relevant substantive expertise.

When do the parties need an expert? When do they want an evaluative mediator, or someone of relevant technical experience who can cast meaningful lights and shadows on the merits of the case and alternative settlements? It may not always be possible to know and evaluate a mediator and fit the choice of mediator to your case. But the wrong mediator may fail to get a settlement another mediator might have finessed.

Problem: Wrong Case

Almost every type of case, from antitrust or patent infringement to unfair competition and employment disputes, is a likely candidate for mediation. Occasionally, cases don't fit the mold, not because of the substance of the dispute, but because one or both parties want to set a precedent. For example, a franchisor that needs a legal precedent construing a key clause that is found in 3,000 franchise agreements might not want to submit the case to mediation. Likewise, an infringement suit early in the life of an uncertain patent might be better resolved in court; getting the Federal Circuit stamp of validity could generate industry respect not obtainable from ADR.

Problem: Omitting Client Preparation

Lawyers should educate their clients about the process and the likely questions the mediator will ask. At the same time, they need to understand that the other party (rather than the mediator) should be the focus of each side's presentation. [Note: Tom Arnold gives more detailed advice about client preparation later in this chapter.]

Problem: Not Letting a Client Open for Herself

At least as often as not, letting the properly coached client do most or even all of the opening, and tell the story in her own words, works much better than lengthy openings by the lawyer.

Problem: Addressing the Mediator Instead of the Other Side

Most lawyers open the mediation with a statement directed at the mediator, comparable to opening statements to a judge or jury. Highly adversarial in tone, it overlooks the interests of the other side that gave rise to the dispute. Why is this strategy a mistake? The "judge" or "jury" you should be trying to persuade in mediation is not so much the mediator as the adversary. If you want to make the other party sympathetic to your cause, most often at least it is best not to hurt him. For the same reason, plenary sessions should demonstrate your client's humanity, respect, warmth, apologies, and sympathy. Stay away from inflammatory issues, which are better addressed by the mediator in private caucuses with the other side.

Problem: Making the Lawyer the Center of the Process

Unless the client is highly unappealing or inarticulate, the client should be the center of the process. The company representative for the other side may not have attended depositions, so is unaware of the impact your client could have on a judge or jury if the mediation fails. People pay more attention to appealing plaintiffs, so show them off.

Prepare the client to speak and be spoken to by the mediator and the adversary. He should be able to explain why he feels the way he does, why he is or is not responsible, and why any damages he caused are great or only peanuts. But he should also consider extending empathy to the other party.

Problem: Failure to Use Advocacy Tools Effectively

You'll want to prepare your materials for maximum persuasive impact. Exhibits, charts, and copies of relevant cases or contracts with key phrases highlighted can be valuable visual aids. A ninety-second video showing one or more key witnesses in depositions making important admissions, followed by a readable-sized copy of an important document with some relevant language underlined, can pack a punch.

Problem: Timing Mistakes

Get and give critical discovery, but don't spend exorbitant time or sums in discovery and trial prep before seeking mediation. Mediation can identify what's truly necessary discovery and avoid unnecessary discovery.

One of my own war stories: With a mediation under way and both parties relying on their perception of the views of a certain neutral vice president who had no interest in the case, I leaned over, picked up the phone, called the vice president, introduced myself as the mediator, and asked whether he could give us a deposition the following morning. "No," said he, "I've got a board meeting at 10:00." "How about 7:30 A.M., with a one-hour limit?" I asked. "It really is pretty important that this decision not be delayed." The parties took the deposition and settled the case before the 10:00 board meeting.

Problem: Failure to Listen to the Other Side

Many lawyers and clients seem incapable of giving open-minded attention to what the other side is saying. That could cost a settlement.

Problem: Failure to Identify Perceptions and Motivations

Seek first to understand, only then to be understood. [B]rainstorm to determine the other party's motivations and perceptions. Prepare a chart summarizing how your adversary sees the issues: Part of preparing for mediation is to understand your adversary's perceptions and motivations, perhaps even listing them in chart form. Here is an example, taken from a recent technology dispute:

Plaintiff's Perceptions:	*Defendant's Perceptions:*
Defendant entered the business because of my sound analysis of the market, my good judgment and convictions about the technology.	I entered the business based on my own independent analysis of the market and the appropriate technology that was different from plaintiff's....
Defendant used me by pretending to be interested in doing business with me.	Plaintiff misled me with exaggerated claims that turned out to be false.
Defendant made a low-ball offer for my valuable technology. Another company paid me my asking price.	I made plaintiff a fair offer; I later paid less for alternative technology that was better.

Problem: Hurting, Humiliating, Threatening, or Commanding

Don't poison the well from which you must drink to get a settlement. That means you don't hurt, humiliate, or ridicule the other folks. Avoid pejoratives like "malingerer," "fraud," "cheat," "crook," or "liar." You can be strong on what your evidence will be and still be a decent human being. All settlements are based upon trust to some degree. If you anger the other side, they won't trust you. This inhibits settlement.

The same can be said for threats, like a threat to get the other lawyer's license revoked for pursuing such a frivolous cause, or for his grossly inaccurate pleadings. Ultimatums destroy the process and destroy credibility. Yes, there is a time in mediation to walk out — whether or not you plan to return. But a series of ultimatums, or even one ultimatum, most often is counterproductive.

Problem: The Backwards Step

A party who offered to pay $300,000 before the mediation, but comes to the mediation table willing to offer only $200,000, injures its own credibility and engenders bad feelings from the other side. Without some clear and dramatic reasons for the reduction in the offer, it can be hard to overcome the damage done. The backwards step is a powerful card to play at the right time — a walk away without yet walking out. But powerful devices are also dangerous. There are few productive occasions to use this one, and they tend to come late in a mediation. A rule of thumb: Unless you're an expert negotiator, don't do it.

Problem: Too Many People

Advisors — people to whom the decision-maker must display respect and courtesy, people who feel that since they are there they must put in their two bits worth — all delay mediation immeasurably. A caucus that with only one lawyer and vice president would take twenty minutes, with five people could take an hour and twenty minutes. What could have been a one-day mediation stretches to two or three.

This is one context in which I use the "one martini lunch." Once I think that everyone present understands all the issues, I will send principals who have been respectful out to negotiate alone. Most come back within three hours with an oral expression of settlement. Of course, the next step is to brush up on details they overlooked, draw up a written agreement and get it signed. But usually those finishing touches don't ruin the deal.

Problem: Closing Too Fast

A party who opens at $1 million and moves immediately to $500,000 gives the impression of having more to give. Rightly or wrongly, the other side probably will not accept the $500,000 offer because they expect more give. By contrast, moving from $1 million to $750,000, $600,000, $575,000, $560,000, $550,000, sends no message of yield below $500,000, and may induce a $500,000 proposal that can be accepted. The "dance" is part of communication. Skip the dance, lose the communication, and risk losing settlement at your own figure.

Problem: Failure to Truly Close

Unless parties have strong reasons to "sleep on" their agreement, to further evaluate the deal, or to check on possibly forgotten details, it is better to get some sort of enforceable contract written and signed before the parties separate. Too often, when left to think overnight and draft tomorrow, the parties think of new ideas that delay or prevent closing.

Problem: Breaching Confidentiality

Sometimes parties to mediation unthinkingly, or irresponsibly, disclose in open court information revealed confidentially in a mediation. When information is highly sensitive, consider keeping it confidential with the mediator. Or if revealed to the adversary in a mediation where the case did not settle, consider moving before the trial begins for an order in limine to bind both sides to the confidentiality agreement.

Problem: Lack of Patience and Perseverance

The mediation "dance" takes time. Good mediation advocates have patience and perseverance.

Problem: Misunderstanding Conflict

A dispute is a problem to be solved together, not a combat to be won.

Questions

3. Have you made any of Tom Arnold's errors in an exercise in this course?
4. Which errors are you most likely to make in an actual case?

5. Can you recast Arnold's errors as statements about how to be effective in mediation?

B. Entering the Process

1. Whether to Mediate

The first strategy issue in mediation advocacy is whether to mediate at all. Although we have emphasized what mediation can contribute to bargaining efforts, it is not appropriate for every case or at every stage of a dispute. Arnold, for example, suggests that mediation may not make sense if one side would benefit greatly from obtaining a precedent to set a pattern for future disputes — and, of course, is confident that it will get a favorable one. John Cooley gives other criteria for whether or not to mediate.

❖ John Cooley, Mediation Advocacy
NITA 38-39 (2002)

[The following are] some situational indicators favorable to a mediated settlement of a dispute. The presence of only one of these indicators (and the absence of any unfavorable indicators) may be sufficient to trigger scheduling of mediation.

- The parties and counsel are agreeable to participating in the mediation process and desire a prompt settlement.
- The parties will have to maintain a direct or indirect relationship after resolution of a dispute.
- Sufficient discovery has occurred to make settlement discussions meaningful.
- The parties desire to minimize litigation costs.
- In addition to or instead of damages, the parties desire a remedy that is non-monetary or one that the court cannot provide.
- The parties wish to avoid establishing a judicial precedent or a judgment.... The parties or their lawyers have difficulty initiating negotiations with the other side, lack adequate negotiation skills, or are deadlocked....
- The parties have differing appraisals of the facts of a case.
- Resolution requires complex trade-offs.
- The parties want the matter settled confidentially.

[By contrast, the] presence of one of these indicators could be a sufficient basis to decline using mediation to resolve a particular dispute.

- A party cannot effectively represent its best interests and will not be represented by counsel at the mediation sessions.
- The parties have a history of acting in bad faith in negotiations.
- A party seeks to establish legal precedent or a judgment with preclusive effect.
- Significant parties are unwilling to mediate.

- The parties are engaged in a dispute directly affecting the public interest, and the government is not represented.
- A party is threatening to press criminal charges.
- One or more parties stand to gain from a strategy of delay.
- A party needs more formal discovery to obtain necessary information....
- The parties have rigid assessments of the law applicable in the case and desire the court to decide who is right and who is wrong, legally.
- A third party neutral needs to make an immediate decision to protect the interests of a disputant or of the public.

It is worth bearing in mind that Cooley's factors apply mainly to decisions about whether to use mediation for the purpose of settling a dispute. Lawyers sometimes elect to mediate for other reasons, such as to set up an efficient discovery plan or to improve the parties' overall relationship. The fact that a settlement does not appear realistic at a certain point, in other words, is not always a reason to reject mediation.

2. *When to Mediate*

Assuming that mediation is appropriate, when is the right time to undertake it? Sometimes there is no choice: Parties may be required to mediate by a contract clause or court order, and in such circumstances the issue of timing is academic. If a disputant does have a choice, however, the issue is an important one. To answer the question, you and your client must again consider your goals for the process. If your primary objective is to solve a problem or restore a relationship, it is usually best to mediate as soon as possible. If not, the parties' positions are likely to harden, and one of them may replace the relationship with a new one, making a repair nearly impossible.

If relationships are not a priority, then the issue of timing is more complex. By delaying mediation, an advocate may be able to improve her client's bargaining position, for instance, by winning a round in court. But in doing so the client will incur costs, and her opponent may react in kind. As we know, the U.S. legal system does not ordinarily allow litigants to recover their legal expenses and makes no provision for the nonlegal costs of conflict. As a result, parties must "swallow" any expenses that they incur in an effort to improve their bargaining position. The phenomenon of loss aversion then becomes an even greater obstacle to agreement.

Disputants tend to enter legal mediation at particular points along the litigation continuum, in particular when they face either a sharp increase in cost or the risk of a significant loss in adjudication. Natural points for mediation are before a formal legal action is filed, after preliminary discovery, in the shadow of a significant court ruling, and shortly before trial.

Before a Formal Legal Action Is Filed

A supplier and customer involved in a dispute over the quality of goods supplied under a contract, for example, may opt to mediate to minimize the damage to a profitable relationship and avoid the expense of hiring outside law firms. Likewise, a discharged employee may decide to mediate before filing a charge of discrimination with a state agency, to avoid the inflamed feelings that often result from such a step. Whenever disputants decide to enter mediation before filing a lawsuit, they accept a trade-off: Each side has less information about the case, but also has avoided the cost of litigating to obtain it. Parties appear to be electing to enter mediation before filing suit with increasing frequency.

After Preliminary Discovery

Parties may file suit and undertake some discovery — for example an exchange of documents — but enter mediation at the point they face more costly and adversarial processes such as depositions. In essence, the parties' common wish to avoid a higher level of conflict serves as a "settlement event." Thus Jeffrey Senger of the U.S. Justice Department has written that:

> One approach...is to follow the 80-20 rule: 80 percent of the relevant information that parties learn from discovery often comes from the first 20 percent of the money they spend. Tracking down the last, difficult-to-obtain data is the most expensive part of discovery....If parties conduct initial core discovery, they may find all they need to know in order to resolve the case appropriately. Following this approach, parties can agree to take abbreviated depositions of the key witnesses and then proceed to ADR. If necessary, they also may serve certain essential interrogatories and requests for production of vital documents. Often this will give them everything they need to determine their negotiation position with reasonable accuracy....(Senger 2004)

In the Shadow of a Significant Ruling

Parties sometimes elect to mediate when they are approaching a significant stage in the court process, such as a motion for summary judgment. In such situations, each side knows that its bargaining position will either improve or deteriorate, depending on the court's decision. One might think that if one side were willing to mediate because it fears a loss, its opponent would refuse in hope of obtaining a gain. As we have seen, however, humans are generally much more sensitive to losing than to winning, and as a result both parties in a case are often motivated to mediate at the point they face the risk of a significant loss in adjudication.

Shortly Before Trial

This has been the traditional point at which to pursue settlement, either through direct bargaining or mediation, for several reasons. First, as trial approaches, attorneys must prepare intensively, imposing higher costs on them or their clients. Second, trial represents the ultimate win-or-lose event, triggering feelings of loss aversion. Finally, there are cultural assumptions about the "right" time to broach settlement: In the legal community, this used to mean that mentioning mediation early in a case was considered a sign of weakness, while raising the issue on the eve of trial was acceptable, an assumption that no longer appears to be true.

3. How to Initiate the Process

In the past, lawyers were often reluctant to propose mediation, out of concern that an adversary would see it as a sign of weakness. That attitude has largely disappeared — as one litigator remarked in Chapter 5, many lawyers now find it easier to propose mediation than to suggest direct negotiation. Lawyers have several options for initiating the process.

Point out that Settlement Discussions Are Inevitable

Given the phenomenon of the "vanishing" civil trial described in Chapter 1, settlement discussions are nearly inevitable at some point. You like to litigate — it's what you do for a living. But given that the parties will be talking settlement sooner or later in any event, why not do it now and save everyone the distraction and expense of litigation?

Rely on a Policy

If a lawyer represents an organization that has a uniform policy of exploring ADR early in every dispute, she can cite the policy as the reason for suggesting mediation. The most prominent example is the "CPR Pledge," which appears at *www.cpradr.org*. More than 4,000 companies have signed this pledge, and 1,500 law firms have signed a similar commitment to explore ADR with their clients in appropriate cases.

Cite a Rule

Some court systems require counsel to discuss ADR or to make a good-faith effort at settlement in every case. Even if no judicial mandate exists, lawyers may consider contacting an ADR administrator or clerk of court and ask that the judge in the case suggest mediation to both sides.

Invite a Third Party to Take the Initiative

Another way to have a third party play "matchmaker" is to ask a private neutral to approach an adversary and advocate mediation. Although the opponent will probably know that opposing counsel initiated the contact, this allows lawyers to avoid the burden of "selling" the process to a reluctant adversary.

So far we have assumed that the issue is to persuade one's opponent to mediate. In some situations, though, the major obstacle is one's own client. In the words of one litigator:

> There are no hard and fast rules as to when that perfect moment has arrived to mediate, [but] one point is clear. Before you begin, recognize that the first obstacle to starting the dialogue early may well be your own client, particularly if you have not represented him in the past. He may wonder if you lack confidence in yourself or the case if you push for settlement too early. On the other hand, if you don't mention settlement to the more sophisticated client, he may well wonder whether you are looking to "milk" a case that will likely never be tried. As such, begin with the adversary only after you have reached a consensus with your own client.... (Stern, 1998)

C. Structuring the Mediation

How mediation is structured is often crucial to its success. In each case an advocate must think about the following issues.

1. Selecting a Mediator

The most important issue in arranging for mediation, apart perhaps from agreeing on who will attend the process, is to select the right neutral. We have seen that mediators vary in characteristics such as the breadth or narrowness of their approach, substantive expertise, and willingness to use facilitative or evaluative techniques. When selecting a legal mediator, you will typically be able to choose among former or practicing litigators, transactional lawyers, and ex-judges, as well as professionals in fields ranging from psychotherapy to civil engineering. Your goal should be to select a neutral with qualities that match the needs of your case.

One approach is to think about what barriers are making it difficult to negotiate directly with the other side. The answer will give you an insight into what qualities a neutral will need to help you overcome them. If, for example, the key problem is that your opponent has an abrasive or insulting manner, then a mediator with strong process skills may be the best choice. If your own client needs "cover" to justify a compromise to an outside constituency, then an evaluative neutral may be helpful. If the parties are very angry or need to repair their relationship, then a neutral with skills in counseling may be what is called for. In many situations more than one barrier exists, calling for a mediator with a blend of abilities.

❖ **David S. Ross, Strategic Considerations in Choosing a Mediator: A Mediator's Perspective**

2 J. Alternative Disp. Resol. in Emp. 7 (Spring 2000)

Because the mediation process is only as effective as the mediator who manages it, choosing the right mediator is critical. The mediator selection process demands a thoughtful balancing of many criteria, including

- Mediation experience
- Mediation process skills
- Substantive expertise
- Reputation for neutrality
- Creativity
- Strong interpersonal skills and an ability to connect with people, and
- The ability to help parties reach agreement

Since every case is different, it makes sense to prioritize these criteria based on the needs of the case and parties. . . .

Substantive Expertise

People often ask whether they should choose a mediator with substantive expertise or one with strong process skills. A short answer is "both." A longer answer is that in most employment disputes, process skills count as much or more than substantive expertise. However, more mediators are specializing in specific substantive areas [such as] employment law, so parties now can more easily choose a mediator with both substantive expertise and process skills.

References

Participants should take the time to speak directly with individuals — ideally both lawyers and principals — who have worked with a proposed mediator to learn their candid assessment of the mediator's strengths and weaknesses, mediation style, and overall effectiveness. Most mediators provide references upon request. If they do not, then press the mediator to do so.

Opposing Counsel's Recommendations

What should you do if opposing counsel proposes a mediator? There may be a strong instinct to reject such a proposal. My experience suggests that sophisticated lawyers should seriously consider mediators proposed by opposing counsel, honestly hashing out the advantages and disadvantages of various candidates. . . .

Attorneys should consult with their clients when choosing a mediator . . . Encouraging client participation in the mediator selection process empowers clients. Finally, and perhaps most importantly, it builds trust in the attorney-client relationship and in the mediation process, promoting a sense of shared responsibility in making mediation work.

—————————————

Assuming you have identified the skills you want in a mediator, how can you determine whether a particular candidate possesses them? Common sources include recommendations from colleagues, references, and the opposing party's suggestions. In addition, companies and law firms that engage regularly in mediation sometimes create private data banks with information about their experience with various neutrals. Some organizations and government agencies develop rosters of mediators who are approved to handle their cases. Mediators also provide prospective clients with information. Such documents typically emphasize the neutral's qualifications, but advocates may be able to read between the lines to identify potential gaps as well. In addition, most mediators are willing to talk informally with attorneys who express interest in hiring them.

Example: In the student death case described in Chapter 5, counsel for both sides gave careful thought to selecting the mediator. Defense counsel decided to allow the Kruegers to select the neutral. In part this was because the Kruegers insisted on the right to do so, and in part because the defense respected the plaintiff counsel's ability to choose wisely. The Kruegers selected a mediator who regularly handled personal injury cases for claimants, but they had other concerns as well. It was important that the mediator be willing to work with counsel to customize the process, and that he or she be respected by the defense. Plaintiff counsel also knew that the discussions would be extremely emotional — in the course of the process both the lawyers and parties found themselves in tears — and it was therefore crucial that the mediator have the ability to absorb and manage intense anger and grief. The mediator's final qualification was unique: Counsel learned that he had once lost a college-age son himself.

Questions

6. Texas mediator Eric Galton has suggested that transactional lawyers are better advocates in mediation because "they negotiate better, more creatively and are more acutely aware of business solutions which may be advantageous to their clients."
   (a) Assuming that this is true, what types of legal disputes would a transactional lawyer be best suited to mediate?
   (b) What might you sacrifice by selecting a transactional lawyer rather than a litigator as your mediator?
7. The other side in a case proposes as a mediator someone with whom they have mediated more than a dozen times. What should you do in response?
8. If you wished to propose a mediator with whom you had worked repeatedly, what would be the best way to do so?
9. You represent a party in an exercise assigned by your teacher. You have agreed to mediate and are now in the process of selecting a neutral. What qualities would you look for in a mediator for your case? If you can obtain biographies of mediators in your area, review some and prioritize the candidates in terms of attractiveness.

2. Ensuring the Presence of Necessary Participants

We know that mediation is an intensely personal process. As a result, the presence of the right people is perhaps the single most important factor in its success. Who these people are in a particular case will depend again on your objectives.

- If the primary goal is to repair a personal relationship, then the presence of the principals themselves, to talk out their problems and regain the ability to relate productively with each other, is usually essential.
- If the parties' relationship is attenuated, as, for example, in the case of a rent dispute between a corporate landlord and a former commercial tenant, the presence of principals may be less important.
- If the objective is to work out an imaginative solution, then it is important that the participants be capable of thinking "outside the box" and know enough about the parties' interests to identify and flesh out useful options. Working out a novel solution to a business dispute, for instance, may require executives rather than lawyers.
- If the only goal is to settle a legal claim on the best possible monetary terms, as is true in many negligence cases, then the primary concern is probably that the bargainers arrive at the table with sufficient authority.

❖ Jerry Spolter, A Mediator's Tip: Talk to Me!
The Recorder 4 (March 8, 2000)

This may come as a surprise to even the most seasoned mediation participants, but there is nothing wrong with communicating ex parte with a mediator or prospective mediator. In fact, it's usually the smart and right thing to do to secure the best result for your client. So don't be bashful. Talk to your mediator.

A recent mediation session I conducted highlights what can happen when you leave your mediator in the dark. Everything went great for about five hours.... The joint session was textbook material, with lots of helpful information exchanged; the private caucuses peeled away postured "positions" to reveal the parties' real interests. And then it happened: Although the physician accused of malpractice was in the room, the doc wouldn't make a move until his personal attorney gave the OK.

Unfortunately, the personal attorney was on a chairlift in the Sierra with a dead battery in her cell phone. And since this was a malpractice case requiring the doc's consent, "my" mediation was suddenly in trouble. To make matters worse, the doc's insurance representative had to consult two "invisible-hierarchy" decision-makers to discuss increasing authority.

If only I had received a "heads up" beforehand, we could have resolved the authority problems in advance and taken advantage of the momentum we had generated that day to settle the case. (Instead, the parties are now scurrying around trying to acquire the necessary authority to put Humpty-Dumpty back together again.)....

There is a good deal that lawyers can do beforehand to ensure that the right people are at a mediation.

Parties

If the parties are individuals, then they should be personally present. Corporations and other organizations, however, must act through agents. Some corporate representatives are positively harmful to the settlement process. An example would be an executive who had a personal stake in defending the decision at issue in the dispute. Others may lack the right kind of expertise; an outside litigator, for instance, might be a good representative in a process that turns on the trial value of a claim, but wrong for a mediation focused on resolving an employee's grievance and bringing her back to work.

When parties are represented by agents, and especially when a nonparty such as an insurer is involved, advocates face a challenge to ensure that the people who come to the table have the authority to make the decisions needed to resolve the case. Negotiators routinely claim to have "full authority," but in practice their ability to agree is usually limited. Bargainers may arrive at mediation with:

- "best-case" authority (the ability to accept the terms their side believes that their opponent *ought to accept*),

- "reasonable" authority (their estimate of what the opponent at the end of the day *will agree to*), or
- "worst-case" authority (the ability to agree, if necessary, to an outcome very close to the other side's *current offer* going into mediation).

In practice, disputants usually conceal or misrepresent their authority, for fear that it will be taken as their "bottom line." It is often useful, however, to touch on the issue with an opposing negotiator, and perhaps to ask about his role in the organization, in order to estimate his ability to make decisions.

Advisors and Stakeholders

People other than parties may also play key roles in decision making at mediation. A husband, for instance, may look to his wife for advice, or a company may be unable to make a deal without permission from its insurer. There is no easy way to resolve this issue. Wise lawyers know that they may need to bargain for the presence of the right person, and that the mediator can help with the process. In asking a neutral for assistance in securing the presence of key decision makers, lawyers benefit from several forces. First, having agreed to mediate, disputants usually feel an interest in establishing a good relationship with the mediator. Mediators, too, acquire a stake in the process, and have a bias toward inclusion. Better, a typical legal mediator will think to ask for the presence of a person who later proves unnecessary rather than to find oneself lacking a key decision maker at crunch time. Advocates can take advantage of their opponent's wish to humor a mediator and the neutral's own investment in the process by agreeing to mediate and then enlisting the neutral's help to shape the field of bargaining.

> *Example:* A high-tech company was suing a former employee who had left and then recruited her software team to join her at a competitor. For technical reasons the new employer was not a party to the litigation, although it had agreed to indemnify the employee for any liability in the matter. The plaintiff company and the former employee agreed to mediate, but the competitor's general counsel refused to attend, arguing that her company was not a party. In response, the plaintiff lawyer first agreed to mediate and then lobbied the mediator to secure the presence of the missing lawyer. He began his effort by stressing to the mediator how important the general counsel would be to the success of "our" process. The general counsel eventually agreed to join all sessions of the mediation by conference call, and her presence proved crucial to reaching agreement.

For more examples of how counsel can work with mediators to ensure the presence of key people, see the discussion of the premediation stage in Chapter 6.

Questions

10. Neutrals come to mediation from very different careers. What background might make a mediator either more or less willing to take active steps to bring the right people into the process?
11. How could you test for this quality when selecting a neutral?

3. Drafting an Agreement to Mediate

Lawyers who undertake private mediation processes usually enter into written agreements that set out the ground rules for the process, and court-affiliated programs typically deal with such issues through a combination of agreements and program rules. Attorneys can deal with the following issues through a mediation agreement:

- Who are the parties?
- What rules of confidentiality will apply, and who will be bound by them?
- Who will pay the cost of mediation?
- Under what conditions can the mediator evaluate legal issues in the case?
- How can a party terminate its participation?
- Can the mediator be called to testify in a later proceeding?
- Is the mediator liable for wrongful or negligent acts?
- What will be the status of ongoing litigation while the mediation occurs?

Examples of commercial and family mediation agreements appear in the Web Appendix.

4. Influencing the Format

Mediation can occur in a wide variety of formats. The parties, for example, can choose to meet entirely in joint session or rely heavily on caucusing. They can bargain with each other directly or through attorneys. The best format for a particular case depends on your overall goal.

- In a case focused on relationship repair, you will probably want the clients to have as much opportunity as possible to communicate directly. It may make sense, for instance, to arrange for the principals to talk without counsel present, or perhaps to remain in joint session throughout the process.
- In a highly emotional case, it may be important for a party to meet with the mediator ahead of time to begin venting, and to carefully structure the party's interactions with the other side.
- In factually complex cases, it may be necessary to arrange for enough time for each side to present a lengthy opening statement, perhaps supported by computerized exhibits or comments from an expert.

These issues are discussed in more detail below. For now, it is important to bear in mind that experienced advocates often ask for changes in the usual format of commercial mediation. If you see a reason to vary the format, you should alert the mediator to this before the process begins.

5. Planning for Court-Connected Mediation

The discussion to this point has assumed that you have the freedom to design an effective mediation process in conjunction with the mediator and the other party. Sometimes, however, your client may be required to engage in mediation by a contract clause. More often the court in which your case is pending will require litigants to go through mediation as a precondition to trial. Many state and federal courts have mandatory mediation programs. They are most prevalent in family disputes, but have become common in general civil litigation as well. Thus, for example, states such as Florida, Texas, and California require most civil cases filed in their courts to go through mediation.

Courts may order mediation but leave process choices to the parties, with court rules available only as a default mechanism. Many jurisdictions, however, channel cases into court-connected programs, assign mediators, require principals to attend, and impose other significant restrictions on the process. Litigants may have the option to opt out of restrictions by agreement, but in the context of adversarial litigation this can be difficult to accomplish.

If you have a case that is subject to mandatory mediation, whether by contract or court rule, you will need to consider the following questions, in addition to the general issues that arise in planning for any mediation. The most important are:

- Is the mandated mediation process adequate?
- If not, how should you respond to it?

In considering the adequacy of the process, several issues are likely to arise that are peculiar to mandatory programs:

- Will you have a role in choosing the neutral? Some programs require parties to select a mediator from panels that consist of attorney-mediators with varying levels of experience. Others assign a mediator, sometimes a full-time court employee, to each case. Some programs and clauses give parties the option to select a private mediator. Contract clauses sometimes designate a named individual as the neutral.
- Who will be required to be present at the session? As we will see in Chapter 13, many courts require each party to send a representative with "full settlement authority." This can create serious problems for organizations that have large numbers of cases pending in different court systems.
- Will you have an opportunity to brief the mediator in advance? Some programs have no restrictions, while others bar parties from submitting statements or talking with neutrals in advance.
- Will you be required to pay for the process? Some programs are free, relying on volunteer attorney-mediators; others use private neutrals who charge market prices; and still others require parties to pay mediators, but at below-market rates.
- Will you be required to mediate within a specific time frame? Court processes can range from a one-hour process with the option to extend the time by agreement, to a full-day commitment. If the process is time-limited, the mediator is likely to feel pressure to produce progress quickly, leading her to forego interest-oriented questioning in favor of "cutting to the chase."
- What confidentiality guarantees does the program offer? This issue is also discussed in more depth in Chapter 13.
- Can you change the structure of the process by agreement with the other side? If so, will the other side agree to the changes you seek?

If you do not want to mediate, or conclude that the mandated process is inadequate, you should consider these questions:

- Is it possible to opt out of the process, for example by applying for an exemption?
- If not, what is the minimum you have to do to comply with the mandate? Some programs, for example, require parties to participate in "good faith."
- Are there penalties for nonparticipation or noncompliance? For example, if you fail to send a representative with settlement authority, will the court impose costs or attorneys' fees? Will the mediator report to the court concerning your cooperation? Will the mediator give the court a recommendation about how the court should rule on unresolved issues, as is done in some divorce mediation programs?

To obtain information about these issues you may wish to:

- Talk with colleagues or a local lawyer who has participated in the program.
- Review the program brochure and rules.
- Talk with the program administrator.
- Talk with opposing counsel.

We discuss the policy issues presented by mandatory mediation, the legal issues raised by such programs, and examples of court-connected mediation in Chapters 12, 13, and 15.

D. Preparing to Mediate

Once advocates have agreed on an overall structure for mediation, they should focus on how they will participate in the process. This requires planning not only what the lawyer will do, but also the roles of the client and other members of the team. Preparation includes at least three areas: developing a negotiation plan, exchanging information, and coaching clients about what to do and say.

1. Developing a Negotiating Plan

Texts often speak of the art of "mediation advocacy," but you now know that the process consists primarily of informal negotiation. Lawyers usually make an opening statement at the outset of the process, which is a form of advocacy, but the rest of the mediation is typically taken up with discussions and bargaining. You should therefore plan for mediation in much the same way that you would for a direct negotiation. The points made in Chapter 3 about preparation for negotiation apply here as well. You will wish, for example, to consider each side's alternatives to agreement, principles that you can cite and those that your opponent will rely on, the parties' underlying interests, and potential options for settlement. If your primary goal is to obtain the best possible monetary outcome, your plan will be similar to that of a competitive bargainer. If you see the purpose of the process as solving a common problem, then you are likely to focus on the parties' interests and cooperate in finding ways to address them. Whatever your goal, however, you will need to modify your approach to bargaining to take advantage of the special aspects of mediation. The readings below look at mediation planning from several perspectives.

a. A Mediator's Perspective

What constitutes a "winning" strategy in mediation, and is it possible that the other advocate could play a role in achieving it? Consider this advice from a commercial mediator.

❖ **Jeffrey G. Kichaven, How Advocacy Fits in Effective Mediation**
17 Alternatives 60 (1999)

Clients and attorneys generally have one of two conceptions of what it means to win in mediation. Some define winning as "clobbering the other side." Others see it as "the satisfaction of our own needs," regardless of whether the other side suffers along the way. In the litigation context, and in many others, clients often start out in a "clobbering" mode. They may believe they have been "done wrong," and want revenge. And more revenge. And more.

This is a serious problem for lawyers. Such a client is almost never satisfied with the result, with the process, or with counsel's performance, because the other side, no matter how badly clobbered, rarely has suffered enough. A vengeful client . . . has a hard time planning, in advance, the specific result to be achieved or the goal against which success or failure will be measured. No matter what happens to the other side, it could always have been worse! These clients believe that their attorneys have failed them. Yet the lawyers have done all that they can. Far better is the situation in which the client focuses on the satisfaction of his or her own needs. This client is better able to give clear instructions and if the client's own goals are satisfied, it doesn't matter very much whether the other side suffers a lot, a little, or even at all.

Mediation has an important role in the pursuit of this second concept of the win . . . In the hands of skilled mediators and counsel, the process can be designed to minimize the incentives to clobber and enhance the likelihood that the parties will engage in goal-oriented, client-satisfying negotiation.

In mediation after mediation, clients and lawyers come to change their negotiating tune. The desire for revenge is trumped by a desire for finality: A desire to eliminate the newly perceived enhanced risks of continued litigation; to eliminate the certainty of the mental, emotional and financial drains of conflict; and to get on with one's career and life with a "bird in the hand" settlement. . . . The key to all this, however, is profoundly counterintuitive. In mediation, your effectiveness as an advocate will vary in direct proportion to that of opposing counsel, not the inverse proportion you might expect in the generally "clobbering" mode of traditional litigation.

In this sense, you and opposing counsel have become each other's best friends. You have given each other's clients what you often cannot give your own: The means by which one can achieve a balanced perspective . . . with the craving to clobber taking a back seat. Let's face it: It's tough for a lawyer to break bad news to his or her own client. It's tough on clients, too, to go beyond denial, even when that bad news is broken with candor and compassion. Yet in virtually every unsettled case, bad news needs to be broken and accepted. In some cases, it's the other side that needs it. In others, it's your side. In most cases, there's plenty of bad news to go around.

In mediation, you and opposing counsel have found uniquely qualified messengers to deliver this essential communication — each other. The mediator works along with you to make sure that the bad news is not only delivered to your client, but also received. Effective mediation advocates, therefore, must be able to hold both conceptions of "the win" in mind simultaneously, side by side, each in its appropriate place, each conception taking the forefront when appropriate.

Question

12. What could you do as an advocate to enhance the likelihood that the other side's arguments would help to educate your own unrealistic client?

b. A Litigator's Viewpoint

The following suggestions about preparation come from a civil litigator.

❖ Robert M. Smith, Advocacy in Mediation: A Dozen Suggestions
26 San Francisco Att'y 14 (June/July 2000)

Your strongest ally, if you can make him or her an ally, is the mediator. It is the mediator's neutral voice that is most powerful in carrying your argument to the other side. This is true even if the mediator asks a lawyer to put on the chalkboard the strongest points of the case, then unveils the board to the other side.

The mediator knows you — indeed, everyone — is trying to manipulate, or con, him or her. Manipulation is as much a given as the coffee machine. But often — perhaps usually — the mediator is aware of the con. Good advocates know when to stop the con, show some trust, and make a straighter, and more reasonable, argument. Honesty can buy an advantage.

Play the Odds

When you go to a commercial mediation, there is, statistically, close to an eighty-five percent chance of settling the case. This means you should probably prepare as if the mediation session will be the last step in the case, and prepare your client accordingly. To tell the client, for example, that we are all just going through the motions and then find yourself in serious end-game bargaining is not prudent.

Black-Tie Affair

Often — we all know this — lawsuits bobble along like a play in search of a theater; they need a defining event before both parties and lawyers get serious.

Mediation is an event — probably the event. If the mediator is effective, everyone will focus on the matter in a way that they haven't before.

The Art of Scribbling

This is the time to do your best brief. Mediators read them — they get paid to. And this may be all they know about the case before you troop in. The mediator is likely to ensure that the parties, as well as the lawyers, see the brief and consider your most forceful arguments, or what a neutral sees as your most forceful arguments. It may be worth considering their impact on the plaintiff or the defendant when sections are pointed out to them.

Sharing Can Be Beautiful

You might consider whether you want to give a copy of the brief to the other side, as well as to the mediator. But you can give only a portion of the brief to the other side — or the whole brief, with only a secret annex going to the mediator (for instance, "I think the claims rep was himself a party to a similar squabble two years ago"). The process is what you make of it. Flexible, it bends to your imaginative sculpting.

We Don't Accept Cash Here

Some have pointed out the power of an apology, appropriately timed and tendered. But advocacy may also involve asking for a non-economic concession — even one you know you likely won't get; it may put other demands in a new, or reframed, perspective.

About Reframing

Once discussions have foundered, the mediator knows that the parties are not likely to move on their own. It is up to the mediator to step back and find a new perspective or approach. You should anticipate the possible reframing, or you may not like the suddenly unfamiliar perspective. Be reframed, not hung.

A las Cinco de la Tarde

"At five in the afternoon" is a repetitive line in a poem by Federica Garcia Lorca. It has to do with a death, not mediation. But I sometimes think of it when discussions bog down after hours of negotiation because it is about five in the afternoon that the role of poetic imagination is sometimes called into play in mediations. You hope the mediator did not lose his or her imagination in the second year of law school; part of what you are paying for is creativity. But when the clock strikes — or beeps — in a soundless room, your own imaginative suggestion may prove sublime advocacy.

---

c. A Problem-Solving Approach

The following reading is addressed to problem-solving advocates, but many of the points apply to other forms of mediation as well.

❖ Harold Abramson, Mediation Representation: Advocating in a Problem-Solving Process

NITA 221-222 (2004)

[*Note:* Professor Abramson recommends that advocates begin their preparation by analyzing the overall nature of the dispute, doing any necessary research, and resolving issues of structure such as who will attend. Having done this, lawyers should prepare for the actual process of mediation by considering the following issues.]

...Identify three components of the mediation representation formula: interests, impediments, and ways the mediator might contribute to resolving the dispute.

1. Goal:
   Identify Interests to Meet: Your Client's
   Identify Interests to Accommodate: The Other Side's
2. Goal: Identify Impediments to Overcome....
3. Identify Mediator's Possible Contributions to Resolving the Dispute.

Approaches to Dispute

You want the mediator to use the following approaches [select among the options for each item]:

* Manage the process by primarily facilitating, primarily evaluating, or following a transformative approach.
* View the problem broadly or narrowly.
* Involve the clients actively or restrictively.
* Use caucuses extensively, selectively, or not at all.

Useful Techniques

You want the mediator to use his or her techniques to [select one or more]:

* Facilitate the negotiation of a problem-solving process.
* Promote communication through questioning and listening techniques.
* Deal with the emotional dimensions of the dispute.
* Clarify statements and issues through framing and reframing.
* Generate options for settlement (e.g., brainstorming).
* Separate process of inventing settlement options from selecting them.
* Deal with power inequalities.
* Overcome the impediments to settlement.
* Overcome the chronic impediment of clashing views of the court outcome.
* Close any final gaps (consider your preferred methods for closing gaps).
* Deal with _____ ....

Questions

13. Assume that you are a competitive advocate in an exercise assigned by your teacher. Your goal is to get the best possible money outcome for your client. How would you answer the questions on Professor Abramson's checklist?
14. Now assume that you have a problem-solving orientation in the same case. How would your answers change?

2. *Exchanging Information*

One of the key aspects of any negotiation is exchanging information, and one of mediation's effects is to enhance the flow of data between the parties. This process often begins well before disputants actually meet to mediate. As an advocate, you will need to think about two types of information:

• What information does your client need to make a good settlement decision?
• What information will help your adversary to agree to the outcome you are seeking?

If necessary, you should be prepared to enlist the mediator's help in persuading the other side to provide you with data. The neutral may also be able to help you explain to your own client why in this context it is a good idea to give an opponent some "free discovery."

What information is relevant depends again on your goals. If the process turns on money, then legal evidence and arguments are likely to be key. If your purpose is to repair a relationship, knowing the "why" behind a disputed action will be important. If the objective is to create a new business arrangement, then financial data may be more useful. As a rule, negotiations that focus on imaginative options require a broader base of information than discussions that revolve solely around money.

a. Exchanging Data with the Other Party

Disputants usually need less data to mediate effectively than they would require to try the same case. Still, especially if parties mediate early in a dispute, one side may lack information that is necessary to make an informed decision. Without that information, the party may not be able to assess the value of its litigation alternative or determine whether an imaginative option is viable. An insurance adjuster, for example, may not be able to obtain the authority needed to settle a claim without documents verifying the plaintiff's medical expenses, while a plaintiff lawyer might be unable to accept a reasonable settlement offer without assurances that there is no "smoking gun" in the defendant's files.

In litigation there is ordinarily no reason for a party to show its hand to an adversary, but in mediation disputants know that providing information will increase their chances of reaping a good settlement. Equally important, they know that the mediator is present to help ensure that the exchange will be mutual. As a result, parties in mediation often provide each other with surprising amounts of information.

> *Example:* A large computer manufacturer asserted a claim against its chip supplier, arguing that the chips had an unreasonably high rate of failure, requiring the manufacturer to make expensive repairs to servers in the field. The parties agreed that the problem existed, and that it was caused by defects in the compound used to finish the chips. The chip maker had bought the compound from a reputable supplier and had no way to foresee the problem. Still, the computer manufacturer asserted a right to be compensated for its costs, relying on a document whose interpretation the chip maker hotly disputed.
>
> Inside counsel for the two companies agreed to meet informally to mediate the claim. When they exchanged mediation briefs, however, it quickly became apparent that the manufacturer's multi-million-dollar claim was both unclear — the chip maker could not understand how losses had reached such a level — and impossible for the chip maker to satisfy — it would go bankrupt if it had to pay such an amount.
>
> With the mediator's assistance, the parties agreed to postpone the mediation for a month and exchange data. The manufacturer agreed to supply documents verifying its damage claim, and the chip maker undertook to provide information about its financial situation. The chip maker also volunteered data about products under development, so that the manufacturer could consider taking part of a settlement in the form of discounts on future purchases.

Questions

15. What types of data gathered before mediation might help an advocate avoid the "twenty common errors" described earlier by Tom Arnold?
16. Assume that you are the lawyer in an exercise assigned by your teacher. What additional information, beyond the facts stated in the problem instructions, would help you mediate well? What data might the other attorney ask you for?

b. Educating the Mediator

In small cases and court-connected programs, neutrals sometimes arrive at mediation knowing almost nothing about the dispute. In privately conducted mediations, however, lawyers typically make an effort to orient, and begin to persuade, the neutral in advance. Premediation communications can take at least three forms: written statements, organizational discussions, and private conversations.

Written Statements

Parties commonly give a mediator written statements, sometimes called mediation "briefs" or "submissions," to read in advance. As they prepare their statements, advocates should consider:

- Is it better to prepare a statement, or use an existing document? A customized document has obvious advantages, but particularly in smaller cases, it is appropriate to use an existing document or pleading that summarizes the party's views.
- Is it preferable to submit the statement on an ex parte basis, or exchange it with opposing counsel? Mediators usually prefer that lawyers exchange statements, so that they are free to discuss the points one side makes with the other. Even if you exchange statements, however, you are ordinarily free to write or call the neutral to discuss sensitive issues privately.

What should be in the mediation statement? A mediator is likely to be interested in knowing, among other points:

- How did the dispute arise?
- What are the key factual and legal issues?
- What nonlegal concerns are present?
- What barriers have made direct bargaining difficult? Are there personal or emotional issues?
- What is the status of any legal proceedings? Is there a history of bargaining?
- Who are the key decision makers in the dispute?

Organizational Discussions

In complex cases, mediators often schedule joint meetings with counsel to discuss organizational questions, such as who will be present at the mediation. Such meetings usually occur by conference call, but they are sometimes convened in person. Organizational meetings are typically limited to lawyers, but clients and experts may occasionally participate as well.

Private Conversations

Mediators sometimes take the initiative to talk with advocates before a mediation session. Such conversations typically occur over the telephone, but may occur in person. Mediators use these private conversations to ask about hidden obstacles, fill factual gaps, or simply listen to disputants vent. For examples of the questions that a sophisticated neutral would be interested in having answered in a premediation statement or might ask in a conversation, see Professor Aaron's reading at the start of Chapter 7.

Attorneys often do not ask for a premediation conversation with the neutral, or if they do, devote it primarily to repeating legal points made in their written statements. This is usually a mistake. Apart from the fact that the mediator may already have read the briefs, lawyers will have a chance to make their legal arguments during the process itself. At this stage many mediators want to know about issues that typically do not appear in the briefs, such as nonlegal obstacles, what the participants are like, and potential options for resolving the case. Premediation private conversations provide an exceptional opportunity for advocates to shape a mediator's "take" on a dispute.

Another alternative is for a lawyer and client to meet personally with the neutral before the "formal" process begins. An advocate might seek out a meeting for these reasons, among others:

- To build a relationship with the neutral.
- To permit a client to begin the process of working through her emotions or to allow the client to get to know the mediator.
- To present sensitive data or proposals.
- To allow the mediator to meet with a key witness or decision maker who will not be present at the mediation itself.

For example, in the student death case in Chapter 5, plaintiff counsel arranged for the student's parents to have breakfast with the mediator before the mediation session began. The purpose of the encounter, which had been cleared with the defense, was to allow the plaintiffs to begin to get to know the neutral, and also to let them start the process of expressing their anger and grief over their son's death before they met with representatives of the university.

Questions

17. You are representing a party in an exercise assigned by your teacher. What might be helpful for you or your client to tell the mediator in a private conversation before the process begins?
18. You have sent your mediation statement to your adversary and the mediator. The other side now sends its confidential statement to the mediator alone. What can you do in response? How might you have avoided this problem?

3. Preparing the Client

As we have noted, mediation is in essence a process of negotiation, but one that varies in significant ways from direct bargaining, requiring different preparation of clients. Attorneys usually conduct direct negotiations outside their clients' presence, often without even meeting face-to-face. In mediation, by contrast, both clients are ordinarily physically present, and the mediator has direct conversations with them. In addition, in the typical caucus-based mediation, disputants spend much of their time isolated from each other, interacting through the neutral rather than directly. Because of these structural differences, lawyers need to cover the following topics, in addition to the issues they would address when preparing a client for a direct negotiation.

- How the mediation process will differ from negotiations to which the client is accustomed.
- The background, personality, and likely approach of the mediator, including the potential for changes in style, for example from an empathic to an evaluative approach.

- The likely format of the process and potential variations in it — for instance, the possibility that the client will be invited to meet privately with the other principal.
- The confidentiality rules that will apply to the process, as well as possible gaps and exceptions in them.
- What role the client should play in the process. In particular,
  —What questions the client should expect from the mediator.
  —What the client should be prepared to say, and when the client should remain silent.
  —What the other side may say and do.
  —How the lawyer and client should coordinate. The client should know, for instance, that it is entirely permissible for the client or the lawyer to ask the mediator to leave the room so that they can talk privately.
- What role the lawyer will play in the process. An advocate should be sure that the client understands that while their overall goal — getting the best possible outcome — will remain the same, she will adapt her tactics to the special nature of mediation. In particular,
  —The attorney will probably take a different tone than she would in a courtroom or direct bargaining session. In particular, the presence of the mediator may call for a more conciliatory stance.
  —The lawyer may also "pull punches" in order not to antagonize the other side while they explore a possible deal.
  —The lawyer may not mention certain key evidence in order to save it for trial.

The following reading gives more specific advice about how to prepare for mediation.

❖ **Thomas Arnold, Client Preparation for Mediation**
15 Corp. Couns. Q. 52 (April 1999)

In adjudicative processes (both arbitration and court trials), it is common for the advocacy to be an attack upon the good faith, integrity, and alleged wrongs of the other.... Necessarily that attack angers the other party, stirs up animosity, and interferes with any settlement effort.

In mediation the intent is to move the parties together, to treat the dispute as a problem to be solved together by respectful partners rather than a combat to be won. It is not the neutral but the other *party* and counsel that are the critical persons to be persuaded. So you don't hurt or disparage them: You seek out, you court, their good will and understanding. From this and other differences between mediation and adjudicative processes, you will see that advocacy and exhibit preparation . . . are poles apart as between mediation and adjudication. In this paper I list key client and some lawyer preparation pointers for mediation.

Who Represents the Client?

Who is the choice client representative for this mediation? A bellicose, unforgiving, inflexible, arrogant, and/or big-risk-taking personality? A wet rag personality who might give away the store? A person whose concessions at the mediation inherently imply criticism of his own prior actions, or his boss's prior actions? A temperate-mannered somebody who knows the subject matter, knows the values of the likely trade-outs? An open-minded person with quiet courage but no arrogance? Merely discussing these considerations and what available person is the best client representative with the client contact . . . becomes importantly educational . . . as to how he should undertake to conduct himself. . . .

First Impression

Upon arrival at the mediation, [the client should be cautioned to] be friendly and respectful, and attempt to build trust with the adversaries. Most settlements involve some degree of trust between client to client, client to counsel, counsel to counsel . . . so it is important to start developing trust at the first opportunity. . . .

Confidentiality

Acquaint the client with the rules and realities of confidentiality. Emphasize what not to say in plenary session, and that it's okay simply to decline to answer some questions. Only some, not all, disclosures in mediation are confidential . . . Once learned in a mediation, . . . information can still be discovered by regular discovery processes and used, even though it may not be attributed to the . . . mediation.

Consider Strengths and Weaknesses

Counsel in a preparation session should have the client write down all of the weaknesses and strengths in his/her case, and discuss and evaluate each with counsel. It is important that counsel strain hard to be objective. . . .

Don't Argue

The client should be cautioned not to argue with the other party or try hard to "win" the . . . case. The stock in trade in most legal negotiation is the other party's (and your own) risk of a substantial loss at important expense. But arguing hard and aggressively to get an admission . . . is usually counterproductive. Just be sure the other party truly knows their risks. . . .

Know Which Questions to Answer

The client should be advised to answer questions from the other lawyer without exaggeration, honestly, carefully, and correctly. And he or she should also know which questions to quietly, simply decline to answer. Some lawyers try to use mediation as if it were primarily a discovery tool. You must make material disclosures for the process to work, but you don't have to tell the other side everything (for example, information subject to the attorney-client privilege). . . .

Become Familiar with "The Dance"

Plan with the client how you might handle the first . . . rounds of offers and counter-offers to convey subliminal messages. Plan not to be disturbed by an outlandish initial offer by the other party, but to turn it to . . . advantage by showing how ridiculous it is. . . .

Consider Speaking Out

When the parties can understand the issues, as is usual in commercial and many other disputes, encourage them to speak up during the mediation and participate in the negotiation.

End the Battle within the Camp

Within a "party" there often are many constituencies . . . with different interests or viewpoints, for example, a partner, the vice-president . . . , the union, the board, the marketing manager. They may be represented at the mediation by one, two, or three persons, or some of them by no one . . . Not infrequently, the most important and destructive disputes are between constituencies on the same side. In multi-faction situations, counsel and the client business representatives at the mediation must each be sure to address all internal disputes before they face the other side.

Don't Look Like a Klutz

This goes for you and the client, but the client is more likely to need the reminder. It is important to show the client off in the mediation as someone who would be an appealing witness in any court process, should mediation fail. People pay more to, and accept less from, a party with jury appeal.

Be Prepared for Down Time

There is often some idle time during mediation, while the other party meets with the mediator in private caucus, so the client should bring work or reading material. . . .

Plan for a Long Session

Let the client know that it will be necessary to make sure work and children are taken care of all day — until 7:30 in the evening or later, if need be. It is a good idea to talk to the mediator in advance about termination times. Some mediators like the pressure of late hours and work on past midnight if there is even a little movement in parties' positions; some quit at 6:00 P.M. no matter what is going on.

Bow Out Gracefully

Advise your client that when the process ends, you should each shake hands with your opposite number and say "Thank you," even if there's no settlement. Many settlements follow shortly after a mediation, when the right flavor is left in the mouth of an adversary.

Conclusion

By their very nature . . . , mediation processes depart fundamentally from the adversarial nature of litigation. But in at least one respect, they do resemble litigation: They call for very careful, thoughtful, thorough preparation....

Questions

19. What aspects of the mediation process do you think a typical plaintiff in a personal injury case is unlikely to understand? What might a business executive find surprising about the mediation of a contract dispute?
20. Tom Arnold's underlying theme is that a lawyer needs to prepare a client differently for mediation than for litigation. Which of his suggestions would you *not* follow if you were preparing a client for a court hearing?
21. Any advice must be adapted to the needs of specific situations. As one example, Arnold advises that clients be told to assume an "empathetic" role. In what kinds of disputes would empathy be likely to be productive? Are there situations in which it might be the wrong emotion to show?
22. Which aspects of Arnold's advice are unique to mediation, as opposed to points that apply equally to direct negotiation?

CHAPTER
11

Representing Clients: During the Process

We now turn to the point in the mediation process at which the parties and mediator convene together to talk and bargain. This is what many lawyers think of as the "actual" mediation, although by now you know that effective advocacy begins well before the parties meet in person. We have seen that commercial mediation tends to follow a joint-session-plus-caucusing format, while family and problem-solving mediators are much more likely to keep disputants together.

There is relatively little written about advocacy outside commercial mediation. This may be due to the fact that in the traditional family-mediation format lawyers are available for consultation but do not participate directly in the mediation session. "No-caucus" and "transformative" mediation also emphasize direct party-to-party communication, with lawyers either absent from the process or playing a subsidiary role. We therefore discuss advocacy in the context of civil, nonfamily mediation, the form of the process in which lawyers are most likely to play a significant role.

A. Joint Meetings

1. The Opening Session

a. Should There Be an Opening Session?

Most mediators prefer to begin the process with an opening session attended by all the disputants. Lawyers, however, regularly suggest to mediators that the parties dispense with the opening stage and go directly into caucuses. Each side already knows the other's arguments, they say — What benefit could there be to repeating them? Or, they warn, the session will simply inflame their clients. Moreover, time is limited: Why not get to the bargaining?

There is often some truth to each of these concerns. Still, however repetitive or uncomfortable an opening session may appear, you should be extremely reluctant to ask that it be omitted entirely. An adversary's comments may offend your client (and vice versa), but the experience of speaking directly to an opponent often helps disputants to let go of emotions that would otherwise impair their decision making later in the process. Allowing a party to listen directly to an adversary's evidence and arguments can also help to bring reality to later discussions, giving each side a better appreciation of what it will face if the case does not settle. And after a time, even angry listeners usually become more calm. Mediators find that it is almost always useful to hold at least one joint meeting early in the process.

If you do have a reason for avoiding a joint meeting, raise this with your mediator in advance. Before doing so, however, carefully examine the pros and cons. Remember that you have the option to request that an opening session be restructured, and consider options that fall between cancellation and the "usual format." You might, for example, ask that the session be limited to presentations by experts or comments by executives.

Question

1. Can you think of any type of dispute in which an early joint meeting is likely to be counterproductive? What format would you advocate using instead?

b. What Role Will You Take in the Session?

You can have a variety of goals for a joint meeting. Even if your objective is solely to get the best possible monetary outcome, you will usually not want to exchange offers during the opening session. Too often, offers made directly by one side to another are reactively devalued. Instead, your strategy should be to create the conditions for successful bargaining later in the process. You can do this in several ways.

Foster a Working Relationship

Advocates and clients can use an opening session, and perhaps also the casual conversation that sometimes occurs as people assemble, to foster a better working relationship with an opponent. This does not necessarily mean repairing a past connection, although that might be desirable. Instead the goal is typically more modest — to create a basis for the parties to bargain effectively later on. Disputants can do this, for example, by demonstrating that they are serious about settlement and are willing to make principled compromises to reach one. Alternatively, a lawyer can use an opening session to help an emotional or angry participant work through difficult feelings.

Gather Information

Lawyers can also use the opening session to gather information. In a joint meeting, unlike discovery or court proceedings, disputants can talk informally with each other. Attorneys and clients also have the opportunity to observe the lawyer and witnesses for the other side, and perhaps also the chance to speak directly with the opposing principal. (The other side, of course, will have the same opportunity to "size up" you and your client.)

Focus the Discussion on Key Issues

Skilled lawyers use the opening session to focus discussion on the issues that are most helpful to their case or that create a platform for effective bargaining. If, for example, an advocate wants to emphasize the evidence (or lack of it) supporting the damage claims in a case, she can alert the mediator beforehand that this issue is significant to her client and then focus attention on it through her comments. If the attorney's primary goal is to explore an interest-based solution, she can use the opening session to send signals about this as well — or prime the mediator to raise the issue as his own idea. Neither side can control the agenda of an opening session, but attorneys who take the initiative can influence the content of such discussions significantly.

Persuade an Opponent

Finally, lawyers use the opening session to persuade their opponents to compromise. They focus their advocacy on the opposing decision maker, knowing that they will have other chances to talk with the mediator, but the opening session may be their only opportunity to speak directly to the other party. The goal will usually be to convince the other side that it is in its own best interest to compromise. Opponents are more likely to do so if they believe that;

- You are serious about seeking a settlement.
- You are open to options that will advance their interests.
- If discussions fail, you have a good alternative to settlement.
- You are willing to compromise, but will accept impasse sooner than agree to an unfair result.

c. What Role Will Your Client Take?

Most lawyers are inclined to take the lead in the opening session, treating it as a kind of informal pretrial hearing. As we have already noted, however, clients can play crucial roles in these meetings as well.

Should the Client Speak in the Opening Session?

As a general rule, clients should be active in joint meetings. Opponents tend to "tune out" what an opposing attorney says, but they are usually very interested in hearing from the opposing principal. Mediators also seek out contact with parties and therefore pay especially close attention to what they say. For these reasons, statements from principals are likely to have a greater impact than the same words spoken by an attorney. By participating effectively in a joint session, parties can significantly affect how opponents view them as witnesses, future partners, or negotiators.

- In personal injury and employment cases, in which the plaintiff's pain and suffering or emotional distress is often an important element of the claim, a plaintiff who can persuasively describe how he has suffered increases the settlement value of the claim. In general, whenever a person is likely to be a significant witness in a future adjudication, his presentation in mediation will affect the other side's estimate of the value of the case.
- When parties wish to repair a relationship, as in some business cases, or the principals cannot avoid relating with each other, as is true of many cases involving children, one party's participation in mediation can significantly affect the other side's willingness to settle on terms that maintain a working relationship. Again, statements made by one party directly to another almost always have greater impact than comments made through a lawyer or mediator.
- Parties can often articulate their interests more persuasively if they speak themselves.
- If one side doubts an opponent's commitment to settling, he may be able to dispel those concerns in the opening session.

All this assumes, of course, that a client presents himself positively. If a party is obnoxious, inarticulate, or unappealing, then his participation will lower an opponent's opinion of his case and hurt his bargaining objectives. In such situations the client should remain silent if possible.

How Should the Client Present Herself?

In the course of preparing a client, advocates should again stress that mediation is an informal process that combines discussion with bargaining, and the party should therefore speak in a conversational tone. In general, speakers should focus on the person who seems to be the key decision maker, or perhaps the most persuadable listener.

If the speaker is focusing on background facts that are familiar to the other side, he should address the neutral. If the issue involves past incidents between the principals, or the party is attempting to explain a misunderstanding, to apologize, or to empathize with an adversary, he should speak directly to the concerned person. If the purpose is to show the client's effectiveness as a witness, then it is appropriate to address both the other side and the mediator.

If, however, the speaker has decided that it is necessary to make an accusation, for example, that the other side has committed fraud, listeners will probably feel less "assaulted" and find it easier to listen if the speaker directs her comments toward the neutral. Finally, mediators with backgrounds as judges sometimes prefer that participants use a settlement-conference format and speak directly to them.

Question

2. You represent a company that vacated commercial space because of dissatisfaction with the condition of the building. Your client is being sued by a corporate landlord for rent due under the lease. Both sides have agreed

to mediate. Apart from the basic issue of liability, which you see as a 50–50 proposition, you believe that the landlord ignored its responsibility to maintain the building, and as a result would not be awarded much even if it did establish a technical violation of the lease. How can you best use the opening session to make the landlord aware of its risk at trial?

2. Other Joint Formats

We have seen that commercial mediation typically relies on extensive private caucusing. The caucus format can be useful, but it also imposes significant limitations. Advocates should not let themselves fall into caucusing as a matter of routine without thinking about whether other formats might be more effective. Caucusing is most useful when disputants want to focus primarily on legal issues and monetary offers, or when they are too emotional, inarticulate, or unskilled in bargaining to interact effectively.

If, however, parties wish to repair a relationship or work out inventive solutions, direct discussions, perhaps moderated by the mediator, are often more effective because they allow the people who are most concerned or knowledgeable about a situation to talk directly with each other. Even when a case is "only about money," it may be useful for representatives of each side to talk directly in order to resolve emotional issues, address complex factual issues, or deal with misunderstandings. The flexible nature of mediation allows participants to change its structure on an ad hoc basis. Again, this creates opportunities for sophisticated counsel to use the process to advantage. Consider this example:

Example: A manufacturer and a trucking company had a productive relationship for more than a decade, with the trucker distributing the manufacturer's products throughout the southern United States. Then their relationship somehow went sour. The manufacturer eventually sued the trucking company, claiming that it had fraudulently inflated its costs by overstating mileage and had padded its bills for loading. After two years of angry litigation, the parties agreed to mediate.

The mediation process began with an unusual twist, however. The plaintiff's lawyer contacted the mediator ahead of time to suggest that he ask the defense to dispense with the usual opening statements by lawyers, and instead have the two CEOs meet privately with each other. The mediator contacted defense counsel, who agreed, subject to the neutral being present during the conversation.

At the outset the two executives and the mediator retired to a room, leaving the lawyers behind. The manufacturer's CEO opened the discussion by retracing the companies' initial good relationship and their later problems. He suggested that the breakdown had been provoked in part by a wayward manager, whom he had hired away from the trucker but had recently let go for poor performance. The executive then made a settlement offer. The defendant's CEO thanked him, and said that he needed to run it by his lawyers. The parties then engaged in several hours of tough but productive bargaining, reducing their initial $900,000 gap to $30,000 — a demand of $300,000 against an offer of $270,000. At that point, however, the defense dug in and refused to make another offer.

As the mediator searched for ways to break the impasse, the defendant CEO suddenly pulled a quarter out of his pocket. "See this?" he asked. "You check — It's an honest quarter. I'll flip him for it!" "For what?" said the neutral. "The 30," he replied. "Let's see if he's got the ****s to flip for it!" The mediator looked at the trucker's lawyer: Was this serious? The attorney shrugged his shoulders: "It's OK with me. Why don't you take Jim down and present it to them. But you should do the talking; Jim's feeling really frustrated by all this." Why not? the mediator thought — it was better than anything he had to suggest.

The neutral led the defendant CEO into the plaintiff's conference room and, with a smile, said, "Jim has an idea to break the deadlock. It's kind of...unusual, but you might want to listen to it." In a calm voice and without anatomical references, the CEO repeated his coin-toss offer. The plaintiff executive grinned. "OK," he said, "But you didn't answer my last move, so the real spread is 50, between my 320 (his last offer before dropping to $300,000) and your 270." They argued over what should be the outcomes for the flip, showing some exasperation but also bits of humor. When the discussion stalled, the mediator suggested options to keep it going ("Why not give the 20 to charity?"), but in the end they could not agree and the defendant CEO walked out. As he left, the mediator followed him down the hall. "Suppose I could get him to drop to a flat 290," he asked. "Would that do it?" As it turned out, it would.

In this example both sides' initiatives proved important to settlement. The plaintiff lawyer's proposal that the mediation begin with a principals-only meeting created an informal connection between the executives that helped them to get over difficult points later on. And the defendant CEO's idea of a coin toss (which the mediator later learned had been suggested by his lawyer) was key to shaking the parties out of their impasse.

As this example demonstrates, even in a process in which the parties are separated in caucuses, lawyers can advance their client's interests by arranging meetings of subgroups of disputants. The mediator will usually be present to moderate such sessions, but this is not always true: In a case described later, the plaintiff's inside counsel asked to meet privately with the defendant's CEO, outside the presence of both the lawyers and the neutral. Good mediators readily agree to adjourn from caucusing to allow people to talk directly with each other. Effective lawyers are not afraid to ask a mediator to vary the usual format of the process. They understand that mediation is inherently a fluid process, and that mediators are working for the parties, not the other way around.

B. Caucusing

Because caucusing is so common in civil mediation outside the family law area, attorneys and mediators whom you encounter in practice are likely to expect to spend most of the time in caucuses. As a result, you will need either to take action in advance to obtain modifications in the caucus format, or plan to reap the greatest advantage from using it.

To make the best use of caucuses, you will have to prepare in two ways. First, you will need to adapt your direct bargaining tactics to the special structure of caucusing; second, you will need to deal with the mediator differently from the way you respond to opponents. If, for example, opposing counsel asks your client a question, you would ordinarily feel free to cut him off or step in and answer the question yourself. But if a mediator asks your client the same question in the privacy of a caucus, the considerations are quite different. You may be more willing to have your client answer a mediator's question. But even if you are reluctant, you may let the client respond in order not to offend the neutral. The nature of caucusing typically changes over the course of a mediation, and we therefore discuss early and later caucusing separately.

1. Early Caucuses

During the early caucuses of a mediation, you are likely to have some or all of the following goals:

* Relationships:
  —Develop a good working relationship with the mediator.
  —Not harm, and perhaps improve, your relationship with the other side.
* Legal issues:
  —Focus the participants' attention on your issues.
  —Gather data needed to bargain and provide the other side with information it will need to move in your direction.
  —Persuade the other party and the neutral that you have a good alternative to settling.
* Interests:
  —Identify nonlegal barriers that have made settlement difficult.
  —Focus the mediator on your interests and identify the key concerns of the other side.
* Bargaining:
  —Start the process of exchanging options.
  —Encourage the mediator to pursue interest-based options as well as money offers.

Of these possible goals, we focus on two: using mediation to facilitate exchanges of information and to initiate bargaining.

a. Exchanging Information and Arguments

Sophisticated negotiators often spend a good deal of time exchanging information and feeling each other out before making explicit offers. Because legal mediation is at heart a process of negotiation, it is not surprising that good advocates and mediators use caucusing to facilitate the flow of information. A lawyer might, for example, tell a mediator what she wishes the neutral to stress when the mediator talks with an opponent in the other caucus, as well as questions that she needs answered.

Neutrals, for their part, understand that disputants often come to mediation without data that they need to make settlement decisions, and that good lawyers will work to get points across to an adversary through the mediator. Indeed, to the extent that a party's "questions" are implicit arguments, mediators are often willing to transmit them to encourage the listener to reassess the value of his case. To understand how lawyers use mediation to convey questions and arguments, consider the following.

A few years ago one of the authors filmed a series of role-plays in which professional mediators and litigators tried to settle a case. The experiment was based on a manufacturer's claim against a supplier for selling a defective product. The manufacturer also sued the supplier's insurer, alleging that the insurer had acted in bad faith by refusing to make an offer to settle the claim, and asked for treble damages for this alleged violation. The insurer's counsel argued that his client had based its decision on the report of an independent expert, which appeared to be a convincing defense to the allegation of bad faith. Still the treble-damages claim hung over the case, inflating the plaintiff's monetary demands and discouraging the defense from making a serious settlement offer. Toward the end of the defense's first caucus meeting with the mediator, defense counsel decided to highlight this issue:

Defendant's inside counsel: We hope you'll raise with them that we see the crux of settlement as hinging on the fact that we don't see any evidence to support their case on treble damages. . . .

Mediator: But if they do have evidence, that might influence your bargaining position?

Counsel (smiling): Yes, and if they don't, we hope it influences theirs.

The mediator got the message, and raised the issue during his meeting with the plaintiff side.

Mediator: Suppose an outside expert reports that she found nothing in the insured's product that could have caused the damage and the insurer then denies the claim on that basis. If all that is true and the expert is credible, how would you then get the insurer into the case?

Plaintiff counsel: Well, it's a problem, no question about it.

Mediator: What percentage chance would you place on the bad faith claim?

Counsel: Twenty-five percent.

At the conclusion of this discussion the plaintiff team agreed to discount the bad faith claim heavily. What the defense counsel obtained by making this request of the mediator was to focus his discussion with the plaintiff on her preferred issue. She also benefited from the inclination of the plaintiff counsel to be candid with the neutral.

Problem

You represent the defense in the mediation of an employment discrimination case. A typical plaintiff's claim for damages in such a case consists of lost wages, out-of-pocket expenses, and emotional distress. Of these, the item that is often the largest, and the most subject to dispute, is emotional distress.

Here the plaintiff is demanding $200,000 in emotional distress damages, but you think it is highly unlikely that he will recover more than a modest amount because he never sought medical care for the condition. Also, there are no egregious facts, such as being ordered out of the building by a guard, that a fact finder would think likely to trigger serious distress.

You are in the first round of caucusing. The mediator is coming in to meet with you and your client and will then meet with the plaintiff. Outline how you would raise the distress issue with the mediator.

b. Initiating Bargaining

Depending on the circumstances, an advocate in mediation may decide to focus either on money bargaining or creative solutions. The format allows lawyers to advance either of these goals.

Interest-Based Bargaining

We know that interest-based bargaining is desirable. One practical problem for advocates, however, is that even when they wish to explore nonmonetary terms, they are often reluctant to do so for fear of signaling that their client is not committed to its monetary position. This is particularly true of plaintiffs because they are typically the ones seeking damages. Defense lawyers, by contrast, tend to be receptive to imaginative terms, because they see them as a substitute for paying money.

Mediation can allow a lawyer to have it both ways. He can press "publicly" (in communications sent through the mediator or made in joint session) for the best possible money outcome, while asking the neutral "privately" (through a premediation talk or caucus discussion) to explore nonmonetary options.

> *Example:* A large manufacturer sued a supplier of chemicals, alleging that the defendant's product was defective and had caused an unacceptable rate of failure in its products. The supplier was interested in restoring its business relationship with the manufacturer. Not only had the relationship been a source of substantial profit, the supplier knew that if the manufacturer resumed using its products it could not continue to denigrate the defendant's reputation.
>
> Because the plaintiff knew that the quality failure had been a one-time event, it was not necessarily opposed to this. Still, it was wary of talking about a new relationship because it badly needed a cash infusion, and feared that the defense would seize on a "win-win" solution involving providing products at a discount to avoid offering cash. To deal with this problem, the manufacturer's lawyer continued to press for a large money component in any settlement, but at the same time indicated to the mediator privately that her client would not object to a new contract as long as it was not a substitute for a cash payment.

A "Hard" Bargaining Strategy

One rarely mentioned aspect of mediation is that it offers protection to parties who opt for a competitive approach, as well as to negotiators pursuing creative solutions. Indeed, the mediation process allows counsel to take tougher stands than would be possible in direct negotiation. Because mediation is more complicated to arrange than an ordinary bargaining session, participants are more reluctant to walk out in response to an "insulting" proposal. More important, a mediator will work to "scrape the other side off the ceiling" when it erupts at an opponent's stubbornness. Lawyers sometimes take advantage of this dynamic to play "tough cop," knowing that good mediators will instinctively take on a "good cop" role to keep the process alive.

> *Example:* A manufacturer was in a dispute with its insurer over the insurer's refusal to pay nearly a billion dollars in claims against the manufacturer. The parties agreed to go to mediation. The insurer's CEO prepped intensively for the process, planning to have a point-by-point discussion of the merits with the manufacturer's representatives. When the parties convened in joint session and the CEO tried to discuss the case, however, the plaintiff's inside counsel said that he wasn't interested. He had listened carefully to his litigation team's analysis, he said, and saw no point in having a debate. The lawyer went on to say that he would not make any concessions at all on the claim until the insurer agreed to pay the full amount that he believed was due under an "incontestable" section of the policy. That amount, counsel said, was slightly under $130 million.
>
> The mediation was held in a conference room at an airport, and in a direct negotiation, the insurer's team would very likely have been on the next flight out. The manufacturer's lawyer knew, however, that the mediator would respond to his tactic by cajoling, even begging, the CEO to ignore his opponent's obnoxiousness, look at the big picture, examine the legal risks — and put up a very large amount of money. And that is exactly what happened. After hours of talking, the CEO strode into the manufacturer's conference room, wrote "100" on the board, and walked out. Now it was the neutral's job to convince the plaintiff team that although a hundred million dollars might seem paltry in light of its claim, from the insurer's perspective it was a huge step forward. To counter reactive devaluation, he stressed that the right way to assess the offer was to count up from zero, rather than down from the original demand.
>
> Months later the case settled. The turning point came when the manufacturer's counsel — the same lawyer who had refused to discuss the merits with the CEO — intervened to make an unusual request. He asked the mediator to invite the executive to meet him in the lobby of the hotel where the mediation was being held. As the neutral and the lawyers sat in conference rooms, reading newspapers and speculating about what might be going on, the two key players sat down over coffee and cut a deal.

As these examples illustrate, sophisticated counsel can use mediation to enhance both cooperative and competitive bargaining strategies. They can privately encourage a mediator to raise creative options while adhering to a monetary demand, or pursue a genuinely competitive strategy secure in the knowledge that their mediator will work to keep the process from falling apart. Good advocates should also keep in mind that the mediator will be interpreting their position and viewpoint to the other side, and offer suggestions to the neutral about what they want her to say about them in the other room.

2. *Later Caucuses*

As caucusing progresses, the tactics of the disputants and the mediator are likely to evolve. Advocates will continue to probe for information, explore interests, and argue the merits, but as the process continues these aspects usually become less dominant. For one thing, the parties will return to the issues repeatedly, making continued discussion seem repetitive. As a result, during the later stages of a mediation that emphasizes monetary demands, caucuses are likely to become progressively shorter as both sides focus on bargaining. In a creative process, parties often shift their attention gradually from identifying and communicating interests to devising options to satisfy them. In this kind of process caucuses are likely to remain relatively long, but their focus is likely to be on crafting terms to produce the best possible fit of the parties' concerns.

Mediators are also more likely to express opinions as mediation continues. In part this is because as neutrals gather more information, they become increasingly confident about their assessment of the participants and the obstacles to agreement. Parties also typically become more receptive to a mediator's advice; they come to appreciate that the mediator has genuinely listened to their concerns. From the answers he brings back after each round of caucusing, they know that the mediator has communicated their views clearly to the other side. Competitive bargainers in particular are likely to become more receptive to a mediator's advice when they realize that their positional tactics are likely to lead to an impasse. As mediators become more active in the process, advocates should consider modifying their own tactics in response.

a. Facilitating Bargaining

One option is to ask the mediator to assess the emotional "temperature" in the other room, or predict how a counterpart is likely to react to a proposal. Lawyers can also seek to take advantage of the mediator's special status to enhance the effectiveness of their offers.

Obtaining Information

One of the paradoxes of mediation is how mediators are expected to treat information that they gather during private caucuses. On the one hand, caucus discussions are confidential. On the other hand, one of mediation's key purposes is to foster better communication, and as long as the parties are separated in caucuses, this can only happen if the mediator conveys information between them. How can an advocate take advantage of this seeming contradiction?

In practice most lawyers in mediation designate very few facts as confidential, and appear to expect a mediator to reveal at least some of what they say in private caucus. For example, a plaintiff lawyer might tell a mediator, "$500,000 is as low as we'll go at this point. You can tell them 500." The attorney knows that the neutral will interpret this to mean that she can tell the other side that the plaintiff is reducing his demand to $500,000, and also that the plaintiff will probably be willing to go further ("at this point") if the defendant makes an appropriate response.

Experienced lawyers know, in other words, that although mediators will not report sensitive data to the other camp, they will usually feel some license to go beyond simply repeating what a party says, to interpret its general intentions. Unless instructed otherwise, a mediator will convey this information as his own impression, not attributing it to the speaker. The result resembles the way government officials sometimes float trial balloons to the press on a "background" basis. This approach has two advantages. First, the listener may be left a bit unsure of what signal has been given, giving the sender leeway either to reinforce or back away from its message in light of the response. Second, the fact that the mediator is the one making the interpretation makes it appear less manipulative, and therefore less subject to reactive devaluation, than if the lawyer had given the signal directly. Advocates should therefore consider what they want a mediator to say about their attitude and offer in the other room, and state their wishes to the neutral.

Advocates should also consider whether to ask the mediator about the other side's state of mind. If, for instance, a plaintiff seems agitated during an opening session, defense counsel might later ask the mediator, "Has Smith calmed down?" or "If his lawyer recommends a deal, do you think he'll listen?" Alternatively, a lawyer might ask a mediator to collect specific information, such as whether the other side has retained an expert. Lawyers can also ask mediators to explore an adversary's reaction to a potential deal without disclosing their own interest in it.

Questions about what the other side is thinking pose tricky ethical and practical issues for mediators because of the paradox mentioned previously. But that does not mean that counsel should not ask them. Lawyers should be aware, however, that if they ask a neutral for information about their opponent, the neutral may interpret this as permission to provide the other side with the same kind of data about the questioner. As in direct bargaining, in other words, information exchange is often a two-way street. That does not mean, however, that asking questions is not helpful, and mediation can amplify the effectiveness of doing so. To take advantage of the mediator's ability to gather and convey information during the caucusing process:

- Ask the mediator questions about the other side's current attitude and intentions.
- Discuss with the mediator what he will say to your opponent about you.
- Use the mediator as a sounding board for how a potential offer will be received.

Questions

You are in the late afternoon of a mediation of a commercial contract dispute. You and your client have become very frustrated with the slow pace of the bargaining and the defendant's lack of realism. You began with an offer of $5 million, and your most recent proposal was $2.75 million, with a final "bottom-line" target of $1.9 million. The defense opened with an offer of $200,000 and has been inching up, their last move being only from $650,000 to $700,000.

3. In a private conversation while the mediator is out of the room, your client tells you that he is willing to drop to $2.5 million, but that unless the defendant's next offer "hits seven figures" (i.e., $1,000,000) he's inclined to pack up and leave. How might the mediator help you here? What should you and/or your client say to the neutral?
4. Assume that the mediator comes back 30 minutes later with a defense offer of $900,000. What should you do now?

Using a Mediator's Neutrality

As we have seen, mediators have a key advantage that is not available even to the best advocate: the simple fact that they are seen by disputants as neutral. Although the phenomenon of reactive devaluation makes humans instinctively suspect anything that is proposed by an opponent, mediators can potentially deliver bargainers from its impact. Take, for example, a situation in which a defendant is stubbornly clinging to an offer of $75,000. The mediator could say to the plaintiff, "You know, I think that if we could ever get them up to $100,000, it would be worth serious consideration. . . . What do you think?" By phrasing the issue in this way, the neutral has done two things. First, she has presented the offer as hypothetical — it is not yet "cursed" by the fact that the defendant is actually willing to make it. Second, she has tentatively endorsed its reasonableness. If the plaintiff buys into the potential offer, the mediator will have partially "inoculated" it against being devalued if it materializes.

Good lawyers instinctively work to take advantage of the mediator's neutral status. In one of the role-plays in the experiment described previously, for instance, defense counsel's initial response to a high plaintiff demand was to propose that his client provide the plaintiff with future product at a discounted price, but no actual cash. As he made this offer the lawyer was being imaginative, but he also was offering no money so as to deflate the plaintiff's expectations.

Mediator: I've told you that the plaintiff is willing to move significantly from their opening demand. This isn't just the mediator reading tea leaves — they gave me explicit permission to tell you that. . . . But if I go back now and say, "They're willing to give you a discount but . . . *that's it*," we will have a big problem and a short afternoon, I think. . . . But I could be wrong.

Outside counsel: David, we need you to be more . . . *creative* than that. The challenge is going to be to sell [the plaintiff's vice president] on the idea that he can go to his father-in-law with this offer and look like a hero rather than a bum. . . .

To avoid reactive devaluation, the defense attorney also tried to induce the mediator to take responsibility for his proposal.

Mediator: That's going to be a hard sell. . . . But Steve, if that's the way you think is the best way to move this forward, then I'll try it.

Outside counsel: No, I don't think that *those* words are the best way, and I don't think that's the way you would phrase it. I'm confident that you would say to them that you decided after talking to us that it wasn't fruitful to talk in terms of how many dollars we would give them to settle — that *you* came up with the suggestion for a discount program. . . .

Mediator: Well, I'll phrase it however I'm going to phrase it.

In this instance, defense counsel was not able to persuade the mediator to assume authorship of the proposal, probably because the neutral was justifiably concerned that he would seriously damage his credibility if he endorsed an offer that the plaintiff saw as unfair. But the lawyer was not bashful about asking, and in the end he got an excellent result for his client.

> *Example:* A federal government lawyer was willing to settle a weak claim against an insolvent bank for a few cents on the dollar. He was concerned, however, that his agency superiors might refuse to approve the deal. To deal with this, the lawyer asked the mediator to prepare a written case evaluation that he could use as "cover" for his decision to compromise. To avoid the evaluation being used against him if the settlement were not approved, he secured the agreement of the bank's attorney that the mediator would not provide the written evaluation to him, only to the government.

Counsel can take advantage of a mediator's perceived neutrality by:

- Asking a mediator to deliver unwelcome information to the other side.
- Suggesting that a mediator offer a party's proposal or argument as his own.
- Requesting a neutral to certify the fairness of a proposal, either to the other side or to an outside constituency.

Using a Mediator to Carry Out Uncomfortable Tasks

Mediators are freer to use unorthodox tactics to solve bargaining impasses because they needn't worry about maintaining a judge's reserve or showing a litigator's resolve. Attorneys can take advantage of this by asking mediators to take on difficult tasks.

> *Example:* Two brothers were fighting over the business empire of their deceased uncle. Following years of inconclusive court proceedings, the two agreed to mediate. The parties went through a difficult first day, in part because the mediator encountered ambivalence from the plaintiff: He would make a decision, then backpedal after the neutral left the room. The defendant's lawyer became angry over this, and the mediator hinted at what was happening.
>
> The defense counsel told the mediator that the plaintiff couldn't decide anything without first talking to his wife. Unfortunately, the wife was not at the mediation; to alleviate the family's dire financial needs she had taken a job as a bookkeeper at a local store. "Why don't you go talk to her before we meet tomorrow?" the lawyer suggested. With the assent of the plaintiff's attorney, the mediator agreed to do just that.
>
> Early the next morning the neutral drove out to the store, walked down to the basement, and amid boxes of auto parts sat down to talk with the plaintiff's wife. After listening to a tearful story of betrayal and sacrifice, he suggested that she accompany him to the mediation — it was her family's future that was

being discussed, after all. She agreed and rode with the mediator to the mediation site. In the ensuing hours the wife proved to be more decisive than her husband, and also better with numbers. The case settled, but absent an outside-the-box suggestion from counsel, and a mediator's freedom to respond to it, the process would almost certainly have foundered.

Example: In yet another case, a defense lawyer berated a mediator in front of his client for "mistakenly" communicating a concession to the other side — a move that counsel in fact had told the neutral to make, but that his client had apparently balked at accepting. The mediator apologized for the misunderstanding, but the offer broke the deadlock...and the lawyer later complimented the neutral for his effectiveness.

Mediators can take on a wide variety of unusual roles to support the settlement process. They might range from counseling a distraught litigant, to delivering a "hard sell" to a stubborn executive, to acting as the scapegoat for a difficult compromise. If a mediator does not see the need or seems reluctant to take on such a role, however, counsel should take the initiative to ask.

Questions

5. Is there any reason that you as an advocate would feel reluctant to ask a mediator to take the kinds of initiatives described previously?
6. What kind of background would make a neutral more likely to take such initiatives? Less open to doing so?

b. Impasse-Breaking Techniques

Each of the techniques described thus far can help an advocate to achieve more than might be possible through direct negotiation. Suppose, however, that despite a lawyer's best efforts the bargaining process hits an impasse. The reasons can be complex. Negotiations may become stalled because of a process issue such as lack of authority, psychological factors such as loss aversion, merits-based problems like misevaluation of the chances of winning in court, or other obstacles. Impasses occur most frequently when negotiators focus narrowly on monetary solutions, but they are possible even during interest-based bargaining. Two parties may agree, for example, that it would be desirable to restore their business relationship, but reach a stalemate trying to decide how to share the costs and rewards of the new arrangement. When an impasse does occur, advocates can often take advantage of a mediator's assistance to resolve it.

put opinions in question form

Ask the Mediator for Advice

Mediators are experienced negotiators. More important, they have a unique opportunity to observe and talk candidly with both sides and, at least until the end of the process, are not under pressure to express an opinion themselves. As the process goes on, they often acquire a great deal of information about each party's state of mind, approach to bargaining, and priorities for settlement. A mediator will not help one side obtain an advantage over an opponent, and settlement-oriented neutrals do have an interest in seeing each side compromise as much as possible. But when the negotiation process bogs down, advocates should consider asking the mediator for advice about how to restart it. Lawyers can also use a mediator to educate an unsophisticated or emotional client, or to present difficult truths about what is achievable and what it is not. Possible questions for the mediator are:

- What seems to be the obstacle here? What can we do to resolve it?
- Would a gesture toward the other side help?
- Is a new combination of terms likely to get a positive response?
- Are other process options available?

Retry an Earlier Step

Many of the interventions discussed in Chapters 7 through 9 can be useful at the end of the process as well as early on. The concept of returning to a tactic may seem strange — after all, if a particular approach wasn't successful when the participants were fresh, why should it be productive when everyone is tired and frustrated? Necessity, however, can be the mother of invention, in mediation as elsewhere. For example, would a brainstorming session produce new ideas? Does a review of disputed facts appear capable of helping? A party who rejected an option early in the process may become more open to advice as time goes on. As a result, the fact that a particular step has been taken earlier in the process, either with or without success, does not mean that it cannot be used again.

Arrange a Discussion Among a Subset of Participants

A variant of retrying a prior technique is to go to a different format. You will recall, for example, that in the "hundred-million-dollar offer" case, the same lawyer who during the opening session had flatly refused to discuss the legal merits with the defendant's CEO asked weeks later to talk with him privately — and resolved the case. In the "$30,000 coin-toss" mediation, defense counsel asked the mediator to arrange for his client to meet for a second time with the plaintiff's executive, an encounter that led to a solution.

Most common is for a person on one team to talk with his counterpart on the other side: VPs with VPs, experts with experts, and so on. Such discussions can produce genuine insights. Even when this does not occur, however, a new exchange may provide a party with an excuse — a "fig leaf," one might say — to take a step that it knows is necessary to revive the process. By demanding a meeting, even an inconclusive one, a bargainer can feel that he has sent a signal that further concessions will not be easily obtained.

Make a Hypothetical Offer

Counsel who will not make a unilateral concession will sometimes authorize a mediator to make an offer in a hypothetical, or "if...then," format. The motivation can be to test the waters, probe the other side's flexibility, and/or ensure that a potential move will be reciprocated. For instance, a lawyer might say to the mediator, "Given the other side's refusal to go below 250, I cannot see us going beyond 100. However, you could tell them that you think you could get us to 125 if they would respond by breaking 200."

The hypothetical formula gains added impact if it is presented as a final resolution of the case rather than simply as a new move. By proposing an actual settlement, bargainers take advantage of the "certainty effect" described in Chapter 4 — the fact that disputants will often make a special effort if they can achieve complete peace. An advocate wishing to take this approach might say, "You can tell them that if they could only get to 150, you have some optimism that you could convince my client to go there — but only if it would settle the case, once and for all." Such hypotheticals can sometimes short-circuit impasses caused by positional bargaining.

Ask the Mediator to Intervene

If other steps are not effective, lawyers can ask a mediator to intervene directly in the process. Good mediators will delay doing so for as long as possible, knowing that disputants may be alienated by the perception that the neutral is "taking over" the process, or because the mediator wants to avoid asserting control for philosophical reasons. Still, many commercial mediators will intervene actively in a case when the bargaining process appears to be seriously stalled.

If an advocate wants a mediator to adopt a restrained role in the face of impasse, she should make her preference known early in the process. Alternatively, if a lawyer wants the neutral to become more active, she should say that. We discuss next three of the most common interventions used by mediators to resolve impasses — confidential listener, evaluation of the merits, and a mediator's proposal. We also suggest ways in which lawyers can use each tactic to best advantage.

Ask for Confidential Listener

Sometimes each side in mediation will refuse to move to a reasonable position until its adversary has done so. The result is an "After you, Alphonse . . . No you, Gaston . . ." situation in which both sides remain stuck, but the mediator is fairly sure that each would be willing to compromise further. In such situations a mediator may offer to play "confidential listener." This involves asking each side to disclose to him privately how far it would go to settle the case. The mediator can then make a judgment about the real gap between the parties.

At one time participants in mediation tended to assume that unless the parties' confidential positions were identical or very close, the mediation would end. This put considerable pressure on each party to give the mediator its "last and best offer." In modern practice, however, both lawyers and mediators are likely to assume that the purpose of the confidential listener technique is for the neutral to form a better estimate of the actual gap between the parties. People

(handwritten margin note, vertical: "Ask what I want to look for now. Never a bottom line")

now appear to approach the confidential listener on the assumption that the mediator will not end the process even in the face of a large gap.

The first question about the confidential listener technique is whether you wish the mediator to use it. If so, you should suggest it; if not, you should ask the neutral to hold off. Sophisticated lawyers sometimes ask, for example, that a mediator delay doing so for a time, so that the parties can continue to exchange offers. The next question is how to use the technique to best effect. Lawyers should keep in mind that at this point they are in what amounts to a three-sided negotiation, with their opponent and with the mediator. The neutral, one must remember, is not on anyone's side: His goal is simply to obtain a settlement.

Mediators usually do not expect the tactic to settle a case, although they would be delighted if it did. Rather, their goal is to get a more realistic offer from each side. Once both sides have given their response, the neutral usually gives the litigants an assessment of the situation; for example, "You're still a considerable distance apart, but I think it's worth continuing." In addition, neutrals will sometimes ask both parties for permission to disclose their confidential responses on a mutual basis, so that both can form a better estimate of the distance between them.

What should you as an advocate tell a mediator who is playing confidential listener? Unless you are in a situation in which a mediator states explicitly that he wants each side's true bottom-line number *and* you believe that he really means it — that unless the parties' positions either touch or come very close, the mediator will terminate the mediation — it is not wise to give your client's actual final terms. Doing so will place you at a disadvantage in the next stage of the process, in which the parties are asked to continue to bargain, and may lead your client to prematurely dig into an unrealistic position. For these reasons, experienced mediators often avoid asking litigants for a bottom-line number at all. Professor Marjorie Aaron's practice, for instance, is to ask disputants instead for their "next-to-last number"; this sends a signal that she does not want them to commit to a "final" offer.

For a competitive bargainer, the challenge in the confidential listener process is to make an offer high or low enough to set up a favorable compromise, but realistic enough to motivate the other participants to continue. A principled bargainer, by contrast, will gravitate toward a proposal that is solidly based on neutral criteria, but may also leave some room to move. A cooperative bargainer will be inclined to answer the mediator honestly and to consult with the neutral about steps to keep the process alive. Parties can also sometimes couple a response with an indication of their intentions. The explanation can be either for the mediator's private information ("Our number is $100,000. That's as far as we're willing to go at this point. Let's see what they come back with.") or for the other side ("Tell them $100,000 is as far as we're willing to go until they move below $200,000.").

One final point: If a neutral does ask flat out for your "bottom line," how should you respond? If you are cooperative and fully trust the neutral, you can answer with complete candor. In other situations, you may want to adopt this response, suggested by litigator David Stern:

> Based on what we currently know about the case and taking into account the arguments, we believe that the offer we have made is the best we could make.

Obviously, we would like to pay less and [they] would like to receive more, but what we might like is not the issue. If you can give me a principled reason why my client should consider paying more, we will consider it; otherwise, we don't believe that any further adjustments are warranted.

[By this response,] you are conveying at least two messages. First, you are flexible. Second, your flexibility is based on principle — meaning the value of the case — not demands, extortion or other extraneous factors. With this response, you have left the door open for dialogue and you have moved the dialogue to the plane of principle rather than petulance (Stern 1998).

Ask for Evaluation

If shuttle diplomacy fails, lawyers often ask mediators to evaluate the legal merits of a case. As we have suggested, evaluation is a controversial technique but can be useful, not only with opponents but also with clients. Whenever, for example, an advocate stops a mediator in the hall and suggests that he give the client his "thoughts" about the case, the neutral knows that he is being enlisted in the difficult task of client education and management.

In the large majority of situations, evaluation will focus on the legal issues in the case — who is likely to prevail in court, what the damages are likely to be, and similar issues. It is possible, however, to have a mediator evaluate broader issues as well. If, for example, a disputant is suspicious that its adversary will not carry out a proposed settlement, the mediator could assess the risk on the basis of his discussions with the opponent or his experience in other cases.

Before requesting a mediator's evaluation on a legal issue, an attorney should ask himself two basic questions. First, is the primary obstacle to settling this case really a disagreement about the outcome in court, or some other issue that evaluation can address? As we have seen, the real barriers to settlement often lie in issues other than the legal merits. Second, if a mediator does evaluate the merits, is the advocate confident that the result will be helpful — that is, will he get the opinion he wants?

Once a lawyer has decided to seek an evaluation, the next issue is how to structure it so as to maximize the chances of a helpful result. The first issue is what data the mediator will consider. Bear in mind that a mediator's views about a case are usually based solely on the briefs and documents he sees, augmented by personal observations of the people present at the mediation. This has two implications:

- Like trial, mediation has a "primacy" effect: Evidence and people whom the mediator actually observes tend to be more vivid, and thus have more impact on her decision making, than data that the neutral merely hears about. Actual documents and face-to-face encounters with potential witnesses are thus likely to have much more impact on a mediator's opinion than evidence summarized in a brief.
- There is also a "melding" effect: When a mediator cannot personally observe a witness, she must place the person in a category ("nurse," "retired accountant," etc.), then make an assumption about how a fact finder would react to a typical member of that group.

As a result, if you want a mediator to give full weight to a witness or a piece of evidence, you should make a special effort to place it directly in front of the neutral. In a construction case, for example, you might ask the mediator to visit the site so that he has a vivid image of the project when he evaluates legal claims arising from it. You may also want to have a mediator meet a key witness. In mediation, unlike a court proceeding, you can arrange for a private meeting without incurring an obligation to expose the witness to your opponent.

You should also take care to ensure that the mediator takes the time required to give your evidence adequate consideration. Don't assume, for example, that a mediator will read every document you give him. Mediators often receive thick piles of paper that they must review without knowing what will turn out to be relevant later in the process. If a neutral is busy or concerned about keeping down costs, he is likely to skim through voluminous materials and wait for the parties to tell him what is important. In addition, mediators are often reluctant to take long breaks in the midst of mediation to review evidence, for fear of losing momentum. If you have documents that are important to a mediator's evaluation, tell the neutral what you would like him to focus on, provide a highlighted copy of the key passages, and ask him to examine the evidence carefully before opining. A mediator assisted in this way is less likely to jump to an erroneous conclusion.

A second crucial question is what, exactly, you want evaluated. Don't simply say "the case." Ten years ago mediators routinely provided global opinions about the likely outcome if a dispute were adjudicated. Increasingly, however, mediators think of evaluation simply as a means to jump-start a stalled negotiation — more like filling a "pothole" in which the "settlement bus" has gotten stuck than building a road to a predetermined destination. Often a prediction limited to a single issue is enough to put the parties back on the path to settlement. The question then is: What specific aspect of the case do you want evaluated?

Finally, as discussed in Chapter 9, you should not expect every evaluation to take the form of an explicit opinion. Good mediators see evaluation as a spectrum of interventions rather than a single event. They rely on pointed questions, raised eyebrows, and other "shadow" techniques, much more than explicit statements, to nudge negotiations back on track. When an advocate hears a mediator make such comments, he should realize that the evaluation process is under way, but in a form less likely to provoke resentment than an explicit conclusion.

Ask for a Mediator's Proposal

In this method, discussed as part of the "basic mediative strategy" for commercial mediators in Chapter 5, the neutral suggests a set of terms to both parties under the ground rule that each litigant must tell the mediator privately whether it will agree to the proposal if the other side does so. If both say yes, there is a settlement. But if either party rejects the proposal, it never learns whether its opponent was willing to agree. Parties thus know that they can achieve complete peace by saying yes, but that if the effort fails, their bargaining position will not be compromised.

In formulating a proposal, mediators typically try to "balance the pain" that each party will have to bear to accept it (although some neutrals base the proposal solely on their estimate of the likely outcome in adjudication — see Contuzzi 2000). One concern is that mediator's proposals have a take-it-or-leave-it quality: Once made, a proposal will tend to "set in cement," in the sense that both parties will resist agreeing to terms less favorable than the neutral has recommended. As a result, if a mediator proposes terms that are even minimally acceptable to a party in light of the costs of litigation, it will feel significant pressure to accept it.

However, a mediator's proposal has some major advantages. For one thing, it allows a party to test a potential settlement without indicating to the other side that it is willing to compromise. In addition, the technique often works — parties often will go to great lengths to accept a proposal because it holds out the promise of settling the dispute, while at the same time protecting their bargaining positions if it does not. If, however, an advocate believes that he can induce the other side to accept terms more favorable than those the mediator will propose, it is usually not in his client's interest to have the mediator make one. Advocates might also wish to talk with the mediator about what standard he will use in setting the terms: balancing the pain that each side must go through to settle, predicting the outcome in court, or something else?

If There Is No Agreement, Ask the Mediator to Continue

If a case does not settle at the mediation session, what should an advocate do? One option is to try again later. A mediator's task is to keep working for settlement until the parties tell him unequivocally to stop, and he sees no plausible way to change anyone's mind.

This was brought home by a comment made by defense counsel to one of the authors at the end of a long case. The mediator had continued to work after each attorney had told him privately that the case could not settle. Finally, however, the parties did reach agreement. As the mediator went over the terms, defense counsel suddenly exclaimed, "They kept beating you up and you just kept going. You were like . . . like . . . the *Energizer Bunny!*" At first, the mediator found the idea of being compared to a drum-beating pink rodent a bit insulting. But as he thought more about it, the comparison was apt. A mediator's job is to keep advocating settlement until the parties tell him unequivocally to stop, and he sees no way to change anyone's mind.

The corollary is that if a neutral does not appear ready to take the initiative, a good advocate will prod her to do so. Neutrals' spirits, like those of other humans, occasionally flag, and some have a narrow conception of their role. A polite reminder that you are counting on a mediator to pull a settlement out of her hat will often encourage the neutral to make further efforts. Consider this example, related by mediator Benjamin Picker:

An inventor sued a company for patent infringement. The company hired a large law firm to represent it. It was aware, however, that litigation costs in such a case could easily exceed $1 million, and in the meantime its business strategy would be in limbo. The company therefore decided to explore settlement, and it designated a separate lawyer in the firm as "settlement counsel," responsible for seeking an agreement while his colleagues focused on litigating. The lawyer suggested early mediation. The plaintiff agreed, and the parties selected a retired judge as mediator.

At the end of the first day of mediation, notwithstanding a defense offer of several million dollars, the mediator indicated that the parties were far apart and recommended that the process end. Settlement counsel suggested, however, that the mediator instead ask the plaintiff to think about how he would spend the millions of dollars that were on the table, and adjourn the process for a week. The hope was that loss aversion would set in, making the plaintiff reluctant to risk money that was already "his." At the second session, the parties reached agreement.

Questions

7. Parties are mediating a dispute concerning the amount due from a commercial real estate developer to a building contractor under a "cost-plus" contract. You represent the developer. The contract provides that the contractor will be reimbursed for its reasonable costs plus a 10 percent profit. The project is complete and all issues have been resolved except one: The contractor has demanded that the developer pay for the cost of benefits in a tax-sheltered retirement plan accrued by the contractor's employees while they were working on the project. Your client believes that the contract, which is silent on the issue, does not call for reimbursement of employee expenses other than wages and usual fringe benefits such as medical care. The mediation proceeds through an opening session and a lengthy series of caucuses. The law and facts relevant to the issue are exhaustively discussed, but the parties see no reasonable prospect of agreeing on the merits. You privately evaluate the likely outcome in court at a $650,000 verdict for the contractor, with a high verdict of $1 million and a low of zero. You also expect the future defense costs in the case to be roughly $75,000. Your client is reluctantly prepared to offer up to $600,000, and if absolutely necessary would go to a maximum of $700,000. He has no interest in working with this contractor again. During the afternoon the process gradually focuses on exchanges of money offers. The offers are as follows:

Contractor's demand:	Developer's offer:
$1.5 million	$100,000
$1.3 million	$100,000
$1.25 million	$250,000
$1.2 million (with difficulty)	$275,000
Remains at $1.2 million	Defendant refuses to "bid against myself"

(a) Assuming that the only term at issue is money, what should the developer do?
(b) Suppose that your client sees a possibility of using the contractor to do approximately $200,000 worth of work on another property. What process would you recommend?

8. You represent the plaintiff in an employment dispute. It is five in the afternoon, and you have been mediating for nearly eight hours. You began with a demand of $1.5 million, and in response the defendant offered $25,000. After laborious bargaining, you have dropped to $400,000. You need at least $350,000 in a cash settlement, but could conceivably go to $200,000 if your client were offered a good job back at the company. Unfortunately, the defendant is only at $100,000, having moved there from a prior offer of $85,000. Your client is feeling very frustrated and has told the mediator this. The mediator has gone back to the defense and returned.

   (a) Assume that the defendant suggests that the mediator play "confidential listener," and you agree. What should you tell the mediator?

   (b) Assume instead that the defense suggests a "mediator's proposal." Should you agree?

If Negotiations Fail

Sometimes settlement is genuinely unachievable. Even in such situations, a mediator can be of use, by helping counsel to design an efficient process of adjudication. A mediator might, for example, facilitate negotiations over a discovery plan. Or the neutral could broker an agreement on an expedited form of arbitration. To take advantage of mediation even when settlement is not possible:

• Ask the mediator to contact the parties periodically to urge further negotiations.
• Ask the mediator to facilitate agreement on an efficient process of adjudication.

How should an advocate leave an unsuccessful mediation process? Litigator David Stern offers the following advice:

At some point, hours or days after you have started, the mediation process will end. If it ends with an agreement, that is fine. But if you can't reach agreement, accept that as well. Parties and lawyers often get desperate as the mediation nears conclusion, but the dispute remains unsettled. It is possible, but exceedingly unlikely, that the mediation is the last chance to settle the case. More likely, there will be multiple opportunities — at deposition, at court-ordered settlement conferences, before trial, during trial, even after trial and appeal — to settle. As such, do not despair or let your client despair if you walk away without a deal. Not all cases should be settled, and almost none should be settled on any available terms. Most will eventually settle one way or another, so if you can't settle at the mediation, ask yourself what benefits you can achieve before you part ways.

Occasionally, you can agree to keep talking. Sometimes that dialogue will depend on one side or the other developing more information. Or it might depend on how well a witness does at a deposition or whether a particular motion is granted or denied. Search for partial agreements if feasible, or part company respectfully, so that the possibility of future negotiation remains open. In all likelihood, settlement will eventually occur and both you and your client will benefit if you keep that probability in mind.

Too often attorneys treat the mediation process simply as a safe place in which to conduct positional bargaining, trading arguments and offers until they reach impasse. At that point mediators take over the process by making settlement recommendations or offering evaluations. We hope you appreciate that whatever approach you take to bargaining, the mediation process has a great deal to offer you. Lawyers who approach mediation actively, looking at the mediator as a consultant, resource, and potential ally, use the process to best effect and are able to obtain optimal outcomes for their clients.

PART
IV

PUBLIC POLICY, ETHICS, AND LAW

CHAPTER
12

Public Policy and Ethical Issues

A. Policy Issues Regarding the Use of Mediation

An unstated assumption of the readings to this point is that settlement is desirable, and that because mediation assists parties to settle, it is a good thing. But is this always true? Respected thinkers have questioned the presumption that all cases should settle, or that all settlements should be mediated. A particular focus of concern is court policies that require the use of mediation in family disputes. This section explores these issues.

1. Should Some Cases Not Be Settled?

❖ **Owen M. Fiss, Against Settlement**
93 Yale L.J. 1073, 1073-1078, 1082-1090 (1984)

In a recent report to the Harvard Overseers, Derek Bok called for a new direction in legal education. He decried "the familiar tilt in the law curriculum toward preparing students for legal combat," and asked instead that law schools train their students "for the gentler arts of reconciliation and accommodation." He sought to turn our attention from the courts to "new voluntary mechanisms" for resolving disputes. In doing so, Bok echoed themes that have long been associated with the Chief Justice and that have become a rallying point for the organized bar and the source of a new movement in the law. This movement is the subject of a new professional journal, a newly formed section of the American Association of Law Schools, and several well-funded institutes. It has even received its own acronym — ADR (Alternative Dispute Resolution).

The movement promises to reduce the amount of litigation initiated, and accordingly the bulk of its proposals are devoted to negotiation and mediation prior to suit. But the interest in the so-called "gentler arts" has not been so confined. It extends to ongoing litigation as well, and the advocates of ADR have sought new ways to facilitate and perhaps even pressure parties into settling pending cases....

The advocates of ADR are led to support such measures and to exalt the idea of settlement more generally because they view adjudication as a process to resolve disputes. They act as though courts arose to resolve quarrels between neighbors who had reached an impasse and turned to a stranger for help.

Courts are seen as an institutionalization of the stranger and adjudication is viewed as the process by which the stranger exercises power. The very fact that the neighbors have turned to someone else to resolve their dispute signifies a breakdown in their social relations; the advocates of ADR acknowledge this, but nonetheless hope that the neighbors will be able to reach agreement before the stranger renders judgment. Settlement is that agreement. It is a truce more than a true reconciliation, but it seems preferable to judgment because it rests on the consent of both parties and avoids the cost of a lengthy trial.

In my view, however, this account of adjudication and the case for settlement rest on questionable premises. I do not believe that settlement as a generic practice is preferable to judgment or should be institutionalized on a wholesale and indiscriminate basis. It should be treated instead as a highly problematic technique for streamlining dockets. Settlement is for me the civil analogue of plea bargaining: Consent is often coerced; the bargain may be struck by someone without authority; the absence of a trial and judgment renders subsequent judicial involvement troublesome; and although dockets are trimmed, justice may not be done. Like plea bargaining, settlement is a capitulation to the conditions of mass society and should be neither encouraged nor praised.

The Imbalance of Power

By viewing the lawsuit as a quarrel between two neighbors, the dispute-resolution story that underlies ADR implicitly asks us to assume a rough equality between the contending parties. It treats settlement as the anticipation of the outcome of trial and assumes that the terms of settlement are simply a product of the parties' predictions of that outcome. In truth, however, settlement is also a function of the resources available to each party to finance the litigation, and those resources are frequently distributed unequally. Many lawsuits do not involve a property dispute between two neighbors, or between [a major corporation] and the government . . . , but rather concern a struggle between a member of a racial minority and a municipal police department over alleged brutality, or a claim by a worker against a large corporation over work-related injuries. In these cases, the distribution of financial resources, or the ability of one party to pass along its costs, will invariably infect the bargaining process, and the settlement will be at odds with a conception of justice that seeks to make the wealth of the parties irrelevant.

The disparities in resources between the parties can influence the settlement in three ways. First, the poorer party may be less able to amass and analyze the information needed to predict the outcome of the litigation, and thus be disadvantaged in the bargaining process. Second, he may need the damages he seeks immediately and thus be induced to settle as a way of accelerating payment, even though he realizes he would get less now than he might if he awaited judgment. All plaintiffs want their damages immediately, but an indigent plaintiff may be exploited by a rich defendant because his need is so great that the defendant can force him to accept a sum that is less than the ordinary present value of the judgment. Third, the poorer party might be forced to settle because he does not have the resources to finance the litigation, to cover either his own projected expenses, such as his lawyer's time, or the expenses his opponent can impose through the manipulation of procedural mechanisms such as discovery. It might seem that settlement benefits the plaintiff by allowing him to avoid the costs of litigation, but this is not so. The defendant can anticipate the plaintiff's costs if the case were to be tried fully and decrease his offer by that amount. The indigent plaintiff is a victim of the costs of litigation even if he settles.

There are exceptions. Seemingly rich defendants may sometimes be subject to financial pressures that make them as anxious to settle as indigent plaintiffs. But I doubt that these circumstances occur with any great frequency. I also doubt that institutional arrangements such as contingent fees or the provision of legal services to the poor will in fact equalize resources between contending parties. . . .

Of course, imbalances of power can distort judgment as well: Resources influence the quality of presentation, which in turn has an important bearing on who wins and the terms of victory. We count, however, on the guiding presence of the judge, who can employ a number of measures to lessen the impact of distributional inequalities. He can, for example, supplement the parties' presentations by asking questions, calling his own witnesses, and inviting other persons and institutions to participate as amici. These measures are likely to make only a small contribution toward moderating the influence of distributional inequalities, but should not be ignored for that reason. Not even these small steps are possible with settlement. There is, moreover, a critical difference between a process like settlement, which is based on bargaining and accepts inequalities of wealth as an integral and legitimate component of the process, and a process like judgment, which knowingly struggles against those inequalities. Judgment aspires to autonomy from distributional inequalities, and it gathers much of its appeal from this aspiration. . . .

The Lack of a Foundation for Continuing Judicial Involvement

The dispute-resolution story trivializes the remedial dimensions of lawsuits and mistakenly assumes judgment to be the end of the process. It supposes that the judge's duty is to declare which neighbor is right and which wrong, and that this declaration will end the judge's involvement. . . . Under these assumptions, settlement appears as an almost perfect substitute for judgment, for it too can declare the parties' rights. Often, however, judgment is not the end of a lawsuit but only the beginning. The involvement of the court may continue almost indefinitely. In these cases, settlement cannot provide an adequate basis for that necessary continuing involvement, and thus is no substitute for judgment.

The parties may sometimes be locked in combat with one another and view the lawsuit as only one phase in a long continuing struggle. The entry of judgment will then not end the struggle, but rather change its terms and the balance of power. One of the parties will invariably return to the court and again ask for its assistance, not so much because conditions have changed, but because the conditions that preceded the lawsuit have unfortunately not changed. This often occurs in domestic-relations cases, where the divorce decree represents only the opening salvo in an endless series of skirmishes over custody and support.

The structural reform cases that play such a prominent role on the federal docket provide another occasion for continuing judicial involvement. In these cases, courts seek to safeguard public values by restructuring large-scale bureaucratic organizations....

The drive for settlement knows no bounds and can result in a consent decree even in the kinds of cases I have just mentioned, that is, even when a court finds itself embroiled in a continuing struggle between the parties or must reform a bureaucratic organization. The parties may be ignorant of the difficulties ahead or optimistic about the future, or they may simply believe that they can get more favorable terms through a bargained-for agreement. Soon, however, the inevitable happens: One party returns to court and asks the judge to modify the decree, either to make it more effective or less stringent. But the judge is at a loss: He has no basis for assessing the request. He cannot, to use Cardozo's somewhat melodramatic formula, easily decide whether the "dangers, once substantial, have become attenuated to a shadow," because, by definition, he never knew the dangers....

Justice Rather Than Peace

The dispute-resolution story makes settlement appear as a perfect substitute for judgment, as we just saw, by trivializing the remedial dimensions of a lawsuit, and also by reducing the social function of the lawsuit to one of resolving private disputes. In that story, settlement appears to achieve exactly the same purpose as judgment — peace between the parties — but at considerably less expense to society. The two quarreling neighbors turn to a court in order to resolve their dispute, and society makes courts available because it wants to aid in the achievement of their private ends or to secure the peace.

In my view, however, the purpose of adjudication should be understood in broader terms. Adjudication uses public resources, and employs not strangers chosen by the parties but officials chosen by a process in which the public participates. These officials, like members of the legislative and executive branches, possess a power that has been defined and conferred by public law, not by private agreement. Their job is not to maximize the ends of private parties, nor simply to secure the peace, but to explicate and give force to the values embodied in authoritative texts such as the Constitution and statutes; to interpret those values and to bring reality into accord with them. This duty is not discharged when the parties settle.

In our political system, courts are reactive institutions. They do not search out interpretive occasions, but instead wait for others to bring matters to their attention. They also rely for the most part on others to investigate and present the law and facts. A settlement will thereby deprive a court of the occasion, and perhaps even the ability, to render an interpretation. A court cannot proceed (or not proceed very far) in the face of a settlement. To be against settlement is not to urge that parties be "forced" to litigate, since that would interfere with their autonomy and distort the adjudicative process; the parties will be inclined to make the court believe that their bargain is justice. To be against settlement is only to suggest that when the parties settle, society gets less than what appears, and for a price it does not know it is paying....

I recognize that judges often announce settlements not with a sense of frustration or disappointment, as my account of adjudication might suggest, but with a sigh of relief. But this sigh should be seen for precisely what it is: It is not a recognition that a job is done, nor an acknowledgment that a job need not be done because justice has been secured. It is instead based on another sentiment altogether, namely that another case has been "moved along," which is true whether or not justice has been done or even needs to be done. Or the sigh might be based on the fact that the agony of judgment has been avoided. . . .

The Real Divide

To all this, one can readily imagine a simple response by way of confession and avoidance: We are not talking about *those* lawsuits. Advocates of ADR might insist that my account of adjudication, in contrast to the one implied by the dispute-resolution story, focuses on a rather narrow category of lawsuits. They could argue that while settlement may have only the most limited appeal with respect to those cases, I have not spoken to the "typical" case. My response is twofold.

First, even as a purely quantitative matter, I doubt that the number of cases I am referring to is trivial. My universe includes those cases in which there are significant distributional inequalities; those in which it is difficult to generate authoritative consent because organizations or social groups are parties or because the power to settle is vested in autonomous agents; those in which the court must continue to supervise the parties after judgment; and those in which justice needs to be done, or to put it more modestly, where there is a genuine social need for an authoritative interpretation of law. I imagine that the number of cases that satisfy one of these four criteria is considerable; in contrast to the kind of case portrayed in the dispute-resolution story, they probably dominate the docket of a modern court system.

Second, it demands a certain kind of myopia to be concerned only with the number of cases, as though all cases are equal simply because the clerk of the court assigns each a single docket number. All cases are not equal. The Los Angeles desegregation case, to take one example, is not equal to the allegedly more typical suit involving a property dispute or an automobile accident. The desegregation suit consumes more resources, affects more people, and provokes far greater challenges to the judicial power. The settlement movement must introduce a qualitative perspective; it must speak to these more "significant" cases, and demonstrate the propriety of settling them. Otherwise it will soon be seen as an irrelevance, dealing with trivia rather than responding to the very conditions that give the movement its greatest sway and saliency. . . .

[In] fact, most ADR advocates make no effort to distinguish between different types of cases or to suggest that "the gentler arts of reconciliation and accommodation" might be particularly appropriate for one type of case but not for another. They lump all cases together. This suggests that what divides me from the partisans of ADR is not that we are concerned with different universes of cases — that Derek Bok, for example, focuses on boundary quarrels while I see only desegregation suits. I suspect instead that what divides us is much deeper and stems from our understanding of the purpose of the civil law suit and its place in society. It is a difference in outlook.

Someone like Bok sees adjudication in essentially private terms: The purpose of lawsuits and the civil courts is to resolve disputes, and the amount of litigation we encounter is evidence of the needlessly combative and quarrelsome character of Americans. Or as Bok put it, using a more diplomatic idiom: "At bottom, ours is a society built on individualism, competition, and success." I, on the other hand, see adjudication in more public terms: Civil litigation is an institutional arrangement for using state power to bring a recalcitrant reality closer to our chosen ideals. We turn to the courts because we need to, not because of some quirk in our personalities. We train our students in the tougher arts so that they may help secure all that the law promises, not because we want them to become gladiators or because we take a special pleasure in combat.

To conceive of the civil lawsuit in public terms as America does might be unique. I am willing to assume that no other country — including Japan, Bok's new paradigm — has a case like *Brown v. Board of Education* in which the judicial power is used to eradicate the caste structure. I am willing to assume that no other country conceives of law and uses law in quite the way we do. But this should be a source of pride rather than shame. What is unique is not the problem, that we live short of our ideals, but that we alone among the nations of the world seem willing to do something about it. Adjudication American-style is not a reflection of our combativeness but rather a tribute to our inventiveness and perhaps even more to our commitment.

❖ Jethro K. Lieberman and James F. Henry, Lessons from the Alternative Dispute Resolution Movement

53 U. Chi. L. Rev. 424, 432-435 (1986)

. . . Critics of ADR, like Owen Fiss, suggest that ADR proponents mistake the function of courts as "mere" dispute resolvers. By diverting cases from courts, society loses the benefit of court-sanctioned judgments. . . .

Fiss also argues that advocates of ADR have an unstated political agenda: to keep the activist state from meddling with powerful private economic interests. Finally, Fiss suggests that settlements lack the legitimacy of cases fully adjudicated to judgment.

Four responses to this critique are in order. One short answer to Fiss is that most ADR proponents make no claim for shunting all, or even most, litigation into alternative forums. The ADR movement . . . does not suppose that every legal dispute has a non-judicial solution. Indeed, the ADR literature recognizes that some types of cases are not suited to resolution outside the courtroom, including particularly cases in which the plaintiff seeks a declaration of law by the court. Fiss overlooks this accepted limitation of ADR because he assumes, at least implicitly, that all cases resemble *Brown v. Board of Education*. But, of course, they do not. It seems obvious that large classes of cases are not so consequential, and do not call for the definitive ruling of a judge or the imprimatur of an official organ of the state. Automobile accidents, uncontested divorces, breaches of contract, and other common types of suits do not cry out to be memorialized in the official reports, and, in any event, most are settled far short of trial.

A second response to Fiss's critique is that his "conspiracy theory" of ADR is dubious. Many people who seek to use ADR are scarcely "powerful" economic interests — ADR is not limited to adoption by Fortune 500 companies. Moreover, ADR does not dispense with community norms. All dispute resolution takes place with an eye toward existing alternatives — including litigation. Finally, the choice to employ ADR is made by parties who have determined that the injustice resulting from delay and the prohibitive costs of pursuing a case through the courts (direct expenditures for lawyers and expenses, as well as significant indirect expenditures, like lost opportunity costs) far outweigh any putative injustice stemming from the decision to forgo judgment by the court.

A third response to Fiss is that not all questions need to be answered. An open society needs the tension of open questions; parties who settle do not thereby foreclose answers at some later time when matters of principle are truly at stake and the issues cannot be compromised. . . .

Finally, Fiss's position is seriously weakened by his failure to offer proof that court judgments are more just. He says, for example, that "[a]djudication is more likely to do justice than conversation, mediation . . . or any other contrivance of ADR, precisely because it vests the power of the state in officials who act as trustees for the public, who are highly visible, and who are committed to reason."

Does ADR reach a just result or merely an expedient one? How can one measure the justice of a private settlement? The question is important, but it has not been well discussed in the ADR literature — no doubt because it is so difficult a proposition to test. Whatever the answer, it seems fair to ask the same questions of courts. In theory, courts are committed to reason, but in practice much stands in their way. Some judges are dispassionate and disinterested seekers after justice, but not all are. And all judges are busy; it is a fair assumption that they do not have sufficient time to devote to any single case. Moreover, the maneuvering of partisan lawyers alone is often enough to ensure that justice will *not* be done.

A perhaps more controversial response to Fiss's argument about the quality of outcomes is that in certain important classes of cases — cases involving public institutions like schools, hospitals, and prisons (the very cases that particularly interest Fiss) — courts themselves invoke processes that are firmly lodged in the ADR arsenal. Stories that describe litigation over unconstitutional prison conditions, inhumane mental hospital conditions, and segregated schools frequently depict the judge acting as mediator, helping the parties to negotiate the remedy the court will impose by consent decree. If the courts themselves find these processes useful or even necessary, chances are good that the same processes can be as beneficial when invoked outside.

Questions

1. Do you find Lieberman and Henry's response to Fiss convincing? Why or why not?
2. Would you carve out certain areas, or types of disputes, as inappropriate for settlement? Which ones?
3. If you would allow settlement in certain types of cases but only subject to special conditions, what conditions would you impose?

❖ **Richard Delgado, ADR and the Dispossessed: Recent Books About the Deformalization Movement**

13 Law & Soc. Inquiry 145, 145-151, 153-154 (1988)

Early writing on Alternative Dispute Resolution (ADR)...was almost uniformly congratulatory. The movement appealed both to the technocratic-managerial instincts of the right and moderate center, as well as to the desire of many on the political left to avoid the polarization, contentiousness, and all-or-nothing character of formal, in-court justice. Drawing support from across the spectrum, the ADR movement grew rapidly. More recent writings about ADR have been more nuanced. Several respected writers have criticized the politics of ADR or questioned its ability to deliver the promised benefits. At the same time, the proponents' claims have become more modest and less global....

Many of ADR's claims rest on user satisfaction surveys. Yet...satisfaction is a measure of the discrepancy between what a disputant expects and what he or she gets. Since ADR frequently draws only on those who want informality, it is not surprising that they are satisfied when they receive it....When, due to subtle or not-so-subtle pressures, unwilling disputants are brought before a deformalized forum, the forum typically cools out their expectations long before a result is reached....

There are only a handful of basic ways in which our society responds to insoluble social problems — ones that, like blacks' demands for justice, women's claims for comparable worth, consumers' demands for well-made, reasonably priced goods, workers' demands for a larger share of the industrial pie, and everyone's desire for a safe, nonpolluted environment, cannot be solved at an acceptable cost.

If those agitating for reform are aroused and united, we cannot dismiss their problem as a nonproblem or the claimants as nonpersons (as we once did with slaves or do today with children and the insane). That would simply inflame them further. The only solution is to seem to be addressing the problem, but without doing anything that threatens the status quo too drastically....

[One] approach is to enlarge the problem — to concede its existence but insist that it is much broader than most realize, that its solution entails expanding the context and taking account of a multitude of factors....When "the problem" is transformed into something so complex and multifaceted that no simple legal formula can encompass it, it is also likely that no single remedy — such as an injunction or damages — can solve it. Instead, we must strive to avoid simplistic win-lose thinking and look for creative solutions that maximize many variables at once. Equally important,...[s]ince dozens, perhaps hundreds, of details are relevant to a case's resolution, the likelihood that identical cases will recur is remote. Therefore, we can dispense with stare decisis, the rule of law, written opinions, and judicial review....

The movement toward alternative dispute resolution illustrates [this] approach...It is an excellent way of seeming to be doing something about intractable social problems while actually doing relatively little....[P]roblems are not faced, responsibility is diffused, grievants are cooled out, while everyone leaves thinking something positive has been done.

Some grievances will not succumb to burial. They will retain their sharp edges despite being embedded in a mass of extraneous detail. The grievant will decline

ADR's demand for peace, for compromise, and insist that his or her problem be dealt with in accord with justice. In disputes of this type — ones that retain their initial polarity — a second problem with ADR emerges....

Formal adjudication contains a multitude of rules and practices the effect, and sometimes intent, of which is to constrain bias and prejudice. These range from rules dealing with disqualification of judges and jurors for bias, to rules that protect the jury from prejudicial influence... Moreover, studies indicate that simply becoming a member of a jury has a fairness-inducing effect on jurors, causing them to display a greater degree of impartiality and fairness than they ordinarily do in daily life....

... [P]rejudice is widespread in American society — surveys and polls indicate that most Americans harbor some degree of prejudice toward members of groups other than their own.... The expression of prejudice is far from simple, however, and certainly not automatic.... The formalities of a court trial are calculated to check prejudice. The trappings of formality — the flags, black robes, the rituals — remind the participants that trials are occasions on which the higher values of the American Creed are to preponderate, rather than the less noble values we embrace during times of intimacy... [They] also encourage minority-race persons to press their claims more forthrightly....

... ADR can, by expanding disputes beyond recognition, cause them to lose their urgency and sharp edges. When ADR cannot avoid dealing with sharply contested claims, its structureless setting and absence of formal rules increase the likelihood of an outcome colored by prejudice, with the result that the haves once again come out ahead....

Questions

4. In what types of cases is it most likely that the concerns set out by Professor Delgado would arise? Why?
5. Could mediation procedures be modified to take account of these concerns without losing the essential character of the process? How might this be done?

2. Should Some Disputes Not Be Mediated?

a. Issues of Gender, Ethnicity, and Culture

❖ **Michele Hermann, New Mexico Research Examines Impact of Gender and Ethnicity in Mediation**
1 Disp. Resol. Mag. 10-11 (Fall 1994)

Professors and students from the University of New Mexico Schools of Law and Sociology are collaborating on a research project... to study the effects of race and gender on mediation and adjudication of cases in Albuquerque's small claims court. This court, the Bernalillo County Metropolitan Court, is a non-record court with jurisdiction to hear civil cases in which the amount in controversy is $5,000 or less. All three judges are male; one is African American, one is Hispanic American, and one is European American. . . . The court contracts with a local mediation center to operate the court's mediation program, under which all civil filings are screened . . . and about one-third of the cases are referred to mediation.

The research project randomly assigned more than 600 cases to either adjudication or mediation, and tracked both the case results and the participants' reactions. . . . The study sought to evaluate results in mediation and adjudication by using two measures: (1) an objective formula for outcome . . . and (2) subjective measures of satisfaction. . . .

Perhaps the most startling finding is that in the objective outcomes of both adjudicated and mediated cases, disputants of color fared worse than did white disputants. These disparate results were more extreme in mediated than in adjudicated cases. An ethnic-minority plaintiff could be predicted to receive eighteen cents on the dollar less than a white plaintiff in mediation, while an ethnic-minority respondent could be predicted to pay twenty cents on the dollar more. When examining how the ethnicity of the co-mediators affected outcomes, the study found that when there were two mediators of color, the negative impact of the disputant's ethnicity disappeared. The ethnicity of the mediators did not change the objective outcomes of white disputants' cases.

The negative outcomes found for ethnic minority participants were not replicated when the data were analyzed for gender. For the most part, neither the gender of the claimant nor that of the respondent had a statistically significant effect on monetary outcomes in either adjudicated or mediated cases, except that female respondents did better in mediation than male respondents, paying less than their male counterparts.

The examination of procedural and substantive satisfaction produced interesting contrasts to the objective outcome analysis. Despite their disparately poorer outcomes, ethnic minority disputants were more likely to express satisfaction with mediation than were white disputants. Female disputants, on the other hand, were more likely to express satisfaction with adjudication. Indeed, white female respondents, who had the most favorable objective outcomes in mediation, reported the lowest level of satisfaction. Furthermore, compared to other mediation respondents, white women were less likely to see the mediation process as fair and unbiased. Women of color, on the other hand, reported the highest level of satisfaction with mediation, despite their tendency to fare the worst in objective outcomes as either claimants or respondents.

The evidence that disputants of color fare significantly worse in mediation than do white participants raises important questions about whether the traditional mediation process is appropriate in disputes involving ethnic minorities, as well as members of other groups who are traditionally disempowered in American society. . . .

It is far from clear, however, that bias, prejudice, and cultural blindness are the only explanation for the results of the UNM study. The underlying effects may be considerably more complex. . . . Similarly, the fact that white women fare well in small claims mediation does not dispel the concerns raised by scholars . . . about gender bias in other forums, such as family court. . . . In the meantime, mediation and other dispute resolution programs need to pay serious attention to the potential impact of power imbalances between and among parties who are in dispute, and should not assume that mediator neutrality will guarantee fairness.

Questions

6. If the conclusions of the New Mexico study are correct, can you think of any safeguards that might reduce the risk of disparate results in small claims mediation? In the mediation of family disputes?
7. Can you suggest any reason why minorities might be more satisfied with mediation despite receiving less favorable results?
8. The federal courts for the District of Columbia and the Northern District of California have created panels of lawyers to represent pro se parties in ADR (Stienstra et al. 2001).
   (a) Would legal representation in mediation resolve any of the issues identified by Delgado?
   (b) Would providing representation to minority participants resolve the problems suggested in the New Mexico study? Why or why not?
9. Some courts do not refer pro se parties to mediation in situations in which the other side is represented by counsel. Do you agree with this policy? What are its advantages and disadvantages?

❖ **Sina Bahadoran, A Red Flag: Mediator Cultural Bias in Divorce Mediation**

18 Mass. Fam. L.J. 69-73 (2000)

Scenario One: An American wife and her Albanian husband are participating in divorce mediation. The couple shares a four-year-old daughter. During mediation, the wife alleges that her husband sometimes acts inappropriately with their daughter — one time fondling her genitalia. The mediator asks the husband about the wife's allegation and the husband responds that it is true.

Scenario Two: An American man and his Danish wife are involved in a divorce mediation. The couple shares a 14-month-old son. During mediation, the husband alleges that on several occasions his wife left their son outside in his stroller, while she went into diners to have lunch.

Scenario Three: An American woman and her Iraqi husband are participating in divorce mediation. The couple shares a nine-year-old daughter. During mediation, the wife accuses the husband of being violent and aggressive with their daughter. The wife also expresses fear over her husband's renewed interest in Islam.

In each of the above scenarios a mediator, as currently trained, would be unprepared to adequately handle these situations. In other words, mediation would be inappropriate. Scenario One is based on the incident involving Sadri Krasniqi of Plano, Texas. After fondling his daughter during a basketball match, Krasniqi was charged with sexual abuse and lost custody of his daughter. Eventually, five years later, charges against him were dropped after the prosecutors became aware that the idea of parent-child sex is so unimaginable in Albania that parental fondling is acceptable behavior.

Scenario Two is based on the case of Annette Sorenson, a Danish woman who left her 14-month-old daughter outside while she went into a diner to have lunch. Sorensen was jailed and charged with child endangerment. Only later was she freed after authorities learned that "parking," or leaving children in their strollers outside of stores, is common behavior in Denmark.

Scenario Three is a fictitious situation in which the foreign spouse would be just as disadvantaged as in the first two scenarios, not because of *actual* cultural differences, but rather because of *perceived* cultural stereotypes....

American Collective Unconscious: Cultural Myths and Stereotypes.... A non-American spouse entering divorce mediation will face a great many cultural myths and stereotypes....The cultural myths that surround people of various ethnicity and nationality vary greatly, but all are unified by a common theme: cultural inferiority.

...Parent-child suicide, religious fanaticism, barbarity, laziness, wife beating, forced marriage, and female genital mutilation are just some of the images associated with non-European immigrants....Arab Muslims are seen as irrational beings, incapable of achieving cultural or intellectual success....With Asian cultures, the myths take on a different quality. Asians are often seen as the "model minority."...Although intended to be complimentary to Asian-Americans, the "praise" can go too far. Most Asians are seen as being fungible....In contrast to the "model" minority status associated with Asians, Latinos are often relegated to the bottom of the minority hierarchy: laziness, alcoholism, criminality, and gang culture are just a few of the myths....[G]iven the cultural myths and stereotypes that pervade the American collective unconscious, the informal nature of mediation creates an atmosphere that is particularly prone to bias....

Power and Danger of Narrative in Mediation. Much of the power of mediation comes from its opportunity for divorcing spouses to tell their own stories. Each spouse is the director, producer, and actor....Despite the benefits of the narrative style, it is also at the center of the problems with mediation. Mediation is essentially a struggle between two opposing narratives. The prevailing narrative sets the context for all of the subsequent descriptions. Minority spouses will have more negative cultural myths aligned against them and will be disadvantaged in their ability to compete for narrative preeminence....

Imagine a scenario where the Iraqi husband and his American wife are seeking mediation for their divorce. The couple has a nine-year-old daughter and is in a heated disagreement as to custody. One portion of the mediation revolves around an incident where the husband smacked their daughter's hand for misbehaving. In the wife's description, she will assign her husband the role of the violent, strict middle-easterner and herself and her daughter as the innocent victims of his rage. The husband will try and reconfigure the wife's "primary narrative." He will explain that the young girl had repeatedly misbehaved and that he lightly slapped her hand after several previous admonitions. In his narrative, the husband will assign himself the role of the "good" loving father and his wife as the unresponsive, distant mother who allows their daughter to be spoiled.

...The conversational narrative in this case is created from fragments of larger cultural stereotypes....Each spouse will attempt to manipulate the conversation by relying on as many positive cultural stereotypes about their identity group and negative ones about their spouse as possible....The mediator sits in the middle of the competing stories as they circle around her. She must choose one....Her choice will not be explicit, but she will offer more credence to one narrative over the other. The mediator enters meditation with his or her own selected conscious and unconscious cultural stereotypes. As the mediator listens to each spouse's perception of reality, she filters all of the narratives through her own individual (experiential) and cultural (identity group) filter. The effects of the narratives will be greater if they are of a subliminal rather than overt nature....

Questions

10. Do you think that cultural myths are widespread enough to pose a serious problem in mediation? Is the problem likely to be more serious in court-affiliated programs or in private mediation? In what areas are problems most likely to occur?
11. You are the lawyer for a client from an Arabic culture who is involved in a parenting dispute that is going to mediation. How might you monitor whether your mediator is allowing stereotypes to influence her approach to the case?

b. Mandatory Mediation of Family Disputes

As we will see in Chapter 15, most state court systems now require litigants to go through mediation before obtaining access to a judge, and the most popular area for mandatory mediation has been family disputes. Mandatory mediation raises special questions, however, particularly when intimate relationships are involved and the participants do not have lawyers. The following reading argues against the use of mandatory mediation in such situations. As you read it, ask yourself these questions.

Questions

12. To what extent do the concerns raised by Professor Grillo exist if mediation is voluntary?
13. To what extent do they exist if the parties have access to lawyers?

14. If parties to domestic relations cases are not required to mediate, what is most likely to happen in such disputes?

❖ **Trina Grillo, The Mediation Alternative: Process Dangers for Women**

100 Yale L.J. 1545, 1547-1557, 1559-1564, 1572-1576, 1581-1586, 1597-1599, 1609 (1991)

There is little doubt that divorce procedure needs to be reformed, but reformed how? Presumably, any alternative should be at least as just, and at least as humane, as the current system, particularly for those who are least powerful in society. Mediation has been put forward, with much fanfare, as such an alternative. The impetus of the mediation movement has been so strong that in some states couples disputing custody are required by statute or local rule to undergo a mandatory mediation process if they are unable to reach an agreement on their own....

[S]tudies have shown that mediation clients are more satisfied with their divorce outcomes than persons using the adversary system. Although there are significant methodological problems with each of these studies, the existence of substantial client satisfaction with some models of mediation cannot be completely discounted.

Nonetheless, I conclude that mandatory mediation provides neither a more just nor a more humane alternative to the adversarial system of adjudication of custody, and, therefore, does not fulfill its promises. In particular, quite apart from whether an acceptable result is reached, mandatory mediation can be destructive to many women and some men because it requires them to speak in a setting they have not chosen and often imposes a rigid orthodoxy as to how they should speak, make decisions, and be. This orthodoxy is imposed through subtle and not-so-subtle messages about appropriate conduct and about what may be said in mediation. It is an orthodoxy that often excludes the possibility of the parties' speaking with their authentic voices.

Moreover, people vary greatly in the extent to which their sense of self is "relational" — that is, defined in terms of connection to others. If two parties are forced to engage with one another, and one has a more relational sense of self than the other, that party may feel compelled to maintain her connection with the other, even to her own detriment. For this reason, the party with the more relational sense of self will be at a disadvantage in a mediated negotiation. Several prominent researchers have suggested that, as a general rule, women have a more relational sense of self than do men, although there is little agreement on what the origin of this difference might be. Thus, rather than being a feminist alternative to the adversary system, mediation has the potential actively to harm women.

Some of the dangers of mandatory mediation apply to voluntary mediation as well. Voluntary mediation should not be abandoned, but should be recognized as a powerful process which should be used carefully and thoughtfully. Entering into such a process with one who has known you intimately and who now seems to threaten your whole life and being has great creative, but also enormous destructive, power. Nonetheless, it should be recognized that when two people themselves decide to mediate and then physically appear at the mediation sessions, that decision and their continued presence serve as a rough indication that it is not too painful or too dangerous for one or both of them to go on. . . .

The Rise of Mandatory Custody Mediation in California

The movement for voluntary mediation of divorce disputes began several decades ago as lawyers and therapists offered to help their clients settle their cases in a nonadversarial manner. . . . As mediation caught on, it began to be heralded as the cure for the various ills of adversary divorce. . . . Consumers, however, were not embracing the mediation cure. . . . In order to bypass this consumer resistance, some state legislatures established court-annexed mediation programs, requiring that couples disputing custody mediate prior to going to court. . . .

Local courts [in California] have the option of requiring mediators to make a recommendation to the court regarding custody or visitation. If the parties do not reach an agreement, the mediator may also make a recommendation that an investigation be conducted or mutual restraining orders be issued. More than half of California counties have opted to require mediators to make such recommendations. . . .

The Betrayal of Mediation's Promises: The Informal Law of Mediation

The good woman: She comes into mediation ready to be cooperative. She does not deny her feelings, but does not shift them onto her children. She realizes her problems are her problems, that she should not use the children as a way of solving them, and that it is critically important that her husband stay involved in the lives of the children. She does not play victim, but realizes what she is entitled to and insists on it calmly. She is rational, not bitter or vengeful, and certainly not interested in hurting her husband. She understands that she played a role in whatever harms he inflicted on her, since in a family no one person is ever at fault.

The bad woman: She is bitter and wants revenge for things that have happened to her in the past. She fights over the most trivial, petty things. She is greedy and ready to sacrifice her children as a tool against her husband. She is irrational and unwilling to compromise. When a specific, focused response is called for, she responds by bringing up a completely unrelated matter. It is hard to keep her on track. She keeps venting her anger instead of negotiating constructively.

In even the most mundane settings there develops a type of informal law, shared expectations that there is a right way of acting, that departures from this way are wrong, and that an offender should be sanctioned. . . . The norms that govern microlegal systems are unwritten and often not consciously perceived, but they are always present. . . . Persons in the midst of a divorce often experience what seems to them a threat to their very survival. Their self-concepts, financial well-being, moral values, confidence in their parenting abilities, and feelings of being worthy of love are all at risk . . . They are especially vulnerable to the responses they receive from any professional with whom they must deal. Against this backdrop, mediation must be seen as a relatively high-risk process. [T]he parties are extremely sensitive to cues as to how they are supposed to act; they will look to the mediator to provide these cues. Mediators are often quite willing to give such cues, to establish the normative components of the mediation, and to sanction departures from the unwritten rules. The informal sanctions applied by a mediator can be especially powerful, quite apart from whatever actual authority he might have. These sanctions might be as simple as criticizing the client for not putting the children's needs first, or instructing her not to talk about a particular issue. . . .

The Promise to Contextualize Decisionmaking: Principles and Fault in Mediation

. . . The informal law of the mediation setting requires that discussion of principles, blame, and rights, as these terms are used in the adversarial context, be deemphasized or avoided. Mediators use informal sanctions to encourage the parties to replace the rhetoric of fault, principles, and values with the rhetoric of compromise and relationship. For example, mediators typically suggest that the parties eschew the language of individual rights in favor of the language of interdependent relationships. They orient the parties toward reasonableness and compromise, rather than moral vindication. The conflict may be styled as a personal quarrel, in which there is no right and wrong, but simply two different, and equally true or untrue, views of the world.

(1) Are All Agreements Equal? . . . Sometimes, however, all agreements are not equal. It may be important, from both a societal and an individual standpoint, to have an agreement that reflects cultural notions of justice and not merely one to which there has been mutual assent. Many see the courts as a place where they can obtain vindication and a ruling by a higher authority. It is also important in some situations for society to send a clear message as to how children are to be treated, what the obligations of ex-spouses are to each other and to their children, and what sort of behavior will not be tolerated. Because the mediation movement tends to regard negotiated settlements as morally superior to adjudication, these functions of adjudication may easily be overlooked.

(2) Conceptual Underpinnings: Family Systems and Circular Causality. On a more theoretical level, the reluctance to discuss principles is based on the view, held by most mediators, that the family is a self-contained system. Under this view, all parts of the family are equally implicated in whatever happens within it. Each part of this system is simultaneously a cause for, and an effect of, all the other parts . . . Causality is circular; that is, "[n]o specific situation or person is considered the antecedent, cause, or effect of [the] problem. . . ."

Although this systems approach can be a useful one in understanding how families and other social organizations work, it has some serious shortcomings. Most critically, it obscures issues of unequal social power and sex role socialization . . . It is typical for mediators to insist that parties waste no time complaining about past conduct of their spouse, eschew blaming each other, and focus only on the future. For example, one of the two essential ground rules mediator Donald Saposnek suggests a mediator give to the parties is the following:

> There is little value in talking about the past, since it only leads to fighting and arguing, as I'm sure you both know . . . Our focus will be on your children's needs for the future and on how you two can satisfy those needs. . . . [U]nless I specifically request it, we will talk about plans for the future. . . .

The Promise to Include Emotion and the Suppression of Anger

Another criticism of the traditional adversary method of dispute resolution is that it does not provide a role for emotion.... Although mediation is claimed to be a setting in which feelings can be expressed, certain sentiments are often simply not welcome. In particular, expressions of anger are frequently overtly discouraged. This discouragement of anger sends a message that anger is unacceptable, terrifying and dangerous. For a person who has only recently found her anger, this can be a perilous message indeed....

At a recent meeting of a mediation group, a nationally known mediator was a moderator at a round table discussion. In the course of the discussion, a participant stated that she thought one of the problems that divorcing couples had was that they had never learned to fight with each other in a productive way. Several of those present, including the moderator, objected to the word "fight." The speaker tried to make her point more palatable by substituting the words "handle conflict." But this modification was not enough. There was general agreement that we should talk instead about "problem-solving"....

[T]here are other forces which may intensify this dynamic of suppression. Mediators working under time pressures recognize that it takes time to express anger, and its full expression might, indeed, jeopardize a quick settlement. More significantly, there are substantial societal taboos against the expression of anger by women, taboos which have particular force when the disputant is a woman of color....

Mandatory Mediation and the Promise of Self-Determination...

Often, the time allotted to a mandatory mediation is short. Frequently, an entire mediation is expected to take place in an hour or less. Some take place in the hallways of the courthouse. Given these conditions, it is impossible for the state to ensure that an adequate process is being offered even in cases in which people have chosen it. Where the process is inadequate, its imposition is even more troubling.

Moreover, a person married to a liar or con artist knows that that person is often more persuasive than someone telling the truth. In a relationship in which the wife has been abused, for example, the abuser will often appear dominant, charming, agreeable, and socially facile in comparison to his less assertive wife.... Of course, liars show up in court, too; but in an informal process where nothing they say can be disproved, they are in a much stronger position. In sum, a person might decide against mediation because she knows the spouse is not capable of working honestly and productively within the process. Forcing mediation can produce a situation in which the parent with the fewest scruples wins.

A substantial proportion of women who file for divorce state that they do so, at least in part, because they have been the victims of domestic violence. ... Mediation where abuse has occurred is troubling even when mediation is voluntary. Mandatory mediation programs, however, do not always permit abused parties to opt out. Moreover, even where such an exception to the mediation requirement exists, the abused spouse might have trouble showing she is entitled to it....

Choice of Mediator: Partiality and Unacknowledged Perspective

Typically in mandatory mediation, the participants cannot choose their mediator or, at best, have a very limited choice of mediators.... Mediators, however, exert a great deal of power....

Exclusion of Lawyers

In California, lawyers typically are excluded from mediation sessions, and the parties are required to speak for themselves, whether or not they wish to do so. Some argue that exclusion of lawyers contributes to client empowerment. In evaluating whether their exclusion actually furthers client empowerment, it is useful to consider the reasons why a person engaged in a divorce might want the services of a lawyer....

Lawyers as Protectors of Rights. A lawyer who is excluded from the mediation sessions may be hampered in protecting her client's rights, particularly if custody is ultimately to be litigated in court. For example, privileged or irrelevant material, which the lawyer does not believe should be disclosed, may mistakenly be revealed in mediation. Once such privileged information is disclosed, it is often impossible to keep it out of a later court proceeding....

Lawyers as Providers of Insulation. Lawyers serve another function in the divorce process, that of insulating the parties from the hand-to-hand combat and self-help that the rule of law is intended to avoid. The presence of a lawyer means that a party does not have to face his adversary directly if he does not wish to do so. Mediation is often put forward as a method of empowering the parties to a dispute, but the words "Don't call me, call my lawyer" are sometimes the most empowering words imaginable. Mandatory mediation, even absent the pressure to reach an agreement that exists when a recommendation to the court can be made, prevents lawyers from performing this protective function....

There are, then, many good reasons why a party might choose not to mediate. While some argue that mediation should be required because potential participants lack the information about the process which would convince them to engage in it voluntarily, this is not a sufficient justification for requiring mediation. If the state were committed only to making sure that disputants become familiar with mediation, something less than mandatory mediation — such as viewing a videotaped mediation or attending an orientation program — could be required, and mediators would certainly not be permitted to make recommendations to the court. That more than the simple receipt of information is required under a statutory mediation scheme demonstrates a profound disrespect for the parties' ability to determine the course of their own lives.... The legislative choice to make mediation mandatory has been a mistake.

... The adversary system admittedly works poorly for child custody cases in many respects. There are, however, some ways to avoid damaging custody battles under an adversary system, such as enacting presumptions that make outcomes reasonably clear in advance, court-sponsored lectures on settlement, and joint negotiation sessions with lawyers and clients present. When in court, lawyers could be held to higher standards with respect to communicating with their clients, and judges could refrain from speaking to lawyers when their clients are not present. . . .

The only reason to prefer mediation to other, more obvious alternatives is that the parties may, through the mediation process, ultimately benefit themselves and their children by learning how to communicate and work together. Whether this will happen in the context of a particular mediation is something only the parties can judge. . . .

Notes and Questions

15. Your local family court has decided that it should impose protective rules to ensure that litigants are not subject to undue pressure to settle in its mandatory mediation program. It has asked you for advice:
    (a) In what situations should the rules apply?
    (b) What specific protections would you suggest?

The issues raised by the use of mandatory mediation in domestic relations cases do not necessarily apply to other types of civil litigation. Thus Professor Roselle Wissler, for example, found in a study of two state court mediation programs that "the manner in which the case entered mediation produced few differences in parties' assessments of the mediator, the mediation process, and the outcome" (Wissler 1997). See, to the same effect, Stienstra et al. (1997).

c. Domestic Violence Cases

Mandatory mediation is particularly controversial when a case involves possible spousal abuse. Many would foreclose even "voluntary" mediation in such cases. In the following reading, an experienced mediator presents a contrarian view.

❖ Ann L. Milne, Mediation and Domestic Abuse
In Divorce and Family Mediation, Guilford Press
304-331 (J. Folberg et al., eds. 2004)

There are nearly 6 million incidents of physical assault against women reported every year, and 76% of these are perpetrated by current or former husbands, cohabiting partners, or dates. . . . Changes in the law and the increased media attention given to domestic abuse have sensitized the public to this formerly private issue. In contrast, the use of mediation has increased significantly as a less-public forum to resolve disputes between former spouses. Courts in at least 38 states have mandated that parents be referred to mediation when they are disputing custody or parental access schedules.

. . . The juxtaposition of strengthened court and legal interventions in domestic abuse cases with the expanded use of mediation has resulted in considerable controversy. . . . Current arguments about the use of mediation in domestic abuse cases . . . do not focus so much on the mediation process itself, but rather on the nature of domestic abuse and the concerns endemic to these cases. *Mediators should take these public policy concerns seriously....*

In Support

Most mediation proponents agree with the following guidelines:

- Some cases involving domestic abuse are inappropriate for mediation.
- Screening is necessary to determine which cases are appropriate.
- Mediators must be well trained in the dynamics of domestic abuse.
- Participation in the mediation process must be safe, fair, and voluntary.
- Victims of abuse should not be required to mediate.

Given these guidelines, proponents of making mediation available in cases of domestic abuse generally start with the argument of the "BATMA": What is the couple's "best alternative to a *mediated* agreement" ... In short, if mediation is not used, then what? It is argued by both social science experts and legal scholars that mediation is more appropriate and effective than the adversarial process, even in cases of domestic abuse. Some have said that the adversarial process exacerbates the dynamics between partners when abuse is a factor by escalating the conflict and reinforcing the power and control differential and the win/lose aspects of the relationship ... Few judges and lawyers have expertise in the subject of domestic abuse, whereas many mediators have had training in it....

Reframing the Debate

...As in any conflict, the framing of the issues is critical in order to adequately address [these concerns]. Rather than framing the question, *Should mediation be used in cases involving domestic abuse?*, a more useful framing of the issue would be: *What process can we develop that will best help individuals who have been involved in an abusive relationship address the issues between them, so that they can move on with their lives without violence and without the need for ongoing court and legal interventions?* ...

When providing mediation to batterers and victims, the following are excluded from the list of topics to be addressed:

- We are not mediating whether or not the abuse occurred....
- We are not mediating reconciliation....
- We are not mediating fault and blame....
- We are not mediating punishment and consequences....
- We are not mediating dropping of charges, protective orders, or restraining orders. ("Do this, then she will drop the abuse charges.")
- We are not mediating contingencies or leveraging of issues...
- We are not mediating court orders.
- We are not mediating threshold issues.

With the above procedural ground rules in place, the following areas can be effectively mediated:

Terms of Living Apart. Matters such as establishing a date for moving out, determining who is going to live where, division of household accessories, establishing a parenting schedule, and payment of household expenses are all day-to-day living arrangements that parties may need to address. The judge often does not have the time to take up each of these individual issues, and paying lawyers to negotiate them can be too costly for many....

Property Division. Mediation can be a very helpful process for dividing up personal possessions such as furnishings, household supplies, photographs, books, tools, and all the other sundry things that family members need to manage their daily lives.

Financial Support ... Use of Clothing and Toys ... Activities With the Children. Mediation can be a very useful forum in which to share information about what activities the children would enjoy as well as to resolve disputes regarding activities of which a parent disapproves. Is it OK to take the children hunting? To a friend's home? To the corner tavern? ...

School Contact. Is it OK for a parent to stop by the school to say hello to a child or to chat with the teacher? ... Will both parents participate in children's sporting and other school events? ...

Child-Care Arrangements. How will child-care decisions be made? ... If a parent is called away from home, will the other parent be given the first opportunity to babysit? ...

Research Findings

Quantitative longitudinal research on the impact of mediation in cases of domestic abuse is lacking.... [S]tudies found that mediation was associated with a greater reduction in physical, verbal, and emotional abuse than lawyer-assisted settlement.... For the growing unrepresented or pro se population of litigants, mediation may be the only consumer support available, short of litigation. Outcome studies on the impact of precluding mediation would be very illuminating.

"Confessions of a Mediator"

I have been a mediator for more than 30 years and have worked in both a court-connected setting and a private practice. Over time I have come to several personal conclusions and observations about my own practices when mediating cases involving allegations or instances of domestic abuse:

I Am Far More Controlling of the Process. Whereas I normally espouse a mildly directive, facilitative style, when I am mediating in a case known to me to include allegations or instances of domestic abuse, I often find that I must be far more controlling of the process.... At the same time, I need to avoid becoming enmeshed in an arm-wrestling contest with the batterer, who may attempt to take over the process....

Judgment is Important. The role of the mediator is typically described as that of a nonjudgmental neutral party.... However, when mediating in cases of possible or known domestic abuse, ... [t]he mediator must continually reevaluate whether this case is appropriate for mediation and whether he or she has the skills needed to work effectively with this couple.

Forget the Balancing Act. Terms such as *maintaining balance, power balancing,* and *level playing field* are often used when describing the mediation process. However, when mediating in a case involving issues of domestic abuse, I find that I am "off-balance" much of the time because I am challenged to keep control of the process.

The Process Is Less Collaborative and More of a Facilitated Negotiation. ... The parties focus more on their separate interests and solutions rather than the mutual interests that I tend to focus on when abuse is not a factor.

Short-Term Agreements. One of the incentives to using mediation in cases involving concerns about domestic abuse is the ability to put in place agreements of a short-term nature and revisit and revise them as needs dictate. Predictability and steadfastness are not often present with these couples. Putting together agreements or court orders that apply over the long haul is often counterproductive. ...

Need for Reliable Resources. The need to establish a scaffolding of support can be very important when mediating in domestic abuse cases. The support of the parties' attorneys, victim and batterer advocates, counselors, and a safety plan can all work together to facilitate the success of the mediation process.

Watch Your Language. Colloquialisms that I use in everyday speech can often take on unintended meanings with domestic abuse partners. Using expressions such as "Can you live with that?," "It strikes me that ...," or "Please cut that out," would be insensitive and inappropriate with couples who have abuse issues. ...

Sweat Equity Is a Fact of Life. I usually tell my mediation students that I know something is wrong when I am working harder than the clients. I have found that, when mediating in cases where abuse concerns have been raised, my skills are challenged, there is a level of stress not found with non-abuse cases, and I work *hard* to ensure that the mediation process is serving the interests and safety of both parties.

Conclusions

The question of whether or not mediation is appropriate in cases of domestic abuse must be reframed to focus on finding an answer to the question of what kind of system we could design that would provide a safe and secure decision-making process for spouses and parents in dispute. Although a traditional mediation process may not offer the protection necessary in domestic abuse cases, dismissing mediation outright may also be a mistake. The development of hybrid mediation models that embody the self-determination principles of the mediation process while also addressing power, control, coercion, and safety issues must be the goal.

Questions

16. Does Milne's model accommodate Grillo's concerns? Overall, which approach seems most appropriate?

17. Assuming Milne's model could work in the right circumstances, is it practical to implement in court programs, even on a voluntary basis? What assurances would you need to support such a program in your local family court?

18. If you favor excluding cases involving allegations of abuse from court programs, would you also favor barring such cases from going to private mediation on a voluntary basis?

d. Termination of Parental Rights

Mediation is also used in disputes over state efforts to terminate parental rights, an area that also raises very serious policy issues. Consider the following case.

❖ *In the matter of T.D., Deprived Child, et al. v. State of Oklahoma, et al.*

2001 Okla. Civ. App. 92 (2001)

COLBERT, J.:

Mother, Pamela Dawn LaTray, appeals the district court's order terminating her parental rights in T.D. and awarding custody to Father, Sean Loftin. The issue on appeal is whether the district court erred in terminating Mother's rights based on the terms of a mediation agreement between Mother, Father, the District Attorney, and attorneys representing T.D.

Mother is the biological mother of T.D . . . and Father is T.D.'s biological father. Although Mother and Father cohabited at the time of T.D.'s birth, they separated when T.D. was approximately 8 months old. Mother moved to Oklahoma with T.D., and Father was unable to locate them until T.D. was 3 years old. Mother subsequently married Damien C. LaTray, Sr., and T.D. lived in their home, along with LaTray's biological son. [In] 1997, the State of Oklahoma filed a petition seeking the adjudication of T.D. as deprived. The petition included allegations of physical abuse, exposure to sexual activity, domestic violence, and substance abuse. T.D. was removed from Mother's home and placed with Father and his wife. Mother stipulated to the allegations in the petition [and a few months later the] State filed an amended petition . . . seeking the termination of Mother's parental rights.

. . . Mother and her attorney met in mediation with Father, Father's attorney, an assistant district attorney, and three attorneys representing T.D. Following a full day of mediation, they executed an agreement in which Mother agreed to voluntarily relinquish her parental rights to T.D. on [several conditions. The] district attorney [also] agreed that "no act of omission or commission committed by" Mother or her husband occurring before the date of the mediation conference would be used as a basis for terminating their parental rights in [the Mother's second] baby. The district court accepted the mediation agreement . . . without comment. . . .

[A few months later] the Department of Human Services (DHS) filed a report with the district court recommending that T.D. remain with Father and his wife in their home and that Mother's parental rights be terminated. The report stated that efforts to reunite T.D. with his Mother had failed and that "[T.D.] continues to have behavioral problems associated with the abuse he has endured." The report included the following information: In the past, [Mother and her husband] have participated in swinger magazines and at the Centerfold Club. [They] also appeared on the Jerry Springer television program in the past displaying their untraditional lifestyle.

On February 25, 2000, the independent assessment of Karen S. Baumann, a psychologist, was filed with the district court in partial satisfaction of the mediation terms. Dr. Baumann reported that . . . "T.D. was diagnosed with post traumatic stress disorder, general anxiety disorder, and attention deficit disorder with hyperactivity. [Father and his wife] appear to be emotionally stable and loving parents."

Mother contends on appeal that the district court erred in enforcing the mediation agreement.... Certainly, mediation is encouraged by Oklahoma courts. However, the use of mediation in a proceeding involving the termination of parental rights for cause has not been considered in any published Oklahoma case of which this court is aware.

... Oklahoma's legislature, in constructing the current statutory scheme, has not contemplated the use of mediation in the context of a state-initiated effort to involuntarily terminate parental rights, and this court is troubled by its use. *Parental rights are fundamental rights* ... The courts will apply the tests of strict judicial scrutiny to a state law which interferes with the exercise of fundamental rights and liberties explicitly or implicitly protected by the Constitution.

We have applied "strict judicial scrutiny" to this mediation process and find that it is seriously lacking in protecting the fundamental due process rights of an individual whose parental rights are in danger of termination. [T]his process lacked a significant procedural protection — that the trial court found a factual basis for its determination that Mother knowingly and voluntarily agreed to the *full and final* relinquishment of her parental rights in T.D. *One of our concerns with this mediation agreement is that it purports to release Mother from all accrued and future child support obligation. Such contracts have generally been held to be against public policy. Second, the terms of this agreement indicate that Mother was trying to protect her parental rights in a newborn baby. The idea of the district attorney trading the rights of one child to be raised in a safe and loving environment for the similar rights of another, younger child would seem to run counter to the public policy of this state.*

This also raises the question of Father's place in this proceeding. Oklahoma law *requires that the trial judge verify, on the record, that the relinquishing parent has been informed of the consequences of her action, answered certain required questions, and has agreed to the full and irrevocable relinquishment of her parental rights.* [Emphasis in original.]

There is nothing in the record before this court... to indicate that those procedural safeguards were observed in this case. Although Mother was represented by counsel... ultimately, Mother's full understanding and acceptance of the results of her agreement are not reflected in the record before us. They must be before this termination can be upheld....

GOODMAN, P.J., dissenting:

I would not permit mediation of a non-voluntary proceeding by the State to terminate the rights of a parent to a child.

Questions

19. Should mediation be permitted at all in proceedings to terminate parental rights?
20. If so, are the procedural assurances suggested by the majority adequate? What would you require? If you conclude that mediation should not be permitted, would it change your opinion if studies showed that on average parents fared no better, and perhaps worse, in cases that were not mediated?

B. Ethics Issues for Advocates and Neutrals

Lawyers may engage in mediation either as advocates or as neutrals. Some attorneys play both roles, maintaining an active law practice and also accepting assignments as a mediator. The ethical issues for each role are different, and we discuss them in turn.

1. Advocates in Mediation

We have seen that advocates in mediation act primarily as negotiators. The rule that governs lawyers as negotiators is ABA Model Rule 4.1, which does not mention mediation. The ABA has proposed changes to the Model Rules through its Ethics 2000 (or "E2K") Commission. The E2K recommendations would change lawyers' obligations in the arbitration process by defining the arbitrator as a "tribunal" to which counsel owe a heightened duty of candor. (See E2K Report, Rules 1.0(m), 3.3, on the book Web site.)

The proposed changes do not, however, grant similar status to mediators. Neither the current nor the proposed rules require attorneys to be more truthful with mediators than with opponents in direct negotiation. In the view of Dean James Alfini, the effect of the proposed changes is that mediation

> would appear to fall into a gap (or black hole) between the formal proceedings contemplated by Rule 3.3 [Candor Toward the Tribunal] and the informal settings contemplated by Rule 4.1 [Truthfulness in Statements to Others]....Thus, lawyering activities in mediation would appear to be governed by the permissive Rule 4.1...which provides an inadequate ethics infrastrucure to support the settlement culture that has developed over the past 20 years....The rules should be re-drafted to hold lawyers to a higher standard of conduct [in mediation]....(Alfini 2001)

Professor Cooley has similarly written that "As long as there are not uniform ethical standards defining truthfulness in mediation, lawyer-mediators and mediation advocates will have the unfettered capacity to practice their showmanship and produce their 'magic' effects by any method they wish" (Cooley 1997).

Although ethical canons say nothing on the subject, other standards may apply to a lawyer in mediation. For one thing, many court-connected ADR programs impose standards of conduct on participants, such as the obligation to mediate in good faith. Lawyers who engage in private mediation also often sign agreements that commit them to standards of conduct, for example to appear with full settlement authority. Finally, as we saw in the context of direct bargaining, advocates often voluntarily choose to observe standards higher than the minimum requirements of the Model Rules. Attorneys may do so because their personal values call for a cooperative approach to bargaining, or for practical reasons such as the wish to maintain good professional relation-ships within their community. Special issues may arise, however, when advocates bargain in the context of mediation. These are discussed below.

a. Candor Toward the Mediator

We saw in Chapter 11 that bargaining in mediation is unique because it is often three-sided. At times disputants are negotiating directly with their opponent, using the mediator simply as a better channel of communication ("Tell them that we won't move into six figures until . . ."). Attorneys adopting a competitive bargaining approach, however, often also negotiate with the neutral. Here are two examples:

Mediator: "I understand that your current offer is $10,000, but can you give me a private indication of where you'd be willing to go if the plaintiff dropped its demand significantly?"

Lawyer: "Well, if they drop to six figures, I would recommend. . . ."

Mediator: "I am going to ask each side to tell me confidentially how far they would go to get a final settlement in this matter. . . ."

Lawyer: "The absolute bottom dollar we can take in this case is. . . ."

Should lawyers be more candid with a mediator than with an adverse party? While there is no legal obligation to bargain differently, there are practical reasons why an advocate might do so. First, if a mediator adopts a cooperative approach, disputants might feel a natural inclination to reciprocate. A lawyer might also opt to treat a mediator well, in the hope that she would reciprocate by exercising her influence over the process to the client's benefit.

Problem 1

You represent the employer in a bitterly contested case involving an executive fired from a Silicon Valley company. The parties have bargained fiercely for several hours. For the past hour they have been at an impasse. The mediator now offers to make a mediator's proposal in an effort to break the deadlock. You ask for a few minutes to confer privately with your client, the company's CEO. After batting the idea back and forth, the CEO says, "I don't think we can live with that, but let's say 'yes' and see if the plaintiff bites. Nothing's final until it's signed anyway." You fear that the CEO is simply testing the waters and will renege if the employee accepts the deal.

(a) Can you indicate that your client assents to the proposal? Would doing so violate the Model Rules?
(b) Suppose that the CEO's tactic will achieve her goal, but will impair your credibility with the mediator in future cases. Does this change the analysis?
(c) Under the law of confidentiality in your jurisdiction, can anyone be compelled to testify concerning your client's response to the mediator's proposal?

Problem 2

Assume the same facts, except that the CEO thinks that the plaintiff's entire case is bogus. She does not authorize you to make any settlement offer, and tells you to go to mediation "just to see where they're coming from." The president will be available by telephone, but has given no indication that she will authorize you to make a settlement offer.

(a) If the mediation agreement commits the parties to bargain "in good faith," is your client violating it?
(b) Do you owe the mediator or the other party any obligation to disclose your situation?
(c) If you disagree with this approach, how would you explain your viewpoint to the client?

b. Obligations to Other Parties

The Model Rules of Professional Conduct impose few obligations on a lawyer vis-à-vis an adversary party. However, lawyers in mediation may have, or feel, other responsibilities. Consider the following problems.

Problem 3

You are a lawyer preparing for your first mediation with mediator Alvarez, who began her practice as a neutral about a year ago, after a long career as a civil litigator. She had an excellent reputation as a lawyer and did well with a small personal injury case that you mediated with her six months ago. You ran into Alvarez on the street a few weeks ago, and she mentioned her interest in doing another case with you. A long-term client, a casualty insurer, has asked you to mediate a major tort case. You recommended Alvarez as a possibility, and it appears that she would be acceptable to the plaintiff's counsel. As you are preparing to call the mediator to make final arrangements, your contact at the insurer calls and says: "Tell her we're a major player in the market. If she gets a good result on this one, we'll think strongly about sending her more cases."

(a) Under the Model Rules, the sample commercial mediation agreement in the Web Appendix, or any other applicable standard, is it improper for you to pass along this comment to Alvarez? Why or why not?
(b) If you say something to the mediator, how will you phrase it? If not, what if anything will you say to the adjuster?

Problem 4

You practice as a litigator in a small firm and are representing a plaintiff in an automobile tort case. The defendant is insured by a major insurance company. Given the market power of the insurer, you are concerned that the mediator might be less than fully neutral. Is there anything that you can do to alleviate your concern? Is there any risk to your proposed course of action?

c. The Duty to Advise Clients About ADR

An increasing number of jurisdictions require lawyers to advise clients about the nature of alternative dispute resolution and the potential for using it in their dispute. For example, Colorado (via the bar association), Arkansas (by statute), and Ohio, New Jersey, and Massachusetts (through court rules), each require attorneys to give such advice. Several federal and state courts have adopted similar rules. Comments to the ABA's Ethics E2K proposals concerning advice to clients also mention ADR, stating that, "In general, a lawyer is not expected to give advice until asked by the client. . . . [W]hen a matter is likely to involve litigation, it may be necessary . . . to inform the client of forms of dispute resolution that might constitute reasonable alternatives to litigation . . ." (E2K Report, Comments to Rule 2.1).

Questions

21. The Colorado Bar's Code of Ethics states that lawyers should "advise the client of alternative forms of dispute resolution that might reasonably be pursued to attempt to resolve the legal dispute or to reach the legal objective sought." Draft the key points you would mention about ADR if you were meeting with a secretary at a local manufacturing company who had just retained you to sue the company for sexual harassment that created a hostile work environment, forcing her to leave her job.
22. What, in practical terms, does the Colorado rule require an attorney to do? Could a lawyer comply with the rule by giving a one-sentence definition of mediation and saying that it would be a waste of time in this particular case? If so, does the rule have any value?

2. *Concerns for Mediators*

There is no empirical evidence that mediators often engage in misconduct. Professor Michael Moffit has observed that: "Despite the thousands, if not millions of disputants who have received mediation services, instances of legal complaints against mediators are extraordinarily rare." His exhaustive survey yielded only one reported case in the past quarter century in which a verdict had been entered against a mediator for improper conduct, and that result was overturned on appeal. The cost of mediator malpractice insurance is also very low. In 2005, for example, a large insurer offered a million-dollar liability policy for mediators in most states for a premium of less than $600 per year. Such rates could not be offered if there were a significant number of claims requiring a defense, much less a money payment.

The absence of lawsuits against mediators does not necessarily mean that they do not commit misconduct, however. Many neutrals operate under civil immunity conferred by the rules of court-sponsored programs or by mediation agreements. Even if a mediator is not immune from suit, it is likely to be difficult as a practical matter for a plaintiff to prove a causal connection between a mediator's misconduct and an ascertainable monetary loss (Moffit

2003b). How could a complainant show, for example, that a mediator's misconduct caused it to settle on different terms or led to a worse outcome at trial?

Even allegations of mediator misconduct are relatively unusual. In Florida during the late 1990s, for example, state courts were sending more than 100,000 cases per year to mediation. Florida maintains a board to investigate complaints against court-certified mediators, but over its first eight years of operation the Board received an average of only six complaints per year (Bergman and Bickerman 1998). Formal complaints against mediators thus appear to be extremely infrequent — although this is admittedly only a minimal measure of ethical behavior.

Several ADR organizations have promulgated codes that are intended to guide mediators in resolving ethical issues. But unless a mediator is part of a panel affiliated with a court or another organized program, the absence of licensing means that she will not be subject to binding rules akin to the canons of ethics for lawyers. In the interest of advancing the field, and recognizing the value of self-regulation as a way to avoid bureaucratic controls, the American Arbitration Association, the American Bar Association, and the Association for Conflict Resolution joined together to draft a voluntary ethical code, known as the Standards of Conduct for Mediators (Model Standards). The Uniform Mediation Act (UMA) also requires the disclosure of mediator conflicts of interest, and individual states and ADR programs have promulgated rules for mediators that incorporate ethical norms.

The Model Standards, the UMA, and other prominent ethical standards for mediators appear on the book Web site, and excerpts are set forth below. Please consider them and answer the questions that follow.

❖ Excerpts from the Model Standards of Conduct for Mediators (2005)

Standard I: Self Determination

A. A mediator shall conduct a mediation based on the principle of party self-determination. Self-determination is the act of coming to a voluntary, uncoerced decision in which each party makes free and informed choices as to process and outcome. Parties may exercise self-determination at any stage of a mediation, including mediator selection, process design, participation in or withdrawal from the process, and outcomes....

B. A mediator shall not undermine party self-determination by any party for reasons such as higher settlement rates, egos, increased fees, or outside pressures from court personnel, program administrators, provider organizations, the media or others.

Standard II: Impartiality

A. A mediator shall decline a mediation if the mediator cannot conduct it in an impartial manner. Impartiality means freedom from favoritism, bias or prejudice.

B. A mediator shall conduct a mediation in an impartial manner and avoid conduct that gives the appearance of partiality....

Standard III: Conflicts of Interest

A. A mediator shall avoid a conflict of interest or the appearance of a conflict of interest during and after a mediation. A conflict of interest can arise from involvement by a mediator with the subject matter of the dispute or from any relationship between a mediator and any mediation participant, whether past or present, personal or professional, that reasonably raises a question of a mediator's impartiality....

Standard IV: Competence

A. A mediator shall mediate only when the mediator has the necessary competence to satisfy the reasonable expectations of the parties....

Standard V: Confidentiality

A. A mediator shall maintain the confidentiality of all information obtained by the mediator in mediation, unless otherwise agreed to by the parties or required by applicable law.

B. A mediator who meets with any persons in private session during a mediation shall not convey directly or indirectly to any other person, any information that was obtained during that private session without the consent of the disclosing person....

Standard VI: Quality of the Process

A. A mediator shall conduct a mediation in accordance with these Standards and in a manner that promotes diligence, timeliness, safety, presence of the appropriate participants, party participation, procedural fairness, party competency and mutual respect among all participants....

Standard VII: Advertising and Solicitation

A. A mediator shall be truthful and not misleading when advertising, soliciting or otherwise communicating the mediator's qualifications, experience, services and fees....

Standard VIII: Fees and Other Charges

A. A mediator shall provide each party or each party's representative true and complete information about mediation fees, expenses and any other actual or potential charges that may be incurred in connection with a mediation....

B.... A mediator should not enter into a fee agreement which is contingent upon the result of the mediation or the amount of the settlement....

Standard IX: Advancement of Mediation Practice

A. A mediator should act in a manner that advances the practice of mediation....

❖ Excerpt from the Uniform Mediation Act

Section 9. Mediator's Disclosure of Conflicts of Interest, Background

(a) Before accepting a mediation, an individual who is requested to serve as a mediator shall:
  (1) make an inquiry that is reasonable under the circumstances to determine whether there are any known facts that a reasonable individual would consider likely to affect the impartiality of the mediator . . . and
  (2) disclose any such known fact to the mediation parties as soon as is practical before accepting a mediation.
(b) If a mediator learns any fact described in subsection (a)(1) after accepting a mediation, the mediator shall disclose it as soon as is practicable.
(c) At the request of a mediation party, an individual who is requested to serve as a mediator shall disclose the mediator's qualifications to mediate a dispute. . . .

Note: UMA Sections 4–8 contain substantive prohibitions against a mediator's disclosure of information about the process.

❖ Excerpt from ABA Model Rules Professional Conduct (2004)

Excerpt from Rule 1.12 Former . . . Mediator or Other Third-Party Neutral

(a) Except as stated in paragraph (d), a lawyer shall not represent anyone in connection with a matter in which the lawyer participated personally and substantially as a . . . mediator . . . unless all parties to the proceeding give informed consent, confirmed in writing.
(b) A lawyer shall not negotiate for employment with any person who is involved as a party or as lawyer for a party in a matter in which the lawyer is participating personally and substantially as a judge or other adjudicative officer or as an arbitrator, mediator or other third-party neutral. . . .
(c) If a lawyer is disqualified by paragraph (a), no lawyer in a firm with which that lawyer is associated may knowingly undertake or continue representation in the matter unless:
  (1) the disqualified lawyer is screened from any participation in the matter and is apportioned no part of the fee therfrom; and
  (2) written notice is promptly given to the parties and any appropriate tribunal to enable them to ascertain compliance with the provisions of this rule. . . .

Questions

23. Any standard of conduct embodies a vision of what the mediation process should be. Can you classify the vision implicit in the Model Standards in terms of mediator styles — broad or narrow? Facilitative or evaluative/directive?

24. Do the Model Standards appear to discourage any particular approach to mediation?

The Model Standards embody core values of mediation, such as party self-determination, mediator impartiality, and the maintenance of confidentiality, and for that reason are fairly noncontroversial. The fact that rules are widely accepted does not mean, however, that they are easy to apply in practice. Most ethical codes are clear about what a mediator must do in egregious situations, such as when she discovers that a case involves a family member or close friend. Good mediators, however, have little difficulty deciding how to behave in such cases. Far more difficult are situations in which two ethical principles, each of which is valid in itself, come into conflict, and there appears to be no way to satisfy both. To understand how this can occur, consider the following problems.

a. Issues of Fairness

Among the most serious problems are issues of fairness. They arise most often in cases in which the disputants are proceeding pro se. Such situations present a tension between Sections I, II, and VI of the Model Standards.

Problem 5

In a private mediation of a divorce case, the husband appears without a lawyer and the wife has counsel. As the process goes forward, the husband becomes progressively more upset, sometimes making illogical arguments and reversing decisions that he had previously made. The mediator suggests to the husband that the mediation be adjourned so that he can rest and consult a lawyer, but the husband expresses a strong wish to "get it over with." He tells the mediator privately that "outside factors" make it important that he resolve the case quickly. The husband will not explain what they are, but the mediator suspects that he has formed a new relationship and is anxious to get out of his old one. The wife's counsel, sensing this, drives a very hard bargain, demanding that she receive 50 percent more alimony than court guidelines would suggest and three-quarters of the marital estate. The process continues for several hours. The husband becomes increasingly upset but refuses to stop. At one point, late in the afternoon during a private caucus, he says to the mediator in an agitated tone, "This can't go on any longer! I guess I've got to take their offer."

(a) What provisions of the Model Standards apply to this situation?
(b) How should the mediator respond? What problems could arise if the husband signs an agreement?

Problem 6

A volunteer mediator is handling landlord-tenant cases in a community mediation program. A case is referred over by a court clerk. The defendant is a tenant facing eviction who is proceeding pro se. The landlord is a corporation represented by counsel. The tenant seems to have little understanding of what will happen in court if he does not settle. At one point shortly before lunch, the landlord offers a "final deal": He will allow the tenant two more months' occupancy, provided that all past rent is paid, the future rent is put into escrow, and the tenant agrees now to the entry of judgment for eviction at the end of the two months. The landlord's representative states that if the plaintiff does not accept the offer by 2 P.M., he will go back to court and ask the judge to rule on his request that the tenant be ordered to vacate the premises within seven days.

The tenant is unsure what to do, and in a private caucus asks the mediator, "Are they right about the law here? What do you recommend?" The mediator privately believes that if the tenant offers to pay rent into escrow, it is very likely that the court will give him at least six months to move, although for a judge to grant the landlord's request is not inconceivable.

(a) Which of the Model Standards apply? What do they counsel the mediator to do?
(b) Is it significant that this case was referred to mediation by a court?

b. Questions of Competence

Mediators sometimes encounter cases in areas in which they have not practiced or previously mediated — indeed, if their practices expand such situations are quite likely. What obligation does a mediator have to disclose her lack of expertise to disputants? Article IV of the Model Standards and Section 9 of the UMA each deal with this issue. Consider this situation.

Problem 7

You are a litigator with ten years' experience who occasionally acts as a mediator. You have handled a total of 15 mediations as a neutral and participated in dozens more as an advocate. You have been asked to mediate a bitter employment dispute involving an employee who says that she was sexually harassed by her supervisor and that management knew of the problem but "swept it under the rug." You do not handle employment cases and have never mediated one, but you do read summaries of decided cases that are printed in your local legal newspaper, and these include court decisions in employment cases, among others.

(a) Do the Model Standards or the UMA require you to make any disclosure?
(b) Draft an outline of what you would tell the parties if you do make a disclosure.

c. Repeat-Player Concerns

To be successful as a mediator one must have clients, and busy neutrals rely on repeat business. One national organization of mediators estimates, for example, that two-thirds of the revenue of their successful panelists comes from cases involving lawyers who have mediated with that neutral at least three times during the past year. When does repeat business create unhealthy dependence? Mediator David Geronemus comments that:

> [F]ull-time mediators need to be careful on a variety of fronts as they face the continuous need to generate new cases to keep their dockets full....Good mediators undoubtedly will have repeat business. And we need to engage in marketing activities. But unless we are careful to fulfill our disclosure obligations, and to make sure that no one client becomes too large a share of our practice, parties will lose confidence in the process. (Geronemus 2001)

Sections II and III of the Model Standards and Section 9 of the UMA may apply to a mediator in such situations; other standards may apply to advocates.

Problem 8

Assume that you are a mediator and have mediated three cases involving Attorney Okawa. In each case the result was a settlement satisfactory to both sides, and at least one of the opposing lawyers in those other cases has selected you as a neutral again. Okawa now calls and asks you to mediate another case. He says that he has just about persuaded the other party to use you, but has not mentioned to them that he has previously mediated with you because it would require discussing the earlier cases, which his clients strongly want to be kept confidential. He asks that you not mention the prior mediations to the other party.

(a) What do the Model Standards require of you?
(b) What should you do?

d. Differences Between Attorney and Client

At times a mediator is dealing with people who are on the same side of a dispute but have widely divergent viewpoints. An attorney, for example, may not appear to be "on the same page" as her client about the risks of litigation or whether to take an offer. Ethical standards for both lawyers and mediators state that in such situations the client's wishes govern. However, parties often hire lawyers precisely because they have more experience and better judgment in highly charged legal situations, and many lawyers feel that clients some-times become too emotional to recognize a good offer when it appears. And, it must be noted, mediators know that attorneys rather than clients are their primary source of referrals in legal cases. Sections I, III, and VI of the Model Standards for Mediators, among others, and Section 1.2 of the Model Rules for lawyers, may apply to such situations. Consider the following problem.

Problem 9

Two parties have gone through nine hours of difficult mediation in a product liability case. The plaintiffs have alleged that their infant daughter died because of defects in a baby carriage manufactured by the defendant. The plaintiff couple is represented by experienced counsel and has held up well to the stress of the process. The maker of the carriage is represented by its CFO and outside counsel. The mediator's impression is that the CFO is being unrealistic about the company's legal exposure. The mediator has tried to bring other company officials into the case, but without success.

At 6 P.M. the mediator brings another offer to the defense, which is promptly rejected. At this point the neutral says to the defense team that although she's willing to keep talking, they appear to be close to deadlock and it may make sense to adjourn for the day. As the neutral leaves the room, defense counsel says she's going to the restroom. In a private conversation in the hallway, she asks the mediator to "get tough" with her client. The CFO, she says, has a visceral dislike of the plaintiff's lawyer. He is letting his determination to beat the other guy lead him into a position that is against the company's best interests. This is her firm's first case with this client, and she does not have the clout to make him listen to advice herself.

The neutral respects counsel's reputation as an advocate and privately agrees with her assessment of the situation. On her return she asks the defense team if it would be helpful for her to give her impressions of how a court would view the case if it had to be tried. The defense lawyer promptly responds that they would welcome her thoughts. The mediator delivers a hard-hitting evaluation that represents her honest assessment, emphasizing some jury sympathy factors that she believes the CFO is ignoring. The CFO does not respond to the mediator's comments, but appears to be a bit taken aback. The bargaining process resumes, and the disputants continue without a dinner break, munching on fast food. At 9:30 P.M., after several lengthy caucuses, the CFO agrees to essentially the same proposal that the mediator had brought to him at 6 P.M.

(a) Did the lawyer act unethically in saying what she did to the mediator?
(b) Did the mediator act improperly in her response? Why or why not?

Problem 10

Assume the same situation as in the prior problem, but that the reason for the CFO's refusal, in counsel's judgment, is that he is seriously overconfident about the company's chances of prevailing in litigation. The lawyer again meets the mediator in the hallway. She says that she selected the neutral, a retired judge, primarily for her credibility on legal issues and asks her to "bring out your gavel" and give her client a "hard" evaluation of the company's chances of success in court. It is clear to the mediator that the counsel wants her to give a reasoned evaluation, but also to emphasize the risks of continuing in litigation. Would such a request be more or less troublesome than the prior problem?

e. Improper Conduct by Litigants

Ethical standards instruct mediators to support the parties' right to self-determination. But what should a mediator do if she learns that one party is acting improperly vis-à-vis another party, or that both parties are considering terms that appear likely to harm the interests of a person who is not represented in the process? Family mediators may confront the latter problem when parents, to satisfy other goals, agree to a visitation arrangement that is likely to create serious difficulties for their children. In commercial mediation the problem is more likely to arise when disputants create value for themselves by cheating an outsider — often the Internal Revenue Service. Mediators may not be asked to contribute ideas in such situations, but they are typically called on to carry proposals back and forth, advocate their acceptance, and act as scribes for memoranda that memorialize dubious arrangements. Several provisions of the Model Standards may apply in these situations. Consider the following examples.

Problem 11

You are mediating a divorce case in which the parents are negotiating over custody and visitation of their two young children. As is common in family mediation, the process is occurring entirely in joint session, and lawyers are not present. You have stated that you will not talk with a party unless the other is present. However, after one session the wife returns to pick up a hat that she had left behind and, as she is leaving, mentions, "You know, I've just gotten a really attractive job offer, so I'm going to move out of state in two months. But I can't tell Jim — we've almost agreed on everything. If he knows I'm moving 2,000 miles away, it'll blow everything up. Let's just work out the custody and visitation and all, and then I'll deal with it."

Your impression is that the husband is conceding much more than he otherwise would on issues such as support, and has agreed to grant the wife sole legal custody of the children, in return for her agreement to generous visitation arrangements.

(a) What should you do in this situation?
(b) Does it matter if the mediation is being conducted under the auspices of a court-connected ADR program?

Problem 12

You are mediating a family dispute in which one of the spouses is self-employed. As part of the process the parties are mediating alimony, support for their seven-year-old child, and a division of assets. You have asked each spouse to prepare a financial statement, which they have exchanged. As the mediation goes forward, stray comments by the husband make you strongly suspect that he is hiding substantial cash income that is not reflected on his financial statement. What should you do?

Problem 13

A terminated executive has been mediating with his former employer for ten hours. After fierce bargaining in which the mediator has used her entire "bag of tricks," the defense has come painfully to a final offer of $180,000, but the plaintiff refuses to accept less than $200,000. A key issue, from the plaintiff's perspective, is that he needs to come out of the process with $100,000 in the bank, net of his attorney's one-third contingency fee. Since the primary claim is for lost pay, however, any settlement will be treated by the company as back pay and therefore will be subject to payroll withholding. The effect is that the plaintiff would net only about $70,000, well below his minimum requirement. The plaintiff also has asserted a vague claim for emotional distress, but federal law bars plaintiffs from receiving settlement money tax-free unless an injury is physical in nature. "Mere" emotional distress is not sufficient to avoid a tax bite.

Suddenly the plaintiff attorney asks the mediator to take an idea to the defense: In a spell of depression caused by the firing, he now remembers, the plaintiff suffered from erectile dysfunction. Counsel didn't make it an explicit part of the claim because of the embarrassment factor, but it's there and it was a physical injury. The lawyer, with her client's approval, proposes allocating most of the settlement to this injury, allowing the plaintiff to receive his $100,000.

(a) Is there a problem for the mediator in presenting this idea to the defense?
(b) Assume that the mediator does so. Defense counsel laughs and says that this is the first she's heard about this malady. However, if the plaintiff says that he's dysfunctional, that's his problem. She says the proposal is OK with her client, as long as the plaintiff certifies the condition and assumes any risk that the IRS will contest it. The lawyers ask you to write down the terms they dictate summarizing the deal. Does this pose a problem for you as mediator?

3. Combining Practice as an Advocate and a Mediator

Experienced lawyers increasingly seek to combine their practices as litigators with work as mediators. There are pluses and minuses to such a combination. Experienced attorneys find it refreshing to take on new roles, and if a lawyer is thinking of changing careers, such an approach allows her to explore being a neutral without "quitting her day job." Even if an attorney decides to continue to practice law, experience as a mediator is likely to enhance her effectiveness as an advocate in the process.

a. Conflicts of Interest

One major issue for lawyers who alternate between the roles of advocate and neutral is the potential for conflicts of interest — the possibility that a party in a mediated case will be a past or future legal client of the mediator-lawyer. This is a particular concern in large law firms, where a lawyer-neutral's partners may be concerned that a single modestly compensated mediation will disqualify the entire firm from representing the party in a much more lucrative matter in the future.

Standards for neutrals call for disclosure in such situations. Model Standard III requires disclosure of "all actual and potential conflicts that are reasonably known to the mediator and could reasonably be seen as raising a question about the mediator's impartiality." If the conflict "might reasonably be viewed as undermining the integrity of the mediation," the Standards require a mediator to recuse herself. The UMA relies on disclosure: Section 9(a) requires a neutral "to make an inquiry that is reasonable under the circumstances to determine whether there are any known facts that a reasonable individual would consider likely to affect the impartiality of the mediator [including] an existing or past relationship with a mediation party or foreseeable participant . . ." and disclose any such facts if they exist. The UMA does not impose disqualification on the lawyer or her firm, but Section 9(d) does bar violators from asserting the mediation privilege.

The ABA's E2K Report deals explicitly with conflicts between roles, stating that "a lawyer shall not represent anyone in connection with a matter in which the lawyer participated personally and substantially as a . . . mediator. . . ." The rule goes on to provide that "If a lawyer is disqualified . . . no lawyer in a firm with which that [lawyer-mediator] is associated may knowingly undertake or continue representation in that matter unless" the lawyer-mediator is screened from knowledge or fees associated with the case, and the parties to the mediation are notified of the situation (E2K Report, § 1.12 [a, c]). The issue is also addressed by other codes of ethics, in particular the CPR-Georgetown Rule (on the book Web site).

Question

25. A lawyer-mediator has no current or past attorney-client relationship with the parties in a case she is mediating, but she knows that lawyers in another department of her firm have approached the defendant in the case about serving as outside counsel. The firm has never received a case from the defendant, but hopes to represent it in the future.
    (a) What do the above standards require of the lawyer?
    (b) Must she disqualify herself as mediator?
    (c) If she mediates the case, is her firm disqualified from representing the party as counsel?

b. Role Confusion

The very fact that a mediator is an attorney may lead pro se litigants to believe that the neutral will provide them with legal advice. The E2K report proposed the following rule to deal with this issue:

> *Rule 2.4(b)* . . . A lawyer serving as a third-party neutral shall inform unrepresented parties that the lawyer is not representing them. When the lawyer knows or reasonably should know that a party does not understand the lawyer's role in the matter, the lawyer shall explain the difference between the lawyer's role as a third-party neutral and a lawyer's role as one who represents a client.
>
> *Comment:* . . . Where appropriate, the lawyer should inform unrepresented parties of the important differences between the lawyer's role as third-party neutral and a lawyer's role as a client representative, including the inapplicability of the attorney-client evidentiary privilege. . . .

Questions

26. In what types of disputes is the danger of confusion between the role of counsel and mediator likely to be greatest?
27. Assume that you are a lawyer who has agreed to mediate a dispute between a quarry and neighbors who are complaining about noise and dust from its operations. The company is represented by its business manager, the neighbors by a committee of three laypeople.
    (a) Draft a statement that you could make to the participants to explain your role.
    (b) When and how would you deliver it?
28. Consider these situations:
    (a) Lawyer-mediator Garcia successfully mediates a case in which Allen sued Thompson. A month later, Allen approaches Garcia and asks her to represent her in a matter not related to the dispute that was mediated. Can Garcia accept the case? Must she follow any special procedure? Does it matter whether the matter, although unrelated in terms of subject matter, involves Thompson in any way?
    (b) Suppose that Allen instead approaches Garcia's law partner, Black, to represent her in the new case. What, if anything, is required then?
    (c) What if Thompson asks Garcia to represent her in pursuing a third-party defendant in the *Allen v. Thompson* dispute? The activities of the third party were discussed during the mediation, but the third party was not involved in the mediation process. Does Allen have to consent? If so, why?
    (d) Lawyer-mediator Horwitz conducts a one-hour orientation session about the mediation process for a couple who are considering divorce, but they decide not to go ahead with the mediation. Two months later the wife asks one of Horwitz's partners to represent her in the divorce, which is contested. Is the lawyer disqualified from doing so? Should she be? (See *Bauerle v. Bauerle*, 615 N.Y.S.2d 954 (1994), *later opinion* 616 N.Y.S.2d 275 [1994].)

The role of a mediator is inherently ambiguous, and ethical standards that apply to the role tend to be stated in general terms. This leaves even conscientious neutrals in doubt about what they should do in particular situations, particularly when the ethical principles that apply to a given situation appear to conflict. We hope to have convinced you that being an ethical mediator or lawyer is a process of continuing self-examination rather than a matter of learning a set of rules, and that you will continue to explore these issues for the rest of your professional life.

CHAPTER

13

The Law of Mediation

A. Confidentiality

One of the key attractions of mediation for both parties and lawyers is that the process is confidential. Participants in mediation regularly sign agreements in which they commit not to disclose to outsiders anything communicated during the process. In addition, states and the federal government have given mediation varying levels of confidentiality protection. Sometimes, however, participants in mediation seek to disclose, or outsiders attempt to discover, what occurred during the process.

Disputes over mediation confidentiality arise in two different ways. First, litigants sometimes attempt to take confidential information from the mediation process and use it in another context, usually in court. ("Isn't it true that in mediation you admitted that . . . ?"). We refer to these as "litigation" breaches. A second type of confidentiality issue arises from allegations by disputants that the mediation process itself went awry ("Your Honor, I signed the agreement at 2 A.M., but I wasn't thinking clearly. The mediator just wouldn't let me go home!") This latter category can be thought of as "supervisory" intrusions, because confidentiality is being invaded allegedly to protect the mediation process itself. To understand how confidentiality issues arise in various contexts, consider the following problems.

Problem 1

You represent a St. Louis company, Bates, Inc. Bates is a "headhunter" firm that fills executive positions for corporations. A year ago Bates contracted with a Chicago software consultant, Alpha Websites, to develop a Web site for Bates. A key goal for Bates was that its clients be able to advertise openings without revealing their identity, and that candidates be able to input personal data online in confidence. One function of the new software was thus to screen out conflicting requests (e.g., an executive applying for an opening at a company where he is currently working). The site was to be developed over six months for a total fee of $150,000.

Bates reports that the transaction was a disaster. The developer took nearly a year to deliver the site, and the security provisions proved to be porous. Clients complained that candidates could determine who was advertising, and some people found themselves applying to their current employer, causing embarrassment for all concerned. Bates estimates that it lost at least a million dollars in business as a result of the Web site problems.

You filed suit against Alpha in federal court in Illinois, and a few months later accepted an invitation from Alpha's counsel to go to mediation. The mediation was governed by a confidentiality agreement. After several hours of mediation you deadlocked, with your client at $350,000 and Alpha at $50,000. In an effort to break the impasse, the mediator offered both sides a tentative opinion that while Bates had a good case on the contract, the site was now up and running fairly smoothly, and that given the language of the contract he did not think the court would grant a recovery on the lost profits claim. He recommended a settlement at $125,000. You declined this proposal, feeling that the evaluation was unrealistic and that the neutral was "bending" his evaluation to produce a number that Alpha would accept.

Three months later, you are called into a status conference with the judge presiding over the case. He asks both sides if they have explored settlement. You mention the unsuccessful mediation. The judge asks if the mediator gave an evaluation of the case. You say that the discussions were confidential, but the Alpha lawyer says, "Yes, Judge. Do you want to know what it was?" The judge nods affirmatively.

(a) What should you do?
(b) Is there anything you could have done in advance to prevent this situation?

Problem 2

Assume that at a settlement conference in the Bates-Alpha case, the presiding judge suggests that the litigants participate in mediation. Bates is willing, but Alpha declines. The judge says that in his experience mediation is often beneficial, and exercises his authority to order the parties to mediate. Rules of the court's mediation program require that participants mediate "in good faith" and bring with them "full settlement authority." Three weeks later Bates and Alpha appear before a court-appointed mediator. Bates is represented by its CFO and outside counsel, Alpha by an associate from its outside law firm. In its opening statement Bates indicates that while it believes strongly in its case, it is willing to consider a reasonable compromise. Alpha argues that there is no basis for liability and that Bates's damage claims are wildly inflated.

After four hours of mediation Bates, which entered the mediation demanding $750,000, has dropped to $450,000. Alpha, which had made no offer before the mediation, offers $5,000, then $10,000, and then refuses to move further. In a caucus discussion with the mediator, Alpha's counsel reveals that she has no authority to go beyond $15,000, since that is all the company thinks the claim is worth, and that any offer above $100,000 would have to be approved by the defendant's board of directors. Bates does not know about this conversation, but tells the neutral that it strongly suspects that Alpha never gave its negotiator "real" settlement authority.

A week later, Bates files a motion for sanctions with the judge, charging that Alpha's conduct at mediation violated the court's ADR program rules. Bates subpoenas the mediator to testify at the hearing on its motion.

(a) How should Alpha respond to Bates's claim that it violated program rules?
(b) How should it respond to the mediator subpoena?

1. How Important Is Confidentiality to Mediation?

❖ Lawrence R. Freedman and Michael L. Prigoff, Confidentiality in Mediation: The Need for Protection

2 Ohio St. J. Disp. Resol. 37-38 (1986)

Confidentiality is vital to mediation for a number of reasons:

Effective mediation requires candor.... Mediators must be able to draw out baseline positions and interests, which would be impossible if the parties were constantly looking over their shoulders. Mediation often reveals deep-seated feelings on sensitive issues. Compromise negotiations often require the admission of facts which disputants would never otherwise concede. Confidentiality insures that parties will voluntarily enter the process and further enables them to participate effectively and successfully.

Fairness to the disputants requires confidentiality. The safeguards present in legal proceedings, qualified counsel and specific rules of evidence and procedure, for example, are absent in mediation . . . Subsequent use of information generated at these proceedings could therefore be unfairly prejudicial, particularly if one party is more sophisticated than the other. Mediation thus could be used as a discovery device against legally naive persons if the mediation communications were not inadmissible in subsequent judicial actions. . . .

The mediator must remain neutral in fact and in perception. The potential of the mediator to be an adversary in a subsequent legal proceeding would curtail the disputants' freedom to confide during the mediation. Court testimony by a mediator, no matter how carefully presented, will inevitably be characterized so as to favor one side or the other. This would destroy a mediator's efficacy as an impartial broker.

Privacy is an incentive for many to choose mediation. Whether it be protection of trade secrets or simply a disinclination to "air one's dirty laundry" in the neighborhood, the option presented by the mediator to settle disputes quietly and informally is often a primary motivator for parties choosing this process.

Mediators and mediation programs need protection against distraction and harassment. Fledgling community programs need all of their limited resources for the "business at hand." Frequent subpoenas can encumber staff time, and dissuade volunteers from participating as mediators. . . .

There is a consensus that some degree of confidentiality in the process is appropriate, but commentators do not agree on how strong the protection should be. In particular, some question whether mediation requires a formal legal privilege. Consider the following.

❖ Scott H. Hughes, A Closer Look: The Case for a Mediation Confidentiality Privilege Still Has Not Been Made

5 Disp. Resol. Mag. 14-15 (Winter 1998)

Consider the case of the manipulating minister: At a small women's college, a minister with the campus ministry seduces a naive young coed into a sexual relationship. When she attempts to break off the relationship, the minister responds with harassment. She subsequently sinks into a deep depression and drops out after her first semester. Several months later, she confides in her sister, who promptly relays the sordid tale to their mother.

The family's attorney files suit and commences discovery, from which she learns about an earlier incident involving the same minister while at the college's sister institution. Finding that the previous dispute had been settled through mediation, the attorney issues a subpoena for the mediator and his notes. During a caucus with the mediator, it seems, the minister stated that his supervisors had been aware of his illicit urges for some time. The mediator, joined by the church and the minister, seeks to quash the subpoena by asserting the privilege contained in the state mediation act. Does the need to encourage settlement outweigh the victim's rights to this information? I think not.

[Or] consider the case of the disputant in duress: During a mediation, one party complains of chest pains and fatigue, only to be told by the mediator that he cannot leave the mediation session until a settlement has been reached. The disputant subsequently signs a settlement, but tries to have it set aside during a subsequent action for specific performance. The adverse party contends that the mediation privilege prohibits an examination of the communications that took place during mediation, preventing the assertion of such a defense. Mediation privileges would foreclose disputants from raising this or many other contract defenses. . . .

Over the past two decades we have witnessed a vast proliferation of mediation statutes throughout the United States, many of which contain privileges shielding the mediator and/or the parties from the disclosure of events that take place during mediation, thus shrouding mediation proceedings in a veil of secrecy. . . . Before rushing to create another privilege that may preclude the law's traditional right to "every person's evidence," we should take at least one more close look at the social and legal cost of such a privilege. If that important step is taken, it will become apparent that the benefit of the mediation privilege does not justify its cost.

To begin with, it should be noted that there is almost no empirical support for mediation privileges. For example, no data exists to show a difference in growth rates or overall use of mediation services between jurisdictions with privileges and those without such protections, or from within any jurisdiction before and after the creation of a privilege. . . . Moreover, there is no empirical work to demonstrate a connection between privileges and the ultimate success of mediation. Although parties may have an expectation of privacy, no showing has been made that fulfilling this expectation is crucial to the outcome of mediation....

[T]o assess the overall value of mediation privileges, it is important to weigh any gains that would be attributable to mediation against their cost. Privileges sacrifice potentially important evidence for subsequent legal proceedings and restrict public access to information that may be necessary to a democratic society. Of course, finely detailed exceptions to a mediation privilege could be crafted that would help overcome many problems. However, numerous exceptions could well lead to an unpredictable privilege that would be more detrimental than no privilege at all.

Until [an] empirical connection can be made, the arguments in favor of mediation privileges should not overcome the historical presumption favoring the availability of "every person's evidence."

Questions

1. Who do you find more persuasive — Freedman and Prigoff, or Hughes?
2. In the absence of a legal privilege, what can a lawyer do to increase the likelihood that mediation communications will be kept confidential?
3. The introduction to Chapter 5 lists several ways in which a mediator can facilitate settlement, including:
   - Helping to ensure the presence of key decision makers at the table.
   - Allowing disputants to present arguments, interests, and feelings directly to their opponent.
   - Moderating negotiations, coaching bargainers, and reframing positions.
   - Assisting each side to reassess its litigation option.
   - Helping participants to focus on their underlying interests.
4. For which of these functions is the assurance of confidentiality most significant?

2. Sources of Mediation Confidentiality

There are five primary sources of rules governing confidentiality in mediation:

- Rules of evidence
- Privileges
- Confidentiality statutes and rules
- Mediation agreements
- Positive disclosure obligations

a. Rules of Evidence

Virtually every jurisdiction has adopted a rule of evidence to protect the confidentiality of settlement discussions. The key federal provision is Federal

Rule of Evidence (FRE) 408.[1] About two-thirds of the states have evidentiary rules patterned on FRE 408. The first point to note about Rule 408 is that it is a rule of evidence, not a guarantee of confidentiality. Rule 408 is intended to limit what litigants can offer in evidence in a court proceeding, not what parties or observers can disclose in any other context. The rule does not, for example, apply to discovery depositions, nor does it limit what a person can say in a conversation or a media interview. In addition, FRE 408 and its counterparts typically apply only to court proceedings. They may therefore not be effective in less-formal forums such as administrative hearings and arbitrations; whether a mediation conversation will be admissible in another forum will depend on its rules and the philosophy of the presiding officer.

Even in court, Rule 408 may not prevent information about settlement discussions from being disclosed. The rule and its state counterparts cover only evidence that a person offered or agreed to accept "valuable consideration" to compromise a claim, not everything said in settlement discussions. Thus, for example, the rule does not protect a trade secret disclosed in mediation from being introduced into evidence unless it formed part of an offer to settle. Indeed, even an offer of compromise is not necessarily sacrosanct under Rule 408, because the rule has many exceptions. The rule applies, for example, only if an offer of compromise is introduced for the purpose of proving a party's "liability for or invalidity of the claim or its amount." Confidential information offered for another purpose is not protected by the rule. A litigant might avoid Rule 408, for example, by arguing that it is introducing evidence of an offer to show that a witness is biased, or that a party did not bargain in good faith.

Other uncertainties arise from the fact that only the person against whom evidence is being offered can make a Rule 408 objection. The rule, in other words, is designed to prevent a party from being shot in court with a "gun" that it provided to the other side during settlement discussions, not to help nonparties or mediators keep discussions confidential. Finally, a rule of evidence can often be hard to enforce, since parties who evade it ordinarily risk at most a judicial reprimand.

b. Privileges

Twenty-five states now have statutes that apply generally to mediation, and most of the rest have laws that cover the use of mediation in specific types of cases or settings, such as environmental disputes or court-connected programs. Of the 25 states with general statutes, most have created formal legal

---

1. The text of the rule is as follows:

Rule 408. Compromise and Offers to Compromise. Evidence of (1) furnishing or offering or promising to furnish, or (2) accepting or offering or promising to accept, a valuable consideration in compromising or attempting to compromise a claim which was disputed as to either validity or amount, is not admissible to prove liability for or invalidity of the claim or its amount. Evidence of conduct or statements made in compromise negotiations is likewise not admissible. This rule does not require the exclusion of any evidence otherwise discoverable merely because it is presented in the course of compromise negotiations. This rule also does not require exclusion when the evidence is offered for another purpose, such as proving bias or prejudice of a witness, negativing a contention of undue delay, or proving an effort to obstruct a criminal investigation or prosecution.

privileges. It is important to bear in mind the following distinction: Although a privilege bars evidence from being admitted in adjudication, it does not bar persons from disclosing the same information outside of court. By contrast, a statute providing "confidentiality" would ordinarily bar the release of information in all contexts. A privilege is less subject to evasion than an evidentiary rule such as FRE 408, however, because privileges bar admission of evidence regardless of the purpose for which it is offered. Violations of privileges may also give rise to a cause of action for damages.

To understand the level of protection offered by a privilege in any particular setting, a lawyer should consider the following issues:

- What privilege applies to the process?
- What does it cover? Litigation testimony only, or disclosure in any context?
- In what phases of the process does the privilege apply?
- Who can invoke it?
- Is it subject to any exceptions or exclusions?

What Privilege Applies? Courts almost always apply their own rules of evidence, but this is not true of privileges. Thus, if a mediation takes place in State A, but the case later goes to trial in State B, choice of law principles will often determine which state's mediation privilege is applied. Indeed, as Professor Ellen Deason has commented, "Mediation confidentiality would make an ideal poster child for the shortcomings of choice-of-law" (Deason 2002b).

A few federal courts have recognized a mediation privilege as a matter of federal common law, but there is no general federal mediation privilege. FRE 501 authorizes courts to apply either state or federal privileges in a federal case. The absence of a general federal privilege makes it difficult to predict how confidential communications will be treated in federal proceedings.

What Is Covered? In What Phases of the Process? As we have noted, some privileges apply only to testimony given during litigation, while other privileges impose confidentiality in noncourt settings as well. What phases of the mediation process are covered by the privilege also varies from state to state and is sometimes poorly defined. A particular privilege may, for example, apply only to the mediation session itself, not to conversations and e-mails between counsel and the neutral before and afterward.

Who Holds the Privilege? Only persons designated as "holders" of a privilege are entitled to invoke it. Typically the parties to a case hold the privilege and thus can prevent disclosures about the mediation process. The mediator, however, may not be entitled to use the privilege as a shield, just as lawyers are not usually permitted to invoke the attorney-client privilege unless their client elects to do so. Thus, if a neutral is called to testify about what occurred during a mediation, he may well have to ask a party to protect him from testifying. This is not always true, however; California, for example, requires the mediator's as well as the parties' consent for anyone to testify as to the content of a mediation and bars testimony from mediators (Cal. Evid. Code §§ 1122, 703.5).

Is the Privilege Qualified or Absolute? What Exceptions Apply?   Some states have adopted mediation privileges that are absolute, meaning that they contain no stated exceptions. Other privilege statutes allow or even require mediators to breach confidentiality in certain situations, for example, to report evidence of a felony, threats of harm to children, perjury, and other matters. Even when privileges are absolute on their face, courts sometimes create exceptions as a matter of common law.

c. Confidentiality Statutes and Rules

As noted, roughly half of the states have enacted statutes governing mediation. Many of these go beyond establishing an evidentiary privilege to make the entire mediation process confidential. A Massachusetts statute, for instance, states that any communication during a mediation, as well as the mediator's work product, "shall be confidential," as well as inadmissible in adjudication, and California statutes similarly provide that the mediation process shall be "confidential." (See Mass. Gen. Laws ch. 233, § 23C; Cal. Code §§ 1115–1128.)

Neither Congress nor the federal courts have provided any general guarantee of confidentiality to mediation. However, provisions exist in a variety of specific statutes. For example, the Administrative Dispute Resolution Act of 1996, 5 U.S.C. § 574, provides that neutrals and parties in mediations of administrative cases "shall not voluntarily disclose or through discovery or compulsory process be required to disclose any dispute resolution communication." The ADR Act of 1998, 28 U.S.C. § 652(d), requires that federal district courts adopt local rules to provide for the confidentiality of ADR processes that occur within their programs. Parties are thus more likely to find confidentiality protected in a federal court if they mediate under the aegis of a federal court program than if they use a private process.

State court and private mediation programs also typically provide that mediations held under their auspices will be confidential. The rules of such programs often do not specify, however, what is meant by confidentiality. In one sense a party's incentive to comply with the rules of a court-affiliated program is strong, because litigants may be concerned that if they violate a rule, they will incur the wrath of the judge who will hear their case. This is not to say, however, that a party will have a legal cause of action or other remedy if an opponent violates a confidentiality rule.

d. Mediation Agreements

Mediation agreements offer the best opportunity for a lawyer to tailor confidentiality protections to the needs of particular cases. An agreement is a contract, however, and thus is subject to the limitations inherent in any contractual undertaking. First, agreements bind only those who enter into them, not nonparties. In the case of mediation, this means that outsiders to the process, such as third-party litigants, are not constrained by the parties' mediation agreement. Second, if a breach does occur, a party's only remedy is usually to sue for monetary damages, if any can be proved. Even in the unusual situation in which a litigant knows of an impending violation and is able to seek a court order to prevent it, a judge may refuse to enforce the obligation out of concern that a contract not to provide evidence in court violates public policy. This said, however, practicing neutrals report few, if any, complaints from parties that an opponent violated a confidentiality agreement

e. Positive Disclosure Obligations

Public policy sometimes weighs against secrecy concerning settlement negotiations. Many states, concerned that secret settlements have operated to hide serious social problems — for example, that confidential agreements settling individual sexual abuse and toxic tort cases have delayed authorities from discovering the extent of these problems — have considered statutes that would bar courts from ordering certain kinds of settlements to be sealed. Some states also have decisional law or statutes that require persons who become aware of certain offenses to report them to authorities. Thus, for example, some jurisdictions require therapists to report potential harm that they learn about from clients (see *Tarasoff v. Regents of Univ. of Cal.*, 17 Cal. 3d 425 (1976)), and many states require mediators to report instances of child abuse. Finally, both individual states and the federal government have enacted "sunshine laws," which require that certain meetings involving government officials be open to the public. As a result, when environmental and regulatory issues are mediated, the process may have to be open to outside observers.

3. Examples from Practice

As we have discussed, most attempts to penetrate the confidentiality of mediation occur either because a litigant is seeking to use information that was revealed in mediation in court, or because a mediation participant is alleging that the process itself was defective. We consider each category in turn.

a. Use of Mediation Information in Litigation

❖ *Rojas v. Superior Court of Los Angeles County*
33 Cal. 4th 407 (2004)

CHIN, J.:

We granted review in this case to consider the scope of Evidence Code Sec. 1119(b), which provides: "No writing . . . that is prepared for the purpose of, in the course of, or pursuant to, a mediation . . . is admissible or subject to discovery. . . ." In a divided decision, a majority of the Court of Appeal held that application of this statute is governed by the same principles that govern application of the work product privilege [and] classified raw test data, photographs, and witness statements as . . . material that is not protected. We conclude that the Court of Appeal's interpretation . . . is contrary to both the statutory language and the Legislature's intent. We therefore reverse the . . . judgment.

Factual Background. Julie Coffin is the owner of an apartment complex in Los Angeles that includes three buildings and a total of 192 units. In 1996, Coffin sued the contractors and subcontractors who built the complex . . . alleging that water leakage due to construction defects had produced toxic molds and other microbes on the property. . . . In April 1999, the litigation settled as a result of mediation. . . .

In August 1999, several hundred tenants of the apartment complex filed the action now before us against [Coffin and] numerous . . . entities that participated in development or construction of the complex. Tenants alleged that defective construction had allowed water to circulate and microbes to infest the complex, causing numerous health problems. They also alleged that all defendants had conspired to conceal the defects and that they (Tenants) had not become aware of the defects until April 1999. Tenants served [a] request for production of all photographs . . . taken . . . during the underlying action. . . . Coffin asserted that, under section 1119, the requested documents were not discoverable. . . .

On March 7, 2002, Judge Mohr denied Tenants' motion . . . explaining: "The plaintiffs say that they need these photos and there's no other evidence of the conditions as they were at that time and in those places, and defendants are saying these photographs were created for mediation purposes. . . . They're clearly protected by the mediation privilege. This is a very difficult decision . . . because it could well be that there's no other way for the plaintiffs to get this particular material. On the other hand, the mediation privilege is an important one, . . . and if courts start dispensing with it by using the . . . test governing the work product privilege, . . . you may have people less willing to mediate."

Discussion. As we recently explained, implementing alternatives to judicial dispute resolution has been a strong legislative policy since at least 1986. Mediation is one of the alternatives the Legislature has sought to implement. . . . One of the fundamental ways the Legislature has sought to encourage mediation is by enacting several mediation confidentiality provisions. [C]onfidentiality is essential to effective mediation because it promotes a candid and informal exchange regarding events in the past. This frank exchange is achieved only if participants know that what is said in the mediation will not be used to their detriment through later court proceedings and other adjudicatory processes.

The particular confidentiality provision at issue here is section 1119(b), which provides: "No writing . . . that is prepared for the purpose of, in the course of, or pursuant to, a mediation or a mediation consultation, is admissible or subject to discovery, and disclosure of the writing shall not be compelled, in any arbitration, administrative adjudication, civil action, or other noncriminal proceeding. . . ." The Court of Appeal's holding directly conflicts with the plain language of these provisions. . . . [Section 1120 of the

Code] does not, as the Court of Appeal held, support a contrary conclusion. As noted above, section 1120(a), provides that "[e]vidence otherwise admissible or subject to discovery outside of a mediation . . . shall not be or become inadmissible or protected from disclosure solely by reason of its introduction or use in a mediation. . . ." Read together, sections 1119 and 1120 establish that a party cannot secure protection for a writing — including a photograph, a witness statement, or an analysis of a test sample — that was not "prepared for the purpose of, in the course of, or pursuant to, a mediation" simply by using or introducing it in a mediation. [The statutory scheme] prevents parties from using a mediation as a pretext to shield materials from disclosure.

The Court of Appeal's holding is also inconsistent with the relevant legislative history. . . . [The California Law Reform Commission], in making its recommendation regarding mediation confidentiality, . . . chose language expressly designed to give a mediation participant who takes a photograph for purpose of the mediation "control over whether it is used" in subsequent litigation, even where "another photo" cannot be taken because, for example, "a building has been razed or an injury has healed." The Legislature adopted the Commission's recommendation and enacted the mediation confidentiality provisions in substantially the form the Commission proposed. . . . The Court of Appeal's conclusion that photographs and videotapes taken for purposes of mediation are not protected under section 1119 is inconsistent with this legislative history. . . . More broadly, the Court of Appeal's construction is inconsistent with the overall purpose of the mediation confidentiality provisions. . . .

For all of the above reasons, we conclude that the Court of Appeal erred in holding that photographs, videotapes, witness statements, and "raw test data" from physical samples collected at the complex — such as reports describing the existence or amount of mold spores in a sample — that were "prepared for the purpose of, in the course of, or pursuant to, [the] mediation" in the underlying action are . . . discoverable "upon a showing of good cause."

[T]he Legislature did expressly enact other exceptions to section 1119's protection, [such as for] settlement agreements made or prepared "in the course of, or pursuant to, a mediation." Under [maxims] of statutory construction, if exemptions are specified in a statute, we may not imply additional exemptions unless there is a clear legislative intent to the contrary. Here, there is no evidence of a legislative intent supporting the "good cause" exception the Court of Appeal majority read into the statute. [A]s Judge Mohr observed, "the mediation privilege is an important one, and if courts start dispensing with it by using the . . . test governing the work-product privilege, . . . you may have people less willing to mediate." The judgment of the Court of Appeal is reversed.

Questions

4. The California Supreme Court in *Rojas* refused to allow judicially created exceptions to the state's mediation privilege statute. Suppose, however, that you were a legislator considering the issue. Would you support a law giving materials prepared for mediation absolute protection, or the narrower protection available under the "work product doctrine" that governs materials lawyers create in preparation for trial? Why?

5. Can you think of any other situations in which the interest in mediation confidentiality should give way to the needs of the justice system or other social needs?
6. Is the effect of the *Rojas* decision that the defendant Coffin, having created the photographs, can use them but the plaintiffs cannot? If so, is that fair? If not, should she be permitted to do so? Why?
7. If you conclude that *Rojas* bars all parties to a case from introducing data created for a mediation in court, how would you handle this situation: The plaintiff lawyer in a California personal injury case creates a video that shows a "day in the life" of his seriously handicapped client to dramatize the extent of the plaintiff's injuries to the insurer and the neutral in a mediation process. The mediation, however, is not successful. The plaintiff later seeks to introduce the same video at trial. The defense objects, citing the statute at issue in *Rojas*. Assuming that a video is a "writing" for purposes of the statute, how should the court rule? Is your result fair? Can you suggest any changes to the statute to deal with this issue?

One of the strongest arguments for allowing a party to disclose information revealed in a mediation in a subsequent proceeding involves criminal law enforcement. The following case illustrates one way that the issue can arise.

❖ *Byrd v. The State*
367 S.E.2d 300 (Ga. App. 1988)

[Byrd was accused of stealing property from Graddy. He participated in pretrial mediation and agreed to pay $800 in restitution. Byrd failed to make the payments required by the mediated settlement, criminal charges were reinstated, and he was convicted. Byrd appealed on the ground that statements he had made during mediation were introduced against him at trial.]

BEASLEY, J.... Appellant alleges error [by the trial court] in allowing evidence concerning a mediation proceeding.... [T]he parties were directed to the Neighborhood Justice Center of Atlanta, Inc., by the state court before which the criminal charge was first pending. The purpose was to facilitate a civil settlement for the dispute by way of the mediation process provided by that agency. The criminal charge, brought by warrant, remained pending, to await the outcome of the settlement efforts. If they were successful, the state court would entertain dismissal of the criminal charges. If not, the latter would proceed. After about eight months elapsed without appellant's compliance with the mediated agreement, he was indicted and bound over to superior court for trial.

By allowing this alternative dispute resolution effort to be evidenced in the subsequent criminal trial, the trial court's ruling eliminates its usefulness. For no criminal defendant will agree to "work things out" and compromise his position if he knows that any inference of responsibility arising from what he says and does in the mediation process will be admissible as an admission of guilt in the criminal proceeding which will eventualize if mediation fails... Federal Rule of Criminal Procedure 11(e)(6)... protects statements and conduct made in negotiations and plea bargains in criminal cases except in very limited circumstances....

In the instant case, as is standard in these referrals, defendant's mediation-related statements and actions were not made with any warning of rights against self-incrimination, and yet they were prompted by court action, itself creating a close procedural tie. A serious Fifth and Fourteenth Amendments *Miranda* problem is created by the admission of the objected-to evidence. This differs from the situation in *Williams v. State*, 342 S.E.2d 703 (Ga. App. 1986), in which a privately-negotiated agreement, not instigated at court direction during criminal proceedings, was ruled admissible.

Just as a withdrawn plea of guilty "shall not be admissible as evidence against [a defendant] at his trial," so too must be the words and actions which defendant undertakes in an effort to comply with the court's direction that mediation be pursued to resolve the pending criminal matter.

A new trial is required because we cannot conclude that the inadmissible evidence did not contribute to reaching the verdict.... Judgment reversed.

SOGNIER, JUDGE, dissenting:

I respectfully dissent. "Any statement or conduct of a person, indicating a consciousness of guilt, where such person is, at the time or thereafter, charged with or suspected of the crime, is admissible against him upon his trial for committing it."... The mediation proceedings in this case occurred while appellant was under criminal charges, and his conduct in signing a mediation agreement acknowledging his liability is conduct indicating a consciousness of guilt. Hence, under the rule...the evidence was admissible as bearing on appellant's guilt or innocence. Accordingly, I would affirm appellant's conviction....

Questions

8. Do you agree with the majority or the dissent in *Byrd*? Does it make a difference that Byrd failed to comply with the agreement he made in mediation?

9. Would it be better policy to give a *Miranda*-type warning to all defendants in such mediations, then to permit the use of any statements that they make?

10. The court says that an admission by someone in Byrd's situation presents different issues from one made by a party in a private mediation process. Should a defendant's admissions during a noncourt-sponsored process be admissible?

11. If a defendant cannot be "hoist with his own petard" by using statements he makes in mediation against him, is it also improper to invade confidentiality when it is the defendant who asks for disclosure? In one case a defendant charged with attempted murder claimed that he had acted in self-defense. To support his defense he sought to introduce into evidence threatening statements made by the alleged victim during the mediation of an earlier altercation between them. Should defendants be barred from using such evidence? (See *State v. Castellano*, 400 So. 2d 480 (Fla. App. 1984).)

Problem 3

Assume that you are counsel for the defendant Alpha in the Alpha-Bates case mentioned at the start of this chapter. In the course of mediation you argued that Bates should accept a reasonable settlement, because as a practical matter your client could never pay a six-figure judgment. In response to a request for substantiation, you provided the mediator with an asset-liability statement for Alpha. The mediation failed and the parties returned to court. Two days later Bates moves for a $250,000 attachment against Alpha's bank account, including with its motion copies of the asset-liability statement that your client provided in mediation.

(a) How should you respond on behalf of Alpha?
(b) Is there anything that you could have done, before or during the process, to make admission less likely?

Problem 4

Seven years ago you represented a young man, James Connor, who said that he had been sexually abused ten years before by the minister of his church. The abuse occurred when your client was 12 years old, during outings of the church's youth group. It appeared to be a difficult case to prove because of the absence of objective evidence and the time that had elapsed since the incidents, but you gave notice of your intent to sue the minister and the church official who oversaw his work. Shortly afterward the church agreed to mediate the matter. In the course of the mediation, the supervisory official offered your client a heartfelt apology and swore that this kind of abuse would never happen again. The church made what you thought was a good monetary offer; however, it was conditional on Connor signing a confidentiality clause that barred him from ever discussing the case. Connor decided to accept the offer, and the settlement was finalized.

Over the past month your local newspaper has published a series of dramatic stories alleging a widespread pattern of sexual abuse by clergy. One of the stories said that the same minister who abused your client had been sued several other times, and that two months after the settlement in your case the church had transferred him to a different community, where he continued his pattern of abuse. Connor has just called you. He is outraged by the stories, and even more so by the church's violation of its promise to him. He wants to talk to a reporter about what happened in his case, including the promise he was given in mediation.

(a) What advice should you give to Connor? What are the potential consequences of his talking with the reporter?
(b) Assume that your client has said nothing yet, but that a lawyer has subpoenaed him to testify at a deposition in another case brought against the same minister. The lawyer plans to ask about what occurred during Connor's mediation. What advice should you give Connor?
(c) If Connor refuses to answer questions at the deposition and the lawyer seeks a court order compelling him to testify, how should the court rule?

b. Supervisory Intrusions into the Process

To this point we have focused on the confidentiality issues that arise when a litigant discloses confidential mediation information for an ulterior purpose — usually to support a position in court. The other major category of confidentiality disputes involves claims that the mediation process itself went awry. In these situations a litigant is typically alleging either that mediation was thwarted because an opponent did not participate in good faith, or that the process itself was badly flawed, making a resulting settlement invalid. This second type of claim poses a conflict between a court's need to gather evidence in order to supervise the process and the interest in preserving its confidentiality. In the following case, a judge grapples with these issues.

Questions

As you read the *Olam* case, consider these questions:

12. Are you persuaded by the judge's decision? What factors seem most significant to it?
13. If you were a lawyer practicing in the court that decided *Olam*, would the decision affect the advice you give to clients about what to say or do during mediation?
14. Would the decision affect your willingness to recommend that a client enter the court's mediation program?

❖ *Olam v. Congress Mortgage Co.*
68 F. Supp. 2d 1110 (N.D. Cal. 1999)

BRAZIL, UNITED STATES MAGISTRATE JUDGE:

The court addresses in this opinion several difficult issues about the relationship between a court-sponsored voluntary mediation and subsequent proceedings whose purpose is to determine whether the parties entered an enforceable agreement at the close of the mediation session. As we explain below, the parties participated in a lengthy mediation that was hosted by this court's ADR Program Counsel — an employee of the court who is both a lawyer and an ADR professional. At the end of the mediation (after midnight), the parties signed a "Memorandum of Understanding" (MOU) that states that it is "intended as a binding document itself. . . ." Contending that the consent she apparently gave was not legally valid, plaintiff has taken the position that the MOU is not enforceable. She has not complied with its terms. Defendants have filed a motion to enforce the MOU as a binding contract. One of the principal issues with which the court wrestles, below, is whether evidence about what occurred during the mediation proceedings, including testimony from the mediator, may be used to help resolve this dispute. . . .

Facts. The events in the real world out of which the current dispute arises began unfolding in 1992, when Ms. Olam applied for and received a loan from

Congress Mortgage in the amount of $187,000. The 1992 loan is secured by two single-family homes located in San Francisco and owned by Ms. Olam. Eventually she defaulted. Thereafter, Congress Mortgage initiated foreclosure proceedings. [Mrs. Olam later sued the mortgage company, alleging violations of state and federal consumer laws, and the case went through discovery.]

At the final pretrial conference, the court asked plaintiff's counsel whether there was any meaningful possibility that a mediation would be useful. [Both sides subsequently agreed to mediate.] The mediation continued throughout the day and well into the evening. Sometime around 10:00 P.M. [the mediator and counsel went into another room] to type up what they believed were the essential terms of a binding settlement agreement. At approximately 1:00 A.M., when the mediation concluded, Ms. Olam and her lawyer, and [the defendant] signed the MOU.

[Later on the same day, counsel confirmed the settlement with the court.] At approximately 1:45 P.M. [that day], plaintiff telephoned my chambers. She was referred to the mediator. . . . [M]ore than seven months after the mediation, defendants filed a Motion to Enforce the Original Settlement . . . Ms. Olam, through [a] new attorney, filed her "Opposition" to the defendants' motion to enforce. [One ground] for opposition was that at the time she affixed her name to the MOU (at the end of the mediation) the plaintiff was incapable (intellectually, emotionally, and physically) of giving legally viable consent. Specifically, Ms. Olam contended that at the time she gave her apparent consent she was subjected to "undue influence" as that term is defined by California law.

[P]laintiff alleges that at the time she signed the MOU she was suffering from physical pain and emotional distress that rendered her incapable of exercising her own free will. She alleges that after the mediation began during the morning of September 9, she was left *alone* in a room *all* day and into the early hours of September 10, while all the other mediation participants conversed in a nearby room. She claims that she did not understand the mediation process. In addition, she asserts that she felt pressured to sign the MOU — and that her physical and emotional distress rendered her unduly susceptible to this pressure. As a result, she says, she signed the MOU against her will and without reading and/or understanding its terms.

[The court determined that California law, rather than federal law, governed the issue of mediation confidentiality.] California has offered for some time a set of strong statutory protections for mediation communications. If anything, those state law protections might be stronger than the [federal] protections offered through the relevant local rule of the Northern District of California or through any federal common law mediation privilege that might have been emerging when the mediation took place in this case.

As we noted earlier, the plaintiff and the defendants have expressly waived confidentiality protections conferred by [California law.] Both the plaintiff and the defendants have indicated, clearly and on advice of counsel, that they want the court to consider evidence about what occurred during the mediation, including testimony directly from the mediator. . . .

The Mediator's Privilege. [U]nder California law, a waiver of the mediation privilege by the parties is not a sufficient basis for a court to permit or order a mediator to testify. Rather, an independent determination must be made before testimony from a mediator should be permitted or ordered.

... First, I acknowledge squarely that a decision to require a mediator to give evidence, even *in camera* or under seal, about what occurred during a mediation threatens values underlying the mediation privileges. [T]he California legislature adopted these privileges in the belief that without the promise of confidentiality it would be appreciably more difficult to achieve the goals of mediation programs. While this court has no occasion or power to quarrel with these generally applicable pronouncements of state policy, we observe that they appear to have appreciably less force when, as here, the parties to the mediation have waived confidentiality protections, indeed have asked the court to compel the mediator to testify — so that justice can be done.

... [O]rdering mediators to participate in proceedings arising out of mediations imposes economic and psychic burdens that could make some people reluctant to agree to serve as a mediator, especially in programs where that service is pro bono or poorly compensated. This is not a matter of time and money only. Good mediators are likely to feel violated by being compelled to give evidence that could be used against a party with whom they tried to establish a relationship of trust during a mediation... These are not inconsequential matters.

... But the level of harm to that interest likely varies, at least in some measure, with the perception within the community of mediators and litigants about how likely it is that any given mediation will be followed at some point by an order compelling the neutral to offer evidence about what occurred during the session.... [T]his case represents the first time that I have been called upon to address these kinds of questions in the more than fifteen years that I have been responsible for ADR programs in this court. [M]y partially educated guess is that the likelihood that a mediator or the parties in any given case need fear that the mediator would later be constrained to testify is extraordinarily small.

The magnitude of the risk to values underlying the mediation privilege that can be created by ordering a mediator to testify also can vary with the nature of the testimony that is sought. [E]vidence about what words a party to the mediation uttered, what statements or admissions that party made ... could be particularly threatening to the spirit and methods that some people believe are important both to the philosophy and the success of some mediation processes.

[W]e turn to the other side of the balance. The interests that are likely to be advanced by compelling the mediator to testify in this case are of considerable importance. Moreover, as we shall see, some of those interests parallel and reinforce the objectives the legislature sought to advance by providing for confidentiality in mediation. The first interest we identify is the interest in doing justice. Here is what we mean. For reasons described below, the mediator is positioned in this case to offer what could be crucial, certainly very probative, evidence about the central factual issues in this matter. There is a strong possibility that his testimony will greatly improve the court's ability to determine reliably what the pertinent historical facts actually were [and to do justice.]

... In sum, it is clear that refusing even to determine what the mediator's testimony would be, in the circumstances here presented, threatens values of great significance.

[The Court decided that the mediator's testimony might be sufficiently important to justify an *in camera* exploration of what he would say. After the hearing, the Court decided] that testimony from the mediator would be crucial to the court's capacity to do its job.

The Evidentiary Hearing. The court held the evidentiary hearing. We heard testimony and considered documentary evidence about Ms. Olam's medical conditions, the events of September 9–10...and various post-mediation events related to the purported settlement. All the participants in the mediation testified, as did the physician who was treating plaintiff during the pertinent period. We took [the mediator's] testimony.

Conclusion. Because plaintiff has failed to prove either of the necessary elements of undue influence, and because she has established no other grounds to escape the contract she signed...the court GRANTS defendants' Motion to Enforce the settlement contract that is memorialized in the MOU.

Questions

Recall that in *Rojas v. Superior Court*, the California Supreme Court rejected a litigant's effort to intrude into the mediation process for purposes of discovery.

15. Which is more likely to promote effective mediation, the approach adopted by the court in *Rojas* or the one favored by the *Olam* judge?
16. Would the *Rojas* decision make you, as a California lawyer, more or less likely to advise clients to participate in mediation?

4. Confidentiality in Caucusing

So far we have discussed confidentiality only in terms of disclosures that are made to persons outside the mediation process. In caucus-based mediation, however, there is an additional layer of privacy: Mediators typically assure disputants that if they request that information disclosed in a caucus be held in confidence, the mediator will not disclose it to their opponent. As we have seen, however, one of a mediator's key functions is to facilitate communication between parties to a dispute. What is the appropriate balance between confidentiality and communication in caucus-based mediation? Consider how you would respond to the following situations, gathered from actual cases by Professor Marjorie Aaron.

Problem 5

You are plaintiff's counsel in the mediation of a commercial contract case. After hours of bargaining, the parties are stuck, with the plaintiff at $240,000 and the defendant at $90,000. The mediator proposes to play "confidential listener," and asks for the absolute lowest dollar number that you would accept to settle the case. The mediator also asks you for a "public" offer that he can convey to the other side. You tell the mediator that your client will never accept less than $150,000 to settle, and authorize him to communicate to the other side a new demand of $225,000.

When the mediator conveys the $225,000 figure, the other side expresses frustration. "They've hardly moved at all," says counsel. "It looks like they won't go any lower than $200,000 to settle, and we're just not going to go that high. The very most this case is worth is 150. We'd be prepared to go to $100,000 at this point, but it's probably a waste of time. I hate playing games — what will it take? Should we just pack up and leave?"

(a)   The mediator says to the defense, "I think I can get them to 150, if I can tell them that that will truly settle it — Are you saying that 150 would do it?" Has he broken his pledge of confidentiality to you?

(b)   Suppose you had told the mediator that your bottom line was $175,000, but the mediator suspects from observations of your client's body language that he would in fact go as low as $150,000. Can the mediator say, "They're hanging tough at 225, but I think I can get them to 150. If I can do that, will it settle the case?" Does it depend on whether the mediator "read" your client's intentions correctly?

Problem 6

You are representing the complainant in the mediation of a discrimination case. After the legal arguments have been aired in joint session, the mediator moves both sides into private caucusing. The mediator spends a great deal of time with you and your client, who is decidedly "dug in" and unwilling to see any weakness in his case or the need to lower her settlement expectations. Although you are well known as a zealous advocate, in this case you see reasons to reach a reasonable settlement. In a hallway conversation you indicate to the mediator that you are aware of the problems in the case and support his efforts to bring your client into a zone of reality.

In the mediator's caucus with the defense side, counsel expresses frustration at the lack of progress. "I bet the problem is the lawyer here. I've litigated with her before," he complains. "She is just hell-bent on getting a high number. This is a political cause for her, but we're not going to cave to meet her agenda." His anger toward you seems to be driving his resistance to further movement.

What, if anything, can the mediator appropriately say about your or your client's attitude toward the case?

5. Proposals for Change

The Current State of Protection

How serious is the problem of mediation confidentiality in practice? From the discussion above and the varying responses of courts, it is plain that significant gaps and ambiguities exist in mediation's "confidentiality safety net." Indeed, there is disagreement among academics about how much confidentiality protection the process needs. But although court cases over confidentiality issues exist, they appear to represent only a miniscule fraction of all disputes that are mediated. Private mediators report, for instance, that they rarely hear parties complain about breaches of confidentiality. Similarly, the judge in *Olam* commented that in the more than 15 years he had spent supervising the Northern District of California's mediation program, he had never before encountered a case in which parties sought a mediator's testimony.

Why do disputes over confidentiality arise in such a small percentage of mediated cases? The large majority of cases that go to mediation reach an agreement, and even those that do not settle are very unlikely ever to go to trial. If a case is never adjudicated, then the parties have less reason to breach confidentiality in order to bolster their arguments. It also appears that when people enter into a clear commitment to keep information confidential, they consistently honor their agreements, either as a matter of morality or because they are afraid of the possible consequences of a violation. The remedies for confidentiality violations may be uncertain, but as Professor Ellen Deason has observed, disputants' *"perception* of confidentiality is [what is] of central importance" (Deason 2002a). Also, as we have seen, when the mediation process focuses on distributive bargaining, disputants are less likely to reveal sensitive information in the first place. Finally, we should bear in mind that to the extent that mediation brings a sense of peace to a situation, the process itself may induce participants to treat rules with respect. Whatever the cause, parties' compliance with confidentiality obligations appears to be higher than a purely tactical analysis would suggest.

Reported cases involving confidentiality arise largely in the context of court-connected mediation. This may be because parties are often compelled to participate in court programs, while they usually enter private mediation voluntarily. A person unhappy to be in a process is probably less likely to respect its rules. Also, litigants are probably more apt to complain, and judges to impose sanctions, when a problem arises in a court-affiliated context.

A Response: The Uniform Mediation Act

What level of protection should be given to confidentiality in mediation? Assuming that confidentiality is necessary, the lack of uniformity among jurisdictions, and the resulting uncertainty about what rule will apply to a given mediation, may be retarding the growth of the field. One possibility is for the states to adopt a uniform confidentiality statute. To this end, the National Conference of Commissioners on Uniform State Laws has proposed a Uniform Mediation Act (UMA) for adoption by the states. (The complete text of the UMA appears in the Web Appendix.)

If the UMA is enacted on a widespread basis, confidentiality rules will become more uniform from one state to another, and the likelihood that federal courts will develop a uniform rule may also increase.

Section 4(a) of the Act creates a legal privilege for communications made during mediation: A communication that falls within the UMA is not "subject to discovery or admissible in evidence" in a legal proceeding (§ 4(a)). The UMA thus prevents the use of mediation communications in adjudicatory proceedings. The statute does not provide complete confidentiality, however, only a privilege; it leaves disputants free to disclose mediation information in contexts other than litigation, for example in a conversation with a friend or to the media. (See comments to UMA § 8.) For this reason, disputants in a UMA jurisdiction who wish to ensure that their mediation communications remain confidential outside legal proceedings must enter into private confidentiality agreements. Sample agreements that include confidentiality provisions appear in the Web Appendix.

The UMA also contains several exceptions to its ban on disclosure in litigation. Sections 5 and 6(a) of the UMA permit a court to order a disclosure of mediation communications about:

- Agreements signed by all parties.
- Documents required to be kept open to the public.
- Threats to commit bodily injury or crimes of violence.
- Plans to commit or conceal an ongoing crime.
- Information needed for a mediator to respond to claims or charges against him.
- Situations involving child abuse and neglect.

Section 6(b) of the UMA creates an additional exception to confidentiality in situations where a tribunal finds that a party has shown that:

- Evidence is not otherwise available,
- There is a need for the evidence that substantially outweighs the interest in protecting confidentiality, and
- The mediation communication is sought or offered in a court proceeding involving a felony or litigation over a contract reached in mediation (but in the latter situation the mediator cannot be compelled to testify).

The UMA has provoked disagreement within the mediation community. Some commentators argue that its provisions are inadequate because they do not cover out-of-court disclosures, while others consider the UMA's restrictions excessive. In addition, some mediators and lawyers who practice in states that have strong mediation confidentiality rules object to "watering down" their existing protections in the interest of national uniformity. As of this writing, it is not clear how widely the UMA will be adopted.

B. Enforcement of Participation in Mediation

1. Agreements to Mediate

Parties entering into relationships, particularly ones that are lengthy or complex, are increasingly likely to include in their agreements a clause obligating them to mediate any dispute that may arise as a result of their interactions. Businesses entering into commercial supply contracts or divorcing parents with young children, for instance, can expect to encounter changes in circumstances over the term of their agreement and may wish to create a process to address such changes. Agreements to mediate are also required by law in some states; Arizona and Washington, for example, require divorcing parents who seek court approval of certain kinds of child custody and visitation arrangements to include ADR provisions in their plans.

The first question raised by an agreement to mediate is what it obligates the parties to do. For instance, what constitutes "good-faith bargaining" and what does it mean to come to mediation with "full settlement authority"? A party who does not wish to mediate might also assert contractual defenses such as lack of assent or misrepresentation. It seems most likely that such defenses will be raised by consumers, who are increasingly subject to compulsory ADR clauses imposed through adhesion contracts. Such issues arise most often in the context of arbitration. However, a mediation clause that imposed significant costs on consumers could also raise serious questions.

There have been few reported cases concerning compliance with private agreements to mediate. This may reflect the fact that parties who contract to mediate usually carry out their obligation. The presence of an ADR clause may also prompt disputants to enter into direct negotiations, making mediation unnecessary. Even when a disputant does not wish to mediate, it may conclude that it is easier to go through a mediation session than to litigate over it, or a party confronted with an opponent who refuses to mediate may conclude that a compelled process would be meaningless.

Questions

In the early 1990s, a large California bank instituted a multistep ADR program for many of its customers. The program required consumers to mediate any dispute they might have with the bank. Under the program, professional mediators would be provided through either of two prominent ADR organizations. Many of these mediators charged hundreds of dollars per hour for their time. Consumers were obligated to pay half of the cost of mediation, although the program allowed them to apply for an exemption from the payment obligation. The plan also stated that neither party could leave mediation until the mediator had made a finding that there was "no possibility of resolution without pursuing the adjudicatory phase."

17. If you were a customer with a claim against the bank, would you challenge this program? What grounds might there be to do so?
18. Is the program likely to create practical problems for the mediators in it?

2. Mandates to Mediate

a. Issues of Court Authority

Many court systems, impressed with the potential of mediation, have decided to make participation in the process mandatory. Courts sometimes do so in the belief that disputants and counsel are unfamiliar with the benefits of mediation and need to be compelled to "try some." Other courts impose such requirements out of concern that the parties most in need of mediation — or those most likely to consume judicial resources unnecessarily — will not enter the process voluntarily. Thus many states require parents involved in a child visitation or custody dispute to mediate before seeking orders from a court.

Early in the development of court-connected mediation, commentators were concerned that it might be unconstitutional for a court to order parties into ADR — for example, that such a requirement might interfere with provisions in many state constitutions that give citizens a right of free access to justice. Courts, however, have upheld mediation mandates against arguments that they violate constitutional guarantees, probably because participation in mediation is inherently no more burdensome than other steps in the litigation process, such as compelled appearance at depositions (see Golann 1989).

The fact that mandatory ADR is constitutional, however, does not mean that a particular court has the authority to order it. Courts ordinarily derive their authority from specific sources, such as constitutional provisions and statutes. Many federal courts, for example, base orders compelling litigants to mediate on formal plans and court rules adopted pursuant to the Civil Justice Reform Act of 1990, 28 U.S.C. §§ 471–482, or the ADR Act of 1998, 28 U.S.C. §§ 651–658. The 1998 Act, in particular, bars federal courts from forcing parties to arbitrate but says nothing about requiring litigants to mediate, which has been interpreted to mean that federal courts may adopt rules providing for mandatory mediation.

Can a federal court that has not adopted a rule pursuant to these statutes nevertheless order parties to mediate as a matter of "inherent judicial power"? On the one hand, the Seventh Circuit Court of Appeals has ruled that a federal court can use its inherent power to force parties to attend a pretrial settlement conference. (See *Heileman Brewing Co. v. Joseph Oat Corp.*, 871 F.2d 648, 650 (7th Cir. 1989) (en banc).) On the other hand, both the Sixth and Seventh Circuits have ruled that federal courts cannot rely on inherent powers to force litigants to engage in "summary jury trials," an ADR process that involves an abbreviated trial to a jury with a nonbinding verdict, usually followed by mediation. (See *In re NLO, Inc.*, 5 F.3d 154 (6th Cir. 1993); *Strandell v. Jackson County*, 838 F.2d 884 (7th Cir. 1987).)

The First Circuit Court of Appeals, in the case of *In re Atlantic Pipe Corp.*, 304 F.3d 135 (1st Cir. 2002), confronted the issue of whether a federal district court may use its inherent powers to order a party in a civil case to participate in and pay for mediation. The case involved a complex construction dispute with many parties. The Court of Appeals confirmed the inherent power of a trial judge to order mediation over a party's objection, to require the objector to pay part of the cost of the process, and to name as a mediator a private neutral nominated by one of the parties. The court expressed concern, however, over the lack of any restrictions on the process, particularly in light of the mediator's quoted rate of $9,000 per day, and remanded the case to the trial court for further orders.

Question

19. Assume you are a law clerk to the trial judge in *Atlantic Pipe*. What conditions might you add to the mediation order to meet the First Circuit's concerns?

b. Good-Faith Bargaining Requirements

If a court has the power to order disputants to mediate, should it require them to satisfy any minimum standard of conduct? If the adoption of rules is any guide, the answer is plainly yes. Professor John Lande has found that at least 22 states have "good-faith bargaining" requirements for mediation, and that 21 or more federal district courts and 17 state courts have local rules imposing such duties on disputants, usually in connection with a court ADR program. The problem is that virtually none of these rules defines what constitutes "good faith" in mediation, or its absence. According to Professor Lande, the reported cases on good-faith obligations break down as follows:

- Failure to attend mediation at all.
- Failure to send a representative with adequate settlement authority.
- Failure to submit required memoranda or documents.
- Failure to make a suitable offer or otherwise participate in bargaining.
- Failure to sign an agreement.

In practice courts have found it easiest to sanction objective conduct, such as a party's failure to appear or file a statement. Judges have found it much more difficult to determine whether a party has made a "suitable offer" or sent a representative with "adequate settlement authority." There are only a few cases in which sanctions based on subjective conclusions about misconduct in mediation have been upheld on appeal (Lande 2002).

Attempts to regulate parties' conduct during mediation raise difficult issues. To begin with, a court would have to define the meaning of "good faith." In many cases the court would also have to take evidence about what had been said or done during the mediation process itself, raising the confidentiality concerns discussed previously. Assuming that enforcement were feasible, many argue that good-faith bargaining requirements are in inherent conflict with a key value of mediation. In the words of the first principle of the Model Standards of Conduct for Mediators, "Parties may exercise self-determination at any stage of a mediation, including... participation in or withdrawal from the process." If parties have the unfettered right to make their own decisions about mediating, however, how can any specific level of participation be required? At the same time, if parties are ordered to mediation by a court and one party expends substantial resources to comply, should its adversary be permitted to nullify the process by failing to prepare or refusing to bargain? The following questions illustrate the issue.

Questions

20. Consider again the problem at the start of this section, in which Alpha's counsel offered $10,000 in response to the plaintiff lowering its demand from $750,000 to $450,000.
    (a) If applicable rules require that the parties "bargain in good faith," has Alpha complied?
    (b) Does anything else that Alpha did or failed to do in that process strike you as "bad faith"?
21. Consider the situation of defense counsel in the following California case: A court-appointed master ordered the parties to engage in a five-day mediation process of a complex construction defect claim. Knowing that such claims necessarily involve expert testimony, the neutral instructed each side to bring its experts to the process. The neutral's charges and the plaintiff's cost for assembling its experts for mediation totaled nearly $25,000. Defense counsel, however, arrived 30 minutes late for the first session and appeared alone. Asked about his failure to bring his client or his experts, he said, "I'm here, you can talk to me." (See *Foxgate Homeowner's Association, Inc., v. Bramlea California, Inc., et al.*, 25 P.3d 1117 (Cal. 2001).)
    (a) Did the defense counsel's actions in this mediation constitute bad faith? Why, exactly?
    (b) The mediator in *Foxgate* reported to the court that defense counsel took this approach because he believed that his pending motion for partial summary judgment would substantially reduce the value of the plaintiff's claims. Does this justify the lawyer's strategy?
    (c) The neutral also reported that in his opinion, the defendant had sufficient time to present the motion before the mediation but had not done so. How relevant is the mediator's opinion on this issue?

The fact that mediation often leads people to change their minds makes it particularly important that the persons who attend have the authority to adopt new positions. If a negotiator ultimately decides that a difficult compromise is appropriate, for example, he needs the authority to implement his judgment.

Recognizing this, mediation agreements and program rules usually require that if a party does not appear personally — impossible for a corporation — it must send a representative who has "full" or "adequate" settlement authority. This raises another issue of "good-faith participation" in mediation, the problem of invading confidentiality, discussed earlier. There is also the issue of defining what is meant by full or adequate authority. Consider, for example, the following case, and as you read it, ask yourself the following questions.

Questions

22. If the authority that the defendant brought to this mediation was not adequate, what would have been sufficient?

23. If you were counsel to a corporation whose business required it to mediate cases around the country, what practical problems might a "full authority" rule present for you?

❖ *Nick v. Morgan's Foods of Missouri, Inc.*

270 F. 3d 590 (8th Cir. 2001)

Gee Gee Nick, a Kentucky Fried Chicken employee, filed a district court complaint against her employer, Morgan's Foods, alleging sexual harassment. Following a scheduling conference, the parties were ordered to participate in the federal court's Alternative Dispute Resolution ("ADR") process pursuant to its local rules, which provided in part: "Duty to Attend and Participate: All parties, counsel of record, and corporate representatives or claims professionals having authority to settle claims shall attend all mediation conferences and participate in good faith." (Court rules also required that each side file a memorandum with the mediator in advance, but Morgan Food's lawyer did not do so because, the court said, he "believed it was unnecessary and a waste of time.")

The mediation conference was attended by Nick, her court-appointed counsel, Morgan's Foods' outside counsel, and the local regional manager. The manager's settlement authority was limited to $500. Any decision to change the company's settlement position had to be made by its general counsel, . . . who was in Connecticut and only available by telephone. During the mediation, Nick twice made offers of settlement that were rejected without counteroffers. The mediation was terminated shortly thereafter. The neutral informed the district court of the minimal level of Morgan's Foods' participation in the ADR process. In response, the trial court . . . sanctioned Morgan's Foods $1,390 [in costs], . . . its outside counsel $1,390 [as well, and] ordered the company to pay a $1,500 fine. . . . In its Memorandum and Order, the Court explained why personal attendance at a mediation session is a sine qua non:

"For ADR to work, the corporate representative must have the authority and discretion to change her opinion in light of the statements and arguments made by the neutral and opposing party. Meaningful negotiations cannot occur if the only person with authority to actually change their mind and negotiate is not present. Availability by telephone is insufficient because the absent decision-maker does not have the full benefit of the ADR proceedings, the opposing party's arguments, and the neutral's input. The absent decision-maker needs to be present and hear first hand the good facts and the bad facts about their case.

"Instead, the absent decision-maker learns only what his or her attorney chooses to relate over the phone. This can be expected to be largely a recitation of what has been conveyed in previous discussions. Even when the attorney attempts to summarize the strengths of the other side's position, there are problems. First, the attorney has a credibility problem: the absent decision-maker wants to know why the attorney's confident opinion expressed earlier has now eroded. Second, the new information most likely is too much to absorb and analyze in a matter of minutes. Under this dynamic it becomes all too easy for the absent decision-maker to reject the attorney's new advice, reject the new information, and reject any effort to engage in meaningful negotiations.

"It is quite likely that the telephone call is viewed as a distraction from other business being conducted by the absent decision-maker.... [The] easiest decision is to summarily reject any offer and get back to the business on her desk....

"Morgan's Foods' lack of good faith participation in the ADR process was calculated to save Morgan's Foods a few hours of time in preparing the mediation memorandum and to save its general counsel the expense and inconvenience of a trip to attend the mediation. The consequence of Morgan's Foods' lack of good faith participation in the ADR process, however, was the wasted expense of time and energy of the Court, the neutral, Nick, and her court-appointed counsel. If Morgan's Foods did not feel that ADR could be fruitful and had no intention of participating in good faith, it had a duty to report its position to the Court and to request appropriate relief. Morgan's Foods did not do so and sanctions are appropriate to remedy the resulting waste of time and money."

[The court affirmed the sanctions ordered by the trial judge.]

Questions

24. You are counsel to Morgan's Foods. Another employee has filed a claim similar to Nick's, and it has been referred to the same mediation program. What do you need to do to comply with the court's rule?
25. In a case involving an East Coast computer company's claim that a Silicon Valley firm had improperly "stolen" its development team, the defendant's general counsel refused to travel to a mediation session in New York. At the mediator's request, however, she did agree to be present on a conference phone during all of the joint meetings and throughout each caucus that the mediator held with her side. Does that level of presence meet the objections of the *Nick* court? What are the potential drawbacks to such an arrangement?
26. Florida, one of the most active states in promoting court-related ADR, requires litigants to appear at mediation, and defines appearance to mean that: "[The] party or a representative with full settlement authority is present along with the party's counsel, if any, and a representative of the insurance carrier with full authority to settle up to the plaintiff's last demand or policy limits, whichever is less...." Assume that you are the national litigation counsel for a Fortune 500 company with operations in Florida that occasionally result in cases being filed against your company, and you are required to mediate under this rule.
    (a) Could your local outside counsel appear at a court-connected mediation in Florida without a company representative, if he had full authority to bind your company?
    (b) What practical problems would this rule create for you? Can you think of any steps that would lessen them?

In response to the difficulty of defining and enforcing "good-faith" requirements, some have argued that such rules should be discarded. Professor Lande, for example, warns that

Sanctioning bad faith in mediation actually may stimulate adversarial and dishonest conduct....[It] might also encourage surface bargaining...Because mediators are not supposed to force people to settle, participants who are determined not to settle can wait until the mediator gives up....Similarly, tough mediation participants could use good-faith requirements offensively to intimidate opposing parties....[Innocent] participants may have legitimate fears about risking sanctions when they face an aggressive opponent....[In addition, a] good-faith requirement gives mediators too much authority...to direct the outcome in mediation....

He has proposed that litigants instead be given education about the value of interest-based processes, and that courts limit themselves to enforcing objective standards of conduct, such as a requirement that parties appear at mediation for a minimum period of time (Lande 2002).

Problem 7

Two companies are in mediation. In the underlying lawsuit, the plaintiff has alleged that the defendant knowingly violated a franchise agreement. The "hard" damages in the case, computed on the basis of the franchisee's minimum purchase requirements, are about $100,000. However, the plaintiff has also claimed $500,000 in lost profits and made an initial settlement demand of $600,000. It appears to the franchisee's lawyer that her client has about a 50–50 chance of being found liable under the contract and having to pay the hard damages, but that the risk that her client will be liable for lost profits is virtually nil. Applying the 50 percent risk factor to the hard damages, the defense therefore assesses the value of the case at $50,000. The parties agree to mediate.

In a first caucus meeting with the mediator, the plaintiff's lawyer says that while its demand is "negotiable," it will not make any concessions until the defense puts a "significant offer" on the table. The defense lawyer informs the neutral that he will not make any offer at this point because the plaintiff is "on another planet." He tells the mediator that it's his job first to bring the plaintiff into a zone of reality, and $600K is not it. The mediation agreement commits the parties to "engage in good-faith bargaining." Is either the plaintiff or the defendant violating its obligation? If so, why?

3. Enforcement of Mediated Settlements

Mediation is a voluntary process, but if it is successful then the parties usually enter into a binding contract — a settlement agreement. Even settlements, however, may provoke new controversies over issues such as the following:

- Did the parties actually reach a final agreement? If so, what were its terms?
- Should the agreement be invalidated on grounds such as duress, mistake, unconscionability, or lack of authority?

a. The Existence of an Agreement

Good practice calls for parties who settle in mediation to memorialize their agreements in writing. To ensure that this occurs, mediation texts counsel neutrals, however late the hour or strong the settling parties' wish to depart, to push the disputants to sign a memorandum that summarizes the settlement before they leave. Sometimes, however, the parties do not execute an agreement, or it is later attacked as incomplete.

Most courts test mediated settlements by the standards that apply to contracts generally. If an agreement is oral, the first issue is whether it complies with the applicable statute of frauds. Courts in several states have held oral mediated settlements to be enforceable contracts, and although there are few reported cases, it appears that federal common law also permits enforcement of oral settlements. Where a court has refused to enforce an oral agreement reached in mediation, it has usually been because the state has imposed procedural rules that go beyond the requirements of the common law of contracts. Florida, Washington, and Texas, for example, mandate that pending court cases may be settled only through a written document signed by the parties or their counsel (Cole et al. 2001).

As we have seen, virtually every state has rules intended to guarantee the confidentiality of mediation. Some state privilege laws contain explicit exceptions that permit the introduction of evidence of oral settlements, and other statutes, although absolute on their face, have been interpreted to permit such testimony. In many states, however, it is not clear whether disputants may testify about the existence of an oral settlement, or whether the mediator can be called as a witness on the issue. Sections 4(a) and 6(a) of the Uniform Mediation Act prevent participants from testifying about agreements reached in mediation, but exempt agreements that are signed and in writing or electronically recorded from the restriction. The net effect of the UMA is thus to bar enforcement of purely oral settlements, but permit enforcement of written ones.

b. Grounds for Invalidation

Suppose, following a successful mediation process, that the lawyers draw up a settlement agreement and the parties sign it. Is that enough to ensure that a settlement will be enforced? Generally the answer is yes, but not always. Again there are potential concerns. Some of these are formal in nature. First, settlement agreements must contain the essential terms of the parties' bargain. Where, for example, a settlement provides that "the parties shall exchange mutual releases," a court would probably find the language sufficient to form a binding agreement. If, however, a settlement states that a defendant will make payments "in installments" but does not specify a schedule, a challenge would be more likely to succeed. In addition, some jurisdictions impose special requirements on mediated agreements. A California statute, for instance, requires that for evidence of a mediated agreement to be admissible over objection, the document must either state that it is admissible or intended to be enforceable, or words to that effect, or be offered to show illegality (Cal. Evid. Code § 1123). A few jurisdictions also require that mediated settlements of pending litigation be approved by a court.

The most serious basis for invalidating mediated settlements is a substantive one: that the process of mediation itself was so deficient that any resulting agreement is invalid. On the one hand, the presence of a neutral person would seem to make it less likely that a "bad" settlement would result. On the other hand, aspects of the process that are intended to push litigants to confront unpleasant realities may also create stress that inhibits good decision making. An example is the *Olam* case, above, in which an individual who remained in mediation for many hours and agreed to a late-night settlement later claimed that she did so under duress.

Questions

27. Is the UMA provision allowing the introduction of evidence about written or recorded settlements, but not oral ones, justified? Why or why not?
28. Do you agree with the California law requiring that mediated agreements, but not directly negotiated ones, state that they are admissible or intended to be enforceable in order to be introduced into evidence?
29. Are there particular circumstances in which a mediated settlement should be subject to special scrutiny? When?
30. When a mediated agreement is challenged on grounds such as duress or misrepresentation, should the court apply a different standard than it would to a settlement reached through direct negotiation? Why or why not?

❖ *Christian Cooper v. Melodie Austin*
750 So. 2d 711-715 (Fla. App. 2000)

HARRIS, J.:

Cooper appeals a final judgment which adopted a mediation agreement Cooper alleges was obtained by extortion and was the basis for [a] contempt citation.... During the course of a lengthy mediation, it is undisputed that the wife sent Cooper the following note:

> If you can't agree to this, the kids will take what information they have to whomever to have you arrested, etc. Although I would get no money if you were in jail — you wouldn't also be living freely as if you did nothing wrong.‡

Relatively soon thereafter, the parties "settled" their property matters.

... In the midst of extended negotiations before the mediator, the wife sent the husband a note that constituted classic extortion. However, the wife convinced the [trial] judge that the note was merely a "wake-up" call and did

---

‡ [Footnote to court opinion] The crime threatened to be reported by the wife was Cooper's photographing a nude, underage girl. Cooper, who had experienced firsthand the law's disapproval of this practice on an earlier occasion, was aware that in going through his property, the wife's children had found a photograph taken by him of a young woman who indeed looked under age. It was not until shortly before this action for relief from judgment was filed that Cooper tracked down the woman and verified she was "of age" at the time the photograph was taken.

not influence the agreement subsequently reached. The court relied on two established facts to reach this conclusion. First, the husband did not immediately accede to the wife's demands but continued to negotiate for a period thereafter. Second, the husband did not seek relief from the extortionate agreement until after his efforts to reconcile with the wife failed. Even accepting these facts as true, we cannot agree that they negate the effect of extortion when reviewing the remainder of the record.

The husband testified, without contradiction, that the result of the mediated agreement was that the wife received $128,000 in marital assets while the husband received $10,000.... This grossly unequal distribution speaks volumes about the effect of the extortionate note sent by the wife....

In this case, the wife's "wake-up call," which demanded the husband either give in to her demands or go to jail, was clearly extortionate and her presentation of the extorted agreement to the court was a fraud on the court making the trial court an instrument of her extortion. Mrs. Cooper should not profit from her actions. Nor should this Court, or any court, ignore them.

GRIFFIN, J., dissenting:

This is not the first time an appellate court has been unable to overcome the urge to trump factual findings of a trial judge with which the panel violently disagrees, nor will it be the last. But it is awkward when it happens.... *How*, the majority asks incredulously, could the trial judge have allowed himself to be hoodwinked in this fashion? After reading the transcript of the hearing, it is clear to me that Judge Hammond simply did not believe Mr. Cooper. This is important because there are only three items of evidence to support Mr. Cooper's claim of duress: (1) the threat; (2) the apparent uneven distrib-ution of assets; and (3) Mr. Cooper's testimony that the reason he entered into the agreement was because of the threat.

The lower court so much as said it did not find Mr. Cooper to be credible. First of all, Mr. Cooper, who has a bachelor's degree and a master's degree in business, both from Duke University... testified repeatedly that he had no idea of the value of the marital assets. [T]he evidence, in fact, showed that he had a very good idea of what the marital assets were....

There was direct conflict between Mr. and Mrs. Cooper concerning Mr. Cooper's response to her threat. She testified that his response was that he was not scared, that the kids did not "have anything" and that he knew that he "owed it to her to put her through school."... As the lower court succinctly said: "The former husband knew that the photographs in his possession were not illegal."

There is also the fact that Mr. Cooper, his free will forborne due to his "fear of arrest," continued to negotiate the agreement for another two and one-half hours[, securing substantial changes in the terms of a promissory note to the wife].... The fact that he received all of the benefits of the mediation agreement as adopted by the Final Judgment, made all alimony payments ..., received back all of the personal property he was concerned about, [and] continued his pursuit of the Former Wife are not the actions of a man who was subject to extortion, coercion or duress.... We should affirm.

Question

31. If Mr. Cooper's counsel thought that his client was feeling extorted during the mediation, what should he have done?

C. Certification and Licensing

There is a continuing debate about whether mediators should be either certified or licensed. Licensing is an official act carried out by a government agency, whereas certification can be done by either an official organization such as a court program or a private association. The two options have different implications. Licensing is more restrictive, since only persons who obtained a license could mediate the types of cases covered by it (e.g., family disputes). Certification has less effect: It prevents neutrals from working in settings in which the certification is required (e.g., a particular court program), but not from mediating in general.

Mediation licensing does not exist — there is no equivalent to bar membership, or even a driver's license, for neutrals. A child can act as a mediator (many students do, in fact, mediate peer disputes in schools). This reflects the history of mediation, which was fueled in large measure by frustration with the conventional legal system and peoples' wish to find new ways to approach disputes. The idea of creating licensing systems for mediators, with the need for agencies to define "good" practices and test for them, strikes many in the field as antithetical to their basic values. There is also concern that government regulation of ADR would stifle its creativity. Finally, there is little empirical evidence that licensing or certification is needed, leading many to say, "If it ain't broke, don't fix it!"

Most of the court systems and private organizations that offer mediation do, however, impose standards for admittance to their panels. The effect is that certification standards have become widespread, especially in connection with court-connected mediation programs. The popularity of certification in court settings probably reflects the view that courts, as official institutions, should take responsibility for the quality of mediators who practice under their aegis. However, there is no national, or in many cases even statewide, uniformity in the standards for certification even where they exist. The following articles discuss whether a wider, more consistent system for certifying mediators should be created.

Juliana Birkoff and Robert Rack with Judith M. Filner,
Points of View: Is Mediation Really a Profession?

8 Disp. Resol. Mag. 10-21 (Fall 2001)

[T]here has been a push for quality assurance by developing credential programs for mediators. Skeptics have said that the drive toward credentials comes from the desire of some practitioners to reduce competition. Others have urged resistance to this impetus to create qualifications, claiming it is elitist and exclusionary. Some further assert that creating qualifications will limit the diversity of the field. Advocates, however, perceive a need and responsibility to protect consumers from incompetent mediators, to enhance the credibility and status of the field, and to address the need for agencies, courts, and other referral sources to assure the quality of the services provided.

Skeptics and advocates alike puzzle over how qualifications can be related to performance, whether credential programs assure quality, and whether or not the field of mediation is sufficiently mature to define what mediation is, what mediators do, and what they have to know to serve competently. While the discussion continues, various states and agencies are, in fact, establishing qualifications and standards. And, the field is maturing . . . The interview that follows . . . frames the quality assurance discussion.

JMF: So . . . is mediation a profession?

JB: Yes, I think mediation is a profession or is becoming a profession. When I began my research, I did not expect to find [this]. . . .

BR: I certainly think most mediators are professional in the sense that they are committed to their work. . . . But I think mediation is bigger than a profession and I resist the temptation to try to capture and contain it. We've seen mediation explode in use throughout society. . . . I see it as a broad social movement. . . .

JMF: . . . If mediation is a profession, how do we, as a field, as practitioners, as program directors, assure quality or address issues of quality practice?

JB: Credentialing is a way that professionals try to define what they do and distinguish it from what other professions or occupations do. For me, it is not so important to look at credentialing. Rather, it is important to look at the body of knowledge that a mediator uses to do the work, to practice. . . .

BR: . . . I see the heart of good mediation as skillfully facilitating communication and effectively infusing strained relationships with goodwill. The most essential "knowledge" for a mediator seems to me to be an understanding of human nature and human behavior, especially under stress and in conflict. That knowledge can be largely intuitive, and developed through experience. We may one day have such a precise understanding of human behavior that we can write it down and require mediators to commit it to memory, like biology, laws, and accounting rules for doctors, lawyers, and accountants. And we might then be able to measure a mediator's ability to apply that knowledge. But I doubt that will happen anytime soon.

JB: Let me clarify; mediators do not develop their unique knowledge by studying literature. This is why so few mediators find that going to M.S. or Ph.D. programs improves their skills as mediators. Mediators develop their knowledge by doing the work. . . .

BR: The first thing I look for in new mediator candidates is a kind of life stance — an inclination to see the validity in apparently conflicting points of view and to seek synthesis, rather than domination by any one of those views. The second thing I look for is experience that demonstrates a skillful articulation of that inclination . . . So I'd say that mediation is a life skill first. . . . Daniel Bowling and David Hoffman published an article in . . . which they concluded that a mediator's mere "presence" is a major ingredient in the mediation dynamic . . . I completely agree. Now, how do we "credentialize" that?

JB: While I understand where Bob is coming from, it sounds like he believes that being artistic and creative has no place in a profession. . . . Professional knowing is not only tacit theory but also the intuition, skill, and experience of trained and talented individuals who know how to apply that knowledge. . . .

JMF: One of the reasons mediators talk about assuring quality is that there is poor
practice out there....

JB: I guess I would ask what proof exists, besides rumors and anecdotes, that there is a
need to protect the public. This is often an argument that beginning professions use
to protect their insecure control of their work...However, I do believe that the
mediation organizations should promote standards of practice and require a
commitment from members to abide by the standards of practice.

BR: I agree with almost everything Juliana has said. If participants understand the
very basics of mediation, it's really pretty hard for a mediator to do much harm...I
believe the focus and responsibility for resolution should remain on the parties and
there already is a tendency for many disputants to hand over that responsibility to
the mediator. I hate to give any more authority or stature to the mediator than is
absolutely necessary....

JMF: Finally, I see a strong, albeit disorganized and informal, move toward
credentialing....

JB: It is significant that people are representing themselves as professional
mediators....This says more about the ways we as a society judge the effectiveness
of lawyers and therapists than it does about the benefits of having a conflict
resolution profession.

BR: I understand the disdain for charlatans, the frustration over not being able to
do anything about incompetent people in our field, and the feeling of responsibility
for assuring quality. It's just that we have no reason at this time to believe we know
how to legislate for the selection of good mediators and the screening out of bad
ones....

...There are things that can be done to advance the quality ball without
legislating requirements for everyone. First, let's...let [private associations]
experiment with qualifications and see if they can find some that really make a
difference....This field is still hot and is still evolving rapidly. My vote remains that
we not try to freeze it with mandatory qualifications or performance standards until
we know it will make a significant and positive difference.

❖ James E. McGuire, Certification: An Idea Whose Time Has Come

10 Disp. Resol. Mag. 22-23 (Summer 2004)

Is mediation a profession? If it is, what are the requirements to be a
professional mediator? Who should do the certifying? These seemingly simple
questions have been part of the mediation dialogue in the United States for
more than 25 years....

Why Certify Any Mediator? Mediators not only want to be competent,
they want to be perceived as competent. Currently, mediators do so by
collecting credentials: training programs taken, panels joined, articles written,
and for those with actual experience, number of cases mediated. While not
ensuring competence, credentialing creates a competitive advantage for a
mediator.

In order to secure the credential of participating on a panel, taking the
sponsor's training course is often a prerequisite. Training programs can be
a major source of revenue for the sponsor and a significant burden for
potential mediators. Moreover, multiple, repetitive, mandatory entry-level
training programs exist within most states and practice areas. Certification
may provide an answer to the frustration these duplicative requirements
present....

As legislators begin to codify mediation confidentiality . . . some are asking the basic hard questions: Who are these mediators? How do they get trained? What safeguards exist to ensure that the mediators are trustworthy? An additional reason for considering voluntary mediator certification is recognition that if mediators do not create a certification process, others will and it may not be as voluntary or nuanced and flexible as the field would desire. . . .

How to Become Certified. The exact contours of a certification program will be determined through the current collaborative process between [the Association for Conflict Resolution, many of whose members are not lawyers, and the American Bar Association.] A likely model is [a] two-step process . . . : preparation and submission of a "portfolio," which, if accepted, qualifies the applicant to sit for an examination to become a certified mediator. The portfolio is a paper submission documenting 100 hours of training and relevant course work, including a minimum of 80 hours in mediation process skills. The portfolio must also document at least 100 hours as an active mediator within the last five years. Letters of recommendation, evidence of professional liability insurance, and disclosure of disciplinary matters complete the portfolio requirements.

A candidate with an acceptable portfolio would then take a written examination. The examination itself would be prepared by an independent professional. The exam is intended to test awareness of mediation principles, approaches, and relevant techniques. [T]here is likely to be no provision for reviewing an actual demonstration of mediation skills. Such live evaluations are difficult to develop and expensive to administer. This is especially true where the goal is to avoid having certification itself become an economic barrier to entry into the mediation field.

Who Certifies? The development and successful implementation of certification standards is most likely to succeed if it is a multi-organizational effort. . . . [N]either lawyers nor the ABA "own" the mediator certification process. . . . Though there can be no guarantee of success, any other approach may well be a guarantee of failure.

Questions

32. Assume that you wish to become a mediator and can meet the qualifications described by James McGuire. Would you favor having your state adopt a credentialing program like the one outlined in his article, or the "hands-off" approach advocated by Juliana Birkoff and Robert Rack?
33. Most mediators of legal cases in superior and federal courts are selected by lawyers. In such situations, who would a credentialing requirement protect?
34. What is gained or lost if regulation of mediators is limited to certification, rather than a licensing system like bar membership?

PART
V

APPLICATIONS

CHAPTER
14

Specific Applications

Mediation is used in a wide variety of subject areas. From its traditional roots in family, union, and construction disputes, it has expanded to employment, environmental, high-tech, and even criminal cases. The application of mediation to specialized fields raises issues of process design, and also poses the question of whether the process is appropriate for every kind of dispute. The following readings explore these issues.

A. Family Disputes

1. What Is Unique About Family Mediation?

Family disputes involve several factors that make them different from other civil cases. Among them are

Intense Emotions. Marriage is perhaps the most intimate relationship that human beings can enter. People often define themselves around being a husband or wife, and divorce thus strikes at the very heart of their sense of identity and self-worth. This is likely to provoke feelings more intense than those found in almost any other kind of conflict. Marital discord can also trigger deep and sometimes irrational emotions that stem from each spouse's own childhood.

Continuing Relationships. Ordinarily when people fall into disagreement, they have the option to separate from each other. But if a couple has children, they usually cannot completely dissociate, even when they divorce. Instead ex-spouses remain connected to each other in their roles as parents, often for many years. Divorced parents must find ways to share their children's physical presence, financial responsibility for their expenses, commitment to teaching and socializing the child, and a variety of other tasks. People often find it difficult to cooperate on these issues even when they are happily married. If both parties seek custody, or if a spouse decides to use the children as a weapon in the marital conflict, the difficulties created by an unwanted relationship over parenting will multiply.

Impact on, and Participation by, Children. While children are young, parents can usually enforce decisions about their upbringing. This raises a concern that a spouse who is desperate to escape a marriage or not thinking clearly may sacrifice a child's best interests to his or her own. For teenagers, a different problem arises. Older children often have strong wishes about where they want to live and how they want to lead their lives. They can become third-party players in disputes over custody and visitation, rejecting agreements that have been worked out by their parents and further complicating the process of settling such cases.

Potential for Physical or Emotional Abuse. In domestic conflicts, unlike most civil disputes, there is a real possibility that criminal acts, in the form of physical or emotional abuse, will occur. Even when victims do not complain, society has a strong interest in preventing such acts and in protecting an abused spouse from giving away rights. This issue is especially acute in states that require couples to engage in mediation as a precondition to gaining access to court, an issue discussed in Chapter 11.

Lack of Legal Counsel. Despite the fact that family disputes involve some of people's most basic rights, divorcing spouses are less likely than most litigants to obtain legal advice. Business disputants typically have the resources to obtain counsel, and in personal injury cases contingent fees and insurance can provide access to lawyers. Family disputes, however, involve disagreements between individuals who often have neither assets nor insurance to cover legal costs. There is a serious risk that participants in family mediation will not get good legal advice, making it difficult for them to negotiate effectively and putting the mediator in an awkward position as well.

Although these factors greatly complicate the use of mediation in family cases, the consequences of litigating such disputes can be horrific. Legal proceedings are often deeply destructive, creating rather than healing emotional scars. They can also exhaust a family's financial resources at the very time that its expenses are increasing because of the need to establish a second household. Legal battles over custody and visitation, in particular, often have a severe impact on children. For these reasons, as the use of mediation grew, family disputes were among the first areas to which it was applied. Today, most states have statutes and policies governing family mediation and mandate that parties involved in disputes over child custody or visitation go through mediation before entering a courtroom.

As we have seen, the process of family mediation differs from traditional civil or commercial mediation in several respects. The parties generally remain together throughout the process rather than separating into private caucuses. Attorneys are ordinarily not present, although parties may consult them between sessions. Because many couples have issues about custody and visitation, there is more need for the process to be interest based and future oriented. Family mediations often are not one-day affairs, but rather extend over a period of weeks or months. Finally, perhaps due to the strong emotional issues present in such cases, most family mediators have in the past been mental health professionals, although the proportion of attorney-mediators in the field is increasing.

2. *The Process*

Given the special characteristics of family disputes, it is not surprising that the process differs from general civil mediation. The following is an edited transcript of a mediation session that occurred at the outset of a divorce case. As you read it, think about these questions.

Questions

1. How does this process differ from examples you have seen of commercial mediation?
2. What might have happened in this case if the parties had not gone to mediation?
3. Some commentators criticize this mediator's technique, seeing him as maneuvering disputants into going in a certain direction rather than helping them make decisions for themselves. Do you see any evidence of this in the transcript?
4. Like many mediators in this field, John Haynes was not a lawyer, instead holding a doctorate in the social sciences. Do you think his background has any impact on how he mediates?

❖ **John Haynes, Mediating Divorce: Casebook of Strategies for Successful Family Negotiations**
Jossey-Bass 50 (1989)

Transcript and Annotations*

Mediator: [Your] counsel has asked you to come today to see if we can work out an agreement that is appropriate for both of you and in the best interest of Sarah and Daniel. I wonder if you could tell me a little bit about what's happened in the last month.[1] Perhaps if I could ask you to begin, Debbie, in terms of where the children are living currently and what the arrangements are.[2] Then we can see what differences there are between you and see where we go from there.

Debbie: Well, the children are with me in the matrimonial home. Michael left a month ago, and I have let him see the children on several occasions.[3] But the children aren't happy seeing their father. They said they don't want to see him. They are very

---

* The footnotes to this reading contain comments of the mediator as he reviewed the transcript of the session. They set forth why he made certain interventions and his assessment of what the disputants were feeling at the time.

1. I open with this information question about the events of the last month to focus on what is current and avoid drifting into the past and the marriage. The body language of the couple throughout the session is very revealing. Michael is very closed when I talk to Debbie and tends to open when I talk to him. Debbie looks away from Michael and down [at] the floor when Michael says something she does not like. Michael frequently turns away from both Debbie and the mediator, gazing at the wall.

2. A focused question, directed at Debbie, is designed to limit the amount of space for a marital fight to develop. This future-oriented question sets the agenda for the session.

3. "I have let" indicates that Debbie believes she has the power in the situation. If Michael agrees with this assessment, it will provide me with some power-balancing information.

unhappy about the separation.[4] When they come home, they're very upset. They're crying, and it takes me hours to settle them down. I just don't know how they're going to cope with this.

Mediator: So they're currently living in the family home with you, and they're spending time with their dad.[5] Michael, what is your feeling?

Michael: I think that Debra's a little . . . ah . . . she doesn't have a grasp on the situation. I've seen these kids now five times over the past month. They are happy to come with me; we have a good time. We've done a lot of things together; they enjoy being with me. They're obviously at strain, because when I was living at home they were seeing me daily, constantly. . . . I don't think that Debra is helping them at all. I'm having a great difficulty in coming back and watching her dissemble. When I bring the kids back home, she starts. . . .

Mediator: How old are the children?[6]

Michael: Five and seven.

Mediator: Five and seven, and the older one is . . .

Michael: Daniel.

Mediator: Daniel is seven and Sarah is five. Okay. It's not unusual for them to have this tension and lots of crying when they go back and forth. . . . So it's perfectly possible for them to have a good time when they're with you, Michael, but also express real concerns and reservations when they're with you, Debbie. That's not an unusual situation. Let me just see now what's the difference between you. What is it that brings you here?

Michael: Well, the difference basically is this: Debra says that I can be a part-time parent and I can see my kids every second weekend from Saturday morning until Sunday night, if I see them alone and so long as she maintains control over it.

Mediator: What does Michael want?

Michael: These are my children. I am one-half of their parents. I want the kids half-time. When we were living together, I was spending most of the time with the children.

Mediator: So you'd like to have the children spend half of the time with you and half the time with Debbie.[7]

Michael: I think so. I don't see that it's inappropriate in our circumstance.

Debbie: I don't think he wants to see the children. I think he's using that.[8]

Mediator: What do you want, Debbie? . . .

Debbie: I want him to come back. My children are devastated. I'm devastated. . . . We had plans for us and for our children, and he's destroyed that. He's giving me no reason. All of a sudden, after fifteen years of marriage, he says that's it, I can't stand it any more. And I think you should know he's seeing someone else, and he's exposing our children to that other person. . . .[9]

4. Debbie's complaint about Michael is diffuse as she stakes out a tough opening position, defining the problem as the children's unhappiness, which can be solved only by a change in Michael's behavior, as defined by Debbie.

5. This summary of the factual content makes no comment on Debbie's charges, so as not to solidify her position. If the mediator comments or argues with her about this, she will have to defend her position and thereby become more "wedded" to it.

6. As Michael continues his complaints, I cut through the "feelings" with a factual (closed) question on a different subject. This process interruption breaks the cycle Michael is about to launch.

7. The summary of Michael's proposal reframes it, to help Debbie hear that under his proposal she would also have them half of the time. She probably heard only that he wanted them. By pointing out the "half-full glass," the mediator facilitates the bargaining.

8. Debbie ignores the reframing of Michael's statement.

9. Debbie sends two messages: She wants Michael back, and he is seeing another woman. I develop a hypothesis that the fight is over the other woman and devise questions to test my hypothesis.

Mediator: Help me understand, Debbie, what it is you are looking for me to do. . . .

Debbie: Well, I'm here because I don't want to go through the court system. If we're going to separate, I don't want a lawyer or judge shoving an agreement down my throat.

Mediator: That's wise. So, what you want me to do is mediate . . . ?

Debbie: Yes.

Mediator: . . . I'm not going to work with you to get back together.[10] If you want to do that, there are other people competent at doing that. That's not my area. . . . What I'm going to do is to help you define the problem between the two of you, see what options there are to solve that problem, and help you solve that problem in a way that's mutually acceptable to you, and in the best interests of Sarah and Daniel. . . .

Mediator (to Michael):   So you'd like to have them. Right? You'd like to have them half of the time.[11]

Michael: Yes.

Mediator: Debbie, if you were to structure the arrangement for the parenting, how would you structure it?[12]

Debbie: Well, I think the children need a home. . . . And I don't think he's prepared to give them the proper kind of a home. . . .

Mediator: . . . That's an issue; we will deal with it because it's obviously an issue between you. But assuming that was not an issue, then how much time would you want Sarah and Daniel to spend with their daddy?

Debbie: The children love their father, and I don't want to keep the children away from their father. I suppose if we could sort out other problems, I would want him to see them as much as he could and as much as their schedules would allow.[13]

Michael: . . . She's misrepresenting me to the children on a constant basis. She tells them that I'm sick, she tells them that I'm depressed, she tells them that poor daddy doesn't know what he's doing, poor daddy has a mean friend, poor daddy has a friend who's taking your daddy away from you.

Mediator: It's very, very hard when you get divorced, isn't it? To deal with all of the emotions and all of the things that happen.[14]

Michael: She's a professional woman, she's a smart lady. I have a lot of respect for her. She moves in those circles, she knows what she's doing. . . .

Debbie: Well, I don't see how the children can live one week here and one week there. I think it will be too hard on them. I don't think he's being fair to them. He's the one that broke up this family. . . .

Mediator: Are there any other problems?

Debbie: I don't think they should be exposed to this woman.[15]

Mediator: Okay . . . you're living with somebody, Michael?

Michael: No. I have a relationship with a woman I've come to know over the last period of time. And I can honestly say this isn't the reason that I left. The reason I left is that I was sitting at home and dying, waiting to die in that house. I was sitting at home looking after the kids. Mommy's got a meeting. Mommy's at the hospital. . . . They need their mother, they love their mother. But . . . all of a sudden I'm a bad bastard. . . .

10. I clarify my role, disclaiming responsibility for repairing the marriage.

11. The restatement of the content of Michael's proposal is designed to redirect the discussion and to emphasize "half."

12. Debbie is asked for the first position statement. Given their respective positions and the fact that hers is unlikely to be supported by community norms, I decide to look for the first concession from her.

13. Debbie makes the first significant move, acknowledging Michael's father role. She picks up my language, moving from the spousal to the parenting designation.

14. I let Michael ventilate. . . . I empathize with Michael . . . to re-engage him in the process.

15. I continue probing until all the issues are on the table. This helps to test my hypothesis and determine the order of priority of the issues. Debbie restates an untenable demand, confirming my hypothesis.

Mediator: I'm hearing Debbie say that. I'm also hearing her say they love their father and they need their father and she would like to work it out so they could be with their father.[16] That's what I'm hearing on two levels ... and those are the issues that we need to focus on and get some agreement on.... What would you like?[17]

Debbie: Well, I don't think he should be sleeping — letting his girl friend sleep overnight, and sleeping in the same bedroom with her with our children in the house. I don't think it's right.

Mediator: Let me ask you now: A question, if ... excuse me just one second, but what is her name?

Michael: Jocelyn.

Mediator: Jocelyn. If Jocelyn is not sleeping over, would you feel comfortable working out some arrangement for the children?[18]

Debbie: I'd feel more comfortable. I'd be more comfortable, as well, if he had a house not too far from ours, so the children could go back and forth on their bicycles....

Michael: Tell him about what sort of car I should drive. Tell him about where I should take the kids on the afternoons. Tell him about....

Mediator: And you, Michael, would like to make your own decisions about these issues?

Michael: Of course. This is ridiculous....

Mediator: Okay, so you've been living apart for a month. You're both angry with each other, and that's perfectly legitimate, and that's perfectly normal, too.... Although, interestingly enough, so far today I've not heard any serious differences emerge between you as father and mother. There's a lot as wife and husband — there you're way apart — but not as mother and father. I'm wondering now where you want to go....

Debbie: He's a good father. He's been a good father. I can't deny that. The children love him and he loves the children.

Mediator: In the short run, Michael, could you agree that Jocelyn would not sleep over when the kids are with you?

Michael: What's the short run?

Mediator: Two months.... Give the children a sort of chance to settle in.

Michael: I can live with that. I don't know if Jocelyn can, but I can live with that....

Mediator: All right. Debbie, if, for the next two months, when the children were with Michael ... she's not sleeping over, ... how would you then feel about sharing the parenting? ...

Debbie: Well, I want the children to see their dad, but why does she have to be along? ...

Mediator: There's a lot of work to be done by all of us in terms of working out all of the details.... I'm wondering if we could move for just the next two months, in a sense of trying to get a little space for both of you as we think through all of the issues.

Debbie: Well, maybe if he would agree not to hold her hand and kiss her in front of the children — that's just his friend, that's what he's told them....

Mediator: Okay, so you're saying that if Michael would agree not to be physically affectionate with Jocelyn while the children are there, you'll feel comfortable moving off your position and sharing time for the children with both of you.

Debbie: I'm not saying fifty-fifty, but ... I'd try.

Michael: I'll live with it.

16. Michael moves from talking to me to talking directly to Debbie. Therefore, I permit him to continue ... even though he begins to ventilate. Michael sends a message to Debbie that she will not be displaced. The mediator considers this directional information, indicating where Michael might move in the negotiations.

17. I am using a particularly gentle tone of voice as I pursue this line of questions and providing Debbie with a face-saving way out.

18. A reframing into a future goal, not a current impediment, in an effort to decouple the issue from Jocelyn.

Mediator: All right. Let's then do that for the next few weeks. Let's review it along the way, and let's get back together next week to talk about some of the other issues that are going on between you, so that we can try to get the children clearly out of the middle of your fight as spouses. Okay?

Debbie: Thanks.

The Mediator's Concluding Thoughts

It could be argued that Michael lost in this settlement. He did not achieve the 50–50 shared parenting he sought, and he did give up his girlfriend when the children slept over. It could also be argued that I had a major role in shaping the agreement. These observations are true — in the short run. Note, however, that I sought the agreement only for a couple of months; it was not a permanent agreement. I did not make a moral judgment about Jocelyn's sleeping with Michael; I made a practical one. Debbie was incapable of dealing with her displacement by Jocelyn as wife, and her possible displacement by Jocelyn as mother, while she was still dealing with her loss of Michael.... What this couple needed was a brief respite from the battle, to give them a chance to organize their lives for the next two months.... Mediation is situational.... The agreement provided them with a breathing space in which to collect themselves and sort out the more serious emotional issues.

---

3. Policy Issues

The special characteristics of family disputes raise important policy issues. The reading that follows offers a viewpoint on several of these questions. As you read it, ask yourself these questions.

Questions

5. Should family mediation be barred or restricted when one or both participants do not have a lawyer?
6. Does this depend on whether the case arises in a court system that mandates mediation of disputes over custody and visitation?
7. Are there any steps that could alleviate your concerns?

❖ Jay Folberg, Divorce Mediation: The Emerging American Model

Paper presented at Fourth Annual Conference of the International Society for Family Law, Harvard University (June 1982)

Issues Relating to Divorce Mediation

The very elements that make divorce mediation so appealing compared to the adversarial model also create its dangers and raise substantial issues not yet resolved. Because mediation distinguishes itself as an approach that recognizes divorce and family disputes as both matters of the heart and of the law, there exist issues of how emotional feelings are to be weighed against and blended with legal rights and obligations and what are appropriate subjects for mediation. Because mediation is conducted in private and is less hemmed-in by rules of procedure, substantive law, and precedent, there will remain the question of whether the process is fair and the terms of a mediated agreement are just. This concern for a fair and just result has particular applicability to custody and child support provisions because mediated bargaining occurs between parents, and children are rarely present or independently represented during mediation.

Because mediation represents an "alternative" to the adversarial system, it lacks the precise and perfected checks and balances that are the principal benefit of the adversary process. The purposeful "a-legal" character of mediation creates a constant risk of overreaching and dominance by the more knowledgeable, powerful, or less emotional party. Some argue that the "a-legal" character of divorce mediation requires all the more careful court scrutiny before mediated agreements are approved and incorporated into a decree. Others argue against court review of mediated agreements. They reason that if the parties have utilized mediation to reach agreement, there is no need for the expense, delay, and imposition of a judge's values — all features of the judicial review process. Questions about the enforceability of agreements to mediate as well as the enforceability of mediated agreements cannot long be avoided.

Fairness. In considering whether mediated settlements will be fair and just, we must ask "compared to what"? We know that the great majority of divorce cases currently go by default. The default may be a result of ignorance, guilt, or a total sense of powerlessness. The default may also be a result of an agreement between the parties on distributional questions, eliminating the need for an appearance. The question persists in our present dispute resolution system of whether such agreements are the result of unequal bargaining power due to different levels of experience, patterns of dominance, the greater emotional need of one divorcing party to get out of the marriage, or a greater desire on the part of one of the parties to avoid the expense and uncertainty of litigation. The present "adversarial" approach does not require the adverse parties to be represented, nor does it impose a mediator or "audience" to point out these imbalances and assure that they are recognized by the parties, as mediation should attempt to do. Pro se divorce is increasingly popular and sanctioned by our present system in which there need be no professional intervention prior to court review. Mediation, at least, provides a knowledgeable third party to help the couple evaluate their relative positions so that they may make reasoned decisions with minimal judicial intrusion.

The most common pattern of legal representation in divorce is for one party to retain an attorney for advice and preparation of the documents. The other party will often negotiate directly with the moving party's attorney or retain an attorney to do so without filing an appearance. If a second attorney has not been retained, the unrepresented party will often consult with an attorney to determine whether the proposed settlement is "fair enough" not to contest and if all necessary items have been covered or discussed. The reviewing attorney serves as a check, informing the client of any other options to the suggested terms and whether the points of agreement fall within acceptable legal norms. The likelihood of a different court outcome than the proposed agreement is weighed against the financial, time, and emotional expenses of further negotiation or litigation.

A similar pattern of independent legal consultation could, and should, be utilized for review of mediated agreements. Current mediation practice, influenced by ethical restraints, is to urge or require that each divorcing party seek independent legal counsel to review the proposed agreement before it is signed. Though the criteria for independent attorney review of a proposed mediated agreement are not clear, the purpose of the review is no less clear than it is under the present "fair enough" practice. The initial mediated agreement is formed in a cooperative environment with the assistance of a neutral person who serves as a check against intimidation and overreaching. Independent legal review by an attorney for one spouse pursuant to a "fair enough" standard should assure at least as great a fairness safeguard as the common reality of our present adversary system. When both parties to the mediation obtain independent legal review, as they should be encouraged to do, there is a double-check of what is fair enough. In some complex cases, other professional review, such as that of a CPA, may be necessary for still another opinion and double-check. . . .

Protection of Children. When divorce involves minor children, some argue that the state has a responsibility for the children beyond encouraging the speedy, private settlement of disputes between parents. The state, however, under the well-developed doctrine of parens patriae has a responsibility for the welfare of children *only when parents cannot agree or cannot adequately provide for them.* Divorce mediation begins with the premise that parents love their children and are best able to decide how, within their resources, they will care for them. . . .

A mediated agreement is much more likely than a judicial decision to match the parents' capacity and desires with the child's needs. Whether the parents' decision is the result of reasoned analysis or is influenced by depression, guilt, spite, or selfishness, it is preferable to an imposed decision that is more likely to impede cooperation and stability for the child. In any event, a resolution negotiated by attorneys, reviewed by a court, or litigated before a court, is no more likely than a mediated settlement to disclose which outcomes are the result of depression, spite, guilt, or selfishness. . . .

The principal protection that the mediator can offer the child is to ensure that the parents consider all factors that can be developed between them relative to the child's needs and their abilities to meet those needs. The mediator should be prepared to ask probing and difficult questions and to help inform the parents of available alternatives. The mediator's ethical commitment, however, is to the process of parental self-determination and not to any given outcome. . . .

The Continuing Role of Courts and Attorneys. Increased use of divorce mediation does not remove the courts from the divorce process and would not entirely eliminate adversarial proceedings. We know that some cases cannot be settled or mediated. There must be a fair and credible forum with procedural safeguards and rules to assure the peaceful resolution of disputes for parties who are unable to recognize the benefits that may come from a less coercive process. The threat of court litigation, with all of the human and material expense that it requires, may be the very element that will help some parties cut through their egocentric near-sightedness to see that their self-interests, as well as the interest of the family, may be promoted through mediation rather than a court fight. . . .

Conclusion. Divorce mediation has been touted as a replacement for the adversary system and a way of making divorce less painful. Though it should be available as an alternative for those who choose to use it, it is not a panacea that will create love where there is hate, nor will it totally eliminate the role of the adversary system in divorce. It may, however, reduce acrimony and post-divorce litigation by promoting cooperation. It may also lessen the burden of the courts in deciding many cases that can be diverted to less hostile and less costly procedures. . . .

B. Employment Cases

One of the fastest growing areas of mediation practice is employment disputes. These range from contract claims by terminated executives to discrimination charges lodged by hourly employees. In the excerpt that follows, practicing mediators analyze the special issues likely to arise in such cases.

❖ **Carol A. Wittenberg, Susan T. Mackenzie, and Margaret L. Shaw, Employment Disputes**

In D. Golann, Mediating Legal Disputes 441-456 (1996)

The use of mediation to resolve employment disputes is on the rise. Increasingly, federal district courts are referring discrimination cases to mediation, and administrative agencies charged with enforcing anti-discrimination laws are also experimenting with mediation programs. Mediation is well-suited to resolving employment disputes for a number of reasons.

Emotionality. Employment disputes usually involve highly emotional issues. It is said that loss of one's job is the third most stressful life event, next only to the death of a loved one and divorce. Whether one's livelihood is at stake, as in a wrongful termination case, or the issue involves a professional relationship that has gone awry, as in a sexual harassment claim, the dispute occurs in a charged atmosphere. A mediator can help parties vent their anger and frustrations in a nonjudgmental setting that allows them to feel that their positions have been heard and to move on to a more productive, problem-solving viewpoint.

One of us, for example, had the experience of being asked by a plaintiff after several hours of mediation if a one-on-one meeting with the mediator was possible, and counsel agreed. After telling the mediator that she reminded her of a former boss who had been an important mentor, the plaintiff talked about how upset the case had made her. She also talked about how much the negotiations over dollars were leaving her feeling disassociated from the process, and from what she was personally looking to accomplish. The mediator was able to help the plaintiff identify her feelings, think through what she really wanted out of a resolution, and work within the process to accomplish that result. The case settled shortly after their caucus.

Confidentiality. The privacy and confidentiality that mediation affords may be especially important to employees and employers alike. For example, in many of the sexual harassment cases that we mediate a primary focus of the claimant is to have an unpleasant situation stop, stop quickly, and stop permanently. Individual respondents, unless they are looking for vindication, may also want to put the incident behind them and get on with their lives, while employers, for their part, are almost always interested in confidentiality. This is particularly true in discrimination cases, since publicity about claims can affect a company's reputation in the marketplace. Employers are also concerned that without confidentiality, settlements will create precedents or "benchmarks" for future plaintiffs, or encourage "me-too" complaints.

Creativity of Outcomes. Mediation's creativity is particularly important in employment disputes, where the impact of the controversy can have profound effects on the parties' lives. We find that in many of the litigated disputes we mediate, non-legal and non-monetary issues are as significant a barrier to resolution as the financial and legal aspects of the case. For example, in one age discrimination claim we mediated, the settlement called for the employee to retain his employment status without pay for a two-year period, so as to vest certain benefits afforded retirees. In a gender discrimination case, the terms involved keeping the employee on the payroll for a period of time with a new title to assist her in securing alternative employment. In a breach of contract case involving a senior executive, part of the settlement involved a guaranteed loan to invest in a new business.

Cost Savings. Practical considerations also make mediation of employment disputes an attractive alternative to litigation. The process is likely to be much less expensive than litigation, or even arbitration. One attorney who frequently represents plaintiffs in discrimination cases observed that, as of the mid-1990s, the litigation cost of a discrimination claim to individual claimants was roughly $25,000, as compared to $1,000 to $3,000 for mediation. A study in the early 1990s estimated the cost to defend a single discrimination claim at $81,000, a figure that is now almost certainly much higher.

Note also that the monetary cost of litigation does not take into account the indirect, personal, and emotional costs of a court proceeding to all parties. All workplaces have informal information channels; we often hear from individual mediation participants about the disruptive effects of the case on fellow employees. For instance, at one company with which we worked speculation was rampant about who would be let go or reassigned in the event the case resulted in the reinstatement of a discharged employee.

Speed. Mediation is also likely to be significantly faster than litigation. This is of particular importance in the employment context, given the dramatic increase in anti-discrimination claims. In our experience, mediation of a routine employment case involving an individual claimant generally can be concluded in one or sometimes two days. Although some parties are unable to reach complete closure in the mediation sessions, often additional follow-up telephone conferences with one or both parties will bring about a settlement. An evaluation of the EEOC's pilot mediation program, for instance, showed that mediation resolved charges of discrimination less expensively and more quickly than traditional methods, with closure in an average of 67 days as opposed to 294 days in the regular administrative process.

Questions. Are there disadvantages to mediation in the context of employment disputes? Of course there are, although we believe that some of the "dangers" are often overemphasized. Some employers are concerned that the availability of mediation will encourage frivolous complaints. Others are concerned that mediation simply adds a layer of time and expense when a case does not settle. Certain attorneys have also expressed a concern that an opposing party might merely be using mediation as a form of discovery. There are, of course, specific cases that are inappropriate for mediation, cases that upon analysis are without any apparent merit and call for the employer to take a firm stance.

Challenges for the Mediator

There are some distinctive characteristics of employment cases that can challenge a mediator and require special approaches.

Disparity in Resources. While parties in other kinds of cases may have unequal resources, in employment disputes a lack of parity can make it difficult even to get the parties to the table. Employment claimants are often out of work, or face an uncertain employment future. They may balk at the added expense of a mediator, particularly when the outcome is uncertain. While some employers will agree to pay the entire mediation bill as an inducement to a plaintiff to participate, others are concerned that without some financial investment a plaintiff will not participate in the process wholeheartedly. In these circumstances, we have found several approaches effective. If, for example, the employer is worried about the employee's investment in the process, the mediator can explore the nature of that concern and determine whether verbal representations by the claimant or claimant's lawyer might allay them. As an alternative, a mediator can suggest having the employer assume most of the cost, while requiring the employee to pay something toward it.

Timing. The timing of mediation can affect both the process and its outcome. Where it is attempted shortly after a claim has been raised, the claimant may need extra help in getting beyond feelings of anger or outrage, while an individual manager or subject of a claim may feel betrayed. If little or no discovery has occurred, the lack of information about the facts on the part of one or both parties can hamper productive negotiations. At the other extreme, when a case has already been in litigation for an extended period of time, positions can become hardened and the parties even more determined to stop at nothing short of what they perceive to be "justice."

For instance, in one case we handled, an age discrimination claim referred by a court, the plaintiff's attorney had done little investigation prior to the mediation and thus was unaware of circumstances that called into question the plaintiff's integrity during his final year of employment. Assisting the attorney to become more realistic about the chances for a recovery at trial became the challenge of this mediation. In another case that involved a sexual harassment claim, outside counsel for the employer, who had recommended mediation, was unaware of some of the conduct of the individual manager who was the subject of the allegations. That case required us to mediate between the employer and the manager, the individual manager and the claimant, and the claimant and the corporate entity as well.

Imbalances of Power. In certain employment disputes, such as those involving sexual harassment claims, a perceived or real imbalance in the power relationship between the parties may itself constitute an impediment to settlement. We have found that as a general proposition, particularly in dealing with an individual who feels at a power disadvantage in mediation, movement is better accomplished by pulling rather than by pushing. For example, in one case where the facts underlying the claim were perhaps unconscionable but not legally actionable, helping the claimant to recognize the benefits of moving forward with her life was more effective than trying to convince her that she had a weak case.

When an issue of power imbalance is articulated or apparent, it is helpful to take the time to consult with the parties before the "real" mediation begins in order to structure the process. We typically discuss, for example, whether the complainant or the attorney wants to make an opening statement. We have observed that complainants who prepare a statement for the initial joint session tend to feel a sense of control and dignity in the process that is not otherwise possible. At times, having a family member or close friend attend a session is helpful. We also attempt to establish in advance whether it will be necessary to keep the complainant and individual respondent apart at least initially. We routinely schedule premediation conference calls with all persons involved in the case to work through these kinds of issues.

Desire for Revenge. Complainants who feel they have been wronged will sometimes look for a way to make the employer or the individual charged with harassing or discriminatory behavior "pay." Such a focus on revenge can present a major obstacle to settlement. There is no simple way to deal with this in mediation. Sometimes, particularly in cases where the complaint has already prompted the employer to take preventive measures, explaining the full impact that the complaint has already had on workplace policies or on the careers of others can help the complainant change to a posture more conducive to resolution. Another approach may be to have the individual respondent contribute out of his or her own pocket to a financial settlement.

Negotiation by Numbers. In some employment mediations, one or both parties may become fixed on a settlement figure and refuse to budge. Finding a new framework for analysis that appears objectively fair can help parties stuck on numbers save face and ultimately agree on a different figure to settle the case.

Personal and Emotional Issues. At times both parties will fail to realize that a nonlegal problem is the root cause of an employment dispute. For example in one case we handled, a personality conflict between the head of accounting and his most senior employee had festered for years. The working relationship between the two had deteriorated to the point that they routinely hurled racial and sexual epithets at one another. At that point, management could see no alternative to dismissing one or both of them. With the mediator's assistance, each party was able to shift focus from placing blame on the other to recognizing their mutual interest in continuing to be employed, and mutually acceptable procedures for personal interaction in the office were identified and reduced to writing. During the mediation, the parties also came to recognize that a contributing, if not overriding, cause of the deterioration of their relationship was an outstanding loan from the department head to the bookkeeper. While the department head had treated the loan as forgiven years ago, in reality the bookkeeper's failure to repay it had continued to bother the department head. The resolution included a repayment schedule for the loan.

"Outside" Barriers to Resolution. In some employment cases, the real barrier to resolution may be an individual who is not a direct party to the dispute. For instance, in one case we mediated involving a disability claim by an airline manager, it became clear that his spouse, who was also present, was so angered by what she perceived as unconscionable treatment that she urged rejection of all settlement offers as insulting. The mediator dealt with this situation by recognizing the spouse's feelings and helping her understand that her anger was fueled at least in part by resentment over the amount of time her spouse had spent on his job rather than with his family. The spouse was also given an opportunity to air her position directly to the corporate representatives. Once she had done this, she was able to reorient her focus from the past to the future, and the elements of a mutually acceptable package fell into place.

Questions

8. What style would you look for in an employment mediator?
9. Would a caucus or no-caucus model be more likely to be effective in such cases?
10. You may remember that the U.S. Postal Service has used a form of transformative mediation in employee disputes. Why do you think that two styles as different as conventional commercial and transformative mediation have each enjoyed success in this area?
11. The U.S. Equal Employment Opportunity Commission, in an effort to address lengthy delays in processing complaints, has adopted a policy of active and early promotion of mediation of all employment claims filed with the Commission. Do you see any dangers in the EEOC policy? Any advantages for parties?

C. Environmental and Public Controversies

❖ **Gail Bingham, The Environment in the Balance:**
   Mediators Are Making a Difference

   2 AC Resol. 21 (Summer 2002)

[T]he number and magnitude of environmental disputes is rising, and finding solutions only gets more difficult...there are many reasons why environmental and other public policy disputes are difficult to resolve....For a mediation process to be successful, it must be designed with these challenges in mind.

Multiple Forums/Changing Incentives. Frequently, the same or related [environmental] issues may be the subjects of simultaneous action at different levels of government and in one or more administrative, legislative, or judicial forums. Disputing parties may have different advantages in different forums, creating conflicting views about the best process to use. A mediated negotiation is just one more choice among competing forums.

Multiple Parties/Issues. Because environmental disputes typically affect large numbers of interested parties and involve a multiplicity of issues, organizing the negotiation process may prove to be extremely difficult. Sometimes coalitions can be formed, allowing several parties to be represented by one negotiator. At other times, one must design ways to have conversation in large groups....

Institutional Dynamics. Environmental and resource management conflicts are more often played out between organizations or groups than between individuals. Therefore, the individuals at the table must get proposals ratified by others who are not participating directly....

Complex Scientific and Technical Issues. [P]arties to environmental disputes are often confronted with large volumes of information that require broad-based expertise and may be subject to honest differences of opinion....

Inequality of Resources. Mediation processes are resource intensive in the sense that the parties take the time to negotiate with one another up front, and need funds for travel expenses, information collection, evaluation, and expert advice. While government agencies and private corporations are generally well funded and represented by paid staff, other parties may lack the necessary financial and technical resources....

Public/Political Dimension. Environmental disputes generally involve public issues, addressed in public forums, with laws, governmental institutions, and the media all playing a significant role. Any mediation process must therefore respond with sensitivity to the press and open meeting laws and must attempt to arrive at outcomes that can withstand public scrutiny....

Questions

12. What qualities would you look for in selecting a mediator for an environmental dispute, as compared with an employment case?
13. Would the basic mediative strategy described in Chapter 5 have to be modified to deal with an environmental controversy? In what respects?

One of the unique aspects of public controversies is that it is often difficult to identify all of the "parties" to the dispute. Public disputes may simmer in the community at large, and first become visible through discussions in community centers, city council meetings, and the news media rather than in formal court proceedings. In such situations, in addition to the challenges outlined by Gail Bingham, a mediator must determine who the key disputants are and develop a consensual framework in which they can communicate and bargain effectively. This task is known as "convening," and the overall resolution process as "consensus-building." The word "consensus" reflects that the goal in these processes is not necessarily to achieve agreement among all the participants, but rather to develop a solution agreed to by a large enough majority to give confidence that it will be successfully implemented.

❖ Chris Carlson, Convening
In The Consensus Building Handbook 169-173 (2000)

When someone *convenes* a meeting, he or she typically finds appropriate meeting space, invites people to attend, and perhaps drafts an agenda. In a consensus building process, however, which may involve multiple meetings over the course of weeks, months, or years, convening is a more complex task. In this context, convening typically involves

- assessing a situation to determine whether or not a consensus-based approach is feasible
- identifying and inviting participants to ensure that all key interests (i.e., stakeholders) are represented;
- locating the necessary resources to help convene, conduct, and support the process; and
- planning and organizing the process with participants or working with a facilitator or mediator to do so.

It may be helpful to think of convening as Phase 1 in a consensus building process, which is followed by Phase 2, the actual negotiating or consensus building phase. . . .

The Importance of Convening: Two Examples

How the convening steps are carried out, and who carries them out, can have an impact on whether or not a consensus process will be successful. The parties who serve as convenors, whether they are government agencies, private corporations, nonprofit organizations, or individuals, need to be viewed as credible and fair-minded, especially in those cases in which issues are contentious or parties are distrustful of each other. At the community level, consensus processes are often sponsored and convened by a local leader, an organization, or a steering committee made up of representatives of different groups. At the state and federal levels, government agencies or officials often serve as sponsors, and sometimes as convenors. Let us look at two examples illustrating the importance of effective convening — (one convened by an individual, the other by a federal agency.

A Community Collaboration Gets Off on the Right Foot. In the first example, a diverse conflict over logging practices and their impact on endangered species was under way in a rural community in southern Oregon. By the early 1990s, there had been numerous skirmishes between environmental interests and timber industry supporters over logging in the Applegate Valley. In 1992, the listing of the northern spotted owl on the federal endangered species list led to an injunction prohibiting logging on federal lands. There were bitter and sometimes violent protests. Yet, in the midst of the crisis, some representatives of industry and environmental groups were able to negotiate land exchanges and timber sales. These agreements seemed to signal the possibility that a consensus building approach might be useful for developing a longer-range plan for the watershed.

A local environmentalist who had been one of the architects of the earlier cooperative effort served as the sponsor and convenor. He put together a proposal to use a consensus building approach to develop a comprehensive ecosystem management plan. He distributed his proposal to all the involved and affected stakeholders. He then shuttled back and forth among them, discussing and revising the proposal, and got their agreement to start meeting. The participants included most of the major interests: government agency staff, environmentalists, timber industry representatives, farmers and ranchers, and a variety of other local residents.

The convenor decided that rather than begin with a formal meeting, complete with flip charts and facilitators, he would host a potluck at his home. The first meeting was spent reaching agreement about how the process would be organized and developing ground rules. The partnership rapidly took shape, and after several months of meetings, the group arrived at an agreement on basic objectives.

After a promising beginning, the Applegate Partnership got swept up in the national politics surrounding the spotted owl issue in Oregon. All the outside attention and publicity caused the partnership to founder, but it managed to survive because participants continued to see a need for building consensus on plans and actions to serve the community's interests. The partnership has been able to develop consensus on projects to restore watersheds, improve agricultural irrigation practices, and initiate economic development projects in the community. By almost any assessment, this convening led to successful outcomes.

A Federal Agency Convenes a Similar Process That Fails. Our second example came about as a result of the Applegate experience. Word spread quickly about the success of the Applegate Partnership. Federal officials caught wind of Applegate's success, and Interior Secretary Bruce Babbitt dropped in on one of the partnership meetings. What he saw fit nicely into the administration's plans for resolving the spotted owl issue: Getting communities involved in working out how federal policies could be implemented locally. The federal government decided that there were 10 communities in which it wanted to stimulate similar partnership efforts.

However, when the federal agency tried to convene local groups and get them to form partnerships, it failed. In each case, stakeholders attended one or two meetings, but were not willing to commit to a longer-term, consensus building process. One probable reason for the failure was that the agency's attempts were made unilaterally, without consulting local stakeholders about what should be discussed and what it would take to make the discussions "safe" for participants, among other things. When the federal government organized meetings, stakeholders came, but they participated only grudgingly. They felt compelled to be there to protect their interests.

When asked, the participants revealed a variety of concerns about how the process had been planned and convened by the federal government. They were concerned, for example, about the federal government's motives, the balance of power at the table, and the availability of resources to enable all groups to participate on an equal footing. Because these questions were not addressed during the convening stage, the groups were ultimately unable and unwilling to form partnerships to work toward consensus on watershed management....

What made the difference in these two cases? The difference was not in *who* carried out the convening role. Federal agencies can convene processes just as successfully as individual community members. The difference in this case lay in how the convening role was handled....

D. Intellectual Property Disputes

Technology Mediation Services, High Tech and Intellectual Property Disputes

http://www.technologymediation.com/hightech (2004)

About Mediating Intellectual Property Disputes. Mediation is not just for simple contractual disputes. Indeed, complex intellectual property matters may be resolved best through mediation. An intellectual property dispute may be especially ripe for mediation if any of the following factors exist.

One Or Both Parties May Have an Interest in Cost Control. Most intellectual property matters are expensive to litigate. It is not unusual for a patent infringement dispute to cost each side well over $1 million through trial, and such cases are often appealed, adding more to the cost. Moreover, they often are settled via business agreements. Much of the cost of extensive discovery, trial preparation, voluminous exhibits, expert witness testimony, and diverted executive time can be spared by using mediation at an early stage to craft an appropriate settlement.

A Business Resolution May Solve the Legal Dispute. A mediator can help the parties craft a variety of business arrangements, such as licensing (or cross-licensing) agreements, joint ventures, distributor agreements, usage phase-out agreements, etc., which may lay the groundwork for future business. A mediated agreement may extend well beyond the subject matter of the pending lawsuit and accommodate larger business interests.

The Decision Maker May Misunderstand the Law or Technology. If the judge, jury or arbitrator may have trouble understanding intellectual property law issues such as prior art or doctrine of equivalents, or the underlying technology, it may be best to avoid the possibility of being handed a "poor" decision. The parties can keep control of the outcome by mediating, rather than relinquishing the decision to a third party.

The Defendant May Feel Disadvantaged in the Forum Chosen by the Plaintiff. In complex intellectual property matters, a defendant may need lots of time (and money) to prepare its defense and cross-claims alleging invalidity of the patent, trademark, or copyright. If time is short, such as in investigations before the U.S. International Trade Commission, or in federal courts such as the "rocket docket" of the Eastern District of Virginia, it may be better to settle a dispute than to defend under such constraints. Similarly, a defendant may prefer not to defend in a jury trial in the plaintiff's "home" court, or in a jurisdiction with precedent favorable to the plaintiff. Mediation offers a sensible way to end the dispute before it's too late.

The Useful Life of the Subject Matter May Be Depleted Before the Litigation Is Over. Any "hot" products or technologies are covered by patents, trademarks or copyrights, and by virtue of their appeal become subject to infringement. But how good is a favorable judicial decision if the patented technology already has been superceded by another patent, or if last season's most popular toy now sits on the shelf, or if some other copyrighted software game now heads the "top 10" sales list? Mediation can resolve the dispute quickly, while the product is still commercially viable.

One or Both Parties Are Concerned About Disclosure of Confidential Information. Many intellectual property disputes, particularly alleged trade secret misappropriation, involve confidential business and technical information. Mediation avoids disclosure of such sensitive information, to the public and to your adversary. Everything said in mediation is protected as confidential settlement discussions, and cannot be introduced in litigation or disclosed in public. Additionally, a party can disclose certain information in confidence to the mediator, who will not transmit it to the opponent.

Why Use a Technology Mediator Instead of a General Mediator? Disputes that involve specialized industries or complex technology benefit from having a mediator that understands the context in which the dispute arose, and/or the technology involved. A mediator knowledgeable about high tech businesses and their problems can delve right into the issues, without expending a lot of time learning about them. In patent, trademark or copyright disputes, it is useful to use a mediator experienced in intellectual property law, who will be familiar with the legal and factual issues related to, e.g., prior art, doctrine of equivalents, and likelihood of confusion. The mediator will know who needs to be included in the mediated settlement. The mediator will have a real-world context for the parties' positions, and won't be easily persuaded by a party's legal bluster or alleged inability to comply with a standard request. Moreover, prior experience will enable the mediator to make suggestions to facilitate resolution, or to offer a realistic evaluation of the parties' chances of success outside of mediation.

Questions

14. Given the advantages of mediation in this area, why do you think that every high-technology dispute that cannot be settled through direct negotiation is not mediated?
15. If you were counsel to a company that had a claim against a competitor for infringement of a biotech patent and wished to try mediation, but the only available mediators had either strong process skills or extensive technical knowledge, but not both, which type of mediator would you choose? Is there a way to obtain the presence of both qualities?

E. Criminal Matters

One of the most controversial uses of mediation is in criminal cases. The vast majority of criminal charges, ranging from small misdemeanors to capital cases, are plea bargained — that is, negotiated by prosecutors and defense counsel — rather than tried. Mediation has not, however, been used with any frequency to assist the process of plea bargaining. At the same time, the use of mediation is expanding in other areas of the criminal justice system, raising both exciting possibilities and troubling issues of justice.

Questions

16. As prosecutors and defense counsel negotiate plea bargains in criminal cases, what obstacles might they encounter? Could mediation be useful in overcoming these obstacles?
17. Why do you think lawyers in the criminal justice system so rarely use mediation to help work out plea bargains?

1. Potential Charges

❖ **Christopher Cooper, Police Mediators: Rethinking the Role of Law Enforcement in the New Millennium**

7 Disp. Resol. Mag. 17 (Fall 2000)

In the 21st century, it is time for new and fresh police strategies. One such strategy is mediation of interpersonal disputes by patrol police officers.... The patrol police officer is often the first person to respond to many of American society's interpersonal squabbles, including disputes between neighbors, siblings, and customers and merchants. Many of these disputes are marked by flared tempers or chaos.... Mediation by a patrol officer need not be carried out in an office. It can be conducted on a basketball court or in a parking lot, for example. It can be done standing up or sitting down....

For calls-for-service involving an interpersonal dispute in which there are no grounds to arrest or to cite a party for a law violation, mediation by a police officer often is a sensible approach.... When police officers apply this approach to conflict, citizens make fewer repeat calls-for-service, including 911 calls.... Whereas poor conflict resolution skills and unsystematic approaches by an officer can escalate disputes, using a systematic dispute resolution process such as mediation is less likely to have such a negative effect....

Poor relations, particularly between people of color and police, are at epidemic levels throughout the United States. The relationship is strained in part by police who act as arbitrators in situations in which citizens have a legitimate expectation that they should be empowered to help themselves. ...It makes good sense to provide police officers with the professional skills they need to empower others.... Mediation by patrol officers champions community policing objectives by providing ... self-empowerment to citizens, who should expect contemporary law enforcement officers to function as a police service, rather than a police force.

Question

18. Does the use of informal mediative techniques by police officers pose any dangers?

2. Victim-Offender Cases

Although mediation is rarely applied to plea bargaining, it does appear to be taking root at a different phase of the process — post-sentencing encounters between victims and offenders. Here the issue is not the defendant's guilt, but rather how she and the victim will deal with what has happened. As we have seen, mediation can be used to help people change their perspectives and even to restore ruptured relationships. In the criminal context, however, such efforts are much more controversial. As you read the following excerpt, ask yourself these questions.

Questions

19. For what purpose is mediation being used here?
20. If you were designing a victim-offender program, would you have all criminal cases be eligible for the program? Would you exclude some categories of cases? Which ones?

❖ **Marty Price, Personalizing Crime: Mediation Produces Restorative Justice for Victims and Offenders**

7 Disp. Resol. Mag. 8-11 (Fall 2000)

Our traditional criminal justice system is a system of retributive justice — a system of institutionalized vengeance. The system is based on the belief that justice is accomplished by assigning blame and administering pain. If you do the crime, you do the time, then you've paid your debt to society and justice has been done. But justice for whom? . . .

Because our society defines justice in terms of guilt and punishment, crime victims often seek the most severe possible punishment for their offenders. Victims believe this will bring them justice, but it often leaves them feeling empty and unsatisfied. Retribution cannot restore their losses, answer their questions, relieve their fears, help them make sense of their tragedy or heal their wounds. And punishment cannot mend the torn fabric of the community that has been violated. . . .

Focus on Individuals, Healing. Restorative justice has emerged as a social movement for justice reform. Virtually every state is implementing restorative justice at state, regional and/or local levels. . . . Instead of viewing crime as a violation of law, restorative justice emphasizes one fundamental fact: crime damages people, communities, and relationships.

Retributive justice asks three questions: who did it, what laws were broken and what should be done to punish or treat the offender? Contrast a restorative justice inquiry, in which three very different questions receive primary emphasis. First, what is the nature of the harm resulting from the crime? Second, what needs to be done to "make it right" or repair the harm? Third, who is responsible for the repair? . . .

As the most common application of restorative justice principles, VOM [victim-offender mediation] programs warrant examination in detail. These programs bring offenders face to face with the victims of their crimes with the assistance of a trained mediator, usually a community volunteer. Victim participation is voluntary in most programs.

In mediation, crime is personalized as offenders learn the human consequences of their actions, and victims have the opportunity to speak their minds and their feelings to the one who most ought to hear them, contributing to the victim's healing. Victims get answers to haunting questions that only the offender can answer. The most commonly asked questions are "Why did you do this to me? Was this my fault? Could I have prevented this? Were you stalking or watching me?" Victims commonly report a new peace of mind, even when the answers to their questions were worse than they had feared.

Offenders take meaningful responsibility for their actions by mediating a restitution agreement with the victim to restore the victim's losses in whatever [way is] possible. Restitution may be monetary or symbolic; it may consist of work for the victim, community service, or other actions that contribute to a sense of justice between the victim and offender.

Fulfilling Restitution. . . . There are now more than 300 programs in the United States and Canada and more than 700 in England, Germany, Scandinavia,

Eastern Europe, Australia, and New Zealand. Remarkably consistent statistics from a cross-section of the North American programs show that about two-thirds of the cases referred resulted in a face-to-face mediation. More than 95 percent of the cases mediated resulted in a written restitution agreement. More than 90 percent of those restitution agreements are completed within one year. In contrast, the rate of payment of court-ordered restitution is typically only from 20 to 30 percent. Recent research has shown that juvenile offenders who participate in VOM subsequently commit fewer and less serious offenses than their counterparts in the traditional juvenile justice system. . . .

Careful Preparation Required. Mediation is not appropriate for every crime, every victim, or every offender, Individual, preliminary meetings between mediator and victim, mediator and offender permit careful screening and assessment according to established criteria. . . . At their best, mediation sessions focus upon dialogue rather than the restitution agreement (or settlement), facilitating empathy and understanding between victim and offender. Ground rules help assure safety and respect. Victims typically speak first, explaining the impact of the crime and asking questions of the offender. Offenders acknowledge and describe their participation in the offense, usually offering an explanation and/or apology. The victim's losses are discussed. Surprisingly, a dialogue-focused (rather than settlement-driven) approach produces the highest rates of agreement and compliance.

Agreements that the victim and offender make together reflect justice that is meaningful to them, not limited by narrow legal definitions. [T]he overwhelming majority of participants — both victims and offenders — have reported in post-mediation interviews and questionnaires that they obtained a just and satisfying result. Victims who feared re-victimization by the offender before the mediation typically report that this fear is now gone.

Forgiveness is not a focus of VOM, but the process provides an open space in which participants may address issues of forgiveness if they wish. Forgiveness is a process, not a goal, and it must occur according to the victim's own timing, if at all. For some victims, forgiveness may never be appropriate. Restorative justice requires an offender who is willing to admit responsibility and remorse to the victim. . . .

Different Concept of Neutrality. Neutrality, as understood in the mediation of civil disputes, requires that the mediator not take sides with either party. Judgments of right and wrong are not within the mediator's role. The mediation of most crime situations, however, presents a unique set of circumstances for a mediator and the concept of neutrality must be different. In the majority of criminal cases, the parties come to VOM as a wronged person and a wrongdoer, with a power imbalance that is appropriate to this relationship. The mediator balances power only to ensure full and meaningful participation by all parties. . . . The mediator is neutral toward the individuals, respecting both as valuable human beings and favoring neither, but the mediator is not neutral regarding the wrong. . . .

Most victim-offender programs limit their service to juvenile offenses, crimes against property, and minor assaults, but a growing number of experienced programs have found that a face-to-face encounter can be invaluable even in heinous crimes. A number of programs have now mediated violent assaults, including rapes, and mediations have taken place between murderers and the families of their victims. Mediation has been helpful in repairing the lives of surviving family members and the offender in drunk-driving fatalities. In severe crime mediations, case development may take a year or more before the mediation can take place.... In cases of severely violent crime, VOM has not been a substitute for a prison sentence, and prison terms have seldom been reduced following mediation....

What Can We Learn? What can attorneys and other dispute resolution professionals learn from the philosophy and successes of restorative justice? Our system, which settles most cases without trial, does so with adversarial assumptions as its foundation. Each attorney is expected to maximize her client's win at the expense of the other attorney's client's loss. In the majority of cases, the clients of both attorneys (and often the attorneys, as well) feel like losers in the settlement....

Our system of money damages and financial settlements for losses and injuries has a faulty assumption at its core. We give lip service to the truth that "no amount of money can right this wrong," then we conclude that the only available measure of amends is the dollar! In contrast, a basic principle of restorative justice is that a wrong creates a singular kind of relationship — an obligation to personally right that wrong.... The most important lesson learned from restorative justice practice may be the realization that the key to justice is found not in laws but in the recognition and honoring of human relationships.

Question

21. Criminal prosecutions serve important public functions. Which of these functions may not be fulfilled when cases go into a VOM program?

F. Deal Mediation

You now understand, as many practicing lawyers do, the potentially significant role that a mediator can play in resolving disputes, enhancing communication, and even repairing relationships. It should therefore come as no surprise that some have theorized about — and in some cases implemented — efforts to apply the same principles at points "upstream" from active disputes. The following reading asks whether mediators could be as helpful in creating deals as they are in resolving disagreements over them.

❖ **Scott R. Peppet, Contract Formation in Imperfect Markets: Should We Use Mediators in Deals?**

38 Ohio St. J. on Disp. Resol. 283 (2004)

[M]any of the same barriers to negotiation that plague litigation settlement exist in commercial transactions, particularly during the closing stage of a deal when lawyers attempt to negotiate terms and conditions. [A] transactional mediator could help lawyers and clients to overcome such barriers. By a "transactional mediator," the author means an impartial person or entity that intervenes in a transactional negotiation pre-closing to facilitate the creation of a durable and efficient contract.

In one experiment, for example, small teams of experienced executives were given detailed information about two simulated companies. They were then assigned to represent one company or the other and asked to evaluate the companies and negotiate a merger. Although agreement was possible, only nine of the twenty-one pairings reached agreement. In addition, the executives disagreed wildly about the relevant valuations — selling prices ranged from $3.3 million to $16.5 million. This suggests that occasionally transacting parties fail to "close the deal" because of strategic posturing. [Moreover], as in litigation, transacting parties may fail to find [the most efficient] agreements.... Interest-Interestingly, the researcher in this corporate acquisitions experiment re-ran the simulation offering each negotiating pair the service of a trained mediator, but not requiring that they use the mediator. Those executives that made use of the mediator reached more efficient contracts than those that did not.... [M]edia-M]ediators should [also] theoretically be able to help merging companies resolve disagreements over "social issues," such as how to name the post-merger corporation, how to resolve status and position questions (e.g., who will be CEO), and where to locate the new company's headquarters.

Howard Raiffa also suggests that a mediator might serve as a "contract embellisher" in transactions. [A]t the start of bargaining a mediator could privately interview each party about its needs, priorities, and perceptions. The mediator would lock away that information and the parties would be left alone to negotiate a deal. At the conclusion of their negotiation, but prior to closing the deal, the intervenor would return [and] try to use his private information about the parties' interests to craft a superior deal. He would then show his substitute agreement to each party privately. If both sides agreed that the mediator's suggestion was superior to their own contract, the substitution would be made. There would be no haggling about the terms of the mediator's proposal — it would be a take-it-or-leave-it situation.

[U]nder what market conditions [will] the argument that "mediators add value..." hold? In a bilateral monopoly, there is only one seller and only one buyer. In other words, there is no market to establish a market price... [T]he outcome of bilateral monopoly bargaining depends on the negotiators' ability to wield bargaining power and invoke procedural and substantive norms of bargaining to their advantage. [A] competitive market, by contrast,...will discipline negotiators to bargain reasonably....

[However,] a complex deal often takes on bilateral monopoly characteristics at certain stages of the deal's life cycle. [P]roblems may arise at any of four stages of a transaction — matching, pricing, closing, and renegotiation — but they are likely to increase in intensity as a transaction progresses towards closing and renegotiation.

In complex transactions, lawyers, accountants, bankers, and other agents are generally brought in to assist in the closing stage. Lawyers in particular are needed to draft legal language for an acquisition agreement or other contract....A lawyer-mediator might prevent the parties' lawyers from blowing up the deal unnecessarily, and, perhaps more importantly, from reaching an inefficient set of contract terms. Although the bargaining about a single contract term may be largely distributive, contracting attorneys can generally create value by trading between terms....

Empirical analysis of contracts shows that parties often do not trade risk in complex — yet value-creating — ways. Instead, in many domains contracts are simpler than one might expect. Various explanations have been offered for this simplicity. . . . [One possible] explanation is that the threat of strategic behavior prevents parties from complex contracting. To create a tailored term requires disclosing information about one's interests and preferences. This again permits exploitation. In the absence of trust, parties may resort to a standard term to minimize this risk.

A mediator might help the parties to overcome these strategic difficulties, thereby permitting more complex contracting. Again, a mediator can solicit and compare information from each side, potentially finding value-creating trades. The mediator might test the viability of various packages . . . , asking each side in confidence which of several sets of terms the party would accept, but not revealing the origin of the various packages. . . .

[Besides helping the parties to overcome strategic barriers to transactions, mediators can also help them to overcome psychological barriers.] A neutral is in an ideal position to identify self-serving assessments by one or both parties. At a substantive level, if the neutral has sufficient expertise she can check each side's assumptions about "what's fair" and keep the parties from locking in to diverging stories about how a transaction should be priced or closed. Moreover, the mediator may be able to offer a neutral assessment or fair proposal that the parties will adopt. . . . At a procedural or process level, a neutral can also help the parties avoid spinning very biased interpretations of how their bargaining is unfolding.

Negotiating parties must constantly assess information received from the other side. [A] neutral can help parties to overcome reactive devaluation in transactional bargaining by either adding noise to the parties' communication or proposing solutions of her own. Adding noise may be as simple as raising Party A's proposed solution privately with Party B without telling B that the idea came from Party A. If B assumes that the idea originated with the neutral, B may be more willing to consider it on the merits.

A neutral may be less susceptible to the endowment effect than a partisan agent, and therefore able to help parties to overcome it. For example, a neutral may be able to provide both sides with market information against which they can test their (biased) evaluations. . . . A lawyer-neutral might be familiar with the legal norms in a given context and be able to point the parties towards compromise legal language. Rather than start with a standard form or with a first draft, which would typically become the original endowment against which the parties compared, the neutral could manage the negotiation process so that the parties instead would work collaboratively to build a contract draft from framework through to completion.

In addition to managing information exchange and helping parties to overcome these cognitive and social psychological biases, a neutral can help parties to manage emotional and relational difficulties in their negotiations. This may facilitate trust and permit more efficient outcomes.

. . . To some extent, agents such as investment bankers and lawyers already serve to mediate emotional conflicts during mergers, acquisitions, and other transactions. A neutral sometimes has an advantage over an agent in this regard, however. An agent may naturally take his client's perspective. . . . In strategic situations it is easy to assume that when the other bargainer "starts high" or "holds out," they do so because they intend to harm you or to treat you unfairly. Bargainers are less likely to attribute such actions to the exigencies of circumstance. By screening some overly opportunistic offers and at times sending fuzzy rather than clear information between the parties, a mediator can blunt such emotions and thereby keep the negotiations on track. Over time, avoiding emotional disagreements may help the parties to establish trust. This not only leads to more amiable negotiations, but also has serious substantive benefits. If the parties trust each other they may be better positioned to find value-creating solutions to their substantive differences. They may be able to rely more on informal agreements rather than contractual obligations and may be more flexible in the face of unexpected bumps in the road. Perhaps most importantly, they may avoid the destructive cycle of misattributions that can lead parties to "blow up" a deal or reach [an inefficient] agreement.

Question

22. Why do you suppose deal mediation is not more popular?

G. International Mediation

Until now we have discussed mediation almost entirely as an American phenomenon. In fact, however, people across the world have turned to third parties to assist them in resolving disputes. International mediation is best known in the context of disputes involving nation-states. Theodore Roosevelt, for example, won the Nobel Peace Prize for his work as mediator of peace talks between Russia and Japan, and Jimmy Carter is remembered for facilitating the Camp David accords between Egypt and Israel. Mediation has also produced settlements between warring factions in Northern Ireland, Bosnia, and other regions.

Mediation is not nearly as well established in private international disputes. But the growth of legal mediation in the United States and the rapid rise of world trade raise questions: Do other countries use mediation in their own legal systems — for example, do the British use mediation to resolve domestic lawsuits in their courts? How often is mediation applied in disputes between citizens of different nations? Are there significant differences between mediation as practiced in international disputes and the processes we have described in the preceding chapters?

1. Foreign Legal Systems

The use of mediation in legal disputes varies greatly from country to country. As a result, no single statement about its prevalence is possible. In countries with common-law legal systems, particularly Canada, Great Britain, and Australia, mediation has become quite popular. England, for instance, now requires that many civil cases go through mediation before proceeding to trial.

In the civil-law countries of continental Europe, there is growing interest in mediation, but to date it has not yet been applied broadly except in a few specialized areas such as family law. The same is true of most of the rest of the world. Some suggest that because civil-law systems do not allow extensive motion practice or discovery, parties are not as motivated by the need to avoid legal expense as in the U.S. legal system. Overcrowded court dockets appear to be the primary impetus for experimentation with mediation in civil-law countries. In Italy, for example, the fact that a typical case requires approximately ten years to proceed from filing to final judgment has stimulated business interest in mediation (DePalo and Hurley 2005). The process is also being explored as a method to reduce delay in Russia and some eastern European countries.

2. International Legal Disputes

Mediation can also be used to resolve disputes between citizens of different countries. Parties to international contracts are understandably reluctant to litigate in a foreign court system, and typically specify that disputes will be resolved by arbitration. Although international business contracts rarely refer explicitly to mediation, international arbitrators have long followed the custom of seeking to "conciliate" cases. The following readings explore the different forms that these processes can take in an international business deal, and what they mean when implemented by neutrals of different cultures.

❖ Jeswald Salacuse, Mediation in International Business
In J. Bercovitch, Studies in International Mediation 213-224 (2002)

...The International Deal: A Continuing Negotiation

All international transactions are the product of negotiation — the result of *deal-making* — among the parties. Although lawyers like to think that negotiations end when the participants agree on all the details and sign the contract, this view hardly ever reflects reality. In truth, an international deal is a *continuing negotiation* between the parties to the transaction as they seek to adjust their relationship to the rapidly changing international environment...in which they must work.... In the life of any international deal, one may therefore identify three distinct stages when conflict may arise and the parties rely on negotiation and conflict resolution to achieve their goals: *deal-making, deal-managing*, and *deal-mending*. Within the context of each of these three kinds of negotiation, one should ask to what extent third parties, whether called mediators or something else, may assist the parties to make, manage, and mend productive international business relationships....

Deal-Making Mediation

The usual model of an international business negotiation is that of representatives of two companies from different countries sitting across a table in face-to-face discussions to shape the terms of a commercial contract. While many transactions take place in that manner, many others require the services of one or more third parties to facilitate the deal-making process. These individuals are not usually referred to as "mediators." They instead carry a variety of other labels: consultant, adviser, agent, broker, investment banker, among others....

Although it could be argued that consultants and advisors should not be considered mediators since they are not independent of the parties, a close examination of their roles...reveals that they exercise a mediator's functions...[I]n most cases, one of the principal assets of deal-making mediators is the fact that they are known and accepted by the other side in the deal.

Deal-Making Mediation in Hollywood. The acquisition in 1991 by Matsushita Electric Industrial Company of Japan, one of the world's largest electronics manufacturers, of MCA, one of the United States' biggest entertainment companies, for over $6 billion illustrates the use of mediators in the deal-making process. Matsushita had determined that its future growth was dependent upon obtaining a source of films, television programs, and music — what it termed "software" — to complement its consumer electronic "hardware" products. Matsushita knew that it could find such a source of software within the U.S. entertainment industry, but it also recognized that it was virtually ignorant of that industry and its practices. For Matsushita executives, embarking on their Hollywood expedition may have felt almost interplanetary....They therefore engaged Michael Ovitz, the founder and head of Creative Artists Agency, one of the most powerful talent agencies in Hollywood, to guide them on their journey.

After forming a team to assist in the task, Ovitz...first extensively briefed the Japanese over several months, sometimes in secret meetings in Hawaii, on the nature of the U.S. entertainment industry, and he then proceeded to propose three possible candidates for acquisition, one of which was MCA. Ultimately, Matsushita chose MCA, but it was Ovitz, not Matsushita executives, who initiated conversations with the MCA leadership, men whom Ovitz knew well. Indeed, Ovitz assumed the task of actually conducting the negotiations for Matsushita. At one point in the discussions, he moved constantly between the Japanese team of executives in one suite of offices in New York City and the MCA team in another building, a process which one observer described as "shuttle diplomacy."...Although Matsushita may have considered Ovitz to be their agent in the talks, Ovitz seems to have considered himself to be both a representative of Matsushita and a mediator between the two sides.

Because of the vast cultural and temperamental differences between the Japanese and American companies, Ovitz's strategy was to limit the actual interactions of the two parties to a bare minimum....He was not only concerned by the vast differences in culture between the two companies but also by the greatly differing personalities in their top managements. The Japanese executives, reserved and somewhat self-effacing, placed a high value on the appearance if not the reality of modesty, while MCA's president was an extremely assertive and volatile personality. Like any mediator, Ovitz's own interests may also have influenced his choice of strategy. His status in the entertainment industry would only be heightened by making a giant new entrant into Hollywood dependent on him and by the public image that he had been the key to arranging one of the biggest deals in the industry's history....

... Eventually the talks stalled over the issue of price, and meetings between the two sides ceased. At this point, a second deal-making mediator entered the scene to make a crucial contribution. At the start of the negotiation, Matsushita and Sony together had engaged Robert Strauss, a politically powerful Washington lawyer who had been at various times U.S. Ambassador to the Soviet Union and U.S. Trade Representative, as "counselor to the transaction." Strauss, a member of the MCA board of directors and a close friend of its chairman, was also friendly with the Matsushita leadership and did legal and lobbying work in Washington for the Japanese company.... Strauss' close relationship to the two sides allowed him to act as a trusted conduit of communication who facilitated a meeting between the top MCA and Matsushita executives...[H]e apparently gained an understanding of the pricing parameters acceptable to each side and then communicated them to the other party.... In the end, as a result of that meeting, the two sides reached an agreement by which Matsushita acquired MCA.

[A]lthough Matsushita did succeed in purchasing MCA, the acquisition proved to be troubling and ultimately a disastrous financial loss for the Japanese company. One may ask whether Ovitz' strategy of keeping the two sides apart during negotiations so that they did not come to know one another contributed to this unfortunate result. It prevented the two sides from truly understanding the vast gulf which separated them and therefore from realizing the enormity and perhaps impossibility of the task of merging two such different organizations into a single coordinated and profitable enterprise.

Other Deal-Making Mediators. An opposite mediating approach from that employed by Ovitz is the use of consultants to begin building a relationship between the parties *before* they have signed a contract and indeed before they have actually begun negotiations. When some companies contemplate long-term relationships...they may hire a consultant to develop and guide a program of relationship building, which might include joint workshops, get-acquainted sessions, and retreats, all of which take place before the parties actually sit down to negotiate the terms of their contract....

... Sometimes persons involved in the negotiation because of their technical expertise or specialized knowledge may assume a mediating function and thus help the parties reach agreement. For example...local lawyers or accountants engaged by a foreign party to advise on law or accounting practices in connection with an international negotiation may assume a mediating role in the deal-making process by serving as a conduit between the parties, by suggesting approaches that meet the other side's cultural practices [or] by explaining why one party is behaving in a particular way....

Deal-Managing Mediation

Once the deal has been signed, consultants, lawyers, and advisers may continue their association with one or both parties and informally assist as mediators in managing conflict that may arise in the execution of the transaction.... Once top management of the two sides have reached an understanding, they may have to serve as mediators with their subordinates to get them to change behavior and attitudes with respect to interactions at the operational level. . . .

Deal-Mending Mediation

The parties to an international business relationship may encounter a wide variety of conflicts that seem irreconcilable. . . . A poor developing country may stop paying its loan to a foreign bank. Partners in an international joint venture may disagree violently over the use of accumulated profits and therefore plunge their enterprise into a state of paralysis. Here then would seem ideal situations in which mediation by a third party could help in settling conflict. In fact, mediation is relatively uncommon once severe international business conflicts break out. To understand why, one must first understand the basic structure of international business dispute settlement.

International Commercial Arbitration

Nearly all international business contracts today provide that any disputes that may arise in the future between the parties are to be resolved by international commercial arbitration. . . . Thus in the background of virtually all international business disputes is the prospect of binding arbitration if the parties, alone or with the help of a third person, are unable to resolve the conflict themselves.

Arbitrating a dispute is not, however, a painless, inexpensive, quick solution. Like litigation in the courts, it is costly, may take years to conclude, and invariably results in a final rupture of the parties' business relationship. . . . [Arbitrators sometimes seek to play a mediating role. Their usual strategy] is to give the parties a realistic evaluation of what they will receive or be required to pay in any final arbitration award.

Mediation in International Business Disputes

Traditionally, companies engaged in an international business dispute have not actively sought the help of mediators. . . . With increasing recognition of the disadvantages of arbitration, some companies are beginning to turn to more explicit forms of mediation to resolve business disputes.

Conciliation. One type of deal-mending mediation used occasionally in international business is *conciliation*. . . . While the conciliator has broad discretion to conduct the process, in practice he or she will invite both sides to state their views of the dispute and will then make a report proposing an appropriate settlement. The parties may reject the report and proceed to arbitration, or they may accept it.

In many cases, they will use it as a basis for a negotiated settlement. Conciliation is thus a kind of non-binding arbitration. Its function is predictive. It tends to be rights-based . . . Conciliators do not usually adopt a problem-solving or relationship-building approach . . . The process is confidential and completely voluntary . . . Thus far few disputants in international business avail themselves of conciliation. . . .

❖ **M. Scott Donahey, The Asian Concept of Conciliator/Arbitrator: Is It Translatable to the Western World?**

10 Foreign Investment L. J. 120-128 (1995)

In various Asian countries, there is a profound societal and philosophical preference for agreed solutions.[1] Nevertheless, such generalizations are often necessary when comparing one cultural system to another. Rather than a cultural bias toward "equality" in relationships, there exists an intellectual and social predisposition towards a natural hierarchy which governs conduct in interpersonal relations. Asian cultures frequently seek a "harmonious" solution, one which tends to preserve the relationship, rather than one which, while arguably factually and legally "correct," may severely damage the relationship of the parties involved.

Where the Westerner will segregate the function of facilitator from that of decision-maker, the Asian will make no clear distinction. The Westerner seeks an arbiter that is unconnected to the parties to the dispute, one whose mind has not been predisposed by previous knowledge of the dispute or the facts which underlie it, a judge who is prepared to "let the chips fall where they may." On the other hand, many Asians seek a moderator who is familiar with the parties and their dispute, who will not only end their state of disputation but assist the parties in reaching an agreed solution, or, failing that, will find a position which will not only be one that terminates their dispute, but one that will allow the parties to resume their relationship with as little loss of "face" as possible. Thus, the distinction between the function of the arbitrator and that of the conciliator is blurred.

Clearly, as there is increased interaction in the forms of tourism and trade between the Western world and Asia, differences between the two cultures have diminished and will continue to diminish. We in the West tend to view this process as one in which the Asian countries are influenced by our economic and political systems and become more "Westernized." Our western pride and predispositions often do not permit us to recognize the degree to which we have been influenced and changed by the Asian cultures with which we have come in closer contact. . . .

Within the Confucian tradition, there is a concept known as "li," which concerns the social norms of behavior within the five natural status relationships: emperor and subject, father and son, husband and wife, brother and brother, or friend and friend. *Li* is intended to be persuasive, not compulsive and legalistic, a concept which governs good conduct and is above legal concepts in societal importance. The governing legal concept, "fa," is compulsive and punitive. While having the advantage of legal enforceability, *fa* is traditionally below *li* in importance. The Chinese have always considered the resort to litigation as the last step, signifying that the relationship between the disputing parties can no longer be harmonized. Resort to litigation results in loss of face, and discussion and compromise are always to be preferred. Over time the concepts of *fa* and *li* have become fused, and the concept of maintaining the relationship and, therefore, face, has become part of the Chinese legal system. . . .

---

1. The author recognizes that the generalizations in which he engages tend to explain away the complexities and vast difference that exist in any nation or culture[,] and [thus those generalizations] are inherently suspect.

Adjudication is an act-oriented process...In contrast, since conciliation/ mediation is a "person-oriented" one, it is non-adversarial and set in a warm and friendly air of informality unbound by technical rules of procedure. Furthermore, while the nature of the adjudicative process requires that evidence and arguments presented by one party be made in the presence of the adverse litigant, separate conferences with the parties have been found to be an effective tool of conciliation. It is less important, in conciliation proceedings, to be accurate in finding the truth of the issues than to know what values are held by the parties so that a "trade-off" may be effected that will restore the disrupted harmonious relationship.

In Japan, as well, permitting a relationship to fall into a state of disharmony is culturally unacceptable: In Japan...the existence of a dispute may itself cause a loss of "face," and submission of a dispute to a third party may carry with it some sense of failure. . . . Thus, if there is one principle which can be said to lead to the combining of the role of arbitrator with that of conciliator it is that of preserving the harmonious relationship between the parties to the dispute. This principle is one that is frequently cited by Western arbitral institutions in promoting the use of commercial arbitration over litigation. . . .

Perhaps the foremost proponent of the practice of combining the role of conciliator and arbitrator...is the People's Republic of China. While no written rules have ever sanctioned or even described the practice, Chinese arbitrators and practitioners both practice and espouse the combination of mediation and conciliation: Arbitration and conciliation are interrelated and complementary with one another. They are not antagonistic and do not exclude each other. . . .

It is important to understand that the Chinese combination of arbitration and conciliation occurs during the ongoing process of arbitration. The arbitrator, after taking some evidence and hearing some witnesses, might attempt to conciliate the differences and, if efforts at conciliation fail, return to the receipt of evidence and the hearing of witnesses, ready to attempt conciliation again at an opportune time during the course of the proceedings. . . . [I]t is unclear whether parties convey information to the arbitrators/ conciliators in confidence during the conciliation phase, and, if so, how it is maintained. . . . This is different from the way that other Asian nations combine the functions of arbitrator and conciliator. . . .

The traditional Western view is that the conciliation process should be separate from the arbitration process and that the same persons who act as conciliators should not act as arbitrators in the same dispute. . . . However, the traditional Western view is changing, largely due to the influence of Asian cultures. . . . A combined conciliation and arbitration process offers significant advantages in reaching an agreed settlement and in preserving existing commercial relations between the parties. It is a system that apparently has worked well in Asia, and we in the West should not shrink from its use. . . .

Questions

23. What approach would you expect from an Asian conciliator: facilitative or evaluative? Narrow or broad?

24. You are involved in an arbitration of a business contract dispute on behalf of a U.S. computer manufacturer who contracted with a Chinese firm to produce silicon chips, paid for and installed the chips in its products, and has since found out that they are unreliable, leading to serious repair costs and lost profits. Your client believes that the Chinese partner failed to comply with the quality requirements because it overstated its expertise in the area and simply did not understand them. The contract gives you the right to recover your damages, but it is not clear how you would enforce an award in arbitration against the supplier. If you know that the chair of the arbitration panel is a Chinese attorney,
    (a) What, if anything, would you say to the neutral about the possibility of conciliation before the process begins?
    (b) What instructions would you give your client about how to act during conciliation?

H. Online Mediation

One development in mediation does not involve a new subject area, but rather the use of technology to enhance its impact. Mediators already use conference calls to allow people to talk without meeting in person. Law firms and businesses use videoconferencing to bring people together visually, and nothing prevents mediators from doing so as well. The Internet offers potentially huge savings in the transaction costs of conducting a mediation — assembling the parties and lawyers at one physical location and keeping each side "on call" while the mediator meets with the other party. It seems only a matter of time before electronic media revolutionize our approaches to resolving disputes, along with most other aspects of modern life.

So far, however, online mediation has not been widely used in disputes handled by lawyers. One reason is that meeting face-to-face is an important aspect of mediation, because so much of communication between people occurs through their tone of voice, facial gestures, and body language. Although disputants separated in caucuses cannot exchange such information, they communicate directly with the mediator, and most neutrals consider the ability to talk face-to-face with parties to be crucial to their effectiveness. Electronic communication thus eliminates one of the most important qualities of conventional mediation.

There is also the psychological reality that meeting in person forces disputants to go through trouble and expense — clearing schedules, traveling to a site, and remaining isolated for hours. Requiring parties to attend in person thus forces them to take the process seriously, demonstrates to each side that its opponent is also committed to seeking a resolution, and marks mediation as a "settlement event."

Perhaps as a result of these factors, efforts by private companies to establish e-mail or computer-based settlement systems between lawyers and adjusters in personal injury cases have not yet been widely adopted, and even videoconferencing in large disputes appears to be infrequent. The large majority of mediations in which lawyers appear continue to involve face-to-face meetings between the disputants and a neutral. In smaller cases, or where parties are in different countries, however, typical commercial mediation is often not feasible. Here e-mail and other computer-assisted techniques can make the process much less expensive and more practical to conduct. In the following reading, Colin Rule describes the potential of online dispute resolution (ODR) in such disputes.

❖ Colin Rule, Online Dispute Resolution

Adapted from Online Dispute Resolution for Business: B2B, E-commerce, Consumer, Employment, Insurance, and Other Commercial Conflicts (2002)

Dispute resolution and information technology have combined into an important new tool, a new system, a new way of doing business which is more efficient, more cost effective, and much more flexible than traditional approaches. The tool is called Online Dispute Resolution, and it combines the efficiency of alternative dispute resolution with the power of the Internet to save businesses money, time, and frustration.

Online dispute resolution is not tied to geography, so disputants can reach resolution even if they are located on different continents. ODR can move to resolve matters before they escalate, so that disputants can quickly resolve the matter and get back to business. ODR is not tied to particular bodies of law, so there is no need for each side to retain expensive legal counsel to learn the legal structure of the other side's country. ODR can be priced much more reasonably than legal options, and even less than the cost of a single plane ticket. ODR can also leverage expertise from skilled neutrals around the world, ensuring that the participants will get a fair hearing, from someone who has knowledge and experience in the matter at hand. ODR enables businesses, governments, and consumers to achieve the best resolution possible in the shortest amount of time.

These advantages apply to all kinds of disputes. Intellectual property disputes, insurance claims, and B2B and B2C e-commerce matters are all good fits with the power of ODR. Some disputes are over more abstract issues not related to monetary payments, like privacy or workplace conflict. For example, ICANN (the Internet Corporation for Assigned Names and Numbers) faced monumental problems when they decided to build a global process to handle domain name disputes. What courts should govern the matter? What laws should apply? No one country has the jurisdiction over domain names, it is a truly international system. ICANN solved the problem by creating a global domain name dispute resolution process, the UDRP, administered by a variety of ODR providers. Over the past three years this process has resolved thousands of disputes all over the world, none of which have ever been appealed in a courtroom. Soon similar ODR systems will be created for a wide variety of areas, such as insurance, commerce, privacy, government, workplace, and finance.

[T]he rapid growth in online-only disputes has cast the shortcomings of court litigation in even starker contrast. Legal systems are tied to geography almost by definition. In the U.S., lawyers are only admitted to the bar on a state-by-state basis, facing penalties if they even offer legal advice to clients in other states. Enforcement of court decisions involves jails and policemen that also only operate in a particular geographic area.

It is obvious that transaction partners who meet on the web can take little comfort from the redress options provided in the face-to-face world. You can't merely re-create offline judicial mechanisms online and expect them to work, with e-judges making e-rulings enforced by e-police running e-jails. The model doesn't work, on a fundamental level, when participants in the system can change their identity as easily as they change their email address. It might work to hunt down the odd international criminal who shuts down the stock exchange with a virus, but there's no way law enforcement is going to be able to get every fraudulent seller on eBay, especially when they may be on the other side of the planet.

The delays of face-to-face processes also hamper their applicability to online transactions. Over the web, consumers and businesses expect that any service they need should be available online, 24 hours a day. Courts, in contrast, have long been designed to involve delays, ornate filing requirements, and strict procedural rules, to deter potential users from being cavalier in their decision to file new cases. If two businesses engage in a trans-boundary transaction that goes awry they have no interest in waiting months for an offline dispute resolution body to initiate a process to resolve the dispute. They want to get the matter resolved as quickly as possible so that they can get back to doing business.

Simply put, offline courts do not work for online disputes. Courts can operate as an effective safety net for those cases that involve criminal wrongdoing, or where the parties are unwilling to use a non-public forum, or when they put the highest priority on due process and precedent. But for a huge number of cases that are cropping up online, where the value under dispute is less than likely legal bills, or where both parties truly participated in the transaction in good faith, online dispute resolution is the best solution.

In response to these conclusions, the consensus behind online dispute resolution is growing rapidly. International organizations (the OECD, the Hague Conference on Private International Law, the European Union), consumer groups, governmental bodies, professional associations and business organizations have all issued recommendations calling for online dispute resolution. While there is some debate about how to ensure that online dispute resolution services are fair to consumers, or how best to oversee online dispute resolution service providers, there is no debate over whether or not online dispute resolution is the best option for providing redress on the Internet.

Online dispute resolution is the future. Businesses that integrate it into the way they do business will reap rewards in the form of greater efficiency, cost savings, happier employees, protection from liability, and more loyal customers. Those businesses that ignore it will continue to be drawn into expensive and inefficient legal proceedings that breed ill will and sap competitive strength.

One prominent example of ODR is SquareTrade, which has achieved prominence as the mechanism for online negotiation and mediation of disputes between buyers and sellers on eBay. SquareTrade's system has a growing range of applications, including eBay, Yahoo!, Google, the Federal Trade Commission's *www.econsumer.gov* program, and the California Association of Realtors. Since February 2000, it has handled over 1.5 million disputes online, with participants representing 120 different countries. As of 2004, SquareTrade had a volume of approximately 80,000 new online case filings a month. SquareTrade claims success rates of over 80 percent when both parties participate in online mediation, and over 98 percent follow-through on settlement agreements. More than 80 percent of buyers and sellers report satisfaction with their experience.

If you encounter a problem with goods purchased through the "eBay" Web site, a few clicks direct you to "A Simple 4-Step Process to Resolve Disputes" — a process that, like the underlying transaction, is all online. Here is eBay's description of the process:

> *Step 1: File a case.* On the SquareTrade website (*http://www.squaretrade.com/odr*) a buyer or seller clicks "File a Case" and fills out a short online form designed to identify the problem and its possible resolutions.
>
> *Step 2: SquareTrade notifies the other party.* SquareTrade contacts the other party via an automatically generated email and provides instruction on responding to the case. The case and all related responses appear on a password-protected Case Page on the SquareTrade website.
>
> *Step 3: The parties discuss their issues directly in direct negotiation.* Once each party is aware of the issues, they first try to reach an agreement using SquareTrade's Direct Negotiation tool. This initial phase of the service is a completely automated web-based communications tool and is currently free of charge to all users. Using SquareTrade's secure Case Page, the parties try to reach an agreement by communicating directly with each other. The other option is to have a SquareTrade mediator guide the process.
>
> If the parties cannot resolve the case through Direct Negotiation, they can request the assistance of the mediator in developing a fair, mutually agreeable solution. [At the time this book went to print, eBay subsidized mediators' services. As a result, the cost to consumers for professional assistance was only $30 for ordinary consumer disputes and $100 for passenger vehicle disputes.] The mediator's role is to facilitate positive, solution-oriented discussion between the parties. He or she does not act as a judge or arbitrator. The mediator will only recommend a resolution if the parties request it.
>
> *Step 4: The case is resolved.* The parties may either reach a Settlement Agreement independently during Direct Negotiation, or with the assistance of a SquareTrade mediator.

Questions

25. You have been consulted by a client who has bought an antique mandolin on eBay for $250 and, on receiving the instrument, has found that it is in much poorer condition than the seller had represented. She wants to return the mandolin and get her money back. Would you recommend the SquareTrade system to her? What concerns, if any, would you have about it?

26. You are consulted by a business client who purchased a computer server system from an out-of-state supplier in a private transaction for $75,000. The system is dysfunctional, and the client believes that the seller defrauded him by not revealing that the system would only function with customized software, which would require an additional $15,000–$20,000 to create. Even with this software, the client says, the system will not handle the volume of data that he has to process, contrary to assurances given during the sales process. He wishes to revoke the transaction. He has heard about the SquareTrade system and wonders if it would make sense to use it. Assuming that SquareTrade would take the case, what would you advise your client, and why?

Court-Connected Mediation

Much of the early impetus for applying ADR in legal disputes came from judges concerned about overloaded dockets. It is not surprising, therefore, that courts throughout the United States have established dispute resolution programs, and legislators have also supported court-connected ADR. Congress, for example, required in the ADR Act of 1998, 28 U.S.C. § 651(b), that every federal district court in the nation implement a dispute resolution program. Modern ADR programs cover general litigation as well as special categories such as family and small claims cases. Programs are most common at the trial level, but exist in appellate courts as well.

The primary reason that courts have embraced mediation is to relieve their dockets of unwanted cases. In the words of one Texas judge, "I am interested in mediation because the cases settle earlier, and that gives me more time to be a judge, to spend that time I can gain to improving the quality of justice in my court" (Bergman and Bickerman 1998). Although their primary motivation is usually to reduce backlogs, courts divert cases to mediation for other reasons as well. Some cases involve complex continuing relationships, such as disputes between parents over visitation rights to their children. Adjudication is often ineffective to resolve such disputes, and litigation is beyond the financial means of many individuals. Court personnel also find such disputes frustrating and personally demanding. Family and neighborhood disputes, for example, often provoke raw emotions that defy rational analysis. Along with small claims and prisoners' rights suits, they also frequently involve pro se litigants who place extra burdens on court staff.

Court-connected mediation thus raises important policy issues, which involve designing programs not simply to yield the greatest benefit to the system, but also to ensure fairness to participants. This chapter describes how court-connected programs are structured and explores the process issues they present.

A. Issues of Program Design

1. What Goals Should a Program Seek to Achieve?

What should be the purpose of a court-connected mediation program? Although many judges have embraced mediation as a means to reduce delay, the evidence that it does so is conflicting. For example, a study of six federal court programs that used mediation as one ADR technique did not find statistically significant evidence that the programs affected the duration of cases (Kakalik et al. 1996). On the other hand, studies of one federal and a group of state courts found that mediation programs did significantly reduce the length of cases and a California study found similar results (Stienstra et al. 1997; Stipanowich 2004). (Abstracts of these and other studies of court-related ADR programs can be found at *http://www.caadrs.org.*)

The differences in study results may be due to the great variations in how individual courts design and implement their programs. Some courts, for example, do not send cases to mediation until after discovery is complete, greatly reducing the ability of the programs to cut cost or delay, and some courts have initial timeframes for mediation as short as one hour, too little time to apply the techniques described in this book. Given these variations, it is not surprising that results are mixed. But whether or not court-sponsored mediation consistently reduces delay, there may be other reasons to support its use.

❖ Wayne D. Brazil, Why Should Courts Offer Non-Binding ADR Services?

16 Alternatives 65 (1998)

[T]here is no one method of procedure that works best for resolving . . . every kind of dispute. . . . In some cases, the parties' dominating concern will be with trying to establish the truth. They will want to use the process that is most likely to generate historically accurate factfinding, regardless of other considerations. . . . Traditional adversarial litigation may well best meet the needs of such parties.

But for parties to whom other values or interests loom larger, other processes are likely to deliver more valued service — and are more likely to result in consensual disposition. . . . To some parties, relationship-building . . . may be of prime importance. . . . In some cases, what the parties care most about are feelings. . . . In some disputes, it is the quality and character of communication that matters most — or that holds the most promise of delivering constructive solutions. . . . It follows that if our judicial system is to be responsive to the full range of interests and needs that cases filed in our courts implicate, then the system cannot offer only one dispute resolution method. . . .

One role of public courts in a democratic society is to try to assure that it is not only the wealthy or the big case litigants who have access to appropriate and effective dispute resolution processes. Poor litigants, and parties to cases without substantial economic value, should not be relegated by our judicial system to the often-slow and disproportionately expensive procedures of traditional adversarial litigation. To force poor people and small cases into that system can be tantamount to denying them access to any system at all. . . .

A related consideration supporting court sponsorship of ADR begins with the observation that some litigants and lawyers might have greater confidence in the integrity of an ADR process and the neutral when the ADR services are provided or sponsored by a court than when they are provided in a wholly private setting. When the service provider is a public court, for example, there is no occasion for the concerns that have surfaced about the possible influence...of large companies that are current or potential sources of considerable repeat business....

[In addition,] active participation in designing and implementing ADR programs provides courts with opportunities to gain insight that they can use to improve their handling of traditional litigation. [A] thoughtfully monitored ADR program can develop...insights into negotiation dynamics that can be shared with judges who host settlement conferences, enhancing the skills...that judges can bring to their work as settlement facilitators....

Unhappily, there is a risk that courts could be tempted to permit institutional selfishness to infect the thinking that drives their program design. Some judges and judicial administrators, for example, might be attracted to ADR only or primarily as a docket reduction tool, [posing] serious threats to fairness or other values that ADR should be promoting. There also is a risk that some judges and administrators could try to use ADR programs as dumping grounds for categories of cases that are deemed unpopular, unimportant, annoying, or difficult.

Questions

1. Would a traditional trial-oriented judge disagree with the arguments that Judge Brazil makes for court-connected mediation? Which ones?
2. Brazil promotes mediation as a means of securing justice for poor people. Commentators such as Richard Delgado, however, have raised concerns that ADR provides second-class justice to the disadvantaged. What aspects of the process does each side focus on?
3. One study found that attorneys permitted to choose from among several ADR processes were more likely than attorneys who did not have a choice to report that the ADR process lowered litigation costs, reduced the amount of discovery and number of motions, was fair, resulted in settlement, and had benefits that outweighed the costs (Stienstra et al. 1997). What downside might there be to permitting attorneys to choose among court ADR processes?

Professor Nancy Welsh has delved deeply into some of the fairness concerns raised by Judge Brazil, focusing on what ordinary people mean by "justice" and whether court-connected ADR programs deliver it. In doing so, she distinguishes between "procedural" justice, which refers to disputants' feelings about the process of ADR, and "distributive" justice, which focuses on their assessment of outcomes. This reading focuses on procedural justice.

❖ Nancy A. Welsh, Making Deals in Court-Connected Mediation: What's Justice Got to Do with It?

79 Wash U. L. Q. 787, 817-26 (2001)

Researchers have found that procedural justice matters profoundly. Disputants' perceptions of the justice provided by a procedure affect their judgments of the distributive justice provided by the outcome, their compliance with that outcome, and their faith in the legitimacy of the institution that offered the procedure. Disputants use the following indicia to assess procedural justice:

- whether the procedure provided them with the opportunity to tell their stories,
- whether the third party considered their stories, and
- whether the third party treated them in an even-handed and dignified manner.

The procedures used in socially-sanctioned dispute resolution processes assume such significance because disputants seek personal and pragmatic reassurance. Disputants need to believe that they are valued members of society and that the final outcome of a dispute resolution process will be based on full information. . . .

The Effects of Procedural Justice

Although issues of procedural justice often do not attract as much public attention as concerns about distributive justice, research has shown that when people experience dispute resolution and decision-making procedures, they pay a great deal of attention to the way things are done [i.e., how decisions are made] and the nuances of their treatment by others. As a result, perceptions of procedural justice profoundly affect people's perceptions of distributive justice, their compliance with the outcomes of decision-making procedures and processes, and their perceptions of the legitimacy of the authorities that determine such outcomes. Perhaps surprisingly, perceptions of distributive justice generally have a much more modest impact than perceptions of procedural justice.

Research has repeatedly confirmed that people's perceptions of procedural justice mediate or influence their perceptions of distributive justice. Disputants who believe that they have been treated in a procedurally fair manner are more likely to conclude that the resulting outcome is substantively fair. In effect, a disputant's perception of procedural justice anchors general fairness impressions or serves as a fairness heuristic [heuristic is a social science term for a mental shortcut]. Further, research has indicated that disputants who have participated in a procedure that they evaluated as fair do not change their evaluation even if the procedure produces a poor or unfair outcome.

The perception of procedural justice also serves as a shortcut means of determining whether to accept or reject a legal decision or procedure. Disputants who believe that they were treated fairly in a dispute resolution procedure are more likely to comply with the outcome of that procedure. This effect will occur even if outcomes do not favor the disputants or they are actually unhappy with the outcomes.

Disputants' perceptions of the procedural justice provided by a decision-making authority also affect the respect and loyalty accorded to the authority. This effect is particularly strong for the courts. Thus, litigants' reactions to the institution of the judiciary and their compliance with decisions arising out of court-mandated procedures do not depend simply (or even primarily) upon whether they feel that they won or lost their cases. Rather, litigants' reactions depend largely upon their "experience of legal procedures."

Process Characteristics That Enhance Perceptions of Procedural Justice

Several rather specific process characteristics enhance perceptions of procedural justice. First, perceptions of procedural justice are enhanced to the extent that disputants perceive that they had the opportunity to present their views, concerns, and evidence to a third party and had control over this presentation ("opportunity for voice"). Second, disputants are more likely to perceive procedural justice if they perceive that the third party considered their views, concerns, and evidence. Third, disputants' judgments about procedural justice are affected by the perception that the third party treated them in a dignified, respectful manner and that the procedure itself was dignified. Although it seems that a disputants' perceptions regarding a fourth factor — the impartiality of the third party decision maker — also ought to affect procedural justice judgments, it appears that disputants are influenced more strongly by their observations regarding the third party's even-handedness and attempts at fairness.

Through a long series of experiments involving many different settings and situations, disputants' opportunity for voice has been found to reliably affect perceptions of procedural justice. When disputants feel that they have been allowed a full opportunity to voice their views, concerns, and evidence, the disputing process is seen as fairer and the outcome is more likely to be accepted. Concerns regarding the opportunity for voice apply in a variety of settings, including the courtroom, arbitration proceedings, contacts with the police, political decision making, and decision making in work organizations. Even in countries where the judicial systems typically use nonadversarial procedures, citizens often prefer procedures that allow a full opportunity for voice. Perhaps most surprisingly, both field and laboratory studies have demonstrated that the opportunity for voice heightens disputants' judgments of procedural justice even when they know that their voice will not and cannot influence the final outcome.

These research results are helpful as we consider the application of procedural justice to court-connected mediation, but they raise several important questions: What counts as a full opportunity for voice? How much freedom and time must disputants be given? What represents sufficient control by disputants over the presentation of their views, concerns, and evidence? Can an agent's presentation fulfill the disputants' opportunity for voice? Many of the procedural justice studies deal with these questions, directly or indirectly....

The other three process characteristics that influence procedural justice judgments center upon the behavior of the third party. In particular, disputants assess the extent to which the third party hears and considers their presentations, treats them with dignity and respect, and tries to be fair and even-handed. Disputants seek assurance that the decision maker has given adequate consideration to their presentations. Apparently, while disputants care very much about having the opportunity for voice, they also wish to know that they have been heard. In one study examining citizens' interactions with police and judges, researchers found that the effect of providing an opportunity for voice was significantly enhanced if citizens also believed that the police and judges considered their views before they made decisions. Indeed, a third party's behavior, including the third party's consideration of the disputants' views, independently affects perceptions of procedural justice and acts as a filter for and an amplifier of the disputants' subjective assessments of their control over both the outcome and the process within a particular procedure.

Disputants' perceptions of procedural justice also are influenced by how the third party interacts with them on an interpersonal level ... For example, in one study comparing litigants' reactions to the third-party processes of trial, arbitration, and judicial settlement conferences, the litigants gave much higher procedural justice rankings to trial and arbitration, even though these proceedings required the litigants to surrender decision-making control. Most litigants perceived trial and arbitration as dignified and careful. In contrast, settlement conferences were more likely to strike litigants as undignified and contrary to the litigants' sense of procedural fairness.

Dignified and respectful treatment demonstrates to citizens that authorities recognize their own role as that of public servants and recognize the role of citizens as clients who have a legitimate right to certain services. Interestingly, while authorities' politeness and respect for citizens' rights have been found to influence all citizens' perceptions of procedural justice, some research suggests that minority group members particularly value the existence of these qualities in their interactions with authorities.

Significantly, several studies have shown that disputants value these process characteristics as much as, or even more than, control over the final decision (also termed "decision control"). Disputants particularly have identified the opportunity for voice as just as valuable as decision control ... [This] is consistent with other studies that have found that disputants' procedural justice judgments are affected much more strongly by variations in process control than by variations in decision control.

Ultimately, the procedural justice literature highlights the need to focus not solely on the fairness of outcomes, but also on the fairness of procedures. Further, the literature suggests that disputants are less concerned about receiving formal due process during their experiences with the courts than they are about being treated in a manner that is consistent with their everyday expectations regarding social relations and norms.

Questions

You are an advisor to a court seeking to design a mediation program for disputes in which only about half of the participants will be represented by a lawyer.

4. What do the procedural justice findings suggest about how the program should be designed in terms of structure — format, length of sessions, and physical facilities — and the selection and training of mediators?
5. Can you suggest specific problems that the program should avoid?

2. How Should Services Be Provided?

The goals of promoting settlement and satisfying litigants' interests are not necessarily contradictory, but varying goals are likely to lead to different program designs. A program focused on stimulating settlements at minimal cost, on the one hand, might encourage participants to "cut to the chase." A program whose goal was to address parties' underlying interests, on the other hand, would be more likely to plan for longer sessions, which would probably increase its cost.

One key issue is who will mediate court-sponsored cases. Most court programs rely on panels made up of neutrals with limited training and experience, usually practicing attorneys who often serve on a volunteer basis. This approach allows courts to offer ADR services at low cost and build support for mediation in the private bar. The services themselves, however, vary widely in quality. A second option is to create a roster of professional neutrals. Such panels are more consistently competent because the participants have been tested by the market. Professionals, however, are likely to require payment for their services. Some courts seek to achieve both goals by using professionals but requiring them to contribute their initial time on each case without charge or to work at reduced rates. Finally, some courts, particularly in the federal and family court systems, use full-time employees as mediators. These neutrals may be lawyers, magistrates, or senior judges, and may have the advantage of receiving training and being able to devote substantial time to each case. However, the "full-time employee" model requires the court to bear most or all of the cost of providing neutrals and may make it difficult for litigants to avoid a mediator whom they consider ineffective.

Cases in court-connected programs may be selected by litigants, judges, or court screeners. Courts vary widely as to when they order or permit cases to go into mediation. Empirical research has not resolved whether earlier or later mediation is more effective in terms of settlement rate, but the general trend is to mediate disputes earlier in their lives.

In summary, courts that offer mediation services face the following issues of program design:

1. Will participation in the program be voluntary or mandatory?
   - If mandatory, will the mandate apply to all cases or only a subset of them?
   - If a subset, will it be defined by the type of case, the parties (e.g., pro se versus represented litigants), the amount in controversy, or some other criterion?
   - If voluntary, will entry be by referral only, or will litigants be allowed to opt in?
2. How will neutrals be selected?
3. How much time will be allowed for the process? Can the time be extended by agreement?
4. How will program costs be covered?
   - Will neutrals be paid?
   - Will participants be charged? On what basis?
   - Will waivers be available to indigents?
5. What level of attendance will be required?

- Will individual parties be required to attend in person?
- Will corporate parties be required to send a representative with a specific level of authority (e.g., "full" authority)?
6. What level of participation will be required?
   - Will parties be required or permitted to file written materials?
   - Will disputants be allowed to contact mediators in advance?
   - Will disputants be required to adhere to a standard of conduct (e.g., to "mediate in good faith")?

Problem

Investigate a mediation program offered by your local courts. How does the program deal with the issues listed here?

B. Models of Court-Connected Programs

Almost every state and federal court system has a mediation option or requirement. To give you a sense of the forms these programs can take and the issues they confront, this section provides descriptions of several state and federal programs.

1. State Trial Courts

❖ **Nancy A. Welsh and Barbara McAdoo, Alternative Dispute**
Resolution in Minnesota — An
Update on Rule 114

In Court-Annexed Mediation: Critical Perspectives on State and Federal Programs
203-212 (1998)

When Rule 114 [requiring litigants to engage in mediation in most state civil cases] arrived on the Minnesota legal scene in July, 1994, it took many attorneys by complete surprise.... Today, largely as a result of Rule 114, nearly 80 percent of Minnesota's attorneys report that they are using ADR to help resolve their civil cases filed in trial courts, and a majority of the state's attorneys indicate that they would continue to use ADR even if Rule 114 were repealed....

Rule 114's Unique Approach. [T]he ADR Task Force struggled mightily with the question of whether or not to make ADR *mandatory* in all civil cases. The experience of other jurisdictions was instructive. In those jurisdictions where ADR was totally voluntary, parties used ADR rarely or not at all. In jurisdictions that made ADR mandatory for certain classes of cases, there was not always a good "match" between a case and the ADR process used to attempt resolution of the case.

Therefore, the ADR Task Force recommended an approach which institutionalizes *consideration of ADR* in every case. Basically, early in the life of a case, attorneys and parties are required to think and talk about ADR. They are given overwhelming discretion and creative freedom in selecting an ADR process, the ADR neutral, and the timing of the ADR process. And, to ensure that attorneys and parties take advantage of this window of opportunity, Rule 114 and its enabling legislation supply judges with a "stick." Simply, judges have the authority to order parties into non-binding ADR processes against their will. This provision has helped to ensure that attorneys and parties actively investigate and select ADR processes . . . Generally, the court exercises this discretion within the first 90 days after a case has been filed. However, the Rule provides the court with the authority to issue an order for non-binding ADR at any time, upon its own initiative or pursuant to a party's motion. . . .

An Infrastructure of Qualified ADR Neutrals. . . . The Rule also recognizes the need to ensure that qualified neutrals are available to support the creative and appropriate application of Rule 114. . . . [Neutrals selected by parties] tend to be lawyers and litigators, and, most importantly, to have substantive experience in the field of law related to the case. . . .

Paying for ADR. When Rule 114 was being developed, it was very clear that Minnesota's judicial system could not assume responsibility for paying for ADR services. . . . The Rule provides that the parties will pay for the services of an ADR neutral. . . .

On-Going Evaluation and Monitoring. This is an area of concern for Minnesota. [T]here is no on-going monitoring or required party evaluation process to assure the quality of the ADR neutrals. . . .

Effect of Rule 114 on the Use of ADR Processes. Recent research indicates that Rule 114 has had a dramatic effect in increasing the use of ADR in Minnesota's courts. The overwhelming majority of the attorneys who responded to the Rule 114 Questionnaire — more than 80% — reported that they had used an ADR process for their civil cases in the past two years. . . .

❖ **Mike Amis et al., The Texas ADR Experience**

In Court-Annexed Mediation: Critical Perspectives on State and Federal Programs 369, 376-378 (1998)

The Dallas Experience. Court-annexed mediation seemed to take off in Dallas County in 1989. Now, nine years later, on any given day, dozens of cases are being mediated in the county, with the use of mediation having spread to all civil, family, and probate courts. Virtually all types of cases have proven to be appropriate, from the large, complex commercial or injury case to the neighborhood dispute. . . . Overcrowded dockets, Rambo litigation, with widespread client dissatisfaction, particularly in the business sector, paved the way for a new day: Our existing jury system was wonderful when it worked, but it was not functioning very well. The courts were overburdened, and no settlement system was in place....

It is our belief that the transformation which took place in Dallas can occur in any community with certain fundamental elements in place....[A rule] that provides for court-ordered mediation, giving counsel an opportunity to reasonably object, is crucial....Our experience is that busy lawyers, perhaps worried that suggesting mediation will be construed as a sign of weakness, need a mandatory referral, the proverbial "two by four on the head of the donkey to gain attention." The mandatory orders, in turn, paved the way for voluntary efforts; attorneys, with credibility, can advise their clients that the Order is coming....

The ripple effect of the [many] lawyers trained in mediation skills serves to change the litigation landscape for the better....Some attorneys now have participated in hundreds of mediations as advocates. Experienced mediators are currently serving on the bench....Dallas has a mature court-annexed mediation system....

❖ **Sharon Press, Florida's Court-Connected State Mediation Program**

In Court-Annexed Mediation: Critical Perspectives on State and Federal Programs 55-59 (1998)

Mediation is on the rise in Florida. Statistics of court-connected mediation programs from 1988 to 1996 indicated an increase from approximately 10,000 cases to more than 74,000 documented cases mediated annually....In 1997...Florida had 12 Citizen Dispute Settlement Center programs, 34 county programs, 23 family programs, 13 circuit programs, 12 dependency mediation programs, and one appellate mediation program....In toto, we estimate that more than 100,000 cases are diverted from the traditional court process to mediation each year....[This figure does not include private mediations that are scheduled without court involvement.]

Currently, there is a trend in Florida toward greater freedom of choice. Although courts still retain the authority to mandate that parties attend mediation, more parties, through their attorneys, are selecting mediation before receiving a court order....

Questions

6. What appear to be the key differences among the state court programs described above?
7. Regarding the Texas comment about applying a "two by four on the head of the donkey," who is the donkey here? Is there any downside to this approach to encouraging use of mediation?
8. A court has been requiring parties to participate in ADR for several years, and as a result the local bar has become very familiar with how mediation can be used to resolve disputes. The court has asked you whether as a matter of policy it should now drop its requirement and allow parties to decide voluntarily whether to use ADR. What would you recommend? What are the arguments pro and con?

2. Federal Trial Courts

As we have noted, federal law requires every federal district court to institute an ADR program for civil cases, and many courts require parties in selected cases to go through dispute resolution. Most courts allow litigants to choose among ADR processes. With the possible exception of the traditional settlement conference, mediation is the process most often chosen.

One example of a trial-level ADR program is the program offered by the federal court for the Western District of Michigan (see *http://www.miwd. uscourts.gov/adr*). In 2004 the court referred slightly more than 450 civil cases to ADR. Of those, about 250 were sent to judicial settlement conferences and 150 to mediation.[1] However, litigants who were referred to mediation were much more likely to carry out the process than parties referred to settlement conferences. Moreover, mediations produced agreements at a much higher rate than did settlement conferences. Results such as this, as well as how litigants and attorneys feel about participating in mediation, have fueled mediation's popularity in federal ADR programs.

While most federal courts rely on practicing lawyers and neutrals to mediate cases, some employ full-time court employees or magistrates as mediators. The following reading describes one court's experience with a full-time neutral.

> ❖ Donna Stienstra, Demonstrating the Possibilities of Providing
> Mediation Early and by Court Staff: The Western
> District of Missouri's Early Assessment Program

**In Court-Annexed Mediation: Critical Perspectives on State and Federal Programs
251-254, 261-267 (1998)**

In early 1991, a group of attorneys in Kansas City, Missouri met to consider how their local federal court could best help litigants resolve their disputes. From the attorney's deliberations emerged a new and innovative ADR program, the Early Assessment Program [EAP]. Unique among federal district courts, this program relies not on private sector mediators but on a mediator who is a member of the court staff. Also unlike many other federal district court programs, in this one the ADR session occurs very early in the case. . . .

Why did Missouri Western adopt the Early Assessment Program? [T]he advisory group had studied the court's caseload and overall condition and had concluded that delay was not a serious problem in the district. . . . Nonetheless, both the judges and advisory group believed that cases could — and should — be resolved earlier and that by doing so litigation costs might be lowered. . . .

First, they decided that cases should be required to participate in some form of ADR and that a variety of ADR options should be available to

---

1. Eighty percent of the cases referred to mediation went through with the process, versus only 47 percent of those referred to settlement conferences. Of the cases that completed a process, 67 percent of mediated cases, but only 46 percent of conferenced cases, settled.

litigants...Second, to provide assistance much earlier in a case, the judges and attorneys determined that the initial event — labeled the "early assessment meeting" — should be held within 30 days after completion of responsive pleadings. Third, the judges and attorneys agreed that clients should be required to attend the initial meeting....

Nature of the first EAP sessions. As originally designed, the program expected attorneys to come to the first EAP session to engage in a discussion about the case and to make plans for discovery and the use of ADR. (In practice, however, most parties have asked the EAP administrator to serve as mediator, and most have proceeded to mediation at the first EAP session. Thus, [the program] in actuality provides a fairly classic form of mediation. And it provides this service shortly after a defendant is engaged in the case....[The typical case takes several hours and in] the unusual case, the program administrator and parties will have spent a day together....

Earlier case resolution and more settlements. Judging by the most objective of measures — the number of days from filing to termination — the Early Assessment Program results in earlier case resolution. Cases that are required to participate in the program terminate in 7.0 months while those not permitted to participate terminate in 9.2 months. [T]he reduction is greatest for contract and, especially, civil rights cases....

Possible reductions in litigation costs. In moving cases to earlier dispositions, the court and advisory group attorneys hoped the EAP process would also reduce litigation costs...a little over two-thirds of the attorneys who participated in an EAP session reported that the EAP reduced litigation costs. The median estimated savings per party was $15,000...although they come at a cost to the court of about $700 per case. Caution must be used, however, in reaching conclusions about the EAP's effect on costs....

Ways in which the EAP is helpful in a case... Over three-quarters of the attorneys who participated in an early assessment meeting reported that the session encouraged the parties to be more realistic about their positions. [One attorney, for example, commented that the sessions allowed clients to] "gain a personal impression of the opposing party, counsel...." Another said that, "There are times the client does not want to hear what their lawyer is telling them. Having a third party...give his thoughts on the case can certainly get the client's attention and bring them back to earth."

Timing of the EAP session. Of particular interest are the attorneys' responses regarding the timing of the EAP session. Conventional wisdom holds that meaningful settlement discussions cannot occur until some discovery has been done. However, in this court where the ADR process occurs very early, only 11% of the attorneys reported that it began too early in their case....

Question

9. What are the potential pluses and minuses of using full-time court employees or judges, rather than a panel of trained lawyers, as the neutrals in a court-affiliated program?

3. Small Claims Sessions

Mediation has also been extended to cases in which lawyers are not usually present. The following reading describes its use in small claims sessions.

❖ **Susan E. Raitt, Jay Folberg, Joshua Rosenberg, and Robert Barrett, The Use of Mediation in Small Claims Courts**

9 Ohio St. J. Disp. Resol. 55, 62-63, 80 (1993)

Numerous factors have led to the development of mediation programs in small claims courts over the past decade. First there are the cost savings for the courts themselves. Mediators can clearly reduce the amount of judge time the court must assign to small claims calendars by settling a substantial percentage of trial ready cases.... Second, mediation benefits the disputants. Because mediation is less confrontational and less formal, it can provide a forum where a party will be more relaxed and have a greater opportunity to explain her or his side of the case. In explaining their positions to a third-party neutral, the parties can vent their pent-up feelings....

Mediation may be able to help smooth out the potential one-sidedness of cases filed by more "sophisticated" businesses. The perception is that businesses that file large numbers of small claims cases have become very professional in the way they adjudicate [such] cases.... It is also hoped that by increasing the use of mediation in small claims cases, the collectability of judgments may be enhanced. [If so,] plaintiffs who would expect to win at trial stand to benefit from mediation as well....

Overall, mediation programs in the small claims court appear to be quite successful in settling a substantial percentage of contested cases before trial.... Successful mediation programs are more labor-intensive than the relatively short hearings in adjudication of small claims. In many mediation programs the labor comes exclusively or primarily from volunteers.

---

4. Appellate Courts

❖ **Dana Curtis and John Toker, Representing Clients in Appellate Mediation: The Last Frontier**

1 JAMS Alert No. 3, 1 (December 2000)

These days mediation of disputes in trial courts is commonplace. Yet mediation of appeals is relatively rare, even though each circuit of the U.S. Court of Appeals has long maintained staffs of mediators and some state appellate courts have mediation programs. [In] the Ninth Circuit, the eight full-time...mediators helped parties settle over 600 cases last year. [And more] than forty percent of cases sent to mediation in [a California state court appellate program] have settled.

...The introduction of mediation into the appellate process requires appellate lawyers to take on the role of counselor in the broadest sense. Lawyers must analyze cases not only from a *legal* viewpoint, but also from a *human* and *business* perspective. They need to help their clients make good decisions regarding not only whether, but also how, to proceed. The consideration of mediation should be part of that process....

The similarities between mediation of appellate cases and other matters far exceed the differences. Nevertheless, understanding the distinctions will help you do a better job of representing your clients in appellate mediation.

1. *There's already a winner and a loser.* As counsel for the appellant, it may be that you have not considered mediation of appeals because it doesn't occur to you that the respondent, as the victor, would be willing to accept a compromise instead of an appellate decision. There are a number of reasons why a respondent may be willing to accept a compromise instead of [a] decision. Essentially, they boil down to a five little words: risk, cost, time, life, and gain.

Risk	Appellate courts can be unpredictable, even in cases that seem open and shut. Appeals from judgments entered as a matter of law, such as summary judgments...are particularly risky because the appellate court reviews these appeals de novo. The reversal rate in these cases is approximately 30 percent...
Cost	Appeals can be very expensive. A five-day trial can translate into a $30,000 appeal with transcript production and briefing. If the appellate court reverses the judgment, the case may be remanded to the trial court for further costly proceedings. A reasonable compromise may be in the best interest of all parties.
Time	It likely is in the interest of a respondent to have a judgment satisfied sooner rather than later....
Life	There comes a time for many litigants...when they just want to end the pain and get on with their lives.
Gain	Mediation offers creative solutions outside of the litigation box....

2. *The participants may be less optimistic about resolution.* Generally, parties in appellate mediation have had a number of failed negotiations and are therefore more discouraged about settlement than they were at the beginning of the dispute. And they also suffer from the skepticism discussed above, that is, why would the winner want to sit down at the mediation table?

3. *Paradoxically, the law and evaluation of the legal issues by the mediator may not be as important to settlement as it was before trial....* Mediator evaluation of the merits of the case may not play an important role as it does in other litigated cases [because] parties have already had an evaluation by a judge or a jury, and at least one of them is not convinced it was right.

4. *The relationships between the parties may be more strained.* A contested trial court proceeding that has been resolved in favor of one of the parties never *enhances* the relationships between them. If they were antagonistic before litigation, parties often are bitter enemies by the time of the appeal. In selecting a mediator for an appeal, you'll need to consider the mediator's

ability to manage high conflict and create a positive environment for problem solving.

5. *Lawyers and clients both have problems with cognitive dissonance* between their negotiating positions before and after the trial court decision. Failing to settle earlier for a greater/lesser amount before the court decision may make it more difficult for the client to enter into a settlement that differs greatly from the earlier offer or demand. You may also struggle with your failure to have settled for more/less before the decision.... If you can't put aside the previous settlement proposal, and your regret at having passed it up, you may not be able to advise your client rationally....

Question

10. You are advising a legislative committee in your state that wishes to conduct a three-year project to test the usefulness of court-connected mediation. The committee has only enough funds to create pilot programs in two court departments. It must choose among the small claims, district (smaller cases), superior (larger cases), family, juvenile, and appellate courts. Which two departments would you advise the committee to select for funding? Why?

CHAPTER
16

Mixed and Changing Roles

Thomas J. Stipanowich

A. The Use of Mixed Processes: Med-Arb

Suppose that mediation does not produce a settlement. Is the only alternative to abandon settlement efforts and enter a separate adjudicatory process — either court or arbitration? Or is there a third way? In fact, disputing parties sometimes opt for a format in which a single neutral plays more than one role in a dispute, first nonbinding, but if that fails, a binding one. The most common mixed process is known as "med-arb." Here a person acts as mediator in the usual manner but, if the process fails to achieve a settlement, then "morphs" into the role of arbitrator in a binding, adjudicatory proceeding.

It is worth taking a moment to consider the vast difference between the roles of mediator and arbitrator. Although the parties may circumscribe an arbitrator's powers by agreement, in the typical commercial case the arbitrator is in effect a private judge. As a result, for the same person to act both as a mediator and arbitrator requires her to assume, successively, very different, almost contradictory mindsets toward a case. It is also important to appreciate the finality of the arbitration process. Students are often surprised to learn that except in extraordinary cases, proof that an arbitrator has misinterpreted the law or misunderstood the facts is *not* adequate grounds for a court to overturn the decision. As a result, successful appeals from arbitrators' decisions, or "awards," are quite rare.

There are nevertheless situations in which experienced litigators opt to have one person take on both roles. Indeed, mixing processes is quite common in other cultures: Recall, for example, how Asian arbitrators routinely interrupt arbitration processes to attempt to mediate disputes, returning to their arbitral role if conciliation is not successful.

Although commentators have expressed concerns about neutrals wearing multiple hats, the reality is that a significant percentage of active arbitrators and mediators sometimes serve in roles very different from the ones to which they were initially appointed. Recently a group of 128 commercial and employment mediators was queried about how frequently they change hats. They responded as follows:

When initially appointed as a mediator, I have arbitrated issues at the request of the parties when mediation failed to resolve them:

Always	Often	About half the time	Occasionally	Never
1	3	0	45	78

I have mediated issues at the request of the parties even though I was initially appointed as arbitrator:

Always	Often	About half the time	Occasionally	Never
1	3	3	46	69

Attorneys representing clients in mediation or arbitration are likely to be confronted with the option of employing a neutral in multiple roles, either as a matter of initial planning or midway through the course of a proceeding. It is therefore important to understand the relevant practical, legal, and ethical concerns raised by the use of the med-arb process.

1. Concerns About Med-Arb

Some neutrals regularly employ med-arb to resolve contractual disputes, and some institutional sponsors of ADR offer med-arb procedures. Advocates of such approaches argue that having a single neutral serve in both roles avoids the necessity of having to educate two separate neutrals about the same case, saving time and money. They also reason that if the parties are aware that their mediator will render a final and binding decision if a dispute is not settled, they will be encouraged to resolve the matter in mediation.

Despite the arguments put forward in favor of med-arb, many lawyers oppose mixing these roles. They argue, first, that the approaches of mediators and arbitrators are fundamentally incompatible: The arbitrator's interaction with the parties is confined to adversary hearings in which parties present and contest evidence. By contrast, mediation usually involves extensive ex parte communications with disputants. Parties who know that their mediator will become the ultimate decision maker should mediation fail may be less candid in communicating with her, undermining an important feature of the process. Moreover, there is always the possibility that the mediator-turned-arbitrator's view of the issues will be affected by information imparted confidentially that has never been subjected to cross-examination or rebuttal. Another concern is that the "big stick" wielded by a mediator-arbitrator will undermine party self-determination, especially if the intervener "telegraphs" her own views of the issues in dispute. Finally, many mediators have little or no experience conducting an arbitration hearing and may not be competent to take on this role.

If parties do wish a neutral to serve in mixed roles, they must address waiver issues, in particular the right of a party to challenge an arbitration award on the ground that the neutral had ex parte contacts with the other litigant. Otherwise a med-arb arrangement may simply set the stage for a later motion to disqualify the arbitrator or vacate the arbitration award. This difficulty is exemplified by *Township of Aberdeen v. Patrolmen's Benevolent Association*, 669 A.2d 291 (N.J. S. Ct., App. Div. 1996), a decision regarding a med-arb arrangement in a public employment contract. When negotiations over a new collective bargaining agreement between the township and the police officers' union reached an impasse, the union petitioned for the initiation of arbitration. Prior to the start of hearings, the parties agreed to have the arbitrator attempt to mediate the dispute. When mediated negotiations fell apart, the case went to arbitration. The arbitrator rendered an award in favor of the union, largely on the basis of the township's shifting positions during mediation.

Although state law permitted med-arb, the court struck down the award on the basis that the arbitrator had improperly relied on information gained during the course of mediation and not presented in the arbitration hearing. The court reasoned that "parties should feel free to negotiate without fear that what they say and do will later be used against them," and that "[m]ediation would be a hollow practice if the parties' negotiating tactics could be used against them by the arbitrator in rendering the final decision." For the same reason that "it would be unthinkable for a trial court to base its decision on information disclosed in pretrial settlement negotiations," the court ruled that mediated negotiations preceding arbitration should be protected.

With these concerns in mind, consider your approach to the following scenarios based on actual cases.

Problem 1

You are representing a party in an arbitration proceeding before a panel of three neutral arbitrators in a significant commercial case. During a break in the prehearing conference that arbitrators typically hold with both sides, the chair states her sense that the circumstances might lend themselves to mediation. You would rather not mediate, because the strength of your case lies in your witnesses, and mediation will not allow them to be presented to full advantage. The other lawyer says, "That sounds like an excellent idea, Your Honor." What should you say or do?

Problem 2

You have been appointed to arbitrate various issues associated with a corporate "divorce." After several arbitration sessions have been held, the parties jointly inform you that they have discussed settlement and believe it would be productive to mediate. Given your familiarity with the issues and their comfort with you as a neutral, they ask you to act as mediator. What will you do?

2. The Need for Precision in Specifying Roles

Efforts to structure a workable and enforceable ADR agreement are sometimes undermined by a lack of precision. Such issues are particularly acute when a single individual is assigned multiple roles, or when the neutral's role may be characterized in more than one way.

These concerns are illustrated by *Ex parte Industrial Technologies*, 707 So. 2d 234 (Ala. 1997), a case in which a bank filed suit on a promissory note, and the borrower counterclaimed for conversion of certain equipment taken by the bank during collection efforts. Prior to trial the parties agreed to refer the matter to an out-of-court process, described as "mediation or arbitration," with a retired circuit judge named Snodgrass as "mediator/arbitrator." After the parties had engaged in settlement negotiations supervised by Snodgrass, they announced to him that they had entered into a "stipulation of agreement." The agreement acknowledged that the bank had converted the borrower's equipment, called for appraisers to determine the fair market value of the converted property, and provided for Snodgrass to determine the lost rental value of the property during the time it was improperly held by the bank.

Snodgrass subsequently issued an "Order" that directed the bank to pay the lost value of the property during the conversion period, plus the difference between the fair market value of the equipment at the time it was converted and its salvage value at the time of return. The borrower sought to enforce the outcome, which it termed a "binding arbitration order." The bank, however, argued that the proceeding was merely a mediation and that Snodgrass had no authority to issue the order.

The Alabama Supreme Court determined that both the parties' agreement and the subsequent process were fatally flawed. First of all, it was impossible to determine the precise character of the process agreed to by the parties, only that they apparently intended for Snodgrass to determine damages based on an agreed formula. Unfortunately, the court concluded, there was never a meeting of the minds about whether Snodgrass was empowered to award damages, other than to determine the lost rental value of the property. While the lack of precision in tailoring the original ADR agreement might have been overcome by the participants in their subsequent "stipulation of agreement," the second document merely exacerbated their mistakes.

Question

1. The borrower in the Snodgrass case has approached you, asking how it should draft an ADR clause in the future so as to avoid the problems identified by the *Industrial Technologies* court. What suggestions can you offer?

B. Changing Roles

We conclude with a look at important opportunities and challenges confronting lawyers as problem solvers today and in the future. After more than a quarter century of efforts to develop different and more effective ways of managing conflict, lawyers have the opportunity to approach the litigation experience in a wholly new way and achieve more satisfactory results for their clients. As advisors they are ideally poised to bring about a wholesale change in the culture of disputing. Understanding the value of mediation, they can pioneer interventions "upstream," such as the mediation of deals and the facilitation of long-term relationships. As citizens, they can play a leading role in creating a society that is transformed by the application of problem-solving and meditative approaches to individual disputes. As neutrals and as consumers of dispute resolution services, they must also face the challenges of an expanding and increasingly competitive field.

Throughout this book we have noted the primary role that judges have played in reordering the litigation landscape. Here U.S. Magistrate Judge Wayne Brazil considers how, with a different mindset, a well-known legal case might have taken a very different path.

❖ Hon. Wayne Brazil, A Judge's Perspective on Lawyering and ADR
19 Alternatives 44 (January 2001)

I choose . . . to examine a specific case — to search in the social wreckage it represents for lessons about lawyering and ADR — lessons that may apply broadly, from lawyering for the little guy(s) to lawyering in self-perceived cynicism for the largest of economic stakes.

The case is *Anderson v. Cryovac Inc.*, also known as *Anderson v. W.R. Grace, Co. and Beatrice Foods*, but best known, simply, as "A Civil Action." Made famous by a book and movie, this litigation pitted 33 individual plaintiffs against large corporations. The plaintiffs alleged that the defendants had contaminated the local public water supply — and that contamination was responsible for the deaths of five children and for serious injuries and illnesses suffered by other children and by adults. My interest here is not in how the case was litigated, but on how it wasn't lawyered. With the benefit of hindsight, disengagement, and the considerable developments in ADR since the mid-1980s (when the case was tried), I would like to use this case to make an argument about what really good, really professionally responsible lawyering should be all about — and to show how essential a problem-solving spirit, aided by ADR processes, is to lawyering that aspires to deem itself "the highest quality."

Many of the plaintiffs in "A Civil Action" had suffered in the most severe of ways — physically and emotionally. They felt confused, alone, and betrayed — even though they weren't sure by whom. Some probably felt, at some level, guilty and responsible for the terrible things that their children and they had suffered. They remained both afraid and angry. They wanted answers. Why did this happen? Who was really responsible? Can anything be done about the present and the future? They wanted help dealing with the consequences of their tragedies. They wanted restoration of and to their community.

Lawyers with insufficient vision might say that the plaintiffs were naive to think that they could achieve these kinds of ends through the legal system. Certainly the system as it was actually used by the lawyers who handled the case, traditionally and narrowly over a period of eight years, delivered precious little toward these ends. The transaction costs (not counting a dime of settlement money) were well above $15 million. But the huge investment of money and time yielded a judgment and a settlement that brought no answers to the biggest questions, no emotional healing, no restoration of community, no repair of severely damaged good will, and addressed only modestly the plaintiffs' need to respond financially to the consequences of their injuries (each plaintiff received through settlement about $100,000).

Really good lawyers, however, would have understood that in the aftermath of the tragedy there was an opportunity to build — to use ADR to create new, long-range value of great significance. What could have been? Let's look at the situation primarily through the eyes of the defendant corporations. Even if the only value that really mattered to the defendants was profit, a good lawyer would have counseled them to move in a very different direction — and to use ADR to do so.

The defendants knew that the U.S. Environmental Protection Agency had designated the accused area as a Superfund site and had been investigating the extent and sources of the obvious contamination for some time before the lawsuit was filed. The defendants knew that they were required by law to cooperate fully with the EPA investigation. The defendants knew that there was a substantial possibility that the EPA would order them to contribute toward the cost of clean up. The defendants knew that the U.S. Geological Survey also was studying contamination in the area. And the defendants should have known that if they were not truthful with federal authorities, the U.S. Department of Justice might well intervene. In fact, the Justice Department ultimately indicted one of the corporate defendants for just such untruthfulness — and that defendant ultimately pled guilty.

The defendants also could foresee that a case like this would generate a great deal of press coverage (as it did), and that the defendants would not be favored in the sympathy slant (77% of people polled in surveys taken as the trial date approached believed that the corporate defendants were responsible for the deaths of the children). Moreover, two of the three companies that ended up being pulled into the case knew they would remain in the community — that they would employ local workers, work with local politicians, and need local services.

Given these circumstances, a good lawyer would have counseled his or her client to use an ADR process early in the pretrial period — well before most of the litigation transaction costs were incurred and before the litigation process further alienated the plaintiffs and rigidified their positions. The goal would be to use ADR to explore what was most important to the plaintiffs themselves (as opposed to their lawyers), to de-demonize the defendants, and to reach out to the plaintiffs in a constructive and civic spirit that might make it possible to work out a settlement that would simultaneously save the defendants money and yield potentially huge public relations benefits.

A good lawyer would have urged each corporate defendant to send its chairman or its CEO to the ADR session — to demonstrate graphically that the company understood the gravity of the losses that plaintiffs had suffered. This was a big case — economically, "politically," and emotionally. Direct participation by the highest level corporate officers was fully justified (by financial considerations alone) and would have improved the odds, considerably, that the companies' presentations would elicit favorable responses from the plaintiffs.

A good lawyer would have advised the representative of the company to begin the [mediated] session by listening to the plaintiffs — actively, openly, and sympathetically. After listening, the CEO or chairman would seek an opportunity to speak directly to the plaintiffs (in the presence of their lawyers and the neutral) and would communicate, gently, the following messages and proposals. He would begin by telling the plaintiffs how sorry he and his company were about what had happened to them. Then he would say that he really doesn't understand what the causes were of these tragedies — but that he wants to. He would explain that the scientists who advise him do not think that chemicals from his operations reached the wells or caused the illnesses, and he would emphasize that he and his staff never would have permitted the operations to proceed if he had known that they would cause such effects. But he would concede that no one knows enough about the sources of these kinds of illnesses to be completely sure — so one of his goals will be to support the effort to learn from these tragedies.

He would propose doing that in two ways. One would be to cooperate fully with the EPA and all other governmental agencies who are investigating these matters. He would promise that his company would open its records and provide the authorities promptly with all the information and other forms of assistance they might seek. The second way his company (along with the other defendants) would support the search for answers would be to contribute several million dollars directly to support research into the possibility that there are environmental causes of leukemia. In making these proposals, the spokesman for the company would emphasize that many of the company's valued and longtime employees live here — so it is partly on their behalf that he wants to help find out why this happened. But the spokesman also would emphasize that the company wants to be a responsible and valued member of this community — and thus wants to identify with certainty any aspects of its operations that might cause harm to any other members of the community.

Next, the CEO or chairman would commit the company to contribute its full fair share to the cost of cleaning up the contaminated area. He would say that even though it is not clear that the contamination that has been found caused the cancer, it is clear that the contamination is a legitimate source of concern and must be removed. So the company, the spokesman would say, stands ready to pay (toward the cost of the cleanup) whatever share the government scientists conclude is appropriate. The company representative also would say that the company would do everything it can to speed up the process of making that determination and to press for completion of the cleanup work on as fast a timetable as possible.

To evidence the company's good faith, the representative then would say that none of the commitments just described are contingent on the case settling. The company intends to go forward with them — including the commitment to support the cancer research — even if the parties cannot reach an agreement that would end the litigation.

Finally, the spokesman, on behalf of the defendants as a group, would offer money to help the plaintiffs meet the needs they face. The spokesman would start by acknowledging that no amount of money could adequately compensate for the personal losses that have been suffered — but also that the tragedies have had real and damaging consequences that require resources. The defendants collectively would like to provide some of those resources — and toward that end they are offering the plaintiffs, as a group, $10 million.

Making a package of proposals like this early in the pretrial period would have encouraged a perception that defendants were sincerely sorry about the plaintiffs' losses and wanted not only to act responsibly, but also as real members of a shared community. The likelihood that the plaintiffs would not have responded positively to such an offer is quite small. Good lawyers for them would have encouraged acceptance.

With acceptance of this offer, the defendants would have saved considerable money. They also would have generated considerable positive press and good will — and avoided the years of bad press (to say nothing of the criminal indictment) that accompanied the protracted litigation. Moreover, they would have distinguished themselves from their competitors — encouraging investors to perceive them as possessing especially acute business judgment — and so worthy of investment confidence.

It is clear that there is a very real chance that a scenario like the one described here could have occurred. That real possibility demonstrates, contrary to a high visibility suggestion to the contrary, that statesmanship actually can have a great deal to do with good lawyering. Breadth-of-solution vision can be an essential tool even in pursuing narrow client interests. And a lawyer who cannot help his or her client explore problem-solving solutions simply cannot be considered a wise counselor.

Question

2. Do you think Magistrate Brazil's admonitions are realistic? What barriers might there be — on the defendants' side, the plaintiffs' side, or elsewhere — to successfully executing the scenario he contemplates?

C. Transforming the Community

In this reading former U.S. Attorney General Janet Reno discusses how meditative techniques can have an effect on society that transcends the resolution of individual legal disputes.

❖ Hon. Janet Reno, Promoting Problem Solving and Peacemaking as Enduring Values in Our Society
19 Alternatives 16 (January 2001)

[T]here is an understandable sense of accomplishment and pride within the dispute resolution community. We have witnessed significant growth in the use of dispute resolution by courts, corporations, government bodies, schools and communities. There is much to celebrate. There is also vast, untapped potential for appropriate dispute resolution in so many aspects of society. There are so many ways that dispute resolution can help to improve society's response to conflict. We must all learn how to be effective dispute resolvers and peacemakers. Indeed, our challenge for the 21st century is to make certain that dispute resolution becomes an enduring, ingrained value that is promoted and endorsed in all aspects of our society.

We begin this task by shedding the notion that "cookie-cutter" justice is sufficient, that one size or one process fits all when we deal with disputes. It is neither possible nor appropriate for the courts to serve as the single mechanism for resolving the many kinds of disputes that arise in this complex, busy age. Instead, we need to establish a range of options and processes to resolve disputes. . . .

Our challenge, then, is to engage all sectors of the public in dispute resolution, and to obtain society's recognition that dispute resolution is a necessary life skill at which we should all be proficient, just like math, reading, and spelling. To reach this goal, there are several steps that we must take. First, we must begin with the formal, structured means for resolving conflict in our society, and make sure that the courts have programs to divert those cases into dispute resolution that can and should benefit from facilitated negotiation. . . .

Second, governments, law firms, and frequent litigants should have programs in place to avoid litigation by using dispute resolution at the earliest possible time. . . . I hope that the efforts now being made by the federal government also will contribute to the growing recognition that dispute resolution is a vital skill every lawyer and senior manager must have.

Third, we need to do more with our law schools to promote problem solving in legal education. Our young lawyers need to be educated to recognize that even if the outcome of litigation is relatively certain, there is not always just one right answer to a problem. Our lawyers need to be educated in how not only to root out the facts of a problem, but to understand the context in which the problem arose. We should work with law schools to encourage curricula that include an expanded approach to traditional casebook study of appellate decisions, exposure to interdisciplinary insights, as well as academic courses and clinics that promote crosscutting skills such as negotiation, mediation, and collaborative practices.

Fourth, the use of these skills should not be limited to a select segment of our society. Our schools should teach our children skills in dispute resolution. Through such training, our children can participate in peer mediation programs and, we hope, carry these skills with them to use through later life. It is my vision that every teacher, every school administrator, and every community police officer who comes in contact with young people will be trained in mediation skills to deal with disputes that involve our youth. It is so exciting to see what is going on in schools all across the country when young people gain insight and confidence into genuine, nonviolent problem solving. It truly makes a difference in their lives.

Fifth, we should make use of dispute resolution concepts in creating community courts where justice is approached from a problem-solving perspective, and all relevant players participate in the resolution of a dispute. At the Midtown Community Court in Manhattan, the building contains not only courtrooms but also a social services center, a community service program with mediators, community probation officers, and other services. Local residents, community prosecutors, businesses, and social service providers collaborate with the criminal justice system to provide swift, visible justice that is augmented by drug treatment, health care, employment counseling, education, and other services. By holding defendants immediately accountable for their crimes while, at the same time, addressing the underlying problems that contribute to crime, we improve the community and free other courts to prosecute more serious crime.

Sixth, we must work hard at developing mechanisms that address the impact of technology in conflict resolution. We are communicating ever so rapidly; our economy is truly global, and the possibilities for new types of disputes have expanded exponentially. We must find ways to use these technologies to resolve conflict and to address those types of conflicts that would not have occurred in an earlier age. Each of these steps represents a formidable undertaking. But we know the way, because substantial progress has been made in every one of these areas. What is needed now is the commitment to see all of this as integrated and effective conflict management for our society, where dispute resolution skills for everyone — participants, neutrals, and bystanders — are valued because of their contribution to the overall health of our institutions, organizations, and communities.

D. Mediative Skills as Part of a Legal Career

It is tempting to look at the mediation process solely from the perspective of a neutral, but you now know that lawyers are much more likely to enter the process as advocates. This is particularly true for young lawyers who are in the process of establishing their reputations in the legal community. The fact that an attorney does not embark on a full-time career as a mediator does not, however, mean that she will not benefit greatly from having mediative skills.

The revolution in the management of conflict that inspired this book continues apace. While the future remains uncertain, it is very likely to become even more important for lawyers to provide their clients with a wide range of tools for managing and resolving disputes, particularly mediation. To do this, attorneys will need a thorough appreciation of mediation's appropriate uses as well as its limitations. This is true for attorneys who advise or advocate on behalf of businesses or government institutions, and for those who represent family members, employees, or consumers. We hope that this book has provided you with the fundamental understanding of the mediation process that is essential to modern law practice. If we have not led you to all of the answers, we hope to have equipped you to ask the right questions.

APPENDIX

The appendix to this book is entirely Web based. This makes it possible for students and teachers to download and edit materials to meet their individual needs. To access the Appendix, enter the following URL:

http://www.law.suffolk.edu/pubs/Resolving Disputes

The contents of the Appendix, which will be updated from time to time, are as follows:

Negotiation

- Ethical Guidelines for Settlement Negotiations (ABA)
- Federal Rule of Civil Procedure 68
- Model Rules of Professional Conduct (ABA)

Mediation

- Legislation
  - ADR Act of 1998
  - Uniform Mediation Act (NCCUSL)
- Rules
  - Commercial Mediation Procedures (AAA)
  - CPR Mediation Procedure (CPR)
  - Ethics 2000 ("E2K") Report (ABA)
  - Model Rule of Professional Conduct for the Lawyer as Third-Party Neutral (CPR-Georgetown)
  - 2005 Model Standards for Mediators (AAA, ABA, and ACR)
  - Model Standards of Practice for Family and Divorce Mediators (ACR)
  - Sample Mediation Agreements

BIBLIOGRAPHY AND REFERENCES

Negotiation

BOOKS

Arrow, Kenneth J., et al., eds. (1995) *Barriers to Conflict Resolution*. New York: W.W. Norton.

Axelrod, Robert M. (1984) *The Evolution of Cooperation*. New York: Basic Books.

Babcock, Linda, & Sara Laschever (2003) *Women Don't Ask: Negotiation and the Gender Divide*. Princeton, NJ: Princeton University Press.

Bazerman, Max H., & Margaret A. Neale (1992) *Negotiating Rationally*. New York: Free Press.

Bernard, Phyllis, & Bryant Garth, eds. (2002) *Dispute Resolution Ethics: A Comprehensive Guide*. Washington, D.C.: ABA Section of Dispute Resolution.

Brazil, Wayne D. (1988) *Effective Approaches to Settlement: A Handbook for Lawyers and Judges*. Clifton, NJ: Prentice Hall Law and Business.

Carter, Jimmy (2003) *Negotiation: The Alternative to Hostility*. Macon, GA: Mercer University Press.

Chew, Pat K., ed. (2001) *The Conflict & Culture Reader*. New York: New York University Press.

Cialdini, Robert B. (2001) *Influence: Science and Practice*. Boston: Allyn & Bacon.

Craver, Charles B. (2001) *Effective Legal Negotiation and Settlement*. Newark, NJ: Lexis.

Dawson, Roger (2001) *Secrets of Power Negotiating*. Franklin Lakes, NJ: Career Press.

Deutsch, Morton, & Peter T. Coleman, eds. (2000) *The Handbook of Conflict Resolution*. San Francisco: Jossey-Bass.

Edwards, Harry, & James J. White (1977) *The Lawyer as Negotiator*. St. Paul, MN: West Publishing.

Fisher, Roger, & William J. Ury, with Bruce Patton (1991) *Getting to Yes*. New York: Penguin.

Freund, James C. (1992) *Smart Negotiating: How to Make Good Deals in the Real World*. New York: Simon & Schuster.

Gilligan, Carol (1982) *In a Different Voice: Psychological Theory and Women's Development*. Cambridge, MA: Harvard University Press.

Goodpaster, Gary (1997) *A Guide to Negotiation and Mediation*. Irvington-on-Hudson, NY: Transnational.

Hammond, John S., Ralph L. Keenney, & Howard Raiffa (1999) *Smart Choices: A Practical Guide to Making Better Decisions*. Boston: Harvard Business School Press.

Harr, Jonathan (1996) *A Civil Action*. New York: Vintage Books.

Kolb, Deborah M., & Judith Williams (2000) *The Shadow Negotiation: How Women Can Master the Hidden Agendas that Determine Bargaining Success*. New York: Simon & Schuster.

Lax, David A., & James K. Sebenius (1986) *The Manager As Negotiator: Bargaining For Cooperation And Competitive Gain*. New York: The Free Press.

Lewicki, Roy, et al. (2004) *Essentials of Negotiation*. Boston: McGraw-Hill/Irwin.

Mnookin, Robert H., Scott R. Peppet, & Andrew S. Tulumello (2000) *Beyond Winning: Negotiating to Create Value in Deals and Disputes*. Cambridge, MA: Harvard University Press.

Nelken, Melissa L. (2001) *Understanding Negotiation*. Cincinnati, OH: Anderson Publishing.

Raiffa, Howard (1982) *The Art and Science of Negotiation*. Cambridge, MA: Harvard University Press.

Raiffa, Howard (2002) *Negotiation Analysis: The Science and Art of Collaborative Decision Making*. Cambridge, MA: Harvard University Press.

Schelling, Thomas C. (1960) *The Strategy of Conflict*. Cambridge, MA: Harvard University Press.

Shell, G. Richard (1999) *Bargaining for Advantage: Negotiation Strategies for Reasonable People*. New York: Viking.

Stone, Douglas, Bruce Patton, & Sheila Heen (1999) *Difficult Conversations: How to Discuss What Matters Most*. New York: Penguin Books.

Tesler, Pauline H. (2001) *Collaborative Law*. Chicago: ABA Section on Family Law.

Ury, William (1993) *Getting Past No: Negotiating Your Way from Confrontation to Cooperation*. New York: Bantam Books.

ARTICLES AND CHAPTERS

Adler, Robert S., & Elliot M. Silverstein (2000) "When David Meets Goliath: Dealing with Power Differentials in Negotiations," 5 *Harv. Negot. L. Rev.* 1.

Alfini, James J. (1999) "Settlement Ethics and Lawyering in ADR Proceedings: A Proposal to Revise Rule 4.1," 19 *N. Ill. U. L. Rev.* 255.

Ayres, Ian (1991) "Fair Driving: Gender and Race Discrimination in Retail Car Negotiations," 104 *Harv. L. Rev.* 817.

Birke, Richard, & Craig R. Fox (1999) "Psychological Principles in Negotiating Civil Settlements," 4 *Harv. Negot. L. Rev.* 1.

Brett, Jeanne M. (2000) "Culture and Negotiation," 35 *Int. J. Psychol.* 97, 273, Collected References.

Brown, Jennifer Gerarda (1997) "The Role of Hope in Negotiation," 44 *UCLA L. Rev.* 1661.

Cohen, Jonathan R. (2001) "When People are the Means: Negotiating with Respect," 14 *Geo. J. Legal Ethics* 739.

Cohen, Jonathan R. (2005) "The Immorality of Denial," 79 *Tulane L. Rev.* 903.

Condlin, Robert J. (1992) "Bargaining in the Dark: The Normative Incoherence of the Lawyer Dispute Bargaining Role," 51 *Md. L. Rev.* 1.

Craver, Charles B. (1997) "Negotiation Ethics: How to Be Deceptive Without Being Dishonest/ How to Be Assertive Without Being Offensive," 38 *Tex. L. Rev.* 713.

Craver, Charles B., & David W. Barnes (1999) "Gender, Risk Taking, and Negotiation Performance," 5 *Mich. J. Gender & Law* 299.

Crystal, Nathan M. (1998) "The Lawyer's Duty to Disclose Material Facts in Contract or Settlement Negotiations," 87 *Ky. L.J.* 1055.

Eckel, Catherine, & Philip Grossman (1998) "Are Women Less Selfish Than Men?: Evidence from Dictator Experiments," 108 *Econ. J.* 726.

Galanter, Marc S. (1983) "Reading the Landscape of Disputes: What We Know and Don't Know (And Think We Know) About Our Allegedly Contentious and Litigious Society," 31 *UCLA L. Rev.* 4.

Goodpaster, Gary (1996) "A Primer on Competitive Bargaining," 1996 *J. Disp. Resol.* 325.

Guthrie, Chris (2003) "Panacea or Pandora's Box?: The Costs of Options in Negotiation," 88 *Iowa L. Rev.* 601.

Korobkin, Russell (1998) "Inertia and Preference in Contract Negotiation: The Psychological Power of Default Rules and Form Terms," 51 *Vand. L. Rev.* 1583.

Korobkin, Russell (2000) "A Positive Theory of Legal Negotiation," 88 *Georgetown L.J.* 1789.

Korobkin, Russell, & Chris Guthrie (1994) "Psychological Barriers to Litigation Settlement: An Experimental Approach," 93 *Mich. L. Rev.* 107.

Korobkin, Russell, Michael Moffett, & Nancy Welch (2004) "The Law of Bargaining," 87 *Marq. L. Rev.* 839.

Lubet, Steven (1996) "Notes on the Bedouin Horse Trade or 'Why Won't the Market Clear, Daddy?'" 74 *Tex. L. Rev.* 1039.

Menkel-Meadow, Carrie (1984) "Toward Another View of Legal Negotiation: The Structure of Problem-Solving," 31 *UCLA L. Rev.* 754.

Mnookin, Robert H. (1993) "Why Negotiations Fail: An Exploration of Barriers to the Resolution of Conflict," 8 *Ohio St. J. Disp. Resol.* 235.

Mnookin, Robert H. (2003) "Strategic Barriers to Dispute Resolution: A Comparison of Bilateral and Multilateral Negotiations," 8 *Harv. Negot. L. Rev.* 1 (Spring).

O'Hara, Erin Anne, & Douglas Yarn (2002) "On Apology and Concilience," 77 *Wash. L. Rev.* 1121.

Rosenberg, Joshua D. (2004) "Interpersonal Dynamics: Helping Lawyers Learn the Skills, and the Importance, of Human Relationships in the Practice of Law," 58 *U. of Miami L. Rev.* 1225.

Rubin, Jeffrey Z., & Frank E.A. Sander (1991) "Culture, Negotiation, and the Eye of the Beholder," 7 *Negot. J.* 249.

Salacuse, Jeswald W. (1998) "Ten Ways That Culture Affects Negotiating Style: Some Survey Results," 14 *Negot. J.* 221.

Schneider, Andrea Kupfer (2002) "Shattering Negotiation Myths: Empirical Evidence on the Effectiveness of Negotiation Style," 7 *Harv. Negot. L. Rev.* 143 (Spring).

Sebenius, James K. (2002) "Caveats for Cross-Border Negotiations," 18 *Negot. J.* 122.

Seul, Jeffrey R. (2004) "Settling Significant Cases," 79 *Wash. L. Rev.* 881.

Wetlaufer, Gerald B. (1990) "The Ethics of Lying in Negotiation," 76 *Iowa L. Rev.* 1219.

Wetlaufer, Gerald B. (1996) "The Limits of Integrative Bargaining," 85 *Georgetown L.J.* 369.

White, James J. (1980) "Machiavelli and the Bar: Ethical Limitation on Lying in Negotiation," 1980 *Am. B. Found. Res. J.* 926.

Williams, Gerald R. (1996) "Negotiation as a Healing Process," 1996 *J. Disp. Resol.* 1.

Mediation

BOOKS

Abramson, Harold I. (2004) *Mediation Representation: Advocating in a Problem-Solving Process.* Notre Dame, IN: NITA.

Alfini, James J., & Eric R. Galton, eds. (1998) *ADR Personalities and Practice Tips.* Washington, D.C.: ABA Section of Dispute Resolution.

Ambrose, Stephen E. (1996) *Undaunted Courage.* New York: Touchstone Books.

Bennett, Mark D., & Michele S.G. Hermann (1996) *The Art of Mediation.* Notre Dame, IN: NITA.

Bercovitch, Jacob (2002) *Studies in International Mediation.* New York: Palgrave Macmillan.

Bernard, Phyllis, & Bryant Garth, eds. (2002) *Dispute Resolution Ethics: A Comprehensive Guide.* Washington, D.C.: ABA Section of Dispute Resolution.

Bowling, Daniel, & David Hoffman, eds. (2003) *Bringing Peace into the Room.* San Francisco: Jossey-Bass.

Buhring-Uhle, Christian (1996) *Arbitration and Mediation in International Business.* The Hague: Kluwer Law International.

Bush, Robert A. Baruch, & Joseph P. Folger (2004) *The Promise of Mediation: The Transformative Approach to Conflict.* San Francisco: Jossey-Bass.

Carroll, Eileen, & Karl Mackie (2000) *International Mediation — The Art of Business Diplomacy*. The Hague: Kluwer Law International.

Cloke, Kenneth (2001) *Mediating Dangerously*. San Francisco: Jossey-Bass.

Cole, Sarah R., Craig McEwen, & Nancy H. Rogers (2001) *Mediation: Law, Policy & Practice*. St. Paul, MN: West Publishing.

Cooley, John W. (2000) *The Mediator's Handbook*. Notre Dame, IN: NITA.

Cooley, John W. (2002) *Mediation Advocacy*. Notre Dame, IN: NITA.

CPR Institute of Dispute Resolution (2001) *Into the 21st Century: Thought Pieces on Lawyering, Problem Solving, and ADR*. New York: CPR Institute.

Cronin-Harris, Catherine (1997) *Building ADR into the Corporate Law Department: ADR Systems Design*. New York: CPR Institute.

Erickson, Stephen K., & Marilyn S. McKnight (2001) *The Practitioner's Guide to Mediation: A Client Centered Approach*. San Francisco: Jossey-Bass.

Folberg, Jay, & Alison Taylor (1984) *Mediation: A Comprehensive Guide to Resolving Conflicts Without Litigation*. San Francisco: Jossey-Bass.

Folberg, Jay, Ann L. Milne, & Peter Salem (eds.) (2004) *Divorce and Family Mediation — Models, Techniques and Applications*. New York: Guilford Press.

Friedman, Gary J., & Jack Himmelstein (forthcoming 2006) *The Heart of Mediation: Resolving Conflict Through Understanding*.

Galton, Eric (1994) *Representing Clients in Mediation*. Dallas, TX: American Lawyer Mediation.

Golann, Dwight (1996) *Mediating Legal Disputes: Effective Strategies for Lawyers and Mediators*. New York: Aspen Publishers.

Haynes, John (1989) *Mediating Divorce: Casebook of Strategies for Successful Family Negotiations*. San Francisco: Jossey-Bass.

Katsh, Ethan, & Janet Rivkin (2001) *Online Dispute Resolution — Resolving Conflicts in Cyberspace*. San Francisco: Jossey-Bass.

Kolb, Deborah M., et. al. (1994) *When Talk Works — Profiles of Mediators*. San Francisco: Jossey-Bass.

Kressel, Kenneth, & Dean G. Pruitt (eds.) (1989) *Mediation Research: The Power and Effectiveness of Third-Party Intervention*. San Francisco: Jossey-Bass.

Lang, Michael D., & Alison Taylor (2000) *The Making of a Mediator: Developing Artistry in Practice*. San Francisco: Jossey-Bass.

Moore, Christopher (2004) *The Mediation Process: Practical Strategies for Resolving Conflict*. San Francisco: Jossey-Bass.

Mosten, Forrest S. (1996) *The Complete Guide to Mediation: The Cutting-Edge Approach to Family Law Practice*. Chicago: ABA Section of Family Law.

Niemic, Robert J., Donna Stienstra, & Randall E. Ravitz (2001) *Guide to Judicial Management of Cases in ADR*. Washington, D.C.: Federal Judicial Center.

Ordover, Abraham P., & Andrea Doneff (2002) *Alternatives to Litigation: Mediation, Arbitration, and the Art of Dispute Resolution*. Notre Dame, IN: NITA.

Picker, Bennett G. (2003) *Mediation Practice Guide: A Handbook for Resolving Business Disputes*. Washington, D.C.: ABA Section of Dispute Resolution.

Rule, Colin (2002) *Online Dispute Resolution for Business: B2B, Ecommerce, Consumer, Employment, Insurance, and Other Commercial Conflicts*. San Francisco: Jossey-Bass.

Scanlon, Kathleen, ed. (1999) *Mediator's Deskbook*. New York: CPR Institute.

Senger, Jeffrey M. (2004) *Federal Dispute Resolution: Using Alternative Dispute Resolution with the United States Government*. San Francisco: Jossey-Bass.

Singer, Linda (1994) *Settling Disputes: Conflict Resolution in Business, Families, and the Legal System*. Boulder, CO: Westview.

Slaikeu, Karl A. (1996) *When Push Comes to Shove: A Practical Guide to Mediating Disputes*. San Francisco: Jossey-Bass.

Susskind, Lawrence, Sarah McKearnan, & Jennifer Thomas Larmer (eds.) (1999) *The Consensus Building Handbook: A Comprehensive Guide to Reaching Agreement*. Thousand Oaks, CA: Sage.

ARTICLES AND MONOGRAPHS

Aaron, Marjorie Corman (1995) "The Value of Decision Analysis in Mediation Practice," 11 *Negot. J.* 123.

Aaron, Marjorie Corman (2002) "At First Glance: Maximizing The Mediator's Initial Contact," 20 *Alternatives* 167.

Aaron, Marjorie Corman (2005) "Do's and Don'ts of Mediation Practice," 11 *Disp. Resol. Mag.* 19 (Winter).

Aaron, Marjorie Corman, & David P. Hoffer (1996) "Decision Analysis as a Method of Evaluating the Trial Alternative," in D. Golann, *Mediating Legal Disputes* 307. New York: Aspen Publishers.

Abramson, Harold I. (2004) "Problem-Solving Advocacy in Mediation," 59 *Disp. Resol. J.* 56.

Alexander, Nadja (2004) "Mediation on Trial: Ten Verdicts on Court-Related ADR," 22 *Law in Context* 8.

Alfini, James J. (2001) "Ethics 2000 Leaves Mediation in Ethics 'Black Hole,'" 7 *Disp. Resol. Mag.* 3 (Spring).

Amis, Mike, et al. (1998) "The Texas ADR Experience," in Edward J. Bergman & John G. Bickerman, eds., *Court-Annexed Mediation: Critical Perspective on State and Federal Programs*. Washington, D.C.: American Bar Association.

Arnold, Tom (1995) "Twenty Common Errors in Mediation Advocacy," 13 *Alternatives* 69.

Arnold, Tom (1999) "Client Preparation for Mediation," 15 *Corporate Counsel's Q.* 52 (April).

Bahadoran, Sina (2000) "A Red Flag: Mediator Cultural Bias in Divorce," 18 *Mass. Fam. L. J.* 69.

Belhorn, Scott R. (2005) "Settling Beyond the Shadow of the Law: How Mediation Can Make the Most of Social Norms," 20 *Ohio St. J. on Disp. Resol.* 981.

Berger, Vivian (2003) "Employment Mediation in the Twenty-First Century: Challenges in a Changing Environment," 5 *U. Pa. J. Lab. & Empl. L.* 487 (Spring).

Bingham, Gail (2002) "The Environment in the Balance: Mediators Are Making a Difference," 2 *AC Resolution* 21 (Summer).

Bingham, Lisa (2002) "REDRESS™ at the USPS: A Breakthrough Mediation Program," 1 *AC Resolution* 34 (Spring).

Birkoff, Juliana, & Robert Rack, with Judith M. Filner (2001) "Points of View: Is Mediation Really a Profession?" 8 *Disp. Res. Mag.* 10 (Fall).

Boettger, Ulrich (2004) "Efficiency Versus Party Empowerment — Against a Good-Faith Requirement in Mandatory Mediation," 23 *Rev. Litig.* 1.

Bowling, Daniel, & David Hoffman (2000) "Bringing Peace into the Room: The Personal Qualities of the Mediator and Their Impact on the Mediation," 16 *Negot. J.* 5.

Braz, Avi (2004) "Out of Joint: Replacing Joint Representation with Lawyer Mediation in Friendly Divorces," 78 *S. Cal. L. Rev.* 323.

Brazil, Wayne D. (1998) "Why Should Courts Offer Non-binding ADR Services?" 16 *Alternatives* 65.

Brazil, Wayne (January 2001) "A Judge's Perspective on Lawyering and ADR," 19 *Alternatives* 44.

Brett, Jeanne M., Zoe I. Barsness, & Stephen B. Goldberg (1996) "The Effectiveness of Mediation: An Independent Analysis of Cases Handled by Four Major Service Providers," 12 *Negot. J.* 259 (July).

Bush, Robert A. Baruch (1996) "What Do We Need a Mediator For?: Mediation's 'Value-Added' for Negotiators," 12 *Ohio St. J. on Disp. Resol.* l.

Bush, Robert A. Baruch, & Sally Ganong Pope (2004) "Transformative Mediation: Principles and Practice in Divorce Mediation," in J. Folberg, et al., eds., *Divorce and Family Mediation*. New York: Guilford Press.

Carlson, Chris (2000) "Convening," *The Consensus Building Handbook* 169.

Cheng, Teresa (2004) "Recent Developments in Dispute Resolution in Asia: Beyond Globalization: Issues and Opportunities," 38 *Int'l Law.* 616.

Chester, Ronald (1999) "Less Law, But More Justice?: Jury Trials and Mediation as Means of Resolving Will Contests," 37 *Duq. L. Rev.* 173 (Winter).

Cobb, Sarah, & Janet Rifkin (1991) "Practice and Paradox: Deconstructing Neutrality in Mediation," 16 *Law & Soc. Inquiry* 35.

Coben, James, & Harley Penelope (2004) "Intentional Conversations About Restorative Justice, Mediation and the Practice of Law," 25 *Hamline J. Pub. L. & Pol'y* 235.

Cohen, Jonathan R. (1999) "Advising Clients to Apologize," 72 *S. Cal. L. Rev.* 1009.

Cole, Sarah Rudolph (2000) "Managerial Litigants? The Overlooked Problem of Party Autonomy in Dispute Resolution," 51 *Hastings L.J.* 1199.

Contuzzi, Peter (2000) "Should Parties Tell Mediators Their Bottom Line?" 8 *Disp. Res. Mag.* 30 (Spring).

Cooley, John W. (1997) "Mediation Magic: Its Use and Abuse," 29 *Loy. L. Rev.* 1 (Fall).

Cooley, John W. (2004) "Defining the Ethical Limits of Acceptable Deception in Mediation," 4 *Pepperdine Disp. Resol. L. J.* 263.

Cooper, Christopher (2000) "Police Mediators: Rethinking the Role of Law Enforcement in the New Millennium," 7 *Disp. Res. Mag.* 17 (Fall).

Coylewright, Jeremy (2004) "New Strategies for Prisoner Rehabilitation in the American Criminal Justice System: Prisoner Facilitated Mediation," 7 *J. Health Care L. & Pol'y* 395.

Creo, Robert A. (2001) "Emerging from No Man's Land to Establish a Bargaining Model," 19 *Alternatives* 191 (September).

Curtis, Dana (1998) "Reconciliation and the Role of Empathy," in J. Alfini & E. Galton, eds., *ADR Personalities and Practice Tips*. Washington, D.C.: ABA Section of Dispute Resolution.

Curtis, Dana, & John Toker (December 2000) "Representing Clients in Appellate Mediation: The Last Frontier," 1 *JAMS Alert No. 3* 1.

Davis, Benjamin G. (2005) "International Commercial Online and Offline Dispute Resolution: Addressing Primacism and Universalism," 4 *J. Amer. Arb.* 79.

Deason, Ellen E. (2001) "Enforcing Mediated Settlement Agreements: Contract Law Collides with Confidentiality," 35 *U.C. Davis L. Rev.* 33 (November).

Deason, Ellen E. (2002) "Predictable Mediation Confidentiality in the U.S. Federal System," 17 *Ohio. St. J. on Disp. Resol.* 239.

Deason, Ellen E. (2005) "Procedural Rules for Complementary Systems of Litigation and Mediation — Worldwide," 80 *Notre Dame L. Rev.* 553.

Delgado, Richard (1988) "ADR and the Dispossessed: Recent Books About the Deformalization Movement," 13 *Law & Soc. Inquiry* 145.

De Palo, Giuseppe, & Penelope Hartley (2005), "Mediation in Italy: Exploring the Contradictions," 21 Negot. J. 469.

Donahey, M. Scott (1995) "The Asian Concept of Conciliator/Arbitrator: Is It Translatable to the Western World?" 10 *Foreign Inv. L. J.* 120.

Dunnigan, Alana (2003) "Comment — Restoring Power to the Powerless: The Need to Reform California's Mandatory Mediation for Victims of Domestic Violence," 37 *U.S.F. L. Rev.* 1031.

Edwards, T. Harry (1986) "Alternative Dispute Resolution: Panacea or Anathema?" 99 *Harv. L. Rev.* 668 (January).

Fisher, Tom (2001) "Advice by Any Other Name...," 29 *Conflict Resol. Q.* 107.

Fiss, Owen M. (1984) "Against Settlement," 93 *Yale L. J.* 1073.

Folberg, Jay (1982) "Divorce Mediation: The Emerging American Model," paper presented at the Fourth Ann. Conf. of the Int'l Socy. for Family Law, Harv. U (June).

Folberg, Jay (1985) "Mediation of Child Custody Disputes," 19 *Colum. J. L. Soc. Probs.* 413.

Folberg, Jay (1996) "Certification of Mediators in California: An Introduction," 30 *U.S.F. L. Rev.* 609 (Spring).

Freedman, Lawrence R., & Michael L. Prigoff (1986) "Confidentiality in Mediation: The Need for Protection," 2 *Ohio St. J. on Disp. Resol.* 37.

Fuller, Lon (1971) "Mediation: Its Forms and Functions," 44 *S. Cal. L. Rev.* 305 (February).

Geronemus, David (2001) "The Changing Face of Commercial Mediation," 19 *Alternatives* 38 (January).

Golann, Dwight (1989) "Making Alternative Dispute Resolution Mandatory: The Constitutional Issues," 68 *Or. L. Rev.* 487.

Golann, Dwight (2000) "Variations in Style: How — and Why — Legal Mediators Change Style in the Course of a Case," 2000 *J. Disp. Resol.* 40.

Golann, Dwight (2002) "Is Legal Mediation a Process of Reconciliation — Or Separation? An Empirical Study, and Its Implications," 7 *Harv. Negot. L. Rev.* 301.

Golann, Dwight (2004) "Death of a Claim: The Impact of Loss Reactions on Bargaining," 20 *Negot. J.* 539.

Golann, Dwight (2004) "How to Borrow a Mediator's Powers," 30 *Litig.* 41 (Spring).

Golann, Helaine, & Dwight Golann (2003) "Why Is It Hard for Lawyers to Deal with Emotional Issues?" 9 *Disp. Res. Mag.* 26 (Winter).

Goldberg, Stephen B. (2005) "How Interest-based, Grievance Mediation Performs Over the Long Term," 59 *J. Disp. Resol.* 8.

Green, Eric (1986) "A Heretical View of the Mediation Privilege," 2 *Ohio St. J. on Disp. Resol.* 1.

Green, Eric, & Jonathan Marks (2001) "How We Mediated the Microsoft Case," *The Boston Globe* A23 (November 15).

Grillo, Trina (1991) "The Mediation Alternative: Process Dangers for Women," 100 *Yale L.J.* 1545.

Guthrie, Chris, & James Levin (1998) "A 'Party Satisfaction' Perspective on a Comprehensive Mediation Statute," 13 *Ohio St. J. on Disp. Resol.* 885.

Herman, G. Nicholas (2005) "10 Tools for Mediation Cases," 41 *Trial* 66.

Hermann, Michele (1994) "New Mexico Research Examines Impact of Gender and Ethnicity in Mediation," 1 *Disp. Res. Mag.* 10 (Fall).

Herring, Victoria L. (2004) "Creative Advocacy in Voluntary Alternative Dispute Resolution," 40 *Trial* 40.

Hodges, Ann C. "Mediation and the Transformation of American Labor Unions," 69 *Mo. L. Rev.* 365.

Honeyman, Christopher (1990) "On Evaluating Mediators," 6 *Negot. J.* 23.

Hughes, Scott H. (1998) "A Closer Look: The Case for a Mediation Confidentiality Privilege Still Has Not Been Made," 5 *Disp. Res. Mag.* 14 (Winter).

Hyman, Jonathan M. (2004) "Swimming in the Deep End: Dealing With Justice in Mediation," 6 *Cardozo J. of Conflict Res.* 19.

Izumi, Carol L., & Homer C. La Rue (2003) "Prohibiting 'Good Faith' Reports Under the Uniform Mediation Act: Keeping the Adjudication Camel Out of the Mediation Tent," 2003 *J. Disp. Resol.* 67.

Kakalik, James, et al. (1996) *An Evaluation of Mediation and Early Neutral Evaluation Under the Civil Justice Reform Act*. Santa Monica, CA.: RAND Corp.

Keating, Michael (1996) "Mediating in the Dance For Dollars," 14 *Alternatives* 71 (September).

Kichaven, Jeffrey G. (1999) "How Advocacy Fits in Effective Mediation," 17 *Alternatives* 60.

Kirtley, Alan (1995) "The Mediation Privilege's Transition from Theory to Implementation: Designing a Mediation Privilege Standard to Protect Mediation Participants, the Process and the Public Interest," 1995 *J. Disp. Resol.* 1.

Kloppenberg, Lisa A. (2002) "Implementation of Court-Annexed Environmental Mediation: The District of Oregon Pilot Project," 17 *Ohio St. J. on Disp. Resol.* 559.

Koh, Hea Jin (2004) "Yet I Shall Temper So Justice with Mercy: Procedural Justice in Mediation and Litigation," 28 *Law & Psychol. Rev.* 169.

Kovach, Kimberlee K. (1997) "Good Faith in Mediation — Requested, Recommended, or Required? A New Ethic," 38 *S. Tex. L. Rev.* 38.

Kovach, Kimberlee K., & Lela P. Love (1998) "Mapping Mediation: The Risks of Riskin's Grid," 3 *Harv. Negot. L. Rev.* 71.

Laflin, James, & Robert Werth (2001) "Unfinished Business: Another Look at the Microsoft Mediation," 12 *California Tort Reporter No. 3*, 88 (May).

Lande, John (2002) "Using Dispute Systems Design Methods to Promote Good-Faith Participation in Court-Connected Mediation Programs," 50 *UCLA Law Rev.* 69 (October).

Levi, Deborah (1997) "The Role of Apology in Mediation," 72 *N.Y.U. L. Rev.* 1165.

Lewis, Michael (1995) "Advocacy in Mediation: One Mediator's View," 2 *Disp. Res. Mag.* 7 (Fall).

Liebman, Carol B. & Chris S. Hyman (2004) "A Mediation Skills Model to Manage Disclosure of Errors and Adverse Events to Patients," 23 *Health Affairs* 22.

Lieberman, Jethro K., & James F. Henry (1986) "Lessons from the Alternative Dispute Resolution Movement," 53 *U. Chi. L. Rev.* 424.

Lipsky, David A., & Ronald L. Seeber (1999) "Patterns of ADR Use in Corporate Disputes," 54 *Disp. Res. J.* 66 (February).

Lipsky, David B., & Ronald L. Seeber (1998) *The Appropriate Resolution of Corporate Disputes: A Report on the Growing Use of ADR by U.S. Corporations.* Ithaca, NY: Cornell/PERC Institute on Conflict Resolution.

Love, Lela P. (1997) "The Top Ten Reasons Why Mediators Should Not Evaluate," 24 *Fla. St. U. L. Rev.* 937.

Lowry, L. Randolph (1997) "To Evaluate or Not — That Is Not the Question!" 2 *Resolutions* 2 (Pepperdine Univ.).

Madoff, Ray D. (2002) "Lurking in the Shadow: The Unseen Hand of Doctrine in Dispute Resolution," 76 *S. Cal. L. Rev.* 161.

Matz, David E. (1999) "Ignorance and Interests," 4 *Harv. Negot. L. Rev.* 59.

Max, Rodney A. (1999) "Multiparty Mediation," 23 *Am. J. Trial Advoc.* 269.

McEwen, Craig (1998) "Managing Corporate Disputing: Overcoming Barriers to the Effective Use of Mediation for Reducing the Cost and Time of Litigation," 14 *Ohio St. J. on Disp. Resol.* 1.

McGuire, James E. (2004) "Certification: An Idea Whose Time Has Come," 10 *Disp. Res. Mag.* 22 (Summer).

Menkel-Meadow, Carrie (1999) "Do the 'Haves' Come out Ahead in Alternative Judicial Systems?: Repeat Players in ADR," 15 *Ohio St. J. on Disp. Resol.* 19.

Menkel-Meadow, Carrie (2001) "Ethics in ADR: The Many 'Cs' of Professional Responsibility and Dispute Resolution," 28 *Fordham Urban L. J.* 979.

Menkel-Meadow, Carrie, & Elizabeth Plapinger (1999) "Model Rules Would Clarify Lawyer Conduct When Serving as a Neutral," 6 *Disp. Res. Mag.* 20 (Summer).

Milne, Ann L. (2004) "Mediation and Domestic Abuse," in J. Folberg, et al., eds., *Divorce and Family Mediation.* New York: Guilford Press.

Mnookin, Robert H. (1993) "Why Negotiations Fail: An Exploration of Barriers to the Resolution of Conflict," 8 *Ohio St. J. Disp. Res.* 235.

Moffit, Michael (2003) "Suing Mediators," 83 *B.U. L. Rev.* 147.

Moffit, Michael (2003) "Ten Ways to Get Sued: A Guide for Mediators," 8 *Harv. Negot. L. Rev.* 81.

Nadler, Janice (2001) "In Practice: Electronically Mediated Dispute Resolution and E-Commerce," 17 *Negot. J.* 333.

Nolan-Haley, Jacqueline (1996) "Court Mediation and the Search for Justice Through Law," 74 *Wash. Univ. L. Q.* 47.

Nolan-Haley, Jacqueline (1998) "Lawyers, Clients, and Mediation," 73 *Notre Dame L. Rev.* 1369.

Owen, Rebecca M. (2005) "In re Uncertainty: A Uniform and Confidential Treatment of Evidentiary and Advocatory Materials Used in Mediation," 20 *Ohio St. J. on Disp. Resol.* 911.

Peppet, Scott R. (2004) "Contract Formation in Imperfect Markets: Should We Use Mediators in Deals?" 38 *Ohio St. J. on Disp. Resol.* 283.

Press, Sharon (1998) "Florida's Court-Connected State Mediation Program," in Edward J. Bergman & John G. Bickerman, eds., *Court-Annexed Mediation: Critical Perspectives on State and Federal Programs.* Washington, D.C.: ABA Section of Dispute Resolution.

Price, Marty (2000) "Personalizing Crime: Mediation Produces Restorative Justice for Victims and Offenders," 7 *Disp. Res. Mag.* 8 (Fall).

Raitt, Susan E., Jay Folberg, Joshua Rosenberg & Robert Barrett (1993) "The Use of Mediation in Small Claims Courts," 9 *Ohio St. J. Disp. Res.* 55.

Reichert, Klaus (2005) "Confidentiality in International Mediation," 59 *J. Disp. Resol.* 60.

Reno, Janet (2001) "Promoting Problem Solving and Peacemaking as Enduring Values in Our Society," 19 *Alternatives* 16.

Riskin, Leonard (1993) "Mediator Orientations, Strategies and Techniques," 12 *Alternatives* 111.

Riskin, Leonard (1996) "Understanding Mediator's Orientations, Strategies, and Techniques: A Grid for the Perplexed," 1 *Harv. Negot. L. Rev.* 7 (Spring).

Riskin, Leonard (2003) "Decision-Making in Mediation: The New Old Grid and the New New Grid System," 79 *Notre Dame L. Rev.* 1 (December).

Riskin, Leonard (2003) "Retiring and Replacing the Grid of Mediator Orientations," 21 *Alternatives* 69.

Robinson, Peter (1998) "Contending with Wolves in Sheep's Clothing: A Cautiously Cooperative Approach to Mediation Advocacy," 50 *Baylor L. Rev.* 963.

Rogers, Joshua S. (2004) "Riner v. Newbraugh: The Role of Mediator Testimony in the Enforcement of Mediated Agreements," 107 *W. Va. L. Rev.* 329.

Rosenberg, Joshua D., & Jay Folberg (1994) "Alternative Dispute Resolution: An Empirical Analysis," 46 *Stan. L. Rev.* 1487.

Rosengard, Lee A. (2004) "Learning From Law Firms: Using Co-Mediation to Train New Mediators," 59 *Disp. Resol. J.* 16.

Ross, David (2000) "Strategic Considerations in Choosing a Mediator: A Mediator's Perspective," 2 *J. Alt. Disp. Res. in Empl.* 7 (Spring).

Rule, Colin (2002) "Online Dispute Resolution," adapted from *Online Dispute Resolution for Business: B2B, Ecommerce, Consumer, Employment, Insurance, and Other Commercial Conflicts.*

Salacuse, Jeswald (2002) "Mediation in International Business," in J. Bercovitch, ed., *Studies in International Mediation.* New York: Palgrave Macmillan.

Salem, Richard (2003) "The Benefits of Empathic Listening," Conflict Research Consortium, University of Colorado, *http://www.crinfo.org.*

Schmitz, Suzanne J. (2001) "What Should We Teach in ADR Courses?: Concepts and Skills for Lawyers Representing Clients in Mediation," 6 *Harv. Negot. L. Rev.* 189.

Senger, Jeffrey M. (2002) "In Practice: Tales of the Bazaar — Interest-Based

Negotiation Across Cultures," 18 *Negot. J.* 233 (July).

Seul, Jeffrey R. (1999) "How Transformative Is Transformative Mediation?: A Constructive-Developmental Assessment," 15 *Ohio St. J. on Disp. Resol.* 135.

Silbey, Susan S. (2002) "The Emperor's New Clothes: Mediation Mythology and Markets," 2002 *J. Disp. Resol.* 171.

Slavitt, Evan (2006) "Using Risk Analysis as a Mediation Tool," 2006 *Disp. Resol. J.* 18.

Smith, Robert M. (2000) "Advocacy in Mediation: A Dozen Suggestions," 26 *S.F. Att'y* 14.

Spolter, Jerry (2000) "A Mediator's Tip: Talk to Me!" *The Recorder* 4 (March 8).

Stallworth, Lamont E., et al. (2001) "Discrimination in the Workplace: How Mediation Can Help," *Disp. Res. J.* 35.

Stempel, Jeffrey W. (1997) "Beyond Formalism and False Dichotomies: The Need for Institutionalizing a Flexible Concept of the Mediator's Role," 24 *Fla. St. U. L. Rev.* 949.

Stern, David M. (1998) "Mediation: An Old Dog with Some New Tricks," 24 *Litigation* 31.

Stienstra, Donna (1998) "Demonstrating the Possibilities of Providing Mediation Early and by Court Staff: The Western District of Missouri's Early Assessment Program," *Court-Annexed Mediation: Critical Perspectives on State and Federal Programs* 251.

Stienstra, Donna, Molly Johnson, & Patricia Lombard (1997) "Report to the Judicial Conference Committee on Court Administration and Case Management: A Study of the Five Demonstration Programs Established Under the Civil Justice Reform Act of 1990." Washington, D.C.: Federal Judicial Center.

Stipanowich, Thomas J. (1998) "The Multi-Door Contract and Other Possibilities," 13 *Ohio St. J. on Disp. Resol.* 3.

Stipanowich, Thomas J. (2001) "Contracts Symposium: Contract and Conflict Managment," 2001 *Wis. L. Rev.* 831.

Stulberg, Joseph (1981) "The Theory and Practice of Mediation: A Reply to Professor Susskind," 6 *Vt. L. Rev.* 85.

Stulberg, Joseph (1997) "Facilitative Versus Evaluative Mediator Orientations: Piercing the 'Grid' Lock," 24 *Fla. St. U. L. Rev.* 985.

Susskind, Lawrence (1981) "Environmental Mediation and the Accountability Problem," 6 *Vt. L. Rev.* 1.

Technology Mediation Services (2004) "High Tech and Intellectual Property Disputes," *http:// www.technologymediation.com/hightech.htm*.

Thompson, Leigh, & Janice Nadler (2002) "Negotiating Via Information Technology: Theory and Application," 58 *J. Soc. Issues* 109.

Thompson, Peter (2004) "Enforcing Rights Generated in Court-Connected Mediation — Tension Between the Aspirations of a Private Facilitative Process and the Reality of Public Adversarial Justice," 19 *Ohio St. J. Disp. Resol.* 509.

Wade, John (2004) "Representing Clients Effectively in Negotiation, Conciliation and Mediation of Family Disputes," 18 *Austl. J. Fam. L.* 283.

Waldman, Ellen A. (2004) "Healing Hearts or Righting Wrongs?: A Mediation on the Goals of 'Restorative Justice,'" 25 *Hamline J. Pub. L. & Pol'y* 355.

Weinstein, John (1996) "Advocacy in Mediation," 32 *Trial* 31.

Welsh, Nancy A. (2001) "Making Deals in Court-Connected Mediation: What's Justice Got to Do With It?," 79 *Wash. Univ. L.Q.* 787 (Fall).

Welsh, Nancy A. (2004) "Remembering the Role of Justice in Resolution: Insights from Procedural and Social Justice Theories," 54 *J. Legal. Educ.* 49.

Welsh, Nancy A., & Barbara McAdoo (1998) "Alternative Dispute Resolution in Minnesota — An Update on Rule 114," in Edward J. Bergman & John G. Bickerman, eds., *Court-Annexed Mediation: Critical Perspectives on State and Federal Programs*. Washington, D.C.: ABA Section of Dispute Resolution.

Wissler, Roselle L. (2001) "To Evaluate or Facilitate? Parties' Perceptions of Mediation Affected by Mediator Style," 7 *Disp. Res. Mag.* 35 (Winter).

Wissler, Roselle L. (2002) "Court-Connected Mediation in General Civil Cases: What We Know from Empirical Research," 17 *Ohio St. J. on Disp. Resol.* 641.

Wittenberg, Carol, Susan Mackenzie, & Margaret Shaw (1996) "Employment Disputes," in D. Golann, ed., *Mediating Legal Disputes: Effective Strategies for Lawyers and Mediators*. New York: Aspen Publishers.

WEB SITES

Alternative Dispute Resolution Section of the Association of American Law Schools, *http:// www.law.missouri.edu/aalsadr/index.htm*.

American Bar Association Section of Dispute ✳ Resolution, *http://www.abanet.org/dispute/home* (Professional association of lawyers and law students interested in mediation and other forms of ADR).

Association for Conflict Resolution, *http:// www.acrnet.org* (Professional association for lawyers, law students, and nonlawyers interested in mediation and other forms of ADR).

Center for Analysis of Alternative Dispute Resolution Systems, *http://www.caadrs.org* (Abstracts of empirical studies of court-related ADR programs).

Center for Dispute Resolution, Willamette University College of Law, *http://www.willamette. edu/law/wlo/dis-res*.

Center for the Study of Dispute Resolution, University of Missouri, *http://www.law.missouri. edu/csdr/adr* (References to information and other academic ADR Web sites).

Centre for Effective Dispute Resolution, *http://www.cedr.co.uk* (Information on British and European use of ADR in commercial disputes).

Conflict Resolution Information Source, Conflict Research Consortium, University of Colorado, *http://www.crinfo.org* (Information and referral sources on a wide variety of ADR issues).

CPR Institute of Dispute Resolution, *http://www.cpradr.org* (Information concerning use of ADR in commercial disputes).

Federal ADR Network, *http://www.adr.af.mil./general/guide_adr.doc* (a comprehensive list of ADR Web sites).

Information, Education, and Web Development for Mediation and Mediators, *http://www.mediate.com*.

The Center for Information Technology and Dispute Resolution, *http://www.odr.info*.

Treeage Software, Software for Decision Analysis, Cost Effectiveness, Decision Trees, Markov Models, Influence Diagrams, and Monte Carlo Simulation, *http://www.treeage.com*.

CASES

Byrd v. The State, 367 S.E.2d 300 (Ga. App. 1988).

Christian Cooper v. Melodie Austin, 750 So. 2d 711 (Fla. App. 2000).

Nick v. Morgan's Foods of Missouri, Inc., 270 F. 3d 590 (8th Cir. 2001).

Olam v. Congress Mortgage Co., 68 F. Supp. 2d 1110 (N.D. Cal. 1999).

Rojas v. Superior Court of Los Angeles County, 33 Cal. 4th 407.

In the matter of T.D., Deprived Child, et al., vs. State of Oklahoma, et al.., 2001 Ok. Civ. App. 92 (2001).

VIDEOTAPES AND DVDS (ALL ARE VIDEOTAPES, UNLESS OTHERWISE NOTED)

Representing Clients

Golann, Dwight (2000) "Representing Clients in Mediation: How Advocates Can Share a Mediator's Powers," *http://www.abanet.org/cle* (Unscripted examples of advocates using mediators to advance bargaining goals).

Phillips, John (2003) "Mediation Madness," *http://www.abanet.org/dispute/videos.html* (Examples of good and bad mediation advocacy).

Mediation Skills

Aaron, Marjorie Corman, & Dwight Golann (2004) "Mediators at Work: A Case of Discrimination?" *http://www.pon.org* (Unscripted mediation of an age discrimination case).

CPR Institute for Dispute Resolution (1994) "Mediation in Action," *http://www.cpradr.org* (Mediation of international contract dispute).

CPR Institute for Dispute Resolution (2003) "Resolution Through Mediation," *http://www.cpradr.org* (Mediation of international trademark case).

Golann, Dwight, & Marjorie Corman Aaron (1999) "Mediators at Work: Breach of Warranty?" *http://www.pon.org* (Unscripted mediation of commercial contract dispute).

Himmelstein, Jack, & Gary Friedman (2001) "Saving the Last Dance: Mediation Through Understanding," *http://www.pon.org* (No-caucus mediation of a manager-organization dispute).

JAMS Foundation (2003) (DVD) "Mediating A Sexual Harassment Case: What Would You Do?" *http://www.jamsadr.com* (Vignettes of challenging situations for a mediator).

Mixed Processes

BOOKS AND TREATISES

Costantino, Cathy A., & Christina S. Merchant (1996) *Designing Conflict Management Systems*. San Francisco: Jossey-Bass.

CPR Institute for Dispute Resolution (2003) *How Companies Manage Employment Disputes*. New York: CPR Institute.

Dispute Prevention Through Partnering (1998) CPR Institute for Dispute Resolution MAPP Series.

Scanlon, Kathleen (Supp. 2003) *Drafter's Deskbook — Dispute Resolution Clauses*. New York: CPR Institutes.

Stipanowich, Thomas J., & Peter Kaskell (eds.) (2001) *Commercial Arbitration at Its Best: Successful Strategies for Business Users*. Chicago: American Bar Association.

ARTICLES

Elliott, David C. (1995) "Med/Arb: Fraught with Danger or Ripe with Opportunity?" 34 *Alberta L. Rev.* 163.

Feinberg, Kenneth R. (2001) "One-Stop Shopping: Using ADR to Resolve Disputes and Implement a Settlement," 19 *Alternatives* 59 (January).

Fortier, L. Yves (2001) "International 'E-commercial' Dispute Resolution," 19 *Alternatives* 23 (January).

Niemic, Robert J., et al. (2001) "Matching the ADR Process to the Case," in *Guide to Judicial Management of Cases in ADR*. Washington, D.C.: Federal Judicial Center.

Peter, James T. (1997) "Note & Comment: Med-Arb in International Arbitration," 8 *Am. J. Int'l Arb.* 83.

Reuben, Richard C. (2005) "Democracy and Dispute Resolution: Systems Design and the New Workplace," 10 *Harv. Negot. L. Rev.* 11.

Sander, Frank (1976) "Varieties of Dispute Processing," 70 *F.R.D.* 111.

Sant, John T. (1997) "How Contract Clauses Can Ensure ADR," 15 *Alternatives* 146.

TABLE OF CASES

INDEX